Contents

The Blair Handbook

The Blair Handbook

TOBY FULWILER
UNIVERSITY OF VERMONT

ALAN R. HAYAKAWA

 A Blair Press Book
PRENTICE HALL, ENGLEWOOD CLIFFS, NJ 07632

Library of Congress Cataloging-in-Publication Data

Fulwiler, Toby.
    The Blair handbook / Toby Fulwiler, Alan R. Hayakawa.
        p.   cm.
    Includes bibliographical references (p.) and index.
    ISBN 0-13-953233-1 (case). —ISBN 0-13-954108-X (case : annotated
instructor's ed.)—ISBN 0-13-301409-6 (paper)
        1. English language—Rhetoric—Handbooks, manuals, etc.
    2. English language—Grammar—Handbooks, manuals, etc.
    I. Hayakawa, Alan R.   II. Title.
    PE1408.F78   1994
    808'.042—dc20   93-21423
                                                                     CIP

Publisher: Nancy Perry
Development Editor: Denise Branch Wydra
Production Editor: Susan Brown
Editorial Assistant: LeeAnn Einert
Interior Design and Page Layout: Betty Binns Design
Cover Designer: Wendy Alling Judy
Production Coordinator: Bob Anderson

Acknowledgments
"Communicate." From *Merriam-Webster's Collegiate Dictionary,* Tenth Edition
© 1993 by Merriam-Webster Inc., publisher of the Merriam-Webster ® dictionaries.
Used by permission.
"Communicate." From *Webster's Third New International Dictionary* © 1986 by
Merriam-Webster Inc., publisher of the Merriam-Webster ® dictionaries. Used by
permission.
"Teacher Expressiveness." This citation is reprinted with permission of the American
Psychological Association, publisher of *Psychological Abstracts* and the PsycINFO
Database (Copyright © 1967–1993) by the American Psychological Association. The
screen in reprinted with permission of SilverPlatter Information, Inc. © 1967–1993
SilverPlatter Information, Inc.

Blair Press
The Statler Building
20 Park Plaza, Suite 1113
Boston, MA 02116-4399

 © 1994 by Prentice-Hall, Inc.
A Paramount Communications Company
Englewood Cliffs, NJ 07632

10 9 8 7 6 5 4 3 2 1

ISBN 0-13-301409-6

Prentice-Hall International (UK) Limited, *London*
Prentice-Hall of Australia Pty. Limited, *Sydney*
Prentice-Hall Canada Inc., *Toronto*
Prentice-Hall Hispanoamericana, S.A., *Mexico*
Prentice-Hall of India Private Limited, *New Delhi*
Prentice-Hall of Japan, Inc., *Tokyo*
Simon & Schuster Asia Pte. Ltd., *Singapore*
Editora Prentice-Hall do Brasil, Ltda., *Rio de Janeiro*

Preface

We wrote *The Blair Handbook* to provide student writers with a single resource containing everything they need to know about both the conventions of good writing and the variable processes by which good writing is produced. Too often, handbooks have been little more than compendiums of isolated rules focusing on finished, technically correct products. Not much has been done to teach students how or why to apply these rules to their own writing. Even less has been done to help students write papers ready for final polishing. In other words, what has been missing in handbooks is an honest and uncompromising focus on the process of writing and rewriting.

Although we have very different backgrounds—one as a college writing instructor, the other as a journalist, editor, and writing coach—we've both worked extensively with developing writers. We both know that writers learn not by conforming to requirements or rules but by writing for a purpose, exploring different means of fulfilling that purpose, and analyzing the consequences of the means chosen. This is what we mean by "process"—the set of activities through which texts become better texts and writers become better writers.

We wanted *The Blair Handbook* to complement the process that writers use, not usurp it. We wanted the handbook to be so clear and flexible that all writers, both strong and weak, both experienced and inexperienced, would benefit from using it. We also wanted our handbook to be easy to use; although writing a paper is a lengthy, recursive, and continuous process, using a handbook should not be. Finally, we wanted our handbook to minimize jargon and drills and to emphasize the material that students really need to become more skillful and confident writers—clear explanations of the many language conventions that govern effective prose; practical composing strategies that have proved useful to experienced writers in the past; and friendly guidance through the many expectations surrounding academic and real-world writing tasks.

PRINCIPLES UNDERLYING *THE BLAIR HANDBOOK*

Writing as a process

The organization of *The Blair Handbook* corresponds to the stages of the writing process that real writers typically use. Following an introductory part that provides a context for college writing are five parts that represent the five interrelated but discrete stages of the writing process: planning, drafting, researching, revising, and editing.

- **Part II, Planning.** This part discusses planning as an activity writers engage in whenever they need to figure out what to do next. Topics include purpose, audience, voice, invention and discovery writing, and journals.

- **Part III, Drafting.** This part introduces students to basic drafting strategies such as finding a subject and stating a thesis in the context of specific writing assignments.

- **Part IV, Researching.** This part has a twofold purpose: to introduce students to research methods they can use to enhance all college writing and to guide them through the challenging and exciting task of writing a research essay.

- **Part V, Revising.** This part focuses on perhaps the most demanding and creative stage in the writing process, revision, in which writers grapple with the content and organization of their papers.

- **Part VI, Editing.** This part, the largest in the book, deals with the stage in the process when writers improve not what they've said but how they've said it. "Editing" is divided into subsections on effectiveness, grammar, punctuation, and mechanics.

This organization allows us to contextualize every piece of information within the writing process. In particular, it allows us to present traditional handbook material—information on style, grammar, punctuation, and mechanics—as "editing," the final stage in the writing process.

Finally, a thorough process orientation allows us to devote generous attention to the earlier stages of the writing process. By presenting information and ideas with the level of detail and the context needed to make them truly comprehensible, we give students not only practical advice for approaching their college assignments but also, we hope, the help they need to grow and develop as writers.

Research as an essential part of the writing process

We recognize that research is an essential part of most college writing projects. We also recognize that research is a part of the writing process, not a separate activity. For these reasons, we integrate our ample section on research into the main sequence of the book rather than tuck it away at the end.

The first chapter in this section introduces students to the process of research and offers advice for completing that challenging college writing task, the research essay. The next three chapters guide students through conducting library and field research and then using and documenting the sources they find. The sampler concluding the section includes three complete sample research essays showing both MLA and APA documentation styles.

Students as writers

In *The Blair Handbook*, we do everything we can to get students working on and involved in their own writing as quickly and as often as possible.

Support for choice making, risk taking.   Students cannot become better writers by passively following rules and formats. We stress that writing is a dynamic activity in which the writer continually chooses from a variety of possible options, evaluates the results, and rewrites as necessary. Students learn to decide for themselves which choice will be most effective with their readers and most satisfying to themselves. We outline the possible choices and give students the information and skills to make their own decisions. We also try to give them the freedom they need to experiment, take chances, and try things that may not work.

Activities focused on writing.   Rather than including exercises that drill students on isolated skills, *The Blair Handbook* features meaningful activities that help students work through their own versions of the writing process. Activities within chapters fall into three categories:

■ **Exploration.**   Students explore their experiences as writers, or they examine the writing of other people to see what they can apply to their own work.

■ **Practice.**   Students practice editing techniques on sample texts provided. Most of these texts are passages based on real student essays.

■ **Application.**   Students apply the principles and strategies discussed in the handbook to papers they are currently working on.

In addition, we put imaginative "Suggestions for Writing and Research" at the ends of chapters in the first five parts of the book. These ideas for complete papers include both individual and collaborative assignments.

Plentiful samples of student writing.   Samples of authentic student writing build reader confidence, encouraging students to say, "Hey, I could do that too." *The Blair Handbook* includes the greatest number and variety of freewrites, journal entries, early drafts, and complete essays (nine final drafts in all) of any handbook available.

Hand-edited examples.   Examples in the editing part of The Blair Handbook use handwritten corrections to show students problems and their solutions at a single glance. This format shows students that editing is not a set of rules but a hands-on activity that involves picking up a pencil or sitting down at the keyboard.

Communication as the purpose of most college writing

If college writing is to benefit the student, it must have meaningful communication as its purpose rather than the mastery of required skills and forms.

Emphasis on specific communicative purposes for writing. Describing the dynamics and principles of communication in the abstract does little to help student writers. Instead of presenting a single idealized and decontextualized "essay," in *The Blair Handbook* we focus on specific communicative tasks, each defined by its own purpose: recounting experience, explaining things, arguing positions, interpreting texts, or reflecting on the world.

Emphasis on conventions, not rules.   In *The Blair Handbook*, we explain features of standard, written English as conventions that facilitate efficient communication, not arbitrary rules to be memorized and followed by rote. We stress that while there are no absolute rules that govern all writing, there are conventions that govern writing in specific situations with specific purposes and audiences. We spend less time instructing students in grammar jargon and more time showing students how to identify, analyze, and solve problems that can cause reader confusion.

Emphasis on effectiveness.   Good writing must be more than conceptually sound and grammatically correct. If a piece of writing is to succeed in its communicative purpose, it must also be clear, vital, and stimulating to read—what we call "effective." In *The Blair Handbook,* we show students how to engage and maintain readers' interest by expressing ideas precisely and powerfully. These issues are often slighted or reduced to the status of "style," which implies surface ornament rather than an element essential to good writing. By conceiving of them as effectiveness and stressing their importance to communication, we give students a purpose for and a guide to improving their writing.

Diversity as a reality in contemporary classrooms

As writers and teachers, we know that there are both different pathways to good writing and different requirements for good writing, depending on the situation. Equally important, we recognize that the diversity of students and of classroom methods continues to grow—and that this diversity is a strength. Accordingly, in *The Blair Handbook* we try to build upon this diversity in various ways.

Comprehensive help for those who speak English as a second language.   Over fifty easily identified boxes placed throughout the book contain information not only on correct grammar and word choice but also on aspects of planning, drafting, researching, and revising that sometimes prove troublesome for ESL writers. In addition, a strand of special writing suggestions in the first three parts asks students to draw on their experiences as nonnative speakers and writers as a means of improving their writing.

Both individual and collaborative writing.   Because writing is a social act as well as an individual activity, we include ideas and advice for both individual and collaborative writing throughout the book. Both individual and collaborative possibilities are included in the end-of-chapter assignments and in many in-chapter activities, and the collection of sample research essays in Part IV contains both individually written and collaboratively written papers.

Six types of papers.   In Parts III and IV, we provide detailed information on the six types of essays students are most often assigned in the first-year writing class. Each of these is illustrated by at least one complete sample student paper. For the research essay, we provide three different samples, representing three possible research assignments: an informal "I-search" essay, a literary analysis with secondary sources, and a collaboratively researched and written report.

Both library research and field research.   In Part IV, we stress that profitable research can occur not only in the library but also in the field. We explore in depth two possible field techniques—interviews and site observations—and urge students to look for information wherever their search takes them.

Complete information on writing across the curriculum.   In Part VII, we provide detailed information on the five distinct disciplinary branches that form the context for most college writing outside the composition classroom.

Innovation as a hallmark of contemporary pedagogy

Writing classrooms today may look quite different from those only a decade ago—walk in and you're likely to see students reading drafts to each other in groups, writing in ungraded journals, quietly conversing together around computers, editing each other's work, or brainstorming as a class for a collaborative research project. *The Blair Handbook* includes special emphasis on the soundest of the current trends in writing instruction.

Computers.   Computers have fundamentally changed the way most of us write, especially the way we revise and edit. In *The Blair Handbook*, we discuss the benefits of word processors and urge students to explore and experiment with them. We integrate suggestions for using specific computer techniques and features into the handbook so that they appear wherever they are likely to be most useful. Chapter 15, on library research, includes a complete discussion of computerized databases and on-line catalogs.

Critical reading.   Reading and writing are necessarily complementary processes; if students cannot read critically, they cannot possibly write well. In addition, incisive reading and writing are both essential to the development of critical thinking. Believing that critical reading is therefore a keystone in the development of every student, we present a thorough discussion of it in Chapter 2 and ask students to draw on their critical reading skills repeatedly in the drafting, researching, and revising sections of the book.

Voice.   The concept of voice gives students a way to see themselves in the texts they write. Chapter 6 discusses and analyzes voice, and the drafting, revising, and editing sections of the book repeatedly ask students to consider the voices they hear in their own writing.

Invention and discovery.   Teachers and writers realize that these activities are crucial not only at the beginning of the writing process but also at each step along the way. Chapter 7 first discusses the general idea of invention and then gives specific suggestions for employing various techniques such as freewriting and outlining. Writing activities in the drafting and revising parts of the book then ask students to use these techniques to develop and improve their writing.

Journals. Because writing-to-learn is recognized as an important part of learning to write, a complete chapter (Chapter 8) features ideas for journal writing. We present additional suggestions for journal writing in individual chapter's activities as "Explorations."

Revising. In Part V, we devote four full chapters to the process of revising, which is increasingly recognized as a creative activity essential to the development of good writing. We describe revision as a complex and variable process and give students concrete suggestions for a variety of methods—some conventional and some more innovative—that they can usefully apply to their writing.

SUPPLEMENTS

Print supplements for instructors

■ *Annotated Instructor's Edition for The Blair Handbook,* by Sue Dinitz, Jean Kiedaisch, and Timothy Brookes, a helpful resource with answers for activities, additional activities, teaching tips, ESL advice, background information on writing, and interesting quotations

■ *Blair Resources for Teaching Writing,* individual booklets presenting information on some of the most effective approaches and important concerns of composition instructors today, each written by an expert on the particular topic

> *Classroom Strategies,* by Wendy Bishop
> *Portfolios,* by Pat Belanoff
> *Journals,* by Christopher C. Burnham
> *Collaborative Learning,* by John Trimbur and Harvey Kail
> *Computers and Composition,* by Deborah Holdstein
> *English as a Second Language,* by Ruth Spack
> *Writing across the Curriculum,* by Art Young

Print supplements for students

■ *The Blair Journal Book,* by Sue Dinitz and Jean Kiedaisch, providing sample papers, prompts asking students to analyze the sample papers and leading them through the process of writing their own papers, and space for students to write (Instructor's Manual available)

■ *Editing Activities from The Blair Handbook with Additional Items,* including both the editing activities in the handbook and additional activities, with ample space to edit on the page (Answer Key available)

■ *The Blair Guide to Documentation,* assembling all the documentation information presented in *The Blair Handbook* in one convenient guide

■ *Prentice Hall/The New York Times Supplement,* a   sixteen-page collection of timely articles from the *New York Times,* providing students with examples of rhetorical strategies and springboards for writing

■ *Preparing for TASP with The Blair Handbook*

■ *Preparing for the CLAST with The Blair Handbook*

Software and Audio-Visual Supplements

■ *The On-Line Handbook,* a pop-up and abbreviated version of the handbook

■ *Blue Pencil,* an interactive program that allows students to practice their editing skills on-screen

■ *Bibliotech,* a bibliography generator with MLA, APA, and CBE documentation styles

■ *ABC News/Prentice Hall Video Library for Composition,* a collection of topically arranged clips from news programs that allows students to experience firsthand the vital relationship between traditional written discourse and video compositions (Instructor's Guide available)

ACKNOWLEDGMENTS

To our colleagues nationwide who agreed to share their wisdom on the teaching of writing in The Blair Resources for Teaching Writing: Pat Belanoff, State University of New York at Stony Brook; Wendy Bishop, Florida State University; Chris Burnham, New Mexico State University; Deborah Holdstein, Governors State University; Harvey Kail, University of Maine; Ruth Spack, Tufts University; John Trimbur, Worcester Polytechnic Institute; and Art Young, Clemson University.

To Sue Dinitz and Jean Kiedaisch, colleagues at the University of Vermont, who created *The Blair Journal Book* as an alternative to conventional workbooks, and who carefully composed the Annotated Instructor's Edition with the generous help of the master of arcane anecdotes, Tim Brookes (also of the University of Vermont).

To the many students at the University of Vermont and Michigan Tech who asked and answered questions about learning to write and especially to those who allowed us to reprint their essays, freewrites, and journal entries: Brendan Annett, Julie Conner, Caleb Danilof, Beth Devino, Mari Engel, Angel Fuster, Robert Greene, Rebecca Grosser, Rebecca Hart, John Jacobi, Jeff Kasden, Dawn Luscier, Sandi Martin, Heather Mulcahy, Pat Quinby, Steve Reville, Amanda Robertson, Zoe Reynders, Karen Santosuosso, Lorraine White, Judith Woods, and Scott Yarochuk.

To Nancy Perry, whose vision of contemporary writing instruction founded Blair Press and guided *The Blair Handbook* from inception to completion. Our warmest thanks to Denise Wydra, our savvy, careful, and relentless development editor, and to Sue Brown, our insightful, sharp, and quizzical production editor. Thanks also to LeeAnn Einert, who makes everything at Blair Press run smoothly. We'd like to acknowledge Mark Gallaher, Ellen Darion, and Sylvia Dovner, whose editing saved more than one chapter from disaster, and Barbara Flanagan and Anne Lesser, whose painstaking care and intelligent comments helped give *The Blair Handbook* its final shape. We are also grateful to Joyce Hinnefeld and Pamela Marshall for their indispensable contributions to the book.

To Jan Frodesen, of the University of California, Los Angeles, who offered invaluable assistance in framing the ESL component of *The Blair Handbook*. Thanks, too, to other colleagues who aided us with their helpful recommendations for this part of the book: Betty Bastankhah, San Jacinto College; Valerie Flournoy, Manatee Community College; Kay M. Losey, University of North Carolina, Chapel Hill; Elizabeth Rorschach, City University of New York, City College; and Ruth Spack, Tufts University.

To the many people at Prentice Hall who supported the project and helped bring it to fruition. In particular, we'd like to thank Phil Miller, Publisher for Humanities and Social Sciences; Gina Sluss, Executive Marketing Manager for English; Jan Stephan, Managing Editor for Humanities Production; and Paula Martin, Design Director. We'd also like to thank Betty Binns for giving *The Blair Handbook* a truly distinctive and appealing look. And special thanks to Marlane Mariello, who introduced us to each other and got us started on the project.

To our many thoughtful, critical, and experienced reviewers whose comments guided the major manuscript revisions: Duncan A. Carter, Portland State University; Christine S. Cetrulo, University of Kentucky; Nancy S. Ellis, Mississippi State University; Robert W. Emery, Boston University; Jo Nell Farrar, San Jacinto College; Kristine Hansen, Brigham Young University; Franklin Horowitz, Columbia University; Francis A. Hubbard, Marquette University; Nancy Johnson, University of New Orleans; Tammy R. Jones, Memphis State University; Edward A. Kline, University of Notre Dame; Douglas Krienke, Sam Houston State University; Bill H. Lamb, Johnson County Community College; Sarah Liggett, Louisiana State University; David Mair, University of Oklahoma; Eileen M. Meagher, University of Tennessee, Chattanooga; Libby Miles, Purdue University; Michael G. Moran, University of Georgia; Sheryl Mylan, University of Houston, Downtown Campus; Laura Noell, Northern Virginia Community College; Michael A. Pemberton, University of Illinois, Urbana-Champaign; Mary Ellen Pitts, Memphis State University; Thomas E. Recchio, University of Connecticut; Donnalee Rubin, Salem State College; Charles I. Schuster, University of Wisconsin, Milwaukee; Joyce Simutis, University of Illinois, Urbana-Champaign; Barbara R. Sloan, Santa Fe Community College; William L. Smith, University of Pittsburgh; Jane S. Stanhope, American University; Sally T. Taylor, Brigham Young University; Allysen Todd, Community College of Allegheny County, Allegheny Campus; William J. Vande Kopple, Calvin College; Richard Veit, University of North Carolina, Wilmington; Sam Watson, University of North Carolina, Charlotte; Sara G. Wieland, University of Dayton; Donna Haisty Winchell, Clemson University; and Linda Woodson, University of Texas, San Antonio.

To William A. Hilliard, who gave Alan a desk with a typewriter and a telephone and a chance to stick at a daily newspaper; to John Harvey, news editor of *The Oregonian*, who instilled respect for the language and for a writer's style; and to John A. Kirkpatrick of *The Patriot-News* of Harrisburg, for his support for better news writing. Warmest gratitude to Ichiro Hayakawa and Frederick Romer Peters, who never met but shared a love of the English language that they passed on to their children.

And thanks finally and always to Laura, Megan, and Anna Fulwiler, for their three-year patience with this project.

Toby Fulwiler

Alan R. Hayakawa

The New York Times Program

The **New York Times** and **Prentice Hall** are sponsoring **Themes of The Times,** a program designed to enhance student access to current information of relevance in the classroom. Through this program, the core subject matter provided in the text is supplemented by a collection of time-sensitive articles from one of the world's most distinguished newspapers, **The New York Times.** These articles demonstrate the vital, ongoing connection between what is learned in the classroom and what is happening in the world around us.

To enjoy the wealth of information of **The New York Times** daily, a reduced subscription rate is available in deliverable areas. For information, call toll-free: 1-800-631-1222.

Prentice Hall and **The New York Times** are proud to co-sponsor **Themes of The Times.** We hope it will make the reading of both textbooks and newspapers a more dynamic, involving process.

The ABC News / Prentice Hall Video Library: Composition

Prentice Hall and **ABC News** have joined together to bring the most thoroughly integrated and comprehensive video libraries to the college market. These professional presentation packages offer both feature and documentary-style videos from a variety of ABC's award-winning news programs, including *World News Tonight, Nightline, 20/20, Primetime Live,* and others. Features in the **Composition** Video Library present current topics that can serve as springboards to discussion and writing.

Contents

*The **ESL** symbol indicates sections that have ESL boxes.

II Planning 41

III Drafting 93

IV Researching   181

V Revising   269

Editing for Effectiveness   325

Editing Grammar   465

Editing Punctuation 597

Editing Mechanics   673

VIII A Grammar Reference   801

The Blair Handbook

Writers' Purposes and Processes

You can count on one thing — attending college will mean writing papers. Whether you enroll in a first-year writing class or other courses in the arts and sciences, you'll be asked to write critical essays, research reports, position papers, book reviews, lab reports, essay exams, and sometimes a journal. You may have been given similar writing assignments in high school, so you've had some practice. The quality of writing expected in college will soon put that practice to a test.

This chapter will introduce you first to some of the concerns that students customarily have about writing in college and second to some of the reasons why writing is valued so highly in colleges and universities — as well as virtually everywhere else in the modern world.

Recently we asked a class of first-year students to talk about themselves as writers. Several described where they wrote. Amy, for example, said she did most of her writing "listening to classical music and, if it is a nice day, under trees," while Jennifer felt "most comfortable writing on [her] bed and being alone." Others described their attitudes. John, for example, said he wrote best "under pressure." Becky, however, preferred writing when she "felt strongly or was angry about something," while Kevin "hated deadlines." In fact, there proved to be as many different ways of being writers as there were students in the class. To continue our conversation, we asked more specific questions.

1 **a** **What is difficult about writing?**

Even professional authors admit that writing is not easy. What, we wondered, did first-year college writers find difficult about writing? Were their problems similar to or different from ours? Here is what they told us:

Jennifer: "I don't like being told what to write about."

Amy: "I never could fulfill the page requirements. My essays were always several pages shorter than they were supposed to be."

Jill: "I *always* have trouble starting off a paper . . . and I hate it when I think I've written a great paper and I get a bad grade. It's so discouraging and I don't understand what I wrote wrong."

Jolene: "I get so bent out of shape because I'm sometimes unsure if I need a comma."

Omar: "Teachers are always nitpicking about little things, but I think writing is for communication, not nitpicking. I mean, if you can read it and it makes sense, what else do you want?"

Ken: "Putting thoughts down on paper *as they are in your mind* is the hardest thing to do. It's like music — anyone can play a song in his head, but translating it to an instrument is the hard part."

We weren't surprised by these answers; we too remembered writing in college. We remembered wondering, What *did* teachers want? How long was *enough*? Where *did* the commas go?

■ **WRITING I: EXPLORATION**

What do you find difficult about writing? Do you have a problem finding subjects to write about? Or do you have trouble getting motivated? Or does something about the act of writing itself cause problems for you? Explain in your own words by writing quickly for five minutes without stopping. ESL: Are any of your writing difficulties related to writing in a second language? For example, do you need to translate some ideas from your native language to English? Do problems with grammar or vocabulary make it difficult for you to communicate?

1 b   What do you enjoy about writing?

In addition to the difficulties with writing, we remembered interesting and exciting times as well, so we asked our first-year students whether there was anything about writing that they enjoyed.

Jolene: "If I have a strong opinion on a topic, it makes it so much easier to write a paper."

Rebecca: "On occasion I'm inspired by a wonderful idea. Once I get going, I actually enjoy writing a lot."

Casey: "I enjoy most to write about my experiences, both good and bad. I like to write about things when I'm upset — it makes me feel better."

Darren: "I guess my favorite kind of writing is letters. I get to be myself and just talk in them."

Here again, we weren't too surprised. Then as now we prefer to write about topics that inspire or interest us, and we too find letters especially easy, interesting, and enjoyable.

WRITING 2: EXPLORATION

What do you most enjoy about writing? Is it the subject you're writing about? Is it the chance to communicate with somebody? Is there something about the process of writing that you like?

I C   What surprises are in store?

After talking with first-year students about writing, we asked some seniors about their experiences with writing. To catch their attention, we asked, "What has surprised you the most about writing in college?"

Carmen: "Papers aren't as hellish as I was told they would be before coming to college. In fact, I've actually enjoyed writing a lot of them — especially *after* they were done."

Aaron: "I have gone through many changes, and rather than becoming more complex, my style has become more simple."

Kerry: "The most surprising and frustrating thing has been the different reactions I've received from different professors."

Rob: "I'm always being told that my writing is superficial. That I come up with good ideas but don't develop them."

John: "The tutor at our writing lab took out a pair of scissors and said I would have to work on organization. Then she cut up my paper and taped it back together a different way. This really made a difference, and I've been using this method ever since."

Chrissie: "Sharing papers with other students is oh so very awkward for me. But it's extremely beneficial halfway through the semester when I trust and like my group — it is at this point that we all relax enough to talk honestly about one another's papers."

As you can see, most of our seniors found ways to cope with and even enjoy college writing, and several reported satisfying and profitable experiences sharing writing with each other. We are sorry that some students, even in their last year, could not figure out what their instructors wanted; we think there are ways to do that.

▪ WRITING 3: EXPLORATION

Think about your experience with writing in the last school you attended. What surprised you — pleasantly or not — about the experience? What did you learn or not learn?

I d Why is writing important?

We also asked these seniors why, in their last year of college, they had chosen to enroll in still another writing class. In other words, we wanted to know, "Why is writing so important to you?"

Kim: "I have an easier time expressing myself through writing. When speaking my words get jumbled — writing gives me more time, and my voice doesn't quiver and I don't blush."

Rick: "Writing allows me to hold up a mirror to my life and see what clear or distorted images stare back at me."

Glenn: "The more I write, the better I become. In terms of finding a job after I graduate, strong writing skills will give me an edge over those who are just mediocre writers."

Amy: "I'm still searching for meaning. When I write I feel I can do anything, go anywhere, search and explore."

Aaron: "I'm fascinated with the power of words."

Angel: "I feel I have something to say."

We found ourselves agreeing with virtually all of these reasons. At times writing is therapeutic, at other times it helps us clarify our ideas, and at still other times it helps us get and keep jobs.

WRITING 4: EXPLORATION

Look over the various answers given by the college seniors. Select one with which you especially agree, and explain why this aspect of writing is important to you, too.

I e   What can you learn from the seniors?

Since our seniors seemed to enjoy talking about writing, we asked them to be consultants: "What is your advice to first-year college students?" Here are their suggestions:

Aaron: "Get something down!! The hardest part of writing is starting. Forget the introduction, skip the outline, don't worry yet about a thesis — just blast your ideas down, see what you've got, then go back and work on them."

Christa: "Plan ahead. Although it sounds very dry, planning can make a writing assignment easier than doing laundry."

Victor: "Follow the requirements of the assignment to the T. Hand in a draft for the professor to mark up, then go and rewrite it. Do exactly what is asked, and remember to speak simply, the simpler the better."

Allyson: "Don't think every piece you write has to be a masterpiece. And sometimes the worst writing you do turns out to be the best. Don't worry so much about what the professor says, just worry about how you feel about what you said."

Carmen: "Imagine and create, never be content with just retelling a story. And never be content with your first telling. Dive into the experience deeply and give the reader something to dream about."

Rick: "When someone trashes your writing, thank them and listen to their criticism. It stings, but it helps you become a better writer."

Jason: "Say what you are going to say as clearly and as straight-forwardly as possible. Don't try to pad it with big words and fancy phrasing."

Angel: "Read for pleasure from time to time. The more you read, the better you write — it just happens."

Kim: "When choosing topics, choose something that has a place in your heart."

These are good suggestions to any writers: start fast, think ahead, plan to revise and edit, listen to critical advice, consider your audience, be clear, read a lot. We hope, however, that in-structors respond to your writing in critically helpful ways and don't "trash" it or put it down. Whether or not you take some of the advice will depend upon what you want from your writing: good grades? self-knowledge? personal satisfaction? clear commu-nication? a response by your audience? When we shared these suggestions with first-year students, they nodded their heads, took some notes, and laughed — often with relief.

WRITING 5: EXPLORATION

What else would you like to ask a college senior about writing or writing as-signments? Find a senior and ask. Report back the answer to your class.

		What else **do you want to know** about writing?
1	**f**	

Realizing that our first-year college writers had already re-ceived twelve years' worth of "good advice" about learning to write, we asked them one more question: "What do you want to learn about writing that you don't already know?"

Jolene: "How do I develop a faster way of writing?" (See Chapter 7, "Writing to Invent and Discover.")

Amy: "Is there a trick to making a paper longer without adding useless information?" (See especially Chapter 20, "Limiting and Adding.")

Sam: "How do I learn to express my ideas so they make sense to common intelligent readers and not just to myself?" (See suggestions in Part VI, "Editing.")

Mike: "I want to learn to talk to people comfortably with pen and paper." (See especially Chapters 4, "Writing for a Purpose," and 5, "Addressing Audience.")

Scott: "How can I make my writing flow better and make smooth transitions from one idea to the next?" (See Chapters 25, "Shaping Strong Paragraphs," and 26, "Strengthening Sentence Structure.")

Terry: "I want to learn to like to write. Then I won't put off assignments until the last minute." (See Chapter 3, "The Writing Process," and Part II.)

Jennifer: "I have problems making sentences *sound* good. Can I learn to do that?" (See Chapters 24–32.)

John P.: "I would like to develop some sort of personal style so when I write people know it's me." (See Chapter 6, "Finding a Voice.")

John K.: "I want to become more confident about what I write down on paper. I don't want to have to worry about whether my documentation is correct or my words spelled right." (See Chapters 17, "Using and Documenting Sources," and 50, "Spelling.")

Woody: "Now that I'm in college, I would like to be challenged when I read and write, to think, and ask good questions, and find good answers." (See Chapter 2, "Reading Critically to Write Well.")

Pat: "I don't want to learn nose-to-the-grindstone, straight-from-the-textbook rules. I want to learn to get my mind into motion and pencil in gear." (See Chapters 3, "The Writing Process," and 7, "Writing to Invent and Discover.")

Heidi: "I would love to increase my vocabulary. If I had a wider range of vocabulary, I would be able to express my thoughts more clearly." (See Chapter 31, "Choosing the Right Word.")

Jess: "I'm always afraid that people will laugh at my writing. Can I ever learn to get over that and get more confident about my writing?" (See Chapters 3, "The Writing Process," and 22, "Responding," and be sure that you write what you believe and know.)

We can't, of course, guarantee that if you read *The Blair Handbook* your writing will get easier, faster, longer, clearer, or more correct. Or, for that matter, that your style will become more personal and varied, or that you as a writer will become more confident and comfortable — no handbook can do that for you. Learning to be a better writer will depend upon your own interest, attention, and self-discipline. It will also depend upon the college you attend, the classes you take, and the teachers with whom you study. Actually, whether you read *The Blair Handbook* for class or on your own, if you read it carefully and practice its suggestions, you will find possible answers to all these questions and many more.

We admit that there was at least one concern for which we really had no good response. Jessika wrote, "My biggest fear is that I'll end up one semester with four or five courses that all involve writing and I'll die." Or maybe we do have a response: If you become clear, comfortable, and competent as a writer, you'll be able to handle all the writing assignments all your instructors throw your way. Even if you can't, Jessika, you won't die. It's just college.

■ WRITING 6: EXPLORATION

What else do *you* want to learn about writing? Refer to the table of contents and indicate where in *The Blair Handbook* you think you might find the answer.

SUGGESTIONS FOR WRITING AND RESEARCH

INDIVIDUAL

1. Interview a classmate about his or her writing experiences, habits, beliefs, and practices. Include questions such as those asked in this chapter as well as others you think may be important. Write a brief essay profiling your classmate as a writer. Share your profile with a classmate.

2. Over a two-week period, keep a record of every use you make of writ-

ten language. Record your entries daily in a journal or class notebook. At the end of two weeks, enumerate all the specific uses as well as how often you did each. What activities dominate your list? Write an essay based on this personal research in which you argue for or against the centrality of writing in everyday life.

COLLABORATIVE

As a class or small group project, design a questionnaire about people's writing habits and attitudes. Distribute the questionnaire to both students and faculty in introductory and advanced writing classes as well as classes in other disciplines. Compile the results to compare and contrast the ideas of students at different levels and disciplines. Write a feature article for your student newspaper or faculty newsletter reporting what you found.

2 Reading Critically to Write Well

If people learn to read and write critically, they will have learned to think critically. In fact, the goal of most college curricula is to train students to be critical readers, writers, and thinkers so they can carry those habits of mind into the larger culture beyond college. What, you may ask, does it mean to be critical? How does being a critical reader, writer, and thinker differ from being a plain, ordinary, everyday reader, writer, and thinker?

Being critical in writing means making distinctions, developing interpretations, and rendering conclusions that stand up to thoughtful scrutiny by others. Being critical in reading means knowing how to analyze these distinctions, interpretations, and conclusions. Becoming a critical thinker, in other words, means learning to exercise reason and judgment whenever you encounter the language of others or generate language yourself.

Most of *The Blair Handbook* explores strategies for helping you become an accomplished critical writer. This chapter, however, explores strategies for helping you become a more accomplished critical reader and emphasizes as well the close relationship between critical reading and critical writing.

2 a Reading to understand

Before people can read critically, they need to understand what they're reading. In order to understand a text, readers need to know something about it already. It's virtually impossible to read and understand material that is entirely new. Readers need to understand enough of the text and its ideas to fit them into a place in their minds where it makes sense and connects with other information that they already know. The following example will explain what we mean.

> **ESL** **READING STRATEGIES ACROSS LANGUAGES**
>
> If you learned to read in your native language before learning English, you can use some of the same reading strategies you developed in your native language when you read in English. For example, some features of stories, explanations, or arguments may be the same in English as in your native language. Even if they are different, the strategies you developed in your native language for identifying and understanding the distinctive features of different kinds of texts can probably be used when you read in English as well. Whenever you feel that you do not have a good grasp of the purpose or important features of something you are reading in English, take a moment to reflect on how you would have approached a similar text in your native language, and see if you can use some of the strategies.
>
> You can also take advantage of information you gained through reading in your native language when you read in English. All readers relate new information in a text to what they already know; this helps them understand the text better and allows them to make predictions about what it will contain. As you read, try to be aware of any relevant information you know about the subject, whether you gained this information in English or in your native language.

1 Reading field hockey

Have you ever watched a game for which you did not know the rules? Not long ago we saw a field hockey game for the first time, and for much of the game we were fairly confused. Players ran up and down a field swinging bent sticks at a little hard ball. We guessed — because we knew something of field games like soccer — that the objective was to drive the ball down the field with a stick and hit it into the opponent's net. But we didn't understand why the referee blew her whistle so often, or why the teams lined up in different ways at different times, or what the offensive and defensive strategies were.

In other words, we saw the same game as many fans around us but understood less of it. We were unable to "read" it. However, the more games we saw, the more we understood — about "high sticking," "strikers," "corners," "long and short hits," and the like.

Soon we found ourselves making predictions based on this knowledge, and many of these proved to be correct.

By midseason, we found ourselves correctly anticipating referee calls, second-guessing various offensive and defensive strategies, and understanding scores. When we were puzzled by something, we also learned who among the other fans could help us.

We learned to read this strange text, field hockey, by watching the game closely, by comparing it to what we already knew, by asking questions, by making trial-and-error guesses, and by consulting expert sources.

In the end, we actually learned enough not only to comprehend what we saw, but also to analyze, interpret, and evaluate it as well. We moved, in other words, from mere watchers to critical observers of field hockey.

2 Understanding field hockey

Look again at the strategies we used to understand field hockey.

First, we watched the game closely and *identified* what we saw: we looked at the number of players; their equipment; the size, shape, and markings on the field; the action as the players ran up and down the field hitting the little rubber ball with their bent sticks; and the pauses, interruptions, cheers, and whistles. We noticed that the field resembled a football or soccer field and that at each end of the field was a netlike cage defended by a well-padded player.

Second, we *questioned* what we saw: Why did the players line up in certain ways? What infractions caused the whistle to blow? How did they keep score? How long did a game last? Some of these questions we answered through further observation, some were answered by other fans.

Third, we *predicted* what would happen in the game if our assumptions were correct. We guessed, for instance, that whenever the hard rubber ball was driven into the opponent's net a score would be recorded.

Fourth, we *tested* our predictions and found that, yes, a score was recorded whenever the ball was driven into the opponent's net — with some exceptions. In this manner, through trial and error and correction, we generated our own list of the rules by which field hockey operates.

Finally, by consulting expert sources, we *confirmed* our hunches and found out more about the game. For instance, one time when we saw a ball driven into an opponent's net, a score was *not* recorded; we asked why and were told that a penalty had nullified the score. That made sense since the same thing occurs in football, soccer, and ice hockey, but we had not yet learned to recognize what constitutes a penalty in field hockey.

In other words, the more we observed and studied, the more we understood. The more we understood, the more we could assess what we saw and make critical judgments about it.

3 Reading written texts

The same strategies that taught us to "read" field hockey games apply to reading written texts. To understand a text, you need some context for the new ideas you encounter, some knowledge of the text's terms and ideas and of the rules that govern the kind of writing you are reading.

Imagine reading Mark Twain's novel *The Adventures of Huckleberry Finn* with no knowledge of American geography, the Mississippi River, or the institution of slavery. Imagine reading about the national debt without understanding basic mathematics, principles of taxation, or the meaning of *deficit spending*. The more you know, the more you learn; the more you learn, the more careful and critical will be your reading, writing, and thinking.

Many college instructors will ask you to read about subjects that are new to you; you won't be able to spend much time reading about what you already know. To graduate, you've got to keep studying new subjects that require, first, that you understand what you read and, second, that you can critically assess and write about this new understanding.

If getting a college degree requires that you read one unfamiliar text after another, how can you ever learn to read successfully? How do you create a context, learn the background, and find the rules to help you read unfamiliar texts and in unfamiliar subject areas? Let's look at how this might be done.

4 Understanding written texts

As an experiment, read the following short opening paragraph from an eight-paragraph *New York Times* story titled "Nagasaki,

August 9, 1945." When you have finished, pause for a few moments and think about what you learned from it, how you learned what you learned, and what the rest of the story will be about.

> In August 1945, I was a freshman at Nagasaki Medical College. The ninth of August was a clear, hot, beautiful, summer day. I left my lodging house, which was one and one half miles from the hypocenter, at eight in the morning, as usual, to catch a tram car. When I got to the tram stop, I found that it had been derailed in an accident. I decided to return home. I was lucky. I never made it to school that day.
>
> MICHAITO ICHIMARU

How did you do? It is possible that your reasoning went something like ours, which we have reconstructed here. Note, however, that although the following sequence presents ideas one after the other, that's not what it seemed like when we first read the passage. Instead, meaning occurred in flashes, simultaneously. Even as we read a sentence for the first time, we found ourselves reading backward as much as forward to check our understanding. Here are the experiences that seemed to be happening.

1   We read the first sentence carefully, noticing the year 1945 and the name of the medical college "Nagasaki." Through our prior historical knowledge, we *identified* Nagasaki, Japan, as the city on which the United States dropped an atomic bomb at the end of World War II —though we did not remember the precise date.

2   We noticed the city and the date (August 9) and wondered if that was when the bomb was dropped. We *asked* (silently), Is this a story about the bomb?

3   Still looking at the first sentence, a reference to the writer's younger self ("I was a freshman"), we guessed that the author was present at the dropping of this bomb. We *predicted* that this would be a survivor's account of the bombing of Nagasaki.

4   The word *hypocenter* in the third sentence made us pause again; the language seemed oddly out of place next to the "beautiful, summer day" described in the second sentence. We *questioned* what the word meant. It sounded technical enough to refer to the place where the bomb went off. Evidence was mounting that the narrator may have lived one and a half miles from the exact place where the atomic bomb detonated.

5   In the next to last sentence of the paragraph, the author says that he was "lucky" to miss school. Why, unless something unfortunate happened at school, would he consider missing it "lucky"? We *predicted* that had the author gone to school "as usual," he would have been closer to the hypocenter, which we now surmised was at Nagasaki Medical College.

6   We then *tested* our several predictions by reading the rest of the essay — which you, of course, could not do. They proved correct: Michaito Ichimaru's story is a firsthand account of witnessing and surviving the dropping of the bomb, which in fact killed all who attended the medical college, a quarter of a mile from the hypocenter.

7   Finally, out of curiosity, we looked up "Nagasaki" in an encyclopedia and *confirmed* that 75,000 people were killed by this second dropping of an atomic bomb on August 9, 1945.

You'll notice that in our seven-step example some parts of the pattern of identifying/questioning/predicting/testing/confirming occur more than once, perhaps simultaneously, and not in a predictable order. This is a slow-motion description — not a prescription or formula — of the activities that occur in split seconds in the minds of active, curious readers. No two readers would — or could — read this passage in exactly the same way. However, our reading process may be similar enough to yours that the comparison will hold up: reading is a messy, trial-and-error process that depends as much on prior knowledge as on new information.

Whenever you read new texts or watch unfamiliar events, you make meaning by following a procedure something like we did in these two examples, trying to identify what you see, question what you don't understand, make and test predictions about meaning, and consult authorities for confirmation or information. Once you know how to read successfully for basic comprehension, you are ready to read critically.

■   **WRITING 1: APPLICATION**

In a book you have been assigned to read for one of your courses, find a chapter that has not yet been covered in class. Read the first page of the chapter and then stop. Write out any predictions you have about where the rest of the chapter is going. (Ask yourself, for example, What is its main theme or argument? How will it conclude?) Finish reading the chapter and check its conclusion against your predictions. If your predictions were close, you are reading well for understanding.

STRATEGIES FOR READING TO UNDERSTAND

1. Identify. Read first for what you recognize, know, and understand. Identify what you are reading about. Read carefully, slowly at first, letting meaning take hold where it can.

2. Question. Pause, and look hard at words and phrases you don't know or understand. See if they make sense when you reread them, compare them to what you do know, or place them in a context you understand.

3. Predict. Make predictions about what you will learn next: How will the essay, story, or report advance? What will happen? What theme or thesis will emerge? What might be the point of it all?

4. Test. Follow up on your predictions by reading further to see if they are correct or nearly correct. If they are, read on with more confidence; if they are not, read further, make more predictions, and test those. Trial and error are good teachers.

5. Confirm. Check your reading of the text with others who have also read it and see if your interpretations are similar or different. If you have questions, ask them; if you have answers, share them.

2 **b** **Reading critically**

People read in different ways at different times. When they read a novel for pleasure or a newspaper to learn about current events, they read to find out "what happens." This is reading for understanding. However, when they read a novel to write a paper on it or a newspaper to find evidence for an argument, they must read beyond this literal level of basic facts. They must analyze what they've read and assess the validity of the author's assumptions, ideas, and conclusions. This is reading critically.

The rest of this chapter describes three strategies that lead readers from understanding texts to evaluating and interpreting them: previewing, responding, and reviewing. Although we've broken up the process of critical reading into three separate activities, it will become clear that they seldom occur in a simple one-two-three order.

One of our students, Richard, kept a detailed journal when he read a book titled *Iron John*. Richard shared with us both his thoughts and journal entries, some of which are reproduced here as an example of critical reading.

■ WRITING 2: EXPLORATION

Describe how you read a text when you need to understand it especially well, say, before an examination on it or when you plan to use its ideas in a paper.

■ Previewing

To preview a text, you either look it over briefly before reading it or read it rapidly once through in order to get a general sense of what it says.

First questions

You should begin asking questions of a text from the moment you pick it up. Your first questions should be aimed at finding general, quickly gleaned information, such as that provided by the title, subtitle, and table of contents.

■   What does the title suggest?

■   What is the subject?

■   What does the table of contents promise?

■   What can I learn from the chapter titles or subheads?

■   Who is the author? (Have I heard of him or her?)

■   How current is the information?

You may not ask these questions methodically, in this order, and you don't have to write down your answers, but you should ask them before you read the whole text. If your answers to these questions suggest that a text is worthy of further study, continue with the previewing process.

Here are the notes Richard took in response to his first questions.

The title itself, *Iron John*, is intriguing, suggests something strong and unbreakable.

I already know and admire the author, Robert Bly, for his insightful poetry, but have never read his prose.

The table of contents looks like fun:

1. The Pillow and the Key
2. When One Hair Turns Gold
3. The Road of Ashes, Descent, and Grief
4. The Hunger for the King in Time with No Father
5. The Meeting with the God-Woman in the Garden

Second questions

Once you've determined that a book or article warrants further critical attention, it's very helpful to read selected parts of it rapidly to see what they promise. Skim reading leads to second questions, the answers to which you should capture on note cards or in a journal.

■ Read the prefatory material: What can I learn from the book jacket, foreword, preface?

■ Read the introduction, abstract, or first page: What theme or thesis is promised?

■ Read a sample chapter or subsection: Is the material about what I expect?

■ Scan the index or notes: What sources have informed this text? What names do I recognize?

■ Note words or ideas that you do not understand: Do I have the background to understand this text?

■ Consider: Will I have to consult other sources to obtain a critical understanding of this one?

In skim-reading a text, you make predictions about coverage, scope, and treatment and about whether the information seems pertinent or useful for your purpose.

Here are the notes Richard took in response to his second question.

The jacket says, "*Iron John* is Robert Bly's long-awaited book on male initiation and the role of the mentor, the result of ten years' work with men to discover truths about masculinity that get beyond the stereotypes of our popular culture."

There is no introduction or index, but the chapter notes in the back of the book (260–67) contain the names of people Bly used as sources. I recognize novelist D. H. Lawrence, anthropologist Mircea Eliade, poet William Blake, historian/critic Joseph Campbell, and a whole bunch of psychologists — but many others I've never heard of.

These preview notes confirmed that *Iron John* is a book about men and male myths in modern American culture by a well-known poet writing a scholarly prose book in an informal style. Richard learned that Bly will not only examine current male mythology, but also make some recommendations about which myths are destructive, which constructive.

Previewing is only a first step in a process that now slows down and becomes more time-consuming and critical. As readers begin to preview a text seriously, they often make notes in the text's margin or in a journal or notebook to mark places for later review. In other words, before the preview stage of critical reading has ended, the responding stage has probably begun.

■ WRITING 3: APPLICATION

Select any unfamiliar book about which you are curious and preview it, using the two kinds of questions outlined here. Stop after ten minutes and write what you know about the text.

2   Responding

Once you understand, through a quick critical preview, what a text promises, you need to examine it more slowly. You need to begin the work of evaluating its ideas, assumptions, arguments, evidence, logic, and coherence. You need to start developing your own interpretation of what the text is all about. The best way to do this is to **respond,** or "talk back," to the text in writing.

Respond to passages that cause you to pause for a moment to reflect, to question, to read again, or to say "Ah ha!" If the text is informational, try to capture the statements that summarize ideas or are repeated. If the text is argumentative (and many of the texts you'll be reading in college will be), you need to examine the claims the text makes about the topic and each piece of supporting evidence. (See Chapter 11 for more on arguments.) If the text is literary (a novel, play, poem, or essay), pay extra attention to language features such as images, metaphors, and dialogue. In any text, notice boldface or italicized words — they have been marked for special attention.

Ask about the effect of the text on you: How am I reacting? What am I thinking and feeling? What do I like? What do I distrust? Do I know why? But do not worry too much about answering all your questions. (That's where reviewing comes in.)

Responding can take many forms — from margin notes to extensive journal entries — but it should involve writing. The more you write about something, the more you will understand it. If you own the article or book, write any questions or comments in the margins. If you don't, or in addition to this, try writing in a **journal.** A reading journal gives you a place to record responses to what you read. (See Chapter 8.) Write each response on a fresh page, with the date, the title, and the author noted. In these entries, write any and all reactions you have to the text including summaries, notes on key passages, speculations, questions, answers, ideas for further research, and connections to other books or events in your life. Note especially ideas with which you agree or disagree. Explore ideas that are personally appealing. Record memorable quotations (with page numbers) and why they strike you as memorable.

To read any text critically, begin with pen or pencil in hand. Mark places to examine further, but be aware that mere underlining, checking, or highlighting does not yet involve you in a conversation with the text. To converse with the text, you need to actively engage in one or more of the following three activities: probing, freewriting, or annotating and cross-referencing.

The following brief passage from Bly's *Iron John* is an example of a text that Richard responded to in a variety of ways:

> The dark side of men is clear. Their mad exploitation of earth resources, devaluation and humiliation of women, and obsession with tribal warfare are undeniable. Genetic inheritance contributes to their obsessions, but also culture and environment. We have defective mythologies that ignore masculine depth of feeling, assign men a place in the sky instead of earth, teach obedience to the wrong powers, work to keep men boys, and entangle both men and women in systems of industrial domination that exclude both matriarchy and patriarchy. . . .
>
> I speak of the Wild Man in this book, and the distinction between the savage man and the Wild Man is crucial throughout. The savage soul does great damage to soul, earth, and humankind; we can say that though the savage man is wounded he prefers not to examine it. The Wild Man, who has examined his wound, resembles a Zen priest, a shaman, or a woodsman more than a savage.

Richard's responses to *Iron John* illustrate all three activities; in reality, however, you would probably use no more than one or two of these techniques to critically examine a single text.

Probing

Probing is, in essence, asking deeper questions than those asked during previewing. Here, for example, are the questions Richard raised about the passage from *Iron John*:

> Bly refers to the dark side of men; does he ever talk about the dark side of women? How would women's darkness differ from men's? What evidence for either does he provide?

> Bly suggests that part of men's dark behavior is genetic, part cultural; where does he get this information? Does he think it's a 50/50 split?

> What "defective mythologies" is Bly talking about? Does he mean things like religion and politics, or is he referring to nursery rhymes and folktales?

> Bly generalizes in his opening sentence "The dark side of men is clear" — in most sentences actually. Will subsequent chapters support these statements or are we asked to accept them on faith?

> I like the distinction Bly makes between "Wild" and "savage" men. Did he coin the terms or are they used pervasively in mythology in the same way? I wonder how sharp the line really is between the two.

> When I read further in *Iron John*, will I find the Wild Man in me?

Those are good questions to ask about the passage; however, any other reader could easily think of many more. These questions are "critical" in the sense that they not only request further information from the book but also challenge the author's terms, statements, and sources to see if they will stand up under scrutiny.

The questions are also written in Richard's own language. Using your own words helps in at least three ways: first, it forces you to articulate precisely; second, it makes the question *your* question; and third, it helps you remember the question for future use.

Freewriting

Freewriting is writing rapidly and generally about an idea to see where your mind takes it. Such writing often helps you clarify your own thoughts about the ideas in the text. When you freewrite, write fast to yourself in your own natural style, not worrying about careful sentence structure, spelling, or punctuation. Nobody else need ever read this; its purpose is to help you tie together ideas from your reading with the thoughts and experiences in your own mind. (For more details on freewriting, see 7b.)

In thinking about the passage from *Iron John*, Richard made the following freewriting entry in his journal.

> 9/30 Bly praises the "Wild Man" in us, clearly separating "wildness" from barbarism and savagery — hurting others. Also suggests that modern men are wounded in some way — literally? — but only those who examine their wounds gain higher knowledge. In an interview I once heard him talk about *warriors* — men who seek action (mountain climbing? skiing? Habitat for Humanity?) to feel whole and fulfilled. So men (why not women too?) test themselves — not necessarily against other men — against nature or even themselves. Harvey says sailing is his warrior activity. Is backpacking mine?

Richard's freewrite illustrates the technique: the writer starts reacting to one idea in the text (wildness), moves to another (being wounded), digresses by remembering a TV interview, raises a question (*why not women too?*), and concludes by raising a question about himself (*Is backpacking mine?*). Freewriting raises questions at random and leaves the answers for later.

Annotating and cross-referencing

Annotating, or talking back to a text by writing in the margins, is an excellent way to make that text your own. Annotating is easier if you have your own copy of the text — otherwise you would make your annotations on Post-It notes or in a notebook with page numbers marked. As a critical reader, what would you annotate?

- Points of agreement or disagreement
- Supporting examples
- Extensions and further possibilities
- Implications and consequences
- Personal associations and remembrances

■   Connections to other texts, ideas, and courses

■   Recurring images and symbols

To move beyond annotating (commenting on single passages) to **cross-referencing** (finding relationships among passages), you can use a coding system to show that one annotation or passage is related to another and thus identify and locate patterns in the text. Some students write comments on different features of the text in different colors, reserving green for nature images, blue for important uses of key terms, red for interesting episodes in the plot, and so on. Other students write their notes first and then go back and number them, 1 for plot, 2 for key terms, and so on.

■   **WRITING 4: APPLICATION**

Keep a reading journal for an assigned reading from one of your courses. Be sure to write something in the journal after every reading session, including probing questions and freewriting. In addition, annotate the text and create a cross-referencing system as you go along to see what patterns you can discover. Write about the results of these response methods in your journal: Did they help? Which ones worked best?

3 Reviewing

To **review** you need both to reread and to "re-see" a text, reconsidering its meaning and the ideas you have about it. You need to be sure that you grasp the important points within the text, but you also need to move beyond that to a critical understanding of the text as a whole. In responding, you started a conversation with the text so you could put yourself into the book's framework and context; in reviewing, you should consider how the book can fit into your own framework and context. Review any text you have previewed and responded to as well as anything you've written in response — journal entries, freewriting, annotations, outlines. Keep responding, talking back to the text, even as you review, writing new journal entries to capture your latest insights.

Reviewing will take different forms depending on how you intend to use the text — whether or not you are using it to write a paper, for example. In general, there are two ways to review a text you have read critically — you can evaluate its soundness or significance and you can interpret its deeper meaning.

Reviewing to evaluate

Reviewing to evaluate means deciding whether you think the text accomplishes its own goals. In other words, is the text any good? Different types of texts should be judged on different grounds.

Arguments. Many texts you read in college make arguments about ideas, advancing certain claims and supporting those claims with evidence. At the responding stage, you probably started to identify and comment on the text's claims and evidence. In reviewing, you must examine and evaluate each part of the argument to see whether it is sound. (See Chapter 11 for more on arguments.)

First, is the evidence reliable? Most evidence falls into three categories. A **fact** is something that can be verified and that most readers will accept without further argument. An **inference** is a conclusion drawn from an accumulation of facts. An **opinion** reflects an author's personal beliefs and may be based on faith, emotion, or myth. All three types of evidence have their place in argumentative writing, but the strongest arguments are based on accurate facts and reasonably drawn inferences. Look out for opinions that are masquerading as facts and for inferences that are based on insufficient facts. (See 11e for more on argumentative evidence.)

Second, is each claim supported by evidence? A **claim** is a statement that something is true or should be done. Every claim in an argument should be supported by reliable and sufficient

---

ESL **EVALUATING TEXTS**

If you received reading instruction in your native language, the emphasis of your instruction may have been on understanding, remembering, and applying the information that you read rather than on critically evaluating it. You may have been taught to accept the texts you read as factual; consequently, it may seem strange or even inappropriate for you to evaluate or challenge what you read. If this is the case, you might want to discuss with your instructor this difference between your reading experience in your native language and reading in English. Or you could write about it in your journal.

evidence. If a claim is important or daring, one fact is not enough. Look for any claims that are unsupported or that are supported by insufficient evidence.

Third, do the claims combine to form a logical argument? For an argument to be logical, it must be based on reason, not emotion. It should lead from one step to the next, without any unexplained gaps or mistakes in reasoning. Look for important claims that have not been demonstrated and for gaps or flaws in the logic. (See 11e for more on argumentative logic.)

Informational texts. Reviewing to evaluate informational texts is much like reviewing to evaluate an argument's evidence and claims. You need to make sure that the facts are true, that inferences rely on facts, and that opinions presented as evidence are based on professional expertise. Informational texts don't make arguments, but they do often draw conclusions from the facts they present. You must decide whether there are enough reliable facts to justify these conclusions. Consider also whether you think the author is reliable and reasonable: Is the tone objective? Has all the relevant information been presented? Is this person an expert? (See Chapter 10 for more on the characteristics of informational writing.)

Literature. Literary texts (such as essays, short stories, poems, plays) don't generally make arguments, but they do strive to be believable, to be enjoyable, and to be effective in conveying their themes. One good way to evaluate literature is to reread journal entries in which you responded to the author's images, themes, or overall approach. Then look through the text again — guided by any annotations you've made — and ask whether you think the author's choices were good ones. Look in particular for patterns, for repeated terms, ideas, or images that will help you see the pattern of the text as a whole. Evaluating literature is often very personal, relying on individual associations and responses, but the strongest critical evaluations are based on textual evidence.

Reviewing to interpret

Reviewing to interpret means moving beyond an appreciation of what the text *says* and building your own theory of what the text *means*. An interpretation is different from the text's stated theme or thesis; it's an assertion of what you as a reader think the text is about. (See Chapter 12 for more on interpretation.)

Review any of your journal entries that articulate overall reactions to the writer's main ideas. What did you see in the text? Do you still have the same interpretation? Also reread key passages in the text, making sure that your interpretation is reasonable and is based on the text, and not a product of your imagination.

If you plan to write a critical paper about a text, it's a good idea to confirm your interpretation by consulting what others have said about that text. The interpretations of other critics will help put your own view in perspective as well as raise questions that may not have occurred to you. Try to read more than one perspective on a text. It is better to consult such sources after you have established some views of your own so that you do not simply adopt the view of the first expert you read.

■ **WRITING 5: APPLICATION**

Critically review the same reading assignment you responded to in Writing 4. First, determine whether you should evaluate it, interpret it, or both, given the purpose of your assignment. Review the text by asking the sorts of questions discussed here and then recording a summary of your evaluation or interpretation in your reading journal. Also, write about the results of this process in your journal: Did the notes you took while responding help you review the text? What would you do differently next time?

SUGGESTIONS FOR WRITING AND RESEARCH

INDIVIDUAL

Select a short text. First read it briefly for understanding, to be sure it makes sense to you. Second, read it more carefully according to the critical method described in this chapter. Finally, write a short (two-page) critical review of the text in which you recommend or don't recommend it to other readers. (For more detailed information about writing critically about texts, see Chapter 12.)

COLLABORATIVE

As a class or small group, agree on a short text to read and write about, following the suggestions in the preceding individual exercise. Share reading your reviews in small groups, paying particular attention to the claims and evidence each writer uses. Rewrite your review using the response you received from your group. (For more information about responding to other writers' texts, see Chapter 22.)

3 | The Writing Process

This chapter examines how writers write, from the time they select something to write about; through their efforts at drafting, revising, and editing; until they send their writing out into the world. It also examines strategies to help writers move more quickly and efficiently through these different stages, commonly called the **writing process.**

3 a | Describing writing as a process

Have you ever thought about how you write? What do you do, for example, when you are assigned to write a paper due in one week? Do you sit down that day and start writing the introduction? Or do you sit down but do something else instead? If you don't work on the assignment right away, do you begin two days before deadline, or is your favorite time the night before the paper is due? Do you write a few pages a day, every day, and let your paper emerge gradually? Or do you prefer to draft it one day, revise the next, and proofread it just before handing it in?

What writing conditions do you seek? Do you prefer your own room? Do you like to listen to certain kinds of music? Do you deliberately go somewhere quiet, such as the library? Or do you prefer a coffee shop, a café, or a booth at McDonald's?

With what do you write? Your own computer with WordPerfect or MacWrite, or the school's computer with whatever software is available? Your old Smith Corona portable typewriter, or a pencil on tablets of lined paper? Or do you first write with a favorite pen and then copy the result onto a computer?

Which of the habits or methods described here is the right one? Which technique yields the best results? They all work. There is no single best way to write. Different people prefer and tolerate wildly different conditions and still manage to write well.

> **ESL**
>
> **USING YOUR NATIVE LANGUAGE WHEN COMPOSING IN ENGLISH**
>
> You may want to compose in both your native language and English when working on a writing assignment. For example, you might brainstorm, make notes, or create outlines in your native language, or you could use native-language words or phrases when you're not sure of the English equivalents. Using your native language this way may help you avoid writer's block and develop fluency in English. Periodically you should evaluate the effectiveness   of your composing strategies. For instance, if you find that using a native language–English dictionary often results in unidiomatic constructions, you may want to become more familiar with a good   English–English dictionary.

While there is no one best way to write, some ways do seem to work for more people on more occasions than others. On the one hand, writing is and will always remain a complex, variable, many-faceted process that refuses to be reduced to a step-by-step procedure or foolproof formula. On the other hand, people have been writing since the dawn of history, and during that time some habits and strategies have proved more helpful than others. Learning what these are may save you some time, grief, or energy — perhaps all three.

The rest of this chapter identifies five discrete but overlapping and often nonsequential phases of the process of writing — planning, drafting, researching, revising, and editing — and explains how *The Blair Handbook* is organized to follow this process.

 WRITING 1: EXPLORATION

Answer the questions posed on the opening pages of this chapter: Where, when, and how do you usually write? What are the usual results? With what do you need some extra help? **ESL:**   If you sometimes write in your native language, compare the process you use when writing in it with the process you use when writing in English. Are any parts different? Why do you think this is so?

3 b Planning

Planning involves creating, discovering, locating, developing, organizing, and trying out ideas. Writers plan deliberately when they make notes, turn casual lists into organized outlines, write journal entries, compose rough drafts, and consult with others. They also plan less deliberately while they walk, jog, eat, read, browse in libraries, converse with friends, or wake up in the middle of the night thinking. At its beginning, a writing task has an almost unlimited number of ways of being accomplished, so planning often involves articulating these possibilities and trying some while discarding others. Planning also involves limiting those options, locating the best strategy for the occasion at hand, and focusing energy in the most productive direction.

Planning comes first. It also comes second and third. No matter how careful your first plans, the act of writing usually necessitates that you keep planning all the way through the writing process, that you continue to think about why you are writing, what you are writing, and for whom. When writers are not sure how their ideas will be received by someone else, they often write to themselves first, testing their ideas on a friendly audience, and find good voices for communicating with others in later drafts.

During the planning process for *The Blair Handbook*, for instance, we were both trying out ideas and exploring broadly and

STRATEGIES FOR PLANNING

1. Plan to plan. Make planning a first, separate stage in the writing process.

2. Plan to continue planning while you draft, research, revise, and edit.

3. When you plan, write out crazy as well as sane ideas. While the wild ones may not in themselves prove useful, they may suggest others that do.

4. When stuck for ideas, try to articulate — in writing or speech — how you are stuck, where you are stuck, and why you think you are stuck. Doing so may help you get unstuck.

narrowing our thinking to focus on our *purpose* as writers and the purposes that handbooks serve. We had to consider our *audience* — who uses handbooks. We had to find our *voice* not only as classroom teachers but as writers — would we be friendly and casual, authoritative and serious? We spent some time *inventing and discovering ideas* — figuring out what kind of information you, our readers, require in a handbook, how much of this information we already knew, and where to find what we didn't know.

The chapters in Part II focus on the concerns that most writers face at the initial stages of a writing project: writing for a purpose (Chapter 4); determining who your audience is and how to write to that audience (Chapter 5); finding your voice as a writer (Chapter 6); inventing and discovering ideas through exploratory writing (Chapter 7); and using a journal to help you create and discover ideas (Chapter 8).

■ WRITING 2: APPLICATION

Describe the strategies you commonly use when you plan papers. How much does your planning vary from time to time or assignment to assignment? Now use your favorite planning strategy for twenty minutes to plan one currently assigned paper.

3 **c** Drafting

At some point all writers need to move beyond thinking, talking, and planning and actually start writing. Many writers like to schedule a block of time — an hour or more — to draft their ideas, give them shape, see what they look like. One of the real secrets to good writing is simply learning to *sit down* and write.

Drafting is the intentional production of language to convey information or ideas to an audience. First drafts are concerned with ideas, with getting the direction and concept of the piece of writing clear. Subsequent drafting — which includes *revising* and *editing* — is concerned with making the initial ideas ever sharper, more precise and clear.

While most writers hope their first draft will be their final draft, it seldom is. Still, try to make your early drafts as complete as possible, to compose in complete sentences, to break into paragraphs where necessary, and to aim at a satisfying form. At the same time, allow time for second and third drafts and maybe more.

Sometimes it's hard to separate drafting from planning, researching, revising, and editing. Many times in writing *The Blair Handbook*, we sat down to explore a possible idea in a notebook and found ourself drafting part of a chapter instead. Other times, when we were trying to advance an idea in a clear and linear way, we kept returning instead to revise a section just completed. While it's useful to separate these phases of writing, don't worry too much if they refuse to stay separate. In most serious writing, every phase of the process can be considered recursive — that is, moving back and forth almost simultaneously and maybe even haphazardly, from planning to revising to editing to drafting, back to planning, and so on.

The five chapters in Part III describe strategies for drafting different college writing assignments, including recounting experience (Chapter 9); explaining things (Chapter 10); arguing positions (Chapter 11); interpreting texts (Chapter 12); and reflecting on the world (Chapter 13). Each chapter includes samples of student writing, in both draft and finished stages. While there are more than five kinds of college papers, the approaches to drafting in Part III apply to any number of other writing assignments.

STRATEGIES FOR DRAFTING

1. Sit down and turn on your computer, or place paper in your typewriter, or open your writing notebook and pick up a pen. Sit still and write for half an hour.

2. Plan to throw away your first page. This simple resolution will help you relax, and let the momentum of the writing take over. Later, you may decide to keep some of this page.

3. Compose in chunks. It's hard to write a whole term paper; it's fairly easy to write a section of it; it's easier still to write a paragraph. In other words, even large projects start with single words, sentences, and paragraphs.

4. Allow time to revise and edit Start drafting any writing assignment as soon as you can, not the night before it's due.

■   **WRITING 3: APPLICATION**

Describe the process you most commonly use to draft a paper. Is your way of starting consistent from paper to paper? Now, write the first draft for the paper you planned in Writing 2: sit down, and for half an hour compose as much of the paper as you can, noting in brackets as you go along where you need to return with more information or ideas.

3   d   Researching

Writers need something to write about. Unless they are writing completely from memory, they need to locate ideas and information. Even personal essays and experiential papers can benefit from additional factual information that substantiates and intensifies what the writer remembers.

As a college student, you do a form of **research** every time you write an analysis or an interpretation of a text — reading and rereading the text is the research. You do research when you compare one text to another. You do research to track down the dates of historical events. You do research when you conduct laboratory experiments, visit museums, or interview people in the college community.

Whenever you write about unfamiliar subjects, you have two choices: to research and find things out or to bluff with unsupported generalizations. Which kind of paper would you prefer to read? Which kind of writing will you profit by doing?

The five chapters in Part IV describe how to write papers that require research. We encourage you to consider research as a natural part of almost every writing assignment. However, one common college assignment — the research essay — will require you to do more extensive research, use a more formal style and format, and write a longer paper than most other assignments; Chapter 14 provides guidance on writing research essays. Research for college papers is conducted either in the library (Chapter 15) or out in the field (Chapter 16), and after gathering your information, you'll need to decide how to use and document your sources (Chapter 17). Chapter 18 provides sample research papers written about different subjects, using a variety of styles, formats, sources, and voices.

Because the documentation system appropriate for a paper

> ✔ **STRATEGIES FOR WRITING WITH RESEARCH**
>
> **1.** Consider incorporating research information into every paper you write. For interpretive papers, revisit your texts; for argument and position papers, visit the library. For experiential papers, revisit places and people.
>
> **2.** Research in the library. The library is the informational center of the university; using it well will make all of your writing and learning more substantial.
>
> **3.** Research people. Interview experts to add a lively and local dimension to your papers..
>
> **4.** Research places. Visit settings in which you can find real, concrete, current information.
>
> **5.** Learn to document sources. Whenever you do research, write down *who* (the author or speaker) said *what* (an idea or quote), *where* (publication or site), and *when* (date). Then, as needed, look up the specific forms required in specific disciplines.

depends largely on the discipline in which it is written, *The Blair Handbook* gives specific instructions and models for documenting research papers in Part VII, "Writing across the Curriculum" (Chapters 57–63). In this section, each documentation system is presented within the context of the aims and styles of its discipline: the MLA system for languages and literature, the endnote or footnote system (old MLA) for the humanities, the APA system for the social sciences, and different number systems for the sciences.

■ **WRITING 4: APPLICATION**

Describe the kind of research assignments you have done in the past. Now locate additional research information to add to the paper you began drafting in Writing 3, using any research process with which you are familiar.

3 **e** **Revising**

Somewhere in the middle to later stages of writing, writers revise the drafts they have planned, started, and researched. **Revis-**

ing involves rewriting to make the purpose clearer, the argument stronger, the details sharper, the evidence more convincing, the organization more logical, the opening more inviting, the conclusion more satisfying.

We consider revising separate from editing, yet the two tasks may not always be separable. Essentially, revising occurs at the level of ideas; editing occurs at the level of the sentence and word. Revising means reseeing the drafted paper and thinking again about its direction, focus, arguments, and evidence. Editing involves sharpening, tightening, and clarifying the language, making sure that paragraphs and sentences express exactly what you intend.

In writing *The Blair Handbook*, we revised ceaselessly to get each chapter just right. For instance, this is the third complete revision of this chapter. In our last revision we added research to our description of the writing process and changed the term *invention* to *planning* as a better description of the first stage of the writing process. And we rewrote nearly every paragraph from start to finish.

While it is tempting to edit individual words and sentences

 STRATEGIES FOR REVISING

1. Plan to revise from the beginning. Allow time to examine early drafts from beginning to end for main points, supporting evidence, and logical direction.

2. Revise by limiting your focus. Many first drafts bite off more than they can chew. When you revise, make sure your topic is narrow enough for you to do it justice.

3. Revise by adding new material. An excellent time to do additional research is *after* you've written one draft and can see exactly where you need more information.

4. Revise by reconsidering how you tell your story. Consider the effect other points of view and tenses may have on your subject.

5. Revise for order, sequence, and form. Have you told your story the only way you can, or are there alternative structures that would improve how you tell it?

as you revise, revising first saves time and energy. Revising to re-focus or redirect often requires that you delete paragraphs, pages, and whole sections of your draft — which can be painful if you have already carefully edited them.

The four chapters in Part V recommend making revision a dynamic and aggressive activity. Each chapter covers a different aspect or approach to revising. Chapter 19 discusses the revising process as a whole and recommends some general strategies. Chapter 20 shows you how to limit your focus and add important details. Chapter 21 explains the techniques of switching your perspective and transforming your paper from one form or genre to another. Writing groups and constructive ways to give and receive writing help are examined in Chapter 22.

■ WRITING 5: APPLICATION

Does your usual process for revising a paper include any of the ideas discussed in this section? Describe how your process is similar or different. Now revise the paper to which you added research information in Writing 4, using any revision techniques you are comfortable with.

3 **f** Editing

Whether writers have written three, five, or ten drafts, they want the last one to be perfect. When editing, writers pay careful attention to the language they have used, striving for the most clarity and punch possible. Many writers edit partly to please themselves, so their writing sounds right to their own ear. At the same time, they also edit for their intended readers.

The goal of editing is to improve communication. After you've spent time drafting and revising your ideas, it would be a shame for readers to dismiss those ideas because they were poorly expressed. Check the clarity of your ideas; the logic and flow of paragraphs; the precision and power of words; and the correctness and accuracy of everything, from facts and references to spelling and punctuation.

In finishing *The Blair Handbook*, we went over every word and phrase to make each one expressed our ideas precisely. Then our editors did the same. Then they sent the manuscript to other experts on writing, and they too went over the whole manuscript. Then we revised and edited again.

Because there are so many different things to look for when you edit your writing, the editing section, Part VI, of *The Blair Handbook* occupies more than half the volume. It is organized into several subparts for easy reference. **Editing for Effectiveness** covers strategies for attracting and holding your readers' attention with clear and vital language, paragraphs that flow logically from point to point, sentences that present ideas in a form matched to their content, words that express your thoughts as precisely as possible. **Editing Grammar** shows how to edit writing so that it follows the grammatical conventions of standard English and allows readers to see your ideas clearly, unencumbered by distracting or confusing mistakes. **Editing Punctuation** discusses conventional use of periods, commas, semicolons, colons, quotation marks, and other punctuation marks, and **Editing Mechanics** covers additional conventions of presenting language in written form.

 STRATEGIES FOR EDITING

1. Read your draft out loud. Does it sound right to your ear? Your ear is often a trustworthy guide, alerting you to sentences that are clear or confused, grammatically correct or incorrect.

2. Read your draft with fresh eyes. Try to imagine how your paper will be interpreted by someone who has never seen it before.

3. "Simplify. Simplify. Simplify." Henry David Thoreau offers this advice about both life and writing in his book *Walden*. Simplify words, sentences, paragraphs, the whole paper so that you make your point clearly and directly.

4. Delete unnecessary words. The easiest of all editing actions is to omit words that do not carry their own weight.

5. Proofread by reading line by line, using a ruler to cover the following sentences. This forces your eyes to read word by word and allows you to find mistakes you might otherwise miss. This is important advice even if you use a spell checker on a computer, for it will not catch all mistakes.

■ **WRITING 6: EXPLORATION/APPLICATION**

Do you edit using any of the ideas mentioned in this section? Describe your usual editing techniques. Now edit the paper you revised in Writing 5, referring to Part VI of *The Blair Handbook* as needed.

3 g   Writing with computers

Computers have revolutionized the way writers work. Unlike typewriters, ballpoint pens, or pencils, computers allow writers to change their writing infinitely and easily before the words are ever printed on paper. Writers are not committed to a final version of their text until they print it out — and even then, they can work on it again and again without retyping the whole thing over.

All **word processing programs** work in pretty much the same way: you type the words of your paper on the computer screen and store them in your computer in a **document** or **file** with a brief descriptive name (say, trees.1). When you want to work on the document again, you call it back to the screen. If, after revising the paper, you want to save both the old and the new versions, you can save the revision under a new name (trees.2), which leaves the old one as it was before you revised — should you need to return to it.

Following are several ways that computers can help you in the process of writing. Throughout *The Blair Handbook* you will find suggestions for using computers at each stage of the writing process.

❚ Improve your writing process

Computers make it easier for you to move back and forth freely as you compose. If you are like most writers, you probably jump around, planning, drafting, and researching whenever you need to; computers facilitate this process by keeping everything fluid and endlessly changeable.

2 Create distance

Computers create instant distance from your thoughts, setting them in good-looking electronic type where they seem less personal and easier to revise and edit. Some computers give you access to type styles (fonts), graphic images, and page layouts that can produce professional-looking and visually exciting papers with improved readability and aesthetic appeal. If you are adept at including fancy fonts and graphics in your text, keep in mind that these are no substitute for clear language, logic, and organization.

3 Gain access to the library

Computers equipped with modems can gain access to library information over telephone lines from your home or dormitory room. Instead of traveling physically to locate books, periodicals, and special collections, you can search for, find, and receive printouts from sources within the collections of many libraries.

4 Consult reference sources

Computer programs are becoming more sophisticated and powerful. With a keystroke you can check dictionaries, encyclopedias, thesauruses, grammar books, and style manuals, automatically coordinated with whatever text you are working on. In the future such tools will only become more numerous and better.

5 Write everywhere

Computers are increasingly smaller, more portable, and, at the same time, more powerful. You can take a portable computer that weighs only a few pounds wherever you go. Any machine that makes writing possible anywhere encourages more writing everywhere.

3 **h** Writing in English as a second language

All students in a writing class can grow as writers — those with extensive writing experience as well as those who have never written much. However, those faced with the greatest challenge may be students whose first language is not English. In addition to learning new strategies for composing and new forms for expressing what they know, nonnative speakers must attend to the conventions of language that native speakers take for granted.

Besides possible grammar and vocabulary difficulties, students who grew up speaking another language may have to adjust to the expectations and traditions of the American classroom. For example, American academic prose is often less formal than that in many other countries. Students who have learned to write in more formal systems may find instructors suggesting that they make their writing more lively or personal. Also, while U.S. schools increasingly treat writing as a multiple-draft process, instructors in many other countries may expect a piece of writing to be finished correctly the first time through.

If English is not your native language, the most important thing you can do to improve your writing skills in English is to read, write, speak, and listen attentively to as much English as you can. Use your writing class as a place to try out new ideas about writing, revising, and editing, and don't be afraid to ask your instructor and classmates for help.

Throughout *The Blair Handbook* green boxes provide information about the English language of particular interest to nonnative speakers. The letters "ESL" in green in the table of contents identify each section of the book that includes one of these specially marked boxes. This symbol also appears before the special ESL writing suggestions found in many chapters in Parts I, II, and III. Finally, an ESL index is provided at the back of the book to help you locate topics that you may find helpful.

SUGGESTIONS FOR WRITING AND RESEARCH

INDIVIDUAL

Study your own writing process as you work on one whole paper from beginning to end, taking notes in your journal to document your habits and practices. Write an analytic sketch describing the way you write and speculating about the origins of your current habits.

COLLABORATIVE

With your classmates, form interview pairs and identify local professional writers or professors who publish. Make an appointment with one of these practicing writers, interview him or her about the writing process he or she practices, and report back to the class. Write a collaborative report about writers in your community; make it available to other writing classes or interested faculty.

PART TWO

Planning

Writing doesn't happen accidentally, but on purpose. When you initiate your own writing task, you know why you are doing it. However, when you write in response to assignments, an instructor determines much of your purpose for you. To produce good writing, regardless of who started it, you need to understand and take control of your own purpose.

Think first about the range of purposes that writing serves. People write to discover what's on their minds, figure things out, vent frustrations, keep records, and remember things. They write to communicate information, ideas, feelings, experiences, concerns, and questions. And they sometimes write for the pleasure of creating new forms, imaginary concepts, and vicarious experiences. This chapter examines three broad and overlapping purposes of writing — *discovering, communicating,* and *creating* — and discusses strategies to accomplish each one effectively.

4 **a** **Writing to discover**

Writing helps people discover ideas, relationships, connections, and patterns in their lives and the world. In college, writing can help you discover paper topics, develop those topics, expand and explain ideas, and connect seemingly unrelated material in coherent patterns. In this sense, writing is one of the most powerful learning tools you have.

Writing can do this because it makes language — and therefore thought — visible and permanent. It allows you to examine your ideas from a distance, holding them still long enough to be understood, critiqued, rearranged, and corrected.

Christopher Fry, a playwright, once said, "My trouble is that I'm the sort of writer who only finds out what he is getting at by the time he's got to the end of it." In other words, his purpose and plan become clear only *after* he's written a whole draft; he knows that the act of writing will help him find his way. But rather than considering this inventive power of writing a *problem* — to use Fry's word — you can consider it a *solution* to many other problems. Once you know that writing can generate ideas, advance concepts, and forge connections, then you can use it deliberately and strategically to help you write college papers.

Discovery can happen in all writing. Anytime you write, you may find new or lost ideas, implications, and directions. However, sometimes it pays to write with the specific intention of discovering. **Discovery writing** is often used before actual drafting to explore the subject and purpose of a paper or to solve writing problems once drafting and revising have begun. (See Chapter 7.)

■ WRITING 1: EXPLORATION

Describe one time you used writing for discovery purposes. Did you set out to use writing this way or did it happen more accidentally? Have you used it deliberately since then? With what results?

4 b Writing to communicate

The most common purpose for writing in college is to communicate to an audience. As a college student, you may write comments on papers to friends, essays and exams to instructors, and applications and résumés to potential employers. To communicate, your writing needs to be *clear* — so that others understand you — and *effective* and *correct* — so that they believe you. In college writing, there are several common specific purposes within the general purpose of communication.

Recounting experience. The purpose of recounting experience is to share something about yourself with others, and in the process, teach them something they don't already know. Assignments may ask you to explore personal experiences that were especially meaningful to you. Put your readers in your shoes and make them experience how you were thinking and feeling at the time. (For more on recounting experience, see Chapters 9 and 13.)

Explaining information and ideas. The purpose of explaining information and ideas is to make them clear to somebody who knows less about them than you do. You do this best by stating them simply and providing plenty of details and examples. Pay special attention to the sequence of your explanation — let your readers absorb the idea or information a little at a time. Keep attention focused on the thing you are explaining, and cite sources to explain where the information came from. (For more on explaining, see Chapters 10 and 12.)

Arguing positions. The purpose of arguing is to persuade your readers that your position is the best one. College assignments frequently ask you to explore both sides of ideas, issues, and policies or to explore various interpretations of a text, but then to take a stand on one side. (For more on arguments, see Chapters 11 and 12.)

■ **WRITING 2: EXPLORATION**

List all of the communicative writing you have done in the past two weeks. Who were your audiences? Were all of your acts of communication successful? If not, why not?

4 **c** **Writing to create**

When you write to create, you pay special attention to the way your language looks and sounds — its form, shape, rhythm, images, and texture. Though the term *creative writing* is most often associated with poetry, fiction, and drama, it's important to see any act of writing, from personal narratives to research essays, as creative.

When you write to create, you pay less immediate attention to your audience and subject and more to the act of expression itself. Your goal is not so much to change the world or to transmit information about it, but to transform the experience or ideas into something that will make your readers pause, see the world from a different angle, and perhaps reflect upon what it means. You want your writing itself — not just the information it contains — to affect your readers emotionally or aesthetically as well as intellectually.

In most college papers, your primary purpose will be to communicate, not to create. However, nearly every writing assignment has room for a creative dimension. Be especially careful when writing for emotional or aesthetic effect in an otherwise communicative paper that your creativity serves a purpose and that the communicative part is strong on its own. You want your creative use of language to enhance, not camouflage, your ideas.

1 Intensifying experience

When Amanda recounted her experience picking potatoes on board a mechanical harvester on her father's farm, she made her readers *feel* the experience as she did by crafting her language to duplicate the sense of hard, monotonous work.

> Potatoes, mud, potatoes, mud, potatoes, that was all I saw in front of me. They moved from my right side to my left, at hip level. A conveyor belt never stopping. On and on and on.
>
> The potatoes passed fast, a constant stream. My hands worked deftly, pulling out clods of dirt, rotten potatoes, old shaws, and anything else I found that wasn't a potato. It was October, the ground was nearly frozen, the mud was hard and solid. Cold. Dirt had gotten into my yellow and yet brown rubber gloves, had wedged under my nails increasing my discomfort.

2 Experimenting with form

Keith created a special language effect in an otherwise traditional and straightforward academic assignment by writing a poetic prologue for a research essay about homeless people in New York City. The full essay includes factual information derived from social workers, agency documents, and library research.

> The cold cement
> no pillow
> The steel grate
> no mattress
> But the hot air
> of the midnight subway
> Lets me sleep.

Using the poetic form creates a brief emotional involvement with the research subject, allowing readers to fill in missing information with their imagination. Note, however, that the details of the poem (*cold cement, steel grate, subway*) spring not from the writer's fanciful imagination, but from his research notes and observations.

■ **WRITING 3: EXPLORATION**

Describe one time in which your primary purpose in writing was to create rather than to discover or communicate. Were you pleased with the result?

4 d Approaching assignments

For most assignments in first-year writing classes, the overriding purpose is to communicate. However, there are two other ways in which purpose is involved. First is your instructor's purpose asking you to recount an experience, make an argument, interpret a text, and so on. Second is the purpose you yourself impart to the assignment: even if you know you have to communicate something, you still have to figure out what, in particular, you want to *say* about it. Good papers are written only when writers find a way to achieve their own purposes.

How can you make sure your writing serves both your instructor's purpose and your own? Let's look at two typical writing assignments taken from a first-year writing class.

Assignment 1

Write a personal essay in which you explore a recent personal experience of some significance to you. Write the paper in such a way that your audience understands this event's importance and what you learned from it. After reading your paper, the audience should know more about both you and the experience you describe.

Assignment 2

Write a research essay in which you investigate and report on one of the following: (a) an issue recently reported in the news media that has some local impact, or (b) a local institution, including what it does, how it works, who works there, and what issues concern it. In completing this report, include information derived from library research, site visitations, and expert interviews.

There are at least four steps you should take when considering the purpose of any assignment: (1) find and state the instructor's general purpose, (2) find a specific topic that interests you, (3) find your approach to the topic, and (4) make the topic your own.

1 Find the instructor's purpose

Look at the assignment for key words. First find the **direction words,** verbs that tell what action to perform or nouns that imply a specific activity. Next find the **subject words,** nouns and their adjectives that specify the subject of the assignment. These key words will tell you what your instructor expects you to write about, what the final paper is supposed to accomplish, and what steps you are expected to take in order to write the paper.

In Assignment 1, the direction word is *explore*, which suggests an open approach allowing the writer to investigate the subject and examine different dimensions of it. The subject words are the combination of *personal experience* and *significance*, words that define what is to be explored. The experience also needs to be *recent*. How recent? This is a good question to ask the instructor.

In Assignment 2, the direction words are *investigate* and *report*. Additional words of nearly equal importance are *research*, *visitations*, and *interviews* because they suggest the nature of the investigation. The subject words are *issue* and *institution*. It would be a good idea to explore with your instructor the definition of *institution* — would that include, for instance, the hot dog cart downtown, Woolworth's, and the elementary school?

■ WRITING 4: APPLICATION

Identify the key words in a current writing assignment and write an analysis of how the direction words and subject words determine your purpose.

2 Find a topic

The subject words in an assignment are usually quite broad; they define a set of possible subjects but don't tell you which one to write about. You must select a subject to write about and then narrow it down to a workable topic. **Subjects** are large and inclusive: *sports* or *soccer*. Within each subject there are many **topics:** *the advantage of playing competitive sports in high school* or *the lessons of comradeship learned playing soccer*. Finding a good topic serves both your instructor's purpose (because it will result in a better paper) and your own (because it allows you to influence the direction your paper will take).

First, select a subject that attracts and holds your interest. A subject you find interesting will cause you to ask more and better questions and result in more, not less, involvement in later drafts.

Second, once you've selected your subject, find a topic within the subject that retains your interest but is also manageable. A common problem is attempting to write about every aspect of a subject, but doing so superficially. Narrowing the focus allows for more detailed research and a written product of greater depth.

In Assignment 1, you would limit the experience to something important, but particular. If, for example, you wanted to describe your experience playing high school sports, you could limit the topic to one year rather than four, to one game rather than all season, or to one theme (such as competition) rather than all possible themes (comradeship, team spirit, losing with grace, and so on).

In Assignment 2, if pollution were your issue, you could limit the topic to one kind of pollution (water rather than air), to a specific incident (the closing of a public beach), or to a particular place or time (when a closing occurred). Each act of narrowing offers the opportunity to report more detailed and concrete information.

■ WRITING 5: APPLICATION

For a current writing assignment, select a subject that interests you. Make a list of ten possible topics within the subject. Then write a paragraph on each of the three that interest you most. Select the one that has the most possibilities and begin your writing or research.

3 Determine your approach

A paper needs information and ideas. Exactly *what* information and ideas and exactly *how* you are supposed to find them are determined partly by the assignment as your instructor first stated it — the subject words tell you "what" and the direction words tell you "how." But your approach is also determined by the assignment as you've refined and narrowed it.

To write Assignment 1, you would need to tap into remembered knowledge. This assignment requires organizing your memories in a meaningful way. Though your memory might contain most of what you need, you might also consider revisiting the site of the experience or talking with others involved to retrieve more useful details.

To write Assignment 2, you would need to know about recent issues that will have some impact on a local institution. It may be profitable to read newspapers or listen to the news. (For more information on research, see Part IV.)

■ WRITING 6: APPLICATION

Identify the necessary sources of information for a current writing assignment. What do you need to know to select your topic in the first place? What else do you need to know to complete your paper?

4 Own the assignment

To understand and take seriously assignments given by your instructor, you need to make them your own. One way to own an assignment is to figure out how the assignment benefits you in some way — answers a nagging question, is fun or challenging, helps somebody else you care about. Another way to own an assignment is to break it down to a manageable size so you can handle it with the information and time available.

Always ask yourself whether this paper seems worth doing — not just as a class requirement and not just to satisfy your instructor's expectations, but for yourself. If it doesn't, then you might need to refocus your topic or you might need to find a new angle. If it seems that you might be taking the assignment in a direction your instructor might object to, be sure to check before going too far.

In Assignment 1, you'd need to find an experience you want to explore and that still has something to teach you. For example, writing about the time you sat on the bench during a soccer game might teach you and your readers more than writing about the time you scored the winning goal. You can also make a personal experience paper your own by writing with insider knowledge, including little-known details that will make the events come alive.

In Assignment 2, ask yourself whether the topic will be relevant and interesting to you and to your readers. For example, you might choose a familiar institution (the Registrar's Office) that you can approach from a novel angle (what do the daily operations look like from the perspective of the receptionist?). Or you could find an institution somewhat off the beaten track (the junkyard on

GUIDELINES FOR APPROACHING ASSIGNMENTS

1. Analyze the direction words and subject words that identify your instructor's purpose. If the assignment asks for analysis, be sure your writing stresses the analytical rather than the personal or persuasive.

2. Narrow the topic to one that is both interesting and manageable. Think first of as many possible topics as you can; think second about those that truly interest you; think third about the one you can best manage in the time available.

3. Write from what you know. Plan to research what you don't know. Figure out the best way to collect and organize both kinds of information.

4. Own the assignment by adopting an original approach that will separate your paper from less imaginative ones.

the edge of town) or one that readers might not normally think of as an institution (the pretzel man at the mall).

■ WRITING 7: APPLICATION

Make a current writing assignment your own by adopting one of the strategies described in this section. What works best for you — connecting an assignment to something you are already an expert in or taking on something new about which you have many questions?

SUGGESTIONS FOR WRITING AND RESEARCH

INDIVIDUAL

1. Select a topic in which you are interested and write about it in each of the three modes described in this chapter. First, begin with *discovery* writing to yourself, perhaps in a journal. Second, write a letter to *communicate* with somebody about this interest. Third, write *creatively* about it in a short poem, story, or play. Finally, describe your experience writing in these different modes.

2. Write a letter to your writing teacher in which you explain what makes a good writing assignment and why. Make a proposal for a

writing assignment you would want to do for your writing course. Request a response.

COLLABORATIVE

1. Select a topic that your whole writing group is interested in writing about. Divide your labors so that some of you do discovery writing, some do communicative writing, and some write creatively. With scissors and tape, combine your efforts into a single coherent, creative piece of *collage writing*, making sure that some of every member's writing is included in the finished product. Perform a reading of this collage for the other groups; listen to theirs in return.

2. As a class, research the assignments you were given in high school. Examine old notebooks and papers you have saved for evidence of teachers' instructions. Write a collaborative research essay on the topic "American School Assignments: The Good, the Bad, and the Ugly," in which you describe and analyze what is typical and explain what separates the good from the bad.

Every piece of writing is read by somebody. And whether a piece of writing is "good" is largely a question of how effectively it communicates with those who read it, the audience. To write effectively, you need a sense of who your audience is. You need to know not only that it is "Professor Watkins" or "the readers of the school paper," but also what these people are like: what they know and don't know, what they find interesting or boring, what they expect from writing in general or this paper in particular. Armed with this knowledge, you can improve your chances of effective communication by shaping your writing to suit your particular audience.

Writers and speakers share many of these concerns. Both want to explain their ideas fully in language their audience understands but not to overexplain or to bore the audience. They want to use a tone that seems appropriate for the occasion and to present your ideas in the best possible order. Speakers have one advantage over writers: they can see their audience's reactions from moment to moment. They know exactly when something needs to be explained more carefully or when a humorous story isn't going well. Writers can only imagine the reactions of the people reading their work. To overcome this disadvantage, writers must carefully consider in advance the best way to address their readers.

All college papers are written to at least two audiences: the writer and the instructor. In addition, some college papers are also addressed to classmates. And some of them are published for an even wider public in a student newspaper or literary magazine. While these audiences all need clarity and coherence, honesty and insight, exactly what constitutes clarity or honesty differs from audience to audience.

5 a Understanding college audiences

It might help to think of the different audiences you will address in college as existing along a continuum, with those closest to and best known to you at one end and those farthest from and least known at the other end.

Self ——— Peer ——— Instructor ——— Public

While your particular continuum will always differ from somebody else's, the principle — that you know some audiences better than others — will be the same.

The better you know your readers, the more you know their likes, dislikes, interests, politics, and so on. For example, every semester you go through the process of learning about your instructors. At the beginning, you may be unsure of what your instructors expect from your papers. By the end, though, you know what topics or approaches each one appreciates, what sort of thinking each expects you to demonstrate, even what sort of jokes each one prefers — or whether some of them would rather *not* see jokes in your papers. Similarly, the closer your readers are to you, the more likely you will have beliefs and opinions in common.

This doesn't mean there is no chance of writing effectively to unknown readers or to readers who are unlike you. It only means that you need to take a little more time figuring out what they will respond best to. For any piece of writing you do, take some time early in the process to identify your readers and to think about what they're like. You may want to do some discovery writing to help you record and organize your thoughts about these people. (See Chapter 7.)

■ **WRITING 1: EXPLORATION**

Think back over the past several weeks and list all the different audiences to whom you have written. To whom did you write most often? Which audiences were easy for you to address? Which were difficult? Why? **ESL:** Do you think English-speaking audiences have expectations that differ from the expectations of audiences who speak your native language?

5 **b** | **Shaping writing for different audiences**

To shape your writing for a particular audience, you first need to understand the qualities of your writing that can change according to audience. The context you need to provide; the structure, tone, and style you use; and your purpose for writing can all be affected by your audience. (Structure, tone, and style are important elements of voice. See Chapter 6.)

Context

Different audiences need different contexts (different amounts or kinds of background information) in order to understand your ideas. Find out whether your audience already knows about the topic or whether it's completely new to them. Consider whether any terms or ideas need explaining. For example, other students in your writing group might know exactly who you mean if you refer to a favorite singer, but you might need to identify him or her further in a paper for your instructor. Also consider what sort of explanation would work best with your audience.

Structure

Every piece of writing is put together in a certain way — some ideas are discussed early, others late; transitions between ideas are marked in a certain way — similar ideas are either grouped together or treated separately. How you structure a paper depends in large part on what you think will work best with your particular audience. For example, if you were writing an argument for someone who disagrees with your position, you might begin with the evidence that you both agree with and later introduce more controversial evidence.

Tone

The tone of a piece of writing conveys the writer's attitude toward the subject matter and audience. How do you want to sound to your readers? Do you want them to hear you as friendly? Businesslike? Angry? Serious? Humorous? Puzzled? You may, of course, have a different attitude toward each audience you address. In addition, you may want different audiences to hear you in different ways. For example, when writing to yourself, you won't mind sounding confused. When writing to instructors, though, you will want to sound confident and authoritative.

Style

Style is largely determined by the formality and complexity of your language. Writing ranges from the chatty and casual — full of contractions and sentence fragments — to the elevated and elaborate. You need to determine what style your readers expect and what style will be most effective in a given paper. Fellow students might be offended if you write in anything other than a friendly style, but some instructors might interpret the same style as disrespectful.

Purpose

The explicit purpose of your writing depends more upon you and your assignment than on your audience. (See Chapter 4.) However, certain purposes are more likely to accompany writing to particular audiences than others. Also, there are unstated purposes embedded in any piece of writing, and these will vary depending on who you're addressing. For example, is it important that your readers like you? Or that they respect you? Or that they give you good grades? Always ask yourself what you want a piece of writing to do for — or to — your audience and what you want your audience to do in response to your writing.

1 Writing to yourself

Every paper you write is addressed in part to yourself. However, most papers are also addressed to other people — your instructor, your peers, or a public audience. Journal writing is your opportunity to write to yourself and yourself alone. When you write to yourself alone, you don't need to worry about context, since you are the audience and you know what you know. However, if you make a journal entry that you might want to refer to later, it's a good idea to provide sufficient background and explanation to help you remember the event or the idea described when you turn to it again later.

Similarly, you don't need to worry about structure or organization. In fact, the structure that will occur most naturally will be free association, in which writing down one idea triggers another. You may want to start each journal entry on a new page and to record the date of each one.

In writing to yourself, neither style nor tone matters much. When you are the reader of your own writing, choose words, sentences, rhythms, images, and punctuation that come easiest and most naturally to you. If you want to capture a particular mood or event accurately, however, you may need to make your tone reflect your feeling at the time of the event.

Writers write to themselves in journals for many purposes, from simple reminders to deliberate acts of discovery to the therapeutic venting of frustration. (See Chapter 8.)

2   Writing to peers

Your peers are your equals — people of similar age, background, or situation. Your peers in an academic situation are other students. Some of your assignments will ask you to consider the other students in the class to be your audience. Even though your instructor will still read and evaluate your paper, remember that you are writing to and for your classmates. In fact, part of your instructor's evaluation will probably be based on how well you anticipate and meet the needs of your classmates. Other writing addressed to peers includes written responses to papers shared in writing groups.

The primary difference between writing to yourself and writing to peers is the amount of context you need to provide to make sure your readers understand you. If your paper is about a personal experience, you need to provide the explanations and details that will allow your readers — who did not have your experience — to fully understand the events and ideas you describe. If your paper is about a subject that requires research, you may need to provide background information that makes the topic comprehensible and interesting to your peers.

The overall structure of a paper written with your peers as part of the audience will depend primarily on what sort of paper it is — a personal narrative, an argument, or whatever. However, keep your peers' knowledge and interests in mind when deciding what information to put where. For example, if you are structuring an argument so that it begins with commonly accepted claims and builds to more radical ones, consider carefully which claims your classmates will consider self-evident and which they will need to be convinced of.

In papers addressed to peers, the tone and style are more likely to be friendly and casual than in essays addressed to the instructor alone. Your classmates will respond best to honesty and directness — they will see right through any pretentious or stuffy language. Remember, though, that most papers are addressed to peers only in part; your instructor will still want you to use a tone and style that are appropriate for college writing.

The explicit purpose of writing to peers is usually communication: you either want to let them know your response to their writing or you want to recount an experience, explain an idea or information, or argue a position. The implicit purposes can be quite complex; after all, these are some of the people you will be living with, going to class with, and socializing with for the rest of your college career. In a writing class, the most important implicit purpose is probably to establish a good working rapport with your classmates by being honest, straightforward, and supportive.

3 Writing to instructors

Instructors are among the most difficult audiences for whom to write. First, they usually make the assignments, which means they know what they want and it's your job to figure out what that is. Second, they often know more about your subject than you do. Third, different instructors may have quite different criteria for what constitutes good writing. And fourth, each instructor may simultaneously play several different roles: a helpful resource, a critic, an editor, a coach, and, finally, a judge.

It is often difficult to know how much context to provide in a paper written for an instructor, unless the assignment specifies it. For example, in writing about a Shakespeare play to an English professor, should you provide a summary of the play when you know that he or she already knows it? Or should you skip the summary information and write only about ideas original with you? The safest approach is to provide full background, explain all ideas, support all assertions, and cite authorities in the field. Write as if your instructor needed all this information and it were your job to educate him or her.

When writing papers to instructors, be sure to use a structure that is conventional for the type of paper you are writing. For example, personal experience papers are generally either chronologically arranged or use flashbacks. (The chapters in Part III describe conventional structures for each type of paper discussed there.)

In a writing class, you may encounter some confusion about the proper tone and style to use. Because your instructor is also your coach, you might feel it's appropriate to write in a friendly tone and a casual style. But even the friendliest, most casual instructor may want you to write more conventionally as training for other academic writing. Use a fair, respectful, and authoritative tone and a somewhat formal and sophisticated style.

One of your instructor's roles is to help you learn to write effective papers. But another role is to evaluate whether you have done so and, from a broader perspective, whether you are becoming a literate member of the college community. So your implicit purpose when you write to instructors is to demonstrate your understanding of conventions, your knowledge, your reasoning, and your originality.

Demonstrating your understanding of conventions

The first thing your instructor may notice about your writing is what it looks like: Is it typed or handwritten? Does it have a title page? A title? A name? How long is it? How neat is it? How legible is the handwriting, how accurate the typing? How clear and correct are the first few sentences? Did it meet the deadline? Instructors make these observations rapidly — sometimes unconsciously — before they have finished reading the paper. Such observations, although superficial, often determine your instructor's attitude toward the whole paper. He or she is more likely to look favorably on a paper that is neat and free of spelling and grammatical errors than on one that is wrinkled and full of mechanical mistakes.

Of course, academic conventions require more than a neat appearance and correct spelling and grammar. They also affect your decisions about context, structure, tone, and style. Early in the term, your safest stance is to cover all the traditional bases of good academic writing, demonstrating that you can write about teacher-assigned subjects using a conventional structure and style, providing full explanations, supporting assertions with authority, using specialized terms carefully, and documenting all borrowed information. Later in the term, once you have established your academic legitimacy, your experiments with form, style, theme, and voice may be more readily accepted by your instructor. In truth, many instructors get tired of reading safe prose, written to satisfy requirements; they usually welcome creativity.

Demonstrating knowledge

Your paper must also have substance. Even a good-looking paper must demonstrate what you know and how well you know it. If, for instance, you argue for the reintroduction of wolves into Yellowstone National Park, your instructor will look to see how much you know about wolves and parks. Your instructor will ask: Are the definitions, details, and explanations clear? Are they believable? Where did the information come from? How up-to-date is it? What sources were consulted? How reputable do they seem? Any paper must contain solid information.

You also must demonstrate the knowledge you've gained in your writing class about the writing process itself — your understanding of planning, drafting, researching, revising, and editing, as shown in your paper.

Demonstrating reasoning

Your papers should show your ability to reason logically, support assertions, and be persuasive whether you are writing a personal essay or an argument. In arguing for the reintroduction of wolves into Yellowstone, you would need to demonstrate that there are good reasons for doing so and refute opposing arguments. Your reasoning would show not only in your convincing details but also in the logic that holds your argument together.

Demonstrating originality

No matter what the writing assignment, you can find creative ways of doing it. When assignments are open-ended, do not choose the first topic that comes to mind or that seems easiest to do. Let your mind roam over more unusual ideas. When topics are limited, allow yourself to consider some risky or new approach. When you provide information to support your assertions, dig for something more unexpected than those most commonly known. When you open or conclude a paper, try to surprise your reader.

4 Writing to public audiences

Writing to a public audience is difficult for all writers because it is usually both diverse and unknown. The public audience can include people who know both more and less than the writer; it can contain experts who will correct the slightest mistake and novices who need even simple terms explained; it can contain opponents looking for reasons to argue with you and supporters looking for reasons to continue support. And you are unlikely to know many of these people personally.

You usually have some idea of who these anonymous readers are or you wouldn't be writing to them in the first place. Still, it is important to learn as much more as you can about the beliefs and characteristics they have that may be relevant to the point you intend to make. What is their educational level? What are their political, philosophical, or religious beliefs? What are their interests?

When you don't know who your audience is, you need to provide context for everything you say. If you are referring to even well-known groups such as NCAA or NAACP, write out the full names the first time you refer to them; if you refer to an idea as "postmodern," define or illustrate what the term means. Your writing should be able to stand by itself and make complete sense to people you do not know.

The structure of public writing should be logical and clear; your opening paragraph should get rapidly to the point; your conclusion should be emphatic, perhaps making your strongest point. Your tone will depend on your purpose, but generally it should be fair and reasonable. Your style will depend on the publication you are writing for.

Your explicit purpose for writing to public audiences is usually communicative — to inform them about something they do not already know or persuade them to see something from your point of view. However, your implicit purpose is to demonstrate that you are literate and well educated, which means being sure your ideas are clear and your language is correct.

▮ WRITING 2: EXPLORATION

How accurate do you find the discussion in this section of different college audiences? Describe circumstances that confirm or contradict the description here. If instructors are not your most difficult audience, explain who is.

SUGGESTIONS FOR WRITING AND RESEARCH

INDIVIDUAL

Select a paper written recently for an instructor. Rewrite the paper for a publication, choosing either a student newspaper or local magazine. Before you start writing, make notes about what elements need to be changed: context, structure, tone, style, or purpose. When you finish recasting the paper to this larger, more public audience, send it to the publication.

COLLABORATIVE

In a group of five students, select a topic of common interest. Write about the topic (either as homework or for fifteen minutes in class) to one of the following audiences: yourself, a friend who is not here, your instructor, an appropriate magazine or newspaper. Share your writing with one another and together make a list of the choices you needed to make for each audience.

6 Finding a Voice

Each individual speaks with a distinctive voice. Some speak loudly, some softly, others with quiet authority. Some sound assertive or aggressive, while others sound cautious, tentative, or insecure. Some voices are clear and easy to follow, while others are garbled, convoluted, and meandering. Some create belief and inspire trust, while others do not.

To some extent writers' voices, like their personalities, may be determined by factors beyond their control, such as their ethnic identity, social class, family, or religion. In addition, some elements of voice evolve as writers mature, such as their mode of thought (logical or intuitive) and their political or philosophical stance (liberal or conservative). But writers also exert a great deal of control over their language. They shape the style (simple or complex), tone (serious or sarcastic), and many other elements. The point is to control as many elements of voice as you can.

6 a Defining voice

The word *voice* means at least two distinctly different things. First, it is the audible sound of a person speaking (*He has a high-pitched voice*). Applied to writing, this meaning is primarily metaphoric — unless writers read their work aloud, readers don't actually *hear* writers' voices. Speaking voices distinguish themselves by physical auditory qualities such as pitch (high, low, nasal), pace (fast, slow), tone (angry, assertive, tentative), rhythm (regular, smooth, erratic), register (soft, loud), and accent (southern, British, Boston). Writing voices do much the same when the language on the page re-creates the sound of the writer talking. Careful writers control, as much as they can, the sound of their words in their readers' heads.

Second, voice is a person's beliefs and values (*Her voice needs to be heard*). Every writer's text conveys something of the person behind the words. The self that is conveyed often goes well beyond personality to include the writer's political, philosophical, and so-cial values as well as his or her commitment to certain causes (civil rights, gun control, the environment). In addition, what writ-ers stand for may be revealed in the way they reason about things — in an orderly, scientific manner or more intuitively and emo-tionally.

■ **WRITING I: EXPLORATION**

In your own words, describe the concept of voice. Do you think writers have one voice or many? Explain what you mean.

6 b **Analyzing the elements of voice**

Readers experience a writer's voice as a whole expression, not a set of component parts. However, to understand and gain con-trol of your own voice, it helps to examine the individual elements that combine to make the whole.

1 Tone

Tone is your attitude toward the subject and audience: angry, joyous, sarcastic, puzzled, contemptuous, anxious, respectful, friendly, and so on. Writers control their tone just as speakers do — by adopting a particular perspective or point of view, selecting words carefully, emphasizing some words and ideas over others, choosing certain patterns of inflection, and controlling the pace with pauses and other punctuation.

To gain control of the tone of your writing, read drafts of your paper aloud and listen carefully to the attitudes you express. Try to hear your own words as if you were the audience: How does this writer feel about the subject matter? How does this writer feel about the people being addressed? Decide whether the overall tone is the one you intended, and reread carefully to make sure every sentence contributes to this tone. (See Chapter 28 for more on tone.)

2 Style

Style is the distinctive way you express yourself. It can change from day to day and from situation to situation, but it is somehow always *you*. The style you choose for a particular paper will largely depend on your subject, purpose, and audience for that paper. Style in writing is determined by the level of formality (formal, informal, colloquial) and by the simplicity or complexity of your words, sentences, and paragraphs.

To gain control of the style of your writing, learn to analyze the purpose and audience of your writing. (See Chapters 4 and 5.) Decide how you wish to present yourself, given this purpose and audience, and examine your writing carefully to see that your style suits the occasion.

3 Structure

Structure is the organization of and relationships among the parts within your text: where you start, where you conclude, how things are ordered in between, which ideas are grouped together, how explicit transitions between ideas are. Some pattern or logic — structure — holds together all thoughtful writing and reveals something of the thought process that created it. A linear, logical structure presents you as a linear, logical thinker; a circular, intuitive structure presents you as creative and intuitive.

To gain control of the structure of your writing, outline both before and after you draft and revise so that your outline accurately reflects your reasoning patterns. (For more on outlining see 7f and 19c.) Also consider the structure of your paragraphs and sentences. (See Chapters 25 and 26.)

4 Values

Your **values** include your political, social, religious, and philosophical beliefs. Your background, opinions, and beliefs will be part of everything you write, but you must learn when to express them directly and when not to. For example, including your values would enhance a personal essay or other autobiographical writing, but it may detract attention from the subject of a research essay.

To gain control of the values in your writing, consider whether the purpose of the assignment calls for an implicit or explicit statement of your values. Examine your drafts for opinion and judgment words which reveal your values, and keep them or take them out as appropriate for the assignment.

5 Authority

In writing, **authority** comes from knowledge and is projected through self-confidence and control. You can only exert and project real authority over material you know well, whether it's the facts of your personal life or carefully researched information. The more you know about your subject, the more sure of yourself you will sound, and the more readers will hear authority in your voice.

To gain control over the authority in your writing, do your homework, conduct thorough research, and read your sources of information carefully and critically. (See Chapter 2.)

■ WRITING 2: APPLICATION

Describe your own writing voice in terms of each of the elements outlined in this section (tone, style, structure, values, authority). Then compare your description with a recent paper you have written. In what ways does the paper substantiate your description? In what ways does it differ from your description? How do you account for any differences? **ESL:** Is your writing voice in English different from your writing voice in your native language? If you are aware of any differences, try to describe them in terms of the elements discussed in this chapter. Are there qualities of your voice in one language that you would like to transfer to your voice in the other language?

6 **c** Hearing a range of voices

Looking closely at a few distinct voices focused on a common subject may be instructive. As you read the writing in this section, ask yourself what effect each voice creates and how it achieves that effect.

The following three passages have been taken from texts written by experts about trees. In that sense, they are all explanatory writing, meant to inform curious readers about the characteristics of certain trees. But the voices are quite distinct.

1 Scientific/technical

WHITE OAK (*Quercus alba*) leaves are deciduous, 5 to 9 inches long and 2 to 4 inches wide, with 7 to 9 rounded lobes divided by narrow, variable sinuses often extending nearly to midrib. The oblong acorns are set in a bowl-like cup covered with warty scales. The gray bark is in narrow, vertical blocks of scaly plates. Grows 80 to 100 feet tall and 3 to 4 feet in diameter, with a wide-spreading crown.

C. FRANK BROCKMAN, *TREES OF NORTH AMERICA*

In this passage from a guidebook, Brockman wanted to provide unbiased information about a particular kind of tree and omitted any language that would have led readers away from this purpose. The language — including the precise adjectives (*oblong, vertical, warty*), the mathematical terms, the Latin names, the technical terminology (*deciduous, lobes, sinuses*), and the absence of words that make value judgments — contributes to an objective or neutral style typical of scientific and technical writing. Brockman thus presents his description as beyond debate, totally believable, so there can be no question of authority here. In other words, there really *is* a voice in this passage — the objective voice of scientific certainty.

2 Familiar/informal

White Oak is the best known oak of all. Common throughout New England, its beauty attracted the attention of early colonists. In open places White Oak develops a broad symmetrical crown and majestic appearance. The light gray scaly bark is characteristic; so are the leaves with five to nine rounded lobes. . . . White Oak prefers rich soil but grows slowly. The large painted acorns in shallow cups were eaten by Indians. It is an outstanding lumber tree, used for furniture, boats, and barrels.

HERBERT S. ZIM AND ALEXANDER C. MARTIN,
TREES: A GUIDE TO FAMILIAR AMERICAN TREES

In another guidebook, the writers project a voice that is informed but also informal and familiar. They provide identifying information about the oak itself (the two middle sentences) but also comment on its beauty, majesty, history, and usefulness. Unlike the scientific voice, this friendly and engaging voice makes value judgments freely, calling the tree *beautiful* and *majestic*, the lumber *outstanding*. The simple style and the friendly tone suggest that this guide was written to a young audience.

3 Creative/poetic

> There are two spiritual dangers in not owning a farm. One is the danger of supposing that breakfast comes from the grocery, and the other that the heat comes from the furnace.
>
> To avoid the first danger, one should plant a garden, preferably where there is no grocer to confuse the issue.
>
> To avoid the second, he should lay a split of good oak on the andirons, preferably where there is no furnace, and let it warm his shins while a February blizzard tosses the trees outside. If one has cut, split, hauled, and piled his own good oak, and let his mind work the while, he will remember much about where heat comes from, and with a wealth of detail denied to those who spend the week in town astride a radiator.
>
> ALDO LEOPOLD, *SAND COUNTY ALMANAC*

The voice in this passage is quite different from those in the first two passages. The writer's purpose here is not so much to teach readers to identify oak trees as to reflect on the role of nature in the lives of overcitified people. To do so, Leopold creates a strongly creative and poetic voice, leading first with a teasing riddle — what are *two spiritual dangers in not owning a farm*? He follows with folksy yet carefully crafted parallel answers (*To avoid the first. . . . To avoid the second*). He writes all the while in simple, direct language, with many action verbs (*plant, cut, split, hauled, piled*) and colloquial terms (*lay a split*). This more creative voice suggests that Leopold wants his readers to understand trees emotionally as well as rationally. His voice speaks with an authority not of the laboratory but of a personal life long lived and reflected on.

■ WRITING 3: EXPLORATION

List the nonfiction writers whose voices you remember best. After each writer, list the qualities that seem to make his or her voice distinctive.

6 d Hearing the range of one voice

All writing has a voice, even when it strives for apparent objectivity, as the first excerpt in the previous section does. In college writing, you will need different voices to address different purposes, audiences, and situations. To illustrate this range, we have selected five samples of writing from the portfolio created by Julie during her first semester in a college writing class.

▌1 Private

The first example comes from Julie's journal. In this entry, she writes to herself about her first assignment.

> 10/8   I'm really struggling with my personal experience paper — I can't seem to get a good balance of description, dialogue, and depth — I get carried away with one and forget the others! I'm so frustrated — I'm going to give it one more attempt — I've written more of these drafts than any other paper and I'm getting so sick of it — it seems to be getting worse instead of better. . . .

Julie's journal-writing voice was never meant for publication. It is not carefully crafted or revised like the other examples in this chapter. In fact, there's a raw, unfinished effect with all the dashes. Her entry reads the way personal journals read — private, unedited, off the record, but believably honest.

▌2 Personal

The following is the opening paragraph of a personal experience paper by Julie recounting when she played varsity tennis in high school.

> Bounce. Bounce. Bounce. The sound is driving me insane, but I just can't get the nerve to toss the ball and serve. Am I scared? Yes. Of what, this girl or this match? This girl, this girl scares me. She is a natural talent. How many times is that cross-court forehand shot going to rip past me? Nuts! I am going to lose plain and simple. I'll just have to deal with it.

Julie invites her readers into the inner and usually hidden reaches of her mind with her personal — but not private — voice. This clipped, internal voice sounds authentic and believable (*Am I scared? Yes.*) and invites her audience to identify with her feelings of self-doubt. It is the individual voice of a good tennis player at a vulnerable moment.

3 Informative

This example is taken from the early pages of Julie's research essay focusing on a center for emotionally disturbed children.

> The Huron Center provides residential treatment for a limited number of emotionally disturbed children in the upper Midwest. The Center contains forty-five beds: thirty are reserved for long-term care, generally six months to a year; ten are assessment beds, reserved for stays of up to two months; and five are crisis beds, reserved for stays of ten days or less. The children live together, supervised by twelve staff members.

Julie's voice here is that of a reporter presenting and explaining information; she provides numerical facts in a methodical manner and makes no value judgments. By adopting this neutral voice she puts herself in the background but reveals nevertheless her careful attention to detail and organization.

4 Committed

The following is Julie's concluding paragraph from the research essay on the Huron Center.

> The Huron Center is a haven for needy people who have run out of options for helping their own children. However, the small, dedicated staff is stressed to the limit. They often work sixty-hour weeks, with children whose troubles they do not always understand. Emotionally disturbed children need more, not less, help, but federal funds have dried up. Where will future resources come from? The public must wake up and help the children!

Julie here is an advocate for the plight of the understaffed center; she now uses judgment words (*haven, needy, stressed*) and ends with an emotional plea (*wake up and help the children!*). Her voice is committed, but at the same time it remains precise, controlled, and focused on the facts.

5 Reflective

Julie's final paper was an examination of her own voice as a writer. The following passage appears on the last page of her reflective essay.

During the semester my real growth has been in thinking rather than writing. In my first paper, I had to rewrite and rewrite until readers could actually see me playing tennis. In my research paper I found statistics, interviewed staff members, and gathered evidence to show that the Huron Center was in trouble. In writing these papers, I've learned to slow down my thinking, to review it, to return to it, and make it clearer and clearer and clearer. That's what good writing is really about, isn't it, being clear?

Here Julie leads off with what seems to be a surprising discovery — that she has grown more as a thinker than as a writer. She mulls over her experiences and then concludes whimsically with a rhetorical question aimed as much at herself as at the reader. In the end, her voice is reflective, quite different from either the neutral voice or the committed voice from her research essay, but sharing some traits with the voices of both her journal and her personal essay.

 WRITING 4: EXPLORATION

How would you desribe your own writing voice? How many voices do you have? Explain.

QUESTIONS FOR EXAMINING YOUR VOICE

1. *Tone.* Read drafts aloud and listen to the attitude you hear. Is it what you intend? If not, how could you change it?

2. *Style.* What image of yourself do you create through your language? Is it formal or informal? Complex or simple?

3. *Structure.* What does your structure say about your manner of thinking? Is it careful and tight? Loose and flexible? Logical? Intuitive? Which do you want it to be?

4. *Values.* Do your beliefs show through when you speak on paper? Do you want them to?

5. *Authority.* Where does your writing voice sound especially knowledgeable and confident? Where does it sound tentative and unsure? What can you do to make it more consistently authoritative?

SUGGESTIONS FOR WRITING AND RESEARCH

INDIVIDUAL

1. Read a book or a substantial number of articles by one of your favorite writers of nonfiction. Make notes about the features of voice that you notice; describe them in terms of tone, style, structure, values, and authority. Write a report in which you explain and analyze the writer's voice.

2. Collect and examine as many samples of your past writing as you have saved. Also look closely at the writing you have done so far this semester. Write a paper in which you describe and explain the history and evolution of your voice and the features that most characterize your current writing voice.

COLLABORATIVE

Exchange recently written papers with a partner. Examine your partner's paper for the elements of voice. In a letter, each of you describe what you find. How does your partner's perception of your voice match or differ from your own? Now do individual assignment number 2, including your partner's assessment as part of your analysis.

Writers **invent** when they create new ideas. Writers **discover** when they relocate their own forgotten ideas or learn by reading or listening to others' ideas. Invention and discovery work together by helping writers locate the huge amount of information stored in long-term memory, generate new ideas, and make connections among ideas.

Writers need to do invention and discovery writing in virtually all phases of the writing process: when they limit and focus assignments; when they find topics and approaches to topics; when they develop answers to questions and solutions to problems; and when they figure out openings and conclusions, arrange arguments, and place supporting examples. While the writing techniques discussed in this chapter can be used at any point in the writing process, this chapter focuses on helping you get started at the beginning of a project.

Invention and discovery writing is often the best antidote to "writer's block." It lets you start writing by writing, even when you think you have nothing to say. All writers have had the experience of written language generating or modifying thought. It happens whenever they find themselves writing something they hadn't thought about before they started writing. This occurs because writing lets people *see* their own ideas — perhaps for the first time — and then react to and even change those ideas. When you realize that writing has this potential, then you can use it as a tool for invention and discovery.

▪ WRITING 1: EXPLORATION

Describe the procedures you usually use to start writing a paper. Where do you get the ideas — from speaking? listening? reading? writing? Do you do anything special to help them come? What do you do when ideas don't come?

7 **a**   Brainstorming

Brainstorming is systematic list making. You ask yourself a question and then list a variety of answers. The point is to get down on paper as many ideas or pieces of information as you can. Sometimes you can do this best by setting goals for yourself: *What are seven possible topics I could write about for my paper on pollution?* Sometimes you can do it by leaving the question open-ended: *What are all the sources of lake pollution that I've heard about?* Each item in your list becomes a possible direction for your paper.

By making a list, you let one idea lead to the next. For example, while making a grocery list you may write "eggs" on a piece of paper, which reminds you of "bacon," "bread," and "orange juice." By challenging yourself to generate as long a list as possible, you force yourself to find and record even vague, half-formed ideas in concrete language, where you can examine them and decide whether they're worth pursuing.

Writers brainstorm at different stages to help them decide where to go next. For example, some writers make lists of possible topics to write about. Other writers think through their whole papers by making quick lists of possible approaches, options, and directions.

7 **b**   Freewriting

Freewriting is writing quickly without rules. You depend simply on one word to trigger the next, one idea to lead to another. It is an attempt to find a focus by writing intensely, nonstop, without censoring the words and ideas before you have a chance to look at them. Try the following suggestions for freewriting:

1   Write as fast as you can for a fixed period of time, say five or ten minutes, about whatever is on your mind.

2   Do not allow your pen to stop moving until the time is up.

3   Don't worry about what your writing looks like or how it's organized — the only audience for this writing is yourself.

If you digress in your freewriting, fine. If you misspell a word or write something silly, fine. If you catch a fleeting thought that's especially interesting, good. If you think of something you've never thought of before, wonderful. And if nothing interesting comes out — well, maybe next time. The following five-minute freewrite shows John's attempt to find a topic for a local research project.

> I can't think of anything special just now, nothing really comes to mind, well maybe something about the downtown mall would be good because I wouldn't mind spending time down there. Something about the mall . . . maybe the street vendors, the hot dog guy or the pretzel guy or that woman selling T and sweatshirts, they're always there, even in lousy weather — do they like it that much? Actually, all winter. Do they need the money that bad? Why do people become street vendors — like maybe they graduated from college and couldn't get jobs? Or were these the guys who never wanted anything to do with college?

John's freewrite is a typical one: he starts with no ideas but soon finds some. Notice too that his writing is unstructured; in freewriting a writer covers a lot of mental ground by jumping wherever his or her thoughts lead. This turned out to be an especially useful freewriting exercise — John found himself raising questions about street vendors and ended up doing a paper on the hot dog man.

ESL **FREEWRITING AS A WAY TO DEVELOP FLUENCY**

Writing in a second language can be frustrating when you are trying to pay attention to your ideas, sentence structures, word choices, and so on. Many ESL writers have discovered that freewriting helps tremendously with this problem. If you haven't tried freewriting before, you might find it hard at first not to stop and carefully check each sentence, but with continued practice this activity should help you to postpone editing and improve your fluency in English. If you have access to a computer, try invisible writing, described in 7c.

7 c Invisible writing

An interesting way to freewrite on a computer is to turn down the brightness level of the monitor until you cannot see your words. Then begin writing rapidly, concentrating on the ideas in your head. The advantage of not seeing your writing is that your own words will not distract you. If you are among the many writers who find it easier to return to a draft than to start fresh, with invisible writing you can fool yourself into thinking that you have, in fact, already started your paper: after five or ten minutes of freewriting, when you turn the monitor back on, you will have a text to return to.

7 **d** Looping

Looping or loop writing is an extended variation of freewriting in which you do a series of freewrites, each one focusing more closely on the issue becoming foremost in your mind. To loop, follow this procedure:

1   Freewrite for ten minutes to discover a topic or advance the one you are working on.

2   Review your freewrite and select one sentence closest to what you want to continue developing. Copy this sentence, and take off from it, freewriting for another ten minutes. (John might have selected the sentence *Why do people become street vendors?* for further freewriting.)

3   Repeat step 2 for each successive freewrite to keep inventing and discovering.

Looping focuses freewriting. Its effect is like repeated clustering, explained in 7g.

7 **e** Asking a reporter's questions

Writers who train themselves to ask questions are also training themselves to find information. Reporters train themselves to ask six basic questions, *Who? What? Where? When? Why?* and *How?* Having this regular repertoire of questions will help you discover information. For any paper topic, try asking yourself the following questions:

Who was involved?

What happened?

Where did this happen?

When did it happen?

Why did it happen?

How did it happen?

7 f   Making outlines

Outlines are, essentially, organized lists. In fact, outlines grow out of lists, as writers determine which ideas go first and which later, which have equal weight with others and which need to be subordinated to others. Formal outlines use a system of Roman numerals, capital letters, Arabic numerals, and lowercase letters to create a hierarchy of ideas. Some writers prefer informal outlines, using indentations to indicate relationships between ideas.

When Carol set out to write a research essay on the effect of acid rain on the environment in New England, she first brainstormed a list of areas that such an essay might cover:

What is acid rain?

What are its effects on the environment?

What causes it?

How can it be stopped?

After some preliminary research, Carol produced this outline:

   I. Definition of acid rain

  II. The causes of acid rain

      A. Coal-burning power plants

      B. Automobile pollution

 III. The effects of acid rain

      A. Deforestation in New England

          1. The White Mountain study

          2. Maple trees dying in Vermont

      B. Dead lakes

 IV. Solutions to the acid rain problem

Note how Carol rearranged the second and third items in her original list to talk about causes before effects. The very act of making the outline encouraged her to invent a structure for her ideas. Moving entries around is especially easy if you are using a computer because you can see many combinations before committing yourself to any one of them. The rules of formal outlining also cause you to search for ideas. If you have a Roman numeral *I* you need a *II*; if you have a capital letter *A* you need a *B*. Carol immediately thought of coal-burning power plants as a cause, and then she brainstormed to come up with an idea to pair with it.

Outlines are most useful if you let them grow and develop as you write, changing them whenever new arrangements occur to you.

7 g   Clustering

A clustering diagram is a method of listing ideas in a nonlinear way to reveal the relationships among them. Clustering is

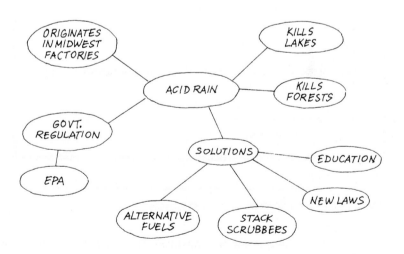

useful both for inventing and discovering a topic and for exploring a topic once you have done preliminary research. To use clustering, follow this procedure:

1 Write a word or phrase that seems to be the focus of what you want to write about. (For her research paper, Carol wrote down *acid rain.*)

2 Write ideas related to your focus in a circle around the central phrase with lines connecting the new ideas to the focus phrase. If one of the ideas suggests others related to it, write those in a circle around it (Carol did this with her idea *solutions*).

3 If one idea (like *solutions*) begins to accumulate related ideas, start a second cluster with the new term in the center of your paper.

SUGGESTIONS FOR INVENTION AND DISCOVERY

1. Brainstorm a list of five possible topics to write about.

2. Freewrite for ten minutes about the most interesting topic on your list.

3. Write invisibly on your computer for ten minutes about your topic.

4. Loop back in your freewriting, selecting the most interesting or useful point, and freewrite again with that point as the focus.

5. Ask the reporter's questions about the topic.

6. Make an outline of a possible structure for your paper.

7. Cluster ideas about your topic and then on a related idea that occurs during the initial clustering.

SUGGESTIONS FOR WRITING AND RESEARCH

INDIVIDUAL

Invent a technique for finding ideas that is not included in this chapter. Write a short section for this chapter explaining the technique, providing samples of it, and giving clear directions to teach other writers how to use it.

COLLABORATIVE

Find a common writing topic by having each person in the group or class select one of the invention and discovery techniques described in this chapter and practice using it for ten minutes. Make a list on the board or on the overhead projector of the topic ideas generated this way. Then ask each individual to select one topic, not his or her own, and write for another five minutes about that topic. Again make a list of topics and the important ideas generated about them. Discuss the ideas together and try to arrive at a consensus on a common writing topic.

Journals allow people to talk to themselves without feeling silly. They help college students figure out and reflect on what is happening in their personal and academic lives. Sometimes students focus their journal writing narrowly, on the subject matter of a single discipline; other times they speculate broadly, on the whole range of academic experience; while still other times they write personally, exploring their private thoughts and feelings. College instructors often require or recommend that students keep journals so they can monitor what and how students are learning. Just as often, however, students require journals of themselves, realizing that journals are useful whether they're handed in or not.

8   **a**   **Understanding journals**

In simplest terms, journals are daily records of people's lives (*jour* is French for "day"). Journals are sometimes called *diaries, daybooks, logs, learning logs,* or *commonplace books.* No matter what you call them, the entries written in them are likely to include whatever thoughts, feelings, or plans are on your mind when you sit down to write. In this sense, a journal can be whatever you want it to be, recording whatever snippets of life you find interesting and potentially useful. Certain characteristics, however, remain true for most journals.

Sequence

Journals capture thoughts sequentially, from one day to the next. Dating each entry allows you to compare ideas to later and earlier ones and provides an ongoing record of your constancy, change, or growth. You thus end up documenting your learning over the course of a semester or a project.

Audience

Journals are written to help writers rather than readers. A journal is a place to explore what's important to you, not to communicate information or ideas to someone else. While you may choose to share entries with readers whom you trust, that is not the reason you keep a journal. An assigned journal may initiate an informal conversation between you and your instructor. As such, it has much in common with notes, letters, and other informal means of communication. In most cases, assigned journals receive credit but not specific grades.

Language

Journal writing is whatever writers want it to be. There are few rules — you should use whatever type of language you feel most comfortable with. (The exception may be an assigned journal.) Your focus should be on *ideas* rather than on style, grammar, spelling, or punctuation. In journal writing, focus on *what* you want to say and use the word, spelling, or punctuation that comes most readily to mind.

Freedom

You should be free to get things wrong in journals and not be penalized, even when the journals are assigned. Used in this way, journals are practice and discovery books — you can put new concepts into your own words, try out new lines of reasoning, and not worry about completing every thought. If something doesn't work the first time, try it again in subsequent entries — or abandon it entirely.

Academic journals differ from diaries, daybooks, and private journals in important ways. Whereas diaries and the like record any and all events of the writer's day, academic journals focus more consistently on ideas under study in college. Academic journals might be described as a cross between private diaries written solely for the writer, and class notebooks, which record an instructor's words. Like diaries, journals are written in the first person about ideas important to the writer; like class notebooks, they focus on a subject under study in a college course.

Diary ————⟶ Academic journal ⟵———— Class notebook

Your journal includes *your* thoughts, reactions, reflections, and questions about your classes and ideas, written in your own language. Think of your academic journal as a personal record of your educational experience.

■ WRITING I: APPLICATION

Describe your experiences with journals. Have you ever kept one for school before? In which class? With what result? Have you ever kept one on your own? With what result? Do you still keep one? What is it like?   **ESL:** Have you ever kept a journal in your native language? What was it like? If you are unfamiliar with journals, what do you think of the idea of journal writing?

8 b Using journals in college

Journals written on many subjects and in many formats can benefit college writers. Academic journals are most often associated with writing classes, but they can be worthwhile for other classes, too. Not only academic journals but also personal journals are useful to college writers because they help students become better thinkers and writers. Double-entry journals are distinguished not so much by their subject matter as by their unique format, which allows writers more easily to make connections between the academic and the personal, the literal and the reflective.

▮ Journals in the writing class

Journals are often assigned in writing classes both to help student writers discover, explore, advance, and critique their writing projects and to help instructors monitor and informally assess students' development as writers.

Use your journal to find topics to write about, to try out introductions and arguments, to record relevant research and observations, to assess how the paper is turning out, and to make plans for what to do next. In the following journal entry, John tells himself what to do in the next draft of a paper describing his coaching of an eighth-grade girls' soccer team.

> 9/16   I'm going to try to use more dialogue in my paper. That is what I really think I was missing. The second draft is very dull. As I read it, it has no life. I should have used more detail.

I'll try more dialogue, lots more, in draft 3. I'll have it take place at one of my practices, giving a vivid description of what kids were like.

I have SO MUCH MATERIAL. But I have a hard time deciding what seems more interesting.

John's entry is an excellent example of a writer critically evaluating himself and, on the basis of that evaluation, making plans to change something.

Use your journal to record regularly what you've learned about writing through class discussions, through reading other student papers, and through reviewing your own writing. Near the end of John's writing course, he reflected in his journal about what he'd learned so far.

11/29   I've learned to be very critical of my own work, to look at it again and again, looking for big and little problems. I've also learned from my writing group that other people's comments can be extremely helpful — so now I make sure I show my early drafts to Kelly or Karen before I write the final draft. I guess I've always known this, but now I actually do it.

■ **WRITING 2: APPLICATION**

Keep a journal for the duration of a writing project, recording in it all of your starts, stops, insights, and ideas related to the project. At the end, consider whether the journal presents a fair portrait of your own writing process.

2 **Journals across the curriculum**

Journals are good tools for learning any subject. They are especially useful in helping you clarify the purposes of a course, pose and solve problems, keep track of readings, raise questions to ask in class, practice for exams, and find topics for paper assignments.

In science or mathematics, when you switch from numbers to words, you often see the problem differently. In addition, putting someone else's problem or question into your own language makes it yours and so leads you one step further toward a solution.

One of the best uses for journals is to make connections between college knowledge and personal knowledge. When you record personal reflections in a literature or history journal, you may begin to identify with and perhaps make sense of the otherwise distant and confusing past. When you write out trial hypotheses based on personal observations in a social science journal, you may eventually discover good ideas for research topics, designs, or experiments.

■ WRITING 3: APPLICATION

Think of any course you are now taking that does not require a journal. Could you find a use for a journal in that class? What topics would you explore?

3 Personal journals

While *The Blair Handbook* emphasizes academic writing, we believe that personal journal writing has many powerful benefits for college writers. In personal journals writers can explore their feelings about college, prospective majors, getting along with a roommate, the frustration of receiving a low grade on a paper, the weekend party, or a new friend. When you keep a journal in a writing class, it's a good idea to mark off a section for personal entries. Whether you share these with your instructor should be up to you.

■ WRITING 4: APPLICATION

Keep a personal journal for two weeks, writing faithfully for at least ten minutes each day. Write about whatever is on your mind. Follow the guidelines for keeping a journal at the end of this chapter. After two weeks, reread your entries and assess the worth of such writing to you.

4 Double-entry journals

Double-entry journals can help you separate initial observations from later, more reflective observations. To make such a journal, divide each page in a notebook with a vertical line down the middle. On the left side of the page, record initial impressions or data observations; on the right side, reflect on the meaning of what you first recorded, either at the same time or later on.

While such notebooks originated in the sciences, allowing lab scientists to collect data at one time and to speculate about them later, these notebooks also serve well in other courses. In an English class, for example, you can make initial observations about

Summary	What I think
pp. 3-12. Celie's mother is dying so her father starts having sex with her. She got pregnant by him twice and he sold both of her babies. Celie's mother died and he got married again to a very young girl. Mr. is a man whose wife died and he has a lot of children. He wants to marry Celie's sister Nettie. Their father won't let him. He says Nettie has too much going for her so he let him have Celie.	Why did Celie's father sell her kids? How could Mr. take Celie if he wanted Nettie so much? I think Celie's father is lowdown and selfish. A very cruel man.
pp. 13-23. Celie got married to Mr. and his kids don't like her and he beats her. While Celie was in town she met the lady who has her kids. She was a preacher's wife. Nettie ran away and came to stay with Celie. Mr. still likes her and puts her out because she shows no interest in him. Celie tells her to go to the preacher's wife's house and stay with them because she was the only woman she saw with money.	I think it's wrong to marry someone to take care of your children and to keep your home clean. I think Celie was at least glad to know one of her children was in good hands. I am glad Nettie was able to get away from her dad and Mr., hopefully the preacher & wife will take her in.
pp. 24-32. Shug Avery, Mr.'s old girlfriend and also an entertainer, came to town. Mr. got all dressed up so he can go see her, he stayed gone all weekend. Celie was very excited about her.	How could he go and stay out with another woman all weekend? Why didn't he marry Shug? Why was Celie so fascinated with Shug?

the plot of a story on the left, while raising questions and concerns on the right, as we see in Susan's entry about Alice Walker's novel *The Color Purple* shown on page 85. In the left column, she recorded the plot; in the right column, she noted her personal reaction to what she was reading.

ESL **JOURNALS FOR SECOND LANGUAGE WRITING**

When you are writing in a language other than your native language, journals can be especially useful. Since you don't have to be concerned with correctness, you can work on developing fluency. A journal is a good opportunity for experimenting with language; you may want to try out new vocabulary or use different kinds of sentence structures.

For an academic journal, your instructor will most likely expect you to do more than summarize assigned reading. Consider using a double-entry journal. Summarize what you have read in one column and then comment on or raise questions about the reading in the column next to it.

To help you develop your English vocabulary, use a journal to keep an ongoing list of new words as described in 31c. This list can include both vocabulary you learn in your classes and words or idioms that you hear outside of class.

■ **WRITING 5: APPLICATION**

Keep a double-entry journal for a two-week period. On one side of the page include notes on books you are reading. On the other side, write your own reactions to these ideas. At the end of two weeks, ask yourself if this technique works for you.

---

8 **c** **Experimenting with journals**

If you are keeping a journal for the first time, write often and regularly on a wide variety of topics, and take risks with form, style, and voice. Notice how writing in the early morning differs from writing late at night. Notice the results of writing at the same time every day, regardless of inclination or mood. Try to develop the habit of using your journal even when you are not in an academic environment. Good ideas, questions, and answers don't always wait for convenient times. Above all, write in your most comfortable voice, and don't worry about someone evaluating you. The following selection of journal entries illustrates some of the ways journals can be used.

1 Planning

Journals can help you plan any project by providing a place to talk it over with yourself. Whether it's a research paper, a personal essay, or a take-home examination, you can make journal notes about how to approach it, where to start, or who else to consult before actually beginning a draft. Here is an entry from Peter's journal kept for his first-year writing class.

> 10/12   Well, I switched my research topic to something I'm actually interested in, a handicapped children's rehabilitation program right here on campus. My younger brother was born deaf and our whole family has pitched in to help him — but I've never really studied what a college program could do to help. The basis of my research will be interviews with people who run the program — I have my first appointment tomorrow with Professor Stanford.

Sometimes planning means venting frustration about what's going wrong; other times it means exploring a new direction or topic. Journal writing is ultimately unpredictable: it doesn't come out neat and orderly, and sometimes it doesn't solve your problem — but it provides a place where you can keep trying to solve it.

2 Learning to write

Part of the content of a writing course is the business of learning to write. You can use a journal to document how your writing is going and what you need to do next to improve it. In the following example, Bruce reflects on his experience of writing a report.

> 10/3   I'm making this report a lot harder than it should be. I think my problem is I try to edit as I write. I think what I need to

do is just write whatever I want. After I'm through, then edit and organize. It's hard for me though.

Bruce chastises himself for making his writing harder than need be and reminds himself about the process he learned in class. Journals are good places to monitor your own version of the writing process and to document what helps you the most.

3 Writing to learn

The act of regular writing clarifies ideas and causes new ones to develop. In that sense, journal writing is an invention and discovery technique. (See Chapter 7.) Julie, who kept a journal about all the authors she studied in her American literature course, noticed a disturbing pattern and wrote in her journal to make some sense of it.

> 5/4   So far, the first two authors we have to read have led tragic, unhappy lives. I wonder if this is just a coincidence or if it has something to do with the personality of successful writers. Actually, of all people, writers need a lot of time alone, by themselves, thinking and writing, away from other people, including, probably, close family members. The more I think about it, writers would be very difficult people to live with, that's it — writers spend so much time alone and become hard to live with.

Julie used the act of regular journal writing to process and figure out ideas, make interpretations, and test hypotheses. To write to learn is to trust that as you write, ideas will come — some right, some wrong; some good, some bad.

4 Becoming political

College is a good place in which to develop a wider awareness of the world, and a journal can help you examine the social and political climate you grew up in and perhaps took for granted. In the following example, Jennifer uses her journal to reflect on sexist language.

> 3/8   Sexist language is everywhere. So much so that people don't even realize what they are saying is sexist. My teacher last year told all the "mothers-to-be" to be sure to read to their chil-

dren. What about the fathers? Sexist language is dangerous because it so easily undermines women's morale and self-image. I
try my hardest not to use sexist language, but even I find myself
falling into old stereotypes.

Jennifer recorded both her awareness of sexist language in society
and her own difficulty in avoiding it.

5   Evaluating classes

Journals can be used to capture and record feelings about
how a class is going, about what you are learning and not learning. In the following entry, Brian seemed surprised that writing
can be fun.

9/28   English now is more fun. When I write, the words come
out more easily and it's not like homework. All my drafts help me
put together my thoughts and retrieve memories that were hidden
somewhere in the dungeons of my mind. Usually I wouldn't like
English, like in high school, but I pretty much enjoy it here. I like
how you get to hear people's reactions to your papers and discuss
them with each other.

Entries like this can help you monitor your own learning process.
Instructors also learn from candid and freely given comments
about the effects of their teaching. Your journal is one place where
you can let your instructor know what is happening in class from
your point of view.

6   Letting off steam

Journals are good places to vent frustration when things
aren't going well — personally or academically. College instructors
don't assign journals to improve students' mental health, but they
know that journals can help. Kenyon wrote about the value of
keeping his journal for one semester.

10/14   This journal has saved my sanity. It got me started at
writing. . . . I can't keep all my problems locked up inside me,
but I hate telling others, burdening them with my problems —
like what I'm going to do with my major or with the rest of my life.

In many ways, writing in a journal is like talking to a sympathetic audience; the difference, as Kenyon noted, is that the journal is always there, no matter what's on your mind.

7   Recording growth

Sometimes it's hard to see how much you've learned until you reread your journal at the end of a term and notice where you began and where you ended. Your writing may have been casual and fast, your thinking tentative, your assessments or conclusions uncertain. But it gives you a record of who you were, what you thought, and how you've changed. Rereading a term's worth of entries may be a pleasant surprise, as Jeff found out.

11/21   The journal to me has been like a one-man debate, where I could write thoughts down and then later read them. This seemed to help clarify many of my ideas. To be honest there is probably fifty percent of the journal that is nothing but B.S. and ramblings to fulfill assignments, but that still leaves fifty percent that I think is of importance. The journal is also a time capsule. I want to put it away and not look at it for ten or twenty years and let it recall for me this period of my life.

■   WRITING 6: APPLICATION

Look over the examples in this section and see if you can think up half a dozen other uses for journals that the section does not cover. Can you provide any concrete examples from your own journal?

SUGGESTIONS FOR WRITING AND RESEARCH

INDIVIDUAL

I. Select a writer in your intended major who is known for having written a journal (for example, Mary Shelley, Ralph Waldo Emerson, Virginia Woolf, or Anaïs Nin in literature; Leonardo da Vinci, Georgia O'Keeffe, or Edward Weston in the arts; B. F. Skinner or Margaret Mead in the social sciences; Charles Darwin or Marie Curie in the sciences). Study the writer's journals to identify important characteristics and the purpose they probably served. Write a report on what you find and share it with your class.

2. Review your journal entries for the past two weeks, select one entry that seems especially interesting, and write a reflective essay of several pages on it. How are they different? Which is better? Is that a fair question?

COLLABORATIVE

Bring duplicated copies of one journal entry written during the term. Exchange entries and discuss interesting features of the entries.

 GUIDELINES FOR KEEPING A JOURNAL

1. Choose a notebook you are comfortable with. A small loose-leaf binder allows you to add, delete, and rearrange entries or share selected samples with an instructor.

2. Consider using a computer. One advantage of computer journals is that they make it easy for you to copy interesting or useful entries directly into the paper you are working on.

3. Date each entry. Also include the day of the week and the time if you like having more complete records. A journal allows you to watch your thoughts change over time.

4. Write long entries. Plan to write for at least ten minutes, preferably longer, to allow your thoughts to develop as fully as possible. The more you write, the more you will find to say.

5. Include both "academic" and "personal" entries. Put a divider in your loose-leaf notebook to separate them.

PART THREE

Drafting

People write about their personal experiences to know and understand themselves better, to inform and entertain others, and to leave permanent records of their lives. Sometimes people recount their experiences casually, in forms never intended for wide circulation, such as journals, diaries, and letters. Sometimes they write in forms meant to be shared with others, such as memoirs, autobiographies, or personal essays. In college, the most common form for such writing is the personal experience essay.

9 a Writing to tell a story

What makes a story worth telling in the first place? Is it the *subject*, so that big subjects such as earthquakes make better stories than small subjects such as pet cats? Is it the *character*, so that lively or quirky personalities are worth hearing about while quiet and normal ones are not? Or is it the *perspective* from which the story is told, so that first person, present tense is superior to third person, past tense? Is it the *setting*, so that exotic locales with lots of palm trees, bamboo huts, and snakes are better than small towns in the Midwest? Is it the *sequence of events*, so that stories with flashbacks are superior to stories told chronologically? Or is it the *theme*, the meaning embedded in the story, so that themes of high drama need be told while common ones do not?

We hope these questions make it clear that good stories can be told about virtually anything. Otherwise the best story would be a tragic adventure taking place during an earthquake on a South Pacific island told through flashbacks by an idiot. Not only can good stories be about any subject, they can be quite simple and can take place in your own backyard. And you can tell them.

Potential stories happen all the time — in fact, daily. What makes them actual is recounting them, orally or in writing, so that they become verbal structures that convey some meaning. Your purpose as a writer is to select events from your life and craft them into a narrative (story) that is informative, lively, and believable, a narrative that will mean something to you and your readers. This is what separates a good story from a simple string of facts.

All narratives, whether fictional stories, news reports, or accounts of personal experience, are made up of the same elements: *Who? What? Where? When? Why?* and *How?* To write your personal experience paper, you must make decisions about each of these elements and then weave them together to create a coherent whole.

■ **WRITING 1: EXPLORATION**

Think about the best stories you have read or listened to. What makes them memorable? What makes them believable? **ESL:** You might want to reflect on stories you have read or heard in your native language.

9 **b** **Finding a subject (what?)**

Subjects for good stories know no limits. You already have a lifetime of experiences to choose from, and each experience is a potential story to help explain who you are, what you believe, and how you act today. Here are some of the topics selected by a single first-year writing class.

- ■ playing oboe in Saturday orchestra rehearsals
- ■ counseling disturbed children at summer camp
- ■ picking strawberries on a farm
- ■ winning a championship tennis match
- ■ ballet dancing before a live audience
- ■ clerking at a drugstore
- ■ finishing second in a sailboat race
- ■ attending a Grateful Dead concert
- ■ trying out for the college volleyball team

- touring Graceland in Memphis
- painting houses during the summer

When you write a paper based on personal experience, your first two questions should be: Which experience do I want to write about? Will anybody else want to read about it? Following are three suggestions for areas to write about and one about an area to avoid. (Chapter 7 describes specific strategies for finding topics.)

1 Winning and losing

Winning something — a race, a contest, a lottery — can be a good subject since it features you in a unique position and allows you to explore or celebrate a special talent. At the same time, the obviously dramatic subjects such as scoring the winning goal in a championship game or placing first in a creative writing contest may actually be difficult to write well about because they've been used so often before — readers have very high expectations.

The sad truth is that in most parts of life there are more losers than winners. While one team wins a championship, dozens do not. This means that there's a large, empathetic audience out there who will understand and identify with a narrative about losing. Although more common than winning, losing is less often explored in writing because it is more painful to recall. So there are fresher, deeper, more original stories to tell about losing.

2 Milestones

Perhaps the most interesting but also the most difficult experience to write about is one which you already recognize as a turning point in your life, whether it's ballet dancing before a live audience for the first time or being a camp counselor. People who explore such topics in writing often come to a better understanding of them. Also, their very significance challenges writers to make them equally significant for an audience that did not experience them. When you write about milestones, pay special attention to the physical details that will make the story come alive for your readers.

3 Daily life

Commonplace experiences make fertile subjects for personal narratives. Describe practicing for, rather than winning, the big game, or cleaning up after, rather than attending, the prom. If you are accurate, honest, and observant in exploring a subject from which readers expect little, you are apt to pleasantly surprise them and draw them into your story. Work experiences are especially fruitful subjects, since you know the inside details and routines that the rest of us can only guess about.

4 A caution about love, death, and divorce

Several subjects that are good to write about extensively in journals are to be avoided in formal papers that will be extensively revised, edited, and scrutinized by classmates and instructors. You are probably too involved in a love relationship to see or portray it objectively; too close to the recent death of someone you care about to render the event faithfully; too angry, confused, or miserable to write well of your parents' divorce. Writing about these and other close or painful experiences can be immensely cathartic, but there is no need to share them with others.

■ WRITING 2: APPLICATION

Make a list of a dozen subjects that you might tell stories about. Think of milestones, moments of special insight, and commonplace events that were instructive or caused change. Share your list with classmates and find out which they would most like to hear about.   **ESL:** You might want to reflect on your experiences learning English or adjusting to a new culture.

9 c Delineating character (who?)

The characters in a good story are believable and interesting; they come alive for readers. In personal experience writing, your main character is yourself, so you must give your readers a good sense of who you are. You accomplish this through the voice in which you speak, the actions you portray, and the insights you share.

1 Voice

When you recount an experience, your language reveals the kind of person you are — playful, serious, rigid, loose, stuffy, honest, warm, or whatever. In the following excerpt, Beth relates her experience playing oboe during a two-hour Saturday morning orchestra rehearsal.

> I love that section. It sounds so cool when Sarah and I play together like that. Now I can put my reed back in the water and sit back and listen. I probably should be counting the rests. Counting would mean I'd have to pay attention and that's no fun. I'd rather look around and watch everyone else sweat.

The self Beth shows here is serious about music — after all, she's rehearsing a difficult instrument on a Saturday morning — but also fun-loving, impish, and just a little bit lazy ("I'd rather look around and watch everyone else sweat"). (For more information on voice, see Chapter 6.)

2 Actions

Readers learn something about the kind of person you are from the actions you take in the course of your story. While the word *action* usually suggests movement of some kind, it can also be very quiet, as Mary demonstrates in relating her experience as a summer camp counselor for emotionally disturbed children.

> Josh looked so peaceful and sweet asleep that it was hard to imagine how difficult he had been all afternoon. He asked me to rub his head so he could fall asleep. I remember that first night hoping that he liked me — at least a little bit. I was so happy that I could give him a week of the love and happiness he couldn't get at home.

Mary's bedside observation shows readers that she enjoys working with children — with Josh in particular — and that she has some insecurities herself about being liked.

3 Insights

One of the best ways to reveal who you are is to show yourself gaining a new insight — a new self-awareness or a new way of seeing the world. While insights can occur for apparently unexplainable reasons, they are most likely to occur when you encounter new ideas or have experiences that change you in some way. Jeff developed a new self-awareness when he participated in Outward Bound, a month-long program that teaches wilderness survival skills.

> Day 13.   After three days of not talking to or seeing one single person, I know the three basic necessities of life. Sorry Dad, they are not Stocks, Bonds, and Spreadsheets. And no, Mom, they're not *General Hospital*, *Days of Our Lives*, and *All My Children*. All I have been doing is melting snow for drinking water, rationing my food so it will last, and splitting dead trees in order to get firewood.

In this passage, Jeff reveals not only his sense of humor but also the conflict between his current bleak, snowy circumstances and his comfortable middle-class upbringing — a conflict that leads him to a new way of seeing himself in the world. (Jeff's paper uses a journal format. See 9d2.)

■ **WRITING 3: APPLICATION**

From your list of possible subjects, select three that caused you to change in some significant way. Write a paragraph on each one, concentrating on portraying yourself in the act of learning something. Select the one that seems most worthy of further exploration and write a few more paragraphs on it.

9 **d**   **Establishing perspective (how?)**

Perspective addresses the question, How close — in time, distance, or spirit — are you to the experience? Do you write as if it happened long ago or yesterday? Do you summarize what happened or put readers at the scene? Do you explain the experience or leave it mysterious? In other words, you can control how readers respond to a story by controlling the perspective, or vantage point, from which you tell it.

Authorial perspective is largely established by **point of view.** Using the **first person** (*I*) puts the narrator right in the story itself, as a participant; this is usually the point of view used in personal experience writing. The **third person** (*he* or *she*) establishes a distinction between the person narrating the events and the person experiencing them and thus tends to depersonalize the story. (See 21b and 28b for more on point of view.)

Tense is the other important element of perspective. It establishes the time when the story happened or is happening. The tense used to relate most of the events in a story is called the governing tense. Personal experience stories are usually set in either the present or the past. (See 21a and 35d–f for more on tense.)

A good approach may be to write your first draft from whatever perspective seems most natural or easy. As the story becomes clearer, experiment with other possible perspectives and see what you gain and what you lose with each.

1 **Once upon a time: past tense**

The easiest and most natural way to recount a personal experience is to write in the past tense. Lorraine uses this perspective in describing an automobile ride with her Native American grandfather to attend a tribal conference.

> I sat silently across from Grandfather and watched him slowly tear the thin white paper from the tip of the cigarette. He gathered the tobacco in one hand and drove the van with the other. I memorized his every move as he went through the motions of the prayer which ended when he finally blew the tobacco out of the window and into the wind.

Although the governing tense for your personal narrative may be the past tense, you may still want to use other tenses for special purposes. Lorraine concludes her five-page narrative with this passage, switching to the present tense in the final sentence. The present tense allows Lorraine to evaluate her past experience from her present perspective.

> That day on the mountain was only the beginnings of our teachings, but it was the most important because it was shared with our grandfather. Though he has now gone to the spirit world, we continue to give thanks for the lessons he taught us.

2 **Being there: present tense**

Using the present tense to recount a personal experience provides the illusion that the experience is happening at the moment, with little time for your reflection. This strategy invites readers to get more involved with your story, since they have to interpret it for themselves. Two ways of using present tense include the **interior monologue,** a fictional device that lets readers hear the writer's uncensored thoughts, and **journal or diary entries,** a format allowing the writer to pretend to describe an experience only a few hours after it happened. Use the interior monologue to describe a short, intense event; use the journal format to provide glimpses of an experience that covers several days or more. (For more information on writing papers in a journal format, see 21d.)

In describing her orchestra rehearsal, Beth writes an interior monologue, pretending that her readers can read her mind. Writers can know firsthand only their own internal monologues — and even these are hard to capture with any authenticity.

> No you don't really mean that, do you? You do. Rats. Here we go . . . Pfff . . . Pfff . . . Why isn't this playing? Maybe if I blow harder . . . HONK!! Great. I've just made a total fool of myself in front of everyone. Wonderful.

Beth talks to herself, answers herself, and, all the time, interacts with the rest of the orchestra. The difficulty in writing an interior monologue is one of balance: to sound as if she is authentically talking to herself, Beth cannot fully describe what she sees and hears; at the same time, in order to help her readers understand, she must provide some clues.

■ **WRITING 4: APPLICATION**

Write one page of your emerging story using the first person, past tense and a second page using the first person, present tense. From which perspective do you prefer to tell the story? Why?

9 **e** **Describing the setting (where?)**

Experiences happen in some place at some time, and good stories describe these settings. To describe a believable physical setting, you need to re-create on paper the sights, sounds, smells, and physical sensations that allow readers to experience it for themselves. Try to include evocative, unusual details that will let your readers know you were really there. In the following example,

Heather describes the farm where she spent the summer picking strawberries.

> The sun is just barely rising over the treetops and there is still dew covering the ground. In the strawberry patch, the deep green leaves are filled with water droplets and the strawberries are big and red and ready to be picked. The patch is located in a field off the road near a small forest of Christmas trees. The white house, the red barn, and a checkerboard of fields can be seen in the distance. It is 5:30 A.M. and the day has begun.

Notice the frequency of sight words, some of which convey the time of day (*there is still dew covering the ground*) while others simply paint a vivid picture of the scene before her (*red strawberries*, *white house*). In addition, Heather uses a metaphor, comparing distant fields to the pattern of a checkerboard.

■ **WRITING 5: APPLICATION**

Describe in detail one of the settings in which your experience took place. Appeal to at least three senses and avoid value judgments.

9 **f** **Narrating a sequence of events (when?)**

In every story, events are ordered one way or another. While you cannot alter the events that happened in your experience, as a writer you need to decide which events to portray and what order to present them in.

1 **Selecting events**

You have dozens of places to start and end any story, and at each point along the way, many possible details and events are worth relating. Your final selection should support the theme of your story. (See 9g.) In your early drafts, you might want to select events by using one of two strategies that writers commonly use to maintain reader interest: showing cause and effect and building suspense.

Some writers recount an experience to show **cause and effect.** In these narratives, writers pair one event (having an accident, meeting a person, taking a journey) with another event or events that it caused to happen (undergoing physical therapy, making a friend, learning a new language).

Suspense occurs when writers raise questions or pose problems that they delay answering or solving. If the writer can make the question interesting enough, the problem pressing enough, readers will keep reading to learn the answers or solutions — to find out, in other words, what happens. Mary's counseling experience raises the question, Will she succeed with this difficult child?

2 Ordering events

The most common way to sequence events is to use **chronological order,** with events presented in the sequence in which they happened. Chronological order can be straightforward, following a day from morning to night as Heather does in her narrative about picking strawberries. Jeff's account of participating in Outward Bound is also organized chronologically to follow the twenty-two days of his actual experience; however, his paper skips some days on which not much happened that was relevant to his theme.

Sometimes the order is deliberately broken up, so that readers are first introduced to an event in the present and then, later in the story, are allowed to see events that happen earlier in time through **flashbacks.** For example, Jeff's paper could start with his first day of solo camping and then flash back to the early days to explain how he got there. Such a sequence has the advantage of stimulating readers' interest by opening with a point of exceptional drama or insight.

■ WRITING 6: APPLICATION

Outline the sequence of events of your story in the order that makes the most sense. Is the arrangement chronological? If not, what is it? How do you decide which event to begin with? Which one to end with?

9 g   Developing a theme (why?)

Perhaps the most important element in a story is its meaning for both writer and reader. Why was this story worth writing or reading in the first place? First drafts of personal experience narratives often do not reveal a clear sense of the meaning of the story, even to the writers themselves. First drafts are for getting the events down on paper so that writers can see what they look like. In subsequent drafts, the meaning of these events — the **theme** — becomes clearer. (For more information on how revision helps themes emerge, see Chapters 19–22.)

In stories, the theme isn't usually explicitly stated in the first paragraph as the thesis statement often is in expository or argumentative writing. Instead, storytellers may create a meaning that is not directly stated anywhere and that becomes clear only at the end of the narrative. Most themes fall into three categories: slices of life, insights, and turning points.

1 Slices of life

Some stories simply let readers see what life is like for someone else. Such stories exist primarily to record the writer's memories and to convey information in an interesting way to readers. Their only theme is, "This is what my life is like." When you finish reading Heather's story about strawberry picking, you have learned a little bit about Heather, life on a farm, and strawberries; but you haven't witnessed major changes or dramatic events. After spending five pages relating a day of hard work, Heather concludes with this paragraph.

> Michelle runs to the car and jumps up and down begging me to let her drive back to the stand. I don't know why, but I let her. As soon as we drive in to the stand, our boss yells, "Girls, go weed the pumpkin patch!" Well, it looks like another hard, sweaty, dirty, full day of working on the farm.

2 Insights

In contrast to the paper that shows a slice of life is the paper relating an experience that led to a new insight. The insight itself is the theme of the paper. Such an experience is deeply significant to the writer, and the writer makes sure that readers see the full value of the experience, usually by explicitly commenting on its meaning. Beth does this at the very end of her paper on her music rehearsal. After using interior monologue for nine paragraphs, in the last paragraph she speaks to readers directly and focuses their attention on the significance of her musical education.

> As hard as it is to get up every Saturday morning, and as hard as it is to put up with some people here, I always feel good as I leave rehearsal. A guest conductor once said: "Music sounds how feelings feel." It's really true. Music evokes emotions that can't be described on paper. Every human feeling can be expressed through music — pride, sadness, love, hatred. Music is the international language. Once you learn it you can't forget it.

3 Turning points

Many themes fall somewhere in between slices of life and profound insights. In fact, many of the best personal experience stories have change or growth as their themes. Such themes are usually implicit rather than explicit; although they may be implied throughout the story, they usually become clear in a single climactic moment or episode that dramatizes the theme. Mary's camp counselor story shows her progress from insecurity to confidence as she wins the heart of a ten-year-old. The following excerpt takes place after she has rescued Josh from ridicule by other campers.

> He ran in and threw himself on my bed, crying. I held him, rubbing his head for over an hour. "I love you, Mary. You're the best big sister in the whole world and you're so pretty! I love you and don't ever want you to leave."

■ WRITING 7: APPLICATION

Freewrite for ten minutes about the meaning of your story as you have written it so far, addressing some of these questions: What have you discovered about yourself? Were there any surprises? Does your story interest you? Why or why not? What do you want readers to feel or know at the end?

9 **h** Shaping the whole paper

The finished draft of Rebecca's personal experience paper, "Nutcracker," takes for its subject the day on which she danced in this famous ballet before a live audience. Rebecca frames the story with her arrival at and departure from the theater, limiting the sequence of events to those that took place in the few hours in between. She relates her story in the present tense to put readers on the scene; the choice of the first person and the backstage setting allow her to give us an insider's view. Details about the preparations backstage create believability and interest. Through ironic observations and bits of internal monologue she reveals important aspects of her character — her anxiety, sense of humor, and love of music. By the end of the eighth paragraph, she comes to the realization that she can perform in front of an audience.

Nutcracker

It's eleven o'clock when my parents drop me off at the side door of the Civic Center Theatre. I enter the studio and walk over to an empty place at the barre. Insulation covers the ceiling, and the concrete walls have no windows. The backstage studio is alive with energy. Today, for the first time, we perform the Nutcracker in front of a real audience. I've danced at school in front of our parents, but never on a real stage, under klieg lights, with hundreds of strangers watching my every move.

Dancers are scattered around the room, stretching, chatting, adjusting shoes and tights. Company members, the professionals who are joining us for this performance, wear tattered leg-warmers, sweatpants which have lost their elastic, and old T-shirts over tights and leotards. Their hair is knotted into buns or, in the case of male dancers, held tight with sweatbands. You can tell the students by the runless pink tights, dress-code leotards, and immaculate hair.

I, along with all the 5A students, wear a royal blue leotard and a thick layer of makeup to soften my face under the harsh lights. Our blue and green chiffon costumes look like something Cinderella would wear, the tiaras on top of our lacquered hair oddly resembling blue mountain ranges.

I glance at one of the mirrors lining the front wall and

sigh in relief. Thank God it's a skinny-mirror. Today of all days, I'm not up to a fat-mirror.

The room becomes silent as Miss Robbins enters the studio. She wears pink tights, black leotard, and a long black ballet skirt. "OK. Are we ready to start the angels' warmup?" Several company members give us sympathetic looks, remembering the days when they were subjected to Miss Robbins. The music from the theater tells us that the tree is growing, and the Nutcracker is about to turn into a prince, and if we don't get moving soon, we'll be onstage with cold muscles.

We are frozen to the floor. I tightly grasp my lyre, remembering the warnings about dropping props, hair falling out, or pointe shoe ribbons hanging. "When any of these things happen to professionals, they are fined." We assume the same expectations apply to us, so we spray our hair and our shoe ribbons until both look painted on. We stand fast, hold on tight, and wait for the fog.

The fog is our cue. I take one last, long breath of clean air as the smoky cloud rolls closer. I bend toward the floor, placing my head on my outstretched leg. The fog comes closer, the lights dim, and my pointe shoe fades out of sight. Why is this stuff called fog anyway? Smog seems more fitting. There has to be a better way to create the fairyland that opens the second act.

Before we suffocate, the stage lights brighten, and my stomach flutters with excitement. The lines from my false eyelashes make a gridlike pattern in my peripheral vision, but I don't seem to mind. We slowly, and ever so angelically, rise out of the fog and begin to dance. Only an occasional cough tells me people are watching. Miss Robbins was right, under the lights you can't see anything. It's no different from an extra bright rehearsal.

The professional dancers fill the stage, looking graceful and elegant in stark contrast to their grubby warmup appearance an hour earlier in the studio. I see fifteen other girls gracefully weaving in and out from each other and know that we're halfway through. We continue to dance as if in a trance.

When our part is over we walk upstage to stand on the stairs that form part of the scenery, holding our lyres and looking pleasant. It's funny, but when I hear the <u>Nutcracker</u> in department stores and restaurants, I want to scream and run away, but here, onstage, the music takes over, and I hope it never ends.

After the second curtain call, the applause fades, and we walk down the cold concrete stairs to our dressing room. I take off my costume, return it to the closet, and put on my cozy sweatshirt and jeans. I scrub off the thick layer of caked-on makeup from my sore face. I rub the soft cream on my face, then sit in front of my mirror and unpin my lacquered hair. Very slowly I brush it in a vain attempt to soften the hair spray.

It's four o'clock and I'm exhausted. I shove my belongings haphazardly into my ballet bag, toss it over my shoulder, and leave by the side door to find my parents. We do another matinee tomorrow, and maybe then I'll get nervous all over again, but, at least for now, it's over.

SUGGESTIONS FOR WRITING AND RESEARCH

INDIVIDUAL

Write a personal experience essay based on Writings 2–7 in this chapter. Try to find a subject that will let you show some change or learning on your part. Plan to write this narrative in several drafts, each one deliberately exploring a different aspect of your experience. Here is a recommended draft sequence:

First draft: Write in your most natural voice and from your most natural point of view, using a chronological sequence of events.

Second draft: Write in great detail about the setting and character (you) so that readers can see, hear, touch, and smell this experience. Concentrate on just one or two scenes in your whole story.

Third draft: Limit the focus of this draft to just one small part of the experience — a day, a few hours, a few minutes. Begin with some dialogue, either something overheard or something you participated in. (See 20b.)

Fourth draft: Write this draft from a different point of view or in a different tense from those you have been using so far. (See Chapter 21.)

Fifth draft: Write a final draft in which you either (1) mix and match elements from your previous drafts, (2) expand on the previous draft you find most pleasing, or (3) write a fresh draft by using insights you gained in the previous writing. Whichever option you choose, attach to your final draft the previous drafts in the order in which you wrote them.

COLLABORATIVE

As a class, write the story of your writing class so far in the semester. Have each class member contribute one short chapter (one page) to this tale. Each member may choose any moment (funny, momentous, boring, routine) and should describe it so that it can stand on its own as a complete episode. Choose two class members to collect all the short narrative chapters and weave them into a larger narrative with a beginning, middle, and end.

GUIDELINES FOR WRITING ABOUT PERSONAL EXPERIENCE

1. Select a subject that interests you but whose meaning still escapes you; the writing will help you capture it.

2. Let your character emerge by showing yourself in action in difficult or complicated situations.

3. Recount your experience from at least two different perspectives to see which one is most effective.

4. In describing your setting, appeal to as many of the five senses as possible.

5. First explain the sequence of events chronologically; then write a draft telling it through flashbacks. Use the order that satisfies you the most.

6. Try to focus and select the events of your story so that your theme emerges without your stating exactly what it is.

10 | Explaining Things

To explain something is to make it clear and understandable. Explanation is perhaps the most fundamental act of communication: if we can't make other people understand our ideas, then we're not communicating at all. Explanations are so important that they are a part of most other types of writing, such as arguments, interpretations, and reflections (see Chapters 11, 12, and 13). In purely explanatory writing, however, the main purpose is to help readers understand something. Such writing can range from a newspaper feature on baseball card collecting to a magazine article on why dinosaurs are extinct, from a textbook on the French Revolution to a recipe for making chili.

10 a | Writing to explain

The purpose of explanatory writing (also called expository or informational writing) is to help readers understand a subject. Explanations can answer a variety of questions.

- What is it?

- What does it mean?

- How does it work?

- How is it related to other things?

- How is it put together?

- Why did it happen?

- What will its consequences be?

Explanatory writing is defined not so much by its subject (which can be almost anything) as by the way the subject is treated. First, explanatory writing commonly uses an objective perspective; that is, it emphasizes the thing explained rather than the writer's beliefs and feelings. Second, explanatory writing focuses on the reader's need for information rather than the writer's desire for self-expression. Third, explanatory writing is usually systematic and orderly, having a stated thesis, clear explanatory strategies, and a logical organizational structure.

Explanatory writing is objective, reader-focused, and systematic because this writing style simplifies an audience's task of reading to understand. If readers have to stumble through a poorly organized explanation or repeatedly sort fact from opinion, they are likely to give up and look for their information elsewhere.

Taking time to analyze your readers is an important part of writing a successful explanation. You need to find out what they know and don't know, what they care about and don't care about. Only by doing this can you be sure that your explanation is focused on information that readers will find useful and interesting. (See Chapter 5.)

In writing classes, explanation usually takes the form of research essays and reports that inform rather than argue, interpret, or reflect. The assignment may ask you to "describe how something works" or to "explain the causes and effects" of a particular phenomenon. (See 4d.) To explain anything successfully, you will need to decide on a topic, have a clear sense of who you are writing to, locate information about your topic, develop a working thesis, use clear explanatory strategies, organize predictably, and write with a focus on the thing being explained rather than on your feelings and opinions about it.

WRITING 1: EXPLORATION

How good are you at explaining things to people? What things do you most commonly find yourself explaining? Is it harder to explain things in writing than in speaking? What is the last thing you explained in writing? How did your audience receive it?   **ESL:** How is explaining things in your native language different from or similar to explaining things in English?

10 b   Finding a topic

You can explain only what you understand yourself. It also helps to write about something you're interested in. Even if you are assigned a subject that isn't particularly compelling, try to narrow the subject to a topic that is more interesting to you than others. For example, the general subject *stereo systems* is so broad that it's hard to know where to begin or what to say. However, a specific aspect of stereo systems, such as compact discs, may interest you; within the subject of CDs, there are probably several topics (their cost, their sound quality, their manufacturing process) that you could write about.

Remember that effective explanations are full of details and carefully developed ideas. This means that even simple explanations may take several pages. For this reason, try to narrow your topic as much as you can. If your topic is too broad, you will need too many pages, or you will have to skip over important points. Even worse, such a topic will probably exhaust both your readers (who are being asked to wade through too much information) and you (who has to find all that information in the first place).

In most instances, an explanatory paper should address one central question, such as *Why do CDs cost more than records?* Of course, there may be other questions to be answered along the way (*How do CDs work? How are CDs made?*), but these are secondary.

Once you have a focused topic on a central question, you need to assemble information. If you're not an expert yourself, you'll need to consult authorities on the topic. Even if you are already an expert, finding supporting information from other experts will help make your explanation clear and authoritative. (See Part IV for more on researching.) Keep your audience in mind as you begin your research. You don't want to waste time researching and writing about things your audience already knows. (See Chapter 5.)

■ **WRITING 2: APPLICATION**

What would you like to explain? For what purpose? To whom? If you're not sure, do some freewriting or journal writing to help you discover a question.

10 **C** **Developing a thesis**

A **thesis** is the writer's declaration of what the paper is about. A good thesis lets readers know what to expect and guides their understanding of the information presented. Because a thesis is important in helping readers understand an explanation, it is usually stated explicitly near the beginning of the paper rather than left implicit or stated only at the end — although in some cases, you may lead up to it step by step and then state it clearly at the end. In explanatory writing, the thesis states the answer to the central question of the paper.

QUESTION Why do compact discs cost so much?

THESIS CDs cost more than records because the laser technology required to manufacture them is so expensive.

If the question you are answering asks What? or How? rather than Why? When? or Who? then your explanation will be clear only after you provide a large amount of varied information. A good thesis for this kind of explanation sums up all the information in a single idea, image, or analogy that gives unity and coherence to your explanation.

QUESTION How are the various offices of the city government connected?

THESIS City government offices are like an octopus, with eight fairly independent bureaus as arms and a central brain in the mayor's office.

You will probably find yourself revising your thesis as you continue to research, draft, revise, and edit your paper. For example, the more you learn about city government, the less your first analogy may seem to explain: you may discover that city government is more like a centipede than an octopus. Throughout the writing process, keep in mind that your first thesis is a **working thesis** and should be tentative, flexible, and subject to change; its primary function is to guide further research and help keep your paper focused.

◾ **WRITING 3: APPLICATION**

Write out a working thesis for the topic you are explaining. If you are addressing a When? or How? question, find a controlling image or analogy that will hold together all of the elements of your necessarily longer answer.

10 d Using strategies to explain

The standard explanatory strategies are defining, describing, classifying and dividing, analyzing causes and effects, and comparing and contrasting. You need to select and use the strategy or strategies that best serve your purpose.

If your paper is on a tightly focused topic and answers a narrow, simple question, you may need to use only one strategy. More often, however, you will have one **primary strategy** that shapes the paper as a whole and several **secondary strategies** that can vary from paragraph to paragraph or even sentence to sentence. For example, to explain why the government has raised income taxes, your primary strategy would be analyzing cause and effect, but you would also need to define terms such as *income tax*, to classify the various types of taxes, and to compare and contrast raising income taxes to other budgetary options. In fact, almost every explanatory strategy makes use of other strategies: it's impossible to describe a process without first dividing it into steps, and a comparison-and-contrast explanation would be useless if it didn't describe the things compared and contrasted.

The primary explanatory strategy you use in a paper will often be determined by the question you are answering.

QUESTION	STRATEGY IN ANSWER
What is it?	Definition
What does it mean?	Definition
What are its characteristics?	Description
How does it work?	Process description
How is it related to other things?	Comparison and contrast
How is it put together?	Classification and division
To what group does it belong?	Classification and division
Why did it happen?	Cause-and-effect analysis
What will its consequences be?	Cause-and-effect analysis

The primary explanatory strategy of your paper and the thesis go hand in hand. It is difficult to develop one without the other. This means that you should expect to reconsider your choice of a primary strategy as you refine your thesis and to reconsider your thesis as you refine your choice of a primary strategy. In your early drafts, focus on using strategies that are appropriate to your purpose and that will be effective with your readers.

ESL VOCABULARY FOR EXPLAINING THINGS

DESCRIPTION

consists of	has
displays	is characterized by

Example: The flower of the tobacco plant has a sweet fragrance.

DIVISION

consists of	can be separated into
can be divided into	is composed of

Example: The curriculum can be divided into the humanities, the social sciences, and the natural sciences.

CLASSIFICATION

can be categorized according to	can be categorized as
can be classified according to	can be classified as
can be grouped according to	

Example: History can be classified as a humanities discipline.

COMPARISON

also	resembles
both . . . and . . .	similar to
like	the same as

Example: Like English, Spanish uses articles before nouns.

CONTRAST

but	on the other hand
however	unlike
in contrast	yet

Example: Unlike English, Spanish does not always state the subject of a sentence.

CAUSE AND EFFECT

as a result	therefore
consequently	thus
for this reason	

Example: Some marathon runners do not pace themselves well, and as a result they may be unable to finish a race.

1 Defining

To define something is to identify it, to set it apart so that it can be distinguished from similar things. Writers need to define all terms that might be unclear to their readers in order to make points clearly, forcefully, and with authority.

Formal definitions are what you find in a dictionary. They usually combine a general term with specific characteristics: *A computer is a programmable electronic device* [general term] *that can store, retrieve, and process data* [specific characteristics]. Another common way to define something is to use a **synonym:** *Computers, high-speed electronic calculating machines, have changed the way people write.* You can also define by **example:** *Small notebook computers, such as Apple's 8 × 12 inch PowerBook, can do virtually everything larger desktop computers can.*

Usually, defining something is a brief, preliminary step accomplished before moving on to a more important part of the explanation. When you need to define something complex or difficult or when your primary explanatory strategy is definition, you will need an **extended definition** consisting of a paragraph or more. This was the case with Mark's paper explaining computers, in which he defined each part of a typical computer system. After defining the central processor unit (CPU), he then defined *computer memory.*

> Computer storage space is measured in units called "Kilobytes" (Ks). Each K equals 1024 "bytes" or approximately 1000 single typewriter characters. So one K equals about 180 English words, or a little less than half of a single-spaced typed page, or maybe three minutes of fast typing.
>
> Personal computers generally have their memories measured in "megabytes" (MBs). One MB equals 1,048,567 bytes (or 1000 Ks), which translates into approximately 400 pages of single-spaced type. A typical personal computer may have one or two megabytes of this built-in storage space.

2 Describing

To describe a person, place, or thing means to create a verbal image so that readers can see what you see; hear what you hear; and taste, smell, and feel what you taste, smell, and feel. In other words, your goal in describing something is to make it real enough for your readers to experience it for themselves. Effective descriptions appeal to the senses.

Good description contains enough detail for readers to understand your subject, but not so much as to distract or bore them. Above all, descriptive details need to be purposeful. Heed the advice of Russian writer Anton Chekhov: "If a gun is hanging on the wall in the first chapter, it must, without fail, fire in the second or third chapter. If it doesn't fire, it mustn't hang either."

To describe how processes work is more complicated than giving a simple physical description: in addition to showing objects at rest, you need to show them in sequence and motion. In other words, a **process description** combines the simple description just discussed with some form of orderly action.

To describe a process, you need to divide the process into discrete steps and present the steps in a logical order. For some processes this is easy (making chili, building a garage). For others it is more difficult, either because many steps are all happening at once or because people really don't know which steps come before others (manufacturing a car, writing a research paper).

In either case, show the steps in a logical sequence that will be easy for readers to understand. Although it is possible to describe a process in reverse chronological order, working from the last event backward to the first, this is far more likely to confuse readers than chronological order. To orient your readers, you may also want to number the steps, using transition words such as *first*, *second*, and *third*. (See 25c.)

In the following example, taken from an early draft of his paper, Keith describes the process of manufacturing compact discs.

> CDs start out as a refrigerator-sized box full of little plastic beads that you could sift your hands through. They are fed into a giant tapered corkscrew — a blown-up version of an old-fashioned meat grinder. As the beads pass down the corkscrew, they are slowly melted by the heated walls.
>
> At the bottom of their descent is a "master recording plate" onto which the molten plastic is pressed. The plastic now resembles a vinyl record, except that the disc is transparent. The master now imprints "pits," rather than grooves, around the disc, the surface resembling a ball of Play-Doh after being thrown against a stucco wall — magnified 5000 times.

3 Comparing and contrasting

To **compare** two things is to find similarities between them; to **contrast** is to find differences. Comparing and contrasting help us understand something better by clarifying both how it is related to similar things and how it is distinctive. College assignments frequently ask you to compare and contrast one thing — whether authors, books, presidents, governments, cultures, centuries, philosophies, or inventions — with another.

The two things compared and contrasted should usually be reasonably similar. You *can* compare apples and oranges, but you'll probably learn more if you compare mandarin oranges with navel oranges. You should also compare and contrast the same elements or feature of each thing. If you describe the digestive system of one frog species, you should be sure also to describe the digestive system of the frog species with which you are comparing it.

There are three common ways to organize a comparison-and-contrast analysis. A **point-to-point** analysis examines one feature at a time for both similarities and differences. A **whole-to-whole** analysis first presents one object as a whole and then presents the other object as a whole; it usually concludes by highlighting important similarities or differences. A **similarity-and-difference** analysis first presents all the similarities and then all the differences between the two things, or vice versa. Use a point-to-point or similarity-and-difference analysis for long explanations of complex things; use a whole-to-whole analysis for simple objects that readers can easily comprehend.

In the following whole-to-whole example, Keith compares and contrasts how records and CDs transmit the information that eventually becomes music.

On a record, the stylus (needle) sits in a spiraled groove and reads the depth and width of the groove, from which it receives its audio signal. However, the depth of the groove is constantly changing by fractions of millimeters due to specks of dust and the wear caused by the needle, which reads not only the music but also the dust and wear, passing along all the sound as "music."

On a CD, however, a laser sends out a beam of light, which bounces off an object, like radar, and returns with a message, which becomes the music. The CD player doesn't read an ever-changing and dirty groove. Instead, it reads either a "yes" or a "no" — a pit or no pit — from the disc. On one CD there are hundreds of thousands of tiny pits. . . . The laser in your CD player reads the distance to the disc to determine if there's a pit, which will be farther away, or not.

As Keith's example shows, most comparison-and-contrast explanations give equal space to each of the two things examined. This is because both are equally important to the writer's point. If you want to focus on one thing but need to explain it in terms of another thing, then you should use an **analogy.** (See 31i.)

Analogies are effective ways of explaining something new to readers because you can compare something they are unfamiliar with to something they already know about. For example, most of us have never seen a heart beating, but we are used to thinking of it as a pump, a device that we have seen at one time or another. Be sure to use objects and images in analogies that will be familiar to your readers.

4 Classifying and dividing

People generally understand short things better than long things and simple things better than complex things. To help readers understand a large and complex topic, often it is effective to use classification and division to reduce it to understandable pieces and to put the pieces in context.

To **classify** something, you put it in a category or class with other things that are like it: *Like whales and dolphins, sea lions are aquatic mammals.* To **divide** something, you break it into smaller parts or subcategories: *An insect's body is composed of a head, a thorax, and an abdomen.* Many complex systems need both classification and division to be clear. To explain a stereo system, for example, you might divide the whole into headphones, record player, graphic equalizers, tape deck, compact disc player, preamplifiers, amplifiers, radio, and speakers. Then you might classify all these parts into a few categories.

Inputs	Radio
	Record player
	Tape deck
	Compact disc player
Processors	Preamplifiers
	Amplifiers
	Graphic equalizers

Outputs   Speakers
                     Headphones

Combining classification and division is particularly important when your division results in a large number of parts or subcategories. Most readers have a difficult time remembering more than six or seven things, so organize a long list into a few logical groups, as in the preceding example. Also be sure that the categories you use are meaningful to your readers, not simply convenient for you as a writer.

5 Analyzing causes and effects

Few things happen all by themselves. Instead, one thing happens because something else happened; then it, in turn, makes something else happen. You sleep because you're tired, and once you've slept, you wake up because you're rested. In other words, you already know about cause and effect because it is a regular part of your daily life. A **cause** is something that makes something else happen; an **effect** is the thing that happens.

When you write a cause-and-effect analysis, usually you know what the effect is and you're trying to explain what caused it: *Why do CDs cost more than records? Why are fish in the lake dying?* The thesis for an explanation analyzing causes should always include the word *because*: *CDs cost more than records because manufacturing costs are higher.* This sort of analysis often forms part of a larger explanation, but entire papers explaining causes are common, too.

You can also start with the cause and try to describe possible future effects: *If billboards were banned from state highways, people would be able to enjoy the countryside again.* Unless there is very sound and widely accepted evidence to support the thesis, however, this sort of analysis will almost always result in argumentative writing. (See Chapter 11.)

In the following example, Tom looks at the shortage of affordable student housing on his campus (the effect) and presents increased enrollment and inadequate planning as the causes.

The university's policy of "delayed retroactive accommodation" has repeatedly affected housing costs. The last university dormitories were constructed and completed in 1978 when the student population was 7400. By 1985 student enrollment had increased to 8100, which put increased pressure on both existing dorms and city apartments adjacent to the university, causing prices in both to increase substantially. By 1991, the student population had increased to nearly 9000, but since no new dormitories were built during this period, demand and prices for student housing skyrocketed.

Tom's explanation illustrates the difficulty of analyzing causes and effects. The causes he presents are reasonable, but many other causes — inflation, high taxes, increased cost of construction materials, increased student vandalism — could also have contributed to the problem. Most complex situations have multiple causes. If you try to reduce a complex situation to just one or two causes, you are making the logical mistake known as **oversimplification.** (See Chapter 11.) To prove his thesis, Tom would have to present considerably more evidence to demonstrate that the causes he proposes are the most important ones and that any others are merely secondary.

▪ WRITING 4: APPLICATION

Decide which of the five strategies described in this section best suits the primary purpose of the explanatory paper you are drafting. Which additional or secondary strategies will you also use?

10 e Organizing with logic

Since the information in an explanatory paper will be new and therefore challenging to readers, a strong, easy-to-follow organization is crucial. If you give your readers a good sense of where you're taking them, they will be more willing to follow you at each step. Make sure your method of organization is clear early in the paper; digress as little as possible.

Your method of organization should be simple, straightforward, and logical, and it should be appropriate for your subject and audience. For example, if you wanted to explain how a CD stereo system works, you could start your paper with a description of putting a CD on a player and end with the music coming out of the speakers, explaining what happens at each step along the way. You could also describe the system technically, starting with the power source and working toward the speakers. You could even describe it historically, starting with components that were developed earliest and work toward those that have been invented most recently. For most readers, the first method of organization would be best because it corresponds to something they themselves have experienced.

■ **WRITING 5: APPLICATION**

Outline three possible means of organizing the explanatory paper you are writing. List the advantages and disadvantages of each. Select the one that best suits your purpose and the needs of your audience.

10 f Maintaining a neutral perspective

Your explanatory writing will usually be clearer if you maintain a neutral or objective perspective, one that emphasizes the thing explained (the object) rather than your beliefs and feelings. This perspective allows you to get information to readers as quickly and efficiently as possible without you, the writer, getting in the way.

Of course, a paper written about stereo systems by a stereo enthusiast would be different from one written by someone who thinks only a live performance is worthwhile; it's never possible to be completely objective. The goal is to be as neutral as possible. Write from the **third-person point of view,** using the pronouns *he, she,* and *it.* Keep yourself (*I*) in the background, unless you have a good reason, such as explaining your personal experience with the subject. It is generally a good idea to avoid the second person as well; however, in some instances, using "you" adds a friendly, familiar tone that keeps readers interested. Present all the relevant information about the topic, both things you like about it and things you dislike. Avoid emotional or biased language. Remember that your goal is not to win an argument but to convey information. (See Chapters 6, 28, and 32.)

■ **WRITING 6: APPLICATION**

Examine the draft you are writing to see if you have maintained as neutral a perspective as possible. Where you find emotional or judgmental words, delete them and write from a less biased perspective.

10 g **Shaping the whole paper**

Keith's complete essay on the high cost of compact discs is presented here. His topic is narrowly focused on one type of sound medium, CDs, and on one feature of that medium, the high cost. His thesis, that CDs cost more than records because their manufacturing costs are higher, evolves throughout the essay and is revealed only at the end, but it is clearly anticipated by the implicit question, Why do CDs cost so much? His organization is simple and easy to follow. First, the whole essay is framed by a description of a reader in a record store wondering why CDs cost more than records. Second, within this frame is a point-by-point comparison of the operational and manufacturing processes of records and CDs. Keith's perspective throughout is that of a knowledgeable tour guide. Although his personality is clear, his biases do not affect the report.

Although the primary explanatory strategy in Keith's essay is an analysis of causes and effects, he uses most of the other strategies discussed in this chapter as well: definition, process description, and comparison and contrast. His essay is most remarkable for its effective use of analogy. At various points, he asks his readers to think of radar, the game of telephone, jimmies on an ice cream cone, corkscrews, meat grinders, player pianos, and Play-Doh.

CDs: What's the Big Difference?

The little package in your left hand says $14.95. The larger package in your right hand says $7.95. The question is, do you want to hear James Taylor in true stereo quality or not? Since you don't want to settle for second best, you nestle the larger LP back between some Disney classics and head to the counter with your new JT compact disc. Wandering out of the store you wonder what, besides seven dollars, was the difference between this little CD and that LP record.

Maybe you've heard the term "digital audio," the type of recording used with CDs, as opposed to "analog audio," used with LPs? If you don't know the difference, read on.

The purpose of your stereo system is to interpret recordings and reproduce them faithfully. Of course, nothing's perfect, so your music always has that quaint amount of background fuzz that never goes away. The fuzz is due to your stereo's misinterpretation of the signal it receives from the magnetic tape or vinyl record.

On a record, the stylus (needle) sits in a spiraled groove and reads the depth and width of the groove, from which it receives its audio signal. However, the depth of the groove is constantly changing by fractions of millimeters due to specks of dust and the wear caused by the needle, which reads not only the music but also the dust and wear, passing along all the sound as "music."

On a CD, however, a laser sends out a beam of light, which bounces off an object, like radar, and returns with a message which becomes the music. The CD player doesn't read an ever-changing and dirty groove. Instead, it reads either a "yes" or a "no"--a pit or no pit--from the disc. On one CD there are hundreds of thousands of tiny pits that resemble those of a player piano scroll, telling the piano which keys to hit. The laser in your CD player reads the distance to the disc to determine if there's a pit, which will be farther away, or not.

What's the difference, you ask, in receiving music from grooves versus pits? Do you remember playing the "telephone game" in fifth grade? You know, the one where someone on one side of class whispers something in your ear and it gets passed along until it gets to the last person, who gets to say what he was told? This is much the way in which your stereo works: the LP or CD is like the first person and your speakers are like the last. In the case of the record, I whisper some line in your ear and you pass it on, but by the time it reaches the last person, it's been twisted about and has a few more words attached. In the case of the CD, I whisper either a "yes" or a "no" and by the time it reaches the last person it should be exactly the same--this is where the term "digital" comes from, meaning either there is a signal (yes) or there isn't one (no). After all, how much can you screw up a yes or a no?

Even when you understand the difference between a CD and a record, you still feel that seven-dollar difference in your pocket. Why does digital cost so much more?

Although a record would be nearly finished at this point, there's still important work to be done on the CD. From here the disc is metallized, a process that deposits a thin film of metal, usually aluminum, on the surface; you see it as a rainbow under a light. Since light won't bounce back from transparent plastic, the coating acts as a mirror to bounce back the laser beam.

The disc is mirrored by a spray-painting process called "sputtering" that must be extremely precise. You couldn't just dip the thing because then the pits would fill in or melt. The clear disc is inserted into a chamber and placed opposite to a piece of pure aluminum called a "target," which is bombarded with electricity, causing the aluminum atoms to jump off and embed themselves onto the surface of the disc, like jimmies to an ice cream cone.

To keep fingerprints from this critical surface, it is coated with a polymer resin--sort of like an epoxy glue. The disc is laid flat, while a mask is laid over the center hole and a thin bead of resin is laid down around the center. Then the disc is "spin-coated" with a fine film of resin, which becomes the outer coating on the CD.

Once the resin is cured by a brief exposure to ultraviolet light, your CD is pretty much idiot-proof. As long as you don't interrupt the light path to the film, your CD will perform perfectly, even with small scratches, so long as they don't diffract the laser beam--and even then you may be able to rub them out smooth with a finger. In no case does anything ever come in contact with the recorded surface.

The CD is finished when it is either stamped or silk-screened with the appropriate logo and allowed to dry. Though all of these steps take a mere seven seconds to produce one CD, with materials costing no more than a pack of gum, the cost of buying and operating one CD-producing machine is close to that of running a small team of Formula 1 racecars.

So next time you walk into Record Land, you know what you are paying for. A CD may be twice as expensive as a record, but the sound is twice as clear and the disc will last forever.

SUGGESTIONS FOR WRITING AND RESEARCH

INDIVIDUAL

1. Write a paper explaining some thing, process, or concept. As a starting point, use an idea you discovered in Writing 2. When you have finished one draft of this essay, look back and see if there are places where your explanation could be improved by using one of the explanatory strategies explained in this chapter.

2. Select a writer of your choice, fiction or nonfiction, who explains things especially well. Read or reread his or her work and write an essay in which you analyze and explain the effectiveness of the explanation you find there.

COLLABORATIVE

Form writing groups based on mutual interests; agree as a group to explain the same thing, process, or concept. Write your explanations separately and then share drafts, comparing and contrasting your different ways of explaining. For a final draft, either (1) rewrite your individual drafts borrowing good ideas from others in your group or (2) compose a collaborative single paper with contributions from each group member.

11 Arguing Positions

Argument is deeply rooted in the American political and social system, where free and open debate is the essence of the democratic process. Argument is also at the heart of the academic process, where scholars investigate scientific, social, and cultural issues, hoping through the give-and-take of debate to find reasonable answers to complex questions. Argument in the academic world, however, is less likely to be about winning or losing — as it is in political and legal systems — than about changing minds or altering perceptions.

Argument as rational disagreement — rather than as quarrels, fights, and contests — most often occurs in areas of genuine uncertainty about what is right, best, or most reasonable. In disciplines such as English, history, and philosophy, written argument commonly takes the form of interpretive arguments, in which the meaning or significance of an idea is disputed. (See Chapter 12 for information on interpretive arguments.) In disciplines such as political science, engineering, and business, arguments commonly appear as position papers.

11 a Writing to change people's minds

Arguments focus on issues about which there is some debate; if there's no debate, there's no argument. College assignments commonly ask that you argue one side of an issue and defend your argument against attacks from skeptics.

A **position paper** sets forth an arguable position on an issue. The position paper is one of the most demanding and, at the same time, most practical forms of argument that you may be assigned in college. A position paper assignment will typically ask you, first, to choose an issue in which you are interested; second, to argue a position on one side or another of the issue; and third, to support your claims with evidence, which you locate through research.

(See 4d for advice about how to approach an assignment.) Understanding position papers and other arguments is easier if we break them down into the following elements.

Purpose

The purpose of argument is to persuade other people to agree with a particular point of view. In the world at large, people argue to get something done: lawyers attempt to win cases; legislators to pass or defeat bills; college committees to ensure a culturally diverse faculty. In your college writing, you attempt to persuade your instructor or classmates to agree that your position is either reasonable or the best one available.

Issue

An issue is something that can be argued about. For instance, *traffic lights* and *cultural diversity* are things or concepts, but not issues. However, they can become issues when questions are raised about them.

ISSUE   Should a traffic light be installed at the corner of Main and 5th streets?

ISSUE   Do American colleges adequately represent the cultural diversity of the United States?

These questions are issues because reasonable people could answer them in different ways; they can be argued about because more than one answer is plausible, possible, or realistic.

Position

Your position is the stand you take on an issue. Virtually all issues can be formulated as yes/no questions; your position, then, will be either *pro* (if the answer is yes) or *con* (if the answer is no).

ISSUE   Should the faculty of Northfield College be more culturally diverse?

PRO   Yes, it should be more culturally diverse.

CON   No, it should not be more culturally diverse.

Claims and counterclaims

When you argue one side of an issue, you make claims that you want your audience to believe. A claim is simply a statement that something is true or should be done. For example, these claims could be made about cultural diversity at Northfield College:

CLAIM   Northfield College fails to provide good education because the faculty is not culturally diverse.

CLAIM   Northfield College should appoint a committee to recruit faculty to ensure more cultural diversity.

Counterclaims are statements made against a particular position.

COUNTERCLAIM   The faculty are good scholars and teachers; herefore, their race is irrelevant.

COUNTERCLAIM   A committee on cultural diversity would be a waste of time and money.

The best arguments provide not only good reasons for accepting a position, but also good reasons for doubting the opposition. Good arguments are made by writers who know both sides of an issue.

Argumentative thesis

The primary claim that you make in your argument is called a thesis. In arguing your position you may make other claims, but they all work to support your thesis.

THESIS   Northfield College should enact a policy to make the faculty more culturally diverse by the year 2000.

CLAIM   The faculty is not culturally diverse.

CLAIM   A culturally diverse faculty is necessary to ensure a good education for today's students.

CLAIM   The goal of increased cultural diversity by the year 2000 is achievable and practical.

Evidence

Once you have formulated a thesis, you will need evidence to demonstrate the reasonableness of your claims. For example, to

support a claim that Northfield College's faculty lacks cultural diversity, you might introduce the following evidence.

EVIDENCE   According to the names in the college catalog, sixty-nine of seventy-nine faculty members are male.

EVIDENCE   According to a recent faculty survey, sixty-five of seventy-nine faculty members are white Caucasian.

EVIDENCE   According to Janet Smith, an unsuccessful job candidate for a position in the English Department, one hundred percent of the faculty hired in the last ten years have been white males.

Most arguments become more effective when they include source material gathered through research. However, shorter and more modest argument papers can be written without research and can profitably follow a process similar to that described here.

▇ WRITING 1: EXPLORATION

An issue debated by college faculty is whether or not a first-year writing course should be required of all college students. Make three claims and three counterclaims about this issue. Then select the claim you most believe in and write an argumentative thesis that could form the basis for a whole essay. **ESL:** Consider similarities and differences in how arguments are developed in English and in your native language. Do arguments in your native language use claims and counterclaims?

▐▐ ▐b▐ Finding an issue

An issue for a position paper should be phrased as a question with a yes or no answer. In selecting an issue, consider both national and local issues. You are likely to see national issues explained and argued on network television, on the front pages of daily newspapers, and in national newsmagazines: Are SATs a fair measure of academic potential? Should handguns be made illegal? Does acid rain kill forests? The advantages of national issues are their extensive news coverage and the likelihood of wide reader interest. The disadvantage is the difficulty in finding a local expert to interview or a site where the issue can be witnessed.

Local issues have an impact on the community in which you live. You will find these issues argued about in local newspapers and on local news broadcasts: Should a new mall be built on the beltway? Should wolves be reintroduced into the nearby national park? The advantage of local issues is that you can often visit a place where the controversy occurs, interview people who are affected by it, and find generous coverage in local news media. The disadvantage is that the subject will not be covered in national news sources.

To write a position paper, you need to select an issue that meets four criteria.

1   It is a real issue, about which there is genuine controversy and uncertainty.

2   You can identify at least two distinct positions.

3   You are personally interested in advocating one of these positions.

4   It is narrow enough to be manageable.

Select an issue you care about. If you do a thorough job on this assignment, you will spend quite a bit of time thinking, researching, and writing about it, so select something that matters to you. Frankly, it's best to select an issue you find interesting but about which you have not fully made up your mind: that way, you will conduct your research with genuine curiosity.

Brendan, who is from Wyoming, chose to write about a local issue that also had broader national implications:

ISSUE   Should wolves be reintroduced into Yellowstone National Park?

■ WRITING 2: APPLICATION

Make a list of three national and three local issues about which you are concerned. Next, select the three issues that seem most important to you and write each as a question with a yes or no answer. Finally, write a paragraph on each issue explaining where you stand on it at this point.

The most demanding work in writing a position paper takes place after you have selected an issue but before you actually write the paper. To analyze an issue, you need to research and describe the context for the issue, identify the arguments on both sides of the issue, and identify the people or groups who make each argument.

In preparing the material for your argument, you must treat both sides fairly, framing the opposition as positively as you frame your position. Think of it as an honest debate with yourself. Adopting a neutral stance toward your material will help you see clearly all the important claims you must refute to write the most persuasive paper possible. You will also have more empathy for the opposition and will therefore qualify your assertions with terms that suggest some room for honest disagreement. For any reader who sees merit in the opposing side, this strategy will be far more persuasive than absolute assertions.

Establishing context

Your first search is usually for the context — social, political, historical, or philosophical — that will allow you, and eventually your readers, to understand the issue. What is this issue about? Where did the controversy begin? How long has it been debated? Who are the people involved?

In this exploratory paragraph, Brendan describes the context for his issue, the reintroduction of wolves to Yellowstone National Park.

> Cattle ranchers killed nearly 81,000 wolves between 1883 and 1918. People believed that if this country was to be domesticated, there was no place for wolves. In 1915 Congress supported the interests of the ranchers and passed legislation for the removal of all wolves from federal lands. Strangely enough, this legislation included national parks, which were originally set aside to conserve wildlife. By 1926 there were no wolves in Yellowstone Park, and within ten years there were no wolves left in the continental United States.

Even in his exploratory writing, Brendan uses a fairly neutral tone, allowing his statistics to tell the story. It's a good idea to use a neutral tone whenever you present the context for an issue in your paper so that your audience witnesses, at the outset, your fairness and reasonableness.

2 Stating the claims for (pro)

List the claims supporting the pro side of the issue. Make each claim a distinctly strong and separate point, and make the best possible case for this position. Here are Brendan's claims supporting the position that *wolves should be reintroduced to Yellowstone National Park.*

a.   Wolves would make the park a complete ecosystem.

b.   Wolves would help control the population of elk, moose, and deer.

c.   The Endangered Species Act of 1973 requires wolves to be restored to federal lands.

d.   Visitors' experience of Yellowstone would be improved.

3 Identifying supporters

After listing the claims for, identify the most prestigious people or groups who make each one. These are the supporters who will add authority and persuasiveness to your argument (if you decide later to take this position) or whose authority and persuasiveness you will somehow have to counteract (if you decide later not to take this position). Here is Brendan's list of supporters.

a.   The National Audubon Society makes the argument that the purpose of national parks is to preserve the wilderness as it was before civilization moved in.

b.   Biologists and ecologists believe that the wolf will once again assume a predatory role in the park.

c.   The National Parks and Conservation Association argues for a strict interpretation of the Endangered Species Act.

d.   In a recent survey, the National Park Service found that seventy-four percent of Yellowstone Park visitors wanted to see wolves.

4 Stating the claims against (con)

List the claims supporting the con side of the issue, the counterclaims. It is not important that you have an equal number of reasons for and against, but you do want an approximate balance. Make the best possible case for this position. Here are the counterclaims Brendan identified.

> a.   Wolves will get out of the park and kill livestock on ranches.
>
> b.   Wolves will reduce the amount of game available to big-game hunters in the Montana-Wyoming-Idaho area.
>
> c.   Wolves will be a danger to people, especially park visitors.
>
> d.   Introduction of the wolf will limit public and commercial use of adjacent federal land and thus hurt area development.

5 Identifying opposition

Now identify the prestigious people or groups who make the counterclaims. Here is Brendan's authority list.

> a.   Sheep and cattle farmers say they fear for their livelihood, knowing that wolves have been proven livestock killers in the past.
>
> b.   Big-game hunters and the Foundation for North American Wild Sheep fear that wolves will kill game outside the park.
>
> c.   Both local citizens and some park visitors believe that wolves harm people, especially children.
>
> d.   Loggers, builders, skiers, and campers believe that the wolf would intrude into land near the park and use of that land for humans would cease.

6 Annotating the references

Now put together, in alphabetical order, the references you consulted during research, briefly identifying each according to the kind of information it contains. The same article may present claims from both sides as well as provide context. Here, for example, is a part of Brendan's reference list:

> Bass, R. (1991, October). The wolves' story. *Outside*, pp. 58–63. [Pro/con/context]

Carey, J. (1987, August-September). Who's afraid of the big bad wolf? *National Wildlife*, pp. 4–11. [Pro/context]

Cohn, J. (1990, October). Endangered wolf population increases; planned reintroduction into old territory raises controversy. *BioScience*, pp. 628–632. [Con/pro]

Edwards, D. (1987, June 13). Recall the wild wolf: recovery plans to reestablish the wolf packs in the wild have diverse groups trapped together in an emotional snare of politics, economics, and law. *Science News*, pp. 378–379. [Context]

Annotating your list of references allows you to check and rearrange your claims at any time during the writing process. In addition, if you use the documentation system that you will use in your final paper, your reference list will be virtually finished. (See Part VII for the documentation systems of various disciplines.)

WRITING 3: APPLICATION

Select one of the issues you are interested in, establish the necessary context, and make pro and con lists similar to those described in this section, including supporters of each position. Make the best possible case for each position.

II d Taking a position

Once you have spread out the two possible positions in the fairest way possible, you need to weigh for yourself which side is the stronger. This is a good time to engage in freewriting or journal writing and to argue with yourself about which position now makes the most sense to you. Write about each position for a page or so to see how it sounds to you, and determine whether you are more persuaded by one or the other. Select the position that you find most convincing and then state the reasons, most compelling reasons last. This will be the position you will most likely defend.

At this point, you need to formulate a **thesis,** a statement of the position you are going to defend.

THESIS   Wolves should be reintroduced to Yellowstone National Park to make the park a complete ecosystem.

Right now, all you need is a **working thesis,** something to focus your efforts in one direction and allow you to continue articulating

claims and assembling evidence. Writers typically revise their theses as they redirect or narrow their paper and find new evidence.

A good argumentative thesis meets the following criteria:

1 It is interesting to you and your intended audience.

2 It can be managed within the confines of the time and space available.

3 It asserts something specific.

4 It proposes a plan of action.

WRITING 4: APPLICATION

Take a position on the issue you have identified. Formulate a working thesis that you would like to support. Test your thesis against the four criteria listed for good theses.

11 e Developing an argument

Your argument is the case you will make for your position, the means by which you will try to persuade your readers that your position is correct. Good arguments need two things: good evidence and effective reasoning.

Assembling evidence

Claims, positions, and theses are meaningless without evidence to support them.

Facts and examples

Factual knowledge is verifiable and agreed upon by everyone involved regardless of personal beliefs or values. Facts are often statistical. These are facts:

Water boils at 212 degrees Fahrenheit.

Northfield College employed 79 full-time faculty and enrolled 1143 full-time students in 1992.

Examples can be used to illustrate a claim or clarify an issue. For example, the general claim that "in most situations wolves pose little threat to humans" would gain force by specific examples of peaceful coexistence between wolves and humans.

Facts and examples can, of course, be misleading and even wrong. For hundreds of years malaria was believed to be caused by "bad air" rather than, as we know today, by a parasite transmitted through mosquito bites; however, for the people who believed the bad-air theory, it was *fact*. Be sure that information you present as factual will be accepted as such by your audience.

Inferences

The accumulation of a certain number of facts and examples should lead to an interpretation of what those facts mean — an **inference,** or **generalization.** For example, if you attend five different classes at Northfield College and in each class you find no minority students, you may *infer* that there are few or no minority students on campus. However, while your inference is reasonable, it is not a fact, since your experience does not account for meeting all the possible students at the college.

Neither a fact nor an inference is better or more important than the other; they serve different purposes. Facts provide information, and inferences give that information meaning. Sometimes inference is all that's available. Statistics describing what "Americans," "college students," or other large groups believe or do are, in fact, inferences about these groups based on information collected from a much smaller number of individuals. To be credible, inferences must be reasonable and based on factual evidence.

Informed opinion

Informed opinions make good evidence; uninformed ones do not. If you say that Jim Smith is the best teacher at Northfield College, this personal opinion would not count for much in determining whether Smith gets tenure. However, opinions informed by either research or expertise would be important. For example, if an opinion about Smith were offered by a researcher who had used a reasonable and generally accepted list of criteria for good teaching to evaluate all the faculty at Northfield, it would be taken more seriously than your personal opinion.

Personal testimony

A kind of evidence that has mixed credibility is testimony based on personal experience. When someone has experienced something firsthand, his or her knowledge cannot easily be discounted — so your opinion that Jim Smith is the best teacher on campus is worth more if you have witnessed the teaching than if you have only heard about it. To use personal testimony effectively, provide details that confirm for readers that you were there and know what you are talking about.

2 Reasoning effectively

To build an effective argument out of your evidence, first take a moment to consider the audience you must persuade. Of course, your most important audience is your instructor, but consider also all those people who would read your position paper if it had a wider circulation. Ask yourself these questions:

- Who are my potential readers?

- What do they believe?

- Where do they stand on the issue?

- How are their interests involved?

- What evidence is likely to be effective with these people?

Once you have a sense of who you're trying to persuade, you can begin to build your argument. First, use **logic.** Make sure each claim and each step in your argument is reasonable and defensible. Make sure you have evidence to support each claim. Present your evidence clearly, make inferences carefully, and avoid errors in logic.

Second, establish your **credibility.** Your audience will reject even the soundest logic if they don't trust you. Show that you've done your homework and used reliable sources. Establish common ground: begin by identifying elements that both you and the opposition agree on. When explaining where you differ with your opponents, state their terms in accurate and neutral language; this way, your arguments cannot be dismissed because you misrepresented theirs. Use an objective and reasonable tone.

Third, appeal to your audience's **emotions.** Telling details, vivid and concrete language, compelling examples, persuasive metaphors, and occasionally a more personal or impassioned tone can help reach your readers' hearts as well as minds.

FALSE ARGUMENTS (FALLACIES)

The following false arguments are often made when a writer does not have enough evidence to support his or her claims. Learn to recognize and avoid them.

1. Bandwagon. Encourages people to accept a position simply because others already have: *More than three-fourths of Americans have already begun to recycle paper and plastics — shouldn't you recycle too?* (Those other people could have made bad decisions.)

2. Begging the question. Treats a questionable statement as if it had already been accepted: *If America is to maintain its position as the foremost military power on the planet, defense spending must be increased.* (Many people would question whether America really should try to maintain its military supremacy.)

3. Does not follow (*non sequitur*). Presents a conclusion that does not logically follow from its premises: *Kathleen Monahan has been an ardent supporter of women's rights, so she will be a good senator.* (Simply because Monahan supports women's rights does not mean she has the skills or knowledge to be a good senator.)

4. False analogy. Uses analogy to show that two things are alike when they are — for the purpose of the argument — different: *Just as the lioness is the one to protect her cubs, so do women bear the responsibility of caring for their children.* (Lions and humans are not alike.)

5. False cause (*post hoc*). Assumes that if one event happened after another, the earlier event must have caused the later one: *Federal spending on schools should be decreased: the last time the government decreased education spending, SAT scores went up.* (There is no clear connection between spending decreases and SAT scores.)

6. False dilemma (*either/or dilemma*). Presents a situation as a dilemma with only two options, when there are actually more: *If we fail to set aside these 30,000 acres as a preserve for the crested loon, the entire population will eventually be wiped out.* (There may be many other possibilities for saving the loon, such as a smaller preserve or a smaller but sustainable loon population.)

7. Oversimplification. Reduces a complex system of causes and effects to an inaccurate generalization: *Ronald Reagan's election in 1980 led to a far more stable economy in the 1980s.* (Reagan's election may have been one factor in the economy of the 1980s, but there were no doubt many other forces at work.)

WRITING 5: APPLICATION

Develop an informal profile of the audience for your position paper by answering the questions posed in this section.

11 f Organizing a position paper

You are now ready to write your paper. The challenge is to prepare a strategy for organizing and presenting your position in the best possible way. Arguments generally use deductive reasoning or inductive reasoning, although many arguments use both to make their cases. Each type of reasoning lends itself to a particular organization: arguments that are primarily deductive are often presented with a thesis-first organization; arguments that are primarily inductive are often presented with a delayed-thesis organization.

1 Deductive reasoning

When you reason deductively, you start with a generalization **(major premise),** add to it a specific case **(minor premise),** and draw a conclusion about the specific case based on the generalization. For example, a deductive argument about the issue of cultural diversity at Northfield College could first assert that *good education is culturally diverse* (major premise), then point out that *cultural diversity is missing from Northfield College* (minor premise), and conclude that *Northfield College does not provide a good education.*

2 Inductive reasoning

To reason inductively, you start with the accumulation of facts and then form a generalization (an **inference**) based on those facts. For instance, the issue of cultural diversity at Northfield College arose from the accumulation of a number of facts indicating that there were few minority group members among either the faculty or the students. *Northfield College lacks cultural diversity* is the generalization based on those facts.

This generalization about cultural diversity is less argumentative than descriptive. To make a position paper more argumentative, you would add to the generalization a chain of deductive reasoning, arguing that the faculty does not provide a good education because it is not culturally diverse.

3 Thesis-first organization

Using this type of organization, writers begin with their thesis and spend the remainder of their essay supporting it and defending their claims against counterclaims.

1 **An issue is introduced as a yes/no question.** This makes clear that there are at least two sides to the issue. (*Should wolves be reintroduced into Yellowstone National Park?*)

2 **A position is asserted as a thesis.** The thesis commonly concludes the paragraph that introduces the issue. (*Wolves should be reintroduced into Yellowstone National Park to restore the natural ecosystem.*)

3 **The counterclaims are summarized.** Squeezing the counterclaim between the thesis and the evidence reserves the strongest places in the essay, the opening and conclusion, for the writer's own position. (See 27a.) (*If wolves are reintroduced into Yellowstone, they will have damaging effects on both the park and the surrounding region.*)

4 **The counterclaims are refuted.** The writer can actually strengthen his or her position by admitting that in some cases the counterclaims might be true. (*The fear of damage is based on commercial interests and old myths.*)

5 **The writer's claims are supported with evidence.** These claims include *because* statements and constitute the longest and most carefully documented part of the essay. (*Wolves should be reintroduced into Yellowstone because they will keep the deer population in check, add excitement for visitors, and fulfill the national park mission.*)

6 **A conclusion broadly restates the writer's position.** The conclusion synthesizes the specific claims into a broad general position. (*Restoring the ecosystem of Yellowstone National Park to its precivilized state is consistent with the mission of the national parks and will be more beneficial than not.*)

There are three distinct advantages to leading with your thesis: (1) Your audience knows where you stand from the first para-

graph on; (2) your thesis occupies the two strongest places — first and last — in the essay; and (3) it is the most common form of academic argument.

4 Delayed-thesis organization

Using this type of organization, a writer introduces the issue, discusses the arguments for and against, but does not obviously take a side until late in the essay. The writer should explain and illustrate his or her position *after* presenting the opposition's position, since placing it at the end will give it more emphasis. The delayed-thesis argument follows this pattern:

1 **An issue is introduced as a yes/no question.**

2 **The claims of the opposition are summarized.**

3 **The claims are refuted.**

4 **The counterclaims (the writer's position) are summarized.**

5 **The counterclaims are supported.**

6 **The conclusion states a thesis based on the counterclaims.**

There are also three advantages to this form of argument: (1) The audience is drawn into the writer's struggle by being asked to weigh the evidence and arrive at a thesis; (2) the audience is kept in suspense about the writer's position; and (3) the audience understands the difficulty in making a decision.

WRITING 6: APPLICATION

Make two outlines for organizing your position paper, one with the thesis first, the other with a delayed thesis. Share your outlines with your classmates and discuss which seems most appropriate for the issue you have chosen.

11 g Shaping the whole paper

Following is the finished draft of Brendan's paper, edited in places to shorten it for illustrative purposes. Brendan uses the thesis-first method of organization, as his instructor specified. Because of the complex nature of Brendan's subject, his position paper relies heavily on research. He adopts the third-person point of view to present his argument in an objective tone, letting the facts, examples, and informed expert opinion make his case for him. He uses the APA documentation style, which is appropriate to his intended major, political science. (For more information on documentation systems, see Part VII.)

The Wolf Should Be Reintroduced into

Yellowstone National Park

Since 1926, there have been no wolves in Yellowstone National Park. The modern wolf inhabited the area of Yellowstone, as well as the greater part of the North American continent, for well over a million years before the Europeans settled the New World. Upon arrival, white settlers began to push the wolf from its natural territory. With the settlers' movement west and with their increased development and agriculture, the wolf's range in the United States rapidly shrank and eventually disappeared.

In recent years there has been a movement to bring the wolf back to Yellowstone Park. A battle is being waged between environmental conservationists, who support the reintroduction of wolves, and sheep and cattle farmers and western hunters, who oppose it. So far, legislators, representing the farmers and hunters, have been able to block the reintroduction of wolves.

The wolf, however, should be reintroduced into Yellowstone to make the park once again a complete ecosystem. Edward Lewis of the Greater Yellowstone Coalition, a regional conservation group, says that "wolves are the missing link" (Edwards, 1987, p. 378). They are the only major species that existed in historical times but is missing now. Wolves would help to balance the ecosystem by preying on deer, elk, and moose. This would reduce the damage that overpopulation of these animals does to the area and would limit the numbers of these species that starve during harsh winters.

Many sheep and cattle ranchers, however, feel that if wolves are reintroduced into the park, they will roam outside the park onto the lands where these ranchers keep their animals and will kill the valuable livestock (Bass, 1991). The fact is that wolves in Yellowstone will have relatively little impact on the livestock industry. Steven Fritts, a U.S. Fish and Wildlife Service ecologist, recently compiled a five-year study on the effects wolves have on livestock (Edwards, 1987). In his research he studied wolves in northern Minnesota. There are 12,000 livestock farms, 230,000 cattle, 90,000 sheep, as well as thousands of turkeys and other domesticated animals in the wolves' territory in Minnesota. According to Fritts's study, only about ten animals are killed each year by wolves, which represents only one-fifth of one percent of farm animals. Similar reductions were projected for deer, moose, and bison, and little or no loss was estimated for bighorn and pronghorn. The report also revealed that the grizzly bear (another endangered species) wouldn't be affected at all. Tom France from the National Wildlife Federation says that wolves can be managed and will enhance the hunting experience (Carey, 1987).

Stephen Kellert, a wolf specialist from Yale University, recently conducted surveys of people's attitudes toward wolves. He says that there is a deep-grained bias toward predators among most ranchers and hunters of the West. These attitudes are not necessarily based on facts, but rather superstition and traditional folklore (McNamee, 1986). Nevertheless, many politicians, senators, and representatives from Wyoming, Idaho, and Montana, including Congressman Ron Marlee from Montana, have an obligation to side with the farmers and hunters whom they represent. Many of these politicians are hunters or were farmers themselves and, therefore, share the same negative feelings about wolves returning. They feel that they must please the people they represent in order to get reelected and keep their jobs, so they are reluctant to side with anyone besides those who are most likely to vote them back into office (Joyce, 1990).

Yellowstone Park alone consists of 2.2 million acres of wilderness; the greater Yellowstone ecosystem consisting of Grand Tetons National Park, seven national forests, and other federal and state land totals about 14 million acres. David Mech, America's leading wolf expert from the U.S. Fish and Wildlife Service, says that Yellowstone "literally begs to have wolves. It's teeming with prey. Wolves would add an element to the ecosystem that would help restore it to a more natural state, and that would allow the public to better enjoy the park" (Cohn, 1990, p. 630). In a recent poll, 74% of Yellowstone's visitors felt wolves would improve the experience of visiting the park (Cohn, 1990). Reasons for this include the fact that wolves are presently not found in the wild anywhere in the United States, with a few exceptions in Canada-bordering states. Many people feel wolves are exciting animals because they have seen the results of studies that have shown how wolves possess many of the family-oriented characteristics that humans value.

The National Park Service is the leading preservation agency in the United States; part of the purpose of the National Park Service is to preserve the natural wilderness as it was before the white settlers disturbed it. Yellowstone is somewhat of a role model for public land management in our times, a symbol of "whole ecosystem management," says William Turnage, the executive director of the Wilderness Society. "Of course the wolf belongs here" (O'Gara, 1986, p. 20).

The Endangered Species Act of 1973 states that federal agencies are to use "all methods and procedures necessary" to restore endangered species that have been driven out, and not just "methods and procedures [that are] convenient, economically painless, and politically expedient" (Williams, 1990, p. 33). The three subspecies of the gray wolf that once occupied the continental United States are listed as endangered. The Endangered Species Act then not only gives the National Park Service the power to work toward the reintroduction of the wolf into areas such as Yellowstone, but also requires it to do so. Today, however, there are no wolves in the park. Conservation organizations, such as the Wilderness Society and the National Parks and Conservation Association as well as the National Park Service, feel that if this issue was worth the time, effort, and money for Congress to pass this act, then it should be enforced. Our leading conservation agency should not be prevented from enforcing this act of Congress.

The reintroduction of wolves into Yellowstone National Park is both an important and a reasonable proposal. In this age of environmental abuse and excessive development by human beings, it seems only appropriate to set aside areas for the complete preservation of nature. Our National Parks are the ideal place for this. The wolf was once an integral part of the Yellowstone environment. Its reintroduction would complete the ecosystem and improve the natural situation. The arguments posed by farmers and hunters are insubstantial. An act of Congress requires government agencies to return the wolf to its original habitat. Why, then, are there still no wolves in Yellowstone?

References

Bass, R. (1991, October). The wolves' story. Outside, pp. 58–63.

Carey, J. (1987, August–September). Who's afraid of the big bad wolf? National Wildlife, pp. 4–11.

Cohn, J. (1990, October). Endangered wolf population increases; planned reintroduction into old territory raises controversy. Bioscience, pp. 628–632.

Edwards, D. (1987, June 13). Recall the wild wolf: recovery plans to reestablish the wolf packs in the wild have diverse groups trapped together in an emotional snare of politics, economics, and law. Science News, pp. 378–379.

Joyce, C. (1990, June 2). Yellowstone lets the wolf through the door. New Scientist, p. 21.

McNamee, T. (1986, January). Yellowstone's missing element.
Audubon, pp. 12–19.

O'Gara, G. (1986, November-December). Filling in a missing link.
Sierra, pp. 20–21.

Williams, T. (1990, November). Waiting for wolves to howl in
Yellowstone. Audubon, pp. 32–34.

SUGGESTIONS FOR WRITING AND RESEARCH

INDIVIDUAL

1. Write a position paper on the issue you have been working with in Writings 2–6. Follow the guidelines suggested in this chapter, using as much research as you deem appropriate.

2. Write a position paper on an issue of interest to your class: consider topics such as (a) student voice in writing topics, (b) the seating plan, (c) the value of writing groups versus instructor conferences, or (d) the number of writing assignments.

COLLABORATIVE

1. In teams of two or three, select an issue; divide up the work so that each group member contributes some work to (1) the context, (2) the pro argument, and (3) the con argument (to guarantee that you do not take sides prematurely). Share your analysis of the issue with another group and receive feedback. Finally, write your position papers individually.

2. Follow the procedure for the first collaborative assignment, but write your final position paper collaboratively.

When you interpret something, you address the question "What does it mean?" When most of us encounter something new and interesting, we try to make sense of it by figuring out how it works, by comparing it to similar things, by analyzing our reactions to it, and by trying to determine why it affects us the way it does. Interpreting things is how we learn to understand and value them.

We usually think of texts as the written material found in books and periodicals. However, virtually all symbolic works can be considered texts open to interpretation — films, music and dance performances, exhibits, paintings, photographs, sculptures, advertisements, artifacts, and even whole cultures. You are probably familiar with the reviews commonly written about these texts, such as a review in a newspaper telling you whether a film is worth seeing. A review is a form of interpretation that not only answers the interpretive question, What does it mean? but also the evaluative question, Is it good? Most interpretive essays in writing classes focus on written texts and are more interpretive than evaluative.

12 a Writing to interpret

A fully developed interpretation *explains* what the text says, in and of itself. It also *argues* for a particular interpretation of the text's meaning, what the text implies or suggests in a larger sense. Our initial reactions to a new text are often a jumble of impressionistic thoughts, feelings, and memories. To write an interpretive essay, you must take the time to analyze this jumble and develop a reasonable, systematic understanding of what the text means and why. Since all texts have more than one possible meaning, you must also make the best possible case that your interpretation is a good one and deserves attention. Like any argument, an interpretive essay should be as persuasive as possible, but it can never be an absolute proof.

Interpretive essays, which are also called critical, analytical, or review essays, are among the most frequent college writing assignments. A typical assignment may ask you to interpret a poem, a story, an essay, a newspaper or magazine article, or even a historical document. Writing a good textual interpretation will draw on all your writing skills. To explain a text, you will usually have to describe its people and situations, narrate its events, and define important concepts or terms. You may also need to analyze the various parts of the text and explain how they work together as a whole, perhaps by comparing the text to others. To argue for your interpretation, you will have to develop a strong thesis and defend this position with sound reasoning. In some cases, you will also be expected to evaluate the text's worth and reflect on its significance to you. (See 4d.)

To explain and demonstrate the art of interpretive writing, we present the following short reflective essay by Angel Fuster, a senior majoring in English and enrolled in an advanced writing class. (Note that the people in this essay use family nicknames to refer to one another. The older brother, Angel, uses the nickname "Mamma" for his sister Angelique; Angelique calls Angel "Chino.") While Fuster's essay is autobiographical and therefore nonfiction, many of the texts you will be asked to analyze in college will be fiction or poetry. But the basic techniques for interpreting works of fiction and nonfiction are the same.

Angelique's Letter
Angel Fuster

-1-

The letter is written on standard grade-school paper, the blue lines far enough apart for any kid to learn on. Her name, "Angelique," at the top of the page, is done in her fanciest style. But the characters are boxy and it looks as though they were done especially slow.

-2-

"Just like a nice restaurant's name," my nine-year-old sister said.

I wanted to say how proud I was that she was learning script, but instead replied, "Yeah, like those restaurants only rich white people go to."

She gazed at her name and smiled wishfully. "Yeah, if I was white, I'd make a restaurant with those letters."

"Don't worry, Mamma, if you go to college like me, you could get whatever you want."

I felt guilty for using her artistically written "Angelique" to teach her about racism, especially since I knew what I had said was a bit oversimplified and inaccurate. But what could I do? How could I ensure that she grows up questioning things? I had to keep her from getting pregnant and dropping out of school as many of her classmates will, as my older sister did, and as my mother before her. And she was already talking about boys.

-3-

The boys loved to talk about Sorada Rodriguez, but none loved her like I did. One day I walked up to her on the playground and, without thinking, took out my pencil and poked her in the thigh.

She was sent to the nurse. I waited after school and told her I was sorry, and she just gave me the worst stare and screamed at me.

I walked her the two blocks to her side of the projects without saying a word. When we got to the empty apartment, I kissed her on the mouth. Then, still without saying a word, she took off her clothes, like in the movies, and I took off mine. I was embarrassed because I had no hair and she had a lot.

-4-

I would have to get Angelique interested in important issues, things that would excite her, make her want to develop her mind so she would grow into a thinking person. My strategy was twofold: I would give her enormous pride in her people, then I would teach her to act on that pride to improve herself. But in order to keep her interested in these issues, I would have to show that they directly affect her, using every opportunity I could to bring up the subject.

-5-

"Chino, play Barbie with me. You could be her," Angelique said, holding up a blond doll dressed in a bikini bathing suit.

"No, I don't want her. I want the one with the black hair. It isn't fair that all the Barbies are blond. Black hair is beautiful too. They don't even make Puerto Rican Barbies."

She studied the long wiry blondness. "I wish they make Puerto Rican Barbies."

I felt like telling her I was only kidding.

-6-

Under "Angelique," her words are written in large print that allows only four or five words to fit between the pink margins.

Dear Chino,
*   How are you doing?*
*   remember you said to write*
*   you a song or a story? Well, I*
*   am goging to write bouth of them.*
*   Are you happy?*

Indeed, I was very happy. My plan to educate Angelique was working. Getting her to write was one step in encouraging her to be a thinking person. I knew that in her grade school, the same one I went to, little encouragement is given to write. From the moment I was assigned my first college paper, I regretted my educational background.

-7-

Why did these white people know how to write so much better than I? Why did they go to the best schools while I went to run-down schools like Seward Park? Why didn't someone encourage me to write?

I would push Angelique as hard as I could. I would get her angry at the injustice around her, make her want to prove herself. If she learned to enjoy writing, I would be that much closer to making her a thinking person.

-8-

She wrote me like I asked her to, at first mostly drawing pictures and writing the standard "How are you doing" and "I miss you." Soon, however, her letters became more substantial. She wrote about the games she played in school, her new shoes, and why she still likes to watch *Ducktails*, even though her classmates say it's a baby cartoon.

-9-

*   do you love scary stoys? Well*
*   you are going to loike this one*
*   get wety here it is "HA" "HA" "HA" "HA"*

*   FRITE NIGHT FOR ANGELIQUE*
*   It all started on Friday mornning*
*   It was 6 am I saw red drops from*
*   my seling! Something is happing in*

the adek I seid. I ran up the stars.
I herd a scem. I opened the door slowly
it was my mom. She was merded she was
stab. She is laing on the floor.
I called Chino. He came in a ower.
Every one we knew was dead. Some one was
kning on the door. It was the mertira.
I kict him in the nust. He drope the
gun and I pict up and seid if you toch
that rabbit your dead. He kick the rabbit.
I shot him in the hart thak his mask off
and it was Chino alalong.

-10-

I was proud of her.	She is learning to be a good writer.
I liked her surprise ending — an unexpected twist.	
	Is the ending a subconscious slip?
Did I push her too hard?	No. After all, is it not I who plays Barbie with her, who encourages her, and who thinks about what is best for her? How could I be choking her?
I am sorry.	But I have to push hard.

-11-

That's What Siste'rs are for
And I neve thought I
felt this way
and I'm glad I got a chanse to say

that I do beleve I love you
and if I should ever go away
Well then close your eye
and trie
the thing we do today
and that if you can remmber
keep smiling, keep shing
Thrus me doling — thats
what sisters for.

-12-

Guilt

■ **WRITING 1: EXPLORATION**

After reading "Angelique's Letter," freewrite for ten minutes about your initial reaction to the text. You may want to consider how your experience is similar to or different from Angel's, and why.

12 b Finding and exploring a topic

To develop an interpretation, you need to read a text carefully — and more than once. The first time (or first few times) you read a text, you will be reading to understand, sorting out what the text says on the literal level. You need to move beyond this, however, to **critical reading,** in which you develop an understanding of the author's larger theme or purpose. (See Chapter 2.)

Pay close attention to the text — every word the author chose, every thing he or she described (or left undescribed) is significant. It is also important, though, to let your own ideas roam freely at this point. Don't try to force every last detail in the text into a tidy pattern; focus on questions, not answers. Freewriting, journal writing, clustering, outlining, and annotating are particularly helpful invention and discovery techniques at this stage. (See Chapters 7 and 8.)

A good topic for an interpretive essay must involve an interesting question that has more than one possible answer. Without the possibility of more than one answer, there is no real interpretation. If the topic is not interesting, you will bore not only your readers but also yourself. Here are some suggestions for finding and exploring topics for interpretive essays.

1 Identify problems or puzzles

Annotate the text by writing down in the margins problems or puzzles you find in the text as you read or discuss it in class. Later you can explore each one to see if a suitable topic emerges. Good topics arise from material that is difficult to understand. Here, for example, are some of the problems or puzzles that could be noted about "Angelique's Letter":

Why does Angel Fuster focus so much on Angelique's writing?

- Why does he include the story about his own early sexual encounter in stanza 3?

- Why does Angelique identify Chino as the murderer in stanza 9?

2 Find patterns of repeated words, ideas, and images

By repeating words, ideas, and images, writers call attention to them and indicate that they are important to the meaning of the text. Often these repetitions form a pattern and are strong enough to suggest a **theme** — a major idea with which the work is concerned. For example, in "Angelique's Letter," the concepts of writing, race, sex, and guilt arise more than once and could be considered themes.

3 Consider the style, organization, or form

Careful writers try to make these elements contribute to the meaning of a text. As a critical reader you should try to decide why the writer made the choices he or she did. For example:

- Why does Fuster number his prose paragraphs as if they were poetic stanzas?

- Why does he arrange stanza 9 in opposite parallel columns?

- What is the effect of including Angelique's letters exactly as she wrote them?

4 Consider the larger context

You can often find an interesting topic by comparing the text with another, either one by the same author or a similar work by a different author. For example, you could compare Fuster's essay with Julia Alvarez's *How the Garcia Girls Lost Their Accents* (1991), which also deals with growing up Hispanic in America. Carefully compare and contrast the texts, looking for clues to why the author you are studying made the choices he or she did. Consider reading what other reviewers or critics have said about the text as well.

■ WRITING 2: APPLICATION

Use at least three of the methods described in this section to find and explore potential topics for a text you are currently reading. Write about the possibilities, but do not, at this time, worry about developing your ideas thoroughly.

12 **C** **Explaining a text** ○

Once you have explored several topics and settled on one, you can begin the task of explaining the text. You need to give your readers a grasp of the text as a whole, so that they can both follow your interpretation and join in the act of interpreting themselves. This process is also valuable because it forces you to reexamine the details of the text.

1 Identify and summarize the text

Your first job in writing about any text is to identify it thoroughly, yet briefly, so that readers know from the start what you are talking about. Identify its author, title, subject, and genre (what type of text it is — essay, poem, novel, and so on).

If the text tells a story, summarize the plot, character, and setting. If the text provides another kind of information (if it is, say, a poem or an argument), summarize the main ideas. In the following paragraph, Bob summarizes "Angelique's Letter":

> "Angelique's Letter," an essay by Angel Fuster, explores one of the many struggles that minority families face in deteriorating inner cities throughout the country. Chino, the author and older brother, would like to see his nine-year-old sister, Angelique, rise above her ghetto education. He does not want her to get pregnant and cut her education short as his mother and older sister did. Nor, however, does he want to stifle her with too much big brother advice.

2 Explain the form and organization

No matter what the text, some principle or plan holds it together and gives it structure. Texts that tell stories are often organized as a sequence of events in chronological order. Other texts may alternate between explanations and examples or between first-person and third-person narrative. You will have to decide which aspects of the text's form and organization are most important for your interpretation. Rebecca explains the unusual stanza organization of "Angelique's Letter":

> After Angelique's scary story, we see both sides of Angel's conscience in an argument made visible by writing it in two columns. On the left is the soft side of him who would like to

praise her. On the right is the voice that wants to control and educate her. He concludes this section with "I am sorry."

3 Describe the author's perspective

Describing the author's perspective provides your readers with clues about the author's theme and purpose. In some cases, you will need to differentiate the author's perspective from those of the characters. "Angelique's Letter," however, is nonfiction, so Angel the author is the same person as the character his sister calls Chino. John attempts to describe Fuster's perspective:

> Angel writes as an angry older brother intent on protecting his sister from the destructive forces of the ghetto. At the same time, he views his attempt to save her as itself destructive. The resulting essay is more confused than revolutionary.

4 Explain the thesis or theme

Tell your readers what the main point of the text is. In fiction, poetry, and reflective essays, the main point usually takes the form of an implicit **theme,** while in most nonfiction it appears as a **thesis,** either stated or unstated. The theme or thesis of a text is different from a reader's interpretation. A theme or thesis is what the text says it is about: *"Angelique's Letter" is about the difficulties of growing up Hispanic in the United States.* An interpretation is the deeper meaning that you, as a critical reader, find in the story: *"Angelique's Letter" is about the author's uneasiness with his well-educated self, which he fears has killed his neighborhood self.*

5 Place the work in a historical, cultural, or biographical context

No text exists in isolation. Each was created by a particular author in a particular place at a particular time. Describing this context provides readers with important background information and indicates which conditions you think most influential. After learning more about the author through an interview, Rebecca describes the circumstances that led to Fuster's essay:

> I particularly liked "Angelique's Letter" because it shows some of the anger and frustration that nonwhite children faced

growing up in the city. Angel drew on his own experience of living in the Seward Park housing project in New York City.

■ WRITING 3: APPLICATION

Look at the text you are now interpreting, and make brief notes about each of the five elements described in this section.

12 d Taking a stand

When you write an interpretation, you not only explain how a text works but also take a stand on what the text means and argue your case as best you can.

■ Understanding interpretive communities

The communities to which you belong shape who you are, how you see the world, and how you respond to it. All of us belong to many communities: families, social and economic groups (students or teachers, rich or poor), organizations (Brownies, Boy Scouts, Democrats, Masons), geographic locales (rural or urban, North or South), and institutions (school, church, fraternity). Those communities that influence you most strongly are your **interpretive communities** — they determine how you interpret the world. People who belong to the same community that you do are likely to have similar assumptions and are therefore likely to interpret things as you would. People who belong to different communities are likely to have perspectives different from yours.

College is, of course, a large interpretive community. It is made up in turn of many smaller communities called disciplines — English, history, chemistry, business, and so on. And within any discipline are several established ways of interpreting texts. Within the field of English literature, for example, there are feminist critics and Marxist critics, scholars who rely heavily on biographical information and those who look at only the words on the page.

When you take a stand in an interpretive essay, you will often do so from the perspective of a traditional academic interpretive community. Take care to follow the conventions of that community. Remember, though, that your views are influenced by many other communities. Acknowledging these other communities — such as class, gender, race, family — and examining how they affect your interpretation can often lead to interesting insights.

2 Choosing a perspective

Many college assignments will ask that you interpret a text objectively — that you focus on the *object* (text) under study instead of the *subject* doing the study (yourself). This would seem to ask you to avoid showing any of those biases that inevitably come with your membership in various interpretive communities. Realistically, however, you can be objective only to a certain degree. What such assignments really ask is that you adopt an **objective stance,** interpreting the text as objectively as possible, trying to see things as they exist apart from your preconceived way of viewing them.

When using an objective stance, write from the **third-person** point of view. Keep yourself and references to yourself out of your writing, and use language that is emotionally neutral and unbiased.

A few college assignments that call for interpretation will ask you to take a **subjective stance.** Such assignments encourage you to acknowledge frankly the interpretive communities to which you belong. Instead of keeping your opinions or emotions out of the paper, you incorporate them as it suits your purpose. A subjective stance can be honest in admitting that complete objectivity is impossible. However, the subjective stance is often distrusted in academic writing because it can divert attention from the object under study and misdirect it toward the writer's self.

When using the subjective stance, write from the **first-person** point of view, but not excessively or in every sentence. Refer to personal experience only when it supports your purpose. Make value judgments, but do so with care, caution, and respect for opposing opinions.

Some of the most readable and honest interpretive writing is a mix of objective and subjective points of view: the writer focuses on the text and supports all assertions with evidence from the text, yet admits his or her own opinions and values at carefully selected points. Frequently, such essays use an objective stance for explaining the text and a more subjective stance for interpreting it. (See Chapter 6 for more on voice; see 28a for more on selecting tone.)

3 Developing and supporting a thesis

The **thesis** of your interpretive essay gives a clear, concise statement of your interpretation. It should answer the question that you identified as the topic of the paper. A good thesis lets readers know what to expect and guides their understanding of the information presented.

QUESTION   Why does Angel Fuster focus so much on Angelique's writing?

THESIS   In "Angelique's Letter," Angel Fuster focuses on education and on writing in particular because he believes they will lead to a better life for Angelique and others like her.

Like an argumentative thesis, an interpretive thesis should answer an interesting question and should be focused enough that you can support it within the confines of your paper. Unlike an argumentative thesis, it does not propose a plan of action; rather, it proposes a way of seeing. A clear thesis helps persuade an audience that your interpretation is careful and reasonable.

Stating your interpretation is one thing, persuading readers to believe it is another. To explore your topic and develop your thesis, you probably marked, collected, and copied passages from your reading. These passages will form the basis for your evidence. In addition, you may want to bring in other expert sources, such as those found through library research or interviews, to support your ideas.

When you draw on other sources to support your view, be careful how you bring that information into your paper. You will need to decide when to **summarize,** when to **paraphrase,** and when to **quote** directly. Regardless of how you bring the outside information into your paper, remember that you must document where each idea came from; to fail to do so is **plagiarism.** (For a complete explanation of using and documenting source material, see Chapter 17.)

WRITING 4: APPLICATION

Write three possible thesis statements about a text you are studying. Identify two quotations in the text that would support each statement. Conclude by freewriting about which thesis you would prefer to write an essay on.

12 e Shaping the whole paper

Angel Fuster's essay "Angelique's Letter" was read and interpreted by a class of first-year students. The assignment was in three parts. The first draft was to be an objective interpretation. The second draft was to be subjective, in the form of a personal letter to the author. And the final draft was to be a revision of whichever interpretation the student preferred. Two final drafts are reproduced here.

1. Objective stance

In Heather's essay, "Slowing Down," the writer herself is not present until the last paragraph, where she felt it necessary to step in personally and affirm her own feelings about the essay. Heather's organization follows Fuster's essay from beginning to end. Because she believes that Fuster's own words convey a great deal of power, she quotes him directly rather than paraphrasing his text; notice that she integrates her quotes smoothly and grammatically with her own sentences.

Slowing Down

"Angelique's Letter" tells a story about how a Puerto Rican college student named Angel decides to see his nine-year-old sister Angelique grow up having pride in herself and her culture, despite the disadvantages she will face because of her race and economic background. Understanding the importance of education and achievement, Angel sets out to instill in his sister a sense of value toward these things, hoping that will help her become all that she is capable of being.

The story begins with young Angelique displaying her excitement about learning. Using her newly acquired ability to write in script, she has written "Angelique" in her "fanciest style" on a sheet of blue-lined notebook paper. Looking for praise from her older brother, whom she calls by the family name Chino, she proudly displays her letter to him. Rather than with praise and encouragement, however, Chino replies sarcastically, "like those restaurants only rich white people go to."

Chino intends his response to provoke thought and encourage his sister to become angry at the system that makes Puerto Ricans second-class citizens. However, Chino appears to worry about his own reaction, as he confesses to feeling "guilty for using her artistically written 'Angelique' to teach her about racism."

These first two passages are important in several ways. First, they show Chino's influence on his younger sister. Second, they introduce Chino's drive to make sure Angelique does not become pregnant and drop out of school "as many of her classmates will." Third, they show Chino's dedication to act on his resolve by turning innocent situations into lessons about ghetto life. Finally, the second passage ends with a clear warning that time is short, "and she was already talking about boys."

Chino's flashback about Sorada Rodriguez illustrates how little time he has to lose if he is going to make a difference in Angelique's life. Girls in this environment are forced to grow up very quickly. Chino has to prevent her from becoming too sexually active, like Sorada, at such a young age if she is to stay in school and do well.

Chino continues with his strategy to ensure that Angelique "grow into a thinking person." He shows how hard he will have to push, "using every opportunity . . . to bring up the subject."

When Angelique offers him a blond Barbie, he replies, "No, I don't want her. I want the one with the black hair." So again he uses her simple game as a lesson in racial discrimination, and again he feels guilty, ending the episode with "I felt like telling her I was only kidding."

When Chino returns to school, Angelique writes to him as he has requested. He knows what it is like to grow up in a poor educational environment. Chino is still "bitter" because the other kids at college went to the best schools and had the best teachers. But his bitterness leads him to push her too hard, too fast, as her scary story "Frite Night" makes clear to him; she has cast Chino in the role of the murderer. On the one hand, Chino is proud of the long imaginative story she has written, but on the other hand he wonders if he is "choking her." He ends his essay with the single word "Guilt"--his clear admission that, despite his good intentions, he is doing his sister wrong.

I do not pretend to understand the situation Chino and his sister are facing, so I really cannot judge whether Chino is right or wrong. His intentions are the best; however, I question whether instilling anger in a young child is a good thing to do. There are other emotions, such as love, that encourage learning and self-improvement. Children need to be children, and childhood is the only time they can be that. There is nothing wrong with educating his sister, but, as Chino realizes himself by the end of his essay, he has to learn where and when to stop. If he doesn't stop, at least he knows he must slow down.

2 Subjective stance

Pat takes a personal approach to finding meaning in Fuster's text. He supports his assertions by sharing relevant elements of his own experiences and also by quoting specific passages from Fuster's text. While Pat's essay is not analytic in a strict academic sense, it does analyze the text in light of his own experience.

Dear Angel,

    I grew up in rural Vermont, a long way from places like Seward Park. My little town is surrounded by high mountains, not tall skyscrapers. But your paper made me think about Bethlehem, Pennsylvania, where I lived before my family moved to Vermont, nine years ago. We lived close to the projects, where both black and Hispanic families lived, and which my parents warned us to stay away from. I wonder what it is like now in my old neighborhood and what the future is of the people who live there. How many children have older brothers looking out for them, wanting them to grow up "questioning things"?

    I learned a lot from "Angelique's Letter," not only about your life, but about mine as well. Though Angelique has formidable obstacles to overcome--especially since she is female--I learned that she has a powerful advocate in you, her older brother. You are a role model for her as well as for all of her friends who are trapped in that system. Your plan to make her a "thinking person" by writing letters is working, even though you worry about pushing her too hard. Remember that in addition to writing "Frite Night" she copied out the song "That's What Sisters Are For" and sent it to tell you she loved you. You have no choice; she does need to read, write, and become better educated to escape her life in the projects.

    I also learned that I take my own educated life for granted. You "regretted [your] educational background from the moment [you were] assigned [your] first college paper." Well, compared to you, I have been handed everything on a silver platter, including a safe, comfortable, middle-class home, college prep classes, and teachers who encouraged me. Reading and writing must have come easy, since I seem to have been doing them all of my life.

    What touches me most is your great concern for Angelique's future. Most people in your situation would be out for themselves and not thinking about what's best for the family they left behind. Instead you are trying to share your success with them, worrying, pushing, and keeping track of enough emotions for two people. Thank you for sharing your story with me.

GUIDELINES FOR WRITING INTERPRETIVE ESSAYS

1. Identify the text fully and correctly.

2. State the thesis of your essay at the beginning or lead up to it and state it at the end — but be sure to state it.

3. Use the third person (objective stance) in most interpretive writing. Use first person when you want to add relevant personal information or are writing deliberately from the subjective stance.

4. Write interpretive essays in a comfortable, semiformal style. Avoid both contractions and pretentiousness.

5. Provide a brief summary of what *happens* in the text, but keep your focus on *interpretation*, or what the text means.

6. When providing evidence for your assertions, quote directly to capture the special flavor of an author. Use summaries and paraphrases for other evidence.

7. Document any assertions not your own or any passages of text that you quote or paraphrase.

SUGGESTIONS FOR WRITING AND RESEARCH

INDIVIDUAL

1. Write the interpretive essay that you have been exploring in Writings 1–4. Write the first draft from an objective stance, withholding all personal judgments. Write the second draft from a subjective stance, including all relevant personal judgments. Write your final draft by carefully blending elements of your first and second drafts.

2. Locate at least two reviews of a text (book, recording, exhibit) with which you are familiar, and analyze each to determine the reviewer's critical perspective. Write your own review of the text, and agree or disagree with the approach of the reviewers you analyzed.

If you have a campus newspaper, consider offering your review to the editor for publication.

COLLABORATIVE

As a class or small group, attend a local concert, play, or exhibition. Have each student take good notes and, when he or she returns home, write a review of this event that includes both an interpretation and a recommendation that readers attend it (or not).

Share these variations on the same theme with others in your class or group and explore the different judgments that arise as a result of different perspectives.

In the scientific sense, *reflection* means the giving back of an image. In the philosophic sense, *reflection* means the act of thinking seriously about something — exploring, speculating, and wondering. Reflective writing raises questions about any and all subjects, reflecting these subjects back to readers to allow a clearer view and expose new dimensions, as if a mirror had been held up before them. Reflective writing allows both writer and reader to consider things thoughtfully and seriously, but it demands neither resolution nor definitive answers.

Reflective essays are the modern form closest to the kind of writing that began the essay tradition some four hundred years ago when French author Michel de Montaigne first published his *Essais* in 1580. An *essai* (from the French, meaning "to try") was a short piece of writing meant to be read at a single sitting on a subject of general interest to a broad spectrum of citizens. Montaigne's essays explored education, truth, friendship, cruelty, conversation, coaches, cannibals, and many other subjects. Essays were never intended to be the last word on a subject, but rather the first thoughtful and speculative word. E. B. White, Virginia Woolf, and George Orwell are among the best known essayists in the twentieth century; among the best known living essayists are Joan Didion, Russell Baker, and Ellen Goodman.

13 a Writing to reflect

When you write to reflect, part of your motivation is to figure out something for yourself, and part is to share your reflections with somebody else. A piece of reflective writing is both *the result of* and *an account of* the act of speculation, and it invites readers into the game of exploration and wonder as well. Such writing is commonly characterized by a slight sense of indirection — as if the writer were in the actual process of examining a subject closely for the first time. This appearance of spontaneity is, of course, an illusion, as most good reflective writing — unlike journal writing — has been thoroughly rewritten, revised, and edited to achieve just the right tentative and spontaneous tone. (See Chapters 6 and 28.)

It is this tone along with the purpose of reflective writing that distinguishes it from other types of writing. In reflective essays, writers ask "Why?": Why do people live and behave the way they do? Why does society develop this way rather than that? Why does one thing happen rather than another? In asking such questions — and offering possible answers — writers try to make sense of the world.

Reflective writing can be on any subject under the sun. However, the subject that causes the reflection in the first place is seldom the actual focus or topic of the essay. The topic of reflective writing is the meaning the writer finds in the subject. In other words, in reflective essays the subject is often treated as a metaphor: the writer observes or experiences something concrete, thinks about it, and then extends that thinking into a more abstract speculation. For example, visiting the library (subject) could stimulate a reflection on knowledge and creativity (topic). The everyday object or experience comes to stand for larger issues and ideas.

Unlike many college writing assignments, reflective essay assignments ask for your opinion. Assignments that contain a direction word such as *imagine, speculate,* or *reflect* invite a kind of writing that features your ability to see a given subject from several sides and to offer tentative answers to profound questions. (See 4d.) For these assignments, it may be important to include factual information; however, such information is background, not foreground material. While reflecting, writers may explain, interpret, or argue; however, neither explanation, interpretation, nor argument is foremost on their minds.

Reflective essays are as varied as the thought processes of the people who write them, but a typical pattern does exist. Many reflective essays describe a concrete subject or actual situation, pause for a moment and focus on the true topic, make a point, and then conclude by coming back to the subject that prompted the reflection.

WRITING 1: EXPLORATION

Describe your past experiences writing reflective essays. Did you enjoy writing them? How did readers respond to them? **ESL:** If you have written reflective essays in your native language, describe some of your experiences with that kind of writing.

13 b Finding and describing a subject

The subject of a reflective essay is the concrete, observable thing or occurrence that prompts you to more abstract reflections. It can be any *person*, any *place*, any *thing* — in other words, everything imaginable is a possibility. To find a subject, start by remembering something that has always interested or puzzled you. You may want to review old journal entries, do some freewriting, or use other discovery techniques to find a possible subject. (See Chapter 7.)

No matter what your subject, begin with concrete description and actual circumstances — a particular concert, a specific case of plagiarism. Record as much detail as you can. Make your subject visible and tangible before considering its more abstract dimensions. If you faithfully record things that readers themselves have seen or can easily imagine, they will be more willing to follow you on your reflective journey. By providing a concrete description before you let readers know what your point will be, you allow them to do some reflection themselves. This in turn makes them more curious to read your reflections.

In your final draft, you will want details that subtly point toward your ultimate point without giving it away: a child's weary expression for a reflection on domestic violence, the spring fashions in a department store window for a reflection on annual rebirth. You will continue the careful layering of details throughout the revising and editing stages. (See also 20d.) For now, collect impressions that seem particularly interesting or meaningful, even if you don't know exactly what they mean.

People

For reflective essays, brief and casual encounters with strangers may work as well as more developed relationships. In fact, reflecting on chance encounters almost guarantees speculative and inconclusive thoughts: Why is she doing that? Where does he live? How are their lives like mine? Reflective writing about people often leads to comparisons with the writer's own circumstances, character, or behavior. What makes such writing especially interesting, of course, is that no two writers who encountered or witnessed the same person would speculate, muse, or wonder in the same way.

In the following passage, Mari writes about a chance encounter one Saturday morning.

> The sign on the front door says the store opens at eight o'clock. It's 7:56, so I put the bag of bottles on the ground.
> An old woman with a shopping cart full of bottles stands in front of the Pearl Street Beverage Mart. Most of her long gray hair is tucked into a Red Sox baseball cap, but some of it hangs in twisted strands about her face. She wears an oversized yellow slicker, a striking contrast against the crystal blue morning sky. She looks at the bottles and her lips are moving as if she's telling them a story.
> Then the bottle lady turns and speaks to me: "These bottles in my cart here, you see which I mean? Well, I'm gonna get five hundred dollars for them and get me a fine stylin' dinner tonight. It's a good thing there's bottles, yes?"

In this early part of her essay, Mari first focuses on locating the circumstance in a particular time and place and on describing the appearance of the woman. She provides enough detail so that readers can see the woman and, perhaps, join the author in asking questions: Why is this woman wearing a raincoat when the sky is blue? Why is she speaking to the bottles?

WRITING 2: APPLICATION

Make a list of people whom you have observed within the past few weeks and who have, for one reason or another, made a sharp impression on you. Did any of them trigger reflective thoughts? What are those thoughts?

2 Places

Places make good reflective subjects; writers can generally return to a place again and again for further information and ideas. You can, of course, reflect on just about any place imaginable, including those in your memories to which you cannot return. But you can also turn to places right under your nose and make something interesting and reflective from those. Reflective essays that begin by describing a physical place often end up focusing on places of the heart, mind, and spirit.

In the following passage, Judith turned the university library into a subject for reflection.

> Inside the smoke-colored doors, the loud and busy atmosphere vanishes, replaced by the soft soothing hum of air conditioning and the hushed sound of whispering voices. The repetitive sound of the copy machine has a calming effect as I look for a comfortable place in which to begin my work.
>
> I want just the right chair, with a soft cushion and a low sturdy table for a leg rest. The chairs are strategically positioned with comfortable personal space around each one, so you can stretch your arms fully without touching a neighbor. . . . People seem to respect each other's need for personal space.

Like her search for the right chair, Judith's description is detailed and concrete. At the same time, she introduces the importance of quiet space to her peace of mind. She concludes with a generalization triggered by the space she describes, hinting at but not stating the topic of her reflection.

■ **WRITING 3: APPLICATION**

Make a list of places that would provide material for a reflective essay. Think about places you've visited recently and those you still have access to. What associations do these places conjure up? What questions do they raise? Write a paragraph each about three of these places and see which offers the best prospect for further writing.

3 Things

Any thing can be a subject for reflection, so long as you treat it accordingly. Perhaps the first things that come to mind are physical objects. But a very different kind of a thing is an event, whether public (a political rally, a basketball game) or private (drinking a cup of coffee, fishing for trout). And a still more abstract kind of thing is a concept (plagiarism, campus parking).

ESL **EXPRESSING REFLECTIONS**

In written English, the following forms are often used to express reflections. They signal that the events or ideas described are possibilities, not certain or actual occurrences.

ADVERBS EXPRESSING UNCERTAINTY

maybe   possibly

perhaps

Example: Maybe next year I will visit the orchard again.

MODAL VERBS

Past	Future
may have	may
might have	might
could have	could
must have	

Example: I could have gone to the beach last week.

THE SUBJUNCTIVE MOOD

Example: If I were ten years old again, I would try to tell her how I feel.

(Note: Remember that the subjunctive is used to express only things that are untrue, not things that are uncertain. See 35h.)

INDIRECT QUESTIONS

Example: Even today I wonder whether the old dog ever made it to safety.

In the following example, Scott opens with a generalized statement about water fountains.

There is something serene about the sound of a water fountain. The constant patter of water splashing into water. The sound of endless repetition, the feeling of endless cycle. . . .

Two paragraphs later, he moves to the campus water fountain.

The fountain pipe has eighty-two nozzles. Two weeks ago, only fifty-five of them were spraying water vigorously, eleven sprayed weakly, and sixteen didn't spray at all. This week eighty-one are spraying; someone has fixed the fountain.

Even though Scott starts with a preliminary generalization, he quickly gives the reader a careful, even technical description. Readers are likely to believe Scott's reflection because he has taken pains to be accurate in his observation, and so they are likely to believe the rest of his account as well. While Scott has made it clear that listening to fountains is peaceful for him, readers still do not know why he chooses to write about them.

WRITING 4: APPLICATION

Make a list of things that interest you or excite your curiosity. Do so either from memory or by walking around your room, house, or neighborhood. Write a paragraph each on three of the things you encounter and see which offers the best prospect for further writing.

13 C Pausing to speculate

The three examples we have seen so far have taken everyday people, places, and things — a bottle woman, a library, a water fountain — as the subjects on which to reflect. The advantage of common over spectacular subjects is that everyone has some experience with them and is automatically curious to see what you make of them. However, your subject alone will carry interest just so far: the rest is up to your originality, creativity, and skill as you present the topic of your essay, the deeper and more speculative meaning you have found.

After introducing your subject, you need to execute a pause, saying in effect, "Wait a minute, there's something else going on here — stop and consider." The pause is a key moment. It signals to the reader that the essay is about to move into a new and less predictable direction.

Often the pause is accompanied by a slight shift in voice or tone as the writer becomes either more personal or more formal, slightly more biased or slightly more objective. The exact nature of your shift will be determined by the point you want to make. (See Chapter 6 and 28b.)

After describing the bottle woman, Mari steps back and shifts from the woman to the common objective that has brought them both to the store, returning bottles for a refund.

> I guess I had never thought about it before, but the world is full of bottles. They're everywhere, on shelves, in trash cans, on park benches, behind bushes, in street gutters. In the modern city, bottles are more common than grass.

By calling attention to her own new thoughts about bottles, Mari causes her readers, too, to think about a world full of bottles and about what, if anything, that may mean.

In the following passage, Scott stops observing the campus water fountain and begins wondering and remembering.

> I'm not sure where my love of fountains comes from. Perhaps it's from my father. When I was very young he bought a small cement fountain for our backyard. Its basin was an upturned shell and there was a little cherubic boy who peed into it.

This pause signals that it is not, in fact, water fountains that are on Scott's mind, but memories of his father.

    ■   **WRITING 5: APPLICATION**

Select one of the topics you explored in Writings 2–4. Once you have described or defined it, create a reflective pause by writing one or two pages about what this person, place, or thing makes you think about.

13 d Making the point

In explanatory, argumentative, or interpretive writing, the point of the paper is commonly stated as an explicit thesis, often in the first paragraph. In successful reflective writing, however, the point may be conveyed only indirectly and nearly always emerges only at the end. That way, readers are themselves drawn into the act of reflecting and become curious to find out what the writer thinks. In other words, reflective writers muse rather than argue. In fact, reflective essays are most persuasive when least obviously instructive or assertive.

Mari concludes her observation of the bottle woman by reporting the shopkeeper's sarcastic response to the woman after he totals the deposits on her bottles.

> "Eight dollars and thirty-five cents, Alice. You must have new
> competition or else bottles are getting scarce. You haven't broken
> ten dollars in days.". . .

As you perhaps suspected, Alice has grossly overestimated the
value of the bottles in her cart. However, this transaction has a
transforming effect on the observer/writer, who now adds her own
bottles to the old woman's pile.

> . . . I realized then that my bottles were more nuisance than ne-
> cessity. They were cluttering up our back hall — the landlord had
> already complained once — and tonight my roommates and I
> were making chicken curry for our boyfriends. That wasn't the
> case with Alice, who seemed to have neither roommate, dinner,
> nor boyfriend.
> "Here you go, Alice. Maybe you can break ten bucks with
> these." I gave them to her freely, at the same time realizing their
> true value for the first time.

Though the essay begins with a narrative about a trip to the bottle
store, it ends somewhere else. Mari is still ignorant of any real details about the woman's life, history, or prospects — though she,
like us, has made educated guesses. Alice remains frozen in the
essay for all time as the "bottle lady." It is what Mari makes of her
that is the real topic of this essay. Mari's encounter with Alice
has caused her to reassess her own relatively comfortable and
privileged life as a college student with her whole future ahead of
her.

Mari's essay is strong precisely because it doesn't hit us over
the head with a message or champion a particular cause. Instead
of writing an editorial about poverty or the homeless, Mari has
raised a question about the relative value of bottles for different
people in a throwaway society.

Scott's essay about water fountains has progressed from
fountains in general to the campus fountain in particular, then to
the memory of childhood fountains, which remind him of his father. Only in the last paragraph does he tell us more.

> My father died just after my twentieth birthday. It was very
> sudden and very surprising and everything felt very unfinished.
> They say I am a lot like him in many ways, but I'm not sure.
> What I do know is that like him, I love the sound of water.

Even at the end, Scott's point emerges by implication rather than explication — he never tells us outright why he began this reflection or what he hopes readers will take from it.

This proved to be an especially difficult topic for Scott to write about; in fact, he may not have chosen "water fountains" had he known in advance exactly where they would lead him. Scott's early drafts focused on water and fountains and people sitting around them — but did not mention his father. A writer may select to write about an object with only a vague idea of why it's attractive, interesting, or compelling. Often it's only through the act of reflective writing that the writer finds out the nature of the attraction, interest, or compulsion.

Remember that reflective essays raise issues but do not need to resolve them. The tradition of essay writing is the tradition of *trying* and *attempting* rather than *resolving* or *concluding*. Ending by acknowledging that you see still other questions invites your reader to join in the search for answers.

At the very end of your essay, it is a good idea to return to the specific person, place, or thing that originally prompted the reflection. This brings about a sense of closure — if not for the topic itself, at least for this particular essay.

MAKING THE REFLECTIVE POINT

1. If you don't know why you selected a certain topic to write about, write several drafts and see if the writing helps the point emerge.

2. If after several attempts you are still uncertain about the point of your reflection, try to answer the question a reader would ask: "What have I learned by reading this?"

3. If you know in advance the point of your reflection, plan carefully where and how you will make it. You may need several drafts to decide whether to make it implicit or explicit.

4. Provide closure. No matter where you have traveled in your reflective essay, it's a good idea, at the end, to return to the specific person, place, or thing that originally prompted the reflection.

■ **WRITING 6: APPLICATION**

Write two conclusions to the reflective essay you have been working on. In one, state your point openly; in the other, let it emerge more gradually and implicitly. Which do you like better? Why?

13 **e** **Shaping the whole paper**

The finished draft of Judith's reflective essay, "Writing in Safety," follows the structure described in this chapter. It opens and closes with a walk to and from the library. It has a loosely narrative pattern and is written in the present tense to convey a sense of the events unfolding as we read them. Her essay does not, however, actually tell a story since nothing happens — unless you count walking and sitting down. The journey emerges as a mental, almost spiritual, quest for safety — safety in which to think and create without fear. At the same time, the physical dimensions of her journey and the attention to descriptive detail make her journey believable.

Writing in Safety

It is already afternoon. I fiddle with the key to lock the apartment door after me. I am not accustomed to locking doors. Except for the six months I spent in Boston, I have never lived in a place where I did not trust my neighbors. When I was little, we couldn't lock our farmhouse door; the wood had swollen and the bolt no longer lined up properly with the hole, and nobody ever bothered to fix it. I still remember the time our babysitter, Rosie, hammered the bolt closed and we had to take the door off the hinges to get it open.

I heft the book bag onto my shoulder and walk up College Street toward the library. As I pass and am passed by other students, I scrutinize everything around me, hoping to be struck with a creative idea for a topic for my English paper. Instead, my mind fills with a jumble of disconnected images, like a bowl of alphabet soup: the letters are there, but they don't form any words. Campus sidewalks are not the best places for creativity to strike.

Approaching the library, I see skateboarders and bikers weaving through students who talk in clusters on the library steps. A friendly dog is tied to a bench watching for its owner to return. Subjects to write about? Nothing strikes me as especially interesting, and besides, my heart is still pounding from the walk up the hill. I wipe my damp forehead and go inside.

Inside the smoke-colored doors, the loud and busy atmosphere vanishes, replaced by the soft soothing hum of air conditioning and the hushed sound of whispering voices. The repetitive sound of the copy machine has a calming effect as I look for a comfortable place in which to begin my work.

I want just the right chair, with a soft cushion and a low sturdy table for a leg rest. The chairs are strategically positioned with comfortable personal space around each one, so you can stretch your arms fully without touching a neighbor. I notice that if there are three chairs in a row, the middle one is always empty. If people are seated at a table, they sit staggered so they are not directly across from one another. People seem to respect each other's need for personal space.

Like a dog who circles her bed three times before lying down, I circle the reading room looking for the right place to sit. I need to feel safe and comfortable so I can concentrate on mental activity. Some students, however, are too comfortable. One boy has moved two chairs together, covered himself with his coat, and is asleep in a fetal position. A girl sits at a table, head down, dozing like we used to do in first grade.

I find my place, an empty chair near a window, and slouch down into it, propping my legs on the low table in front. If my mother could see me, she'd reprimand me for not sitting up straight. I breathe deeply, close my eyes for a moment, and become centered, forgetting both last night's pizza and tomorrow's philosophy exam. I need a few minutes to acclimate to this space, relax, and feel safe before starting my work.

Two weeks ago, a female student was assaulted not far from where I live--that's why I've taken to locking my door so carefully. I am beginning to understand the importance of feeling safe in order to be creative and productive. Here, in the library, I feel secure, protected from real violence and isolated from everyday distractions. There are just enough people for security's sake but not so many that I feel crowded. And besides, I'm surrounded by all these books, all these great minds who dwell in this hallowed space! I am comfortable, safe, and beginning to get an idea.

Hours later--my paper started, my exam studied for, my eyes tired--I retrace the path to my apartment. It is dark now, and I listen closely when I hear footsteps behind, stepping to the sidewalk's edge to let a man walk briskly past. At my door, I again fumble for the now familiar key, insert it in the lock, open the door, turn on the hall light, and step inside. Here, too, I am safe, ready to eat, read a bit, and finish my reflective essay.

GUIDELINES FOR WRITING REFLECTIVE ESSAYS

1. Begin your reflection with something concrete (a person, place, or thing) that interests you.

2. Describe your subject carefully and locate it in a specific circumstance, using sensory details where appropriate.

3. Pause and move deliberately away from your subject to the larger or different issue it brings to mind — the topic of your reflection.

4. Organize your essay to move from the concrete and specific toward the abstract and general.

5. Use a reflective voice — tentative, questioning, gentle — to advance your reflective point.

6. Let your point emerge gently near the end of your essay.

7. Conclude by returning to where your reflective journey began.

SUGGESTIONS FOR WRITING AND RESEARCH

INDIVIDUAL

1. Review your responses to Writings 2–6. Select the reflective possibility that interests you most, and compose a whole essay on the subject. When you have finished, follow the suggestions in the box at the end of the chapter to help you write a second draft.

2. Find an object in your room, dormitory, house, or neighborhood that seems especially commonplace or routine or that you otherwise take for granted (a chair, rug, window, comb, glass, plant, fire hydrant). Describe it carefully, and draft an essay in which you reflect on its possible meaning or value.

3. Look up one of the authors mentioned in the chapter — Michel de Montaigne, Virginia Woolf, Russell Baker, Ellen Goodman — or a similar writer of your choice. Read several of his or her essays; analyze the work in terms of the characteristics of reflective essays described in this chapter. Write a review of this author as an essayist.

COLLABORATIVE

As a class, select a place or event that has reflective possibilities. Have each student write his or her own reflection on the

subject, limiting each reflection to two single-spaced pages. Elect two class members to edit the collection of essays and publish them in bound volumes for the whole class, complete with table of contents, an editors' introduction, and an afterword by the course instructor.

Researching

Before agonizing too long over your next research project, stop to consider what, exactly, research entails. Keep in mind that in your nonacademic life you conduct practical research of one kind or another every time you search the want ads for a used car, browse through a library in search of a book, or read a movie review. You may not make note cards or report the results in writing, but whenever you ask questions and then systematically look for answers, you are conducting research.

In college, the research you conduct is academic rather than practical. In other words, it's designed to result in a convincing paper rather than a purchase or action. Academic research is part of the writing process for most of your papers. You rarely begin writing an explanation, argument, or interpretation already knowing all the facts and information you'll need: to fill in the gaps in your knowledge, you conduct research. However, one particular assignment, the **research essay,** is specially designed to introduce you to the process of conducting research and writing a paper based on research findings. Research essays are generally longer, require more extensive research, use a more formal style and format, and take more time than other papers. We encourage you to use Part IV of *The Blair Handbook* for all papers that require research; it should be particularly helpful when you are writing research essays.

The most meaningful research grows out of your own curiosity and interest: you've thought hard about the questions and you care about the answers. Real research is exciting work. It is when you are assigned research questions you don't care about that research seems dull and mechanical. Yet even then, thoughtful digging into a new subject may turn out to be more interesting than you first imagined.

14 **a** **Understanding research**

An example of practical research

In preparing to write this chapter, we asked ourselves about the last time we did research of a substantial nature. Toby recalled the amount of practical research he did recently when he bought a motorcycle. His current motorcycle was a small BMW that he used for riding to school and taking short trips. It was time, he thought, to buy a new motorcycle big enough for comfortable long-range touring. To find the right machine meant shopping carefully, which meant asking good questions: What kind of motorcycle was best for touring? How large should it be? What make was most reliable? How much would it cost? Who were the best dealers?

Here's how Toby researched his questions about buying a new motorcycle.

- Over a period of several weeks Toby talked to people who knew a lot about motorcycles — some old friends, the mechanic at the shop where his old bike was serviced, a neighbor who owned two different touring machines.

- Toby subscribed to *Motorcyclist* and *Rider* magazines; he found the latter more interesting since it focuses primarily on touring motorcycles. The more he read, the more familiar he became with current terminology (*ABS*, *fairings*), brands (BMW, Harley-Davidson), models (sport tourers, roadsters), and performance data (roll-on speed, braking distance). On a corner of his desk, he piled the most useful magazines with many dog-eared pages.

- Toby looked up back issues of *Rider* magazine in the local library to gain a more historical perspective. He made photocopies of the most relevant articles, underlined key findings, and made notes in the margins of his photocopies.

- Toby visited the local chapter of the BMW Motorcycle Club. Here he met more people who seemed to be expert motorcyclists (all, of course, recommending BMWs) and bought a copy of *BMW Motorcycle Owners of America News*.

- Toby rented the video *On Any Sunday* (1972), considered by many to be the best film ever made about motorcycles, and watched it three times.

■ Toby approached the owner of Frank's Motorcycle Shop and asked about the virtues of certain BMW models on display. He was most impressed by two models, the K75RT and the K100RS, both of which he sat on but did not ride. He left with literature and reread it at home. He wrote in his journal about the dreams motorcycles inspired and the difficult choices they required.

■ Toby visited local dealers who sold Honda, Kawasaki, Yamaha, and Suzuki motorcycles and listened to sales pitches explaining the features of their best touring machines. He found some too racy and others too large, but he still took notes about each to facilitate his comparison.

■ Toby returned to Frank's and test-drove the two BMW models that most interested him: the cheaper K75RT was smoother, but the more expensive K100RS was more powerful. Still he was undecided. He asked about the trade-in value of his old motorcycle. He took notes and made calculations and lay awake at night pondering the possibilities.

■ After weighing the relative merits of smoothness versus power versus money, Toby returned to Frank's Motorcycle Shop and bought the K100RS, receiving an end-of-season discount. Then he retreated into a long Vermont winter and waited for motorcycle season to resume in the spring.

■ WRITING 1: EXPLORATION

What research outside of school settings have you conducted recently? Think about major changes, moves, or purchases that required you to ask serious questions. Choose one recent research activity and list the questions you asked and the steps you took to answer them. Finally, what was the result of this research?

2 Activities in the research process

While the search for motorcycle knowledge is practical rather than academic, it serves nevertheless to introduce most of the activities common to all research projects, argumentative or informational, in school or out.

ı **The researcher has a genuine interest in the topic.** It's difficult to fake curiosity, but it's possible to develop it. Toby's interest in motorcycles was long-standing, but the more he investigated, the more he learned and the more he still wanted to know. Some academic assignments will allow you to pursue issues that are personally important to you; others will require that you dive into the research first and generate interest as you go.

2 **The researcher asks questions.** Toby's first questions were general rather than specific. However, as he gained more knowledge, the questions became more sharply focused and specific. No matter what your research assignment, you need to begin by articulating questions, finding out where the answers lead, and then asking still more questions.

3 **The researcher seeks answers from people.** Toby talked to both friends and strangers who knew about motorcycles. The people to whom he listened most closely were specialists with expert knowledge. All research projects profit when you ask knowledgeable people to help you answer questions or point you in directions where answers may be found.

4 **The researcher visits places where information may be found.** Toby went to dealerships and a motorcycle club, not only to ask questions of experts but also to observe and experience firsthand. No matter how much other people told him, his knowledge increased when he made his own observations. In many forms of academic research, field research is as important as library research.

5 **The researcher examines texts.** Toby read motorcycle magazines and brochures and watched videotapes to become more informed about his subject. While texts are helpful in practical research, they are crucial in academic research.

6 **The researcher evaluates sources.** As the research progressed, Toby double-checked information to see if it could be confirmed by more than one source. In practical research, the researcher must evaluate sources to ensure that the final decision is satisfactory. In academic research, you must evaluate sources to ensure that your final paper is convincing.

7 **The researcher writes.** Toby made field notes, made notes about his library sources, and wrote in his journal. In practical research, writing helps the researcher find, remember, and explore information. In academic research, writing is even more important, since the results must eventually be reported in writing.

8 **The researcher tests and experiments.** In Toby's practical research, testing was simple and fairly subjective — riding different motorcycles to compare the qualities of each. Testing and experimentation are also regular parts of many research projects.

9 **The researcher synthesizes information to arrive at a conclusion.** Toby's synthesized information led to a decision to purchase one motorcycle rather than another. In academic research, your synthesis of information leads not to a purchase but to a well-supported thesis that will convince a skeptical audience that your research findings are correct.

What Toby, as the researcher, did not do, of course, is the step most directly concerned with the subject matter of this handbook — write down the results of his investigation in a formal report. The greatest difference between practical and academic research is that the former leads to practical knowledge on which to act, the latter to theoretical knowledge written for others to read. So, for academic research, there is one more activity to consider.

10 **The researcher presents the research findings in an interesting, focused, and well-documented paper.**

The remainder of this chapter explains how to select, investigate, and write about academic research topics.

■ **WRITING 2: EXPLORATION**

Explain how the research activities described in this section were part of an investigation you once conducted, in school or out. Did you go through the same steps that Toby did? What other activities did you do that are not listed here?

14 b **Managing the research process**

Research essays are usually major projects meant to occupy a span of weeks or months; they usually make a strong contribution to your course grade. Consequently, it pays to study the assignment carefully, begin working on it immediately, and allow sufficient time for the many different activities involved.

1 Understanding the assignment

First, reflect on the course for which the paper is assigned. What is the aim of this field of study? What themes has the instructor emphasized? How would a research assignment contribute to the goals of this course? In other words, before even considering a topic, assess the instructor's probable reasons for making the assignment and try to predict what is expected from your finished paper.

Next, study the assignment directions carefully. Identify both the subject words and the direction words. **Subject words** specify the area of the investigation. **Direction words** specify your purpose for writing — whether you should *explain* or *report* or *argue*, or do something else. (See 4d.)

Finally, examine the assignment requirements: the recommended perspective, the most appropriate style, the preferred format, the sources expected, the documentation system required, the due dates, and the paper length. Thinking about these early on may save time and help avoid false steps. (See Part VII for information on style, format, and documentation conventions in various disciplines.)

2 Developing a research question

Since research essays are among the most lengthy and involved of all college assignments, make the project interesting and purposeful by developing a research question that will be exciting for you to answer. Your instructor may assign a specific topic, or the choice of a topic may be left up to you. If you need to find a **topic,** think about how your interests dovetail with the content of the course. What topics of the course do you enjoy most? What discussions, lectures, or labs have you found most engaging? What has happened recently in the news that both interests you and relates to the course material? Do some freewriting or clustering to find the topic that seems most promising to you. (See Chapter 7.) Be sure to narrow your topic to one that will be interesting to both you and your readers and manageable given the time, space, and resources available.

TOO BROAD	Ben and Jerry's ice cream franchise
TOPIC	The effect of Ben and Jerry's franchise on the Vermont economy
TOPIC	The rapid success of Ben and Jerry's ice cream franchise

Research projects are designed to answer questions, so you need to develop a **research question** about your topic. What makes a good research question? First, it's a question that you really want to know the answer to. Second, it requires more than a yes or no answer. The question "Does my state have a bottle law?" can be answered with one phone call. A better question would be "What are the benefits and liabilities of bottle laws?" Third, it's a question to which you do not already know the answer. If you are knowledgeable about the new state law governing solid waste disposal, you might pursue aspects of the law with which you are not familiar — or a different law altogether. And fourth, it's a question that you have a reasonable chance of answering. If you ask "What effect will a new condominium development have on the environment?" make sure you have access to the people or documents that can provide you with that information.

RESEARCH QUESTION Why has Ben and Jerry's ice cream franchise become such a success?

Whether or not you already have a tentative answer to your research question will determine what type of research you undertake. **Informational research** is conducted when you don't know the answer to the question or have a firm opinion about the topic. You enter this kind of investigation with an open mind, focusing on the question, not on a predetermined answer. In some cases, this kind of research will lead you to an argumentative position; in others you may report the results of your research in an explanatory paper. In either case, you will need eventually to develop an answer to your question — a thesis — and the purpose of informational research is to help you find it. Such research might be characterized as *thesis-finding*.

Argumentative research is conducted to prove a point. You enter the project already knowing your thesis — the answer to your question, the side of the debate you want to support. *Should handguns be abolished? Yes, handguns should be abolished.* You conduct research to further buttress your position. The research question helps focus your energies, but this kind of research is really *thesis-driven*. To be sure, the process of researching may lead to a revised or entirely different thesis; in fact, you should consider any thesis you have in mind at this point a **working thesis,** subject to revision, redirection, and clarification. Nonetheless, your working thesis colors your investigation from the start. (For more on informational and argumentative papers, see Chapters 10 and 11.)

COLLABORATIVE RESEARCH PROJECTS

Of all writing assignments, those involving research profit most from collaboration. If your assignment lends itself to collaboration, and if your instructor approves, find out with which classmates you could work. The following suggestions will aid collaboration.

1. Topics. Either form a group you want to work with and then choose a topic you all want to research, or choose a topic that interests you and see if you can interest others to join you.

2. Size. Small groups (two to three people) work better than large groups because it is easier to find time to meet outside of class and to synthesize the information found.

3. Organization. Divide tasks early in your project, specifying who will do what when. Divide the tasks equitably so that everyone contributes an equal amount. Divide the tasks so that members make maximum use of their different skills, abilities, and interests.

4. Research. Agree to take careful notes on texts or interview subjects and to duplicate the notes so that each group member has full source information.

5. Composing. A whole group writing a single paper can write together by (1) **blending** voices, passing the drafts back and forth, each writer overwriting the others each time; (2) **sequencing** voices, with each writer writing a different section; or (3) **weaving** voices, so that the final product has different writers' voices emerging at different times throughout the paper.

6. Thesis. In the early stages of collaborative writing, each group member should write his or her own version of what the research suggests. These early drafts should be shared, with each writer reconsidering the thesis in light of points made by the other writers.

7. Revision and editing. At the end, responsibilities can be divided equitably according to abilities, with different members volunteering to type, prepare references, edit, proofread, and reproduce the final paper. This is also a good time to even out the workload, if some have done more so far than others.

8. Responsibility and evaluation. If all group members meet their responsibilities and deadlines, all should receive the same grade.

For more information on collaboration, see Chapter 22.

Before you commit to a question or thesis, visit your library and make a quick survey of relevant information there. Locate some of the periodicals in the field and see what kinds of information they contain. Check to see if the book titles in your subject are plentiful and current. You can save yourself a lot of frustration by knowing that periodicals, books, and special collections that you will need are available. If you will need to special order most of your resources, consider a version of your question or thesis for which resources are available in your college library. (For more information on library research, see Chapter 15.)

Finally, ask your instructor to respond to your intended question before you invest too much time in it. Your instructor will help direct you to projects consistent with the goals of the assignment or course and steer you away from questions that are too large or too offbeat.

■ WRITING 3: APPLICATION

Select a topic that interests you and that is compatible with the research assignment. List ten questions that you have about this topic. Freewrite for ten more minutes about the question that most interests you. Why does it interest you? Where would you start looking for answers?

3 Starting a research log

A research log can help you keep track of the scope, purpose, and possibilities of any research project. Such a log is essentially a journal in which you write to yourself about the process of doing research by asking questions and monitoring the results. Questions you might ask include the following:

■ What have I found so far?

■ What do I still need to find?

■ Where am I most likely to find it?

■ Can I articulate my thesis succinctly?

■ What evidence best supports my thesis?

■ What evidence challenges my thesis?

■ If there are contradictions, how should I handle them?

Answering such questions as you visit the library, look for and read sources, review note cards, and write various drafts can make research more efficient. Novice researchers often waste time tracking down sources that are not really useful. Because writing log entries forces you to continually articulate the research project, it can help you better understand *for yourself* what your quest is really about. (See Chapter 8.)

Here, for example, are some entries from a first-year student's research log for an investigation of ozone holes in the atmosphere.

11/12 Checked the subject headings and found no books on ozone depletion. Ref. librarian suggested magazines because it takes so long for books to come out on new subjects. In the General Science Index I found about twenty articles — I've got them all on a printout. Need to come back tomorrow to actually start reading them.

11/17 Conference today with Lawrence about the ozone hole thesis — said I don't really have much of a thesis, rather a lot of information aiming in the same direction. Suggested I look at what I've found already and then back up to see what question it answers — that will probably point to my thesis.

When a project requires you to investigate only a few sources of information, you may choose to keep all your bibliographic and research notes in your research log or just to use a separate part of your class notebook for both notes and log. When keeping notes in a log or notebook, record what you find as if you were keeping separate note cards. (See 15d.) Some students keep their logs on computers. This way, information from log entries can be transferred directly into your draft without recopying.

WRITING 4: APPLICATION

Keep a research log for the duration of your research project. Write in it daily and record everything you think of or find in relation to the project. When your project is finished, write an account of the role the log played.

4 Making a research plan

After you have developed some sense of the range and amount of information available, write out a plan scheduling when you will do what. For example, plan a certain amount of time for trips to the library. If any of the books you need are checked out, allow time for the library to call those in. Arrange needed interviews well in advance, with time to reschedule in case a meeting has to be canceled. And allow enough time not only for writing but also for revising and editing. As you accomplish each task, you may want to check off that item in your plan or note the date. If you find yourself falling behind schedule or discover additional tasks to be accomplished, revise your plan.

■ **WRITING 5: APPLICATION**

On one page of your research log, design a research plan that includes both library and field investigations. In this plan, list sources you have already found as well as those you hope to find.

5 **Consulting a range of sources**

To conduct any kind of research, you need to identify appropriate sources of information, consult and evaluate these sources, and take good notes recording the information you collect. You also need to understand how each source works as evidence.

Primary sources contain original material and raw information. **Secondary sources** report on, describe, interpret, or analyze someone else's work. For example, if you were exploring the development of a novelist's style, the novels themselves would be primary sources and other people's reviews and critical interpretations of the novels would be secondary sources. What constitutes a primary source will differ depending on the field and your research question. For example, the novel *Moby Dick* is a primary source if you are studying it as literature and making claims about what it means. It is a secondary source if you are investigating nineteenth-century whaling and referring to the chapters that describe harpooning for information about what that activity was like.

Most research essays use both primary and secondary sources. Primary sources ground the essay in firsthand knowledge and verifiable facts; secondary sources supply the context for your discussion and provide support for your own interpretation or argument.

Many research essays are based on **library research,** since libraries contain so much of the collective knowledge of the academic community. However, some of the most interesting research essays are based on **field research.** Field research involves first-hand interviews with people who have expert knowledge of your subject. Field research is also what you find simply by being in the field: for example, touring the local sewage treatment plant to see how the treatment actually happens. (See Chapter 15 for more on library research; see Chapter 16 for more on field research.)

ESL **BECOMING AN AUTHORITY**

If you have been educated outside the United States, your instructors may not have emphasized student authority in research writing. You may feel it is inappropriate to "own the topic," especially if the topic is one you don't know much about before researching it.

In U.S. colleges, however, students are expected to develop a sense of authority regarding their topics. This is so that they will be able to present powerful, interesting ideas of their own in their papers rather than repeating what others have said.

Becoming an authority means working hard to become a real expert and to maintain control over your writing project. Keep the following guidelines in mind when writing to develop authority on your topic:

- Learn enough to become the class expert on your topic.
- Read your sources critically, analyzing what they say and why they might be saying it. (See Chapter 2.)
- Control your sources by thinking carefully about which to use in your paper and how to use them. (See 16a and 16b.)
- Make sure your paper includes ideas of your own, not just summaries of what other people have said.

---

6 **Owning the topic**

Whenever you undertake research, you join an ongoing conversation among a select community of people who are knowledgeable about the subject. As you collect information, you too become something of an expert. You become an *author*-ity, gaining an authoritative voice, becoming a stronger, more powerful writer. Plan to become enough of an expert on your topic that you can teach your classmates and instructor something they didn't know be-fore. The best way to exercise your newfound authority is to write in your own words all the major information and ideas connected with your research project, both periodically in journal entries and when you draft. Finding your own language to express an idea makes that idea yours and increases both your understanding of and commitment to the topic.

7 Keeping an open mind

Don't be surprised if, once you begin doing research, your questions and answers multiply and change. Remember that the process of research often circles back on itself. You ask one ques-tion, find the answer to another, pursue that, and then stumble onto the answer to your first question. Be prepared, at times, to travel in circles or find dead ends where you expected thorough-fares — but also thoroughfares where you expected dead ends. Good research will, at some point, become focused research.

For example, say you start out researching local recycling ef-forts, but you stumble upon the problem of finding buyers for re-cycled material. One source raises the question of manufacturing with recycled materials, while another source turns the whole question back to consumer education. All of these concerns are related, but if you attempt to study them all with equal intensity, your paper will be either very long or very superficial. It is wiser to use some information for context, some for the main focus of your research, and some not at all. Follow your strongest interests, and try to answer the question you most care about.

Similarly, what began as informational research may become argumentative, as the process of research turns up information to tip your original neutrality one way or another. Or a research in-vestigation that starts out to prove a thesis may result in a more neutral, informative paper if multiple causes or complications in what had seemed a straightforward case are uncovered.

Research must remain flexible if it is to be vital and exciting; but you also need to conclude your research and write a paper. Keep an open mind, but also keep focusing your topic.

8 Stating a thesis

Whether your research essay makes an argument or reports information, it needs a **thesis.** An **argumentative thesis** states a position on an issue. (See Chapter 11.) An **informational thesis** makes a statement about the information presented in the paper but does not advance one position over another. (See Chapter 10.)

ARGUMENTATIVE THESIS	In order to reduce the annual number of violent deaths in the United States, Congress should pass a law to mandate a waiting period of ten days before all handguns can be purchased in this country.
INFORMATIONAL THESIS	Compact discs cost more than records because the laser technology required to manufacture them is so expensive.

If your research was argumentative, you probably began with a working thesis. If your research was informational, you probably began with a research question, and a thesis evolved as you found answers. In most cases, your final thesis will be based on this working thesis but will be revised according to the information and insights you found through research.

Writing out a detailed thesis statement is an important step in the process of completing a first draft. A good thesis not only helps readers understand your paper, it also helps you organize your thoughts and energies when writing. Look over your research log, notes, journal entries, and any preliminary drafts to remind you of the questions you've asked and the answers you've found. Then try drafting a thesis statement that's as complete, focused, and accurate as possible. Ask yourself the following questions, and revise the thesis as you think necessary:

1   Is it interesting? An informational thesis should answer a question that is worth asking. An argumentative thesis should take a position on a debatable issue and should probably include a proposal for change.

2   Is it precise and specific? Try to sharpen both your understanding of the thesis and the language you use to express it. Don't say *a waiting period* if you mean *a waiting period of ten days*. This will help you define the exact nature of your paper and will result in a final thesis that is more interesting to readers.

3   Is it manageable? You may have collected more information than you can actually write about. If necessary, take this opportunity to narrow both the thesis and the paper you expect to write.

4   Does it adequately reflect your research and the expected shape
     of your paper? Try to state explicitly all the major points you want
     to make in your paper. Consider also whether you have evidence
     or information in support of each point you want to make.

Most research essays are long and complex enough that the
thesis should be stated explicitly rather than left implicit. However, the thesis you include in your paper may be different from
the one you developed to help you write the paper. For example,
after asking the four questions given here, Zoe developed this detailed statement of her thesis.

> To get an internship with a professional photographer in today's
> competitive and heavily commercialized market, you need to sell
> yourself effectively to busy people by developing a small and var-
> ied portfolio, making contact early and often, and demonstrating
> that you understand the unglamorous work involved.

In her paper, however, her explicit thesis focused on only part of
this statement.

> I've learned the steps to setting up an internship: First, establish
> contact through writing a letter and sending a résumé, then push
> your portfolio.

She developed her other points — about the competitive market-
place and the unglamorous work involved in being an assistant —
elsewhere in her paper.

Many research essays give the thesis at the beginning, somewhere in the first or second paragraph, where it acts as a promise
to the reader of what will follow. Some research papers present the
thesis at the end, where it acts as a conclusion or a summary. If
you take the delayed-thesis approach, be sure that the topic and
scope of your paper are clear to readers from the very beginning.

9 Drafting, revising, and editing

Research writing, like all important writing, benefits from the
multistage process of drafting, revising, and editing. In research
writing, however, managing information and incorporating sources
present special problems. When you write your first draft, be sure

you allow time for further research in case it is needed. In addition, be aware that incorporating sources smoothly into your prose may take extra time and require special attention to the conventions of documentation; you will also need to spend more time editing and proofreading than for papers not based on research. (See Chapter 17 for more information on using sources.)

Keep in mind that since you are on your way to becoming an expert on your research topic, you will need to explain, define, and clarify many terms and concepts to your readers, including your instructor, who will know less than you do. You'll also want to make sure that you have remained focused on a topic that appeals to your potential readers. For both these reasons, you may want to ask your classmates and instructor to read and respond to your paper at several points along the way — for example, when you have a detailed outline or thesis, when you have completed your first draft, and when you are ready to edit. (See Chapter 22.)

SUGGESTIONS FOR WRITING AND RESEARCH

INDIVIDUAL

1. Select a research topic that interests you and write an exploratory draft about it. First, write out everything you already know about the topic. Second, write out everything you want to know about the topic. Third, identify experts you can talk to. Finally, make a list of questions you need answered. Plan to put this paper through a process that includes not only planning, drafting, revising, and editing but also locating, evaluating, and using sources.

2. With the research topic you developed in individual assignment 1 in mind, visit the library and conduct a search of available resources. What do you find? Where do you find it? Show your questions to a reference librarian and ask what additional sources he or she would suggest. (Before you go much further, read Chapter 15.)

3. After completing individual assignments 1 and 2, find a person who knows something about your topic, and ask him or her for leads about doing further research: Whom else would he recommend you speak with? What books or articles would she recommend? What's the first thing this expert would do to find out information? (Before you proceed much further, read Chapter 16.)

COLLABORATIVE

1.   Join with a classmate or classmates to write a collaborative research essay. Develop plans for dividing tasks among members of the group.

2.   After completing a collaborative research essay, write a short report in which you explain the collaborative strategies your group used and evaluate their usefulness.

Libraries are the heart — or perhaps the head — of the academic community. Libraries provide the primary knowledge base that allows professors to teach and conduct research in their fields. And libraries provide students with the sources of information that allow them to investigate any area of study.

The modern library is complex and multifaceted; you should visit your college library early and get to know it well. At first, a college library may appear intimidating, but the more you use it, the more friendly it will become.

15 a Planning library research

To learn about the library, you need to go there, walk slowly through it, read the informational signs that identify special rooms and departments, poke your nose into nooks and crannies, and browse through a few books or magazines. If there's an introductory video explaining the library, pause to see it. If there's a self-paced or guided tour, take it. Read informational handouts or pamphlets. Be sure to locate the following:

- The **book catalog,** computerized or on cards, that tells you which books your library owns and where they are located.

- The **book stacks,** where books, periodicals, and pamphlets are stored.

- The **circulation desk,** where you check out and reserve books and get information on procedures and resources.

- The **periodical room,** which houses current issues of magazines, journals, and newspapers.

- The **reference room,** which contains general reference works such as dictionaries and encyclopedias along with guides and indexes to more specific sources of information.

SUGGESTIONS FOR TALKING WITH LIBRARIANS

1. Before you ask for help, try to answer your questions yourself.

2. Bring with you a copy of the research assignment.

3. Be ready to explain the assignment in your own words: purpose, format, length, number of sources, and due date.

4. Identify any special requirements about sources: Should information come from government documents? Rare books? Films?

5. Describe the particular topic you are researching and the tentative question you have framed to address the topic.

6. Describe any work you have done so far: books read, periodicals looked at, log entries written, people interviewed, and so on.

To take full advantage of library resources, keep the following suggestions in mind.

Visit the library early and often. As soon as you receive a research assignment, visit the library to find out what resources are available for your project, and plan to return often. Even if your initial research indicates a wealth of material on your topic, you may not be able to find everything the first time you look. A book you need may be checked out or your library may not subscribe to a periodical containing important information, and you may need to order it on interlibrary loan, a process that takes some time.

Prepare to take notes. If you take careful notes from the sources you find, you will save yourself time and write a better paper. Bring index cards to the library — 3″ x 5″ cards for bibliographical information and 4″ x 6″ cards for notes — from your first visit on. (See 15d for more on note taking.)

Keep a research log. Writing in a research log as you work on your research project will help you find ideas to research, plan your course of action, pose and solve problems related to your topic, and keep track of where you have been so far. (See Chapter 7 and 14b3 for more on research logs.)

Check general sources before specific ones. During your first or second visit to the library, check general sources — dictionaries, encyclopedias, atlases, and yearbooks — for information about your topic. (See 15b.) An hour or two spent with these general sources will give you a quick overview of the scope and range of your topic and will lead you to more specific information.

Ask for help. Talk to librarians. At first you might show them your assignment and describe your topic and your research plans; later you might ask them for help in finding a particular source or ask if they know of any sources that you have not checked yet. Keep in mind, however, that reference librarians are busy people — don't ask questions that you haven't tried to answer for yourself.

■ **WRITING 1: EXPLORATION**

Visit your college library and locate the areas and materials discussed in this section. Then look for a comfortable place, sit down, and write about which of these might be of most use to you as you begin a research project.

15 b   Finding sources of information

Most of the information you need to find will be contained in reference books, in other books, or in periodicals — journals, magazines, and newspapers. Reference books are fairly easy to locate: there are relatively few of them and they are usually placed in one room or section of the library. However, even a moderately sized college library owns hundreds of thousands of books and periodicals. To simplify the researcher's task of finding the relevant ones, **bibliographies** and **indexes** have been developed. These resources either indicate which books or periodical articles have been published on a given topic or attempt to present comprehensive lists of sources in an easy-to-use format. Once you know which book or periodical might be useful, you still need to find it. The library's **catalogs** tell you whether it owns the source. To use these resources efficiently, look for sources of information by using this four-step process:

1   Consult general reference works to gain background information and basic facts. (See 15b1.)

2   Consult bibliographies and indexes to learn which books, periodicals, and articles are relevant. (See 15b2.)

3 Consult your library's catalogs to see if it owns the books and periodicals you want. (See 15b3.)

4 Consult other sources as needed. (See 15b4.)

In most cases, the research source you eventually find will be printed on paper. However, many of the bibliographies and indexes that lead you to these sources will be available in electronic form, either through an **on-line service** (which your library's computers access through a telephone line and a modem) or on a **CD-ROM disc** (a storage device much like a floppy disc, which can be read by a computer). One research tool that is available only in electronic form is the **database,** a large electronic index. Often databases provide summaries or outlines in addition to bibliographic information on the sources they list; occasionally they contain copies of the sources themselves. Databases can be either on-line or on CD-ROM. Many library catalogs today are computerized as well; they are essentially on-line databases.

Searching through electronic indexes, databases, and catalogs is much easier if you have identified the key words for your research topic. A **key word** is an important word describing your topic, either a word for the topic itself, a word for the general subject, or a word describing constituent parts of the topic. Sometimes titles and author names can also be used as key words. For example, key words for a research paper investigating the pottery of Native Americans in the western United States could include *Indian, art,* and *California.* Because a computer can search only for the words you tell it to, the key words you select can mean the difference between success and failure. For example, a search including the word *Sioux* might turn up nothing, but a search including the word *Dakota* (the preferred term for this group) might result in a number of sources. To find good key words for your topic, consult the *Library of Congress Subject Headings.*

Reference works

General reference works provide background information and basic facts about a topic. The summaries, overviews, and definitions in these sources can help you decide whether to pursue a topic further and where to turn next for information. The information in these sources is necessarily general and will not be sufficient by itself as the basis for most research projects; you will need to consult specialized sources as well. General reference works do not make strong sources to cite in research papers.

Specialized reference works contain detailed and technical information in a particular field or discipline. They often include articles by well-known authorities and sometimes contain bibliographies and cross-references that can lead to other sources. Two useful guides to finding specialized reference books are *Guide to Reference Books*, edited by Eugene P. Sheehy (10th edition, 1986) and *Walford's Guide to Reference Material* (4th edition, 1980–86).

While many reference works are published as books, increasingly they are available on CD-ROM. The following lists suggest common and useful references, although there are many more in each category.

Almanacs and yearbooks. Almanacs and yearbooks provide up-to-date information on politics, agriculture, economics, and population along with statistical facts of all kinds.

Facts on File: News Digest (1941–present). A summary and index to current events reported in newspapers worldwide. (Also CD-ROM, 1980–present.)

Statesman's Year-Book (1863–present). Annual statistics about government, agriculture, population, religion, and so on for countries throughout the world.

World Almanac and Book of Facts (1868–present). Reviews important events of the past year and provides data on a wide variety of topics, including sports, government, science, business, and education.

Atlases. Atlases such as the *Hammond Atlas*, the *National Geographic Atlas of the World*, and the *New York Times Atlas of the World* can help you identify places anywhere in the world and provide information on population, climate, and industry.

Biographical dictionaries. Biographical dictionaries contain information on people who have made some mark on history in many different fields; biographical indexes tell you how to locate additional sources.

Contemporary Authors (1967–present). Includes short biographies of authors who have published books during the year.

Current Biography (1940–present). Contains articles and photographs of people in the news.

Who's Who in America (1899–present). The standard biographical reference for living Americans.

Dictionaries. Dictionaries contain definitions and histories of words and information on their correct usage. (See 31b.)

Encyclopedias. Encyclopedias provide elementary information, explanations, and definitions of virtually every topic, concept, country, institution, historical person or movement, or cultural artifact imaginable. One-volume works such as the *Random House Encyclopedia* and *The New Columbia Encyclopedia* give brief overviews. Larger works such as *Collier's Encyclopedia* (24 volumes) and the *New Encyclopaedia Britannica* (32 volumes) contain more detailed information.

Specialized reference works. Although these works provide information that is more detailed and technical than that found in general reference works, you should still use them primarily for exploratory research and background information. Each discipline has many reference works; here is a small sampling.

LANGUAGES AND LITERATURE

Cassell's Encyclopedia of World Literature
Handbook to Literature
McGraw-Hill Encyclopedia of World Drama
Oxford Companion to American Literature

HUMANITIES

Cambridge Ancient History
Dictionary of the Bible
Encyclopedia of American History
Encyclopedia of Philosophy
Encyclopedia of Religion
Encyclopedia of World History
New Grove Dictionary of Music and Musicians
Oxford Companion to Art

SOCIAL SCIENCES

Dictionary of Education
Encyclopedia of Anthropology
Encyclopedia of Crime and Justice
Encyclopedia of Psychology
Encyclopedia of Social Work
International Encyclopedia of the Social Sciences
Political Handbook and Atlas of the World

SCIENCES

Encyclopedia of Biological Sciences
Encyclopedia of Chemistry
Encyclopedia of Computer Science and Technology
Encyclopedia of Physics
Larousse Encyclopedia of Animal Life
McGraw-Hill Dictionary of Science and Technology

BUSINESS

Encyclopedia of Banking and Finance
Encyclopedia of Economics
McGraw-Hill Dictionary of Modern Economics

WRITING 2: APPLICATION

Look up information on your research topic, using at least three of the reference sources described in this section.

2 Bibliographies, indexes, and databases

Bibliographies, indexes, and databases are tools — they help you locate books and periodicals that contain the information you need. Periodicals are magazines, journals, and newspapers, which are published at set periods throughout the year. Periodicals focus on particular areas of interest and their information is more current than that found in books. Because so many periodical issues are published each year and because every issue can contain dozens of articles on different topics, using a periodical index or database is essential to finding the article you need.

Bibliographies

Bibliographies list books alphabetically by title, by author, or by subject. Many books include a bibliography of the works consulted by the author in researching the book; always consult the bibliography of a book you have found helpful. Other bibliographies are published separately as reference tools. Some of the most useful are listed here.

Bibliographic Index: A Cumulative Bibliography of Bibliographies. New York: Wilson, 1938–present. This index lists the page numbers of bibliographies in books over a wide variety of subjects. Such bibliographies provide you with lists of related sources already compiled by another author on a subject similar to your own.

Books in Print. New York: Bowker, 1948–present. The latest edition of this yearly index lists by author, subject, and title all books currently in print. It is also available on-line and on CD-ROM.

MLA Bibliography of Books and Articles in the Modern Languages and Literature (1921–present). It is also available on-line and on CD-ROM.

Paperbound Books in Print. This semiannual index lists paperback books currently in print by author, subject, and title. It is also available on-line and on CD-ROM.

Indexes

Indexes are guides to the material published within works, sometimes within books but more often within periodicals. Each index covers a particular group of periodicals. Make sure that the index you select contains the journals, magazines, and newspapers that you want to use as sources.

Indexes list works alphabetically by author or by subject. To conduct an effective subject search, use the key words you've identified for your topic. Check under every subject heading that might be relevant. Many periodicals use the subject headings in the *Library of Congress Subject Headings,* but others use their own lists.

Most indexes are available both in printed form and in computerized form. Many are also available on microfiche or microfilm — media that simulate the printed page but must be read on special machines. Indexes in book form are usually the most comprehensive; those presented on microfilm, microfiche, or computer usually cover only the past ten or twenty years.

Computerized indexes allow you to focus your search strategy more effectively. By combining key words in certain ways, you can have the computer generate a list of works that closely match your topic. For example, if your research topic is the art of the Dakota Indians, you might try searching for all works with the key word *Dakota* in their subject description. This would result in hundreds of works, a few on art but many others on other topics, such as politics, economics, history, and so on. Something similar would happen if you searched for *art.* But if you search for *Dakota and art* the computer will list only those works with both words in their subject descriptions, a much more useful list, given the research topic. You can also combine key words using *or*. Searching for *Dakota and art or fiction* would result in a list of works that all have the word *Dakota* in their subject descriptions, some of which also have *art* and some of which also have *fiction*.

General periodical indexes. These indexes list articles published in a variety of periodicals of interest to the general public. Some are listed here.

Infotrac. This monthly index is available only on CD-ROM. It contains three separate indexes. The *Academic Index* covers nearly 1000 commonly used scholarly publications. The *General Periodical Index* covers over 1000 general-interest publications. The *Newspaper Index* covers large-circulation newspapers. Many entries include summaries.

New York Times Index (1851–present). This bimonthly index lists every article that appears in the *New York Times*. Short summaries are provided for many articles. It is also available on-line.

Readers' Guide to Periodical Literature (1900–present). This semimonthly index lists articles in over 200 magazines of general interest, such as *Newsweek*, *Popular Science*, and *Rolling Stone*. On-line and CD-ROM versions are also available (1983–present).

Specialized periodical indexes. These indexes list articles in periodicals in specific disciplines or fields of interest. They are usually much more helpful than general indexes for college-level research. Here are some of the most common.

America: History and Life
Applied Science and Technology Index
Art Index
Biological and Agricultural Index
Business Periodicals Index
Dissertation Abstracts International
Education Index
Essay and General Literature Index
General Science Index
Humanities Index
Index to Legal Periodicals
Music Index
Psychological Index
Social Science Index

Databases

Databases are large collections of electronically stored information that function like indexes. Often they provide summaries in addition to bibliographic information on the sources they list; occasionally they contain copies of the sources themselves.

The database most commonly found in college libraries is DIALOG, which keeps track of more than a million sources of information. DIALOG is divided into many smaller, more specialized databases, some 987 of which are listed in the current manual, *DIALOG Blue Sheets*. Some of the most commonly used databases within DIALOG include Arts and Humanities Search (1980–present), ERIC (Educational Resources Information Center, 1965–present), PsychINFO (1967–present), Scisearch (1974–present), and Social Scisearch (1972–present). You must decide which specialized database you need to use before you begin your search.

DIALOG and similar databases are available on-line. To use an on-line database, you will usually need the assistance of a reference librarian, who will ask you to fill out a form listing the key words you have identified for your project. The library is charged a

```
SilverPlatter 3.11    Journal Articles (1/74 - 12/86)    F10=Commands
                                                          F1=Help
........................................................
                                                          1 of 3
TI: Teacher expressiveness:  More important for male teachers than
female teachers?
AU: Basow.-Susan-A.; Distenfeld, -M.-Suzan
IN: Lafayette Coll
JN: Journal-of-Educational-Psychology; 1985 Feb Vol 77(1) 45-52
AB: 55 male and 62 female undergraduates viewed a videotape of a male
or female actor giving a short lecture using expressive or
nonexpressive communication and rated each teacher on a 22-item
questionnaire that yielded 5 factors (Rapport, Student Orientation,
Stimulates Interest, Organization, and Knowledge of Material).
Findings show that the expressive teacher received the highest student
evaluations on the basis of a global evaluation score and on the 5
factor scores.  The nonexpressive male teacher received low ratings
on Organization and Stimulating Interest.  Ss who viewed this tape
also had the poorest performance on a subsequent content test.  Ss who
viewed a nonexpressive female teacher had the highest performance on
the content test.  It is hypothesized that differential attention as a
function of sex-role-appropriate characteristics is a mediating
variable.  It is suggested that in studies of teaching performance and
........................................................
MENU:  Mark Record  Select Search Term  Options  Find  Print  Download

Press ENTER to Mark records for PRINT or DOWNLOAD.
Use PgDn and PgUp to scroll.
```

Partial entry in a CD-ROM database

fee for each search, calculated according to the time spent and the number of entries retrieved. Some libraries have the person requesting the search pay the fee; others limit the time allotted for each search. Be sure to ask what your library's policy is.

Some databases, including some of the specialized databases within DIALOG, are also available on CD-ROM. You can usually search through these databases without the aid of a librarian.

■ WRITING 3: APPLICATION

Use one of the bibliographies, indexes, or databases described in this section to find information on a relevant book or periodical. Locate the work, and take notes on the usefulness of the source and the process you used to obtain it.

3 The library catalog

The **library catalog** lists every book a library owns; many libraries also catalog their periodicals. At one time all catalogs were **card catalogs,** with the information printed on small cards and stored in drawers. Several decades ago, many libraries began transferring their catalogs to more convenient formats: **microfiche** and **microfilm.** These simulate the printed cards in a card catalog but can easily be duplicated and require much less space. More recently, libraries began computerizing their catalogs, which are now known as **on-line catalogs** (or **circulation computers**). Often on-line catalogs can be accessed through telephone lines and modems from locations outside the library.

Regardless of the format, all catalogs provide the same basic information. They list books by author, title, and subject; provide basic information about its physical format and content; and tell you where in the library to find it.

During the course of your research project, you will probably use the library catalog in two different ways. Sometimes you will already know the title of a work you want to find. The catalog can confirm that your library owns the work and can tell you where to find it. At other times, you will use the catalog as you would an index or a database, searching for works that are relevant to your topic; this is called *browsing.* On-line catalogs are particularly good for browsing and usually have several special features designed to facilitate it.

210 **Conducting library research**

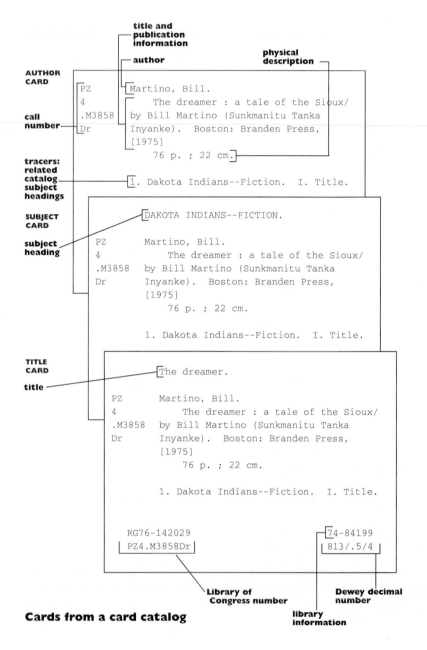

Cards from a card catalog

Even if you discover that your library doesn't own the source you want, don't despair. Many libraries can obtain a work owned by another library through an **interlibrary loan,** although this usually takes a few days. Ask your librarian.

Consulting on-line catalogs

On-line catalog systems vary slightly from library to library, though all systems follow the same general principles. Locating works on on-line catalogs by using author and title information is much like the corresponding procedure with a card catalog, with one important exception: most on-line catalogs allow you to search with partial information. For example, if you know that the title of a novel you'd like to locate begins with the words *Love Medicine* but you can't remember the rest of it, you can ask the catalog computer to search for the title *Love Medicine*. It will present you with a list of all works that begin with those words, including the novel you are looking for.

```
Search Request: T=LOVE MEDICINE
Search Results: 4 Entries Found                           Title Index
------------------------------------------------------------------T257
1  LOVE MEDICINE A NOVEL.  ERDRICH LOUISE <1984>  (BH)

   LOVE MEDICINE AND MIRACLES
2    SIEGEL BERNIE S <1986>  (BH)
3    SIEGEL BERNIE S <1988>  (DA)

   LOVE MEDICINE AND MIRACLES LESSONS LEARNED ABOUT SELF HEALING FROM
       A SURGEONS EXPERIENCE WITH EXCEPTIONAL PATIENTS
4    SIEGEL BERNIE S <1986>  (BH)


-----------------------------------------------------------------------
COMMANDS:      Type line # to see individual record
               O   Other options
               H   Help

NEXT COMMAND:
```

Results of a title search in an on-line catalog

Most on-line catalogs also allow you to perform **key word searches,** much like the searches conducted on computerized databases. The advantage of this kind of search is that the catalog computer can search all three categories (author, title, and subject) at once. To perform a key word search, use the words you've identified as describing your topic, linked by *and* or *or* as appropriate. (See 15b2.) For example, if you're trying to research

fictional accounts of Dakota Indians, you can search for *Dakota Indians and fiction*. The computer will present you with a list of works that fit that description. As with all computer searches, making your key word search request as specific as possible will result in the most useful list.

```
Search Request: T=LOVE MEDICINE
BOOK - Record 1 of 5 Entries Found                          Long View
------------------------- Screen 1 of 1 ------------------------T259
Author:          Erdrich, Louise.
Title:           Love medicine : a novel
Edition:         1st ed.
Published:       New York : Holt, Rinehart, and Winston, c1984.
Description:     viii, 275 p. ; 22cm.
Subjects(LC):    Indians of North America--North Dakota--Fiction.

---------------------------------------------------------------------
   LOCATION:               CALL NUMBER             STATUS:
1. Halley Stacks           PS3555.R42 L6 1984      Not checked out

COMMANDS:        P    Previous screen
                 O    Other options
                 H    Help

NEXT COMMAND:
```

Full information on a book in an on-line catalog

Once you have found your book, you can ask the on-line catalog to provide complete information on it. For the most part, this is the same information you would see in the card catalog. However, many on-line catalogs can also show you circulation information, letting you know whether the book is checked out.

Using call numbers

Once you have determined through the catalog that your library owns a book you want to consult, use the book's call number to locate it in the stacks. Most academic libraries use the **Library of Congress system,** whose call numbers begin with letters. Some libraries still use the older **Dewey Decimal system,** whose call numbers consist entirely of numbers. In either case, the first letters or numbers in a call number indicate the general subject area. Because libraries shelve all books for a general subject area together, this tells you where in the library to find the book you want.

Be sure to copy a book's call number exactly as it appears in the catalog. Most libraries have **open stacks,** allowing you to retrieve the book yourself. One wrong number or letter could lead you to an incorrect part of the library. If your library has **closed stacks,** you will need to give the call number to a librarian, who will retrieve the book for you. If you have given the librarian the wrong call number, you won't get the book you want.

■ WRITING 4: APPLICATION

Use the library's catalog to see what holdings the library has on your topic. Retrieve one of these books from the stacks, and check to see if it contains a bibliography that could lead you to other books. Record these findings in your research log.

4 Other sources of information

Many libraries own materials other than books and periodicals. Often these do not circulate. If you think one of the sources listed here might contain information relevant to your research, ask a librarian about your library's holdings.

Government documents. The U.S. government publishes numerous reports, pamphlets, catalogs, and newsletters on most issues of national concern. Reference books that can lead you to these sources include the *Monthly Catalogue of United States Government Publications* (monthly) and the *United States Government Publications Index,* both available on CD-ROM and on-line.

Nonprint media. Records, audiocassettes, videotapes, slides, photographs, and other media are generally cataloged separately from book and periodical collections.

Pamphlets. Pamphlets and brochures published by government agencies and private organizations are generally stored in a library's **vertical file.** The *Vertical File Index: A Subject and Title Index to Selected Pamphlet Material* (1932/35–present) lists many of the available titles.

Special collections. Rare books, manuscripts, and items of local interest are commonly found in a special room or section of the library.

■ WRITING 5: APPLICATION

Identify one relevant source of information in your library's holdings other than a book or a periodical. Locate it and take notes on the usefulness of the source and the process you used to obtain it.

You will uncover many sources through your library research, but not all of them will be equally useful. So that you don't waste time and energy taking careful notes on sources that contain unimportant or unreliable information, make sure to read each source critically by previewing, responding, and reviewing. (See 2b.)

First, you should **preview** the source quickly to get a general sense of it. Your purpose in previewing is to determine whether the source is related closely enough to your topic to be useful and to decide whether you should read it further. If you decide that your source will probably be useful, you need to read it more carefully and take notes on it. (See 15d.) Critical reading at this stage consists of **responding** — entering into a conversation with a text while you read — and **reviewing** — coming to a critical understanding of the text as a whole.

One critical reading activity, reviewing to evaluate, is particularly important when writing a research essay. Whenever you review to evaluate, you are trying to determine the worth or validity of the text and the information it contains. This is crucial because your final paper will probably require several sources of sound information. If you determine that a source is irrelevant, unreliable, or out of date, you'll need to find a new one. Because you obviously want to know this as soon as possible, make the effort to evaluate each source continually — when reading, when taking notes, and when considering how to incorporate the source into your final paper.

I **Evaluating sources yourself**

The more you research, the more of an expert you become at determining if a source is useful. When in doubt, confer with your instructor or a librarian. Here are some questions to ask yourself.

Subject. Is the subject directly related to my research question? Does it provide information that supports my view? Does it provide helpful context or background information? Does it contain quotations or facts that I will want to quote in my paper?

Author. What do I already know about the author's reputation? Does the book or periodical provide any biographical information? Is this author cited by other sources? Am I aware of any biases that might limit the author's credibility?

Date. When was this source published? Do my field and topic require current, up-to-date sources? Or would classic, well-established sources be more credible?

Publisher. Who published this source? Is it a major publisher, a university press, or a scholarly organization that would subject material to a rigorous review procedure?

2 Using professional reviews

You can get expert help in evaluating books by consulting book reviews. To avoid a hit-and-miss search, consult one of the several indexes that identify where and when a book was reviewed.

Book Review Index. This bimonthly index lists reviews of major books published in several hundred periodicals.

Current Book Review Citations. This annual index lists reviews published in more than 1000 periodicals.

■ WRITING 6: APPLICATION

For at least one source you are considering for your research paper, consult one of the book review indexes listed in this section. Look up some of these reviews and take careful notes.

15 d Taking notes

Taking good notes will make the whole research process easier — from locating and remembering sources to using them effectively in your writing. For short research projects requiring only a few sources, it is easy to take careful notes in a research log or class notebook and refer to them as needed when writing your paper. Or you can use a photocopy machine to copy whole articles or chapters and take them home for further study. However, for any research project requiring more than a few sources, you should

develop a card-based system for recording the sources you consult and the information you find within them.

Bibliographic cards

When you locate a useful source, write all the information necessary to find that source again on a 3″ x 5″ index card, using a separate card for each work consulted. Creating bibliographic cards as you go along will make it easy, at the end, to arrange them in alphabetical order and prepare your reference list. (For complete information on how to record bibliographic information using the appropriate documentation style, see Part VII.)

✔ **INFORMATION TO BE RECORDED ON BIBLIOGRAPHIC CARDS**

FOR BOOKS
1. Call number or other location information
2. Full name(s) of author(s)
3. Full title and subtitle
4. Edition or volume number
5. Editor or translator
6. Place of publication
7. Publisher and date of publication
8. Inclusive page numbers for relevant sections in longer works

FOR PERIODICALS
1. Full name(s) of author(s)
2. Full title and subtitle of article
3. Periodical title
4. Periodical volume and number
5. Periodical date
6. Inclusive page numbers of article
7. Library call number or other location information

PE
1405
.U6
M55
1991

Miller, Susan. _Textual Carnivals._

Carbondale: Southern Illinois UP, 1991

Bibliographic card using MLA documentation style

2 Note cards

Note cards are used to record the relevant information found in your sources. When you write your research essay, you will be working from these note cards, so be sure they contain all the information you need from every source you intend to use. Also try to make them focused on your particular research question, so that their relevance is clear when you read through them later.

To fit as much information as possible on each note card, use 4″ x 6″ index cards. Using different sizes for bibliography cards (3″ x 5″) and note cards will also help keep the two sets separate. A typical note card should contain only one piece of information or one idea. This will allow you to arrange and rearrange the information in different ways as you write. At the top of each note card, identify the source through brief bibliographic identification (author and title), and note the page numbers on which the information appears. Many writers also include the category of information, a particular theme, subject, or argument for which the note provides support. Personal notes, including ideas for possible use of the information or cross-references to other information, should be clearly distinguished from the notes from the source — perhaps by putting them at the bottom in parentheses.

When recording information on your card, you must take steps to avoid **plagiarism.** Do this by making distinctions among quoting directly, paraphrasing, and summarizing. A **direct quotation** is an exact duplication of the author's words in the original source. Put quotation marks around direct quotations on your note cards so that you will know later that these words are the author's, not yours. A **paraphrase** is a restatement of the author's words in your own words. Paraphrase to simplify or clarify the original author's point. A paraphrase must restate the original facts or ideas fully and correctly. A **summary** is a brief condensation or distillation of the main point of the original source. Like a paraphrase, a summary should be in your own words and all facts and ideas should be accurately represented. (See Chapter 17 for more on plagiarism, quotation, paraphrase, and summary.)

Lewis, _Green Delusions_, p. 230

Reasons for overpopulation in poor countries

Some experts believe that birth rates are linked to the "economic value" of children to their parents. Poor countries have higher birth rates because parents there rely on children to work for the family and to take care of them in old age. The more children, particularly sons, the better off the family is financially. In wealthier countries parents have fewer children because they cost more in terms of education and they contribute less.

(Based on Caldwell and Cain — check these further?)

Note card containing a paraphrase

Deciding when to quote, when to paraphrase, and when to summarize in your notes will require judgment on your part. The major advantage of quoting is that it allows you to decide later, in the course of writing the paper, whether to include a quotation or to paraphrase or summarize. However, copying down many long quotations can be time-consuming. Also, simply copying down a quotation may prevent you from thinking about the ideas expressed in a way that will benefit your understanding of the topic. In general, copy direct quotations only when the author's words are particularly lively or persuasive. Photocopying machines make it easy to collect direct quotations, but be sure to highlight the pertinent material or make notes to yourself on the copy so you can remember later what you wanted to quote and why. For ease of organizing notes, many researchers cut out the pertinent quotation and paste it to a note card.

A good paraphrase can help you better understand a difficult passage by simplifying complex sentence structure and vocabulary into language you are more comfortable with. Be careful not to distort the author's ideas. Use paraphrases when you need to record details, but not exact words.

Because a summary boils a source down to its essentials, it is particularly useful when specific details in the source are not important or are irrelevant to your research question. You may often find that you can summarize several paragraphs or even an entire article or chapter in just a few sentences without losing any useful information. It is a good idea to note when a particular card contains a summary so you'll remember later that it leaves out detailed supporting information.

■ **WRITING 7: PRACTICE**

Reread this chapter as though you were researching the question, What are the most important things students need to learn about a library? First, create a bibliographic card for *The Blair Handbook*. Then write the following note cards: (1) a direct quotation; (2) a paraphrase of a passage (two to three paragraphs); (3) a summary of a longer section (for example, 15a or 15b2) in one to three sentences. On the back of each note card, explain why this material was best handled in the manner you chose.

■ **WRITING 8: EXPLORATION**

Describe the most important, useful, or surprising thing you have learned about the library since exploring it as part of your research project. Share your discovery with classmates, and listen to theirs. Are you comfortable in the library? Why or why not?

Research is an active and unpredictable process requiring serious investigators to find answers wherever they happen to be. Depending on your research question, you may need to seek answers by visiting museums, attending concerts, interviewing politicians, observing classrooms, or following leads down some other trail. Investigations that take place outside the library are commonly called **field research.**

Field researchers collect information that is not yet written down. Because the information they collect has not been previously recorded or assessed, field researchers have the chance to uncover new facts and develop original interpretations. To conduct such research, you need to identify the people, places, things, or events that can give you the information you need. Then you must go out in the field and either **observe** by watching carefully or **interview** by asking questions of one particular person. You should take careful notes to record your observations or interviews and critically evaluate the information you've collected.

16 a Planning field research

Unlike a library, which bundles millions of bits of every kind of information in a single location, "fields" are everywhere — your room, a dormitory, cafeteria, neighborhood, theater, mall, park, playground, and so on. Field information is not cataloged, organized, indexed, or shelved for your convenience. Nor is there a reference librarian to point you to the best resources. When you think about making field research a part of your research project, you start out on your own. Successful field research requires diligence, energy, and careful planning.

First, you need to find the person, place, thing, or event most helpful to you and decide whether you want to collect observations, conduct interviews, or do both. Consider your research question as you've developed it thus far. Also consider what sort of information will be most effective in your final paper.

Second, you need to schedule field research in advance and allow enough time for it. People, things, and events will not always hold still or be exactly where you want them to be when it's most convenient for you. Allow time for rescheduling a visit or interview or returning for more information.

Third, you need to visit the library before conducting extensive field research. No matter who, where, or what you intend to collect information from, there's background information at the library that can help you make more insightful observations or formulate better interview questions. (For more information on using libraries, see Chapter 15.)

Finally, you need to keep a **research log** so you can make notes about all the visits, questions, phone calls, and conversations that relate to your research project. (See 14b.) Write in your log as soon as you receive your assignment and at each step along the way about topics, questions, methods, and answers. Even record dead-end searches — to remind you not to repeat them.

■ **WRITING 1: APPLICATION**

In your research log, write about the feasibility of using field research information to help answer your research question: What kind of field research would strengthen your paper? Where would you go to collect it?

16 **b** | **Interviewing**

A good interview provides the researcher with timely, original, and useful information that often cannot be obtained by other means. Getting such information is part instinct, part skill, and part luck. If you find talking to strangers easy, then you have a head start on being a good interviewer — in many respects, a good interview is simply a good conversation. If not, you can still learn how to ask good interview questions that will elicit the answers you need. Of course, no matter how skillful or prepared you are, whether your interview results in good answers also depends on your interview subject — his or her mood, knowledge, and willingness to spend time talking with you.

Your chances of obtaining good interview material increase

when you've thought about it ahead of time. The following guide-lines should help you conduct good interviews.

Select the right person. People differ in both the amount and kind of knowledge they have. Not everyone who knows some-thing about your research topic will be able to give you the infor-mation you need. In other words, before you make an appoint-ment with a local expert because she's accessible, consider whether she's the best person to talk to. Ask yourself (1) exactly what information you need, (2) why you need it, (3) who is likely to have it, and (4) how you might approach them to gain it. Most re-search projects benefit from various perspectives, so you may want to interview several people. For example, to research Lake Erie pollution, you could interview someone who lives on the shore, a chemist who knows about pesticide decomposition, and a vice president of a paper company dumping waste into the lake. Just be sure the people you select are likely to provide you with information you really need.

Do your homework. Before you talk to an expert about your topic, make sure you know something about it yourself. Be able to define or describe your interest in it, know the general issues, and learn what your interview subject has already said about it. This way, you will ask sharper questions, get to the point faster, and be more interesting for your subject to talk with.

Plan appropriate questions. A good interview doesn't follow a script, but it usually starts with one. Before you begin an inter-view, write out the questions you plan to ask and arrange them so that they build on each other — general questions first, specific ones later. If you or your subject digresses too much, your ques-tions can serve as reminders about the information you need.

Ask both open and closed questions. Different kinds of questions elicit different kinds of information. Open questions place few limits on the kinds of answers given: *Why did you decide to major in business? What are your plans for the future?* Closed questions specify the kind of information you want and usually elicit brief responses: *When did you receive your degree? From what college?* Open questions usually provide general information, while closed questions allow you to zero in on specific details.

Ask follow-up questions. Listen closely to the answers you receive, and when the information is incomplete or confusing, ask follow-up questions requesting clarification. Such questions can't be scripted; you've just got to use your wits to direct your subject toward the information you consider most important.

Use silence. If you don't get an immediate response to a question, wait a bit before asking another one. In some cases, your question may not have been clear and you will need to rephrase it. But in many cases your interview subject is simply collecting his or her thoughts, not ignoring you. After a slight pause, you may hear thoughtful answers worth waiting for.

Read body language. Be aware of what your subject is doing when he or she answers questions. Does he look you in the eye? Does she fidget and squirm? Does he look distracted or bored? Does she smile? From these visual cues you may be able to infer when your subject is speaking most frankly, doesn't want to give more information, or is tired of answering questions. ·

Take good notes. Most interviewers take notes using a pad that is spiral-bound on top, which allows for quick page flipping. Don't try to write down everything, just major ideas and telling statements in the subject's own words that you might want to use as quotations in your paper. Omitting small words, focusing on the most distinctive and precise language, and using common abbreviations (like *b/c* for *because* and *w/* for *with*) can make note-taking more efficient.

Also take notes about your subject's physical appearance, facial expressions, and clothing and about the interview setting itself. These details will be useful later in reconstructing the interview and representing it more vividly in your paper.

If you plan to use a tape recorder, ask your subject's permission in advance. The advantage of tape recording is that you have a complete record of the conversation. Sometimes on hearing the person a second time you notice important things that you missed earlier. The disadvantages are that sometimes tape recorders make subjects nervous and that transcribing a tape is time-consuming work. It's a good idea to have pen in hand to catch highlights or jot down questions.

Confirm important assertions. When your subject says something especially important or controversial, read back your notes to check for accuracy and to allow your subject to elaborate. Some interviewers do this as the interview progresses, others at the end.

Review your notes as soon as possible. Notes taken during an interview are brief reminders of what your subject said, not complete quotations. You need to write out the complete information they represent as soon after the interview as you can, certainly within twenty-four hours. Supplement the notes with other remembered details while they're still fresh, by recording them on note cards or directly into a computer file that you can refer to as you write your paper.

ESL **CONDUCTING INTERVIEWS IN ENGLISH**

Interviewing someone in a language other than your native language can be challenging. Before you conduct an interview, consider whether you will feel comfortable taking notes and listening at the same time. If not, and if your interview subject doesn't object, you may want to use a tape recorder.

If you decide to take notes in an interview, develop a list of abbreviations beforehand to facilitate notetaking. Don't hesitate to ask your interview subject to repeat information during the interview, but be polite. It is usually more polite to make a request than to use a command or statement.

LESS POLITE	MORE POLITE
Repeat that statistic.	Could you repeat that statistic?
I don't understand.	Would you explain that to me?

■ **WRITING 2: EXPLORATION**

Describe any experience you have had as either interviewer or interviewee. Drawing on your own experience, what additional advice would you give to researchers setting out to interview a subject?

■ **WRITING 3: APPLICATION**

Whom could you interview to find information useful and relevant to your project? Make a list of such people. Write out first drafts of possible questions to ask them.

---

16 C Observing

Another kind of field research calls for closely observing people, places, things, and events and then describing them accurately to show readers what you saw and experienced. While the term *observation* literally denotes visual perception, it also applies to information collected on site through other senses. The following suggestions may help you conduct field observations.

Select a good site to visit. As with interviewing, observing requires that you know where to go and what to look for. You need to have your research question in mind and then to identify those places where observation will yield useful information. For example, a research project on pollution in Lake Erie would be enhanced by on-the-scene observation of what the water smells, feels, and looks like. Sometimes the site you visit is the primary object of your research, as when the purpose of your paper is to profile the people and activities you find there. At other times the site is chosen to provide supplemental evidence.

Do your homework. To observe well, you need to know what you are looking for and what you are looking at. If you are observing a political speech, know the issues and the players; if you visit an industrial complex, know what is manufactured there. Researching background information at the library or elsewhere will allow you to use your site time more efficiently.

Plan your visit. Learn not only where the place is located on a map but also how to gain access; call ahead to ask directions. Find out where you should go when you first arrive. If relevant, ask which places are open to you, which are off limits, and which you could visit with permission. Find out about visiting hours; if you want to visit at odd hours, you may need special permission. Depending on the place, after-hours visits can provide detailed information not available to the general public.

Take good notes. At any site there's a lot going on that casual observers take for granted. As a researcher you should take nothing for granted. Keep in mind that without notes, as soon as you leave a site you forget more than half of what was there. As with interview notes, be sure to review and rewrite your observation notes as soon after your site visit as possible. (See 16b.)

You can't write everything down, though, so be selective. Keep your research question in mind and try to focus on the impressions that are most important in answering it. Some of your observations and notes will provide the background information needed to represent the scene vividly in your paper. Some will provide the details needed to make your paper believable. Make your notes as precise as possible, indicating the color, shape, size, texture, and arrangement of everything you can.

Use a notebook that has a stiff cover so you can write standing, sitting, or squatting, as a table may not be available. Double-entry notebooks are useful for site visits, because they allow you to record facts in one column and interpretations of those facts in the other. (See Chapter 8.) If visual images would be useful, you can sketch, photograph, or videotape. You can use a tape recorder and speak your notes into it; this way, you will also pick up the characteristic sounds of the site.

■ **WRITING 4: EXPLORATION**

Describe a time when you used close observation in a piece of writing. Was it deliberate or by accident? What was your readers' response?

■ **WRITING 5: APPLICATION**

List at least three sites you could visit that would add relevant information to your study. Then follow the suggestions in this chapter and visit at least one of them.

16 d Thinking critically about field sources

When you've found a potentially useful field source, you need to examine it and assess its value just as carefully as you would a source found in a library. To do this requires critical thinking, a process much like critical reading. (See Chapter 2.) You need to analyze the assumptions and reasoning of the source, determine whether it is reliable and credible, and develop an interpretation of what it means to you and your research question. Ask yourself the following questions.

1 **What is the most important point this source makes?** How does it address my research question? How would I articulate this point in writing?

2 **What evidence did the source provide that supports this point?** Is it strong or weak? Can I use it? Build on it? Should I question it? Refute it?

3 **Does the information support my working thesis?** If so, how? Can I express in writing the precise nature of the support?

4 **Does the information challenge my working thesis?** If so, how? Can I refute the information or contradiction? Or should I revise my thesis to take the new information into account?

5 **Does the information support or contradict information collected from other sources?** How so? How can I resolve any contradictions? Do I need to seek other sources for confirmation?

6 **Is the source reliable?** Does any of the information from this source seem illogical or incredible? Has any of the information been contradicted by a more authoritative source? If so, does this cast all of the information from this source into doubt?

7 **Is the source biased?** Does the interview subject have a reason to be biased in any way? Does he or she have a reputation to protect or a vested interest in the thing I'm researching? Would the selection of a different site have resulted in different information?

■ **WRITING 6: APPLICATION**

Explain how you have evaluated your field sources to assess their accuracy and reliability.

 SUGGESTIONS FOR FIELD RESEARCH PROJECTS

INDIVIDUAL

1. Plan a research project that focuses on a local place (park, playground, street, building, business, or institution) and make a research plan that includes going there, describing what you find, and interviewing somebody. Conduct the research.

2. Plan a research project that begins with an issue of some concern to you. Identify a local manifestation of this issue that would profit from some field research. Conduct the research, using field techniques appropriate to your topic.

COLLABORATIVE

Create a team of two to four classmates who would like to join you in researching the project you planned in individual suggestion 1 or 2. Plan the necessary activities to make this project work. Divide the labor so that each of you brings some information to the group by next week's class meeting. Make a copy of your research information for each group member, including typed transcripts of interviews and photocopies of visual information. You may each write an individual paper based on your collective research, or you may team up and write a longer paper.

Locating potential sources for a research project is one thing; deciding which ones to include, where to use them, and how to incorporate them is something else. Some writers begin making use of their sources in their very earliest exploratory drafts, perhaps by trying out a pithy quotation to see how it brings a paragraph into focus. Others prefer to wait until they have all of their note cards in neat stacks before making any decisions about what to include. No matter how you begin writing with sources, there comes a time when you will need to incorporate them finally, smoothly, effectively, and correctly into your paper.

17 a Controlling your sources

Once you've conducted some research and are ready to begin drafting, you need to decide which sources to use and how to use them. You can't make this decision based on how much time you spent finding and analyzing each source; you have to decide based on how useful the source is in answering your current research question. In other words, you need to control your sources rather than letting them control you.

Papers written in an effort "to get everything in" are *source-driven* and all too often read like patch jobs of quotations loosely strung together. Your goal should be to remain the director of the research production, your ideas on center stage and your sources the supporting cast.

Real research about real questions is vital and dynamic, which means it's always changing. Just as you can't expect your first working thesis to be your final thesis, you can't expect to know in advance which sources are going to prove most fruitful. And don't think that you can't collect more information once you've begun drafting. At each step in the process you see your research question and answer more clearly, so the research you conduct as you write may be the most useful of all.

The best way to ensure that you remain in control is to make an **outline** first and then organize your notes according to it. (If you compose your outline on a word processor, it will be easier for you to make changes later on.) If you do it the other way around — organizing your notes into a logical sequence and then writing an outline based on that sequence — you'll be tempted to find a place for every note and to gloss over areas where you haven't done enough research. By outlining first, you let the logical flow of your ideas create a blueprint for your paper. (Of course, your outline may change as your ideas continue to develop.) If you can't outline before you write, then be sure to begin writing before you arrange your note cards.

Once you've outlined or begun drafting and have a good sense of the shape of your paper, organize your notes. Put bibliographic cards in alphabetical order by the author's last name and arrange your note cards so that they correspond to your outline. Integrate field research notes as best you can, depending on their format. Finally, go back to your outline and annotate it to indicate which source goes where. This will show you if there are any ideas that need more research.

Keep in mind that referring more than two or three times to a single source — unless it is itself the focus of your paper — undercuts your credibility and suggests overreliance on a single point of view. If you find you need to refer often to one source, make sure that you have sufficient references to other sources.

■ **WRITING 1: EXPLORATION**

Describe your experience writing a recent research paper. Were there requirements for using a certain number or kind of sources? Did you or your sources control the paper?

■ **WRITING 2: APPLICATION**

Use your research log to draft a tentative thesis and working outline for your research paper. Then arrange your note cards according to that working outline.

17 b Quoting, paraphrasing, and summarizing

Once you know which sources you want to use, you still have to decide how to use them. The notes you made during your research are in many forms. For some sources, you will have copied down direct quotations; for others you will have paraphrased or summarized important information. For some field sources you may have made extensive notes on background information, such as your interview subject's appearance. Simply because you've quoted or paraphrased a particular source in your notes, however, doesn't mean you have to use a quotation or paraphrase from this source in your paper. Make decisions about how to use sources based on your goals, not on the format of your research notes.

Whenever you quote, paraphrase, or summarize, you must acknowledge your source through documentation. Different disciplines have different conventions for documentation. The examples in this chapter use the documentation style of the Modern Language Association (MLA), the style preferred in the languages and literature. (For more on documentation, see 17c.)

1 Quoting

Direct quotation provides strong evidence and can add both life and authenticity to your paper. However, too much quotation can make it seem as though you have little to say for yourself. Long quotations also slow readers down and often have the unintended effect of inviting them to skip over the quoted material. Unless the source quoted is itself the topic of the paper (as in a literary interpretation), limit brief quotations to no more than two per page and long quotations to no more than one every three pages.

Deciding when to quote

Direct quotations should be reserved for cases in which you cannot express the ideas better yourself. Using only strong, memorable quotations will make your writing stronger and more memorable as well. Use quotations when the original words are especially precise, clear, powerful, or vivid.

- **Precise.** Use quotations when the words used are important in themselves or when they've been used to make fine but important distinctions.

- **Clear.** Use quotations when the ideas would be difficult to paraphrase.

- **Powerful.** Use quotations when the words are especially authoritative and memorable.

■ **Vivid.** Use quotations when the language is lively and colorful, when it reveals something of the author's or speaker's character.

Quoting accurately and effectively

To quote, you must use an author's or speaker's exact words. Slight changes in wording are permitted in certain cases (see next section), but these changes must be clearly marked.

Although you can't change what a source says, you do have control over how much of it you use. Use only as long a quotation as you need to make your point. Remember that quotations should be used to support your points, not introduce them. Be sure that when you shorten a quotation, you have not changed its meaning. If you omit words within quotations for the sake of brevity, you must indicate that you have done so by using ellipsis points. Any changes or additions must be indicated with brackets. (See 49c and 49d for more on ellipses and brackets.)

ORIGINAL

The human communication environment has acquired biological complexity and planetary scale, but there are no scientists or activists monitoring it, theorizing about its health, or mounting campaigns to protect its resilience. Perhaps it's too new, too large to view as a whole, or too containing — we swim in a sea of information, in poet Gary Snyder's phrase. All the more reason to worry. New things have nastier surprises, big things are hard to change, and containing things are inescapable.

STEWART BRAND, *THE MEDIA LAB*

INACCURATE QUOTATION

In *The Media Lab*, Stewart Brand describes the control that is exerted by watchdog agencies over modern telecommunications: "The human communication environment has . . . activists monitoring it, theorizing about its health . . ." (258).

By omitting certain words, the writer has changed the meaning of the original source.

ACCURATE QUOTATION

In *The Media Lab*, Stewart Brand notes that we have done little to monitor the growth of telecommunications. Modern communication technology may seem overwhelmingly new, big, and encompassing, but these are reasons for more vigilance, not less:

"New things have nastier surprises, big things are hard to change, and containing things are inescapable" (258).

Integrating quotations into your paper

Direct quotations will be most effective when you integrate them smoothly into the flow of your paper. Readers should be able to follow your meaning easily and to see the relevance of the quotation immediately.

Using embedded or block format. Brief quotations should be embedded in the main body of your paper and enclosed in quotation marks. A brief quotation consists of four or fewer typed lines according to MLA style guidelines.

> Photo editor Tom Brennan took ten minutes to sort through my images and then told me, "Most photography editors wouldn't take more than two minutes to look at a portfolio."

Longer quotations should be set off in block format. Begin a new line, indent ten spaces (for MLA), and do not use quotation marks.

> Katie Kelly focuses on Americans' peculiarly negative chauvinism, in this case, the chauvinism of New York residents:
>
> > New Yorkers are a provincial lot. They wear their city's accomplishments like blue ribbons. To anyone who will listen they boast of leading the world in everything from Mafia murders to porno moviehouses. (89)

See Chapter 48 for more on punctuating quotations.

Introducing quotations. Introduce all quoted material so that readers know who is speaking, what the quotation refers to, and where it is from. If the author or speaker is well known, it is especially useful to mention his or her name in an introductory signal phrase.

> Henry David Thoreau asserts in *Walden*, "The mass of men lead lives of quiet desperation" (5).

If your paper focuses on written works, you can introduce a quotation with the title rather than the author's name, as long as the reference is clear.

> *Walden* sets forth one individual's antidote against the "lives of quiet desperation" led by the working class in mid-nineteenth-century America (Thoreau 5).

If neither the author nor the title of a written source is well known (or the speaker in a field source), introduce the quotation with a brief explanation to give your readers some context.

> Mary Catherine Bateson, daughter of anthropologist Margaret Mead, has become, in her own right, a student of modern civilization. In *Composing a Life* she writes, "The twentieth century has been called the century of the refugee because of the vast numbers of people uprooted by war and politics from their homes" (8).

Explaining and clarifying quotations. Sometimes you will need to explain a quotation in order to clarify why it's relevant and what it means in the context of your discussion.

> In *A Sand County Almanac*, Aldo Leopold invites modern urban readers to confront what they lose by living in the city: "There are two spiritual dangers in not owning a farm. One is the danger of supposing that breakfast comes from the grocery, and the other that heat comes from the furnace" (6). Leopold sees city-dwellers as self-centered children, blissfully but dangerously unaware of how their basic needs are met.

You may also need to clarify what a word or reference means. Do this by using square brackets. (See 48c.)

UNCLEAR

Observing the remains of earwigs, sow bugs, moths, and spiders, Dillard reminds us that everything is changing, even in death: "Next week, if the other bodies are any indication, he will be shrunken and gray, webbed to the floor with dust."

CLEAR

Observing the remains of earwigs, sow bugs, moths, and spiders, Dillard reminds us that everything is changing, even in death: "Next week, if the other bodies are any indication, [the earwig] will be shrunken and gray, webbed to the floor with dust."

Integrating quotations grammatically. A passage containing a quotation must follow all the rules of grammatical sentence structure — tenses should be consistent, verbs and subjects should agree, and so on. If the form of the quotation doesn't quite fit the grammar of your own sentences, you can either quote less of the original source, change your sentences, or make a slight alteration in the quotation. Use this last option sparingly, and always indicate any changes with brackets. (See 48c.)

GRAMMATICALLY INCOMPATIBLE

If Thoreau thought that in his day, "The mass of men lead lives of quiet desperation" (*Walden* 5), what would he say of the masses today?

GRAMMATICALLY COMPATIBLE

If Thoreau thought that in his day, the masses led "lives of quiet desperation" (*Walden* 5), what would he say of the masses today?

GRAMMATICALLY COMPATIBLE

In the nineteenth century, Thoreau stated, "The mass of men lead lives of quiet desperation" (*Walden* 5). What would he say of the masses today?

GRAMMATICALLY COMPATIBLE

If Thoreau thought that in his day, the "mass of men [led] lives of quiet desperation" (*Walden* 5), what would he say of the masses today?

■ **WRITING 3: APPLICATION**

Read through your research materials, highlighting any quotations you might want to incorporate into your paper. Use your research log to explore why you think these words should be quoted directly.

2 **Paraphrasing**

To paraphrase, you restate a source's ideas in your own words. The point of paraphrasing is to make the ideas clearer (both to your readers and to yourself) and to express the ideas in the way that best suits your purpose.

Deciding when to paraphrase

In taking notes you may have written down or photocopied many quotations instead of taking the time to put an author's or speaker's ideas into your own words. As you draft, however, you should paraphrase or summarize most such information so that your paper doesn't turn into a string of undigested quotations.

Paraphrases should generally re-create the original source's order, structure, and emphasis, and they should include most of its details. This means that a paraphrase is seldom briefer than the original. Use paraphrases only when the original is already quite brief or when you need to present an author's or speaker's ideas in detail; otherwise, use a summary.

Paraphrasing accurately and effectively

Restate the source's ideas, but in your own words. A paraphrase should say neither more nor less than the original source, and it should never distort the meaning of the source. The best way to make an accurate paraphrase is to stay close to the order and structure of the original passage, to reproduce its emphases and details. However, don't use the same sentence patterns or vocabulary or you risk inadvertently plagiarizing the source. (See 17c.)

If the original source has used a well-established or technical term for a concept, you do not need to find a synonym for it. If you believe that the original source's exact words are the best possible expressions of some points, you may use brief direct quotations within your paraphrase, as long as you indicate these with quotation marks.

Keep in mind why you are including this source; this will help you to decide how to phrase the ideas. Be careful, though, not to introduce your own comments or reflections in the middle of a paraphrase, unless you make it very clear that these are your thoughts, not the original author's or speaker's.

ORIGINAL

The human communication environment has acquired biological complexity and planetary scale, but there are no scientists or activists monitoring it, theorizing about its health, or mounting campaigns to protect its resilience. Perhaps it's too new, too large to view as a whole, or too containing — we swim in a sea of information, in poet Gary Snyder's phrase. All the more

reason to worry. New things have nastier surprises, big things are
hard to change, and containing things are inescapable.

STEWART BRAND, *THE MEDIA LAB*

INACCURATE PARAPHRASE

In *The Media Lab*, Brand points out that the "communication
environment" we live within is as complex and vast as any
ecosystem on the planet. Yet no one monitors this environment,
keeping track of its growth and warning us if something is about
to go wrong. This is because the communication environment has
become so large and all-encompassing in such a short time that
we don't worry about it (258).

ESL | **STRATEGIES FOR PARAPHRASING**

Writers who are inexperienced at paraphrasing in English
sometimes paraphrase by substituting synonyms for some of the author's words, keeping the sentence structure and many of the words
the same. This kind of paraphrasing is unacceptable in academic writing; it may be considered a form of plagiarism. (See 17c.) Here are
some suggestions that may help you write effective paraphrases.

1. Before you begin writing a paraphrase of a sentence or passage,
make sure that you understand the author's meaning. Look up in a
dictionary any words you don't know, and ask a native speaker of
English about any idioms or slang with which you are unfamiliar.

2. To write your paraphrase, look away from the original source and
put the ideas into your own words.

3. If you are paraphrasing a passage, don't paraphrase the information one sentence at a time. Instead, try to express the meaning of
the entire passage.

4. Consider the context of the sentence or passage you are paraphrasing. Are there any references that are clear only from the surrounding sentences? Make sure you have given your readers enough
information to understand your paraphrase.

5. Use a thesaurus to find synonyms if you need to, but remember
that not every word listed together in a thesaurus is equally appropriate in every sentence. Use only words you are familiar with.

ACCURATE PARAPHRASE

In *The Media Lab*, Brand points out that the "communication environment" we live within is as complex and vast as any ecosystem on the planet. Yet no one monitors this environment, keeping track of its growth and warning us if something is about to go wrong. This may be understandable, since the communication environment has become so large and all-encompassing in such a short time that we often overlook it. But this is exactly why we should worry: it's the very qualities of being recent, large, and all-encompassing that make this environment potentially so dangerous (258).

▣ WRITING 4: APPLICATION

Read through your note cards for any passages you quoted directly from an original source. Find notes that now seem wordy, unclear, or longer than necessary. Paraphrase notes that you expect to use in your paper. Exchange your paraphrases and the originals with a classmate, and assess each other's work.

3 Summarizing

To summarize, you distill a source's words down to the main ideas and state these in your own words. A summary includes only the essentials of the original source, not the supporting details, and is consequently shorter than the original.

Deciding when to summarize

Use summaries when your readers need to know only the main point the original source makes, not the details of how it makes this point.

You may have taken extensive notes on a particular article or observation only to discover in the course of drafting that all the detail is not necessary, given the current focus of your paper. In such a case, you may be able to summarize your notes in a few sentences that effectively support your discussion.

Keep in mind that summaries are generalizations and that too many generalizations can make your writing vague and tedious. You should occasionally supplement summaries with brief direct quotations or evocative details collected through observation to keep readers in touch with the original source.

> ✓ **QUOTATION, PARAPHRASE, AND SUMMARY**
>
> **QUOTATION**
> - Use the author's or speaker's exact words.
> - A quotation is the same length as the source, although words may be omitted if the omission is indicated with ellipsis points.
> - Use a quotation when the language of the original is particularly precise, clear, powerful, or vivid.
>
> **PARAPHRASE**
> - Put the author's or speaker's ideas in your own words.
> - A paraphrase is usually about the same length as the source.
> - Use a paraphrase when you need to include all or most of the details in the source.
>
> **SUMMARY**
> - Reduce the author's or speaker's ideas to the main points, and express these in your own words.
> - A summary is shorter than the source.
> - Use a summary when you need to include only the essential points in the source.

Summarizing accurately and effectively

Summaries vary in length, and the length of the original source has no necessary relationship to the length of the summary you write. Depending on the focus of your paper, you may need to summarize an entire novel in a sentence or two, or you may need to summarize a brief journal article in two or three paragraphs. Remember that the more material you attempt to summarize in a short space, the more you will necessarily generalize and abstract it. Reduce a text as far as you can while still providing all the information your readers need to know. Be careful though, not to distort the original's meaning.

ORIGINAL

The human communication environment has acquired biological complexity and planetary scale, but there are no scientists or activists monitoring it, theorizing about its health, or mounting campaigns to protect its resilience. Perhaps it's too new, too large to view as a whole, or too containing — we swim in a sea of information, in poet Gary Snyder's phrase. All the more reason to worry. New things have nastier surprises, big things are hard to change, and containing things are inescapable.

STEWART BRAND, *THE MEDIA LAB*

INACCURATE SUMMARY

The current telecommunications networks comprise a nasty, un-changeable, and inescapable environment (Brand 258).

ACCURATE SUMMARY

Stewart Brand warns that we may soon regret not keeping a closer watch on the burgeoning telecommunications networks (258).

■ **WRITING 5: APPLICATION**

Review any sources that you have taken particularly extensive notes on. Would it be possible to condense these notes into a briefer summary of the entire work? Would it serve your purpose to do so? Why or why not?

| **17** | **C** | **Using documentation and avoiding plagiarism** |

Documentation is a systematic method for acknowledging sources. Documentation is also a service to your readers and to later scholars. Knowledge in the academic community is cumulative, with one writer's work building on another's. After reading your paper, readers may want to know more about a source you cited, perhaps in order to use it in papers of their own. Correct documentation helps readers find the source quickly and easily.

Each discipline has developed its own conventions for documentation. The languages and literature use the style recommended by the Modern Language Association (MLA). Other humanities use a system of endnotes or footnotes. Social sciences use the style recommended by the American Psychological Association (APA). Natural sciences use the style recommended by the Council of Biology Editors (CBE) or a related style. You should use the documentation of the discipline for which you are writing; if

you are in doubt, ask your instructor. (See Part VII for complete information on each of these documentation styles.)

You do not need to document **common knowledge,** even if it is mentioned in or by your sources. Common knowledge is information that an educated person can be expected to know or any factual information that can be found in multiple sources. Examples include the dates of historical events, the names and locations of states and cities, the general laws of science, and so on. However, when you read the work of authors who have specific opinions and interpretations of a piece of common knowledge and you use their opinions or interpretations in your paper, you need to give them credit through proper documentation.

ESL   **AVOIDING PLAGIARISM**

If you have attended school and written research papers outside the United States, you may find that the conventions for using quotations and citing sources in U.S. academic writing are stricter than those you are used to. Be sure you understand what plagiarism in the United States is, and do your best to avoid it.

■ Put all quotations in quotation marks and provide source information, even if the quotation is as short as a phrase.

■ Do not use another author's creative ideas in your own paper without citing the source. For example, if an author uses an anecdote or story to explain an idea, you cannot use the same anecdote or story without giving the author credit.

■ Do not use another author's organizational scheme or headings without giving credit to the author. For example, if you were investigating censorship in the media, you would want to avoid identifying exactly the same subtopics in the same order that one of your sources used.

If you aren't sure about what you can use from a source or what you need to cite, ask a tutor or your instructor for help before you turn in your final paper. Also, find out if your school has a booklet on avoiding plagiarism.

Plagiarism is stealing ideas or information from somebody else and passing them off as your own. Whenever you introduce ideas or information from a source into your text, you need to cite the source for those ideas. (See 17d.) Failing to cite a source is an unethical practice and at most colleges is grounds for discipline or even dismissal.

Not all plagiarism is intentional. Many writers are unaware of the guidelines for correctly indicating that they have borrowed words or ideas from someone else. Nevertheless, it is the writer's responsibility to learn these guidelines and follow them.

Keep in mind that when you paraphrase or summarize a source, you need to identify the author of those ideas just as if you had quoted directly. The most common source of inadvertent plagiarism is when a writer paraphrases or summarizes a source but stays too close to the wording or sentence structure of the original, sometimes lifting whole phrases without enclosing them in quotation marks. To avoid plagiarism, use your own words to replace unimportant language in the original, and quote any particularly effective language within quotation marks.

ORIGINAL

Notwithstanding the widely different opinions about Machiavelli's work and his personality there is at least one point in which we find a complete unanimity. All authors emphasize that Machiavelli is a "child of his age," that he is a typical witness to the Renaissance.

ERNST CASSIRER, *THE MYTH OF THE STATE*

PLAGIARIZED PARAPHRASE

Despite the widely different opinions about Machiavelli's work and personality, everyone agrees that he was a representative witness to the Renaissance (Cassirer 43).

ACCEPTABLE PARAPHRASE

Although views on the work and personality of Machiavelli vary, everyone agrees that he was "a typical witness to the Renaissance" (Cassirer 43).

■ **WRITING 6: EXPLORATION**

Read the following quotation from Mike Rose's *Lives on the Boundary*; then explain why each of the three sentences that follow is an example of plagiarism.

"The discourse of academics is marked by terms and expressions that represent an elaborate set of shared concepts and orientations: alienation, authoritarian personality, the social construction of self, determinism,

hegemony, equilibrium, intentionality, recursion, reinforcement, and so on. This language weaves through so many lectures and textbooks, it is integral to so many learned discussions, that it is easy to forget what a foreign language it can be. (192)"

1. The discourse of academics is marked by expressions that represent shared concepts.

2. Academic discourse is characterized by a particular set of coded words and ideas that are found throughout the college community.

3. Sometimes the talk of professors is as difficult for outsiders to understand as a foreign language is to a native speaker.

This chapter provides samples of three research papers, two following Modern Language Association (MLA) format and documentation conventions and one following American Psychological Association (APA) conventions. Each of the student papers has been edited slightly for publication, but remains largely as originally written. Each paper contains annotations explaining the format and documentation conventions. (For a full discussion of these conventions see Part VII.)

18 a Personal research essay: MLA style

The following research essay, "How to Become a Photographer's Assistant," resulted from an assignment asking students to investigate a career interest and report on it in an informal paper. Zoe Reynders writes in her own casual, personal voice yet uses careful library research (and some field research), which she documents according to the conventions of the Modern Language Association (MLA).

Reynder's paper illustrates the simple MLA style of identifying the writer of the paper and other pertinent academic information in the upper left-hand corner of the first page, followed by the title, centered. Page numbers are in the top right corner, without further punctuation or identification. Some instructors want students to put their last names at the top of each page, just before the page number, but others consider this unnecessary. (For an example of a paper that includes a title page and page numbers preceded by the writer's last name — both optional under the MLA system — see 18b.)

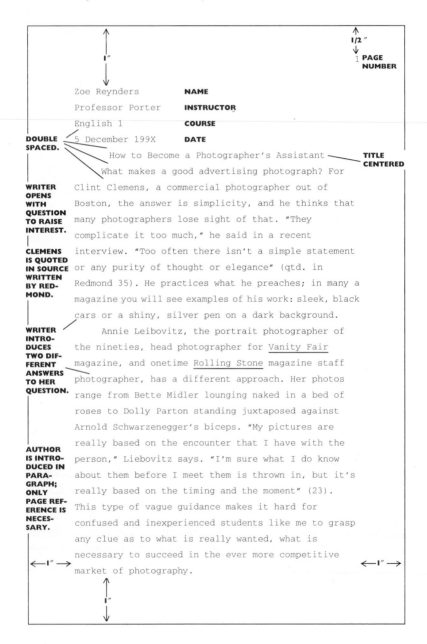

PAGE
NUMBER

1/2 "

1

1"

Zoe Reynders   **NAME**

Professor Porter **INSTRUCTOR**

English 1   **COURSE**

5 December 199X   **DATE**

DOUBLE SPACED.

How to Become a Photographer's Assistant   **TITLE CENTERED**

What makes a good advertising photograph? For

WRITER OPENS WITH QUESTION TO RAISE INTEREST.

Clint Clemens, a commercial photographer out of

Boston, the answer is simplicity, and he thinks that

many photographers lose sight of that. "They

complicate it too much," he said in a recent

CLEMENS IS QUOTED IN SOURCE WRITTEN BY REDMOND.

interview. "Too often there isn't a simple statement

or any purity of thought or elegance" (qtd. in

Redmond 35). He practices what he preaches; in many a

magazine you will see examples of his work: sleek, black

cars or a shiny, silver pen on a dark background.

WRITER INTRODUCES TWO DIFFERENT ANSWERS TO HER QUESTION.

Annie Leibovitz, the portrait photographer of

the nineties, head photographer for Vanity Fair

magazine, and onetime Rolling Stone magazine staff

photographer, has a different approach. Her photos

range from Bette Midler lounging naked in a bed of

roses to Dolly Parton standing juxtaposed against

Arnold Schwarzenegger's biceps. "My pictures are

really based on the encounter that I have with the

AUTHOR IS INTRODUCED IN PARAGRAPH; ONLY PAGE REFERENCE IS NECESSARY.

person," Liebovitz says. "I'm sure what I do know

about them before I meet them is thrown in, but it's

really based on the timing and the moment" (23).

This type of vague guidance makes it hard for

confused and inexperienced students like me to grasp

any clue as to what is really wanted, what is

necessary to succeed in the ever more competitive

←1"→

market of photography.

←1"→

1"

2

WRITER
INTRO-
DUCES
HERSELF
AND HER
PROBLEM.
Here I am then, a lowly college student without access to a good darkroom, having no portfolio to show, attempting to get a commercial photography internship in New York City for the summer as a first step toward becoming a professional photographer. With a little research, however, I've learned the steps to setting up an internship: First, establish contact through writing a letter and sending a résumé, then push your portfolio--mail it, drop it, call, recall, pester. In the process I've also learned that in commercial photography the emphasis is on commercial. Talent alone really isn't enough. If you don't represent yourself correctly, you may never get the chance to show off your photography talents.

FIRST
PERSON
AND CON-
TRAC-
TIONS ES-
TABLISH
INFOR-
MAL
TONE.

This is understandable. An average photo shoot that will cover one full page in a relatively popular magazine can be worth anywhere from $2,000 to $200,000 and can take anywhere from one hour to three weeks to shoot. And the better known you are, the more you can charge, and the more you are used. According to Catherine Calhoun, "The current depressed market . . . is characterized by tried-and-true imagery, slick professionalism, and intense competition." But all this seemed, at first, irrelevant to me. I thought, I'm just in it for the experience, not the money, not the glamour nor the fame. Photography is fun, it is something I enjoy. Wrong.

AUTHOR
IS INTRO-
DUCED IN
SIGNAL
PHRASE.

WRITER
STRUC-
TURES
PAPER AC-
CORDING
TO HER
QUEST
FOR
INFORMA-
TION.

NO PAGE
NUMBER
IS NEEDED
FOR ONE-
PAGE
SOURCE.

FRAG-
MENT IS
ACCEPT-
ABLE IN
INFOR-
MAL
PAPER.

I've already learned that not every aspect of taking photographs is that much fun. "Practically

3

"... every photographer has a preconceived notion of what

he will shoot and what he won't shoot," writes Richard Sharabura in his lively book <u>Shoot Your Way to a $-Million</u>. He continues, "This is probably one of the most common stumbling blocks to financial success" (56). Commercial photographers cannot pick and choose to do only the assignments they want or they would lose clients.

What? You're not interested in shooting a cat food ad? This can deter creative photographers because it seems more obvious today that companies approach advertising conservatively. Special-effects photography and the unconventional photo don't sell products. John Jay, creative director of Bloomingdale's, reiterates this: "There's a lot more money on the line than there used to be. . . . There's not a lot of encouragement for experimentation" (qtd. in Redmond 35).

I've also learned that becoming a photographer's assistant is a creative void and does not entail ever taking any actual pictures. Committing myself to interning this summer won't mean blissful photo shoots with famous people. It

will mean ten hours a day of getting up before the sun, packing photography equipment, carrying supplies, loading cameras, setting up lights, answering phones, and walking someone's dog. Nevertheless, you have to prove that you are also competent. A highly paid photographer is not going to risk having an idiot load preexposed film into a camera. This is where the importance of the

4

portfolio comes in. You are not showing your
portfolio to get a commercial photography job for
yourself . . . you have to demonstrate that you
understand and respect the art of a finely produced
photo.

So, after writing my polite letters to
incredibly famous New York photographers, I next
took about 50 of what I consider my best images to
the leading photographer at the University of
Vermont, in hopes of identifying 10 or 15 of my
pictures that may be portfolio quality. Photo editor
Tom Brennan took ten minutes to sort through my
images and then told me, "Most photography editors
wouldn't take more than two minutes to look at a
portfolio."

**DATE OF
PERSONAL
INTER-
VIEW CAN
BE FOUND
ON
WORKS
CITED
PAGE.**

Again, I became nervous, not because I don't
think I could handle the job, but because of the
strict professionalism of these people. I
question if my photos are strong enough to make
an impact, if I have what it takes to stand apart
from the crowd of would-be photographers. Brennan
chose 12 images he thought would be good. They
do not have a consistent theme or subject;
some are in black and white, others are slides
or color negatives. "What I am looking for are
your photos that show some kind of feeling or
atmosphere," he said. Some of the photos he
chose, I would have too. Others, I wouldn't have
looked twice at. It's clear that I will include
everything from a landscape to a portrait of my
father to pictures of kids, and even an egg. The

**FURTHER
CITATION
OF BREN-
NAN IS
UNNECES-
SARY
BECAUSE
SOURCE IS
CLEAR.**

5

more variety, the better to demonstrate a wide range of skills.

PARA-PHRASED INFORMA-TION IS DOCU-MENTED.

Henrietta Brackman, author of The Perfect Portfolio, carefully outlines how to edit photos for a portfolio: First the work has to be good. (Who could have guessed?) But it is also important to examine every detail, to make sure that the photo is printed and developed at its best and that the picture is intelligible to the eventual viewer. I've done lots of trick photography, but I am going to stick to my traditional photographs. Bob Lynn, the

PARTIAL QUOTA-TION IS WORKED INTO THE SENTENCE IN A GRAMMAT-ICALLY CORRECT WAY.

graphics director of The Ledger-Star, says he "hopes to find surprises, not clichés" (qtd. in Upton 23). I know my photos don't belong in the family album; they are not clichés.

Lost in the technicalities of this whole process, I almost forgot why I really want this internship in the first place—for the practice and hands-on experience. But I hope to learn a more important lesson—to understand how and when to take career chances. An internship, I remind myself, will also make the outside world seem a little less frightening.

WRITER CON-CLUDES WITH HER OWN IDEAS RATHER THAN BOR-ROWED ONES.

So I'll keep sitting around hoping for a break. I can't guarantee that this research method for landing an internship will work; it still remains to be tried and tested. To my knowledge, there is no foolproof formula for a successful start. Like everybody else before me, I'm creating my own method as I go along.

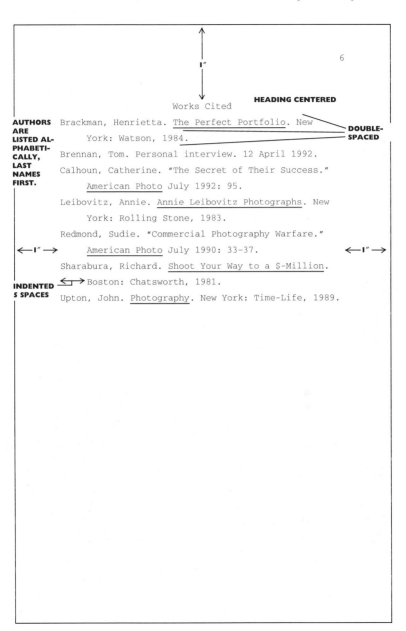

6

|″

HEADING CENTERED

Works Cited

AUTHORS ARE LISTED ALPHABETICALLY, LAST NAMES FIRST.

Brackman, Henrietta. <u>The Perfect Portfolio</u>. New
    York: Watson, 1984.

DOUBLE-SPACED

Brennan, Tom. Personal interview. 12 April 1992.

Calhoun, Catherine. "The Secret of Their Success."
    <u>American Photo</u> July 1992: 95.

Leibovitz, Annie. <u>Annie Leibovitz Photographs</u>. New
    York: Rolling Stone, 1983.

Redmond, Sudie. "Commercial Photography Warfare."

←|″→   <u>American Photo</u> July 1990: 33-37. ←|″→

Sharabura, Richard. <u>Shoot Your Way to a $-Million</u>.

INDENTED 5 SPACES   Boston: Chatsworth, 1981.

Upton, John. <u>Photography</u>. New York: Time-Life, 1989.

18 b Literary research essay: MLA style

In literary research essays, students are expected to read a work of literature, interpret it, and support their interpretation through research. The research in such papers commonly uses two kinds of sources: primary sources (the literary works themselves, from which students cite passages), and secondary sources (the opinions of literary experts found in books or periodicals).

The following paper was written by Andrew Turner in a first-year English class. Students were asked to focus on a topic of personal interest about the author Henry David Thoreau and to support their own reading of Thoreau's work with outside sources.

The Two Freedoms of Henry David Thoreau

TITLE CENTERED, ONE-THIRD DOWN PAGE

by

Andrew Turner

NAME

Professor Stephany

English 2

3 October 199x

INSTRUCTOR

COURSE

DATE

1″

DOUBLE-SPACED

WRITER OPENS WITH THESIS.

WRITER IDENTIFIES TWO WORKS TO BE EXAMINED.

ABBREVIATED TITLE IS USED AFTER WORK HAS BEEN IDENTIFIED BY FULL TITLE.

TITLE IS REPEATED FROM THE TITLE PAGE.

Turner 1

WRITER'S LAST NAME AND PAGE NUMBER APPEAR ON EACH PAGE.

The Two Freedoms of Henry David Thoreau

Henry David Thoreau led millions of people throughout the world to think about individual freedom in a new way. During his lifetime, he attempted to live free of unjust governmental constraints as well as conventional social expectations. In his 1849 essay "On the Duty of Civil Disobedience," he makes his strongest case against governmental interference in the lives of citizens. In his 1854 book <u>Walden, or, Life in the Woods</u>, he makes the case for living free from social conventions and expectations.

Thoreau opens "Civil Disobedience" with his statement that "that government is best which governs not at all" (222). He argues that a government should allow its people to be as free as possible, providing for the needs of the people without infringing on their daily lives. Thoreau explains, "The government does not concern me much, and I shall bestow the fewest possible thoughts on it. It is not for many moments that I live under a government" ("Civil" 238). In other words, in his daily life he attends to his business of eating, sleeping, and earning a living and not dealing in any noticeable way with an entity called "a government."

Because Thoreau did not want his freedom overshadowed by governmental regulations, he tried to ignore them. However, the American government of 1845 would not let him. He was arrested and put in

ONLY THE PAGE NUMBER IS NEEDED WHEN SOURCE IS INTRODUCED IN THE SENTENCE.

SHORT TITLE IS ADDED TO PAGE NUMBER BECAUSE TWO WORKS BY THE AUTHOR APPEAR ON WORKS CITED PAGE.

Turner 2

the Concord jail for failing to pay his poll tax--a
tax he believed unjust because it supported the
government's war with Mexico as well as the immoral
institution of slavery. Instead of protesting his
arrest, he celebrated it and explained its meaning
by writing "Civil Disobedience," one of the most
famous English-language essays ever written. In it,
he argued persuasively that "Under a government
which imprisons any unjustly, the true place for a
just man is also a prison" (230). Thus the doctrine
of passive resistance was formed, a doctrine that
advocated protest against the government by
nonviolent means:

> How does it become a man to behave
> toward this American government today?
> I answer that he cannot without
> disgrace be associated with it. I
> cannot for an instant recognize that
> political organization as my government
> which is the slave's government also.
> (224)

According to Charles R. Anderson, Thoreau's
other writings, such as "Slavery in Massachusetts"
and "A Plea for Captain John Brown," show his
disdain of the "northerners for their cowardice on
conniving with such an institution" (28). He wanted
all free American citizens, north and south, to
revolt and liberate the slaves.

In addition to inspiring his countrymen,
Thoreau's view of the sanctity of individual freedom
affected the lives of later generations who shared

PAGE NUMBER ONLY IS USED BECAUSE THE CONTEXT IDENTIFIES THE WORK.

INDENTED 10 SPACES

QUOTATION OF MORE THAN 4 LINES PRESENTED IN BLOCK FORMAT.

SIGNAL PHRASE INTRODUCED THE NAME OF THE SECONDARY-SOURCE AUTHOR.

PARTIAL QUOTATION IS WORKED INTO SENTENCE IN A GRAMMATICALLY CORRECT WAY.

Turner 3

his beliefs. "Civil Disobedience" had the greatest impact because of its "worldwide influence on Mahatma Gandhi, the British Labour Party in its early years, the underground in Nazi-occupied Europe, and Negro leaders in the modern south" (Anderson 30). For nearly one hundred and fifty years, Thoreau's formulation of passive resistance has been a part of the human struggle for freedom.

WRITER SWITCHES TO DISCUSSION OF A SECOND WORK AFTER DISCUSSION OF FIRST WORK IS COMPLETED.

Thoreau also wanted to be free from the everyday pressure to conform to society's expectations. He believed in doing and possessing only the essential things in life. To demonstrate his case, in 1845 he moved to the outskirts of Concord, Massachusetts, and lived by himself for two years on the shore of Walden Pond (Spiller et al. 396–97). Thoreau wrote Walden to explain the value of living simply, apart from the unnecessary complexity of society: "Simplicity, simplicity, simplicity! I say, let your affairs be as two or three, and not a hundred or a thousand" (66). At Walden, he lived as much as possible by this statement, building his own house and furniture, growing his own food, bartering for simple necessities, attending to his own business rather than seeking employment from others (Walden 16–17).

ABBREVIATED POPULAR TITLE IS LISTED AFTER WORK'S FIRST REFERENCE.

SHORT TITLE IS ADDED TO PAGE NUMBER BECAUSE TWO WORKS BY THE AUTHOR APPEAR ON WORKS CITED PAGE.

IDENTIFICATION FOR WORK WITH MORE THAN THREE AUTHORS.

Living at Walden Pond gave Thoreau the chance to formulate many of his ideas about living the simple, economical life. At Walden, he lived simply in order to "front only the essential facts of life"

PAGE NUMBERS FOR PARAPHRASE ARE INCLUDED.

Turner 4

PAGE NUMBERS ALONE ARE SUFFI-CIENT WHEN CONTEXT MAKES THE SOURCE CLEAR. (66) and to center his thoughts on living instead of on unnecessary details of mere livelihood. He developed survival skills that freed him from the constraints of city dwellers whose lives depended upon a web of material things and services provided by others. He preferred to "take rank hold on life and spend my day more as animals do" (117).

While living at Walden Pond, Thoreau was free to occupy his time in any way that pleased him, which for him meant writing, tending his bean patch, and chasing loons. He wasn't troubled by a boss hounding him with deadlines nor a wife and children who needed support. In other words, he wasn't expected to be anywhere at any time for anybody except himself. His neighbors accused him of being selfish and did not understand that he sought most of all "to live deliberately" (Walden 66), as he felt all people should learn to do.

Then as now, most people had more responsibilities than Thoreau had, and could not just pack up their belongings and go live in the woods--if they could find free woods to live in. Today, people are intrigued to read about Thoreau's experiences and inspired by his thoughts, but few people can actually live or do as he suggests in Walden. In fact, most people, if faced with the prospect of spending two years removed from society, would probably think of it as a punishment or banishment, rather than as Thoreau thought of it, as the good life.

Turner 5

Practical or not, Thoreau's writings about freedom from government and society have inspired countless people to reassess how they live their lives. Though unable to live as he advocated, readers everywhere remain inspired by his ideal, that one must live as freely as possible.

WRITER'S CONCLUSION REPEATS THESIS ASSERTION.

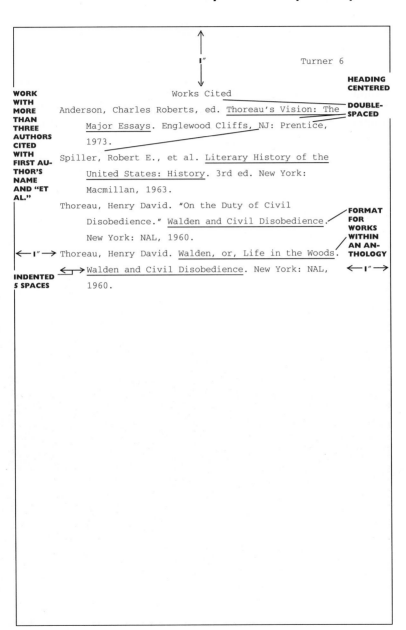

Turner 6

Works Cited

Anderson, Charles Roberts, ed. <u>Thoreau's Vision: The</u>
   <u>Major Essays</u>. Englewood Cliffs, NJ: Prentice,
   1973.

Spiller, Robert E., et al. <u>Literary History of the</u>
   <u>United States: History</u>. 3rd ed. New York:
   Macmillan, 1963.

Thoreau, Henry David. "On the Duty of Civil
   Disobedience." <u>Walden and Civil Disobedience</u>.
   New York: NAL, 1960.

Thoreau, Henry David. <u>Walden, or, Life in the Woods</u>.
   <u>Walden and Civil Disobedience</u>. New York: NAL,
   1960.

HEADING CENTERED

DOUBLE-SPACED

WORK WITH MORE THAN THREE AUTHORS CITED WITH FIRST AU-THOR'S NAME AND "ET AL."

FORMAT FOR WORKS WITHIN AN AN-THOLOGY

←1"→

INDENTED 5 SPACES

18 c   Collaborative research essay: APA style

The following research essay, "New Brew: Vermont's Diverse Beer Culture," is the result of shared research and writing by Pat Quimby and Stephen Reville in a first-year writing class. "New Brew" is documented according to American Psychological Association (APA) conventions and includes a title page, an abstract, and an outline.

ABBREVIATED TITLE (OPTIONAL)

New Brew
1

PAGE NUMBERING
BEGINS ON TITLE
PAGE.

TITLE PAGE IS
CENTERED TOP
TO BOTTOM,
RIGHT TO LEFT,
AND DOUBLE-
SPACED.

New Brew:

Vermont's Diverse Beer Culture

Pat Quimby and Stephen Reville

Professor Fulwiler

English 1

December 3, 199X

TITLE

WRITER(S)

INSTRUCTOR

COURSE

DATE

**IF AN ABSTRACT IS REQUESTED, IT SHOULD BE PRINTED
ON A SEPARATE PAGE FOLLOWING THE TITLE PAGE AND
PRECEDING THE PAPER.**

New Brew

2

HEADING CENTERED

**NO PARA-
GRAPH
INDENT**

Abstract

**DOUBLE-
SPACED**

Beer has a long and diverse history which has been

severely threatened as a result of the

**THE AB-
STRACT
SUMMA-
RIZES
BOTH THE
THEME
AND THE
FINDINGS
OF THE
ENTIRE
PAPER.**

monopolization of the American beer industry by huge

corporate breweries. Recently, however,

microbreweries have begun to challenge the monopoly

of national breweries. These small local brewers who

make alternative beer have found a successful market

niche and begun to turn a profit. This paper

describes how this national trend has affected beer

drinking in the state of Vermont.

IF AN OUTLINE IS REQUIRED, IT SHOULD FOLLOW THE TITLE PAGE AND CONFORM TO TRADITIONAL OUTLINE FORM.   1/2 ″

New Brew

3

1″

Outline   **HEADING CENTERED**

I.   The History of Beer in America   **DOUBLE-SPACED**

    A.   Pilgrims brought beer on the Mayflower.

    B.   Small commercial breweries flourished in
       the nineteenth century.

    C.   Prohibition put small breweries out of
       business, whereas larger breweries
       survived by producing other products.

    D.   After Prohibition, most large breweries
       produced very similar pilsner-style beer.

II.   The Rise of the Microbrewery   **LETTERS INDICATE SUBDIVISIONS AND SMALLER POINTS.**

    A.   In the 1980s, small breweries began to
       flourish again.

ROMAN NUMERALS INDICATE MAJOR DIVISIONS OF THE PAPER.

    B.   Microbreweries offer diverse kinds of
       beer.

    C.   In 1987, the Catamount Brewery opened in
       Vermont and the industry began to expand
       in that state.

    D.   Other small producers include brew pubs,
       bars or restaurants that produce and
       sell their own beers.

    E.   One such brew pub, The Vermont Pub and
       Brewery in Burlington, Vermont, is
       typical in its distinctive beer and
       diverse clientele.

III.   Conclusion

TITLE IS REPEATED FROM THE TITLE PAGE.

New Brew:

Vermont's Diverse Beer Culture

The beer industry in the United States grosses about 40 billion dollars a year. Ninety-nine percent of those profits have been made by enormous corporations such as Anheuser-Busch, Miller Brewing Company, and Coors (Mares, 1984, p. 112). But today, even though dollars are tight and industries are struggling to hold their ground, several microbreweries have gained a foothold in Vermont and they are fighting for their share of the profits (Shaw, 1990). This paper examines the options available to the Vermont beer drinker and explains what distinguishes locally produced beers from their national competitors.

DOUBLE-SPACED

AUTHOR'S NAME, YEAR OF PUBLICATION, AND PAGE NUMBERS ARE INCLUDED IN PARENTHESES.

THE INFORMATIONAL THESIS IS STATED AT THE END OF THE FIRST PARAGRAPH.

The History of Beer in America

THE INFORMATIVE SUBHEADINGS HELP EXPLAIN THE PAPER'S ORGANIZATION.

Understanding the recent interest in locally produced, alternative beers requires first an understanding of some beer history. The earliest proven evidence of the existence of beer dates back over 5000 years to Mesopotamian and Egyptian times where residues have been found in casks and jugs. The Pilgrims brought beer with them on the <u>Mayflower</u>, although apparently not enough of it. According to the captain, they were forced to land at Plymouth, rather than their original destination farther south, because they "could not take time for further search, our victuals being much spent, especially our beer" (Baron, 1972, p. 15).

PARTIAL QUOTATION IS WORKED INTO THE TEXT IN A GRAMMATICALLY CORRECT WAY.

The earliest immigrants to the New World were forced to brew their own beer. George

New Brew
5

Washington, Thomas Jefferson, William Penn, and
Samuel Adams were all home brewers. But eventually
commercial breweries sprang up. At the beginning
of this century there were thousands of breweries
spread all across the country, each brewing
unique styles of beer (Mares, 1984, p. 34). This
practice can still be seen in many European
countries where beer is very much part of the
regional history.

TRANSI-
TION
WORDS
SIGNAL A
CHANGE
IN DIREC-
TION

However, the broad and diverse beer culture
here in America was almost completely destroyed in
1920 by laws prohibiting the sale or consumption of
alcoholic beverages. Prohibition forced all of the
small local breweries and taverns to close, so for
the next fourteen years the only beer in the United
States was illegally smuggled across the border or
secretly and illegally brewed in private homes. In
Vermont, for example, home brewing during
Prohibition was as common as baking bread.
Vermonters made beverages from anything available:
maple sap, spruce needles, herbs, spices, fruits,
and berries (Morris, 1984, p. 25).

The only breweries still in business in
December of 1933, when Prohibition was repealed,
were the largest of the commercial breweries such as
Anheuser-Busch and Miller who had been able to
convert their operations over to other products for
the food industry (Papazian, 1991). According to
Baron (1972), "The kitchen kettle of yesteryear has
given way to the tremendous factory covering several
city blocks" (p. 32). These large breweries became

THE PUB-
LICATION
DATE OF
A SOURCE
IMMEDI-
ATELY
FOLLOWS
THE
AUTHOR
NAME.

New Brew

6

the giants of today's American beer industry without the competition of their small-scale rivals.

And they all brewed essentially the same beer. The warm climate over most of the United States, at least for part of the year, combined with the availability of rice and corn as cheap grains and the economic value of using fewer grains in the brew, suggested a very light-bodied and mild-flavored beer (Roberts & Russett, 1981). The result is what is known as the American light lager or pilsner beer, stemming from a traditional style from the town of Plzen, Czechoslovakia. This style was adopted by all of the major national brands in the United States, leaving only expensive imported or homemade beers for an alternative (Papazian, 1991).

BOTH AUTHORS' LAST NAMES ARE LISTED, JOINED WITH AN AMPER- SAND.

The Rise of the Microbrewery

About ten years ago the movement to bring back the small breweries of the early part of the century began (Morris, 1984, p. 3). Microbreweries, breweries which produce fewer than 30,000 barrels of beer each year, started cropping up across the United States, especially in California and the western states. Jack McAuliffe, one of the pioneers of the microbrewery industry, gave this impression of the changes that were coming in the industry back in 1982:

DOUBLE- SPACED

As the industry continues to shrink, the products you make have to become more and more alike in taste. You want to offend as few people as possible. When you own a large brewery, you can't afford to make specialty

COLON IS USED TO INTRO- DUCE A LONG QUOTA- TION.

beer. In that sense, there is more and more
opportunity for the specialty brewer. In this
country there is a choice of brands, but no
choice of style. People are becoming more
interested in food that tastes different and a
broadened taste will support more specialty
beers. (Mares, 1984, p. 119)

Unfortunately McAuliffe's company, the New Albion
Brewing Company, in California, was unable to make a
profit competing against the national giants, and New
Albion closed within three years. But many others
did survive, companies such as Anchor Brewing Co. in
San Francisco and the Boston Beer Co., brewers of
Samuel Adams. In fact, according to Chris Fisher, a
local home brewer and authority on the industry, "In
the past year the national breweries are down twelve
percent in profits while the microbreweries as a
whole are up about three hundred percent" (personal
communication, October 29, 1992). However, Budweiser
alone still produces more beer in a single day than
all the microbreweries produce in a year (Mares,
1984, p. 121).

According to Shaw (1990), the home brewing
revolution did not begin in Vermont until February
1987 when Stephen Mason and Alan Davis opened
Catamount Brewery, which offered golden lager, an
amber ale, and a dark porter as well as several
seasonal brews. This was only the beginning. In
September 1992, the first Vermont Brewers Festival
was held at Sugarbush Resort. Sixteen breweries
participated and the forty-plus beers present ranged

DOUBLE-SPACED

IN-DENTED 5 SPACES

NO PARAGRAPH IS NEEDED WHEN THE TEXT FOLLOWING THE INDENTED PASSAGE REFERS BACK TO IT.

NAMES SHOULD BE WORKED INTO THE TEXT WHENEVER POSSIBLE TO CLARIFY SOURCE OF INFORMATION.

QUOTATIONS OVER 40 WORDS ARE PRESENTED IN BLOCK FORMAT.

FIELD SOURCE IS IDENTIFIED COMPLETELY HERE, SO NOT INCLUDED ON REFERENCES PAGE.

from American light lagers to German-style bock and everything in between. The beers included such colorful names as Tall Tale Pale Ale, Black Fly Stout, Slopbucket Brown Ale, Summer Wheat Ale, Avid Barley Wee Heavy, and Hickory Switch Smoked Amber Ale.

In addition to new breweries are brew pubs such as McNeill's Brewery in Brattleboro and the Vermont Pub and Brewery in Burlington. These are bars or restaurants that feature their own selection of beers brewed and served in-house only. Greg and Nancy Noonan, the owners of the Vermont Pub and Brewery, will be celebrating the fifth anniversary of their successful venture in December.

According to Greg, their business has been better than they had predicted. He said, "Our first expectations were based on worst-case scenarios" (personal communication, November 17, 1992). In fact, for the Vermont Pub and Brewery there has not been any recession. Greg attributes this success to the consistency of the Burlington economic base and the increase of Canadian tourism: "Our Canadian business doubled or tripled since we opened on November 11, 1988."

FIELD RESEARCH IS SMOOTHLY INTE-GRATED.

The Vermont Pub and Brewery beer selection changes with the seasons, with a core of regular favorites including Burly Irish Ale, Dogbite Bitter, and Smoked Porter. The seasonal specialties range from Oktoberfest in the fall to Maple Ale in the spring. Even the casual observer can see that the patrons at the Vermont Pub and Brewery do not fit

New Brew
9

into any neat categories. Greg described his
intentions this way: "We're not appealing to
primarily blue collar or white collar people, not
any specific age bracket. We're definitely not a shot
and a beer bar. We always knew that we didn't want
to be a college bar."

**THE THE-
SIS IS RE-
PEATED
IN THE
CONCLU-
SION.**

Conclusion

Microbreweries have gone to great lengths to
provide a rich alternative diversity to the normal
pilsner American-style beer offered by the national
breweries. The interest in locally made beer has
found a niche in Vermont. The search for quality and
variety has led the beer drinker away from the
industry giants to the newly established local
alternatives.

268 A sampler of research essays

New Brew

10

HEADING CENTERED   DOUBLE-SPACED

AUTHORS ARE LISTED ALPHABETICALLY.

References

Baker, P. M. (1979). New brewers handbook. Westpoint, MA: Crosby and Baker.

Baron, S. (1972). Brewed in America: A history of beer and ale in the U.S. New York: Arno.

Mares, W. K. (1984). Making beer. New York: Alfred A. Knopf.

INDENTED 3 SPACES

Morris, S. (1984). The great beer trek. Brattleboro, VT: Stephen Greene.

Papazian, C. D. (1991). The new complete joy of home brewing. New York: Avon.

ARTICLE TITLES ARE NOT UNDERLINED AND NOT ENCLOSED IN QUOTATION MARKS.

Roberts, A. K., & Russett, G. H. (1981). The new brewers. National Brewing Digest, 3(4), 129–138.

Shaw, K. (1990, April 12). Micro breweries are hopping in Vermont. The Burlington Free Press, p. 2.

IN BOOK AND ARTICLE TITLES, ONLY FIRST WORDS AND PROPER NAMES ARE CAPITALIZED. BOOK TITLES ARE UNDERLINED.

PERIODICAL TITLES ARE CAPITALIZED NORMALLY. VOLUME NUMBER IS UNDERLINED.

A first draft is a writer's first attempt to give shape to an idea, argument, or experience. Occasionally, this initial draft is just right and the writing is done. More often, however, the first draft shows a broad outline or general direction that needs further thinking, further revision. An unfocused first draft, in other words, is not a mistake, but a start toward a next, more focused draft.

No matter how much prior thought writers give to complex composing tasks, once they begin writing, the draft begins to shift, change, and develop in unexpected ways. In other words, the act of writing itself produces new questions and insights that must be dealt with and incorporated into the emerging piece of writing. That's where active and aggressive revision strategies can help.

For many novice writers, revising is an alien activity that neither makes sense nor comes easy. Experienced writers, though, know that revising is the very essence of writing, the primary way of developing thoughts and preparing them to be shared with others. The rest of this chapter introduces strategies and procedures for effective revision.

19 a Understanding revision

Revising, editing, and *proofreading* are sometimes used to mean the same thing, but there is good reason to understand each as a separate process, each in its own way contributing to good writing. When you **revise,** you reread, rethink, and reconstruct your thoughts on paper until they match those in your mind. Revising is, literally, reseeing your topic, thesis, argument, evidence, organization, and conclusion and making major changes that affect the content, direction, and meaning of your paper. Revising generally takes place at the paragraph level.

When you **edit,** you change your language more than your ideas. You edit after you know what you want to say, testing each word or phrase to see if it is necessary, accurate, and correct. Editing takes place at the level of the sentence or word. The many dimensions of editing, including proofreading, are treated in Part VI.

When you **proofread,** you check very specific sentence elements for correctness: spelling, punctuation, capitalization, and the like. Proofreading is part of the editing process, but it makes most sense to do it at the very end, when you have addressed stylistic and grammatical concerns and simply want to make sure your paper contains no errors that might confuse or distract readers. (See Chapter 56.)

There are two good reasons to revise before you edit. First, when you revise you may cut out whole sections of your first draft because they no longer suit your final purpose. If you have already edited those sections, all that careful sentence-level work goes for naught. Second, if you've invested time in carefully editing sentences, you may be reluctant to cut them — even though cutting may make your paper better. Of course, writers are always circling back through the stages, mixing them up, editing after drafting, revising as they invent, drafting new paragraphs when they only intend to edit. Nonetheless, your work will probably be more productive (and you will probably be happier) if you resist as much as possible the urge to edit before you revise.

Begin your revising process by gaining some distance on your writing. Give yourself a break of a few days between drafting and revising; at the very least, try to wait until the next day. Then scrutinize your paper and ask yourself whether you have accomplished what you set out to do. (See 19b for some basic questions to ask.) After you've examined and questioned your paper, you'll have a better sense of what and where you want to revise.

Revision is a complex and dynamic process. Exactly how to approach it is up to you, of course, but you may want to take advantage of some of the tried-and-true revision strategies described in 19c. These will guide you in thinking profitably about revising and will ensure that your revising is thorough and appropriate. Suggestions for physically keeping track of your revising process are provided in 19d.

WRITING 1: EXPLORATION

Describe one paper that you spent a long time revising. What was the assignment? How did you approach it? Did you plan to revise or did it just happen?

How many drafts did you do? What was the result of this revision work? Were you pleased? Was your audience?

ESL   **REVISING VERSUS EDITING**

As this chapter explains, revising the content and organization of your ideas is different from editing for word choice and grammatical correctness. When a person writes in a second language, it is often difficult to postpone concerns about word choice and grammar. Consequently, ESL writers sometimes try to edit prematurely. Although you may want to do some editing in early drafts, remember that taking time to revise content is very important and that you should work on revision before you do any extensive editing.

---

19 b   Asking revision questions

Learning to revise means learning to ask careful questions about the purpose of your text, the audience for whom it's intended, and yourself as its author. The answers to these questions will help you decide what aspects of your paper to revise.

Ask questions about your purpose

Revising is your last opportunity to modify your paper's purpose. In fact, it's often easier to see your purpose — or lack thereof — most clearly after you have written a draft or two. Return to the basic questions about purpose that you asked during planning:

1   Why am I writing this paper? Do all elements and parts of the paper advance this purpose? If not, why not?

2   What was the assignment? Does my paper fulfill it?

3   What is the aim of the paper? To narrate, explain, interpret, argue, reflect, or something else? Is this what it does?

4   What is my theme or thesis? Have I expressed it clearly?

See Chapter 4 for more on writing with a clear purpose.

Ask questions about your audience

You also need to make sure your paper is aimed accurately at your audience. If in planning and drafting you have been most concerned with gathering information and putting your ideas together coherently, at some point you need to switch your attention to your audience, asking:

1 Who is my audience for this paper?

2 What does my audience know about this subject? Have I told them too much that they already know?

3 What does my audience not know about this subject? Have I given them the context and further information they need?

4 What questions or objections do I anticipate my audience raising? Can I answer any of them before they are asked?

5 Are my tone and style appropriate to this audience?

For more on writing to specific audiences, see Chapter 5.

Ask questions about yourself

Perhaps the best reason for revising is to please yourself. Revise so that when you read the paper you enjoy both its ideas and its language. If you are writing from personal experience, make that experience ring true. If you are writing an argument, develop one you believe in. When you please yourself, you improve your chances of pleasing others as well.

1 Do I believe everything I've written in this paper? If not, why not?

2 What doubts do I have about my paper? Can I still address these?

3 Which passages do I most enjoy reading? How can I make the rest of the paper more like them?

4 Which passages do I find difficult to read? What can I do to change them?

■ **WRITING 2: EXPLORATION**

What additional questions can you think of to guide you in your revising?

19 C Using revision strategies

This section lists more than a dozen time-tested revision strategies that may be useful to you. While they won't all work for you all the time, some will be useful at one time or another. Notice that these suggestions start with larger concerns and progress toward smaller ones.

Some revising strategies are so important that we've treated them in separate chapters. **Limiting** is focusing on a narrow portion of a paper or concept and eliminating extraneous material; **adding** is incorporating new details and dialogue to make writing more vivid and powerful. These are explained together in Chapter 20. **Switching** and **transforming** are more innovative strategies for revision: by changing the tense, point of view, form, or format of a piece of writing, writers can gain insights into their writing and present their ideas in a new light. These are explained together in Chapter 21. **Responding** is a way to incorporate the ideas of thoughtful readers into your revising. Suggestions for sharing your work with others — and for sharing thoughts and questions about the work of others — are given in Chapter 22.

Plan for revising

You cannot revise if you haven't first written or if you write your papers the night before they are due. So plan from the outset to allow time for revising, by planning to write early.

Establish distance

The most important prerequisite for revising well is distance from your first-draft thoughts. Letting your draft sit overnight and returning to it the next day allow you to see it more objectively, more clearly. You'll almost always see places that satisfied you yesterday but now, by the light of a new day, don't. Expect and allow for this possibility so that you welcome rather than dread it. (You can also achieve distance by typing rather than handwriting drafts.)

Reconsider everything

When you return to your draft, reconsider the whole text. Reread the whole paper from the start, and every time you change something of substance reread the whole thing again. Remember that revision is conceptual work in which you try to get your thoughts just right and in the right order. If you change the information on one page, it may change ideas, questions, or conclusions on another page. Finally, if a classmate or instructor has made comments on some parts of the paper and not on others, do not assume that those are the only places where revision is needed.

Believe and doubt

First, reread your draft as if you were a believer (imagine a supportive friend), putting checks in the margins next to passages that create the most belief — the assertions, the dialogue, the details, the evidence. Next, reread your draft as if you were a skeptic (imagine your most critical teacher), putting question marks next to all passages that seem questionable. Review your paper and be satisfied when check marks assure you the paper is on the right track; then review your question marks and answer all the questions a skeptic might have.

Test your theme or thesis

Most college papers are written to demonstrate a particular theme or thesis. Sometimes while writing and revising you generate new ideas, raise new questions, and end up writing a paper quite different from the one you planned to write. Consequently, it's a good idea to return periodically to your theme or thesis and make sure it still corresponds to what you've actually written. If not, you can either realign your paper, making it conform to the theme or thesis you originally envisioned, or change the theme or thesis to reflect the content of your paper.

Evaluate your evidence

To make any theme or thesis convincing, you need to support it with evidence. Check to see if your facts, examples, and illustrations provide that support. Ask the following:

1 Does the evidence support my thesis or advance my theme?

2 What objections can be raised about this evidence?

3 What additional evidence will answer these objections?

For more on evaluating evidence, see Chapters 2 and 11.

Make a paragraph outline

The most common unit of developed thought in a paper is the paragraph, a group of sentences set off from other groups of sentences because they focus on the same main idea. A paragraph outline creates a map of your whole paper, letting you see whether the organization is effective. To make a paragraph outline, number each paragraph and write a phrase describing its topic or focus. Notice if paragraphs that are next to each other discuss similar topics and whether they seem to develop that topic in a logical order. If not, reorganize your outline so your paper proceeds in a clear, logical way. Then do the same with the paragraphs in your paper, making whatever other changes are necessary.

Rewrite openings and conclusions

Papers grow and evolve in many directions. An opening that seemed appropriate in the previous draft may no longer fit. The conclusion that once accurately summed up the paper may not do so now because you've added more ideas or changed the direction. Before you finish revising your paper, examine both its opening and its conclusion to be sure they introduce and conclude as you would like them to. Sometimes writers find their best openings and conclusions by writing fresh ones instead of tinkering with what's there and trying to adjust old constructions. (For more on openings and conclusions, see Chapter 24.)

Play with titles

Make sure your title still matches your revised essay. (Or, if you haven't got a title yet, find one that works.) Remember that titles must catch readers' attention and provide a clue to the paper's content. One good strategy for revising titles is to create a list of five or ten possibilities and then select the most suitable one. Here are some suggestions for finding a good title:

1 Use one good sentence from your paper.

2 Ask a question that your paper answers.

3 Use a strong sense word or image from your paper.

4 Locate a famous quotation or saying that relates to your paper.

5 Write a one-word title (a two-word, a three-word, and so on).

Listen for your voice

Read your paper out loud when it is nearly finished and see if it sounds like you talking. In informal and semiformal papers, your language should sound like you, a real human being, speaking. If it doesn't, can you revise so that it does? In more formal papers, the language should not sound like you talking; if it does, revise to make it more objective.

Let go

The spirit of revision is the welcome acceptance of change, the belief that no matter how good something is, it can always be made better. But many writers become attached to their words, proud to have generated so many of them in the first place, reluctant to abandon them once generated. When writers learn to let go, they have learned to trust that their power, creativity, and authority can generate exciting writing again and again, on demand. Letting go can imply dropping whole sections or even whole drafts.

Consider revising by starting a new second draft. After you have written and reread your first draft, start again as if you had no written draft to tinker with. Sometimes this will generate your best writing, as you automatically delete dead-end ideas and are not constrained from finding better ones. When you let go of one draft on a computer, keep the old one in a backup file just in case you change your mind.

■ **WRITING 3: APPLICATION**

Return to an early draft of a paper and revise it in light of the strategies in this section. Which strategies proved most useful? Do you know why?

19 d Making revision easy

Revising is easier when you use the tools and techniques necessary to keep the process under control. The following suggestions focus on ways to help you keep track of your revising.

Keep a revision notebook

If you normally keep a journal, make a point of writing about revision plans for papers. If you don't keep a journal, consider using a portion of your class notebook for revision suggestions as you work on a paper for that class. Be sure to record both notes about books or articles related to your project and ideas about theme, direction, and purpose. Making time to write about your writing may contribute in surprising ways to the writing itself. (See Chapter 8 for more about keeping a journal.)

Impose due dates

After you write the due date for a final draft on your calendar, add self-imposed due dates for finishing drafting and beginning to revise. If you allow a day or two between your self-imposed due dates, you will be guaranteed the distance you need to revise well.

Type all drafts

Handwriting is too friendly, too familiar, too close for many of us to see clearly. As soon as you are able, put your thoughts into typed words via computer or typewriter. This will give you some distance from your thoughts and allow you to change, expand, or delete them more readily.

Write and rewrite with a computer

It really doesn't matter what brand of computer you use, whether you own it or not, or which word processing system you use. As far as revision is concerned, any computer system makes it easier. When you write with a computer in the first place, all acts of rewriting are easier. You can change your text an infinite number of times before ever printing it out as hard copy. And the computer allows you to move blocks of text — sentences, paragraphs, pages — from one part of your paper to another with ease, which is particularly important during revising.

Read hard copy and save files

If you write and revise on a computer, it's important periodically to print out hard copy of your drafts and read them on paper. This is another technique for gaining distance from your writing. Hard copy also lets you scan several pages at a time and quickly flip pages in search of certain patterns or information.

In addition, when writing on a computer, get in the habit of making backup files of old drafts; if you become unhappy with your revisions, you can always return to the earlier copy. While you will seldom actually return to the earlier version, knowing that it exists will give you peace of mind.

> **REMINDERS FOR REVISION**
>
> **1.** Reread the **assignment** and state it in your own words. Does your paper address it?
> **2.** Restate your larger **purpose.** Has your paper fulfilled it?
> **3.** Consider your **audience.** Have you told them what they want and need to know?
> **4.** Restate the paper's **thesis** or **theme** in a single sentence. Is it stated in the paper? Does the paper support it?
> **5.** List the specific **evidence** that supports this thesis or theme. Is it sufficient? Is it arranged effectively?
> **6. Outline** the paper paragraph by paragraph. Is the development of ideas clear and logical?
> **7.** Return to your **introduction.** Does it accurately introduce the revised paper?
> **8.** Return to your **conclusion.** Does it reflect your most recent thoughts on the subject?
> **9.** Return to your **title** and write five alternative titles. Which is the best one?

WRITING 4: EXPLORATION

Look over the suggestions for revision in this section. Which of them have you used in the past? Which seems most useful to you now? Which seems most farfetched?

SUGGESTIONS FOR WRITING AND RESEARCH

1. Select any paper that you previously wrote in one draft but that you believe would profit from revision. Revise the paper by following some of the revision strategies and suggestions in this chapter.

2. Go to the library and research the revision habits of a favorite or famous writer. If you cannot find such information, interview a professor, teacher, or person in your community who is known to write and publish. Find out about the revision process he or she most often uses. Write a report in which you explain the concept of revision as understood and used by the writer you have researched.

20 Limiting and Adding

In their first drafts, writers often try to cover too much territory in too little detail. Not surprisingly, they end up with drafts that are overgeneralized and not very interesting. Overgeneralization can take many forms, but it usually results from writers doing their best to get information down quickly and make some sense of it. In first drafts of personal experience papers, for example, writers may try to summarize the whole story and its meaning for the reader. In first drafts of argumentative and informational papers, writers may offer capsule summaries of their opinions. These approaches are expected — even necessary — in first drafts, but would seriously damage the effectiveness of the final paper.

The problem of overgeneralization can be combatted with two apparently contradictory revision strategies. **Limiting** is selecting a narrow portion of a paper or concept and eliminating extraneous material. **Adding** is incorporating new details and dialogue to make writing more vivid and powerful. Used together, the strategies of limiting and adding can help turn a bland, overgeneralized first draft into an energetic, focused paper.

20 a Recognizing overgeneralization

The first step in fighting overgeneralization is learning to see it in your own writing. Here, for example, are several typically overgeneralized openings, some of which come from the early drafts of finished essays found elsewhere in this book.

> Life is so full of ups and downs that it sometimes drives me crazy. Last summer was like that, up one week, down the next. Picking eggs every day was so boring, but it was better than picking potatoes, which I did at the end of the summer.

> Last winter I spent nearly a month with the Outward Bound program. This action-packed winter camping trip proved to be

almost more than I could handle. From the tragedy of a close friend nearly drowning to my own experience nearly freezing to death, I discovered a new side of myself and became a new person.

The American timber wolf, the most noble of all North American predators, has been tragically exterminated from every state in the country due to greed, misunderstanding, and fear.

Anybody who has ever tasted a Ben and Jerry's ice cream cone knows that they make the best ice cream in the world. Since Ben and Jerry make their ice cream right here in Burlington, Vermont, we wanted to find out the secret of their success.

These openings provide several clues to the problems typical of first-draft writing: they contain summaries, platitudes, prejudgments, overstatements, misstatements, and misdirection.

Summary. Some of the preceding examples offer a summary rather than particulars about the essay to follow: the ups and downs of a summer, the action-packed trip. While summaries are useful at many points in writing, the particulars and details are more likely to attract and hold attention. Starting an essay with a summary asks readers to take on trust rather than by example that what follows will be interesting and true.

Platitude. When readers are told that life has its "ups and downs" or that an experience made the writer "a new person," they are hearing a platitude, a cliché about life. Platitudes decrease reader expectations for fresh, original insights.

Prejudgment. Some of these passages tell readers how they should feel and react to the information related. The story is either action-packed, a rebirth, or tragic — judgments made for readers by the writer. When writers prejudge an experience or idea, they take the act of interpretation away from readers, unwittingly decreasing readers' involvement in the paper.

Overstatement. Some of the preceding passages make large claims that will be difficult to substantiate: that the wolf is the "most noble of all North American predators," for example. Since critical readers distrust exaggeration, these passages become warnings that the writers' assertions are not to be trusted.

Misstatement. In an effort to make their writing powerful and emphatic, some of these writers have misstated the facts. It is not true, for example, that Ben and Jerry's ice cream is still made in Burlington, since the plant has now moved to Waterbury. Any reader who finds such a misstatement, small in importance though it may be, will read cautiously and skeptically thereafter.

Misdirection. In addition, though you cannot tell it from reading only these openings, some of these writers don't know yet what their theme, thesis, or story really is.

Writers who do not yet know the full extent of their subject see it as if from a distance — and from a distance even cities and mountains look small, well defined, and manageable. Writers have the choice of staying far away, letting the first-draft generalizations stand, and moving on to new subjects or of moving in close, narrowing and sharpening the focus, and adding details. Doing real writer's work means exploring the geography up close, finding out which path, road, sidewalk, or highway to follow home.

The best way to handle overgeneralizations is to get them down on paper where you can examine them. Let the first-draft writing get you started — but don't settle for it. Plan in the second draft to limit your paper and in the third draft to begin building it back up, making it clearer, sharper, more believable each time.

20 b Limiting scope

Writers often overgeneralize in first drafts because their topics are too broad and general. To write about them fully would require a book rather than an essay. One way to fight overgeneralization is therefore to limit the scope of your paper, that is, to limit the conceptual ground you are trying to cover. You can do this by choosing a narrower topic or by choosing a topic that's closer to home; often writers do both at once.

To limit scope by narrowing your topic, try to identify the many subtopics *within* your topic and to find one that especially interests you. Instead of trying to cover endangered wildlife in general, for example, could you limit it to a particular issue, species, or habitat? Or, better still, to a particular issue about a particular species in a particular habitat?

In the first draft of Brendan's argumentative paper about American timber wolves, he had already limited the topic to one species of wildlife in one country. However, even that topic proved too broad. As he read and researched, he further limited his investigation to the reintroduction of wolves into Yellowstone National Park. The final draft of Brendan's paper now begins this way:

Since 1926, there have been no wolves in Yellowstone National Park. The modern wolf inhabited the area of Yellowstone,
as well as the greater part of the North American continent, for
well over a million years before the Europeans settled the New
World. Upon arrival, white settlers began to push the wolf from its
natural territory. With the settlers' movement west and with their
increased development and agriculture, the wolf's range in the
United States rapidly shrunk and eventually disappeared.

(See Chapter 11 for a complete draft of Brendan's final paper.)

You can also limit scope by restricting your investigation to a
local issue or to a local manifestation of a national issue. This will
also allow you to do field research and experience some dimension
of your topic firsthand. (See Chapter 16 for more on field research.)

For example, a collaborative research and writing group that
set out to investigate the Ben and Jerry's ice cream company began by asking broad, general questions about "the secret of the
company's success." However, they quickly decided to limit their
investigation to what they could observe through field research at
local ice cream shops and production facilities. This in turn resulted in a narrower topic, the company's surprising combination
of business success and social responsibility.

■ **WRITING 1: APPLICATION**

Block out a portion of your journal or class notebook to devote exclusively to
the revision of one paper. In this section, try to limit the scope of your paper
first by narrowing the topic and second by choosing something local.

20 **C** **Limiting time and place**

Another way to fight overgeneralization is to limit time and
place. Rather than limiting your paper's topic as an idea or concept, as you do when you limit scope (see 20b), you limit its
chronological and physical boundaries, writing about days rather
than years, neighborhoods rather than cities. Of course, limiting
time and place often results in a more limited scope as well.

Consider, for example, this paragraph from a first draft by
Amanda, a first-year student from Scotland, writing a paper entitled "Waitressing":

> For most of this summer I again worked on the farm, where I removed rotten, diseased potato shaws from a field all day. But I was in the sun all the time with a good bunch of people so it was quite good fun. . . . My waitressing job was nothing to get excited about either. I signed up with an employment agency and got a waitressing job in Aberdeen, a city thirty miles north of our farm. It was only for one week, but I didn't mind — it was the first job that I had got myself and I felt totally independent.

The problem with such writing is not that it is wrong or incorrect but that it seldom makes good reading. Amanda has squeezed into one paragraph two jobs (waitressing and farming), two locations (Aberdeen and the farm thirty miles away), and a whole summer. In order to cover all of this, she only has room for broad generalizations — both in this paragraph and in the rest of her draft.

To limit her paper, Amanda chose one time and place (October on the farm) and wrote about that in the next draft.

> [Picking potatoes] was always in October, so the weather was never very good. It either rained or was windy, often both. Some days it would be so cold that we would lie in between the drills of undug potatoes to protect ourselves from the wind.

As you can see, once Amanda began to *limit* she intuitively began to *add* the interesting specifics and telling details that make writing informative and enjoyable. (See 20d.)

After witnessing the life and energy in her second draft, Amanda revised again, not about what *usually* occurred in October, but about what occurred on one particular day in October.

> Potatoes, mud, potatoes, mud, potatoes, that was all I saw in front of me. They moved from my right side to my left, at hip level. A conveyor belt never stopping. On and on and on.
>
> I bounced and stumbled around as the potato harvester moved over the rough earth, digging the newly grown potatoes out of the ground, transporting them up a conveyor belt, and pushing them out in front of me and three other ladies, two on either side of the belt.
>
> The potatoes passed fast, a constant stream. My hands worked deftly, pulling out clods of dirt, rotten potatoes, old shaws, and anything else I found that wasn't a potato. They were sore, rubbed raw with the constant pressure of holding dirt. They were numb, partly from the work and partly from the cold. It was October, the ground was nearly frozen, the mud was hard and

solid. Cold. Dirt had gotten into my yellow and yet brown rubber gloves, had wedged under my nails increasing my discomfort.

In this draft, Amanda found her story. The idea to limit the time and place had made all the difference, and had Amanda not repeatedly revised her paper, she wouldn't have found the story that most interested her.

 SUGGESTIONS FOR LIMITING

I. Ask yourself what your paper is about; don't settle for first hunches. Try writing in your journal about what your topic means to you personally.

2. When investigating an issue, consider choosing a local topic that will allow you to observe a place and interview the people involved.

3. When writing about something you have experienced personally, consider limiting your paper to one time or one place.

WRITING 2: EXPLORATION

Read again the excerpt from the last version of Amanda's potato paper. Which lines or words stand out as especially strong writing? Explain what makes them strong.

20 d Adding details

Generalization is death to good writing. The problem with most generalizations, including this one, is that everyone has heard them and no one fully believes them. We all hear that there is war in the Middle East, that smoking is hazardous to our health, that the ozone layer is in trouble, and so on. But hearing these generalizations over and over again numbs us rather than makes us more attentive.

What makes people pay attention to these and other issues are the details that bring them to life. Interesting writing teaches readers something they did not already know — something beyond the generalizations they've already heard. When a subject is explored through careful research and exposed through thought- ful writing, readers find themselves learning something new — and wanting to learn more.

Once you have limited your paper's scope, time, or place, two important things will happen: first, you will find more to say of a specific nature, and second, your paper will have more room to in- clude these specifics.

The research team investigating the success of the Ben and Jerry's ice cream company wrote a generalized first draft full of fa- miliar phrases about a good product and happy employees. But after limiting their investigation to local ice cream stores and pro- duction facilities, the team found that they could incorporate the telling details they gathered by observing firsthand.

> Around the corner are five black steps that lead to the up- stairs where the ice cream is sold. At the top of the stairs, next to a white metal wastebasket, is a blue bucket that says "We are now recycling spoons." On every table in the room are napkin dis- pensers saying "Save a tree, please take only one napkin."

On the one hand, this is an example of detailed descriptive writing meant to give readers the feel of the ice cream store. On the other hand, the recycling signs provide readers with concrete evidence that supports the claim that Ben and Jerry's cares about the envi- ronment, an important theme in the research report. Details not only add life, they add power and authority by lending credibility to your assertions.

■ WRITING 3: APPLICATION

Identify a place that contains information relevant to a paper you are writing. If possible, visit this place and describe any concrete details that you find there, especially any that may relate to a larger theme you are developing. If you are writing a paper from memory, close your eyes and visit this place in your imag- ination and describe the details you find there.

20 e Adding quotations

When you add quotations to your writing, you let other people speak in their own words. This is a natural complement to limiting time and place, like putting living characters on sets you have created. Unlike summaries and paraphrases of past action, quotations re-create action as if it were happening at the moment, so that readers become witnesses and interpreters instead of passive recipients of already-digested information. (For more on quotations, paraphrases, and summaries, see 17b.) In many cases, the most powerful quotations are not from written sources but from live people, those who were actually on the scene at the moment. These other voices will enhance and complement your own, making your papers both more lively and more authoritative.

If you are writing about a personal experience, you will probably add quotations in the form of re-created dialogue and interior monologue. Adding **dialogue** requires remembering what was said sometime in the past or, more likely, re-creating or inventing what was probably said. Of course, nonfiction writers are not allowed to create fiction, that is, to invent something that never happened. But they are allowed some license in bringing back the past since nobody remembers *exactly* every word, sentence, or paragraph of conversation. Adding **interior monologue** requires capturing yourself in the act of talking silently to yourself. You won't remember exactly what you thought, but your re-creation should be plausible and should sound like you.

In response to an assignment to write a paper based on a significant personal experience, Karen wrote a first draft describing her whole basketball season in fewer than three pages and concluding with the team playing in the Massachusetts semifinals.

> We lost badly to Walpole in what turned out to be our final game. I sat on the bench most of the time. The coach refused to put me in until the fourth quarter when there were five minutes left and we were already twenty points behind.

As you can see from this example, Karen's first draft included much summary ("We lost badly") and paraphrase ("The coach refused"), storytelling techniques that allow writers to cover ground rapidly but do little to involve readers or create excitement.

In her second draft, Karen limited her paper to the last eight minutes of the final game. She re-created the same scene described above by using dialogue and interior monologue.

> "Girls, you have got to keep your heads in the game. Don't let them get you down," Coach Harding shouted. "You've worked so

hard all season. You are just as good as them, just look at our record, 18–2–0."

"Coach, they're killing us," Allison said. "They're making us look like fools, running right by us. We're down by twenty with eight minutes to go. It's hopeless."

"I don't want to hear anyone talk like that. You girls have worked too hard to give up. You can't quit now."

Yeah, think of every sweat-dripping, physically gruelling, sui-cide-sprinting, drill-conditioning Saturday morning practice this year. ("OK girls, for every missed foul shot it's one full suicide!") Oh, yes, I remember those practice sessions just fine.

This draft puts readers on the bench with Karen, hearing what she heard, experiencing her frustration as she did at the time. (For more of Karen's paper, see Chapter 21.)

If you are writing an explanatory or argumentative paper, you will probably add quotations collected in interviews. **Interviews** are perhaps the most powerful kind of field research. In them, you ask people for their observations, interpretations, and opinions — expert and otherwise — on the issue you are investigating. (For more on interviews, see 16b.)

A group of first-year writing students collaboratively investi-gated the role of the Ronald McDonald House in providing housing for out-of-town parents while their children stayed in local hospi-tals. In their first draft the group reported the following informa-tion derived from newspaper sources:

> The McDonald's corporation actually provided less than 5% of the total cost of starting the Ronald McDonald House. The other 95% of the money came from local businesses and special-interest groups.

By the time they wrote their second draft, however, the group had visited the house and interviewed the director, whose words now add both life and authenticity to their report.

> "Our biggest problem is that people think we're supported by the McDonald corporation. We have to get people to understand that anything we get from McDonald's is just from the particular franchise's generosity — and may be no more than is donated by other local merchants. Martins, Hood, and Ben and Jerry's pro-vide much of the food. McDonald's is not obligated to give us any-thing. The only reason we use their name is because of its child appeal."

In their final draft the writers included both pieces of information, the quotation lending credibility and life to the statistical fact. (For more of this paper, see Chapter 21.)

Whether you are re-creating dialogue or monologue or adding interview material, make sure the quotations serve your purpose and advance the paper in the direction you want it to go. Because the sound of people talking adds life to papers, it is sometimes tempting to keep adding human voices, making the paper lively but sometimes losing the point in the process. Use careful judgment and strive for balance. (For more on controlling your sources and using quotations, see 17a and 17b.)

■ WRITING 4: EXPLORATION

Interview a classmate about anything (favorite food, worst class, last night) for a few minutes and take notes to capture the essence of what he or she says. Now construct a paragraph from these notes. What do you choose to summarize? What do you carefully leave in the person's own language?

SUGGESTIONS FOR ADDING

1. When you visit places, note details that appeal to the senses of sight, sound, touch, smell, and taste. These specific words will help you add convincing details when you write your paper.

2. When you include interview material, be faithful to the character of the person talking.

3. When you re-create dialogue or interior monologue from memory, close your eyes, visualize the experience, and make your re-created words faithful to the spirit of the occasion.

4. Be judicious in your use of details and quotations: summary and paraphrase work well to cover ground or time rapidly or to set up a context for more detailed discussion.

SUGGESTIONS FOR WRITING AND RESEARCH

INDIVIDUAL

1. Write the first draft of a personal experience paper as a broad overview of the whole experience. Write the second draft by limiting the story to one day or less of this experience. Write the third draft by limiting it to one hour. For your final draft, revise the version that most pleases you.

2. Write the first draft of an argumentative or interpretive paper as an overview of the whole issue you intend to deal with. In the second draft write three pages about something you now cover in one page. In the third draft write three pages about something covered in one page in the second draft. For your final draft, revise the version that most pleases you.

3. In revising a personal experience paper, locate a place where you paraphrase yourself or somebody else speaking, and replace the paraphrase with reconstructed dialogue or interior monologue.

COLLABORATIVE

In revising a collaborative paper based on research, locate a place in the paper where interview information would add life or credibility. Find several appropriate people to interview, and add that information to your paper.

21 | Switching and Transforming

Chapter 20 described limiting and adding, two of the most common revising strategies. The strategies described in this chapter are less common but equally capable of advancing a draft. Writers revise by **switching** when they change their paper's tense or point of view. Writers revise by **transforming** when they change the paper's genre from one kind (a report or an essay) to another (a letter or a play).

Both of these revising strategies work according to the same principle. Every type of paper has certain conventions: personal experiences are told in the first person and in the past tense, research essays are objective and formal, and so on. These conventions establish a certain way of seeing; they predispose the reader — and the writer — to interpret and experience the information in a certain way. By changing a mechanical element such as tense or form, writers can provoke a conceptual reassessment both in themselves and in their readers.

These strategies are useful revising tools because they force writers to resee the events in their papers from a different perspective. They are also fun and exciting — which is often what writers need after working long and hard to put together a first draft.

When and under what circumstances should you try switching and transforming? There are no rules, but you might try them whenever your language seems stuffy or boring. Or you might plan from the start to write one draft using a switching or transforming strategy, just to find out what you learn by doing so. You can switch or transform your entire paper or you can use these strategies on a limited part of the paper, to see where it leads you.

It's important to weigh gains and losses whenever you use a radical revision technique such as switching or transforming. Conventions have been developed because they aid reader understanding, and if you disregard the conventions you risk confusing your readers. Always consider whether you have gained more than you have lost, and use a switched or transformed paper for your final draft only when you think it will be effective with your readers (and acceptable to your instructor), not merely when it was fun to write.

The following pages focus on personal experience papers and research essays in particular, but remember that these switching and transforming strategies can be used with any piece of writing. (For more on personal experience papers, see Chapter 9. For more on research essays, see Part IV.)

21 a Switching tense

An interesting technique for switching the way you see an experience, story, issue, or idea is to write a draft in a verb tense different from the tense used in previous drafts. The most common way to recount personal experiences is to use the past tense: *Once upon a time* or *Last night* or *When I visited England.* The past tense is also conventionally used in research essays, both because the events reported have already occurred and because the past tense establishes scholarly distance and detachment. But both personal experience papers and research essays can benefit from being put into the present tense.

Switching in experience papers

Dawn used the past tense in a first draft about her summer experience as a nurse's aide in a hospital.

> Well, I walked into the first room, expecting to see women, but no, there were two men lying in their beds. My face turned red with embarrassment. I didn't expect that I would have to take care of men. So Charlene gave me a washcloth and a towel and told me to wash and dress them. As I washed them, I thought to myself, I can deal with this.

Dawn's past-tense draft recounts her experience in convincing, graphic detail. However, she decided to try another draft in the present tense.

> Up the steps through the big white door again. The foul odor of urine strikes my nose. Sounds quiet . . . of course it is, it's 6:30 in the morning. Time to punch in already! Seems like I just

got here. Another eight hours for a small paycheck. I hope my feet stay under me.

"Dawn, you have assignment five!" yells Terri.

"Gee, thanks. Why do I get stuck with the men's section? Just because I'm younger?"

Dawn uses some of the same material here (being assigned the men's ward) but presents it as if it were just happening, putting readers with her on the ward. Notice that she uses dialogue and internal monologue as a natural way to tell a story in the present tense. This, in turn, adds detail and authenticity to her account. For her final draft Dawn switched her entire paper to the present tense and limited her story to the experiences that happened on one eight-hour shift. (For more on limiting time and place, see 20c. For more on adding dialogue and monologue, see 20e.)

2 Switching in research papers

The following example is taken from a collaborative research essay investigating the effect of lake pollution on city beaches. The paper was based on substantial library and field research, and the early drafts were written in a conventionally formal and objective voice, using the past tense. For a later draft, the team decided to switch to the present tense.

> How do you close down a public beach? You can't barricade the water, can you? But people know the sewage system is dumping raw sewage into the lake, and they won't swim there. The newspaper always calls the contamination "fecal coliform," which according to the dictionary is "bacteria that indicate human waste." But you know what they're talking about.

Switching to the present tense resulted in a number of other changes in perspective and tone, which created a direct, honest student voice. The writers decided to preserve this voice for the introductory part of their paper, since their readers included other students in the class. Most of the twenty pages that follow, however, are written in a conventionally objective manner, usually in the past tense. (For more examples from this paper, see 21b.)

3 Weighing gains and losses

The advantage of switching to the present tense is that it lets you reexperience an event, which in turn allows you to reexamine, reconsider, and reinterpret it — all essential activities for successful revision. The advantage for readers is that the present tense puts them closer to the story, side by side with the writer, and cause them to wonder what will happen next.

The disadvantage is that the present tense makes it difficult for you to reflect on or summarize the experience or information. So long as writers maintain the present tense, they pretend to have no more distance from, perspective on, or understanding of their experience than their readers have. Essays written in the present tense may also seem more fictive and less believable since readers know the experience cannot really be happening at the same time it is being written about.

■ WRITING 1: APPLICATION

Write in your journal about a past experience, using the present tense as if you were reliving what you are writing about. Then reread the passage and describe its effect on you as both writer and reader.

21 b Switching point of view

Switching the point of view means switching the perspective from which a story, essay, or report is related by the writer. For example, in recounting a personal experience, the most natural point of view is the first person (*I*, *we*), with the writer relating each event as it happened to him or her: *On Friday I went to a concert.* In contrast, in recounting the results of research, the most conventional point of view is the third person (*he*, *she*, *it*), with the writer keeping to the background or disappearing completely: *The prison is surrounded by high brick walls.* Sometimes it is useful to switch from the conventional point of view, if only for just a draft — describing a personal experience in the third person or the results of research in the first person. (For more on point of view, see 28b.)

■ Switching in experience papers

Sometimes it is useful for writers to attempt to see themselves and their experience from the outside, as others do. You can do this by simply changing all first-person pronouns to third-person pronouns, so that *I* becomes *he* or *she*. Or you can adopt the role or persona of another person looking at the events and refer to yourself as *he* or *she*.

In the following passage from an intermediate draft, Karen recounts the last few minutes of a basketball game in which her team was competing for the Massachusetts state championship. In previous drafts she told the story from the first-person point of view. (See 20e.) For this draft, she adopts the perspective of the play-by-play announcer and describes her own entry into the game in the announcer's voice.

> Well, folks, it looks as if Belmont has given up. Coach Harding is preparing to send in his subs. It has been a rough game for Belmont. They stayed in it during the first quarter, but Walpole has run away with it since then. Down by twenty with only six minutes left, Belmont's first sub is now approaching the bench.
>
> Megan Sullivan goes coast to coast and lays it in for two. She has sparked Walpole from the start.
>
> The fans have livened up a bit, but oddly they aren't Walpole's fans, they're Belmont's. Cheers for someone named Karen are coming from the balcony. . . . Number eleven, Karen Kelly, replaces Michelle Hayes.

By adding the voice of the announcer, Karen was able to resee and retell her own story with an added bit of drama and suspense. Karen decided to open her final draft from the announcer's point of view and to switch after the first page to the first-person perspective. (This is also an example of transforming, as a personal essay has been changed to a news broadcast. See 21c.)

2 Switching in research papers

Switching point of view can also enhance research writing. The following example is taken from the paper investigating the effect of lake pollution on city beaches. After several early drafts written from the third-person point of view, the research team rewrote the paper as a story told by a fictional narrator using the first person. The research essay begins with an imagined dialogue between two bicyclists riding next to the lake.

> We both started to cycle and I followed her down a path near the lake. "I'm just amazed by the beauty of the water. It is great to see the islands out there in front of us. This is paradise," I said.

"Well, there are some problems with the lake. The sewage treatment plant," she paused and continued, "it's taken a lot of the beauty away."

"What do you mean?" I asked, and she proceeded to tell me this story. . . .

This fictional opening uses the same framing device often used by short story writers and television documentary writers to raise audience curiosity and provide an excuse for telling a story. The remainder of the paper recounts the bike riders' attempt to find out what is wrong with the lake, using a more conventional third-person point of view. (This is also an example of transforming, as a research essay has been partially transformed into a story. See 21d.)

3 Weighing gains and losses

When you switch to unorthodox points of view, you gain distance from your experience or ideas, seeing details and implications invisible before. Your readers gain, too, from the additional

---

GUIDELINES FOR SWITCHING

1. Switch tense and point of view when revising intermediate drafts to create distance and stimulate new insights.

2. Signal changes in tense or point of view within the same piece of writing by clear typographical signals (subheads, indentations, type changes, or white space) or transitional phrases.

3. Switch from past to present tense to create a sense of immediacy, suspense, and surprise. Switch back to past tense to synthesize, summarize, and reflect.

4. Switch your point of view by changing pronouns from third person (*he, she, it*) to first person (*I*). Or create a fictional voice and refer to yourself as *he* or *she*.

5. Keep tense and point-of-view changes in the final draft only when they suit your purpose and are acceptable to your audience. Be careful not to switch back and forth so often within the paper that the effect is confusing rather than clarifying and interesting.

details and insights, from the stylistic and tonal variety that makes technical information accessible, and from the realism of the mixed perspective — which is, perhaps, the fairest representation of reality as we experience it.

If you switch points of view without good reason, however, your writing may appear gimmicky rather than interesting. For example, to narrate life on the urban streets from the perspective of a homeless person may help your readers see the story in a new and useful light; choosing to narrate the same story from the perspective of a fire hydrant or a toy poodle may seem silly.

■ WRITING 2: APPLICATION

Write in your journal about yourself, using the third-person point of view. Then reread the passage and describe its effect on you as both writer and reader.

21 C Transforming experience papers

To transform a text is to change its form by casting it into a new genre. In early drafts, writers often attend closely to the content of their stories, arguments, or reports but pay little attention to the form in which these are presented, accepting the genre as a given. However, recasting ideas and information into different genres presents them in a different light. The possibilities for presenting information in different genres are endless, since anything can become anything else. Consequently, keep in mind that some transformations are useful primarily to help you, the writer, achieve a fresh perspective during the revision process, while other transformations are the best way to present the information to readers.

Personal experience assignments often benefit from transformation. Suppose, for example, that you are writing a paper about a week-long trip you took last year to someplace new and exciting. In your first draft or two you try to recapture the events, scenes, details, and dialogue of this experience, but you pay little attention to the form, since you expect it to be an essay. This may be exactly what you want. However, before calling your paper finished, suppose you recast it as a series of excerpts from an imaginary travel journal kept on the trip, a set of letters back home, or a column for a travel magazine or local newspaper? Each of these transformations can open up new possibilities.

1 Writing journals

In the following example, Mary transformed a personal experience essay into a set of re-created journal entries to capture the immediacy of her experience at a camp for emotionally disturbed children. She took advantage of the informal, conversational language characteristic of journal writing and of the fact that at the end of each entry the writer does not know what will happen the next day. In other words, using the journal genre helped Mary tell her story in a suspenseful manner.

> 8/14   Tomorrow I leave for Camp Daybreak. I thought it was a good idea in May, when I applied for the job, but tonight I'm having second thoughts. I don't know anything at all about emotional disturbances — What will the kids be like? What will the camp be like? How will we be paired with the campers?

Note that in this single entry Mary uses past, present, and future tenses to capture her ambivalent feelings the night before setting off for camp. (For more on switching tense, see 21a.) In other entries, Mary is able to work in the details of people, settings, and events by presenting them as memories of something that happened in the recent past. The journal form encourages informal and conversational language, creates a sense of chronological suspense, is an ideal form for personal reflection, substitutes dates for more complex transitions, and proves especially useful for conveying experience over a long period of time.

2 Experimenting with other genres

In addition to journal writing, you might experiment with these other forms associated with personal experience.

Letters. An experience might be rendered in a lively and interesting way by casting it as an exchange of letters between the writer and a trusted audience. The advantages of this genre are that all readers are familiar with letters and that the writer can adopt a friendly, informal voice, use dates for transitions, and maintain immediacy over a long period of time. The key advantage of a letter exchange over journals is the ease with which other voices (people writing letters in response) can be included.

Poems. The switch to poetic forms offers writers a powerful medium for conveying emotional experiences. The language can be condensed and transitions handled by the stanza form, and there are virtually no rules of form, style, reason, or rhyme governing modern poetry. For novice writers, poems may be especially effective in conveying short, intense experience; it is more difficult for novices to write long poems (more than a page or so) that will sustain readers' interest.

Drama. A personal story can also be told by re-creating the setting where something happened and placing characters, including yourself, in it. In the dramatic genre, writers must convey their meaning through what the characters say out loud since the writer is not allowed to relate what transpires inside the characters' minds. It is an excellent genre with which to create suspense, describe settings in vivid detail, and use the lively language of informal talk to advance your point.

■ **WRITING 3: EXPLORATION**

Describe the genre listed in this section with which you are most familiar and comfortable: journals, letters, drama, or poetry. Are you comfortable as a writer of this form? Why do you think this is so?

21 d   Transforming research papers

In the world outside of college it is common for research information to be reported in different genres to different audiences: a report to a manager, a letter to the president, a pamphlet for the stockholders, or a news release for public media might all contain the same information. Similarly, information collected for a research paper can be presented in a variety of ways. For example, could an argumentative research paper be transformed into a College Bowl debate or a series of letters to the editor of a local paper? Could an informational research paper be transformed into an investigative report for *Newsweek* magazine or a "Reporter at Large" piece for *The New Yorker*? In other words, if you have initially drafted a research report as an academic paper, it might take on new life if you revised it into an alternative genre.

■ Writing scripts

In Chapter 20 we described a group of researchers who wrote about the Ronald McDonald House. Their paper limped through several rather vague and undefined drafts until, in their final draft, they turned it into an imaginary script for the CBS news show *60 Minutes*. Since these first-year writers are not reporters for the television show, the form they chose is, of course, fictional. But the content remains real, consisting of the factual information and statistical data uncovered by both library and local research.

The transformed paper uses a combination of monologue, dialogue, and description. The script opens with a monologue by a fictional "John Smith," who is meant to be a television reporter like Chris Wallace or Diane Sawyer, standing before a camera.

> Smith: Hello, this is John Smith reporting for *60 Minutes*. Our topic this week is the Ronald McDonald House. Here I am, in front of the house in Burlington, Vermont, but before I go inside, let me fill you in on the history of this and many other houses like it.
>
> In 1974, Fred Hill, a Philadelphia Eagles football player, opened the first Ronald McDonald House in downtown Philadelphia. Hill's daughter was suffering from leukemia, so he knew what families with hospitalized children were going through. . . .

When writing for the fictional Smith, the researchers adopted the clear, simple language of TV reporters, which helped them to focus their information. The script also includes dialogue, as Smith learns about the house by going on a walking tour with a volunteer hostess named Robin (a real person) and interviewing her.

Within the script are descriptive scenes called "Camera Eye" that portray the house from the objective view of the TV camera. They are set in italic type to distinguish them from the rest of the script.

> *Toward the back of the house, three cars and one camper are parked in an oval-shaped gravel driveway. Up three steps onto a small porch are four black plastic chairs and a small coffee table. On top of the table is a black ashtray filled with crumpled cigarette butts.*

This procedure both mimics the conventions of *60 Minutes* and allows the writers to accomplish one of their central goals — showing readers what the Ronald McDonald House looks like.

When these writers decided to use the script genre, they were looking for an interesting way to tell a story based on field research. But the new genre raised new questions: How could they make Smith sound like a real reporter? How should they indicate the difference between what a TV audience would hear and what it would see? How should they keep the whole thing moving along? Finding the answers to these questions proved interesting and fun, and the team learned a great deal about presenting information in a powerful, engaging fashion.

2 Experimenting with other genres

Research writing may take innumerable forms. Here are some possibilities.

Stories. One way to present research information in writing is to adopt an obviously fictional form, such as a story, and embed the true information in a made-up setting. For example, the beach pollution research paper (21a2 and 21b2) includes fictional narrators but authentic observations of the treatment plant and interviews with merchants and shoppers.

Books with chapters. Several authors can collaborate on writing a short book with several chapters. Such a form could include a table of contents, preface, foreword, afterword, introduction, and so on. One such example from a recent class was written by four students about the plight of the homeless. Their short book had four five-page chapters, one by each of the four writers, and a collaborative introduction.

Articles for magazines. If you are investigating consumer products, such as VCRs, computers, stereo equipment, motorcycles, and the like, write it as a report for *Consumer Reports*. If you are investigating an issue, write it as an article for *Time* or *Newsweek*.

■ WRITING 4: APPLICATION

Propose a transformation for a research paper you are writing or have recently written. List the advantages and disadvantages of this transformation. Recast your paper (or a part of it) in the new genre and describe the effect in your journal.

> ✔ **GUIDELINES FOR TRANSFORMING**
>
> **1.** Try a new form only when you have time. If it doesn't work, you can still write a final draft in conventional form.
>
> **2.** Don't try to just *imagine* what the new form will do to your ideas — write in it for a while.
>
> **3.** Use a form that complements and enhances the content of the paper. Don't use a new form just for the sake of doing so.
>
> **4.** Be consistent within the form you choose. For example, if you write an article for *Consumer Reports*, follow that publication's style and conventions all the way through.
>
> **5.** Check with your instructor before writing a final draft as a transformation.

SUGGESTIONS FOR WRITING AND RESEARCH

INDIVIDUAL

1. To gain a new perspective on your own personal stories, write the next draft from a third-person point of view, as if somebody else were observing you from the outside looking in, or as if you were watching yourself from a distance.

2. Write a draft of a paper based on either experience or research in which you deliberately weave multiple points of view and tenses. Consider the advantages and disadvantages of this draft before deciding how to proceed in the next one.

3. Select a paper you are writing and rewrite it in a different genre. Before you start writing, make a list of the genres that have the greatest possibilities for your paper so you see the range you have to choose from.

COLLABORATIVE

1. For a class research project, interview college instructors in different departments concerning their thoughts about transforming academic papers into other genres. Write up the results in any form that seems useful.

2. As a class, compile a catalog in which you list and describe as many alternative forms for college papers as you can.

22 Responding

Revision benefits from help. The published writing you read in books, magazines, and newspapers that is signed by individual authors is seldom the result of either one-draft writing or one-person work. This is not to say that authors do not write their own work, for of course they do. But even the best writers revise better when they receive suggestions from friends, editors, reviewers, teachers, and critics about their writing. This chapter explores ways to get help with your own writing and to give help to others with their writing.

22 a Asking for help

Writers can ask for help at virtually almost any stage of the writing process. Sometimes they try out ideas on friends and colleagues while they are still planning or drafting. More often, however, writers ask for help during revision, when they are trying to make their ideas coherent and convincing, and during editing, when they are trying to make their language clear and precise. (See Chapter 23.) In addition, when a draft is nearly final, many ask for proofreading help since most writers are their own worst proofreaders. (See Chapter 56.) Following are some suggestions for getting good help as you revise your writing.

Identify the kind of help you want. When you share a draft with a reader, be sure to specify what kind of reading you are looking for. If you consider your draft virtually finished and all you want is a quick proofreading, it can be very frustrating if your reader suggests major changes that you do not have the time for or interest in. Likewise, if you share an early draft and want help organizing and clarifying ideas because you intend to do major rewriting, it is annoying to have your paper returned with every sentence edited for wordy constructions, spelling, and typographical errors. You can usually head off such miscommunication by being very clear about exactly what kind of response you want. If you *do* want a general reaction, say so — but be prepared to hear about everything and anything.

Ask specific questions. Let your reader know exactly what concerns you most. If you wonder whether you've provided enough examples, ask about that. If you want to know whether your argument is airtight, ask about that. If you are concerned about your tone, ask about that. Also mark specific places in your paper that you have questions about, whether a word, a sentence, or even a paragraph.

Ask global questions. If you are concerned about larger matters, make sure you identify these. Ask if the reader understands and can identify your thesis. Ask if the larger purpose is clear. Ask if the paper seems right for its intended audience. Ask for general reactions about readability, evidence, and completeness. Ask if your reader can anticipate any objections or problems other readers may have.

Don't be defensive. Whether you receive the responses about your paper orally or in writing, pay close attention to them. You have asked somebody to spend time with your writing, so you should trust that that person is trying to be helpful, that he or she is commenting on your paper, not your person. While listening to oral comments, stay quiet, listen, and take notes, interrupting only to ask for more clarity, not to defend what's there. Remember, many first drafts contain information and ideas that are clear to the writer; what you want to hear now is where they are less clear to someone else.

Maintain ownership. If you receive responses that you do not agree with or that you consider unhelpful, do not feel obliged to heed them. It is *your* paper; you are the ultimate judge of whether the ideas in it represent you. You will have to live with the results; you may, in fact, be judged by the results. Never include someone else's idea in your paper if you do not understand it or believe it.

WRITING I: EXPLORATION

Describe the best response to a piece of your writing that you remember. What were the circumstances? Who was the respondent? Explain whether the response was deserved or not.

SUGGESTIONS FOR ASKING FOR RESPONSES

1. Identify what kind of help you want on each particular draft; if you don't, be prepared to hear anything.

2. Ask questions about specific parts that worry you: pages, paragraphs, sentences, words, transitions, introduction, conclusion, title.

3. Ask questions about global issues that concern you: thesis, evidence, purpose, audience.

4. Listen to the responses you receive, ask questions when they're not clear, and avoid being defensive.

5. Own your paper. No matter what responses you receive, it's your paper and you need to be satisfied with it.

22 b Giving constructive responses

When you find yourself in a position to help other writers with their papers, keep these basic ideas in mind.

Follow the Golden Rule. The very best advice to follow when reading others' papers is to give the kind of response that you would like to receive yourself. Remember how you feel being praised, criticized, or questioned. Remember what comments help advance your own papers as well as those that only make you defensive. Keeping those in mind will help you help others.

Attend to the text, not the person. Comment so that the writer knows you are commenting on his or her text and not his or her person. Writers, like all people, have egos that can be bruised easily with careless or cruel comments. Attending to the text itself helps you avoid this problem. Point out language constructions that create confusion, but avoid commenting on the personality or intelligence of the writer.

Praise what deserves praise. Tell the writer what is good about the paper as well as what is not good. *All* writers will more easily accept critical help with weak parts of their paper if they also know that you think there are strong parts. But avoid praising language or ideas that do not, in your opinion, deserve it. Writers can usually sense if your praise is not genuine.

Ask questions rather than give advice. Ask questions more often than you give answers. You need to respect that the writing is the writer's. If you ask questions, you give the writer more room to solve the problems on his or her own. Of course, sometimes it is very helpful to give advice and answers or to suggest alternatives when they occur to you. Use your judgment about when to ask questions and when to give advice.

Focus on major problems first. If you find a lot of problems with a draft, try to focus first on the major problems (which are usually conceptual), and let the minor ones (which are usually linguistic and stylistic) go until sometime later. Drafts that are too marked up with suggestions can overwhelm writers, making them reluctant to turn to the job of rewriting.

■ WRITING 2: EXPLORATION

What kind of response do you usually give to a writer when you read his or her paper? How do you know what to comment on? How have your comments been received?

SUGGESTIONS FOR GIVING RESPONSES

1. Follow the Golden Rule: respond to others as you would have them respond to you.

2. Comment on the text, not the person writing it.

3. Explain what interested you — a specific sentence, paragraph, or page that you found especially strong.

4. Ask questions about what puzzled you. Identify the part of the paper that in your opinion was either confusing or did not advance the writer's goals.

5. Look at the big picture. Focus on major problems first.

22 **c** **Responding in writing**

Responding to writers in writing is both common and convenient. The most common responses that college students receive to their writing are those that teachers make in the margins or at the end of a paper, usually explaining how they graded the paper. Many of these comments — except the grade — are similar to those made by professional editors on manuscripts.

There are many advantages to responses that are actually written on the paper itself. First, writing comments takes less time and is therefore more efficient than discussing your ideas orally. Second, written comments are usually very specific, identifying particular sentences, paragraphs, or examples that need to be changed. Third, written comments leave a record to which the writer can refer later — after days, weeks, and even months — when he or she actually gets around to the rewriting.

There are also disadvantages to writing comments directly on papers. First, unless done with great care, written comments may invite misunderstandings that the respondent is not present to clarify. Second, comments that are too blunt may damage authorial egos — and it's easy to make such comments in writing, when the author is absent. And third, written comments do not allow the writer and reader to clear up simple questions quickly.

In writing classes you will commonly be asked by classmates to read and write comments on their papers. Here are some suggestions to help you do that.

Use a pencil. Too often writers develop negative associations from teachers covering their writing in red ink, primarily to correct what's wrong rather than to praise what's right. If you comment with pencil, the message is more gentle — in fact, erasable — and suggests the thoughts of a colleague rather than the judgments of a grader.

Use clear symbols. If you like, you can use professional editing symbols to comment on a classmate's paper. (They are reprinted in Chapter 56 and on the inside back cover of this book.) Or you can use obvious symbols that anyone can figure out. For example, underline words or sentences that puzzle you and put a question mark next to them. Put brackets where a missing word or phrase belongs.

■ **WRITING 3: EXPLORATION**

Describe your most recent experience in receiving written comments from someone. Were the comments helpful? Did the respondent follow the suggestions given in this section?

22 d Responding through conferences

Most writers and writing teachers believe that one-to-one conferences provide the best and most immediate help that writers can get. Sitting together, you can look at a paper together, read passages aloud, and make both general and specific comments about the writing: "What do you want to leave me with at the end?" or "Read that again, there's something about that rhythm that's especially strong" or "Stop. Right there I could really use an example to see what you mean." Often an oral conference helps as a follow up to written comments.

One advantage of conversations between writer and reader is that one-to-one conferences promote community, friendship, and understanding between writer and reader. Also, conferences can address both global and specific writing concerns at the same time. In addition, conferences allow both writer and reader to ask questions as they occur and to pursue any line of thought until both parties are satisfied with it. And finally, writer and reader can clarify misunderstandings as soon as they arise.

There are, however, a few disadvantages to these kinds of conversations. First, it is harder to make tough, critical comments face to face, so readers are often less candid than when they make written comments. Second, conferring together in any depth about a piece of writing takes more time than communicating through written responses.

The suggestions for making effective written responses also apply to oral conferences. In addition, there are a few other things to keep in mind.

Be relaxed and informal. Finding a comfortable place to have your conference can make all the difference in creating a friendly, satisfying discussion. Don't be afraid of digressions. Very often a discussion about a piece of writing branches into a discussion about the subject of the paper instead of the paper itself. When such talk happens, both writer and reader learn new things about the subject and about each other, some of which circle back and help the writer. Of course, if the paper itself is not discussed at all, the writer may not be helped at all.

Ask questions. If you are the reader, ask follow-up questions to help the writer move the revision along. If you have previously given written responses, most of the conference becomes a series of follow-up questions, and together you can search for appropriate solutions.

Listen. If you are the writer, remember that the more you listen and the less you talk, the more you will learn about your writing. Listen attentively. When puzzled, ask questions; when uncertain, clarify misunderstandings. But keep in mind that your reader is not your enemy and that your work is not under attack, so you do not need to defend it. If you prefer the battle metaphor, look at it this way: good work will defend itself.

■ WRITING 4: APPLICATION

Confer with a writer about his or her paper. Follow the suggestions given in this section. Describe in a journal entry how they worked.

22 e Responding in writing groups

An additional way in which writers receive responses to their work is through writing groups. In writing groups, members both give and receive help with their writing. When a particular writer's work is featured, that writer receives a response from each member of the group; in other sessions, this person becomes one respondent among the others, trying to help another writer move a draft along.

There are many advantages to discussing writing in groups. First, writing groups allow a single writer to hear multiple perspectives on a draft, therefore providing either more consensus or more options for revision. Second, writing groups also allow an interpretation to develop through the interplay of different perspectives, often creating a cumulative response that existed in no single reader's mind before the session. Third, writing groups can give writers more confidence by providing them with a varied and supportive audience. Fourth, when conducted well, writing groups develop friendships and a sense of community among writers and act as a stimulus for doing more writing in the future.

On the other hand, groups that meet outside of a classroom setting can be difficult to coordinate, as they involve people with varied schedules. Also, at the outset, the multiple audiences provided by groups may be intimidating and threatening to a writer.

All of the preceding suggestions about responding to writers also apply, with appropriate and obvious modifications, to writing group responses. But writing groups raise additional questions because they involve more people, require more coordination, take more time, and, for many people, are less familiar. Following are some suggestions for putting together writing groups.

Form a group along common interests. You can create writing groups among classmates, often with your instructor's help, to take advantage of having everyone together at one time in one place working on the same or similar assignments. Over the course of a semester, you may meet together in the same group once every week or two. Writing groups can also be created outside of class by interested people getting together regularly to share their writing.

Focus on the writing. The general idea for all writing groups is much the same: to improve one another's writing and encourage one another to do more of it. Writers share their writing with others in the group, either by passing out copies in advance for silent reading or by reading it aloud during the group meeting, with other group members following along on copies. After members have read or heard the paper, they share, usually orally but sometimes in writing, their reactions to it.

Make your group the right size for your purpose. Writing groups can have as few as three or as many as a dozen members. If all members are to participate, smaller groups need less time while larger groups need more. Groups that meet outside of the classroom have fewer size and time limits, but keep in mind that three hours is long for any meeting and that having more than a dozen members will make it hard for each member to receive individual attention.

Plan how to use your time. Sometimes a meeting is organized so that each member reads a paper or a portion of a paper. At other times a meeting may focus on the work of one member, and members thus take turns receiving responses at different meetings. If papers are to be read aloud, keep in mind that it generally takes two minutes to read a typed, double-spaced page out loud. Discussion and comment time should at least match the oral reading time on each paper. If group members are able to read the papers prior to the meeting, any length paper is fair game, and group time can be devoted strictly to discussion. Independently formed groups should experiment to determine for themselves how much they can read and discuss at each session, perhaps varying the schedule from meeting to meeting.

■ **WRITING 5: EXPLORATION**

Imagine a writing group you would like to belong to. What subjects would you write about? Who would you invite to join your group? How often and where would you like to meet? Explain in a journal entry why you would or would not voluntarily join a writing group.

ESL **PARTICIPATING IN WRITING GROUPS**

As a nonnative speaker of English, you may feel at a disadvantage in writing groups. Keep in mind, however, that participants usually give responses based on the content of a paper, not its grammar or word choice. Like your classmates, you can give valuable responses by pointing out what you think is successful in a paper and by providing suggestions for further developing a topic. As someone with a different cultural background, you may even be able to offer an interesting perspective on a topic that the writer hasn't considered.

SUGGESTIONS FOR WRITING AND RESEARCH

INDIVIDUAL

Recently there has developed a large body of literature on the nature and benefits of peer response. Go to the library and see what you can find about writing groups or peer response groups. Check, in particular, for work by Kenneth Bruffee, Peter Elbow, Anne Ruggles Gere, Thom Hawkins, and Tori Haring-Smith. Write a report to inform your classmates about your discoveries.

COLLABORATIVE

Form interview pairs and interview local published writers about the way in which response by friends, family, editors, or critics affects their writing. Share results orally or by publishing a short pamphlet.

So far *The Blair Handbook* has discussed planning, researching, drafting, and revising — everything involved in getting your ideas onto paper. Beginning with this chapter, we focus on the final stage in the writing process, editing, which involves clarifying ideas as they appear on paper.

Editing is the process of analyzing and improving written language. We have divided this process into steps and arranged them from large-scale concerns to finer points. When you edit, these are the kinds of questions you must answer at each step:

Effectiveness. Is your writing as readable as possible? Are your openings and conclusions clearly and forcefully worded? Do the structure of your sentences and the rhythm of your language support your meaning by helping to emphasize important points? Is each word the best possible choice? (See Chapters 24–32.)

Grammar. Is every sentence logical and complete? Does your choice of verbs and pronouns help clarify your meaning? Are modifiers correctly placed? (See Chapters 33–42.)

Punctuation. Have you used punctuation marks — end punctuation, commas, semicolons, colons, and so on — correctly? (See Chapters 43–49.)

Mechanics. Is every word spelled correctly? Are words capitalized, abbreviated, or italicized according to standard practice? Does your handling of numerals conform to convention? (See Chapters 50–56.)

These divisions are arbitrary of course. As you have seen, most writers plan, organize, research, draft, and revise simultaneously as they write and rewrite. Similarly, they also edit as they revise, and they edit for effectiveness while they are editing for grammar, punctuation, and mechanics. Although we break up the process arbitrarily to discuss it, we recognize that most writers work in circular, not linear, patterns. The chapters that follow detail specific techniques for analyzing and solving writing problems.

| 23 | a | Editing for the reader |

Some writers view editing merely as finish work. Just as a house remains incomplete without plaster, paint, varnish, and door handles, so a paper would seem unfinished without correct grammar, spelling, and punctuation. Yet that analogy, while useful, suggests too narrow a view of the editing process. Editing is a writer's last chance to affect meaning.

Your task when editing is to anticipate how readers will understand your writing. You may find this difficult, since you know what you intend your words to mean even when they do not quite say so. To edit, you must read with the eyes of a reader who has only the words on the page as clues to your intention. You must anticipate any questions your reader would have. This is also the time to identify any lingering questions *you* may have. You must attempt to resolve all such questions by clarifying or correcting the passage.

Putting yourself in the place of the reader is a difficult skill but one that can be developed. To sharpen your editorial eye, try exchanging drafts of a paper with a fellow student and reading each other's work. Note anything that slows the progress of your understanding — a sentence that seems too long, a misspelled word, an illogical sequence of ideas. Notice how such things stand out when you are reading something for the first time. If questions arise while you are reading, jot them down. Then look at the other student's comments on your paper. You may be surprised at the number of questions and suggestions.

To bring the same "fresh eyes" to your own work, try reading it aloud. Listen to yourself as if you were listening to another student's writing. Good writing is clear and compelling when read aloud. Keep the effective passages, and strengthen the weak ones. Another way to create distance is to wait a few hours or overnight between writing the last draft and beginning to edit it. If you use a computer, read from a printout instead of from the screen — changing formats may change the way the words appear and allow you to read with fresh eyes.

23 **b** Understanding the meaning of "error"

Getting facts wrong is one way writers can destroy readers' confidence. A writer who dated Columbus's landing in the New World at 1592 or who identified the North Star as Sirius rather than Polaris would inspire little confidence. Readers also draw conclusions about a writer's reliability based on his or her command of written language. A writer who seems unaware of the rules of writing invites readers' distrust. On the other hand, a writer's command of the language implies mastery of the subject matter.

More importantly, writing problems can make it hard for a reader to grasp meaning. The reader's only tool in interpreting the words on the page is a knowledge of how those words have been used in the past. Every departure from **convention** — the way words are customarily used — presents a challenge to the reader. If that challenge proves too formidable, all but the most dedicated reader will turn to another writer's work or away from reading entirely in favor of, say, watching television or taking a nap.

Some conventions are so widely accepted that they are regarded as **rules.** These rules do not result from any one person or committee deciding what ought to be right and issuing edicts accordingly. On the contrary, the rules are based on many writers' and grammarians' descriptions of how English has been written and spoken in the past.

Rules for spelling and for most punctuation and grammar are so universally accepted that departures from them are considered **errors.** Other conventions are more flexible, such as those related to sentence structure. However, if you stretch the boundaries of what readers expect, you risk being misunderstood or losing the reader's attention. For example, few readers would regard a sentence that has many dependent clauses and phrases hung on it like ornaments from a Christmas tree, each adding its own little highlight, as "wrong," but as it winds its way across the page and onto the next, those readers struggling to follow its convolutions might well, if they paused to think about it, find it turgid, confusing, or boring — indeed not unlike this sentence itself. Editing such a sentence is not a matter of correctness but of judgment about what readers will best appreciate.

Since language is constantly evolving, some conventions have changed over the years. Those described in this book are widely accepted for formal writing, including writing for academic audiences. We point out rules that have fallen into disuse and note distinctions between formal and informal usage.

■ EDITING I: EXPLORATION

Look at the comments and corrections marked on the last draft of a paper handed back to you by your instructor. Which comments concern rules, and which concern conventions? Can you see how the change suggested by each comment would improve communication? If not, why might your instructor have made the comment? If you cannot see any reason for the change, you may want to discuss it with your instructor.

23 c Understanding the editing process

Just as there are many ways to draft a paper, there are many ways to edit one. Nevertheless, most writers find they edit best when they tackle large, general concerns before zeroing in on individual words and sentences. To form good editing habits, try working in the following pattern.

First, quickly read the entire paper to get an overall sense of it and to identify the primary areas for improvement. If you were reading this paper for the first time, would you comprehend its purpose? Every paper should have a single main idea, one central point that all the other points support. Is the main idea of this paper clear? Who is your intended audience? Is your writing appropriate to that audience's level of interest in and knowledge about your topic? Is the language too difficult? Too simple? Make brief notes of any areas that need clarification, but don't get involved at this stage in making corrections.

Then, with a sense of the paper's audience and purpose and with several areas noted for improvement, go back to the beginning. Focus on paragraphs and the paper as a whole, not on individual words. Ask yourself if the main idea of the paper is clear and whether everything in the paper works to support it. Ask whether the main idea of each paragraph is clear, whether each sentence leads smoothly to the next, and whether the paragraph itself flows logically into the next one. (See Chapter 25.) Make sure the opening and the conclusion effectively introduce the paper and sum up your ideas respectively. (See Chapter 24.) Although you may have addressed such questions during revision, it is important to take another look at them at this stage.

Next, read the paper sentence by sentence, preferably out loud. Is the sentence structure varied and interesting? Does it support and help clarify the logical relation of ideas? (See Chapter 26.) Is the language clear? Are any words unnecessary? (See Chapter 30.) Edit the paper to make any changes suggested by these questions.

Now go back and check each sentence for grammatical correctness. (See Chapters 33–42.) Read each sentence word by word — even each word letter by letter — to discover errors of spelling and punctuation and to find unneeded or missing words. (See Chapters 43–56.) Make corrections as you go along.

Finally, read your paper one last time. Pay particular attention to passages you have just edited, making sure you introduced no new errors. Listen mentally to the words you changed to be sure they say what you intend.

23 d Working with others

1 Editing someone else's work

When you edit someone else's writing, it is essential to make your suggestions constructively so that the writer will not feel threatened or defensive. The most effective editing relationship relies not on authority but on cooperation between writer and editor.

The best way to keep your suggestions constructive is to focus first on understanding what the writer is trying to do — his or her purpose — and on the ways in which he or she has succeeded. Perhaps the writing expresses a clear insight or analysis or a compelling personal tone. Identify such strengths so that your other suggestions can help the writer build on them. After you have identified and discussed positive aspects of the writing, it will be easier to talk about things you think the writer needs to clarify or correct. (For more on working with other students, see Chapter 22.)

2 Accepting editorial advice

Almost everyone has had the experience of cringing when handed back a paper covered with curt corrections in red ink. But being edited by others is a fact of life. In college, other students as well as teachers may comment on your writing. If you write for publication or at a job, editors or supervisors will edit your work. As a writer you should accept comments with an open mind, examining them to see how they can benefit your work. Then you can adopt the ones you agree with and discuss the ones you don't. No matter how tactlessly or brusquely an editor communicates, remember that the comments are about a particular draft — not about all your writing and certainly not about you yourself. Try to respond objectively and not defensively. Adopting a professional attitude will facilitate your interactions with those editing your work.

ESL **EDITING OTHER STUDENTS' WRITING**

As a nonnative speaker of English, you may question your ability to edit your classmates' writing. Keep in mind, however, that you probably know more than you think about what makes a piece of writing readable and effective. Also consider that you will often be a part of the audience a classmate wants to reach. As a reader you can offer helpful feedback about clarity of purpose, variety of sentence structure, words or phrases that seem unnecessary, and many other elements of an essay that are discussed in this chapter.

EDITING 2: EXPLORATION

Think of the teacher who has helped you most with your writing. How did he or she express comments and suggestions about your work? How did you respond? Can you also recall an occasion when comments or corrections hurt your feelings? What was the impact on your writing? Were you able to distinguish between the meaning of the comments and their effect on you? How?

23 **e** **Editing with a computer**

A word processing program greatly simplifies the basic operations of editing — adding, deleting, moving, and changing words or groups of words. To edit, you put the computer's electronic pencil point, called the *cursor*, on the spot where you want to add, change, or remove a word. Then you can insert a new word, type over an existing one, or simply delete a word. Most word processors include a search-and-replace feature that allows you to find and change every instance of a word or phrase with a few keystrokes — or to make decisions about each occurrence case by case. Even more powerful is the computer's ability to move chunks of text. By first highlighting a block of text and then telling the computer to move, copy, or delete it, you can rearrange phrases, sentences, and even whole paragraphs with ease.

You store your work in the computer in a document or file with a name of your choosing. When you have finished editing a draft, you can either replace the unedited file with the edited one or save the edited version under a different name, thus preserving both the original and the edited copy. By storing each version of a paper separately, you can gain insight into the successive stages of your creative processes. This practice also frees you from the worry that you can never retrace your steps. Because each version is preserved intact, you can easily compare your most recent work with previous drafts.

Not least important, a computer's ease of printing eliminates the retyping of successive drafts. Because you do not have to re-type an entire paper, you are free to edit and reedit — and then print out — your work as many times as necessary.

Part VI of *The Blair Handbook* offers specific suggestions for editing with computers. To get you started, here are five general ideas for using computers in this stage of the writing process.

1 Change the look of your paper

A computer makes it easy to radically change the appearance of your paper, thus giving you the distance you need to edit your work effectively. Try using the search-and-replace feature to make each sentence start on a new line. This format can help you judge each sentence on its own merits; weaknesses stand out more clearly when not camouflaged within full paragraphs. The format also helps you see a string of short, choppy sentences — or a tangle of long, complex ones.

2 Alternate between hard copy and the screen

Try editing first on a printed-out version of your paper, as you would on any typed draft. Get a sense of the far-reaching changes you have to make, and indicate them in pencil. Then transfer the changes to the computer file. As you do so, you probably will not be able to resist making further changes directly on the screen, where each keystroke provides the instant gratification of neat, orderly type. Try working on both hard copy and on the screen to become familiar with the advantages and disadvantages of each. You will probably find it worthwhile to alternate between the two of them.

3 Print fresh drafts frequently

Writers sometimes reach a point at which, although they know the current draft is not yet *right*, they are not sure exactly what it needs. If you encounter such a block, try entering in the computer any changes you have made and printing out a clean version. Looking at a fresh copy, you will usually get a clearer picture of exactly where you need to go with the next round of editing — and often you will find that things are not so bad as you had feared.

4 Keep a file of personal trouble spots

If you know that you tend to overuse certain words or repeat certain grammatical errors, keep a running list of your personal trouble spots in a separate computer file. Then, when your paper is near completion, consult your list to make sure you have checked the latest draft for these problems. You can also use the search function to help you tackle them. For example, you can find every instance of an overused word and decide whether to replace it, or you can find every semicolon and decide whether you have used it correctly.

5 Use other programs — with care

In addition to the word processing program itself, many software packages are equipped with spell-checking, dictionary, thesaurus, and sometimes even grammar- and style-checking programs. Take advantage of these features, but use them with care. Even the best spell checker cannot tell you whether you've written *two* when you should have written *to*, *dinner* when you should have written *diner*. And no style or grammar checker today can compare with what you can do as an editor.

EDITING 3: APPLICATION

Find out about the possibilities for using computers more extensively in your writing. If you have your own computer, investigate the word processing capabilities of your classmates. Do any of their programs have advantages over yours? Do any of them use particularly helpful computer editing strategies? If you don't have a computer, find out if your college or community has any computers that students can use. How many students take advantage of them? What is the process for getting access to them?

23 f Editing in English as a second language

When editing their work, most native English speakers need guidance at one time or another with the intricacies of the language. Editing can be even more difficult for people who grew up speaking a language other than English because they have had less chance to develop an ear for what sounds right in English.

Certain aspects of English are likely to be particularly confusing to nonnative speakers and writers. For example, the forms and tenses of verbs combine in sometimes infuriatingly subtle ways to convey information about the time at which events occurred:

> By the time the sun *sets* tomorrow, I *will have been walking* for fifteen days.

The first part of the sentence uses the present tense to describe an action in the future; the second part describes an action that began in the past, will continue into the future, but will be finished by the time indicated in the first part (sunset tomorrow).

In seemingly arbitrary ways, adjectives and articles (*the, a, an*) — or their absence — convey significant information about the nouns they precede:

A book is missing from the library.	ONE SPECIFIC BOOK
Books are missing.	AN INDEFINITE NUMBER
The books are missing.	ALL OF THEM
Some books are missing.	BUT NOT ALL
A biology book is missing.	ONE OF SEVERAL
The biology book is missing.	THE ONLY ONE

To edit your writing for issues of this kind, the most important thing you can do is improve your English-language skills in general. You can best gain a masterful command of the language by reading widely, observing how language is used, and examining your own use of English to see how it resembles or differs from standard usage. Of course, this advice applies equally well to native-speaking and second-language students.

In addition, you should read your papers and your instructors' comments carefully to see what nonstandard usages or grammatical errors occur frequently. Once you identify these patterns, edit specifically to find instances of them. The more experience you have in reviewing the rules and applying them, the easier it will be to make the right choice the first time.

Throughout Part VI of *The Blair Handbook*, special green boxes give information and advice on aspects of English that are likely to cause problems for nonnative speakers. The letters "ESL" in green in the table of contents identify each section of the book that includes one of these boxes, and the ESL Index at the back of the book can help you find boxes on particular topics.

23	**g**	Using Part VI of *The Blair Handbook*

Part VI of *The Blair Handbook* can be used in different ways. You may be asked to read several chapters, discuss them in class, and then apply their advice in writing papers for that class. You may also decide to explore the book on your own, looking in the table of contents or the index for issues about which you have questions.

Many college instructors use a handbook like this one to show students how to make their writing stronger. Teachers who must read dozens of student papers a week usually focus their written comments on large-scale issues, such as organization, logical argument, and the development of ideas. Rather than analyze grammatical errors in detail for each student, many instructors simply mark the passages in question and refer students to the appropriate sections of the handbook, like this:

■ What I liked most was/ the opportunity to explore

different kinds of writing.

Not between subject and verb. See commas, 44k

The instructor is suggesting that the student refer to section 44k to review the use of commas, in particular the rule that a comma should not separate a verb from its subject. A student who reads and understands the advice of that section will be less likely to repeat the error.

Your instructor may also simply use a proofreading mark or correction symbol:

■ Every doctor has <u>their</u> own way of working.   *agr*

Proofreading marks and correction symbols are widely used and largely standardized. The correction symbol *agr* in this case stands for *agreement* between a pronoun (*their*) and its antecedent (*doctor*). To see what a symbol means, look it up in the chart on the inside back cover of this book; the chart will refer you to a relevant section of the book. Proofreading marks appear in Chapter 56.

■ **EDITING 4: APPLICATION**

Select two or three comments that were marked on the last draft of a paper handed back to you by your instructor. Use the index or table of contents of *The Blair Handbook* to find out where the handbook addresses these issues, and then read those sections. Were the issues treated as matters of effectiveness, of grammar, of punctuation, or of mechanics? What have you learned that you didn't know before? Use the editing advice in *The Blair Handbook* to edit the relevant sentences and correct any problems.

Editing for Effectiveness

You never get a second chance to make a first impression in writing as well as in life. Your first words are in many ways the most important. The **opening** of an essay must engage, stimulate, and challenge your readers, enticing them to read further. At the same time, the opening must give readers a reliable guide to what will follow: it should introduce the topic and the thesis or main idea and give readers some idea of what you intend to do in the rest of your paper.

An essay's **conclusion** merits equal attention. Because the conclusion is the last thing readers read, it will be the portion of the paper that lingers in the reader's mind, and therefore should be memorable. It is your last opportunity to tie together everything you have covered in your paper and present it in a coherent, tidy package. If you fail to create a clear, strong opening and conclusion, your ideas may be lost to the reader.

On rare occasions, the first words of an essay will spring to mind as you begin to write, the last words will flow effortlessly from the preceding paragraphs, and you will never feel the need to change them. More often, though, you will work and rework your opening and conclusion to get them right. Many writers find it almost impossible to create effective openings and conclusions during the drafting stage; they are still too busy determining what they need to say in the main part of the paper. Instead, they draft a rough opening and conclusion and plan to worry about polishing them during revision, once they have the body of the paper under control. Yet often these writers find themselves at the editing stage still lacking a sound beginning or ending for their paper. If you find yourself in this situation, don't despair: the editing stage is not too late to craft an effective opening and conclusion.

In general, early drafts of openings and conclusions may suffer from two types of weaknesses. First, openings may not compel the reader to read further, and conclusions may miss the opportunity to end with a resounding finale. Second, they may fail to give the reader a reliable guide to reading and understanding the rest of the paper. Openings may be vague and do little to lead readers into the paper; conclusions may repeat generalizations, focus on a relatively minor point, or wander off the subject entirely.

When editing openings and conclusions, keep the following guidelines in mind:

- Make your opening engage readers' interest.

- Remedy weaknesses in your opening.

- Make your conclusion satisfying.

- Remedy weaknesses in your conclusion.

24 a Making openings engaging

There are nearly as many ways to create an engaging opening as there are writers and kinds of writing. The goal is to grab the reader's attention and focus it on the topic, while stating or suggesting the main idea. You must also decide how much of the reader's time you can afford to spend getting started.

In a short essay of two to three pages, you need to start like a sprinter and go flat-out for the full fifty meters. The opening should usually be no longer than one paragraph, which is standard in much college writing. In a longer paper, you can set off at a more leisurely pace. A two-paragraph opening allows you to begin with an interesting anecdote or fact to engage readers' attention in the first paragraph and then comment on it and introduce the thesis in the second paragraph.

In either case, after an opening no longer than two paragraphs, readers should be able to recognize both your **subject,** the general area you are writing about, and your **topic,** the specific idea on which your paper focuses. They should also understand your **main idea,** the central point you will make in your paper. In argumentative and research writing, this is presented in a **thesis,** an explicit statement usually placed in the opening. In personal experience and reflective writing, it is more often an implicit **theme.** Even when a main idea is not explicitly stated or is stated only at the end of a paper, readers should be able to anticipate it after reading your opening.

Here are several techniques for making openings engaging:

- Moving from general to specific
- Making a striking assertion
- Using an anecdote
- Using an interesting detail, statistic, or quotation
- Asking a provocative question

Whatever type of opening you use, be sure it is appropriate to your topic and main idea, and be sure its relevance is clear.

Many opening paragraphs for college papers follow a **general-to-specific pattern** and end by stating the thesis.

> Language is the road map of a culture. It tells you where its people come from and where they are going. A study of the English language reveals a dramatic history and astonishing versatility. It is the language of survivors, of conquerors, of laughter.
>
> RITA MAE BROWN, "TO THE VICTOR BELONGS THE LANGUAGE"

Brown begins with a broad generalization about language, then supports it by explaining more specifically what she means. In the third sentence, she narrows the topic to *the English language*, and in the fourth sentence she states her thesis.

This opening features a **striking assertion,** a statement so improbable or far-reaching that the reader will demand to see proof. After grabbing his readers' attention, the writer directly states his thesis.

> John Milton was a failure. In writing "Paradise Lost," his stated aim was to "justify the ways of God to men." Inevitably, he fell short of accomplishing that and only wrote a monumental poem. Beethoven, whose music was conceived to transcend Fate, was a failure, as was Socrates, whose ambition was to make people happy by making them reasonable and just. The inescapable conclusion seems to be that the surest, noblest way to fail is to set one's own standards titanically high.
>
> LAWRENCE SHANIES, "THE SWEET SMELL
> OF SUCCESS ISN'T ALL THAT SWEET"

This next opening uses an **anecdote,** a brief story about people or incidents that introduces the topic and illustrates the thesis.

Once I met a woman who grew up in the small North Carolina town to which Chang and Eng, the original Siamese twins, retired after their circus careers. When I asked her how the town reacted to the twins marrying local girls and setting up adjacent households, she laughed and said: "Honey, that was *nothing* compared to what happened *before* the twins got there." Get the good gossip on any little mountain town, scratch the surface and you'll find a snake pit!

FRANCIS PROSE, "GOSSIP"

Prose's thesis, that gossip is an inescapable part of communal life, is implicit by the end of this opening.

An **interesting detail, statistic,** or **quotation** can put readers into the middle of an unfamiliar situation, making them eager for the context and explanation you are about to provide.

"Mrs. Tolstoy is your basic L.O.L. in N.A.D., admitted for a soft rule-out M.I.," the intern announces. I scribble that on my patient list. In other words Mrs. Tolstoy is a Little Old Lady in No Apparent Distress who is in the hospital to make sure she hasn't had a heart attack (rule out a myocardial infarction). And we think it's unlikely that she has had a heart attack (a *soft* rule-out).

If I learned nothing else during my first three months of working in the hospital as a medical student, I learned endless jargon and abbreviations.

PERRI KLASS, "SHE'S YOUR BASIC L.O.L. IN N.A.D."

Klass piques readers' curiosity with the unfamiliar jargon in the quotation, but she quickly explains it and, in her second paragraph, identifies jargon itself as the topic of her essay.

The next example provides a few sentences of background information on the paper's topic and then asks readers a **provocative question,** which the thesis will later answer.

Look around you in most locations in the United States and Australia, and most of the people you'll see will be of European ancestry. At the same sites 500 years ago everyone without exception would have been an American Indian or an aboriginal Australian. This is an obvious feature of our daily life, and yet it poses a difficult question, one with a far from obvious answer: Why is it that Europeans came to replace most of the native population of North America and Australia, instead of Indians or native Australians replacing the original population of Europe?

JARED DIAMOND, *THE ACCIDENTAL CONQUEROR*

■ **EDITING 1: PRACTICE**

Edit the following opening paragraph to make it more engaging. More than one edited version is possible. Be ready to explain your editing choices.

Dr. Ravi Batra, an economist at Southern Methodist University, has described a long-term cycle of economic indicators. Those indicators, he believes, forecast a depression in the next few years. The World Futurist Society also predicts a global economic collapse rivaling the Great Depression of the 1930s. Both predictions cite the rash of bank failures in recent years, implying that the first indication of wider economic troubles will be the downfall of financial institutions.

24 **b** Strengthening weak openings

Wanting to sound well informed, scholarly, or self-assured, many writers lapse into wordiness, overgeneralization, and cliché, which — especially in openings — are anything but engaging. Readers are more likely to continue reading if they see that each sentence, each word, is important to the purpose of the writing. To that end, you must edit out any elements that may distract your readers.

■ Being direct

Jana's earlier draft of the opening for a paper about stress rambled before getting to the main point.

> It is a fact that anxiety, stress, and tension exist in us all. Fortunately for us the victims, there are ways to control these emotional states and live a more comfortable life. The most effective way is to replace stress using techniques for relaxation.

Phrases like *it is a fact that, it appears that,* or *it has come to my attention that* serve little purpose other than to preface what is about to be said. When she edited the opening, Jana deleted the sentence that begins *Fortunately for us the victims,* but took its most important idea, *control,* and moved it to the next sentence, where it helps state the thesis more clearly.

> Anxiety, stress, and tension exist in us all. The most effective way to control stress and live a more comfortable life is to use techniques for relaxation.

2 Sharpening focus

If you open with a general statement followed by specifics, beware of the potential trap of a statement too broad to engage readers' interest. Try to limit opening generalizations so that the reader will understand right away what you are talking about. Rodney's draft began with such a broad, safe—and obvious—generalization.

> Watching too much television is bad for you. Many children these days spend more than five hours a day with the television when they could be reading or playing outside. Instead, they are filling their minds with Teenage Mutant Ninja Turtles.

Of course watching *too much* television is bad. The statement is an example of the logical flaw called begging the question: *too much* and *bad for you* say much the same thing. (See Chapter 11.) When he began editing, Rodney decided to turn his broad generalization into provocative questions.

> Many children spend more than five hours a day watching television when they could be reading or playing outside. What effect does television have on these kids? At what levels do those effects appear? In other words, how much TV is too much?

3 Emphasizing the main idea

An opening should move quickly to establish the topic of your paper and tell readers what your point about it will be. Anything that takes readers away from your main idea should be eliminated.

This was Todd's first draft of the opening to his paper on hazing in fraternities.

> "To subject (freshmen, newcomers, etc.) to abusive or humiliating tricks and ridicule." This is how *Random House College Dictionary* defines the word *hazing*. Hazing is practiced by fraternities and sororities on many of the college campuses in the United States. In the past seven years, hazing incidents have killed at least thirty-nine students. Hazing is illegal in nineteen states, and seven more are considering banning it. However, this practice of submitting "pledges" to painful and humiliating ordeals is still

going on. Efforts by colleges and national fraternity organizations to halt the practice seem to have little effect.

When editing, Todd realized that the dictionary definition did little to advance his point and that the string of facts gave no hint of which facts he considered important. The topic of the essay was unclear — was it about hazing, state regulation of hazing, or the dangers of hazing? Todd realized that what he was trying to say was that hazing must stop and that the institutions themselves must be the ones to stop it. He made that his thesis statement and positioned it in a prominent position, at the end of the paragraph. Todd then singled out the most startling statistic and put it in his first sentence where it could help engage readers' attention.

> In the past seven years, hazing at U.S. colleges has killed at least thirty-nine students. The practice is illegal in nineteen states, and seven more are considering banning it, yet new fraternity "pledges" continue to be subjected to pain and humiliation. Despite legal efforts by more than two dozen states to stop it, hazing continues. Colleges, law enforcement agencies, and fraternities themselves clearly must do more to stop the barbaric practice of hazing.

ESL | **CROSSCULTURAL DIFFERENCES IN ESSAY OPENINGS**

Writing instruction in your native language may have emphasized a different approach to writing openings than the one presented here. For example, you may have learned to lead into your thesis less directly or to start with a well-known proverb or saying. Try the following to gain a better understanding about composing introductions in English.

1. Discuss with your instructor or your classmates what you have learned about writing openings in your native country. Try to identify the differences between the way people write in your native language and the way they write in English.

2. Ask a friend or classmate to read and respond to the openings in your drafts before you turn in your final papers.

3. Pay attention to the ways that openings are developed in published works and in your classmates' papers. You might see, for example, that using a proverb or a familiar story as an opening is appropriate and engaging in some contexts but not in others.

■ **EDITING 2: PRACTICE**

Edit the following opening paragraph to strengthen it. More than one edited version is possible. Be ready to explain your editing choices.

Our society today faces many problems. One of these is the problem of high dropout rates among high school students. Several of my friends who dropped out of high school are now happily unemployed or working at dead-end jobs for low wages. In fact, I was almost a dropout myself. I think if administrators could understand the reasons why dropouts leave and why I decided to stay, they might be able to help other students finish school.

■ **EDITING 3: EXPLORATION**

Read several opening paragraphs by an author whose writing you admire, and select one that seems particularly effective to you. What techniques has the author used to engage your attention? How has the author used the opening paragraph to focus your thoughts on the main idea of the piece? Which of these techniques can you use in your own writing?

■ **EDITING 4: APPLICATION**

Read the opening paragraph of a paper you are working on, and evaluate its effectiveness. Will it grab readers' attention? Will it focus the readers' attention on the important ideas in your paper? If not, look for ways to improve the paragraph, whether by using one of the techniques described in 24a or by making the paragraph more direct, more focused, or more emphatic. Edit the paragraph, and then compare the edited version with the original to see how you have improved the effectiveness.

24 c Making conclusions satisfying

An effective conclusion leaves readers satisfied with the discussion and gives them something to think about. Just as there are many techniques for creating engaging openings, there are many ways to construct a satisfying and memorable conclusion. A conclusion usually reminds readers of your main idea or thesis by restating it, usually in slightly shortened form. If you have not yet given readers an explicit statement of your main idea, you should do so in your conclusion. This statement or restatement of the main idea can then be further developed by doing one of the following:

- Asking a rhetorical question
- Summarizing the important points of the paper
- Sounding a call to action
- Speculating about the future

One highly effective strategy is to end with a **rhetorical question.** Brendan concluded his paper with a question meant not to be answered but to ring in readers' ears.

> The wolf was once an integral part of the Yellowstone environment. Its reintroduction would complete the ecosystem and improve the natural situation. The objections of farmers and ranchers can be satisfied through compensation for any losses, which should be small. An existing act of Congress already requires government agencies to return the wolf to its original habitat. Why, then, are there still no wolves in Yellowstone?

Another strategy is a concise **summary** of the important points of the paper, usually concluding with a restatement of the thesis. Brendan's concluding paragraph could have outlined the argument of his essay and then asserted the logical conclusion.

> The wolf was once an integral part of the Yellowstone environment. Its reintroduction would complete the ecosystem and improve the natural situation. The objections of farmers and ranchers can be satisfied through compensation for any losses, which should be small. An existing act of Congress already requires government agencies to return the wolf to its original habitat. There is no excuse for further delay.

In argumentative papers, consider closing with a **call to action.** What was the purpose of marshaling your powers of persuasion if not to mobilize your readers on behalf of change?

> Until the SAT is reformed or abolished, those students who score lower on the test will suffer. They will have a hard time getting into many colleges, even though they may have what it takes to succeed. The emphasis on the test distracts high school students from things that are also important to admission decisions,

such as writing ability, grades, course load, and extracurricular activities. It is time for those who care about justice to see that this system is fixed.

You can also conclude with **speculation** about the future, giving readers a moving vision of the world if action is — or is not — taken. Anthropologist Margaret Mead ends her discussion of capital punishment by presenting a vision of a better future.

> The tasks are urgent and difficult. Realistically we know we cannot abolish crime. But we can abolish crude and vengeful treatment of crime. We can abolish — as a nation, not just state by state — capital punishment. We can accept the fact that prisoners, convicted criminals, are hostages to our own human failures to develop and support a decent way of living. And we can accept the fact that we are responsible to them, as to all living beings, for the protection of society, and especially responsible for those among us who need protection for the sake of society.
>
> MARGARET MEAD, "A LIFE FOR A LIFE"

▇ EDITING 5: PRACTICE

Edit the following conclusion to make it more satisfying. More than one edited version is possible. Be ready to explain your editing choices.

Computers have radically altered our society and will undoubtedly continue to do so. But how far will computers take us? Will we like our destination? From the banking and finance industries to recreation and art, every aspect of our lives has been affected by the ramifications of RAM and ROM. Much as the Industrial Revolution and the Agricultural Revolution did in past centuries, the Computer Revolution will fundamentally transform our culture in ways we cannot yet imagine. The three distinctive characteristics of computer transactions—speed of computation, ease of replication, and access through networking—are unremarkable in themselves, but when combined they change the very nature of information, the currency of our culture. No longer is knowledge accumulated over the centuries, unalterably fixed on pieces of paper, and painstakingly consulted when needed. Today's information resembles a rushing torrent: always changing, impossible to contain or chart, and ready to sweep aside all limits or restrictions.

24 **d** **Strengthening weak conclusions**

An effective conclusion concisely summarizes, yet does not merely repeat, the whole message of the paper. This is your last chance to communicate with your readers: What is it that you most want them to remember? What further guidance can you give them to understanding what you've written? When editing your conclusion, focus on the single most important idea of your paper.

1 **Being direct**

Wordiness is particularly troublesome in conclusions because it undermines the strength and authority of your final sentences and thus weakens the effectiveness of the entire paper. A **transitional phrase** such as *in conclusion, all in all,* or *to sum up* is occasionally useful to signal that a conclusion is approaching, but use such phrases sparingly. You shouldn't have to tell your readers that you've moved on to your conclusion. A conclusion cluttered with transitional phrases suggests that you have little left to say.

A **qualifying phrase** such as *I think* or *I believe* is another sort of wordiness that often gets in the way of a strong conclusion. Using such constructions is entirely appropriate when you need to distinguish your conclusion from someone else's: *While Robinson argues that the data clearly link low-frequency radiation to these illnesses, I would argue that the evidence is far from conclusive.* In most cases, however, readers will assume that the ideas expressed in the conclusion are your own.

Many of the elements Julie recites in summarizing her evidence are other people's opinions or facts she has carefully documented earlier. Thus, qualifying them by *I think* weakens her argument.

> The use of fetal tissue is a very relevant and important issue today. I think that the medical progress we have made is great. I don't think that we would know and understand some of the things that we do if we hadn't taken that first step. It is very important that we go to lengths to study the fetus and reach a higher level of understanding. With this knowledge we can apply new technology to old, unanswered questions. Ten of the thirteen disease-specialized institutes within the National Institutes of

Health have sponsored fetal tissue research. Yet the debate over abortion continues to block essential research. I think now that it is time to demand an end to the political stalemate.

In her editing, Julie collapsed the first two sentences into one. She deleted the vague phrase *a very relevant and important issue* and summarized specific data. By removing *I don't think* and *I think*, she invites her readers to share her conclusion and act on it.

Fetal tissue research has contributed greatly to medical progress. Researchers have learned a great deal about genetic disorders, metabolic diseases, and neurological disorders that otherwise might have gone undiscovered. It is very important that we reach a higher level of understanding of the fetus and its development. With this knowledge we can apply new technology to old, unanswered questions. Ten of the thirteen disease-specialized institutes within the National Institutes of Health have sponsored fetal tissue research. Yet the debate over abortion continues to block essential research. The time has come to demand an end to the political stalemate.

2 Broadening conclusions that are too limited

Take care not to limit the scope of your conclusion unnecessarily. Sylvie had argued in her essay that engineering education was crucial to the economic health of the entire nation, yet in her conclusion she spoke only of its importance in her state.

The College of Engineering is a critical component of the university, the city, and the state. If, as the governor has said, engineering is vital to the state's economy, we cannot afford to diminish the quality of engineering education in the state. We must find the dollars to avoid a shortage of engineers in the state in the coming decades.

Sylvie edited her conclusion to include the national implications of engineering education.

The College of Engineering is a critical component of the university, the city, and the state. As the governor has said, engineering is vital to the state's economy; thus, we cannot afford to diminish the quality of engineering education. Because the program draws students from across the country, its future may well affect the profession nationally as well as in the Mid-Atlantic region. We must find the dollars to avoid a shortage of engineers in the coming decades.

3 Focusing conclusions that are too general

You may want to conclude your essay by raising questions or making generalizations that follow from your discussion. Beware, however, of using your conclusion to answer a question not addressed earlier in your essay or of suddenly broadening the essay's scope.

Kyle's essay discussed his college's requirement that students acquire computers, the educational applications of computers, and the problems students encountered using them. Yet his conclusion wandered off into speculation about the role of computers in every aspect of life.

> People are beginning to wonder where the computer age is taking us. Will computers become a major part of daily life? Will programmable machines make human minds obsolete? One university official seems to think not. "When it comes to just plain living and thinking, the computer is not really much help."

Although the essay showed that computers had indeed become part of daily life at his college, Kyle had not really explored the possible obsolescence of human thought. He decided the idea was too fantastic for speculation in the conclusion of his essay. He edited accordingly.

> Computer literacy has become a necessity. The machines will soon be as prevalent in college as they are in business. Exactly how they will change people's lives remains to be seen, but at least one university official predicts the changes will be more gradual than sweeping: "When it comes to just plain living and thinking, the computer is not really much help."

EDITING 6: PRACTICE

Edit the following conclusion to strengthen it. More than one edited version is possible. Be ready to explain your editing choices.

If the fighting ceases, parents can begin to talk to their children about the divorce and why it happened. From such discussions, children may learn that marriage is not something to rush into, which can be a good thing to learn. As

they grow older, the emotional scar they will carry is knowing that their parents did not have a happy marriage, but I think that can be a good thing as
well as a painful one.

EDITING 7: EXPLORATION

Select an essay that looks interesting to you because of its title but that you
have not read before. First, read the opening paragraph. What can you tell
about the essay from this paragraph alone? What is the topic of the essay?
What will the author's position on this topic be? What is the tone or mood of
the essay? Next, read the conclusion. Do the topic, position, and tone seem
the same as those in the opening? If not, how are they different? Judging only
from the opening and the conclusion, what were the important points made
in the essay? Last, read the entire essay and see how accurate your predictions
were. What do your findings tell you about the author's skill at writing openings and conclusions?

25 | Shaping Strong Paragraphs

Good paragraphing gives readers clues to how to read your paper. The visual pattern of paragraphs on a page helps show the paper's organization: when a new paragraph begins, readers expect a new idea to begin, too. Readers expect that within a single paragraph, each sentence will help develop a single main idea — that the paragraph will be **unified.** They expect that the paragraph will present its ideas in a logical order — that it will be **well organized.** And they expect that each sentence will relate clearly to the sentences around it — that the paragraph will hold together as a single unit, or be **coherent.** If your paragraphs don't satisfy these expectations, readers will have a hard time following your ideas.

Most writers break their work into paragraphs intuitively, without much conscious thought. Look at a draft you have written; you have probably organized the text by starting new paragraphs at places where you leave one thought and begin to develop another. As you edit, make sure you have made the best choices possible. You'll probably find that your intuition has strayed off the mark once or twice. When editing your writing, keep these guidelines in mind:

- Make sure that paragraphs are unified.

- Make sure that paragraphs are well organized.

- Make sure that paragraphs are coherent.

25 a | Ensuring that paragraphs are unified

To evaluate paragraph unity, you must first determine the paragraph's main idea, or **topic.** In college writing, usually that idea should be stated directly, in a **topic sentence.** Sometimes a paragraph's topic can be communicated more subtly. Readers can infer a topic from a series of related sentences that do not include an explicit topic sentence. In either case, a paragraph should contain only one main idea. Anything that does not support or clarify this idea should be eliminated. Sometimes you can simply delete stray words or sentences. If the words or sentences are important, however, you should consider moving them to another paragraph or creating a new paragraph where they will be more effective.

For example, in the following passage Amy identified the first sentence as the topic sentence: *For various reasons, some unhappy couples remain married.* When she read each of the other sentences carefully to see whether they described reasons for staying married, she realized that the fourth sentence was out of place. She decided to move this sentence to the next paragraph, which dealt with a new topic.

■   For various reasons, some unhappy couples remain married. Some are forbidden to divorce by religion, others by social custom. Still others stay together "for the sake of the children." In recent years, psychologists and sociologists have studied families to determine whether more harm is done to children by divorce or by parents who stay together despite conflict. But by staying together, such parents feel, *believing* they are sparing their children the pain of divorce.

In his study of family conflict, Robert S. Weiss found that children in such families were often happiest "when Daddy is at work.". . .

■ **EDITING 1: PRACTICE**

Strengthen the following paragraphs by editing to ensure unity.

A.   College radio stations do not receive lavish gifts, but they are not neglected in the grand sweep of promotions that back college-targeted records. The station I worked at has received everything from posters to gold records to bottles of liquor. Whether the promotions actually get records played is hard to document. The most common gifts are passes to performances and free copies of records.

B.   The idea of planning seems simple enough. Communities are asked to designate areas for specific purposes, such as commercial, residential, or industrial use. The state's new requirement that every city and township formulate a plan may create a shortage of planners. Trying to pinpoint exactly what a planner does is a little more complicated.

■ **EDITING 2: APPLICATION**

Select a paragraph from a paper you are working on. First identify the topic sentence. Then examine each sentence to see whether it directly supports the topic sentence. If there are any sentences or ideas that don't seem to contribute to the main idea of the paragraph, try omitting them. Edit the paragraph by eliminating any other elements that detract from its main point. How does your edited paragraph compare with the original?

25	b	**Ensuring that paragraphs are well organized**

The way you organize your ideas within each paragraph also helps readers understand your writing. Arranging your sentences in a pattern — for example, one that moves from a general statement to specific statements — helps readers follow your ideas. When ideas are presented in no apparent order, readers can be easily confused. When editing for paragraph organization, you must decide where in the paragraph to put the topic sentence and use a recognizable pattern of organization.

1 **Placement of the topic sentence**

Usually a topic sentence is most effective at the beginning of a paragraph. If you find a topic sentence buried in the middle of a paragraph, consider moving it to the beginning.

■ ‸ Edward Lewis of the Greater Yellowstone Coalition, a regional conservation group, views wolves as the missing link: they are the only major native species missing from Yellowstone. Reintroducing wolves to Yellowstone would make the park a complete ecosystem once again. Wolves would help balance the ecosystem by preying on deer, elk, and moose, thus reducing the damage that overpopulation of these animals does to their habitat. Wolf predation would also reduce the numbers of these animals that starve during harsh winters.

Sometimes, as when you want to build to a strong conclusion, you may find it effective to put a topic sentence at the end of the paragraph.

■ Farley Mowat's *Never Cry Wolf* gives readers a greater appreciation for the intelligence, beauty, and dignity of the timber wolf. Perhaps the new understanding gained by reading this book will lead to greater respect for other species and to a stronger determination that they be able to live with dignity, free from human meddling. We recognize that the so-called human characteristics of monogamy, playfulness, and a sense of humor exist in species other than our own. We come to share Mowat's frustration with the narrow-minded "sportsmen" and government officials who continue to slaughter these animals. ∧

2 Standard patterns of organization

The sentences and ideas within a paragraph should follow a logical order, one that is appropriate to the subject and conveys the point of the paragraph effectively. When editing, check each paragraph to make sure the sentences within it are organized logically. If you are using a word processor, you may find it helpful to insert returns so that each sentence begins on a new line. This will make it easier for you to rearrange the order of the sentences and find the best possible organization. You may also want to use the copy function to make several copies of the paragraph so that you can compare different methods of organization.

One common pattern for organizing paragraphs is **general to specific.** You begin the paragraph by stating the principal idea in a topic sentence. The subsequent sentences contain specific examples that support, explain, and expand on that idea.

Many athletes have improved their performance by using steroids. One such athlete is track star Ben Johnson, who won the Olympic gold medal in 1988 in the hundred-meter dash. After a couple of days, Johnson's medal was taken away because he had tested positive for the use of steroids. His steroid use had increased his leg strength and therefore made him a

GENERAL STATEMENT

SPECIFIC EXAMPLE

faster runner. Another example is Benji Ramirez, a **SPECIFIC EXAMPLE** former student at Central State University. He played on the JV team for two years and wanted to be good enough for the varsity squad. He decided to do this by increasing his physical strength, and the method he chose was using steroids. By his senior year, he was a starter on the varsity team.

A **specific-to-general** pattern of organization begins with a series of details or examples and ends with a general statement, the topic sentence. Saving the topic sentence for last gives it more impact than placing it earlier in the paragraph.

I began by oversleeping — somehow I had forgot- **SPECIFIC EXAMPLE** ten to set my alarm clock. Then I had to drink my **SPECIFIC EXAMPLE** morning coffee black and eat my cereal dry because my roommate hadn't replaced the quart of milk she finished yesterday. After missing my bus and arriving late for my first class, I discovered that the history paper I thought was due next week was actually due today. And because my lab partner was still mad at me from the mess I made of things last week, we accomplished almost nothing in two hours. All in all, it was a terrible day.

A discussion of related events can be organized in **chronological** order, the order in which they happened. The topic sentence, a general statement summarizing the events and perhaps interpreting them, can appear at the beginning or end of the paragraph.

Before the arrival of Europeans, Haiti was popu- **EVENT 1** lated by the Arawak tribes. Within fifty years after **EVENT 2** Columbus set foot on the island in December 1492, the Arawaks had nearly died out, victims of disease and enslavement. The Spanish colonists imported **EVENT 3** blacks from Africa to replace the natives as slaves on their plantations. Late in the seventeenth century, the **EVENT 4** island was ceded to France but was the subject of dispute among England, Spain, and France for decades before achieving independence. The population of **GENERAL STATEMENT** Haiti today, predominantly black and French-speaking, reflects that history.

Sometimes paragraphs relating a series of events are better

arranged in **reverse chronological** order, looking back from the most recent to the most distant.

An appeal to logic might be arranged in **climactic** order, beginning with a general statement, presenting specific details in order of increasing importance, and ending with a dramatic statement, a climax.

> Consider the potential effect of just a small increase in the earth's atmospheric temperature. A rise of only a few degrees could melt the polar ice caps. Rainfall patterns would change. Some deserts might bloom, but lands now fertile might turn to desert, and many hot climates could become uninhabitable. If the sea level rose only a few feet, dozens of coastal cities would be destroyed, and life as we know it would be changed utterly.

GENERAL STATEMENT

SPECIFICS IN INCREASING IMPORTANCE

CLIMAX

A physical description can be organized in **spatial** order, moving from one detail to another as the eye would move. As in the chronological paragraph, the topic sentence, a general statement summarizing and interpreting the details, can appear at the beginning or end.

> Above the mantelpiece hung an ancient wheel lock musket that gave every indication of being in working order. A small collection of pewter, most of it dating from the colonial period, was arrayed across the mantel. To the left of the hearth stood a collection of wrought-iron fireplace tools and a bellows of wood and leather with brass fittings. At the right, a brass hopper held several cut limbs of what might have been an apple tree. On an iron hook in the fireplace hung a copper kettle, blackened with age and smoke. The fireplace looked as though it had changed little since the Revolution.

SPECIFICS ARRANGED SPATIALLY

GENERAL STATEMENT

▪ EDITING 3: PRACTICE

Strengthen the following paragraphs by editing to improve organization.

A. The machine sucks the milk out of the cows with a vacuum. The vacuum pulsates so that the cows' teats won't lose circulation. Eight cows were lined up in the milking parlor, chewing their cuds and waiting to be mechanically milked. The workers put a black rubber tube over each teat on each cow's udder and turned on the milking machine. The milk flows through clear plastic hoses into glass jars and is siphoned from there into a tank.

B. After the state legislature passed the Interstate Banking Act of 1987, First State Bank approached state regulators with a plan to merge with the Bank of the Ozarks. Interstate banking is new to the banking industry. Legislation passed before the Great Depression barred interstate banking in an effort to reduce the potential of bank failures and focus banks' investments on their own communities. Given that history, a merger plan like First State's should be evaluated for its effects on local communities and on the stability of the newly created bank.

■ **EDITING 4: APPLICATION**

Make a copy of a paragraph from a paper you are working on, and experiment to find the best possible organization for it. First, disassemble the paragraph so that each sentence stands alone, either by cutting with scissors or by starting each sentence on a new line on the computer screen. Next, find the topic sentence and set it aside. Then play with the order of the sentences until you find one that seems particularly effective; you may want to try some of the patterns of organization discussed in 25b. Next, decide whether the topic sentence belongs at the beginning or the end of the paragraph. Finally, rewrite the paragraph using the new organization, making any necessary changes in wording. How does this edited version compare with the original?

25 **C** **Ensuring that paragraphs are coherent**

1 **Shortening long paragraphs**

In a coherent paragraph, each sentence connects naturally with the surrounding ones in a manner that readers can easily follow. Shortening long paragraphs, using transitional expressions, and deliberately repeating key words can all contribute to coherence.

Long paragraphs often lack coherence. Readers may lose the thread of what you are saying even when the paragraph is unified around a single topic sentence. Breaking a long paragraph into several smaller pieces often results in greater coherence within each of the resulting paragraphs.

■   During a divorce, parents have the ability to shield a child from most of the potential harm. Most couples who stay together believe that the two-parent structure is important to the child's well-being and that changing this pattern upsets a child. [¶]A child's security is based on his or her relationship with each parent individually, according to studies by Judith Wallerstein, who found that stable, caring relationships between a child and each parent are the most significant ingredient in raising a child. If these relationships are maintained, the effect of divorce on a child's emotions is much reduced. Indeed, maintaining even one stable relationship would appear to be better than a weak connection with both parents.[¶]During the early stages of a breakup, both parents are often distracted by other issues. The child may suffer as a result.

An essay consisting of many short paragraphs, however, can seem choppy, and the ideas can appear disconnected. When editing your writing, look for places where several small paragraphs develop what is essentially one idea. They would be better joined into larger paragraphs.

You may want to take advantage of your word processor's ability to quickly reformat text to try out different paragraphing solutions. Try breaking paragraphs into smaller units — groups of sentences or even individual sentences — and then building them back up again. You can use the copy function to make several copies of a passage so you can compare your different solutions.

2 **Transitional expressions**

Transitional expressions connect distinct ideas. They can indicate that one idea expands, exemplifies, qualifies, summarizes, implies, or results from another. They can also contrast, compare, or show relationships in time and space. For example, *earlier* or *afterward* marks a shift in time; *in regard to*, a shift in subject; *in addition* or *by implication*, a logical connection; and *elsewhere*, *above*, or *nearby*, a shift in location.

TRANSITIONAL EXPRESSIONS

EXPANDING
and, also, besides, finally, further, in addition, moreover, then

EXEMPLIFYING
as an illustration, for example, for instance, in fact, specifically, thus

QUALIFYING
but, certainly, however, to be sure

SUMMARIZING
and so, finally, in conclusion, in short, in sum, this experiment shows, thus we see

RELATING LOGICALLY
as a result, because, by implication, for this reason, from this we can see, if, since, so, therefore

COMPARING
also, as well, likewise, similarly

CONTRASTING
but, even though, nevertheless, still, yet

RELATING IN TIME
after, before, between, earlier, later, longer than, meanwhile, since

RELATING IN SPACE
above, adjacent to, behind, below, beyond, in front of, next to, north of, over, through, within

ESL **SUGGESTIONS FOR USING TRANSITIONAL EXPRESSIONS**

You can learn to use transitional expressions effectively by practicing and by paying attention to how others use them in writing. Here are some guidelines for deciding whether you need a transitional expression and which one to use.

1. Shifts that readers may not expect need transitions more than those that are expected. For example, a contrast or contradiction is often unexpected and needs a transition.

The film's plot is very predictable and the characters not especially likable. *Nevertheless,* the movie is worth seeing for the skillful cinematography and fine acting.

Other logical relationships, such as time sequence, are often obvious from the context and do not need a transitional phrase.

The main character of the film moves to Brazil. He finds a job in a large corporation and settles into a routine.

Although you could use then *in the second sentence to signal the time relationship, the reader can infer the sequence easily from the content.*

2. If you use a series of transitional expressions to signal a sequence or to list points, make sure they are parallel. For example, use *first, second,* and *last* to introduce three different points, but don't use *first, in the second place,* and *the last.* If you're not sure which expressions are used together, consult your instructor or a native speaker of English.

3. If you repeatedly use one-word transitions to begin sentences, your writing may sound choppy or monotonous. Try editing your transitions in the following ways.

■ Consider omitting some transitions. (See point number I above.)

■ Put some of the transitional expressions in the middle of sentences: *Keeping a journal is helpful, in addition, because. . . .* If you're not sure where in the sentence a transitional expression can or should go, ask someone for help.

4. Try to use a variety of transitional expressions. Don't use the same ones over and over. For example, instead of always using *first, second,* and *third* to list sequences, consider using *for example, also,* and *finally.*

Wherever your flow of ideas shifts, you should provide smooth transitions. Without them, readers may be confronted with a seemingly unrelated string of facts. Here is a paragraph with no transitional expressions:

> Newspaper and magazine publishing is not usually regarded as cyclic. This recession has cut deeply into advertising revenue. The economy is gathering steam. Classified-ad buyers should return. Display advertising will lag. Publications that have sharply cut their costs should see strong upturns in their profits as advertisers return. The coming year looks rosy.

Here is the same paragraph with transitional expressions added:

> Newspaper and magazine publishing is not usually regarded as cyclic, *but* this recession has cut deeply into advertising revenue. *However*, with the economy gathering steam, classified-ad buyers should return, *although* display advertising will lag. *Meanwhile*, publications that have sharply cut their costs should see strong upturns in their profits as advertisers return. *For them*, the coming year looks rosy.

When you edit, examine each change of subject, time, or setting to see whether you have adequately marked the transition.

Often the changes you make while restructuring paragraphs will necessitate new transitions to help readers understand where your ideas are heading. Look again at the edited example from the paper about divorce, in which one long paragraph was broken into three. To clarify how the three new paragraphs and the sentences within them related to one another, the writer added two transitional sentences.

■   During a divorce, parents have the ability to shield a child

from most of the potential harm. Most couples who stay together

believe that the two-parent structure is important to the child's

well-being and that changing this pattern upsets a child.
     This, however, appears not to be the case.
   A child's security is based on his or her relationship with
 ^

each parent individually, according to studies by Judith Waller-

stein, who found that stable, caring relationships between a child and each parent are the most significant ingredient in raising a child. If these relationships are maintained, the effect of divorce on a child's emotions is much reduced. Indeed, maintaining even one stable relationship would appear to be better than a weak connection with both parents.

The issue during divorce, then, is how well a child can maintain

During the early stages of a breakup, both parents are often
at least one
distracted by other issues. The child may suffer as a result. secure
relationship

The first transitional sentence emphasizes a logical contrast. The second marks a shift of subject.

3 **Using deliberate repetition**

Repeating key words can help create coherence by linking sentences. Key words are usually related either to the topic sentence of the paragraph or to one of the important details presented in support of the topic sentence. Deliberately repeating these key words now and then reminds readers of your main ideas within the paragraph. In the following example, *dispute, opposed,* and the related words *opponents* and *proponents* are all key words reminding the readers of the topic of the paragraph, *the controversy over Northgate Mall.*

> The *controversy* over Northgate Mall has continued for at least five years. The *dispute* has divided the city into two camps. A small group seems *opposed* to the mall, but its members are vocal and energetic. The *opponents* maintain that it would rob trade from existing businesses downtown and contribute to traffic congestion. *Proponents* say that the growth it would bring would be easily manageable.

Be careful, however, not to use too much repetition in a short paragraph or your writing will become redundant.

EDITING 5: APPLICATION

Strengthen the following paragraph by editing to improve coherence. Consider the use of transitional expressions, the order of sentences, and the use of repetition. More than one edited version is possible. Be ready to explain your editing choices.

The number of people accepted at the detoxification center is another issue. If they are violent or if they need specialized medical attention, those brought to the center are not allowed to stay. These policies would seem to restrict the center's effectiveness in reaching everyone who needs help. However, the director, Wanda Rasmussen, defends them as necessary to protect the staff and make sure resources are used efficiently. Others may not have a high enough blood alcohol level to warrant detoxification. About half the people brought to the center are turned away and sent to the "drunk tank" at the city jail.

■ EDITING 6: PRACTICE

Strengthen the following passage by editing to improve its unity, organization, and coherence.

The zoning board rejected the proposal. The plan was the subject of three evenings of raucous debate. Then the city council took it up on appeal. The disagreement continued there for months. Some members said their first responsibility was to promote economic development in any form. The debate on the council reflected the divisions in the community. Growth should be regulated so that it does not harm existing businesses or the city as a whole, others believed. The project was approved two weeks after the new mayor took office. Amanda Robbins campaigned for mayor by rallying downtown businesspeople, historic preservationists, and neighborhood activists against the mall. Council member Steven McMillan ran on a pro-development, pro-mall platform. Both candidates said they wanted voters to end the deadlock on the proposal. The election was won by McMillan.

Grouping ideas into sentences tells the reader how your ideas are related. If each idea is expressed as an individual sentence, it seems separate and unrelated to the others — the reader faces a string of isolated facts rather than a unified passage. **Sentence structure** can clarify the relationships among ideas, first by bringing together closely related ideas and second by indicating how they are related.

Using subordination, coordination, and parallelism can strengthen the structure of sentences and clarify their meaning. Joining sentences or parts of sentences through **coordination** implies that they are of equal importance to the writer's point. Joining them through **subordination** implies that one element is less important than (subordinate to) another. By creating a contrast, subordinating one element also distinguishes another element as more important. By using coordination or subordination to restructure two sentences as one, you can show how their meanings interact.

SEPARATE SENTENCES James Baldwin writes in simple words. His writing conveys deep anger.

COORDINATION James Baldwin writes in simple words, *but* his writing conveys deep anger.

Both ideas are equally important to the writer's point; the conjunction but *emphasizes the contrast between them.*

SUBORDINATION *Although* James Baldwin writes in simple words, his writing conveys deep anger.

By subordinating the clause describing Baldwin's choice of words, the writer emphasizes Baldwin's anger.

Writers use **parallelism** — the repetition of a grammatical structure — to emphasize a similarity between ideas. The repetition may consist of words, phrases, clauses, sentences, or even entire paragraphs. Parallelism creates symmetry and balance, which can both clarify the meaning of a sentence and enhance its elegance.

> *No eye can see, no hand can touch, no tongue can name* the devils that plague him.

When editing your writing, look for places where the relationships between ideas are unclear or misleading. To clarify the relationships, consider the following techniques:

- Relate equal ideas through coordination.

- Combine choppy sentences using coordination.

- Use coordination to create special effects.

- Avoid ineffective coordination.

- Distinguish main ideas from less important ideas through subordination.

- Combine choppy sentences using subordination.

- Avoid ineffective subordination.

- Create parallel structures where needed.

- Use parallelism to create emphasis.

- Correct faulty parallelism.

COORDINATION

26 a Using coordination to relate equal ideas

Coordination implies that ideas should be given equal attention. As you edit your writing, look for places where ideas need to be balanced through coordination.

Two or more sentences, or **independent clauses,** can be combined into a single **compound sentence** in several ways. The most common method is to join the clauses with a **coordinating**

Using coordination to relate equal ideas 355

conjunction (*and*, *but*, *or*, *nor*, *so*, *for*, *yet*) and a comma. Each coordinating conjunction expresses a different relationship; your choice should be based on the meaning you wish to convey.

■ Incoming students must pass a placement examination to meet the foreign language requirement/, ~~Those who fail the test~~ must _or they_ register for an introductory language course.

Another way to coordinate two independent clauses is by using a pair of **correlative conjunctions** such as *both . . . and*, *either . . . or*, or *not only . . . but also*.

COORDINATING CONJUNCTIONS, CORRELATIVE CONJUNCTIONS, AND CONJUNCTIVE ADVERBS

RELATIONSHIP	COORDINATING CONJUNCTIONS
addition	*and*
contrast	*but, yet*
choice	*or, nor*
effect	*so*
causation	*for*

RELATIONSHIP	CORRELATIVE CONJUNCTIONS
addition	*both . . . and*
	not only . . . but also
choice	*either . . . or*
substitution	*not . . . but*
negation	*neither . . . nor*

RELATIONSHIP	CONJUNCTIVE ADVERBS
addition	*also, besides, furthermore, moreover*
contrast	*however, instead, nevertheless, otherwise*
comparison	*similarly, likewise*
effect	*accordingly, consequently, therefore, thus*
sequence	*finally, meanwhile, next, then*
emphasis	*indeed, certainly*

- **Not only did Lavar ~~won~~ win high honors in mathematics and physics ~~.~~, but he ~~He~~ was also recognized for his achievement in biology.**

If you use a **conjunctive adverb** such as *however, moreover,* or *nevertheless* to join two independent clauses, you must also use a semicolon.

- **An Advanced Placement Test score will be accepted ~~.~~; however ~~However~~, the test must have been taken within the last year.**

You can also use a semicolon alone to join two independent clauses, if the relationship between the ideas is apparent.

- **Taking an introductory language course will fulfill the foreign language requirement ~~.~~; the ~~The~~ courses are offered during the fall semester.**

Using coordination to join nouns, verbs, modifiers, phrases, or clauses into **compound elements** allows the writer to combine sentences that would otherwise seem repetitive. (Also see 26h.)

- **The police and the district attorney should be interested in the results of the investigation. ~~The district attorney should also be interested.~~**

When considering whether to use coordination to join two sentences, ask yourself whether the meaning of the sentences is related closely enough to warrant being joined. Then consider whether they are of equal importance to your point. (If not, subordination may work better. See 26e.) Choose the method of coordination carefully to express the relationship you intend between the two ideas. By using coordination skillfully, you can suggest connections, avoid repetition, and enhance readability.

26 b Using coordination to combine choppy sentences

When every idea is expressed in a separate sentence, the result is a choppy, disjointed passage that moves along in baby

Using coordination to create special effects 357

steps rather than at a comfortable stride. Choppy passages leave readers unsure of how the ideas are connected and usually contain needless repetition. When editing a choppy passage, use coordination to connect ideas that are equally important to the point you want to make.

■ To generate electricity, utilities burn tremendous quantities of coal~~, Another fuel widely used is~~ oil/, ~~Many~~ utilities also operate
    and   *but many*
hydroelectric dams.

(Subordination can also improve a choppy passage; see 26f.)

▦ EDITING I: PRACTICE

Edit the following passage, using coordination to relate ideas of equal importance and to combine choppy sentences. More than one edited version is possible. Be ready to explain your editing choices.

The workers were instructed to seal the oiled rags in cans. They forgot to do it. At night the rags caught fire. The fire spread rapidly through the storage area. A smoke detector went off. No one noticed. The alarm was relayed to the fire station. Fire fighters raced to the warehouse. Flames already were darting through the windows. Smoke poured through the ceiling. Glass cracked in the heat. It shattered. The fire commander turned in a second alarm. Another company sped toward the scene.

| **26** | **c** | **Using coordination to create special effects** |

Occasionally repeating coordinate structures can give your writing a rhythm, create a cumulative effect, or build to a climax: *We had no home and no work and no food and no hope.* In one of his essays, E. B. White describes a bareback rider in a circus, circling a ring on horseback again and again. The repetitive coordination emphasizes the rhythm of the scene's action:

> The rider's gaze, as she peered straight ahead, seemed to be circular, as though bent by force of circumstance; then time itself

began running in circles, *and* so the beginning was where the end was, *and* the two were the same, *and* one thing ran into the next, *and* time went round *and* around *and* got nowhere. [Italics added.]

E. B. WHITE, "THE RING OF TIME"

EDITING 2: EXPLORATION

Read the following passage from a personal narrative by N. Scott Momaday. How has Momaday used coordination? How many examples can you find of ideas joined by coordinating conjunctions? By semicolons? Could any of these ideas have been joined in other ways? If they had been, how would the effect of the passage have been different?

"Once there was a lot of sound in my grandmother's house, a lot of coming and going, feasting and talk. The summers there were full of excitement and reunion. The Kiowas are a summer people; they abide the cold and keep to themselves, but when the season turns and the land becomes warm and vital they cannot hold still; an old love of going returns upon them. The aged visitors who came to my grandmother's house when I was a child were made of lean and leather, and they bore themselves upright. They wore great black hats and bright ample shirts that shook in the wind. They rubbed fat upon their hair and wound their braids with strips of colored cloth. Some of them painted their faces and carried the scars of old and cherished enmities."

N. SCOTT MOMADAY, *THE WAY TO RAINY MOUNTAIN*

26 d Avoiding ineffective coordination

1 Illogical coordination

Because coordination implies equal relationships between ideas, misusing coordination can confuse readers. When editing your writing, look for places where coordination sends a confusing message.

Some ideas are not related closely enough to be coordinated meaningfully:

I had eggs for breakfast, and I missed the bus.

If there is a connection between these two statements, it must be explained. Showing cause and effect, for example, is better done with subordination: *Because I took time to cook eggs for breakfast, I missed the bus.* (See 26e.)

Faulty coordination can also imply a connection between ideas that is not simply confusing but inaccurate:

■ The project was a huge undertaking, ~~yet~~ *so* I was exhausted at the end.

The conjunction yet *implies contrast, but contrast between the two clauses is inappropriate. The conjunction* so *properly implies a cause-and-effect relationship.*

2 Overused coordination

Coordination can be overdone, and when it is used too much it begins to sound repetitive, and readers may begin to imagine the voice of a young child speaking in sentences that just go on and on, strung together with *and*, and soon they may get tired or confused or bored, and as a writer you should try to prevent that.

How much is too much? You will have to decide for yourself. Read the sentence aloud — does it strike you as powerful, like the passage quoted earlier from E. B. White's essay? Or as inane, like the deliberate excess of the preceding paragraph? To fix a sentence containing too many coordinate structures, move some elements into separate sentences. You must choose, according to the meaning you intend, which elements belong together and which should stand alone. You must listen to how the whole passage sounds. For example, the preceding paragraph could be rewritten like this:

■ Coordination can be overdone. *When* ~~and when~~ it is used too much it begins to sound repetitive. *Readers* ~~and readers~~ may begin to imagine the voice of a young child speaking in sentences that just go on and on, strung together with *and*. *Soon* ~~and soon~~ they may get tired or confused or bored. *As* ~~and as~~ a writer you should try to prevent that.

If you think you tend to overuse coordination, you may want to use your word processor's search-and-replace function to find every instance of the conjunctions *and, but,* and *or* and underline them, put them in boldface type, or otherwise highlight them. This will allow you to see at a glance how often you have used coordination and will make it easier for you to reconsider the effectiveness of each case.

■ **EDITING 3: PRACTICE**

Edit the following passage to eliminate ineffective coordination. More than one edited version is possible. Be ready to explain your editing choices.

At the start of *The Bridge across Forever,* the narrator is a stunt pilot performing in small towns of the American Midwest, and the narrator and the author seem to have much in common. The author writes about flying, and the narrator takes people for rides in his plane, but he is bored with the routine, but he is convinced that he will find the perfect woman at one of these shows, so he keeps going. Disillusioned at last, he gives up flying to pursue his quest, and he encounters many women, but none of them is the soul mate he is seeking.

SUBORDINATION

26 **e** **Using subordination to distinguish main ideas**

Like coordination, **subordination** joins ideas and implies a relationship between them. In addition, it focuses attention on certain ideas by de-emphasizing, or subordinating, others. When considering subordination as an editing choice, you must think about your intended meaning and desired emphasis. Put the less important idea in a subordinate structure.

NO SUBORDINATION   Tom Peters has become a phenomenon among business writers. He focuses on excellence and quality.

SUBORDINATION   Tom Peters, *who focuses on excellence and quality*, has become a phenomenon among business writers.

This construction emphasizes Peters's status as a phenomenon.

SUBORDINATION   Tom Peters, *who has become a phenomnon among business writers*, focuses on excellence and quality.

This construction emphasizes the focus of Peters's writing.

A subordinate element may appear as a clause, a phrase, or even a single word.

NO SUBORDINATION   The committee selected a plan. It seemed to leave nothing to chance.

CLAUSE   The plan *that the committee selected* seemed to leave nothing to chance.

PHRASE   The plan *selected by the committee* seemed to leave nothing to chance.

WORD   The plan *selected* seemed to leave nothing to chance.

In this series of examples, the subordinated idea (*The committee selected a plan*) grows less and less important grammatically — from clause to phrase to word. The way you subordinate an idea should depend on how important it is to your meaning and flow of your passage. (See 65e and 65f for more about phrases and clauses, respectively.)

A **dependent** or **subordinate clause** contains a subject and a verb but cannot stand alone as a full sentence. A dependent clause is usually introduced by a **subordinating conjunction** such as *although, because, if, since, whether,* or *while* or a **relative pronoun** such as *who, which,* or *that.* Once one of these subordinating elements is added, a clause cannot stand alone. *The train arrived late* is a full sentence, but *When the train arrived late* is not.

Using a subordinating conjunction makes the clause an **adverb clause:**

■ The plan has a chance of success/,It requires the efforts of several people. *[although it]*

■ *[Because one]* ~~One~~ person must be available to explain each course offering to students/,~~Many~~ people are needed. *[many]*

Introducing a dependent clause with a relative pronoun usually makes the clause an **adjective clause.** Relative pronouns include *however, that, what, whatever, which, whichever, who, whoever, whom, whomever,* and *whose.*

■ The gap between rich and poor,has caused great concern among economists. ~~The gap has been widening for nearly twenty years.~~ *[which has been widening for nearly twenty years,]*

■ I have interviewed several economists/ ~~They~~ believe that the gap will continue to grow. *[who]*

Another way to subordinate one sentence to another is to use one as a **noun clause,** that is, to use it as as you would a noun, as a subject or as an object. A noun clause can be introduced by why, what, that, where, whether, or how:

■ The entire department became interested/,~~Other teachers and students wanted to learn about Cate's discoveries~~ *[in what Cate was discovering.]*

SUBORDINATING CONJUNCTIONS

RELATIONSHIP	SUBORDINATING CONJUNCTIONS
cause/effect	*as, because, since, so, so that, in order that*
condition	*if, even if, unless, if only*
contrast	*although, even though, though*
comparison	*than, as though, as if, whereas, while*
choice	*whether, than, rather than*
sequence	*after, as, as long as, as soon as, before, once, since, till, until, when, whenever, while*
space	*where, wherever, whence*

ESL **EXPRESSING LOGICAL RELATIONSHIPS USING SUBORDINATION**

In editing your writing, notice whether you tend to use coordinating conjunctions and conjunctive adverbs to express logical relationships most of the time. If you do, consider using an occasional subordinating conjunction, especially when you have one idea that is related to another but is not as important.

COORDINATING CONJUNCTION	Freud believed that our dreams reflect our unconscious wishes, *but* some psychologists today believe otherwise.
CONJUNCTIVE ADVERB	Freud believed that our dreams reflect our unconscious wishes. *However,* some psychologists today believe otherwise.
SUBORDINATING CONJUNCTION	*While* Freud believed that our dreams reflect our unconscious wishes, some psychologists today believe otherwise.

The following are logical relationships expressed by the three types of connectors. Be careful not to overuse any one type.

RELATIONSHIP	COORDINATING CONJUNCTIONS	CONJUNCTIVE ADVERBS	SUBORDINATING CONJUNCTIONS
Contrast	but	however	while, whereas
Concession	but	nevertheless	although, though
Cause/effect	for, so	therefore, consequently	because, since, so that
Sequence	and	then, later, finally	after, before, until, when

■ ~~There are basic facts~~ we know today about AIDS. ~~They are~~ the
 ^what   ^is
result of years of painstaking research.

When considering whether to use subordination to join two sentences, ask yourself whether the sentences are related in meaning and whether one is less important to your point than the other. (See coordination, 26a, for sentences that are equal in importance.) Use the method of subordination that will most clearly express the relationship you intend between the two ideas. Using dependent clauses, you will be able to build an elaborate structure of information, buttressing main ideas with related but less important ones.

> ✔ **PUNCTUATING SUBORDINATE STRUCTURES**
>
> A dependent clause is not set off by commas if it is **restrictive** — that is, necessary to identify the word it modifies. A **nonrestrictive** dependent clause, one that is not needed to identify the word it modifies, is set off by commas.
>
> **RESTRICTIVE** He likes cats *that seem self-reliant and not too familiar.*
> The dependent clause is restrictive because it identifies particular cats.
>
> **NONRESTRICTIVE** He likes his cats, *which seem self-reliant and not too familiar.*
> The dependent clause is nonrestrictive because *his cats* has already identified the specific cats.
>
> (See 44c for a complete discussion of punctuating clauses and phrases.)

 Using subordination to combine choppy sentences

A series of short, one-idea sentences can sound choppy and disjointed, leaving readers unsure of the connections you intend between ideas. When editing a choppy passage, use **subordination** to connect ideas by emphasizing some and de-emphasizing others. (Coordination can also improve a choppy passage; see 26b.)

In the following paragraph, Dana used subordination to eliminate choppiness.

Although they are quite different restaurants,
∧Arcadia and Canastel have both become popular within the

past year. ~~They are quite different restaurants.~~ To succeed in

New York, a restaurant should not emulate a certain style. ~~It~~ *will respond best if it sets* ~~must set~~ its own style and *excels* ~~excel~~ at it. ~~Customers will respond best to that,~~ Arcadia and Canastel both accomplish this goal, *even though they* ~~They~~ do it in different ways. Canastel creates an environment in which people can feel socially important and at the same time have a good meal, *whereas* Arcadia provides the ultimate in dining within an intimate atmosphere.

For more about using subordination to combine sentences, see 27a and 27b.

■ **EDITING 4: PRACTICE**

Edit the following passage, using subordination to clarify the relationships between ideas and to eliminate choppiness. More than one edited version is possible. Be ready to explain your editing choices.

Ellen Goodman grabs our attention. She does not let it go for an entire article. Her occasional use of wit or irony makes us laugh. Also she makes us aware of problems around us. She offers no solutions. She is not so much trying to change the world single-handed. She is trying to inspire us to set wrongs to right.

26 g **Avoiding ineffective subordination**

1 Illogical subordination

As you edit, watch for inappropriate or illogical subordination, which can confuse readers.

Subordinating the wrong element can change the meaning and logic of a sentence.

INDEPENDENT SENTENCES Some scientists have examined this theory carefully. They have spoken out against it.

INCORRECT SUBORDINATION Some scientists who have spoken out against this theory have examined it carefully.

This wrongly implies that some who oppose the theory have not examined it carefully.

CORRECT
SUBORDINATION   Some scientists who have examined this theory carefully have spoken out against it.

This more clearly states that the scientists who have examined the theory oppose it.

Careless subordination may suggest causal relationships that you do not intend.

■ The nation was plunged into a deep recession, ~~when~~ Ronald Reagan took office in 1981.

which began shortly after

The writer did not intend to imply that Reagan's election caused a recession.

2 Overused subordination

Sometimes you may create passages that rely too much on subordination, which can make them sound insipid, because every point seems to be qualified, while nothing is said directly. When considering whether you have subordinated too much, ask yourself which ideas are most closely related. You can probably leave subordination between them. Ideas with weaker connections probably should be separated into independent sentences. Consider the initial sentence in this paragraph with excessive subordination removed:

■ Sometimes you may create passages that rely too much on subordination. ~~which~~ *This* can make them sound insipid. ~~because every~~ *Every* point seems to be qualified, while nothing is said directly.

If you think you tend to overuse subordination, you may want to use your word processor's search-and-replace function to find all instances of common subordinating conjunctions (*because, if, although*) and relative pronouns (*who, which, that*) and highlight them with underlining or boldfacing. This will allow you to see at a glance how often you have used subordination and will make it easier for you to reconsider the effectiveness of each case.

ESL ## USING SUBORDINATING CONJUNCTIONS

1. When you use *whereas*, *while*, *although*, *though*, or *even though* in a dependent clause to describe contrast or concession, do not use *but* before the independent clause.

■ Although a smile shows happiness in most cultures, ~~but~~ in some it

may be a sign of embarrassment.

2. When you use *because* or *since* in a dependent clause to describe a reason or cause, do not use *so* in the independent clause.

■ Because Rudolf Nureyev defected from Russia, ~~so~~ for many years

he could not return to dance in his native country.

3. *Because* and *because of* are not interchangeable. *Because* is a subordinating conjunction. Use it when your subordinate idea is expressed as a clause with a subject and verb.

      Subject   **Verb**

Because snow peas die in hot weather, you should plant them early in the spring.

Because of is a two-word preposition. Use it when your subordinate idea is expressed as a phrase with no verb.

      Phrase

Because of the hot weather, the peas did not grow well.

4. *Even* cannot be a subordinating conjunction by itself; it can modify a noun (*Even adults can enjoy this cartoon*), a verb (*She can even think in Chinese now*), or an adverb (*He likes to eat pizza when it's cold*).

    Even though is a subordinating conjunction meaning "despite the fact that."

          though

■ Even ⌄ don't play the piano well, I still enjoy taking lessons.

Even if is a subordinating conjunction meaning "whether or not."

        if

■ Even ⌄ it rains tomorrow, the race will be held.

■ **EDITING 5: PRACTICE**

Edit the following passage to eliminate ineffective subordination. More than one edited version is possible. Be ready to explain your editing choices.

The Doors completes what could be termed a sixties trilogy from Oliver Stone, since it differs greatly from *Platoon* and *Born on the Fourth of July*. Stone served in Vietnam, although that part of his work is grounded in personal experience. Because he did not experience the world of the Doors, Stone portrays it as he imagines it was, which makes his work in this film different from the others, although it is less effective and less compelling.

■ **EDITING 6: EXPLORATION**

The following passage describes the influence of politics on the decisions of art galleries such as the Corcoran Gallery of Art in Washington, D.C. How many examples of subordination can you find in the passage? Can you see why the author has used subordination rather than coordination to join ideas?

"Whatever grave reservations regarding Congress may have motivated the directors of the Corcoran, they weakened the entire social fabric by yielding their freedom. Their decision should have been to show the work, whose merit they must have believed in to have scheduled the exhibition. Since then individual members of Congress have revealed themselves as enemies of freedom by letting their aesthetic attitudes corrupt their political integrity as custodians of the deepest values of a democratic society."

ARTHUR C. DANTA, "ART AND TAXPAYERS"

PARALLELISM

26 **h** Creating parallel structures

Parallelism presents similar ideas in a similar fashion to emphasize their similarity. Parallel structures are common in everyday speech as well as in much effective writing.

To die, to sleep. To sleep, perchance to dream.

WILLIAM SHAKESPEARE, *HAMLET*

Do or die.

Where there's smoke, there's fire.

Marry in haste; repent at leisure.

To underscore the similarity of ideas, make sure the elements of a parallel structure are grammatically similar: words paired with words, phrases with phrases, clauses with clauses. The part of speech and the form should be similar, too: possessive nouns paired with possessive nouns, gerunds with gerunds, and so on. (See phrases and clauses in 65e and 65f, respectively, and parts of speech in Chapter 64.)

We saw the frogs *swim, jump,* and *eat.*

Getting into college had been Raymond's first goal, and *getting a 3.0 GPA* was his second.

Some grammatical structures require parallelism: compound elements, comparisons, and lists. If these structures lack parallelism, readers may be momentarily confused. You can use your computer's search function to find every use of common coordinating conjunctions (*and, or, but*), which often signal constructions that should be parallel.

■ Compound elements

Compound elements can be joined by a **coordinating conjunction** (*and, but, or, nor, so, for,* or *yet*) or by a pair of **correlative conjunctions** (*either . . . or, neither . . . nor, not only . . . but also, both . . . and, whether . . . or*). (See 26a.) When editing your writing, make sure that all compound elements are grammatically parallel.

■ He predicted that the day of judgment would cause the earth to shake and ~~wake~~ the dead ⸢to awaken⸣.

■ The school district can afford to make classes smaller, build a new school, and taxes ⸢cut⸣ ~~can be cut~~ too.

■ Wind-generated electric power is not only difficult to capture/ but also ⸢expensive to store.⸣ ~~it must be stored at great expense.~~

2 Comparisons

Because they are presented as equivalent alternatives, elements compared using *than* or *as* should be parallel in grammatical form.

■ Laura likes painting as much as ~~to read.~~ reading.

■ He always believed that effective communication was more a matter of clear thinking than ~~to try to write well.~~ good writing.

3 Lists

Elements presented in a series or list joined with *and* or *or* should be parallel in grammatical form.

■ Her favorite activities were painting, walking, and ~~she liked to visit~~ visiting museums.

26 i Using parallelism for emphasis

Perhaps parallel structures are so common because they are so effective. Few devices give written or spoken language greater power, gravity, and impact than the formal, rhythmic, and forceful words of a well-constructed parallel.

When you edit, consider using a parallel structure to highlight a contrast or to emphasize a major point.

■ With local leaders afraid of the "no-growth" label, the quality of local decision making has clearly declined. The question facing towns like Abilene is ~~whether they will do enough planning to avoid uncontrolled development.~~ not whether they will plan to have no growth but whether they will face growth with no plan.

To give resonance to her conclusion, Lilith used the parallel structure not whether . . . but whether *and added the parallel alternatives* no growth *and* no plan.

To help readers follow a complex thought, many writers use parallel structures inside other parallel structures — like sets of concentric circles. The effect is not only clarity but also the power and grace of a rhythmic chant. Read this example aloud and listen to the rhythm the writer establishes as the parallel structures grow more complex:

> I think a poor life is lived by anyone who doesn't regularly take time out to stand and gaze, or sit and listen, or touch, or smell, or brood, without any further end in mind, simply for the satisfaction gotten from that which is gazed at, listened to, touched, smelled, or brooded upon.
>
> CLEMENT GREENBERG, "THE CASE FOR ABSTRACT ART"

Be careful when using such complex forms of parallelism. The elements of each parallel structure must be carefully matched, and the passage as a whole must warrant the emphasis. (For more on introducing rhythm to your writing, see Chapter 27.)

■ **EDITING 7: EXPLORATION**

The following passage is from an essay on the position of African American women. Where has the author used parallelism? What ideas are emphasized through this use of parallelism? How is the passage as a whole strengthened?

"When we have pleaded for understanding, our character has been distorted; when we have asked for simple caring, we have been handed empty inspirational appellations, then stuck in the farthest corner. When we have asked for love, we have been given children. In short, even our plainer gifts, our labors of fidelity and love, have been knocked down our throats. To be an artist and a black woman, even today, lowers our status in many respects, rather than raises it: and yet, artists we will be."

ALICE WALKER, "IN SEARCH OF OUR MOTHERS' GARDENS"

26 **j** **Making parallel structures complete**

Parallelism is effective because it makes the comparison of words and ideas clear. When the words are not grammatically comparable, however, the ideas seem less similar, and the comparison, instead of being clear and pointed, becomes murky and ambiguous.

To bring faulty parallels into sharp focus, make sure to supply all necessary words. Words commonly omitted from parallel structures are prepositions (*to, for, at*), subordinating conjunctions (*although, since, because*), and relative pronouns (*who, which, that*).

■   The proposal was circulated first to the faculty senate and then
      to
      ∧the administration.

> *Without the second* to, *a reader might think* then the administration
> *was the beginning of a new independent clause, such as* . . . and
> then the administration reviewed it.

■   The researchers tried to ensure that interviewees were represen-
                                              that
      tative of the campus population and ∧their opinions reflected
      those of the whole student body.

> *Without the second* that, *it is unclear whether the clause beginning
> with* their opinions reflected *is part of a parallel structure or a second
> independent clause.*

In some cases, omitting words from parallel structures creates
not faulty parallelism but the stylistic device called elliptical construction. In an elliptical construction, words that readers can be
expected to supply are deliberately omitted to perk up the rhythm
of a passage.

■   Social responsibility is a duty; global thinking ~~is~~ an imperative;
      swift action ~~is~~ a necessity.

Elliptical constructions are an important stylistic device, but
you should use them only when you are certain that they will
cause no confusion. (See 27f for a complete discussion of how to
use elliptical construction.)

■   **EDITING 8: PRACTICE**

Strengthen sentence structures in the following paragraph by using parallelism
and elliptical structures. More than one edited version is possible. Be ready to
explain your editing choices.

The first cut on *Hope Chest* by 10,000 Maniacs uses a reggae sound in the keyboard. It has an insistent bass line and a guitar that sounds like a swarm of mosquitoes. The vocals are so intricately woven that during the bridge, two sets of lyrics are being sung at once. That sound creates the effect of a breakdown. It also creates the impression of the dissolving of structure.

■ EDITING 9: PRACTICE

Edit the following paragraph to correct faulty parallelism. More than one edited version is possible. Be ready to explain your editing choices.

First it rained, then hail was falling, and finally snow came down. As the temperature dropped, we moved our bedrolls closer to the fire, hung blankets over the windows, and more logs were added to the blaze. Nothing seemed to help. The thin walls seemed to invite the cold in. The wind whistled through cracks. The windows rattled in the wind. Snow drifted under the door.

■ EDITING 10: PRACTICE

Edit the following passage to strengthen sentence structure, using coordination, subordination, parallel structures, and elliptical structures as you think appropriate. Many edited versions are possible. Be ready to explain your editing choices.

Whether Hunter S. Thompson's world is reality or imagined, it makes for enjoyable reading. His humor arises from situations that are so frantic or such exaggerations as to be ludicrous. The writing moves from subject to subject, and it mimics the pattern of a drunken or drugged mind. His sentences ramble. His thoughts tumble. His subjects shift like colors in a hallucination. He somehow maintains a sense of reality. Each description and each phrase somehow contain a sharp shard of observation. The reader gets the feeling that his scenes could have happened. Many of them are completely farfetched. He stretches our willingness to believe to the limit. This is the key to Thompson's style.

■ EDITING 11: APPLICATION

Select a page from a draft you are working on, and evaluate it in terms of sentence structure. First, identify all examples of coordination by circling coordinating conjunctions and semicolons. Next identify all examples of subordination by drawing a line under subordinate elements. Are coordination and subordination used where they are most effective? Are there any examples where two ideas would be better joined through another method? Is every conjunction or conjunctive adverb well chosen? Is either coordination or subordination overused? Then look for cases where you have used parallel structures. Are the words and ideas similar enough to be included in a parallel structure? Have you included all necessary words? Find places where you might consider using parallel structures. Edit the page by improving any weak sentence structure you found. How does the edited passage compare with the original?

Effective writing focuses readers' attention on important ideas by putting special stress or **emphasis** on the words that express them. Both the structure and rhythm of sentences can be used to create emphasis.

Sometimes writers find that in trying to make every idea clear and comprehensible, they give each one equal emphasis. Because emphasis works only when more important ideas are contrasted with lesser ones, the result is that none of the ideas is emphasized. **Variety** of structure and rhythm can reestablish emphasis: when one idea is treated differently from those around it, it attracts attention simply because it is different.

Variety not only keeps readers focused on your important ideas, it also ensures that you don't lose their attention altogether. Writing in which all sentences or all paragraphs are the same can be monotonous. Effective writing has a strong but varied rhythm, one that carries the reader along without becoming too predictable. If you edit carefully to achieve emphasis and variety, your writing will be both easier and more pleasant to read.

Emphasis and variety can be established within individual sentences, within paragraphs, and even throughout an entire composition. When editing to achieve emphasis and variety, you can try the following:

- Use the emphatic first and final positions.

- Edit sentence length.

- Vary sentence types.

- Vary sentence openings.

- Use deliberate repetition.

- Create elliptical constructions.

| 27 | a | **Using the emphatic first and final positions** |

One way to emphasize ideas is to position them at a beginning or an end. The first paragraph of an essay, the first sentence of a paragraph, and the first words of a sentence all attract readers' attention. That is why, for example, a thesis statement frequently appears as the first sentence of an essay.

> The single most important and fundamental difference between Chinese and Occidental peoples is undoubtedly the role played by the individual in the society. In the West, we place a strong emphasis on personal achievement, creativity, and initiative. We glory in our individual differences, nurture them, and value them as the essential features that make us unique. Indeed, uniqueness is a goal unto itself in the West; it's vitally important to us that we *not* be exactly like other people.
>
> SCOT SELIGMAN, "SOME BASIC CULTURAL DIFFERENCES"

First words may grab attention, but those that come last have enduring impact. The last words of a sentence, a paragraph, or an entire essay resonate in the reader's mind, lingering to provoke further thought.

ESL **OLD AND NEW INFORMATION IN SENTENCES**

As you edit sentences for emphasis and variety, remember to consider carefully what information you have already given your readers. In an English sentence, information that readers already know — "old" information — is usually presented before new information is introduced. This helps readers see the connection between this sentence and those that precede it.

Most artificial colorings are synthetic chemicals.

Old information   **New information**

These colorings may cause hyperactivity in children.

Early civil rights bills nebulously state that other people shall have the same rights as "white people," indicating that there *were* "other people." But civil rights bills passed during and after the Civil War systematically excluded Indian people. . . . Indians were America's captive people without any defined rights whatsoever.

VINE DELORIA, JR., "CUSTER DIED FOR YOUR SINS"

When editing, look for ways to use the emphatic first and final positions of each paragraph and sentence, especially in your opening and conclusion. (See Chapter 24.)

■ <del>Whatever the rewards</del> The costs of prohibition, <del>its costs</del> will always exceed <del>them.</del> its rewards. Users, who will always exist, are harmed not only by drugs but also by the law. The more effective the law, the more non-users are victimized by crimes committed for drug cash. The higher drug prices go, the more desperate and sophisticated drug gangs become. With a stroke of the pen, society could eliminate drug profits and drug crime.

Editing this conclusion, Darla turned her thesis restatement into a flat, declarative sentence, giving it an authoritative ring. She then moved the phrase with the stroke of a pen *to the emphatic final position.*

■ **EDITING I: APPLICATION**

Select two pages from a paper you are working on. First, underline the first and last sentence in each paragraph. Reading only these sentences, would a reader know what the most important ideas are in each paragraph? Edit each paragraph so that the most important idea is in either the first sentence or the last.

Second, on one of the edited pages, underline the most important element in each sentence — whether this is a thing, an action, or a description. How often does the most important element fall at the very beginning or at the very end of the sentence? How often is it buried somewhere in the middle? Edit each sentence, moving important elements to the emphatic first or final position within sentences wherever possible. How does the edited page compare with the original?

27	b	Editing sentence length

Some writers write short sentences. They seldom use dependent clauses. They rarely use modifiers. They never use verbal phrases. Other writers never use simple sentences when elaborate ones, wreathed like Christmas trees with garlands of dependent clauses, can be substituted, and thus they sometimes keep the reader waiting, hoping — perhaps even praying — eventually to find a period and, with it, a chance to pause for breath.

Short sentences and long ones both have their uses, given a writer's purpose and intended audience. Most good writers mix their sentence lengths. After braving a thicket of elaborate sentences, a reader will be riveted by a plain and direct statement. When you edit, be aware of sentence length: use short and long sentences when each is appropriate, and mix sentence lengths for variety and emphasis if the pattern becomes too predictable.

Many computer style checkers can chart sentence length, giving you a tally of how many words each sentence contains and how many sentences of various lengths you have written. You can develop the same information by using the search-and-replace feature of your computer to start each sentence on a new line. This will let you see at a glance where you have used short sentences and where you have used long ones.

Short sentences

Short sentences sound honest and direct. They have the power to describe intense feelings, impressions, and events. In a series of short sentences, each idea stands alone and asks for the reader's full attention. In the following scene, Richard Rodriguez describes distributing bread in a poor neighborhood in Tijuana. Notice how his brief sentences make his confrontation with hunger and need all the more chilling.

> Five or six children come forward. All goes well for less than a minute. The crowd has slowly turned away from the altar; the crowd advances zombie-like against the truck. I fear children will be crushed. Silent faces regard me with incomprehension. *Cuidado* [careful], damn it!
>
> RICHARD RODRIGUEZ, "ACROSS THE BORDERS OF HISTORY"

To achieve such a dramatic effect, try condensing your ideas into as few words as possible and breaking up long sentences into shorter ones.

■ ~~As soon as~~ I hit the ball and took ~~my first~~ step. ~~my~~ knee collapsed and I was on the ground. ~~in~~ blinding ~~pain~~ I heard my teammates yelling, "Get up! Run!" ~~but~~ I could no more run than ~~I could~~ fly.

Short sentences can also present information clearly and simply. The following example, from a high school civics textbook, discusses the founding of Philadelphia by William Penn.

> From the beginning, Philadelphia was the colony's and the state's largest municipality. A mayor and six aldermen were named by Penn to govern it. Philadelphia became a city in 1691. Penn granted a permanent charter to Philadelphia in 1701. This charter was followed until 1776, when independence was declared for all the colonies.
>
> WILLIAM CORNELL, *UNDERSTANDING PENNSYLVANIA CIVICS*

Presenting one fact at a time in this way may be effective when the information is dense, technical, or potentially confusing. But for less challenging material, a pattern of short, simple sentences may seem too slow or choppy.

2 Long sentences

Most academic writing requires that you elaborate on your ideas and show the connections between them. Long sentences give you room to show the relative importance of ideas through coordination and subordination, thereby enabling you to develop more complex thoughts. (See Chapter 26.)

Notice in the following example that when Barbara turned short sentences into longer ones, she not only made the paragraph less choppy but also made her emphasis more explicit.

■ *Dances with Wolves* is like most good movies. It comes full circle. This circle begins when John Dunbar comes to Fort

Hayes. At first, he only waits for relief to arrive. ~~He~~ *and* looks forward to being joined by the rest of his troop. Over time, though,
he becomes attuned to the ways of the Sioux. ~~The~~ *, so that the* eventual arrival of his troop is not a relief after all. Dunbar has grown to see
through the eyes of the Sioux. ~~He~~ *, and he* recognizes the injustices done
them.

Be careful, however, not to overdo long sentences. When a
sentence covers more territory than a reader can span in a single
stride, when its ideas are dissimilar or weakly connected, or when
it threatens to become confusing or boring, the ideas are probably
better conveyed in several shorter sentences.

3 Mixing short and long sentences

Most academic and professional writers mix long and short
sentences. Such a mix provides variety but it also can help create
emphasis, especially if a pattern of all short or all long sentences
is first established and then broken by a sentence of a very different length. In the following passage from an account about former
hostage Terry Anderson, the author uses the long third sentence
— which stands out by contrast with the short ones — to emphasize a particularly terrifying moment.

> Imagine it. You are chained to a radiator in a bare, dank
> room. You never see the sun. When your captors fear that a noise
> in the night is an impending rescue attempt, you are slammed up
> against the wall, the barrel of a gun pressed against your temple.
> Each day you have 15 minutes to shower, brush your teeth, and
> wash your underwear in the bathroom sink. Your bed is a mat on
> the floor.
>
> SCOTT MACLEOD, "THE LOST LIFE OF TERRY ANDERSON"

You can also create emphasis by changing abruptly from long sentences to a sharply worded, simple sentence that stresses a key
point. The break in rhythm will stop readers in their tracks and
make them notice your point. Try it. It works.

When editing to mix sentence lengths, keep your readers'

needs in mind. Use long sentences to clarify relationships between ideas and use shorter sentences to strengthen a point or break a monotonous pattern.

■ Athletes must decide how they want to perfect their physical condition. The first choice is to do it the old-fashioned way/ ,? ~~This means~~ *by* eating right, running, and lifting. This alternative requires hard work and considerable discipline. The second alternative is to use steroids/ ? ~~These~~ *that* drugs help athletes become strong and fast in a short period of time/ *with little effort.* Obviously, many athletes will resort to this second method. ~~This is because they do not have to exert much effort.~~

■ **EDITING 2: PRACTICE**

Edit the following passage, varying the length of the sentences to improve emphasis and variety. More than one edited version is possible. Be ready to explain your editing choices.

When I heard the mail drop through the slot in the door, my heart leapt. After I practically flew downstairs, I pounced on the mail that lay scattered on the floor. There, finally, was a letter for me from Iowa State University. "Today's the day," I said to myself, "the day that will seal my fate." At last I would have the answer to the all-important question of whether I had been accepted at the school of my choice. I wondered where I would spend the next four years. I wondered if I would be in Ames, Iowa, or home in Deerfield, Illinois. After I took a deep breath and counted to three, I ripped open the envelope.

27 **c** **Varying sentence types**

You can also create variety by using sentences of different types. Sentences can vary by **grammatical type,** by **rhetorical type,** or by **functional type.** (Also see Chapter 66.) Because readers' attention will be drawn to an atypical sentence — a question or command, for instance — varying sentence types allows you to create emphasis within a passage.

Grammatical types

Varying sentence lengths usually also means varying grammatical sentence types: long sentences are usually **compound, complex,** or **compound-complex sentences,** while short sentences are usually **simple sentences.** However, attending to the grammatical type of a sentence apart from its length is also useful, as each type has its own typical pattern and rhythm. Too many sentences of one type will lend a wooden sameness to prose; a variety of types makes prose emphatic and readable.

> Fulghum's book glorifies and celebrates childhood. The adult Fulghum believes that childhood is governed by simple motivating principles: eat, sleep, and play. To Fulghum, children are small gurus, zoos are temples of tranquillity, and playing gets you higher than meditation does.

✔ GRAMMATICAL SENTENCE TYPES

A **simple sentence** consists of a single independent clause:

> Pollution is a growing problem.

A **compound sentence** consists of two or more independent clauses joined by a comma and a coordinating conjunction or by a semicolon:

> Pollution is a problem, and it affects every aspect of our lives.

A **complex sentence** consists of one independent clause and one or more dependent clauses:

> Because the problem continues to grow, our legislature must act before it is too late.

A **compound-complex sentence** contains at least two independent clauses and one or more dependent clauses:

> Pollution must be stopped, and we must take action to stop it, because there is no other way to survive on this planet.

2 Rhetorical types and word order

Within a sentence, should you put the main point first and the subordinate information later? Or should you first establish the context and then deliver the main message? Such decisions refer to **rhetorical sentence types.** The first strategy — placing the main idea first — is called a **cumulative sentence.**

> *Othello smothers* the delicate Desdemona in a fit of anguished passion and boiling fury. *He kills* the person he loves most because he has trusted the lies of the vicious Iago.

The second strategy — which saves its punch for the end — is called a **periodic sentence.**

> In a fit of anguished passion and boiling fury, *Othello smothers* the delicate Desdemona. Because he has trusted the lies of the vicious Iago, *he kills* the person he loves most.

Cumulative sentences often dominate writing because they allow a writer to make a major point, then support it. Yet writing composed solely of cumulative sentences can be monotonous. To break the pattern, consider using a periodic sentence to emphasize a point.

■ *A Small Place* is an unsettling book. In it Jamaica Kincaid discloses shocking details about the tourist paradise Antigua, where she grew up. We see the poor condition of the school, the library, the hospital, and even the government, all problems she links to English and American imperialism. ~~An American reader feels defensive and ashamed~~ when confronted by the consequences of unthinking exploitation, *an American reader feels defensive and ashamed.*

Cumulative sentences put the important information first. Another way to do this is to use **inverted word order,** in which the verb precedes the subject: *Down came the rain.* Although such inversion is fairly uncommon in English, it can be used to strong effect, particularly when the subject includes so many words that the reader is tired of reading by the time the verb shows up.

ESL **INVERTING SUBJECTS AND VERBS**

When you place any of the following structures at the front of a sentence, you must put the subject after the first auxiliary (a form of *have* or *be* or a modal such as *could*) of the independent clause. If there is no auxiliary, then put the subject after the main verb.

ADVERB OF EXTENT OR DEGREE	*So antagonizing* had the speaker been that members of the audience walked out.
NEGATIVE ADVERB OF FREQUENCY	*Seldom* has a verdict created such an outrage among citizens. (Others: *rarely, scarcely, hardly ever, only once*)
OTHER NEGATIVE ADVERBS AND ADVERB PHRASES	*Under no circumstances* should funding for this program be cut. (Others: *in no case, in no way, not until* + [time], *not since* + [time])
CONDITIONAL CLAUSES	*Only if we take measures now* will we rescue our city from urban blight.

When you place the following structures at the front of a sentence, the subject must be put after both the auxiliary (if there is one) and the main verb of the independent clause.

ADVERB OF POSITION	*Behind the sofa* could go the larger of the two bookcases.
COMPARATIVES	*More intriguing than the main plot of the novel* are several of the subplots.
PARTICIPLES WITH MODIFIERS	*Lying on my desk* should be a large sealed envelope.

---

3 **Functional types**

While most writing relies primarily on **declarative sentences** — sentences that make statements — an occasional **question, exclamation,** or **command** can grab the reader's attention and highlight a significant point. (Also see 66a.)

Question

Crime by strangers actually went down in the past decade. But fear of crime by strangers, that other urban cancer, went up. What can we make of the anxiety and the reality? James Fox, a Northwestern University criminologist, believes that "people get their perceptions based on news, not on crime statistics."

ELLEN GOODMAN, "A MURDER IN BOSTON"

Exclamation

Finally, in a paroxysm of therapeutic bullying, the shelter has added a new wrinkle. If you stay more than two days you are required to fill out and then discuss with a social worker a complex form listing what you perceive as your personal failings, goals, and strategies. All of this for men and women who simply want a place to lie down out of the rain!

PETER MARIN, "HELPING AND HATING THE HOMELESS"

Command

Male friendship was still supposed to be a breeding ground for all kinds of upstanding traits — honor, altruism, courage, faith, loyalty. Consider Arthur's friendship with Lancelot, which survived the latter's dalliance with Guinevere. But when two women got together, the best you could hope for, apparently, was bitchiness, and the worst was witchcraft.

BARBARA EHRENREICH, "IN PRAISE OF BEST FRIENDS"

■ **EDITING 3: EXPLORATION**

Extreme examples of periodic and cumulative sentences were once much more common. Here are two excerpts from an essay by the eighteenth-century writer Samuel Johnson in which he relates the demise of an "adventurer in lotteries" — a gambler. Which sentence is periodic, and which is cumulative? What effect does each one have on you, the reader? Try to write sentences modeled on these examples, following their general patterns and rhythms but using different topics.

"As I have passed much of life in disquiet and suspense, and lost many opportunities of advantage by a passion which I have reason to believe prevalent in different degrees over a great part of mankind, I cannot but think myself well qualified to warn those, who are yet uncaptivated of the danger which they incur by placing themselves within its influence."

"My heart leaped at the thoughts of such an approach of sudden riches, which I considered myself, however contrarily to the laws of computation, as having missed by a single chance; and I could not forbear to revolve the consequences which such a bounteous allotment would have produced, if it had happened to me."

SAMUEL JOHNSON, "THE HISTORY OF AN ADVENTURER IN LOTTERIES"

27 d Varying sentence openings

As you edit, consider repositioning modifiers, dependent clauses, and transitional expressions so that some sentences begin with elements other than the subject. Varying sentence openings can create emphasis as well as reduce monotony within a passage by drawing the reader's attention to a sentence structured differently from those around it. It also creates emphasis within a sentence, because the element that is moved to the beginning will receive more attention than it would have received buried later in the sentence. (See 27a.)

Modifiers

■ ~~Doctors~~ *Increasingly, doctors* rely ~~increasingly~~ on advanced diagnostic equipment.

■ ~~Single~~ *Overworked and often underpaid, single* parents/ ~~who are overworked and often underpaid,~~ are among the most marginalized members of society.

Dependent clause

■ *Until researchers learned* ~~Much~~ of ancient Mayan culture remained a mystery *to translate its hieroglyphs, much* ~~,until researchers learned to translate its hieroglyphs.~~

Transitional expression

■ Most teenagers are aware of the dangers of smoking. ~~They~~ *However, they* don't always realize the addictive power of cigarettes/ ~~however.~~

Because they will receive so much emphasis, you must choose carefully the elements you move to the beginnings of sentences.

■ **EDITING 4: PRACTICE**

To improve the emphasis and variety of the following passage, edit it by beginning some of the sentences with an element other than the subject. More than one edited version is possible. Be ready to explain your editing choices.

The College Recruiting Network is a good resource for students and one of the best ways to get a job. The network, provided by campus career development centers, is available across the United States. Forty percent of all students make use of the service, according to studies published last year. Seniors find the network helpful most often, particularly when they don't know what they want to do when they graduate. The network was developed and implemented especially with these students in mind. Students have the opportunity to get involved in the interviewing process early on thanks to the network. Many are, consequently, able to find a job even before they graduate.

27 **e** **Using deliberate repetition**

By deliberately repeating words, phrases, or sentence structures, you link the elements repeated and emphasize them. (See 25c for repetition and paragraph coherence.) Repetition can also create powerful rhythmic effects. A succession of similar phrases, falling on the reader's ear like the sound of waves striking the shore, can be soothing or can build to a strong climax.

The art of writing such prose is difficult to master, perhaps because determining when a rhythm becomes monotonous or when repetition becomes redundancy is a matter of judgment. (See 30d.) When in doubt, err on the side of too little rather than too much repetition. Some writers, rather than repeat the same word or phrase, use slight variations, or *synonyms,* to avoid monotony. Some occasionally omit an expected repetition.

In the following passage, Annie Dillard weaves together repeated words and phrases, creating a rhythm that suggests the sense of serenity she found in the forests of Ecuador.

The point of going somewhere like the Napo River in Ecuador is not to see the most spectacular anything. It is simply to see what is there. We are here on the planet only once, and might as well get a feel for the place. We might as well get a feel for the fringes and hollows in which life is lived, for the Amazon basin, which covers half a continent, and for the life that — there, like anywhere else — is always and necessarily lived in detail: on the tributaries, in the riverside villages, sucking this particular white-fleshed guava in this particular pattern of shade.

ANNIE DILLARD, "IN THE JUNGLE"

To use repetition effectively, look for words, phrases, or structures that are important to your meaning and consider repeating them. Always make sure that the element you have repeated deserves the emphasis and that the rhythmic effect you create is appropriate for your subject and audience.

■ ~~When~~ $\overset{S}{s}$he read to me, $\overset{and}{}$ I ~~could see~~ $\overset{saw}{}$ faraway islands fringed with coconut palms. $\overset{\wedge \ She\ read\ to\ me\ and\ with}{}$ ~~With~~ Jim Hawkins, I shivered in the apple barrel while the pirates plotted. $\overset{\wedge \ She\ read\ to\ me\ and}{}$ I ran with Maori warriors to raid the villages of neighboring tribes. $\overset{\wedge \ She\ read\ to\ me\ and}{}$ I saw Captain Cook slain on a beach of the Sandwich Isles. I saw the Tahitians welcome British sailors. I watched Fletcher Christian mutiny against Captain Bligh, and I marveled that Bligh reached England in an open boat. I heard Ahab's peg leg thump on the deck overhead, and I marveled at the whiteness of the whale.

■ EDITING 5: EXPLORATION

Read the following carefully, identifying as many instances of repetition as you can. How does repetition contribute to the effectiveness of the passage? What ideas are linked? What ideas are emphasized?

"I do not own a horse. I am attached to a truck, however, and I have come to think of it in a similar way. It has no name; it never occurred to me to give it a name. It has little decoration; neither of us is partial to decoration. I have a piece of turquoise in the truck because I had heard once that some of the southwestern tribes tied a small piece of turquoise in a horse's hock to keep him from stumbling. I like the idea. I also hang sage in the truck when I go on a long trip. But inside, the truck doesn't look much different from others that look just like it on the outside. I like it that way. Because I like my privacy."

BARRY LOPEZ, "MY HORSE"

27 f Creating elliptical constructions

In an **elliptical construction,** words that readers can be expected to understand and supply mentally are omitted for the sake of brevity or to create a special rhythm. (See 26j.) The omitted words are almost always dropped from the second part of a compound parallel construction.

■ Her words suggested one thing, her actions ~~suggested~~ another.

Elliptical constructions work only when the words you omit are identical to words that remain.

■ Of Shakespeare's female characters, Lady Macbeth is the most
ruthless, Desdemona and Juliet ⁀are⁀ the most loving, and Portia ⁀is⁀ the
most resourceful.

> *The omitted verbs must match exactly the verb that remains —* is. *But the plural subject* Desdemona and Juliet *requires the verb* are, *so the omitted verbs had to be reinstated.*

Because an elliptical construction enables you to avoid repeating a word or phrase, in a sense it is the opposite of repetition. Like repetition, though, it strongly affects the rhythm and thus the emphasis of a passage. It heightens rhythm by omitting words that would not have been stressed and leaving only the stressed words. But it also syncopates rhythm, so that a word occurs a beat or two sooner than the reader expected. As you edit, look for parallel phrases or clauses that could be strengthened by elliptical construction.

EDITING 6: PRACTICE

Edit the following sentences to create elliptical constructions wherever you think they would be effective. Some sentences can be edited in more than one way. Be prepared to explain your editing choices.

1. In our family, I am the bossy one, Tom is the quiet one, and Cheryl is the friendly one.

2. Whenever we visited our grandparents' farm, we had to weed and prune in the garden until the marigolds were immaculate, the beans were beautiful, and the pea plants were pristine.

3. Our conversation would be on the virtue of hard work; our thoughts would be on the pleasures of a lazy afternoon.

4. Cheryl and I could usually convince Tom that she was too weak for this sort of work and I was too old.

5. By supper time, Tom's eyes were bleary, and his arms were exhausted, but he was happy to have finally finished.

EDITING 7: EXPLORATION

Read the following paragraph carefully, and identify the various techniques the author has used to create emphasis and variety.

"I discovered that I did not like to live on the parlor floor of society. Intellectually I was bored. Morally and spiritually I was sickened. I remembered my intellectuals and idealists, my unfrocked preachers, broken professors, and clean-minded, class-conscious workingmen. I remembered my days and nights of sunshine and starshine, where life was all a wild sweet wonder, a spiritual paradise of unselfish adventure and ethical romance. And I saw before me, ever blazing and burning, the Holy Grail."

JACK LONDON, "WHAT LIFE MEANS TO ME"

EDITING 8: PRACTICE

Edit the following passage to provide emphasis and variety throughout. Be sure that sentences vary in length and type and that not all sentences begin with the subject. Try to make use of deliberate repetition and elliptical construction. More than one edited version is possible. Be ready to explain your editing choices.

Sunday dinner at Grandma's house was about as appealing as a day without recess to me, an energetic nine-year-old. It meant leaving the kids at the playing field at the bottom of the eighth inning. I had to take a bath in the middle of the day and wash behind my ears. The worst thing was that I had to put on my best clothes and try to keep them clean. For me to keep my clothes clean seemed beyond the realm of possibility in those days. My parents would look absolutely delighted as I emerged from the bath every week. I looked, frankly, nothing like myself. My father would exclaim, "She's as clean as a hound's tooth!" Yet I would arrive at Grandma's week after week looking like Raggedy Ann, despite my best efforts. My shirt would inevitably be stained, my stockings would inevitably be split, my shoes would inevitably be scuffed. My mother would look at me in disbelief as I climbed out of the car. She was amazed, no doubt, that such a metamorphosis could have occurred in a twenty-minute car ride. My disheveled appearance, to be honest, never seemed to bother Grandma. She always exclaimed, "Don't you look nice!" I don't know to this day whether she was losing her eyesight or just being kind.

■ EDITING 9: APPLICATION

Select a long paragraph from a paper you are working on, and look for ways to improve its emphasis and variety. First, identify the most important ideas in the paragraph, those that should receive the most emphasis. Are they placed in the first and final positions of the paragraph? Second, count the number of words in each sentence. Do you have a good mix of sentence lengths? Third, identify each sentence according to grammatical, rhetorical, and functional type and determine whether it begins with the subject. Are all your sentences the same in type and word order? Fourth, determine whether you have used any deliberate repetition or elliptical constructions. If not, would either technique be effective? Last, edit the paragraph using the methods described in this chapter. How does your edited version compare with the original paragraph?

The tone of someone's voice can tell listeners whether he or she is angry or conciliatory, confident or hesitant, friendly or hostile, enthusiastic or regretful. Similarly, the **tone** of a piece of writing is the sense it conveys of the writer's attitude toward the subject and the audience. Tone is one important element in **voice,** the sense of the writer as a person that comes through in writing. (See Chapter 6.) It is important that the tone of your writing represent you accurately and be appropriate to your subject and audience. Just as you wouldn't address an auditorium full of people in hesitant whispers, you should not use a breezy, informal tone in formal academic writing.

Tone isn't something you add to writing; it's already there. At the editing stage, you should ask yourself two things about the tone of your writing. First, is it appropriate, given your subject, audience, and purpose? If not, you need to edit to adjust your point of view and level of formality. Second, is your tone consistent? If not, you need to edit your writing for elements that are incompatible with the tone you want to convey.

When editing to improve the tone of your writing, you should do the following:

- Make sure the tone you have established is appropriate.

- Select an appropriate point of view.

- Use the right level of formality.

- Maintain a consistent tone.

28   **a**   **Deciding whether the tone is appropriate**

The tone of writing should convey an attitude that is appropriate to the audience, the subject, and the purpose. Your audience includes the instructor who assigned the paper and sometimes other students as well. Try to imagine them reading your paper, and adjust your tone if you think your readers would get the wrong impression.

The tone of a paper describing personal experience can be informal, as if you were capturing a conversation with a friend or addressing the audience—even the instructor—directly in a friendly manner. (See Chapter 9.) A reflective essay may strike a pensive, questioning, or contemplative tone as you explore the possible meanings of an experience or an event. (See Chapter 13.)

■ My brother and I ~~grew acquainted~~ *became friends* with the other kids who ~~at~~ *went to* ~~tended~~ our elementary school; *I recall that* Tommy even ~~went so far as to ex~~ *swapped* ~~change~~ his favorite slingshot in return for a pet frog.

To explain how something works or interpret a work of literature, you should use an authoritative tone that assures readers of your expertise. (See Chapters 10 and 12.) Avoid unnecessary qualification that makes you sound hesitant and informalities that weaken your authority.

■ What is Title IX? ~~The original name of Beethoven's last sym~~ ~~phony? No. Title IX is~~ *P*art of the Educational Amendments of 1972, *Title IX* ~~that~~ gave women the same rights as men in all aspects of education, including athletics.

In a research essay, your tone should downplay your personal involvement with the subject and emphasize reports or descriptions that could be verified or experienced by other observers (see Part IV.)

■ At the bottom of the vessel ~~I found~~ a thin deposit of reddish-brown crystals. *remained.*

In argument, you can use a dispassionate tone to marshal evidence and appeal to readers' reason, or you can select language that appeals primarily to emotion. (See Chapter 11.) When you edit, check that emotional appeals are not too strident.

ESL

DEVELOPING AN APPROPRIATE TONE FOR ACADEMIC WRITING

You may have noticed that the tone of academic writing in English is sometimes different from that in academic writing in your native language. For example, you may be used to more or less emotion in argumentation than native English speakers use. If your experience learning English has been more oral than written, you may also be unsure about which words and phrases create an informal tone and which a more formal tone.

You can develop your ability to use an appropriate tone in academic English in the following ways.

1. Pay attention to tone as you read; analyze how authors achieve different tones.

2. Make a list of questions about tone to ask your instructor or a tutor. Discuss any differences you have observed between academic writing in your native language and in English.

3. Ask a friend to read your drafts and comment on the tone.

4. Read your writing aloud. Ask yourself what kind of tone you hear, and consider whether the tone sounds appropriate.

5. Start a list of vocabulary that is considered informal (*guy*, *kid*) or slang (*awesome*, *cool*). Consult with your instructor or a tutor about words you're not sure of. Use your list to edit informal words and phrases from your writing when it requires a formal tone.

LeeAnn opened an argumentative paper on conditions in the local jail with first-person observations. When editing, she decided the tone was more appropriate to a personal essay. She edited to downplay her own role and to make the language more formal.

■ In the fading light, the dark, ~~spooky~~ walls of the Dakota County Correction Center loom high above ~~me.~~ *its gate.* Speaking through an intercom, *visitors must* ~~I have to~~ identify ~~myself~~ *themselves* to the guards, who then *admit them to* ~~let me into~~ a locked room monitored by a security camera. *Ahead, a second door opens only after the first is locked. Inside,* ~~The first door clicks shut, and I'm in the slammer. It's~~

the jail resembles

movie

~~just like~~ the set of an old gangster ~~flick~~: concrete floors and iron
bars everywhere.

■ EDITING I: EXPLORATION

Read a few paragraphs from your last three papers. First, try to describe your
tone in each paper. Does your tone vary greatly from paper to paper, or do
you hear a similar tone throughout? Next, try to picture the sort of person
your readers would imagine as the writer of your papers, if they could judge
only from the tone of the papers. Is that image accurate? Is it what you want
them to think? Finally, decide whether you would do anything to change your
tone in these papers. Are there aspects of one paper's tone that you would
like to use in another of the papers?

28 **b**   Selecting an appropriate point of view

The **point of view** establishes the writer's relation to the subject and the audience. Point of view in this sense refers not to the
writer's opinions but to whether the writer's own thoughts, the
reader's reaction, or the subject itself is most important. One principal way in which a writer articulates a point of view is by the selection of a **governing pronoun:** the first person *I* or *we,* the second person *you,* or the third person *he, she, it,* or *they.*

As you edit, make sure that you have used the **first person** to
relate personal reflection and personal experience. The first person
is also appropriate in argumentative and research writing to describe personal observations or conclusions.

I am on the telephone to the emergency room of the local hospital.
My elder son is getting stitches in his palm, and *I* have called to
make *myself* feel better, because *I* am at home, waiting, and *my*
husband is there, holding him. [Italics added.]

ANNA QUINDLEN, "THE NAME IS MINE"

For about a month *I* spent most of each day either on the Peak or
overlooking Mlinda Valley . . . Piece by piece, *I* began to form *my*
first somewhat crude picture of chimpanzee life. [Italics added.]

JANE VAN LAWICK-GOODALL, *IN THE SHADOW OF MAN*

If you want to thrust your readers into the center of the scene or imply a close relationship with them, you can use the **second person** and address the reader directly as *you*.

> Madrid—The window of the hotel is open and, as *you* lie in bed, *you* hear the firing in the front line seventeen blocks away. [Italics added.]
>
> ERNEST HEMINGWAY, *BY-LINE: ERNEST HEMINGWAY*

> How many of *you* have ever wondered where certain slang expressions come from? Like "She's the cat's pajamas," or to "take it on the lam." Neither have I. [Italics added.]
>
> WOODY ALLEN, "SLANG ORIGINS"

You in the sense of "people in general" is not acceptable in formal writing. Try replacing it with an impersonal construction or a more suitable noun or pronoun. (Also see 40d.)

■ To get to the balcony in Paris's famous Opera House, ~~you~~ have
    visitors
    ^
to climb a long flight of stairs.

To focus on your subject rather than yourself or your readers, maintain the **third person** point of view. This is the point of view most widely used in formal academic writing.

> This short lieutenant colonel standing in front of Porter had an ability to convey self-confidence. *He* had also managed to keep *his* khaki shirt and trousers unrumpled, despite the heat, and *he* gave a brisker salute than most officers would have before *he* accepted Porter's invitation to sit down. [Italics added.]
>
> NEIL SHEEHAN, *A BRIGHT SHINING LIE*

Consider which point of view seems appropriate for your essay. In most cases, the purpose of a research essay, a position paper, or a textual analysis is not to describe your personal experience but to record what any investigator would find and think. Stick to the third person, which shifts attention from you to your subject and conveys a sense of objective, scholarly detachment. (See Chapters 10–12 and 14.) If your essay is reflective or drawn from your personal experience, the first person can convey a sense of immediacy and authenticity. Some argument essays can also use the first person. (See Chapters 9, 11, and 13.)

28 c   Achieving the right level of formality

The **level of formality,** sometimes called the **register,** of your writing depends on sentence structure and your use of pattern and rhythm. (See Chapters 26 and 27.) As you edit, check that your level of formality is appropriate.

You use a **familiar** tone in everyday speech but seldom in academic writing. Familiar language includes slang terms, sentence fragments, and even vulgarity without regard to rules or conventions.

> Really got into it with Jones today. The turkey can't see the value in anything. Thinks team sports make kids "aggressors" or some bull like that.

Familiar language also assumes that the audience already knows a great deal about the context—who Jones is, for example.

An **informal** tone is appropriate in a letter to a friend or in a personal experience essay. Writing informally, you give readers more complete context, use complete sentences, and omit slang, but allow your personal feelings to show through.

> I had a real argument with Professor Jones in my behavioral psychology class. He was trying to tell us that team sports teach people to be "aggressive" and "insensitive." He can't see the value in them at all.

Treating the subject of these examples in a **formal** tone for a research paper, you would choose precise language that minimizes the emotional and personal aspects of the dispute. You would write better-developed sentences, eliminate contractions, and use words appropriate to academic readers.

> Citing similarities between sports teams and primitive hunting bands, some scholars, including Professor Wilkin Jones in his writings on Aztec ball games, have suggested that competitive sports breed aggression. Other researchers, however, have found that team sports also foster self-discipline and cooperation.

Striking a level of formality appropriate to your purpose calls for judgment. Most reflective essays, for example, are more formal than personal essays and less formal than research papers. There is room for variation within each category, yet in many cases your editing should steer a middle course, striving for a presentation that is neither too informal nor too formal.

■ *Inevitably,* ~~There's just no way that~~ fans who ~~glom onto~~ Stephen King's lat-
 ^ *suspense novel*   *finish it* ^ *in one sitting.*
est ~~chill-fest~~ will want to ~~put it down until they've inhaled the~~
 ^   ^
~~whole thing~~

■ **EDITING 2: PRACTICE**

Edit the following two paragraphs, adjusting the tone to the appropriate level of formality. The first paragraph is from a paper relating a personal experience; the second is from a formal research paper. More than one edited version of each paragraph is possible. Be ready to explain your editing choices.

PERSONAL EXPERIENCE ESSAY

Who would find it credible that two adults would have trouble convincing one eight-pound feline that the time had come for his annual physical examination? Upon spotting his cage, the cat exits the room as quickly as he can. Under the bed, over the bed, up the staircase, down the staircase, he rushes with extreme celerity from one room to the next, ever eluding our grasp. When his outrageous behavior ceases, and we have him cornered, I stealthily approach him and apprehend him. I loudly proclaim myself triumphant as I deposit him in his place of confinement and secure the top.

FORMAL RESEARCH PAPER

At the Dryden Correctional Center, the guys who run the education department try to prepare the inmates for living on the outside. That way criminals won't (they hope!) turn back to a life of crime. OK. Sounds like a good idea. But how do they do it? Well, they make sure that as soon as the criminals get tossed in the slammer they start getting an education. This is so that they will have a better chance of getting jobs when they get out. The way they figure it is if the criminals get jobs, they won't have to turn to crime to make money. The educational programs are completely voluntary. Lots of the inmates take them, though.

An unnecessary shift in tone will throw your readers off balance; they won't know where your ideas are heading, and they may be reluctant to follow. Be alert to any language that suggests a shift in attitude, level of formality, or point of view.

■ **June Carter Cash's childhood home was filled with music; she is a daughter of early country music's famous singing Carter Family. Her writing style is open and informal, like** ~~a~~ *one* **good friend talking to** ~~you~~ *another* **about her life.**

Although you should avoid arbitrary or accidental shifts in tone, some shifts are necessitated by content. A deliberate shift in tone can be appropriately humorous, moving, or even compelling. In the following passage, Stephen Jay Gould shifts from an amusing story, told in casual language, to an argument based on logic and hard evidence, written in a more formal tone.

> When Muhammad Ali flunked his army intelligence test, he quipped (with a wit that belied his performance on the exam): "I only said I was the greatest; I never said I was the smartest." In our metaphors and fairy tales, size and power are almost always balanced by a want of intelligence. Cunning is the refuge of the little guy. Think of Br'er Rabbit and Br'er Bear; David smiting Goliath with a slingshot; Jack chopping down the beanstalk. Slow wit is the tragic flaw of a giant.
>
> The discovery of dinosaurs in the nineteenth century provided, or so it appeared, a quintessential case for the negative correlation of size and smarts. With their pea brains and giant bodies, dinosaurs became a symbol of lumbering stupidity. Their extinction seemed only to confirm their flawed design.
>
> STEPHEN JAY GOULD, "WERE DINOSAURS DUMB?"

Using a deliberate shift is like telling a joke in front of a group of strangers: you've got to know it's a good joke, and you've got to do it smoothly and with expert timing. If you aren't sure you can pull it off, it may be safer not to try.

■ EDITING 3: PRACTICE

Edit the following passage from a formal literary interpretation, making sure to maintain a consistent, appropriate tone. More than one edited version is possible. Be ready to explain your editing choices.

You can really see the similarities between Shakespeare's *King Lear* and Jane Smiley's novel *A Thousand Acres*. Smiley makes you think of Shakespeare's play on purpose, and she expects you to be with it enough to catch on. You can see the parallels even in the names she gives to her characters. The three sisters in *A Thousand Acres* are named Ginny, Rose, and Caroline. These names make you think of Lear's daughters, Goneril, Regan, and Cordelia. Get it? (The first letters are the same.) In both the play and the novel, one really important idea is how parents and kids get along. In Smiley's story, Caroline, the youngest daughter, doesn't like her father's plan to retire and divide his huge farm among his three daughters, so he chills her. In *King Lear*, Cordelia, also the youngest, won't compete with her sisters in telling her old dad how crazy about him she is just so she can get the largest part of his kingdom. In both works, the two older sisters tell their dad what he wants to hear, but the youngest stands up to him.

■ EDITING 4: APPLICATION

Read through a paper you are working on, paying close attention to its tone. How would you describe the tone? How do your choices of point of view, level of formality, and wording contribute to this tone? Given your subject and your purpose, is the tone appropriate? Have you maintained this tone throughout? If not, do your shifts in tone help the effectiveness of your paper or harm it? As you edit your paper, pay full attention to its tone, keeping the aspects that you like and improving the aspects that you don't like.

What makes writing lively? Why does one writer's prose dull the senses while another's, on the same subject, captures readers' attention? Most readers would find the first of the following examples dull and the second more vivid, effective, and powerful.

> The sky and the sunrise are reflected by the snow. There is a road in front of me that goes down the slope toward the stone formations.

> The snow-covered ground glimmers with a dull blue light, reflecting the sky and the approaching sunrise. Leading away from me the narrow dirt road, an alluring and primitive path into nowhere, meanders down the slope and toward the heart of the labyrinth of naked stone.

> EDWARD ABBEY, *DESERT SOLITAIRE*

How do these passages differ? The first uses general, abstract nouns with few modifiers: *sunrise, road, stone formations.* The second uses **specific, concrete nouns** and **modifiers** that create tangible images: *dull blue light, alluring and primitive path, labyrinth of naked stone.* The first uses weak and static verbs: *is, goes.* The second passage uses **strong verbs** that evoke actions readers can visualize: *leading, meanders.* Finally, while the opening verb in the first passage is passive (are reflected), the verbs in the second passage are all in the **active voice.**

A vital sentence is clear and compelling; it gives readers something interesting to think about. By delighting the imagination, a vital sentence encourages readers to go on to the next sentence, the next idea.

In editing to improve the vitality of your writing, try thinking of each sentence as presenting a story. Like any drama, a sentence has actors and actions; the former is usually a noun, the latter a verb. Make each actor and action as vivid and tangible as possible. Readers should be able to imagine the story unfolding before their eyes. If your sentences don't convey such immediacy and energy, consider the following techniques:

■ Use nouns and modifiers that are concrete and specific.

■ Use strong verbs that express a specific action.

■ Choose carefully between the active and the passive voice.

■ Untangle difficult noun clusters.

29 a Using concrete, specific nouns and modifiers

If a sentence is to tell a story, your first task is to identify the "characters" in it so that readers can recognize them. Whether a character is a person, an object, or an idea, try to describe it so clearly and precisely that you create the same image in readers' minds as you hold in your own. Compare the mental pictures you get from the phrases *an old blue car* and *a rusted, baby-blue Buick.* The first is vague; any of a thousand images could come to mind. The second evokes a specific car.

To determine whether your characters are clearly identified, examine the language you use to describe them. First, is your language abstract or is it concrete? **Abstract** words refer to ideas and concepts that cannot be perceived by the senses: *transportation, wealth, childhood, nutrition.* **Concrete** words name things that can be seen, felt, heard, tasted, or smelled: *cars, dime, child, broccoli.* Second, is the language general or is it specific? **General** words refer to categories and groups: *pets, stores, teachers.* **Specific** words identify individual objects or people: *Rover; Murphy's drug store; my biology professor, Pauline Clay.*

The terms *abstract* and *concrete* are not absolute. Think of them as being ends of a continuum, with many levels of abstraction in between. The same is true for the terms *general* and *specific.*

Abstract

↑　wealth
　　money
　　currency
↓　dollar bills

Concrete

General
▲ college-educated professionals
│ teachers
│ biology professors
▼ my biology professor
Specific

These two ways of characterizing words can overlap. *Music*, for example, is something you can hear and so is concrete, but the word is also a general category embracing everything from Hammer to Handel.

■ Using concrete, specific nouns

Abstract terms make abstract thinking possible: we would be unable to think, speak, or write about *truth*, *insurance*, *constitutionality*, or *political risk* without the words developed for such concepts. Yet writing composed exclusively of abstractions can seem like nothing but "hot air." To revitalize passages containing too many abstractions, consider more concrete nouns that reflect the world of experience.

■ Campus radicalism increased in the 1960s. ~~Protests~~ and ~~antiwar~~ *Sit-ins* *slogans*
~~propaganda~~ were common in those years.

Consider providing an example or definition at the first use of an abstract term. Once you have grounded an abstraction with clear, tangible images, you will be able to use it without wearying your reader. It will have become a recognizable character in your story.

■ Concern about the national debt has resulted in the reduced
— *money the government has borrowed in order to operate* —
availability of guaranteed student loans.

Human thought depends on the ability to make connections between the general and the specific. We absorb specific data through experience and then generalize about our experience: *It has snowed in the winter for the past twenty years, so it will probably snow this coming winter.* Writing consisting only of details and specifics may have difficulty expressing broad or general meanings. Most writers err on the side of too many generalizations, though, so when you edit, look for ways to enliven general terms with specific nouns.

■ Many ~~writers~~ wrote about ~~American cities.~~
     American novelists of the 1920s   *New York City.*

2 Using concrete, specific modifiers

Preferring the specific and concrete to the general and abstract applies also to the selection of modifiers, words and phrases that describe nouns and verbs. Some descriptive modifiers, such as *pretty, dull, dumb, nice, beautiful, good, bad, young, old,* have become almost meaningless through overuse. They paint a very general picture instead of providing vivid, specific information.

ESL   **ORDER OF ADJECTIVES**

There is some flexibility in the order of adjectives preceding nouns, but some types of adjectives typically occur before others. For example, an adjective describing size occurs before one describing color: *the large white house* rather than *the white large house*. The following list and examples show the typical order of adjectives before nouns. (Keep in mind, of course, that you should generally avoid long strings of adjectives.)

1. **Determiner:** *a, the,* her, *Bob's, that, these, a few*
2. **Order:** *first, next, third*
3. **Evaluation:** *good, pretty, happy, interesting*
4. **Appearance — Size:** *big, small, minuscule*
5. **Appearance — Shape:** *oblong, squarish, round*
6. **Appearance — Condition:** *broken, shiny*
7. **Appearance — Age:** *old, young, new*
8. **Appearance — Color:** *blue, green, magenta*
9. **Material:** *wooden, cotton*
10. **Noun used as adjective:** *flower* in *flower garden*

          1   2   6   7   10
One never forgets that first shiny new sports car.

     1   4   5   9
A few large square wooden boxes were stacked on the floor.

ESL **USING ARTICLES WITH NOUNS**

The choice of an article (*a*, *an*, *the*) before a noun depends on the type of noun and the context in which it is used. All nouns are either count nouns or noncount nouns. **Count nouns** can be singular (*island*, *child*, *ratio*) or plural (*islands*, *children*, *ratios*). **Noncount nouns** generally cannot be made plural (*information*, *homework*, *justice*, *success*).

I. You must use an article before a singular count noun unless the noun has a quantifier (*one*) or a possessive (*my*, *her*) before it.

    an island   the child   a ratio

Exceptions to this rule are singular proper nouns, which in most cases do not require an article.

    Italy   Pearl Street   Lake Erie

2. Use *a* or *an* with a singular count noun when you have not specified one particular thing or individual.

> There is *a problem* with this approach.
>> *Readers don't know what the problem is yet.*

> We all appreciate *an understanding friend*.
>> *Any understanding friend, not a particular one.*

3. Use *the* with a singular count noun in the following cases.

■ The noun has already been mentioned.

> There is a problem with this approach. *The problem* is a subtle one.

■ The noun is made specific by modifiers that follow it.

> *The problem* that I see with this approach is a subtle one.
>> *The modifying clause* that I see with this approach *makes it clear that the writer is referring to one specific problem.*

■ The noun is made specific by the context.

> I entered a large lecture hall. *The teacher* was standing behind a podium. *The blackboard* seemed very far away.
>> *In a lecture hall, there is likely to be only one teacher and only one blackboard.*

ESL   **USING ARTICLES WITH NOUNS (Continued)**

■ The noun names a unique person, place, or thing.

> *The moon* was still hovering on *the horizon.*
> *There is only one moon and only one horizon.*

4. Use *the* with plural count nouns in the following cases.

■ The noun is made specific by modifiers that follow it.

> *The novels* that I like best focus on characters rather than on events.
> *The modifying clause* that I like best *makes it clear that the writer is re-ferring to a specific set of novels.*

■ The noun is made specific by the context.

> We saw a play tonight. *The actors* were from London.
> *The context makes it clear that the writer is referring specifically to the actors in the play they saw tonight.*

■ The noun is a proper noun referring to a country or a set of lakes, mountain ranges, or islands.

the United States	the Rocky Mountains
the Great Lakes	the Bahamas

5. Use *some* (*any* in negative sentences) or no article with noncount nouns if the noun is not specific.

They asked for *some information* at the tourist center.

There isn't *any homework* for tomorrow.

The citizens are demanding *justice.*

6. Use *the* with noncount nouns if the noun is specific because it has been previously mentioned, it is clear from the context, or it has modifiers.

We ordered some new skiing equipment. After *the equipment* ar-rived, we decided we didn't need it.

As class came to an end, she passed out *the homework.*

The justice of this verdict is questionable.

Rather than asking readers to accept your impression, give them the concrete, specific details so that they can see things for themselves.

■ ~~Young~~ Madeline was a ~~pretty~~ girl with ~~nice~~ brown eyes.
(handwritten above: Six-year-old ... dimple-faced ... laughing)

■ The city housing manager pointed out a row of ~~old, dilapidated~~ brick houses, *with sagging walls and plywood windows.*
(handwritten above: 1930s)

■ EDITING 1: PRACTICE

Edit the following paragraph by using concrete, specific nouns and modifiers. You may invent and add whatever details you think are necessary. More than one edited version is possible. Be ready to explain your editing choices.

Our college library is really good. Not only does it have lots of books, but it also has plenty of periodicals. Many resources are available to help people with any research we might need to do, and the staff is always ready to give guidance. Last year the library finally finished installing the new computer system. Now we can look up an item in the library from any of the several remote computer terminals located around campus. With just a few keystrokes, we can determine whether the library owns the item and, if so, whether it is available or currently in circulation.

29 b Choosing strong verbs

After you have identified the actors in your sentence, you must describe their actions in equally vivid language. Look for places to use strong verbs that clearly describe an action.

■ Replacing static verbs

Verbs drive sentences the way an engine powers a car. **Action verbs** — verbs that create vivid images — add horsepower to your writing. **Static verbs** — verbs that simply show a state of being, like *be, appear, become, seem, exist* — can leave your sentences underpowered. As you edit, look for static verbs and consider replacing them with action verbs.

■ The outer suburbs of Los Angeles ~~are in~~ *straddle* the hills beyond the San Fernando Valley.

■ This problem will soon ~~become evident.~~ *emerge.*

A form of *be* often precedes a phrase or a clause suggesting or containing a stronger verb that you can make the main verb of the sentence.

■ The most effective writers are those who write as though they were simply talking.

Be particularly sensitive to **expletive constructions** such as *there are* and *it is*. Sometimes you cannot avoid these expressions, but frequently you can find a stronger verb.

■ ~~There are~~ ~~s~~everal moons ~~orbiting~~ *orbit* Jupiter, Galileo found.

When an expletive construction is followed by a dependent clause, you can usually turn the clause's verb into the main verb of the sentence.

USING EXPLETIVE CONSTRUCTIONS

Expletive constructions such as *it is* and *there are* often serve useful functions. They can create emphasis by slightly delaying the subject of the sentence and by allowing more opportunities for parallelism. (See 26h–j.)

It is a far, far better thing that I do, than I have ever done; it is a far, far better rest that I go to, than I have ever known.

CHARLES DICKENS, *A TALE OF TWO CITIES*

Expletives are also necessary in certain expressions about time and the weather.

There were showers this morning, but right now it's sunny outside.

It's five o'clock, sir; it's time to go.

■ ~~There are~~ M̂any people ~~who~~ still believe that Elvis Presley is
alive, even though ~~it is~~ only the tabloids ~~that~~ take such "news"
seriously.

2 Replacing weak action verbs

Not all verbs that describe action spark clear images. Overuse
has exhausted the image-making power of verbs such as *do*, *get*,
go, *have*, *make*, and *think*. As you edit, watch for these weak action verbs and substitute strong verbs whenever possible.

■ She can *handle* ~~do~~ the job.

■ Ozone ~~has~~ *displays* several interesting properties.

Often, a verb that relies on a modifier or other words for its
descriptive power should be replaced.

■ He *scurried* ~~walked quickly~~ from the room.

3 Turning nouns into verbs

The ease with which English words can be changed from one
part of speech to another gives the language a marvelous flexibility. With the help of a suffix such as *-ance*, *-ment*, or *-ation*, verbs
such as *deliver*, *announce*, or *tempt* can become useful nouns: *de-
liverance*, *announcement*, *temptation*.

Yet nouns made from verbs, called **nominals** or **nominalizations,** often conceal the real action of a sentence and require the
use of a static verb such as *have*, *do*, *make*, or *be*. If you have en-
tombed the real action of your sentence in a nominalization, ex-
hume the buried verb to give your prose new life.

■ Few biographies of Roosevelt have *satisfactorily explained* ~~given a satisfactory explanation of~~ the disastrous Yalta conference.

Some nouns and verbs have the same form: *cause*, *dance*,
march, *tie*, *love*, *hate*. If you use them as nouns, then you have to

find new verbs, which are usually weaker. There is no reason to *perform a dance* when you can simply *dance*, no cause to *hold a march* when you can simply *march*.

■ The signs told us to ~~make a~~ detour around the construction.

Nominalizations commonly occur in bureaucratese. (See 30e.)

 CHANGING NOUNS TO VERBS

To enliven your writing, replace these common expressions with the action verbs that are buried within them.

EXPRESSION	BURIED VERB
put forth a proposal	propose
hold a discussion	discuss
formulate a plan	plan
reach a decision	decide
arrive at a conclusion	conclude
hammer out an agreement	agree
hold a meeting	meet
call a strike	strike
make a choice	choose

■ **EDITING 2: EXPLORATION**

Read the following paragraph, which narrates one of the murders committed by Jack the Ripper. What verbs has Colin Wilson chosen to convey the action of the scene? Are they effective? Wilson has used *be* as the main verb of a clause twice in this paragraph. Why do you think he did this?

"They tiptoed down the passageway, and crept into a corner of the yard by the fence. The man moved closer; she was not even aware of the knife he held in his left hand. A moment later she was dead; the first thrust had severed her windpipe. The man allowed her to slide down the fence. He slipped out of his dark overcoat, and bent over the woman."

COLIN WILSON, "THE CRIMES OF JACK THE RIPPER"

■ **EDITING 3: PRACTICE**

Edit the following paragraph by using strong verbs. Make any small changes in wording that are needed for smooth reading. More than one edited version is possible. Be ready to explain your editing choices.

Bilingual education is becoming more of a hot topic of debate every year. Some educators make the argument that young children have a need for linguistic continuity between their homes and their classrooms. There is, in fact, a good deal of evidence that does support this view. These educators are strong advocates of programs that use a child's primary language for most classroom instruction while having him or her learn English as a second language. Over the years, the child is speaking English for more and more of the classroom day, until finally he or she is able to join a mainstream classroom.

29 c Selecting active or passive voice

When a verb is in the **active voice,** the person or thing performing the action is the subject.

Juana reads mysteries.

Juana is the actor performing the action, *reads. Mysteries,* the recipient of the action, is the direct object.

When a verb is in the **passive voice,** the recipient of the action becomes the subject, and there is no object.

Mysteries are read by Juana.

The recipient of the action, *Mysteries,* is the subject of the passive verb *are read.* The actor, *Juana,* appears as an **agent** in a prepositional phrase.

1 Using the active voice to emphasize actors and actions

By focusing on the actor, the active voice usually helps readers visualize the action of a sentence. Active voice sentences usually use fewer words and have a more direct structure than passive voice sentences. For these reasons, the active voice tends to enhance vitality.

■ Andrew Karpinski is the most widely read business writer of our

day. ~~His books have been devoured by~~ M̲illions of executives

412 Building vital sentences

have devoured his ~~books~~,   *His*   *grow*
∧seeking to enhance their management skills. ~~The~~ books ~~are~~
                                                                    ∧   ∧
~~written~~ directly from his years of experience as a consultant.

The habit of relying on the passive appears to be contagious; if your research sources use it extensively, be careful not to let it rub off on your writing.

2 Using the passive voice for special purposes

The passive voice de-emphasizes the actor and highlights the recipient. In some cases, this is very useful. You can use the passive voice to accomplish the following purposes.

To stress results over actions

A $500 million increase in the national debt *was approved* by Congress.

To leave the agent unstated

The city's first shelter for homeless people *was established* in a vacant warehouse.

To establish objectivity in research writing

In the experiment, samples of food *were* first *contaminated* with bacteria. The samples *were* then *irradiated*. The samples *were tested* to see whether the bacteria survived.

To improve flow between sentences

ACTIVE   Two crises threaten the economic security of the nation. Economists, business leaders, and politicians *have documented* the first crisis, which involves the decay of manufacturing industries. They *have* all but *ignored* the second, however.

PASSIVE   Two crises threaten the economic security of the nation. The first crisis, which involves the decay of manufacturing industries, *has been documented* by economists, business leaders, and politicians. The second, however, *has* all but *been ignored.*

ESL **VERBS THAT CAN'T BE PASSIVE, VERBS THAT CAN'T BE ACTIVE**

Not all English verbs can be both active and passive. Verbs that can't be passive are labeled **intransitive verbs** in a dictionary. The verbs *happen, occur, result from, disappear, vanish,* and *die* are a few of those that are sometimes mistakenly put in the passive voice.

▪ The tornado ~~was~~ happened yesterday.

▪ Much improvement ~~was~~ resulted from working with a tutor.

Some verbs followed by objects in active voice sentences (transitive verbs), such as *have, weigh,* and *consist of,* cannot be rephrased in the passive voice either.

ACTIVE New York City has five boroughs.

INCORRECT PASSIVE Five boroughs are had by New York City.

Sentences with **change-of-state verbs** are in the active voice even though no agent of the action is named. Change-of-state verbs are used when the agent is irrelevant. These verbs include *increase, decrease, open, close, develop,* and *change.*

Prices *increased* last week.

My hometown *changed.*

Some of these verbs can also be used as regular verbs in the active and passive voices if the agent is known and is relevant.

ACTIVE Many supermarkets *increased* prices last week.

PASSIVE Prices *were increased* by many supermarkets last week.

Some verbs are used only in the passive voice. These verbs include *be born, be located, be killed, be made,* and *be given.*

PASSIVE The U.S. capital was once located in Philadelphia.

INCORRECT ACTIVE The U.S. capital located in Philadelphia.

■ **EDITING 4: EXPLORATION**

The following passage by James Baldwin makes extensive use of expletive constructions and the passive voice. Read it carefully, and try to decide why the author has used these techniques. Do they influence the meaning of the passage? The effect? Where do they focus your attention? Do they create a particular mood or atmosphere?

"There is a custom in the village—I am told it is repeated in many villages—of 'buying' African natives for the purpose of converting them to Christianity. There stands in the church all year round a small box with a slot for money, decorated with a black figurine, and into this box the villagers drop their francs. During the *carnaval* which precedes Lent, two village children have their faces blackened—out of which bloodless darkness their blue eyes shine like ice—and fantastic horsehair wigs are placed on their blond heads; thus disguised, they solicit among the villagers for money for the missionaries in Africa. Between the box in the church and the blackened children, the village 'bought' last year six or eight African natives."

JAMES BALDWIN, "STRANGER IN THE VILLAGE"

■ **EDITING 5: PRACTICE**

Edit the following paragraph by using the active voice wherever it is effective. Make any small changes in wording that are necessary for smooth reading. More than one edited version is possible. Be ready to explain your editing choices.

We are all affected by pesticides. Hundreds of synthetic chemicals have been developed by scientists to destroy the insects and rodents that are called "pests" by farmers and Sunday gardeners. Once these deadly toxins are used, however, they don't just go away. They are maintained in the environment, where our crops and water supply are contaminated and desirable species of birds and fish are killed off. Ironically, pesticides are even known not to work very well in the first place, since usually a pest population that is resistant to the chemicals is created. And within a few years, it's just as large as ever. Pesticides' effect on the environment and on our lives should be questioned. Perhaps even the right to use them at all should be questioned.

| **29** | **d** | **Untangling noun clusters** |

A remarkable quality of English is its use of nouns as modifiers. Instead of saying *a cabinet for files*, we can say *a file cabinet*. We can also string noun modifiers together. *A metal file cabinet* is far easier to say than *a cabinet of metal for files*.

Like any good thing, noun modifiers can be carried to excess. A long string of noun modifiers, sometimes including adjectives, is called a **noun cluster:** *do-it-yourself home improvement instruction videotape recordings*. Readers encountering a noun cluster must stop and figure out which element is the "real noun" and which elements are modifiers. Vital sentences move readers along quickly and easily, so anything that causes readers to stop and struggle should be eliminated. In editing, untangle noun clusters for your readers by moving some of the noun modifiers to prepositional phrases.

■ Michael Graves's architecture attempts to revitalize a building ^*language of* ~~form~~ language *forms* that was lost during the heyday of International Style modernism.

A special kind of cluster, called a **false title,** is used in front of a person's name: *Texas-style chili cook-off champion Minnie Peppers*. False titles are so called because they are not formally bestowed (unlike, say, *President of the United States*). Like any other noun cluster, long false titles can hurt the vitality of your sentences.

When you encounter a cumbersome false title in your writing, choose the noun that you want to emphasize and put other words that belong together in prepositional phrases.

■ The committee nominated ^*Vernon E. Jordan, an* African American ^civil rights activist ^*lawyer and* ~~and lawyer Vernon E. Jordan, Jr.~~

■ **EDITING 6: EXPLORATION**

Read the following paragraph from Nancy Gibbs's description of modern American zoos. What choices has Gibbs made that give vitality to the passage?

"At some 150 American zoos . . . , the troubles are not very different. The sharks eat the angelfish. The Australian hairy-nosed wombat stays in its cave, and the South American smoky jungle frog hunkers down beneath a leaf, all tantalizingly hidden from the prying eyes of the roughly 110 million Americans who go to zoos every year. Visitors often complain that as a result of all the elaborate landscaping, they cannot find the animals. But this, like almost everything else that goes wrong these days, is a signal that America's zoos are doing something very right."

NANCY GIBBS, "THE NEW ZOO: A MODERN ARK"

■ EDITING 7: PRACTICE

Edit the following paragraph to create vital sentences. You may invent and add any details you think are necessary. More than one edited version is possible. Be ready to explain your editing choices.

Most dog owners don't realize in advance how much time, money, and energy must be spent on a puppy. First, there is housebreaking the puppy and teaching it basic puppy obedience skills: how to accompany its owner while on a leash, how to respond to its name, how to stay near its owner. There are also other things — fetching, standing, and so on. And even when owners have the time for training, they probably don't have the necessary expertise. This means enrollment in expensive obedience school classes is required. Puppies have other expenses as well. Veterinarian visits, food and bedding, leashes and playthings, and grooming — a must for any well-bred dog — are all costly. And at least one nice rug or one pair of shoes must be replaced because a bad dog has chewed through them. Still, as any devoted dog owner will tell you, the expense is justified by the rewards: there's nothing like coming home from a hard day and being greeted by someone who loves you unconditionally and absolutely.

■ EDITING 8: APPLICATION

Read through a paper you are working on, paying close attention to the vitality of your sentences. Have you chosen specific, concrete nouns and modifiers wherever possible? Are your verbs precise? Do they convey action? Have you used the passive voice? If so, do you have a good reason for doing so? Can you find any noun clusters? As you edit your paper, pay full attention to the vitality of the language and sentence structure, keeping the elements that you like and improving those that you don't like.

In most writing situations, the goal is to convey information as clearly and efficiently as possible, and so help the reader absorb information without unnecessary effort. In editing to achieve this goal, you must strive to make your writing **direct** — expressing ideas plainly — and **concise** — using as few words as possible to advance your purpose. By being direct and concise, you avoid vagueness, wordiness, and complexity that can tire or annoy readers.

Making your writing concise and direct may take several editing steps. Some writers call the process *boiling down*, by analogy to the cooking process that turns large quantities of thin broth into hearty, full-flavored soup. The drafts of this book required lots of boiling down. The following is our original draft of a paragraph that appears later in this chapter:

> In a famous piece of advice, public speakers are urged, "Tell them what you're going to tell them, then say it, then tell them what you said." In other words, say the message at least three times so that the audience will understand it clearly. This advice reflects the patterns of spoken language.

The second sentence seemed to do little more than rephrase the first, so we combined it with the third sentence.

■ In~~—other words, say~~ the message ~~at least three times so that~~ the audience ~~will~~ understand it clearly. ~~This advice reflects the patterns of spoken language.~~

spoken language, repeating   will help

With further editing we eliminated other unnecessary words.

■ In spoken language, repeating ~~the message~~ will help ~~the audience~~ understand ~~it clearly~~.

listeners

At every step, we compared the new edited version both with the previous one and with our understanding of what we were trying to say. We guarded against losing meaning, but we were willing to lose subtle shadings if we could state our point more clearly. If you edit relentlessly to eliminate extra words, the number you find may surprise you. Your prose will begin to shine from such polishing.

In editing for conciseness and directness, keep the following guidelines in mind:

- Eliminate vague generalities.
- Remove idle words.
- Simplify grammatical constructions.
- Eliminate redundant words or phrases.
- Avoid pretentious language.
- Minimize euphemism.

30 a   Eliminating vague generalities

Generalizations are broad statements that include little specific detail. By enabling us to express general concepts and to discuss categories, they are essential to abstract thinking. When generalizations become too broad, however, they no longer advance our reasoning; they simply take up space. They become **generalities,** expressing ideas so broad and common as to be obvious: *There are many kinds of dogs.* Some generalities attempt to make a point but result in circular reasoning: *During the harsh winters of the 1870s, the weather was very cold* (a harsh winter is cold by definition). Some are so broad that they don't really say anything at all: *Many factors played a part.*

Such sentences signal only that you will soon come to a point; they don't actually advance the discussion. Because they slow readers down, they may occasionally be useful if your discussion is extremely complex or technical. In most cases, however, eliminating them will improve your writing.

- How did the Ben and Jerry's ice cream franchise become so

successful in only six years? ~~There could be many answers to this question.~~ Fred Lager attributes it to quality, hard work, and being in the right place at the right time.

When you delete a generality, you may have to move some information from it to another sentence.

■ Is college worthwhile? ~~Whether or not to go to college is a decision that many eighteen-year-olds must face after graduating from high school.~~ Each graduate must decide according to his or her finances, other career opportunities, and, most important, personal interests and goals.

Unnecessary generalities can occur anywhere, but look particularly in your openings and conclusions, where you may be struggling to make sweeping statements or impressive summaries. (See Chapter 24.)

30 b Removing idle words

Work to eliminate idle words from your writing. A good test to determine whether a word isn't working is to remove it and see whether the sentence still makes sense. If the meaning is not changed, the word was contributing little.

1 Condensing automatic and wordy phrases

The speech habit of embellishing sentences with unnecessary words too easily becomes a writing habit. It is a fact that most writers do it all the time. For example, in the previous sentence, the introductory words *it is a fact that* add no meaning. Phrases like *it appears that* or *it has come to my attention that* merely preface what the writer is about to say, a sort of authorial "throat-clearing." Most sentences are better off without them.

Think of such phrases as **automatic phrases** that seem to

write themselves but that, when examined, add little if any meaning. They can appear anywhere in a sentence, but they appear
most often at the beginning. When you find an automatic phrase,
remove it and reread the passage. If no meaning has been lost,
read on. If something seems missing, try inserting a condensed
version of the phrase.

■ ~~In order to~~ ^To^ understand the effects of the law, consider the following example.

■ ~~In this day and age~~ ^Today^ children ~~in many instances~~ ^often^ know more
about black holes than they do about Black Beauty.

AUTOMATIC PHRASES

CONSIDER DELETING	OR SUBSTITUTING
it is a fact that	
it is clear that	
there is no question that	certainly
the reason is that	because
without a doubt	surely, certainly
it is my opinion that	I think
beyond the shadow of a doubt	certainly

Wordy phrases can usually be condensed to more concise phrases
or single words. Look for unnecessary uses of the preposition *of*
and for phrases containing *of* that can be reduced to a single
word.

■ They work at a small factory outside ~~of~~ Chicago.

■ The architect had a specific ~~type of~~ construction ^method^ in mind.

Abstract nouns like area, aspect, factor, kind, manner, nature,
tendency, thing, and type are imprecise and can create wordiness.

Often you can delete them, condense them, or find more concrete
substitutes. (See 29a.)

- Lola's job situation was ~~the type of thing that is~~ every working
  woman's worst nightmare.

 WORDY PHRASES

WORDY	CONCISE
most of the people	most people
all of the work	all the work
due to the fact that	since, because
despite the fact that	although
at that point in time	then
communicate to	tell
in this day and age	today
in those days	then
in any case	anyway
in the case of	regarding, concerning
in most instances	usually
in some instances	sometimes
subsequent to	after
in case	if
in the final analysis	finally

---

2 Deleting useless modifiers

Modifiers such as *clearly, obviously, interestingly, undoubt-*
edly, absolutely, fortunately, hopefully, really, and *totally* are often
used to intensify the meaning of a whole sentence, to make it
sound forceful or authoritative. Usually they add little and can be
deleted. Be careful, though, to test for altered meaning.

- The strike against General Motors ~~clearly~~ disrupted production
  of the new Saturn car. It was undoubtedly intended to do so.

  Anna considered, but decided against, deleting undoubtedly. *This mod-*
  ifier tells the reader that the assessment is her own conclusion.

| 30 | C | **Simplifying grammatical constructions** |

To fight wordiness yet another way, consider simplifying grammatical constructions. Changing a **passive voice** sentence to the **active voice** usually shortens it slightly. (See 29c.) Simplify sentences containing **expletive constructions** such as *there were* and *it is* by substituting strong verbs. (See 29b1.)

Also consider shortening dependent clauses to phrases and reducing phrases to single words. A **dependent clause** has a subject and a verb but cannot stand alone as a complete sentence. A **phrase** consists of a group of related words lacking a subject or a verb or both.

When editing to simplify dependent clauses, look especially at modifier clauses — those that function as adjectives or adverbs. A modifier clause usually begins with a relative pronoun such as *which, that, who,* or *whom* or with a subordinating conjunction such as *because, before, when, where, while, if,* or *although.* To shorten a modifier clause to a phrase, try using the past participle of the clause's main verb as the basis of the phrase.

CLAUSE   The research project *that we were assigned to complete* involves a complex experiment.

PHRASE   The research project *assigned to us* involves a complex experiment.

When editing to simplify phrases, look especially at modifier phrases, those used as adjectives or adverbs. They are usually built around a preposition, a participle, or an infinitive: *by the stream, built entirely of logs.* Often a modifier phrase can be turned into a single word.

■   The research project ~~assigned to us~~ involves a complex experiment.
(with handwritten insertion: "assigned" above "research")

In some situations, using the fewest number of words may not be the most effective editing choice. When a noun already is preceded by adjectives or when a modifier phrase itself contains modifiers, take care that you do not create an awkward noun cluster by simplifying too many constructions. (See 29d.)

ORIGINAL   The committee report listed sixteen international dealers who it said illegally sold military weapons.

AWKWARD   The committee report listed sixteen international illegal military-weapons dealers.

BETTER   The committee report listed sixteen international dealers of illegal military weapons.

30 d Eliminating redundancy

In a famous piece of advice, public speakers are urged, "Tell them what you're going to tell them, then say it, then tell them what you said." In speaking, repetition helps listeners understand.

In writing, a certain amount of repetition is important, even necessary. The repetition of words and phrases links sentences and paragraphs, providing continuity. (See 25c.) Repeating a key word or phrase can also help you build a rhythmic pattern to emphasize an idea. (See 27e.)

All that said, there is such a thing as too much repetition. Unnecessary repetition is termed **redundant.** Exactly what constitutes redundancy remains for you to determine. As you edit, evaluate each instance of repetition by using a comparison test. Edit out the repetition and reread the passage, comparing it both to the earlier version and to what you are trying to say. Remember, that in evaluating repetition you are not simply testing for changed meaning; you are trying to determine whether a repetition helps link ideas, sustains an important rhythm, or prevents confusion. If it does none of those things, edit it out.

■ The ~~general~~ consensus ~~of opinion~~ among students was that the chancellor had exceeded her authority.

Eliminate redundancy created by an unnecessary definition.

■ Foresters ~~who study trees~~ report that acid rain is damaging the state's population of hemlocks.

If you find yourself repeating the same word or using a similar one, look for ways to eliminate one.

■ ~~A very high percentage~~ ^About 90 percent^ of the prison's inmates take advantage of the special education program/~~about ninety percent~~.

You can often eliminate ineffective repetition by combining two sentences. (See Chapter 26.)

■ As you edit your writing, be alert to possible redundancy/~~One as kind of redundancy is~~ ^such^ an unnecessary repetition.

REDUNDANT PHRASES

first and foremost	refer back
full and complete	basic fundamentals
past history	initial preparation
round in shape	terrible tragedy
red in color	final result
the general consensus of opinion	free gift
a faulty miscalculation	true facts
old and outdated	completely destroyed

■ EDITING 1: EXPLORATION

Look for examples of writing that contain generalities, idle words, and redundancies. Magazine articles and mass-market nonfiction books are often good sources. Collect two or three examples, and try editing them to make them more concise. You may want to bring your examples and edited versions to class to share with your classmates. Be ready to explain what you found wrong with the originals and how your editing improves them.

■ EDITING 2: PRACTICE

Edit the following passage to make it more concise, eliminating vague generalities, idle words, and redundancies and simplifying grammatical constructions. More than one edited version is possible. Be ready to explain your editing choices.

Many languages have influenced the development of English. The first instance of important influence came from the north in the form of Viking invaders who spoke a Scandinavian language. It appears that when these Vikings settled down and became farmers and traders who were peaceful, they wanted to be able to communicate with and speak to their Anglo-Saxon neighbors. There were several factors involved. Both groups spoke Germanic languages with similar vocabularies but with systems of grammar and inflection that were somewhat different. Clearly the easiest of the ways to smooth communication was for each group to drop the elements of their language that gave the other group difficulty. This explains why it is the case that modern English lacks the elaborate systems of verb endings and gender that characterize and distinguish other Indo-European languages.

30 e Avoiding pretentious language

Some writers believe that to sound authoritative or scholarly they must use technical or obscure language. They write about *institutionalized populations* instead of *people in prison*. Other writers overdecorate their sentences with flowery phrases: *In this sacrosanct institution of higher learning we continually rededicate ourselves to the elevated principle that knowledge is empowering.*

Using needlessly complex language is termed **pretense.** A special class of pretentious language is called **bureaucratese** after the government functionaries who so often use it. Pretentious language may impress readers so much that they stop reading.

Pretentious language often avoids names and personal pronouns and uses the third person and the passive voice. Editing it into plain English sometimes requires that you choose subjects for verbs and find more direct ways of addressing readers.

ORIGINAL   The range of alternative services provided includes examinations to determine visual or auditory impairment and the specification, provision, and instruction in the use of prosthetic devices including corrective lenses and auditory amplification devices.

EDITED   We can examine your eyes and ears, prescribe and sell glasses and hearing aids, and teach you to use them.

PRETENTIOUS LANGUAGE

PRETENTIOUS	PLAIN
client populations	people served
voiced concern that	said
range of selections	choice
minimizes expenditures	saves money
of crucial importance	important
provide an avenue for investigation	be worth investigating
institution of higher learning	college *or* university

30 f Minimizing euphemism

A **euphemism** is a word chosen for its inoffensiveness to substitute for one considered harsh or indelicate. In conversation, social conventions make it difficult to speak of certain subjects, especially money, death, and the human body. For example, many people consider it more delicate to say *I lost my grandmother last week* than *My grandmother died last week.*

Euphemisms are also used by writers or speakers who fear negative reaction to plain talk about bad news. This use is called **doublespeak,** a term coined by George Orwell in his novel about totalitarianism, *1984.* Doublespeak is intentionally misleading. Someone reading of *unemployment compensation reductions* may not understand immediately that *jobless workers will get less money.*

In academic writing, your purpose is to inform, not to obscure or mislead, so your search for a delicate phrase has gone too far when it obscures meaning. Edit to eliminate euphemisms by writing out a more directly worded alternative and reading it in context. Then judge whether you feel comfortable with the more direct wording and whether your audience will be offended by your directness or appreciative of your candor.

■ As a result of ~~the reordering of~~ budget ~~priorities,~~ _{cuts, the} library ~~acquisi-tions~~ will ~~be deferred and maintenance activities suspended.~~ _{stop buying books and cleaning the building.}

ESL IDENTIFYING EUPHEMISMS

Identifying and editing euphemisms can be especially difficult when English is your second language. You may have learned euphemisms in your study of English vocabulary before you learned words that are more basic and direct. Keep in mind that it's often challenging for native English speakers to avoid this kind of language, too. If you're wondering whether a word or expression is a euphemism, try asking your instructor, a tutor, or other students to look at your writing.

▪ EDITING 3: EXPLORATION

Read the following passage, in which humorist Russell Baker lampoons contemporary rhetoric. How many examples of pretentious and euphemistic language can you find? Try editing the passage by replacing each example of pretentious language or euphemism with a more direct expression. Have you got "Little Red Riding Hood" back?

"Once upon a point in time, a small person named Little Red Riding Hood initiated plans for the preparation, delivery and transportation of foodstuffs to her grandmother, a senior citizen residing at a place of residence in a forest of indeterminate dimension.

"In the process of implementing this program, her incursion into the forest was in mid-transportation process when it attained interface with an alleged perpetrator. This individual, a wolf, made inquiry as to the whereabouts of Little Red Riding Hood's goal as well as inferring that he was desirous of ascertaining the contents of Little Red Riding Hood's foodstuffs basket, and all that."

RUSSELL BAKER, "LITTLE RED RIDING HOOD REVISITED"

▪ EDITING 4: PRACTICE

Edit the following passage to make it more concise and direct, eliminating pretentious language, euphemism, or misdirection. More than one edited version is possible. Be ready to explain your editing choices.

The photography exhibit scheduled to appear at the Mainfield Gallery has been postponed because of protests by a local community organization, which has voiced a concern about the photographic depiction of minors au naturel. This is a minority view, however. Moderates who might find fault with photographs showing acts of intimacy between consenting adults see no problem with the scheduled exhibit. And of course, those in the community who firmly espouse the sacred freedom of speech guaranteed by our forefathers would support the exhibit no matter how offensive or injurious to the moral fiber of our young people.

■ EDITING 5: PRACTICE

Edit the following passage to make it more concise and direct. More than one edited version is possible. Be ready to explain your editing choices.

My great-grandfather emigrated from Poland when he was a young man. Several of his cousins already lived in small Pennsylvania mining towns. When my great-grandfather arrived in America, he joined his cousins and began working in the mines. There were several things he found discouraging. The dirty work, which was also dangerous, was far different from the life of agricultural splendor he had expected to lead, but he refused to let these types of circumstances ruin his happiness. It eventually was the case that he brought two of his brothers over to this country, and together the three of them saved money that was sufficient to buy a good-sized farm. By the age of thirty-four, my great-grandfather had once again started a new life: he moved into his farmhouse, married a local woman, and began raising a family that would eventually be blessed by the arrival of fourteen bundles of joy.

■ EDITING 6: APPLICATION

Select a page from a paper you are working on. Examine each sentence carefully, looking for instances of wordy or indirect language. Have you written any vague generalities? Have you used any automatic phrases or useless modifiers? Could any of your sentences be condensed into clauses, your clauses into phrases, or your phrases into words? Are there any redundancies? Have you used any words or phrases that may strike readers as pretentious? Have you tried to soften the facts by using euphemisms? Edit the page to eliminate any problems you found, and then compare the edited version with the original to see how you have improved its effectiveness.

Because English has a particularly rich vocabulary, writers often must choose among many words with similar meanings. For example, the place you live might be your *house, home, residence, abode, dwelling, domicile, habitation, quarters,* or *lodging.* Less formally, it might be your *shack* or *digs.* Eventually you have to choose. Not every word is effective or appropriate in every context. Your goal as a writer is to find the word that conveys precisely the right shade of meaning for the passage you are writing.

As you consider word choice while editing, keep in mind the following guidelines:

- Recognize how the history of English has influenced its vocabulary.

- Use a dictionary and other reference books to learn new words.

- Expand your vocabulary.

- Choose words based on connotation as well as denotation.

- Distinguish among commonly confused words.

- Use standard idioms.

- Use slang, regionalisms, and colloquialisms sparingly.

- Use technical language carefully.

31 a Understanding the history of English

The special richness of the English vocabulary results from the merging of many languages. As waves of invasion and migration have swept over the British Isles in the past three thousand years, each group of new arrivals has brought a language that has blended with existing speech.

In the fifth century A.D., Germanic peoples from northern Europe — the Jutes, Saxons, Frisians, and Angles (for whom England is named) — invaded Great Britain. They brought with them their Germanic language, the basis of modern English (we refer to their early form of English as Old English or Anglo-Saxon). Words that can be traced to this period form a large part of our modern vocabulary: *god, gold, hand, land, under, winter, word.*

In the eighth century, another group of invaders, known as Danes or Vikings, brought their Scandinavian language, Old Norse. Though they came as conquerors, many Danes settled alongside the Angles and Saxons. Loanwords from the Danes include *fellow, hit, law, rag, take, want,* and many words that begin with an *sk* sound (*scorch, scrape, scrub, skill, skirt, sky*).

In 1066 the Normans, from what is now western France, conquered England and brought with them their language, Old French. Following the Norman Conquest, French became the language of the noble classes, of the law, of money, and of learning. The French words *parliament, justice, crime, marriage, money,* and *rent* seeped into common usage, as did *art, ornament, mansion, pleasure, joy,* and thousands more. English retains two sets of words for many kinds of food, an indication of the social distinction between French speakers and English speakers in Norman England. Workers in the farmyard used the English words *pig, deer, sheep, cow,* and *calf,* while the ruling class used French names for the meat prepared for the table: *pork, venison, mutton, beef,* and *veal.* Eventually English became the predominant language among all classes, but by then French words had thoroughly infiltrated its vocabulary.

In the sixteenth century, those interested in classical Greek and Latin learning — history, mythology, and science — brought into English a torrent of new words. From Greek came *democracy, hexagon, monogamy, physics, rhythm,* and *theory.* From Latin came *client, conviction, index, library, medicine, orbit,* and *recipe.* In the nineteenth and twentieth centuries, Greek and Latin roots have continued to provide a wealth of scientific and technical terms, many of which are invented words made up of ancient roots, prefixes, and suffixes: *cholesterol, cyanide, radioactive, telegraph, telephone,* and *television.*

English also has absorbed words from many other languages as its speakers have spread across the globe and as people with other native languages have settled in English-speaking lands. Modern American English includes words from hundreds of languages, including Spanish (*canyon, mustang, poncho, rodeo*), Italian (*balcony, balloon, carnival, ghetto*), Arabic (*alcohol, algebra, candy, lemon*), Hindustani (*bungalow, cot, jungle, loot, shampoo*), Japanese (*kimono, samurai, zen, karate*), and various African languages (*banana, yam, voodoo, jazz, banjo*).

These linguistic riches put at your disposal an array of words with similar meanings. Is a particular man *male, manly, macho, virile,* or *masculine*? Does a particular woman have a *job, employment,* a *profession,* a *vocation,* or a *calling*? The choice depends on the shade of meaning you desire and the effect you want your words to have on your readers.

■ EDITING 1: PRACTICE

For each of the words below, think of as many synonyms and near synonyms as you can. Try to guess which words on your list came from Old English, which from French, which from Latin or Greek, and which from other languages. Use a dictionary to confirm your guesses. You may want to compare your word lists with your classmates'.

> house
> happy
> angry
> light
> street
> walk

31 b Using the dictionary and thesaurus

Writers commonly rely on reference books to guide them in their use of language. Dictionaries and thesauruses can lead you through the maze of similar words. By suggesting even more choices, they also can help you enlarge your own word stock. If you consult them regularly, looking up and noting unfamiliar words, your word skills and your writing will improve.

■ The dictionary

An **unabridged** dictionary offers information on word origins as well as definitions and usage samples. *Webster's Third New International Dictionary* (Springfield, MA: Merriam, 1961), which contains 470,000 words, is among the most widely used. The most comprehensive is the 616,500-word *Oxford English Dictionary*, 2nd ed., 20 vols. (Oxford: Clarendon UP, 1989), which since 1928 has attempted to chronicle the first appearance and usage history of every word in the language. Here is the entry from *Webster's Third*, as it is called for short, for the word *communicate*:

com·mu·ni·cate \ kə'myünə‚kāt, *usu* -ād• + V \ *vb* -ED/-ING/-S [L *communicatus*, past part. of *communicare* to share, impart, partake, fr. *communis* common — more at MEAN] *vt* **1** *archaic* **:** partake of **:** use or enjoy in common **:** SHARE ⟨thousands that ~ our loss —Ben Jonson⟩ **2 a :** to make known **:** inform a person of **:** convey the knowledge or information of ⟨~ the news⟩ ⟨~ his secret to a friend⟩ **b :** IMPART, TRANSMIT ⟨~ his pleasure to us⟩ ⟨an odor *communicated* to one's fingers⟩ ⟨*communicating* the disease to others⟩ **c :** to make (itself) known — used of an intangible ⟨his tension *communicated* itself to his companion⟩ **3** [LL *communicatus*, fr. L] **:** to administer the Communion to (a person) ⟨the priest *communicating* him⟩ **4** *archaic* **:** to put (oneself) into close connection or relationship with — used with *to* **5** *archaic* **:** to give or deliver over (something material or tangible) **:** BE-STOW ~ *vi* **1** [LL *communicatus*, fr. L] **:** to partake of the Lord's Supper **:** receive Communion ⟨Eastern Orthodox Christians ~ in both elements⟩ **2** *obs* **:** to have a common part **:** PARTICIPATE, SHARE **3 :** to send information or messages sometimes back and forth **:** speak, gesticulate, or write to another to convey information **:** interchange thoughts ⟨they *communicated* with each other for years⟩ **4 :** be connected **:** open into each other **:** afford unbroken passage **:** JOIN ⟨the two rooms ~⟩ ⟨the pantry ~*s* with the hall⟩ **5** *philos* **:** to have something logically in common **:** be further specifications of a common universal **:** be overlapping classifications or connotations **6 :** to arouse or enlist the sympathetic interest or understanding — used with *with* ⟨old plays that … have long since lost their ability to ~ with an audience —Wolcott Gibbs⟩

An **abridged** dictionary omits some words and some obsolete or archaic definitions and may be handier to use than a huge unabridged volume. *Merriam-Webster's Collegiate Dictionary*, 10th edition (Springfield, MA: Merriam-Webster, 1993), includes some 170,000 entries with an emphasis on contemporary American usage. *The American Heritage Dictionary*, 2nd college edition (Boston: Houghton, 1991), defines over 200,000 words, putting the most common meaning first. For many entries, it also provides comments on usage from a panel of language experts. The *Random House Webster's College Dictionary* (New York: Random, 1991) lists

over 180,000 entries, also starting with the most common definition. Here is the entry for *communicate* from *Merriam-Webster's
Collegiate Dictionary*:

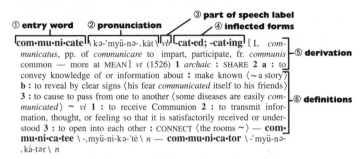

③ **part of speech label**
① **entry word**   ② **pronunciation**   ④ **inflected forms**

com·mu·ni·cate \ kə-'myü-nə-, kät \ *vb* \ **-cat·ed; -cat·ing** [L *com-* ⑤ **derivation**
municatus, pp. of *communicare* to impart, participate, fr. *communis*
common — more at MEAN] *vt* (1526) **1** *archaic* : SHARE **2 a** : to
convey knowledge of or information about : make known ⟨~ a story⟩
b : to reveal by clear signs ⟨his fear *communicated* itself to his friends⟩
3 : to cause to pass from one to another ⟨some diseases are easily *com-* ⑥ **definitions**
municated⟩ ~ *vi* **1** : to receive Communion **2** : to transmit information, thought, or feeling so that it is satisfactorily received or understood **3** : to open into each other : CONNECT ⟨the rooms ~⟩ — **com·**
mu·ni·ca·tee \ -,myü-ni-kə-'tē \ *n* — **com·mu·ni·ca·tor** \ -'myü-nə-
,kā-tər \ *n*

Although specific details may vary, most dictionaries follow a
common format.

The **entry word (1)** is printed in dark type with bars, spaces,
or dots between syllables to show where the word may be hyphenated at the end of a line. If two spellings are shown, the first is
generally more common, although both are acceptable. If two
spellings are dissimilar, entries are cross-referenced.

gaol (jāl) *n. Brit. sp. of* JAIL

A superscript numeral preceding an entry indicates that two or
more words have identical spelling. The words may or may not be
related.

The **pronunciation (2)** is shown in parentheses or set off by
slashes. If two pronunciations are given, the first is generally more
common, although both are acceptable.

A **part of speech label (3),** usually in italic type, appears
next: *n* for noun, *vb* for verb, *vt* for transitive verb, and so forth.

Next may be **inflected forms (4)** — irregular spellings or
forms of plurals for nouns and pronouns, comparatives and superlatives for modifiers, and principal parts for verbs.

The **derivation (5)** of the word from its roots in other languages is set off by brackets or slashes. *OE* and *ME* refer to Old
and Middle English, *L* to Latin, *Gr* to Greek, *OFr* to Old French, *Fr*
to French, *G* to German, and so on.

For the **definitions (6),** the major meanings of a word are
numbered and arranged from the oldest to the most recent or

from the most common to the least common. For some definitions, an example of the word used in a phrase or sentence is enclosed in brackets.

Following the definitions, **synonyms** or **antonyms** are listed for some words, often with a comment describing exactly how the words are similar or different.

For words or meanings not considered standard American English, the following **usage labels** are used:

archaic, for a meaning now used only rarely or only in special contexts: *quotha* for "he said"

colloquial (coll.), for a meaning usually used in speech or informal writing: *oldster* for "elderly person"

dialect (dial.), for words used only in some geographical areas: *nary* for "never" or "not one"

obsolete (obs.), for a sense no longer used that may be encountered in old writings: *nice* for "lewd" or "wanton"

slang, meaning highly informal usage or an unusual sense of an established word: *squeeze,* as in *main squeeze,* for "boyfriend" or "girlfriend"

substandard (substand.), used in some dictionaries for *colloquial,* meaning widely used but not accepted in formal usage: *drownded* for *drowned*

British (Brit.), Irish, Scottish *(Scot.),* and so on, for a word used primarily in a particular area rather than the United States: *lorry* for "motor truck" in Great Britain. Some dictionaries, including *Webster's New World,* use a star (*) to mark Americanisms (*davenport* for "large couch or sofa").

If a term has a special use in a particular discipline, that field is identified before the definition.

rest (rest) *n.* . . . **9.** *Music a)* a measured interval of silence between tones *b)* any of various symbols indicating the length of such an interval

Usage notes following definitions provide information on how the word is used.

andante . . . **2.** moderately slow . . . — often used as a direction in music

Usage notes also indicate that the term may be considered offensive or derogatory or that a usage may be considered incorrect.

2 The thesaurus

A **thesaurus** (the word comes from the Greek for "treasure") lists synonyms for each entry. Many thesauruses list antonyms as well. The most widely used one, *Roget's Thesaurus of English Words and Phrases*, in its 1987 edition lists words in six major classifications, with subdivisions of related concepts under each and cross-references among the subdivisions. A 1992 edition published by Dell, *Roget's 21st Century Thesaurus*, lists words in alphabetical order and includes a concept index.

A thesaurus can help you find the right word for a particular context or level of formality. If you are writing about the final chapters of a novel and you cannot remember the technical term for its ending, look up *ending*. A thesaurus would suggest, among other choices, *conclusion*, *epilogue*, *finale*, and *denouement*, the last of which is a term used in literary analysis. Whenever the thesaurus leads you to an unfamiliar word, look it up in a dictionary to be sure you understand its specific meaning.

3 Specialized dictionaries

Some **specialized dictionaries** provide extensive and detailed information on the vocabularies of various disciplines. For example, if you need terms for the architectural features of medieval cathedrals or the techniques involved in building a modern skyscraper, you might consult the *Dictionary of Architecture and Construction*. Another kind of specialized dictionary covers regional and cultural variations of English. The *Dictionary of American Regional English*, the official dictionary of the American Dialect Society, provides a fascinating survey of American folk speech. (Two volumes of a planned five have been produced.) The *New Dictionary of American Slang* lists words from the fast-changing universe of colloquial English. Etymological dictionaries focus on word origins. Other dictionaries cover major and minor branches of the language, from Canadian to Jamaican and Bahamian English.

■ EDITING 2: PRACTICE

Use a dictionary and a thesaurus to look up any words that seem unfamiliar or that might be misused in the following passage. Edit the passage by substituting more familiar words and correcting any misuses while preserving the intended meaning. Be ready to explain your editing choices.

The role of Emma Woodhouse in Jane Austen's novel *Emma* often receives censure for her supercilious behavior. Many readers consider her attitude toward her neighbors to be unconscionable: she avoids calling on them whenever possible and suffers their visits with scarcely concealed ennui. And it's certainly true that Emma regards all social functions as opportunities to display her better charms and talents. Yet Emma may be understood as Austen's portrayal of an exceptional individual constrained by a mediocre society.

31 c   Expanding your vocabulary

Words are tools of communication. The more such tools you know how to use, the better you will be able to convey your thoughts clearly and precisely. You can enlarge your tool kit of words, your vocabulary, in several ways. If you read and listen actively to the words others use, you will become aware of new words and unfamiliar usages. When you encounter a passage containing a new word, paraphrase it in familiar words. That will help fix the new word in your mind. Here are some other ways to improve your vocabulary.

■ Learning from context

You often can infer the meaning of words from the words around them, the **context.** Suppose you read the following:

> Robin went out looking for mabobs. She knew the best season for them was early in the fall. The first few she found were hard and green, and birds had beaten her to the next bush. Finally she found some lovely ripe ones, just turning blue, and filled her basket with them.

You now know a great deal about *mabobs.* They are found out of doors and they are seasonal. They turn blue as they ripen, birds like to eat them, and they grow on bushes. By now you have probably concluded that *mabobs* must be some kind of fruit. You will be watching at the next reference to see whether or not they are edible.

2 Learning from roots, prefixes, and suffixes

You can find clues to a word's meaning by looking at roots, prefixes, and suffixes. A **root** is a base word, or part of a word, from which other words are formed. A **prefix** is a group of letters attached to the beginning of a root to change its meaning. For example, the word *prefix* consists of a root, *-fix-*, in the sense of "attach," and a prefix, *pre-*, meaning "before." Changing a prefix can dramatically alter the meaning of a word. For example, *democracy* means "rule" (*-cracy*) "by the people" (*demos-*); *autocracy* means "rule by one person"; *theocracy* means "rule by God or divine authority."

A **suffix** is attached to the end of the root. Adding a suffix changes the meaning of the word and often changes the part of speech. For example, the verb *educate* means "to teach or instruct"; the noun *education* means "the process of being taught"; the adjective *educational* means "having to do with education or teaching."

If you learn some common prefixes and suffixes and can spot roots that are related to familiar words, you can make educated guesses about the meanings of words. For example, the words *antebellum*, *bellicose*, and *belligerent* seem to share a root. If you know that *belligerent* means "warlike or at war," you can guess that *antebellum* means "before war" and that *bellicose* means "prone to war or fighting."

Another way to form words is by combining roots. Most scientific and technical words coined since the Renaissance have been made this way. For example, the word *photograph* is composed of the roots *-photo-*, from the Greek word meaning "light," and *-graph-*, meaning "writing." Other root words combined with *-graph-* make *telegraph*, meaning "distant writing"; *phonograph*, "an instrument for recording sound"; and *chronograph*, "an instrument for measuring time." Recognizing common roots like *-chrono-* for time, *-graph-* for writing, *-phono-* for sound, and *-tele-* for distance can help you decipher many new words.

 COMMON PREFIXES

PREFIX	MEANING	EXAMPLE
a-, an-	without	atheist, anhydrous
ante-	before	antecedent
anti-	against	antiwar
auto-	self	autopilot
co-	with	cohabit
com-, con-, cor-	with	compatriot
contra-	against	contradiction
de-	away from, off	deplane
	reverse, undo	defrost
dis-	not	dislike
en-	put into	encode
ex-	out, outside	exoskeleton
	former	ex-president
extra-	beyond, more than	extraterrestrial
hetero-	different	heterogeneous
homo-	same	homogeneous
hypo-	less than	hypobaric
il-, im-, in-, ir-	not, without	illogical, immoral, insensitive, irresponsible
in-	into	inject
inter-	between	intercollegiate
intra-	within	intravenous
macro-	very large	macroeconomics
micro-	very small	microscope
mono-	one	monomania
non-	not, without	nonsense
omni-	all, every	omnipotent
post-	after	postmodern
pre-	before	preheat
pro-	forward	promote
sub-	under	submit
syn-	with, at the same time as	synchronize
trans-	across	transcontinental
tri-	three	triangle
un-	not	unloved
uni-	one	unicorn

COMMON SUFFIXES

NOUN SUFFIXES

SUFFIX	MEANING	EXAMPLE
-ance, -ence	act	adherence
-ation, -ion, -sion,	act	abstention
-tion	state of being	pretension
-er, -or	one who	pitcher
-dom	place	kingdom
	state of being	wisdom
-hood	state of being	manhood
-ism	act, practice	terrorism
-ist	one who	psychologist
-ment	act	containment
-ness	state of being	wildness
-ship	state of being	professorship
	quality	workmanship

VERB SUFFIXES

SUFFIX	MEANING	EXAMPLE
-ate	to make	activate
-en	to make	broaden
-fy	to become	liquefy
-ize	to make into	crystallize

ADJECTIVE SUFFIXES

SUFFIX	MEANING	EXAMPLE
-able, -ible	able to	acceptable
-al, -ial	pertaining to	musical
-ate	having, filled with	passionate
-ful	filled with	fanciful
-ish	resembling	devilish
-ive	having the nature of	votive
-ly	pertaining to	motherly
-less	without	shameless
-like	prone to, resembling	warlike
-ose, -ous	characterized by	morose

ADVERB SUFFIX

SUFFIX	MEANING	EXAMPLE
-ly	in a manner characterized by	easily

Especially in words formed long ago, a root may be spelled in several different ways. Thus *justice* and *jury* are both related to the Latin word *jus*, for "law." Both *transcribe* and *manuscript*, as well as *inscription*, *conscript*, and *scripture*, share the Indo-European root *-skeribh-*, "to cut or incise" and, hence, "to write."

Learning common roots, prefixes, and suffixes can help you decipher unfamiliar words and increase your vocabulary. However, be careful to check your guesses, as appearances can be deceiving. *Indifferent*, for example, does not mean "lacking in difference" or "similar"; it means "unbiased" or "impartial." Guess, but check the dictionary before you write.

3 Keeping a word list

Another technique for learning new words is keeping a list. Reserve a page or two in your journal for a word list, and every time you encounter an unfamiliar word—for example, during a lecture or a conversation—write it down. You might even write down your best guess of the word's meaning. At regular intervals, review the list. Look up the words, and jot down the definitions. Try them out in conversation or in your journal. When you feel sure you have learned them, cross them off the list.

■ EDITING 3: PRACTICE

Using context and your knowledge of prefixes, suffixes, and roots, guess the meaning of the italicized words in the following sentences. Then check the accuracy of your guesses by looking up the words in a dictionary.

1. Eunice acted as though she were a *conscript* when forced to play the role of Madame Bouvard in our production.

2. She would have preferred contributing in some *nondramatic* capacity.

3. Although occasionally *immodest*, Madame Bouvard is still essentially a moral woman.

4. Because of the *proximity* of the furniture and the sets onstage, waltzing around requires a certain amount of *surefootedness*.

5. The script was the result of a collaborative writing project, so the real achievement lay in the *contexture*.

31 d Considering connotations

The direct and literal meaning of a word is its **denotation.** For example, *fragrance*, *odor*, and *smell* denote the same thing: something detected by the sense of smell. But their associations differ. Saying *You have a distinctive fragrance* is quite different from saying *You have a distinctive odor.* *Fragrance* suggests a pleasant sensation, while *odor* suggests an unpleasant one. Such an associated or indirect meaning is a word's **connotation.** As you edit, pay attention to the connotations of your words because they will affect the meaning you convey.

Some words have such strong connotations that using them will make your writing seem **biased.** (See Chapter 32.) Calling someone's hobby a *fixation* or *obsession* rather than just a *pastime* implies that the person is mentally unstable. This characterization will seem unfair unless you can support your implied assertion with credible evidence. When you find words that make your writing seem biased, replace them with more balanced alternatives.

Another way in which connotations differ is in **level of formality.** (See 28c.) Some words are appropriate for informal contexts such as writing about personal experience, while others are appropriate for formal academic writing. Deciding whether you refer to an instructor as a *teacher*, a *professor*, an *educator*, or a *pedagogue* is partly a choice among increasing levels of formality.

■ EDITING 4: PRACTICE

Complete the following passage, choosing one of the two words in each set of parentheses. Be sure the words you choose have the connotations you want. More than one version is possible for some sentences. Be ready to explain your choices.

As a girl, my grandmother worked in a textile mill. Recently she (revealed to/told) me what it was like for her. Every morning she had to feed her (younger/youthful) brother and sister breakfast and then take them to the house of Cousin Sophia, who looked after them. My grandmother was at the (gates/portal) of the factory by 5:25 A.M. If an employee was late, she would (forfeit/lose) half a day's pay. The work was (drab/tedious) and exhausting. My grandmother had to (patrol/watch) and tend the same machine for hours on end, with nothing to (distract/entertain) her but the whirring and clanking of the engines. Her lunch hour was just fifteen minutes long, and she often (toiled/worked) sixteen hours a day.

| **31** | **e** | **Distinguishing among frequently confused words** |

Homonyms, words with the same sound but different spellings and meanings, frequently create confusion. Even experienced writers sometimes use their when they mean *there* or *they're* or confuse *write, right,* and *rite; its* and *it's;* or *principle* and *principal.*

Sometimes the confusion arises from spelling errors. If you drop one letter from *two* or *too,* you may write *to,* and you may miss the error if you are proofreading quickly (so will your computer spell-checking program). As you edit, be aware of potentially confusing words and examine each one to be sure it is used correctly. A list of problem homonyms appears in Chapter 50.

You may also confuse words not because they sound alike but because they are similar in form and somewhat related in meaning. Particularly troublesome offenders include words that can be spelled as one word or two — *every day/everyday, altogether/all together* — and the pairs *sit/set, lie/lay, affect/effect,* and *compose/comprise.*

Remember that *sit* means "to be seated"; *set* means "to put or place": *People sit on their front porches. We set the books on the table. Lie* means "to recline"; *lay* means "to put or place": *I lie down. I lay the mail on her desk.* (*Lie* can also mean "to tell a falsehood.")

With the pair *affect/effect,* normally *affect* is the verb while *effect* is the noun: *Raising prices could affect sales. Raising prices could have a bad effect on sales.* However, *effect* can be a verb meaning "to make happen": *She was able to effect a change in policy. Affect* also has a noun form, used in psychology and the behavioral sciences to mean "an emotion or feeling."

Perhaps no two words are more often confused by professional writers than *compose* and *comprise. Compose,* from French roots meaning "to put together," means "to make up." *Comprise* comes from a French root meaning "to include." Thus *is composed of* means the same thing as *comprises. Comprised of* is always an error.

Fifty states *compose* the United States.

The United States *is composed* of fifty states.

The United States *comprises* fifty states.

If you find that you frequently misuse one of these words, use your computer's search-and-replace function to find all occurrences so that you can evaluate each one. Other problem pairs are listed in Chapter 50 and in the Glossary of Usage.

ESL **FREQUENTLY CONFUSED WORDS AND PHRASES**

The following are some pairs of words or phrases that are often confused by ESL writers.

WORD OR PHRASE	MEANING OR FUNCTION	EXAMPLE
another	an additional one	I lost my library card. May I get *another* one?
the other	the second of two items	We have two cars. One is a station wagon; *the other* is a jeep
few	not many	Frankly, I wouldn't ask him. He usually has *few* good ideas. [He has almost no good ideas.]
a few	some	Why don't you ask him? He always has *a few* good ideas. [He does have some good ideas.]
been	past participle	She's *been* gone all day.
being	present participle	Why do you think she's *being* so difficult?

31 f Using prepositions and particles idiomatically

Idioms are conventional expressions or speech patterns that cannot easily be predicted by rules of logic or grammar. Why do we ride *in* a car but *on* a train? Why do we *take* a picture but *make* a recording? The correct word in each of these cases is determined by what is conventional and customary, by what is idiomatic.

Native speakers of a language seldom have difficulty with its idioms. However, the idiomatic use of prepositions and particles in English sometimes causes problems even for native speakers.

ESL WORD ORDER WITH PHRASAL VERBS

A phrasal verb consists of a verb plus a particle — a word such as *on*, *up*, *by*, or *through*. Both the verb and the particle are needed to convey the full meaning of the phrasal verb: *put on, give up, get by, muddle through.* (See 31f.)

Determining where in a sentence to place the particle of a phrasal verb is sometimes difficult. Here are some guidelines.

Some phrasal verbs are intransitive — that is, they do not take a direct object. The most common phrasal verbs in this category include *break down, come back, come out, come over, pass out* ("faint"), and *play around.* The particle for such a phrasal verb should always come directly after the verb.

The stray dog *came back* the next day.

Some phrasal verbs are transitive — that is, they can take a direct object. The phrasal verbs in this category can be further divided into three types according to whether or not the direct object can come between the verb and the particle.

I. For some transitive phrasal verbs, the particle cannot be separated from the verb by the object. Common verbs of this type include *come across, get on, get off, get over, get through* ("finish"), *look into, run into, see through* ("not be deceived by").

INCORRECT Please *go* this report *over* carefully.

A **preposition**—such as *at, by, for, out,* or *to*—shows the relationship between a noun or a pronoun and other words in the
sentence. Idiomatic usage is the only guide to the correct use of
prepositions with nouns and verbs and in standard expressions
about time and space.

> This novel shows a great similarity *to* that one. The similarity *of*
> the stories is remarkable.

> I will meet with you *in* the evening, *at* sunset.

Particles look like prepositions—common particles include
up, down, out, in, off, and *on*—but they combine with verbs to

---

CORRECT	Please *go over* this report carefully.

2. For some transitive phrasal verbs, the particle may be separated
from the verb by the object. Common verbs of this type include *call
off, cut up, do over, fill out, fill up, find out, give up, look over, leave out,
make up, put on, throw away, turn off,* and *turn on.*

CORRECT	The president *called* the meeting *off.*
CORRECT	The president *called off* the meeting.

If the object of such a verb is a pronoun, however, the particle
must be separated from the verb.

INCORRECT	Why did she *call off* it?
CORRECT	Why did she *call* it *off*?

3. For a few transitive phrasal verbs, the particle must be separated
from the verb by the object. The most common verbs of this type include *get through* ("communicate"), and *see through* ("persevere").

INCORRECT	I tried to *get through* the idea to him.
CORRECT	I tried to *get* the idea *through* to him.

form **phrasal verbs** or **two-word verbs.** Both the verb and the particle are needed to convey the full meaning of a phrasal verb, which may be quite different from the meaning of the verb alone. The meanings of the phrasal verbs in the following sentences, for instance, have very little in common with the verb *to come.*

How did this *come about?* (happen)

Of course, I expected things to *come out* all right. (end)

I was unconscious for a moment, but I soon *came to.* (revived)

The correct particle is determined by the idiomatic construction of the phrasal verb you use.

When editing your writing, watch for idioms with prepositions and particles. Be aware of potential trouble spots; try to make note of how these words are used in standard English, and whenever you are in doubt, consult a dictionary or other reference. If you know that you frequently misuse a particular preposition or particle, use your computer's search-and-replace function to find each occurrence of the problematic construction so you can correct each one.

■ **EDITING 5: PRACTICE**

Edit the following paragraph to make sure that words and expressions are used according to convention. More than one edited version is possible. Be ready to explain your editing choices.

Just a few short years ago, computers were rare as hens' teeth on college campuses. Students had to type their papers or write them with hand, just as they had for generations. Today, however, most of us either own a word processor or have access to one owned by our schools. This has had an enormous affect both on the process we use to create papers and on the papers themselves. Some students still think they can just set down in front of a computer the night before a paper is due, flip a switch, and crank out a paper with no real work. Most of us, however, know the truth of the computer-era saying "Garbage in, garbage out." A computer can do some of the drudgery and can make problem solving more creative, but you still have to put your nose to the grindstone to write a really good paper.

> ✓ **VERB-PREPOSITION IDIOMS**
>
> | | |
> |---|---|
> | amuse | My cousin was amused *by* the clown. |
> | | I was amused *at* my cousin's delight. |
> | | The clown amused us *with* her tricks. |
> | arrive | They arrived *at* the airport. |
> | | They arrived *in* Los Angeles. |
> | | They arrived *on* the scene. |
> | differ | Margot differs *with* Harriet on this subject. |
> | | Each one's opinion differs *from* the other's. |
> | | They differ *over* whether to go skiing. |
> | identify | You can identify her *by* her appearance. |
> | | You must identify her *to* the authorities. |
> | | Do you identify *with* her? |
> | occupy | This room is occupied *by* Mario. |
> | | He is occupied *with* his book. |
> | prejudice | The jury was prejudiced *against* the defendant. |
> | | They were prejudiced *by* improper evidence. |
> | reward | The dog was rewarded *for* its behavior. |
> | | It was rewarded *by* praise. |
> | trust | He trusts *in* you. |
> | | He trusts you *with* his investment. |
> | vary | The colors vary *in* intensity. |
> | | They vary *from* one another. |
> | | People's tastes vary *with* time. |

31 **g** Using slang, regionalisms, and colloquialisms sparingly

Everyday speech is peppered with **slang,** language that originates in and is unique to small groups such as students, musicians, athletes, or politicians. One group's slang may be unintelligible to another. Take, for example, the slang of politics — *spin, sound bite* — or student life — *nerd, grind, flunk.* Some slang words eventually join the mainstream and may even become part of standard English. A *jeep* was originally a general-purpose (*g.p.*) military vehicle introduced in World War II. Now the word denotes a certain type of rugged vehicle driven by average people.

Regionalisms are expressions used in one part of the country but not standard nationwide. The generic word for *soft drink,* for example, varies by region from *pop* to *soda* to *soft drink* to *seltzer.* Some expressions from regional dialects are regarded as **substandard,** not acceptable in formal writing. People in central Pennsylvania, for example, often say *youse* for the plural of *you* and *a while* to mean "while you wait" or "at first," as in *Can I get youse your drinks a while?*

A **colloquialism** is an expression common to spoken language but not usually used in formal writing. For example, the noun *pot* can refer not only to a cooking vessel but also to an illegal drug, the amount of money bet on a hand of cards, and ruination (*go to pot*).

Use slang, regionalisms, and colloquialisms sparingly, if at all. Slang and some regionalisms may not be understood by everyone, and they are frequently too informal for college writing. In descriptions and dialogue, however, they can convey immediacy, authenticity, and unpretentiousness. Colloquialisms also are usually too informal for academic writing, but in some informal contexts—personal experience essays, for example—they may be effective.

■ **EDITING 6: EXPLORATION**

In the following passage, where and how has the author used slang? What effect does it have on the passage? Why do you think she chose to use slang this way?

"Most college students do not live in the plush, comfortable country-clublike surroundings their parents envisage, or, in some cases, remember. Open dorms, particularly when they are coeducational, are noisy, usually overcrowded, and often messy. Some students desert the institutional 'zoos' (their own word for dorms) and move into run-down, overpriced apartments."

CAROLINE BIRD, *THE CASE AGAINST COLLEGE*

31 **h** **Using jargon carefully**

Each discipline develops special terms to express its ideas. Studying biology would be impossible without terms like *mitosis, chromosomes, osmosis,* and *nucleotide.* Literary criticism depends on words like *denouement, character development, motivation, plot,* and *allegory.* Specialized language particular to a field or discipline is called **jargon.**

As you edit, you must decide whether any special terms you have used are appropriate for your audience. For example, a general audience might understand *thigh bone* more readily than *femur,* but an instructor reading a paper on a medical subject would expect you to use the technical term. To a specialized audience, correct and conventional use of technical language helps demonstrate your mastery of a subject and enhances your credibility with your readers. Use of less-technical terms for a general audience shows sensitivity to your readers' needs.

If you adopt jargon for its own sake your writing may end up sounding stilted or pretentious. (See 30e.) As you edit, decide which special terms are essential to your meaning and which are merely for show.

Jargon

It is incumbent on us to challenge the prevailing proposition that critical-theoretical approaches are the most enlightened ways of introducing students to literary experience.

Edited

We should question the widely held idea that using theories of criticism provides the best way to introduce students to literature.

Sometimes the most direct language cannot communicate a complex concept — you need a technical term. In such a case, introduce it in a context that will help the reader grasp its meaning, perhaps with an explicit definition. The following passage was written for car enthusiasts, but not for mechanical engineers, so the writer had to explain clearly the terms *lean* and *stoichiometric.*

> Running an engine *lean* means that there is less fuel in the cylinders than is needed to completely burn all of the available air. With gasoline, 14.7 pounds of air are required to burn 1 pound of fuel. This air-fuel ratio is referred to as *stoichiometric.*
>
> FRANK MARKUS, "LEAN-BURN ENGINES"

■ EDITING 7: PRACTICE

Edit the following paragraph, making sure that slang and technical language are used only where appropriate. More than one edited version is possible. Be ready to explain your editing choices.

Thirty percent of the students interviewed in the study said they owned personal computers and used them regularly to write papers. Many take basic precautions to safeguard their files, such as occasionally backing up on floppies. Most of these said they have learned through experience how important it is to take such steps. Seventy-five percent of those who own computers have trashed a file at one time or another, and almost everyone reported knowing at least one fellow hacker whose hard disk has crashed.

31 **i** **Using figurative language effectively**

Figurative language, which likens one thing to another in an imaginative or fanciful way, can bring freshness, vigor, and resonance to writing. Too much literal language can shackle your prose, tethering it to the hard, dull ground. Figurative language can unchain your thoughts, allowing an occasional leap of the imagination.

Figurative language helps readers understand connections through comparison or analogy. This process is so deeply embedded in our language that we often overlook it. For example, the verb *overlook* in the previous sentence creates a metaphor because it suggests that we can see or fail to see a process the same way that we can see or fail to see a physical object.

Figurative language, however, should be fresh, not hackneyed. You should take care to use it effectively — not for its own sake, as ornament or embellishment, but to help readers understand you.

A **mixed metaphor** combines two or more unrelated images, occasionally with unintended effects. As the old joke goes, keep your eye on the ball, your ear to the ground, your nose to the grindstone, and your shoulder to the wheel; now try to work in that position. Mixed metaphors often occur when a writer unthinkingly strings one cliché after another.

If you find a mixed metaphor, consider eliminating the weaker image and extending the stronger.

■ Jones eclipsed Smith ~~by handing him a whipping~~ in the free-
throw contest, hitting $\overset{a\ shining}{\wedge}$ ten of ten while Smith $\overset{somberly}{\wedge}$ hit but five.

TYPES OF FIGURATIVE LANGUAGE

A **simile** is a comparison that expresses a resemblance between two essentially unlike things, using *like*, *than*, or *as*.

> German submarines swam the seas like sharks, suddenly seizing their prey without warning.

A **metaphor** equates one thing with another.

> Her life became a whirlwind of design meetings, client conferences, production huddles, and last-minute decisions.

An **analogy** uses an extended comparison to show similarities in structure or process.

> The course catalog at a large university resembles a smorgasbord. Courses range from differential calculus to American film, from Confucianism to liberation theology. Students receive little advice as to which classes are the salads, which the desserts, and which the entrees of a college education. Even amid this feast, without guidance a student may risk intellectual malnutrition.

Personification is the technique of attributing human qualities or behavior to a nonhuman event or phenomenon.

> The ship sailed into the teeth of the hurricane.

Deliberate exaggeration is called **hyperbole.**

> No book in the world is more difficult than this economics text. Reading it is absolute torture.

The opposite of hyperbole is deliberate **understatement.**

> With temperatures remaining below zero all day, it will seem just a bit chilly outside tomorrow.

Irony is the use of words to mean the opposite of what they seem to mean on the surface.

> "House guests for three weeks? Terrific."

A **paradox** contains a deliberately created contradiction.

> For a moment after she spoke, the silence was deafening. Then the audience erupted in cheers.

■ **EDITING 8: PRACTICE**

Edit the following paragraph to improve its use of figurative language. More than one edited version is possible. Be ready to explain your editing choices.

Many people object to the television cartoon *The Simpsons* because they say it is over the top, but millions of children watch it with bated breath every week. Critics say shows like this are causing the American family to disintegrate and are teaching children that it is okay not to hit the books. They think that young people want to be like Bart Simpson, who is as proud as a peacock of being a bad student, and that the show is a stumbling block for students who want to be above par. I think it's crystal clear that children can tell the difference between television and reality. When they laugh at Bart talking back to his parents, they are just letting off steam because adults are always laying down the law.

31 j Eliminating clichés

An overused expression or figure of speech is called a **cliché.** The word itself, interestingly, is a metaphor. *Cliché* is a French word for the sound a stamping press makes in a process of making multiple, identical images. In other words, something has become a cliché if it is ordinary, run-of-the-mill, like the following:

the last straw	needle in a haystack
strong as an ox	handwriting on the wall
better late than never	tried and true
lay the cards on the table	hit the nail on the head

To edit a cliché, try improving upon it. Go back to the original image and describe it in new words, make it more pointed with fresh detail, or introduce a play on the too familiar words.

■ Outside, the wind ~~howled~~ *keened as though it had lost a child.*

If you cannot resuscitate the cliché, replace it, striving for directness instead.

■ It was *so* dark ~~as night~~ inside the cave, *that we waited in vain for our eyes to adjust.*

■ **EDITING 9: PRACTICE**

Edit the following passage, making sure that each word is the best one possible. More than one edited version is possible. Be ready to explain your editing choices.

If the nineties have been a golden era for home shopping channels, it has also been one for mail-order catalogs. In the past five years, the number of catalogs delivered to American homes has tripled. Vendors compose not only old favorites such as L. L. Bean and discount electronics distributors, but also newer outfits that have been created merely to take a vantage this trend. According to one survey, the average mail-order catalog junkie receives ten garb catalogs, nine catalogs for housewares and garden equipment, five catalogs for his or her favorite hobby, and six gift catalogs each month. And this doesn't even take into a count the specialized catalogs that focus on children, pets, travel, and any other earmark of a consumer's life that might result in a purchase or two. Mail-order companies sell each other their lists of suckers, so once a consumer receives one catalog, chances are that he or she will be receiving catalogs to life.

■ **EDITING 10: APPLICATION**

Select one page from a paper you are working on. Carefully examine your choice of words, using the dictionary and thesaurus to check any word you aren't sure about. Does each word convey the precise meaning you intended? Do any words have connotations that are inappropriate in context? Have you misused any frequently confused words? Have you used every preposition and particle conventionally? If you have used any idiomatic expressions, are they correctly worded? Have you used any slang, regionalisms, colloquialisms, or jargon? If so, do you have a good reason and are you sure your readers will understand? Edit the page to improve word choices as necessary, and pay close attention to word choice as you edit the rest of the paper.

The structure of language enables us as thinkers, speakers, and writers to move from the general to the specific and back again. Used carefully, **generalization** offers a powerful tool for predicting future experience from the past.

Nevertheless, the process of generalization carries risks. You might generalize from faulty data or use faulty logic. If, for example, a tossed coin comes up tails ten times in a row, you might predict that the next toss will come up tails as well, or that, since tails has come up so many times, it just has to be heads. Either prediction would be illogical; the odds on the next coin toss are exactly the same as the first, fifty-fifty.

Using generalizations about a group of people to predict or describe the behavior or characteristics of an individual is particularly risky. Careless generalizations, especially those based on race, ethnicity, gender, cultural background, age, physical characteristics, or lifestyle, are called **stereotypes.** Many stereotypes in our society have developed in an atmosphere of fear and ignorance, an atmosphere in which people who were "different" were little understood but seen as a threat.

Writers especially should be aware of the extent to which stereotypes are part of language, both in individual terms (*liberal politician, chorus girl*) and in descriptions that rely on stereotypical images (*sleepy Southern town*). Even something as small as referring to a doctor or lawyer as *he* can contribute to a stereotype, such as the image of all doctors and lawyers being men. Language that contributes to stereotypes is called **biased.** Many people — and not just those being stereotyped — find biased language offensive and alienating. Using it may offend your readers and cause them to mistrust your judgment.

When you edit, the following strategies can help you eliminate biased language:

■ Eliminate stereotypes.

■ Use labels that are acceptable to the people under discussion and that are free from negative connotations.

■ Choose nonsexist language.

32 **a** Eliminating stereotypes

Stereotypes are oversimplified generalizations; they frequently involve gender, race, ethnicity, or sexual preference. Many stereotypes attribute undesirable behavior or characteristics to all members of a group. But not all stereotypes seem negative. Expecting someone's racial or cultural background to imply skill in mathematics, for example, may seem positive, but it is still a stereotype. Such assumptions are not only illogical but demeaning, as they substitute a simplistic formula for appreciation of an individual's characteristics, positive or negative.

As you edit your writing, look for sweeping statements, such as *Like most ten-year-olds* (or *suburban families* or *Korean immigrants*). If you find one, ask yourself four questions.

First are you relying on stereotypes rather than on evidence to make your point? Using stereotypes is an easy — but faulty — way to cover a lot of ground quickly. In effect, you say to your readers, "You know what I mean." But your readers may not know what you mean, and, in fact, they may disagree. Second, are you generalizing logically from accurate evidence? Make sure your facts are indeed facts and that you have enough of them to support a broad generalization. Then make sure your conclusions are logically related to your facts. That someone is Canadian and that she behaves in a certain way may both be facts, but it does not necessarily follow that being Canadian *causes* the behavior. Third, are you using generalizations responsibly? Be careful not to use generalizations about a group to predict an individual's knowledge, abilities, attitudes, beliefs, or behavior. For example, anthropologists have suggested that Japanese culture emphasizes group values more highly than Western society does, but that generalization does not support an automatic characterization of any one Japanese person as a conformist. Fourth, do any of your generalizations express stereotypes euphemistically? What seems a positive stereotype often is a slur in disguise, as when a politician praises women for their emotional support and spiritual dedication but means that they shouldn't — or can't — worry about the practical issues of politics and government.

■ Like most ~~teenage~~ *inexperienced* drivers, he didn't know what to do when the car started to skid.

Inexperience, not age, is the reason why he didn't know what to do.

■ ~~Like so many of his race,~~ Michael Jordan is a superbly gifted athlete. His tremendous achievements have provided an inspiration to ~~black~~ *many* children everywhere *, perhaps especially to black children who identify with him.*

Jordan's race is not relevant to his skill as an athlete, and not all the children who admire him are black.

If you find you have used a stereotype, edit your writing to eliminate it. In some cases, you might need to qualify a broad generalization; in others, you might need to replace sweeping statements with relevant, specific evidence. And in still others, you might need to eliminate altogether the stereotypical image or information.

■ Frank Peters, stooped from years in the woods, ~~but still alert,~~ remembers the dry, hot summer of the Tillamook Burn.

The original betrayed the writer's expectation that people of Peters's age should not be still alert.

▇ EDITING I: EXPLORATION

Almost everyone uses stereotypes of some kind in thought patterns. Try to identify stereotypical notions that you hold. For a start, write down what images and ideas spring to mind in response to the following terms:

intellectuals	drug addicts	career politicians
lawyers	BMW drivers	actors
movie producers	chiropractors	churchgoers

How many people do you know in each category? Is your attitude based on your own experience, or does it come from what you have heard or read of other people's attitudes? Do you have similar impressions of everyone you have met in the group, or have you noticed variations?

32 b Using labels carefully

People often speak of themselves in terms of the racial, gender, political, professional, or ethnic group to which they belong. Everyone who communicates, including writers, uses labels to identify such groups: whites, females, Democrats, psychiatrists, Poles. But labels inevitably focus on a single feature and have the potential to offend those who do not want to be characterized in one particular way. Also, some labels are either explicitly or implicitly derogatory because they go beyond simple identification and evoke stereotypes. As you edit, examine any labels you have used for an individual or group. Try to use only those labels acceptable to the members of the group themselves, and avoid labels with negative connotations.

1 Using a group's own labels

Whenever possible, refer to a group of people by the label they themselves prefer. Sometimes this is easy: members of the Rotary Club call themselves *Rotarians*; members of the Ancient Free and Accepted Masons are *Masons*.

With ethnic, racial, or cultural labels, your choices become more difficult. Sometimes even those who belong to a group do not agree on what they should be called. The terms *black*, *Afro-American*, *African American*, and the more inclusive *people of color* all have their advocates, for example, while *Negro* and *colored* have fallen into disfavor. Some people refer to themselves using the term *Hispanic*, others prefer *Latino* and *Latina*, others still *Chicano* and *Chicana*. Many *native Americans* prefer that term to *Indian*. Some *Inuit* insist on that label rather than *Eskimo*. Some people would rather be described as *Asian* than *Oriental*, while others prefer the more specific *Japanese*, *Chinese*, *Korean*, or *Vietnamese*.

Wherever possible, be guided by the preferences of the people you are writing about. If you cannot ask a member of the group, consult a recent dictionary.

■ For centuries, historians have hailed William Penn's treaty as an
  Native Americans.
effort to deal honorably with ~~the Indians~~

It should go without saying that certain racial, ethnic, and other labels are so emotionally loaded that they have no place in academic writing.

ESL **USING LABELS DERIVED FROM ADJECTIVES**

Many labels that describe groups are derived from adjectives: *the wealthy, the poor, the homeless,* and so on. If you have decided that one of these collective nouns is an appropriate reference for a group of people, check to make sure you have used it correctly. Always use the definite article *the* before the noun.

■ The legislature passed a new law to help *the* hearing impaired.

Use a plural verb when the collective noun is the subject.

■ The wealthy in this country *are* going to get taxed more.

Use the collective noun only in reference to a group. A collective noun usually cannot refer to a single person. If you refer to one person in the group, use an adjective + noun construction.

■ We interviewed a homeless *person* about her search for a job.

---

2 Checking labels for negative connotations

Even labels that seem neutral on the surface can hide negative connotations. (See 31d.) For example, the term *AIDS victims* implicitly characterizes the people it refers to as blameless, which may be your intent, but also as helpless, which may not. As you edit, watch for such unnecessary or unintended negative connotations, and substitute more neutral alternatives. Focus whenever possible on people's strengths, referring for example to people who are *living with* cancer or are cancer *survivors* rather than people *suffering from* the disease. Also try to focus on individuals first as people and second as having a particular characteristic: *a woman with quadriplegia* rather than *a quadriplegic*.

People's preferences for certain labels change frequently, as connotations change. People with physical limitations often, but not universally, prefer *disabled* to *handicapped*, a term that at one time seemed more neutral than *crippled*. The continuing attempt to avoid the negative connotations of some terms has resulted in the use of *visually impaired* or *hearing impaired* for *blind* and *deaf* and in such constructions as *differently abled* for *disabled*. Because labels without negative connotations can become cumbersome, such terms are easily lampooned as an excess of "political correctness." Indeed, they often involve a trade-off, costing in directness as much as they gain in sensitivity. When you edit your writing, you must decide where to strike a balance.

If a label has no relevance, consider dropping it.

■ He was a fascinating ~~old~~ man with a lifelong passion for book collecting and fine cognac.

■ **EDITING 2: PRACTICE**

Identify stereotypes in the following passages and describe the ways in which they may be thoughtless or offensive. If any useful information is conveyed by a particular passage, edit it to communicate the information in a way that is not offensive. Be ready to explain your editing choices.

1. The biggest menace on our highways is teenagers and old folks.

2. No matter how reliable your housekeeper may seem, it's best not to give her a key to your house. It could easily end up in the hands of a drug-addicted grandson.

3. Children of recent immigrants are generally either underachievers or overachievers.

4. The husband in the movie is a typical accountant: bland, boring, and conventional. His flaky, astrology-obsessed wife is pure Californian.

5. The willingness of Japanese workers to value team effort above individual reward gives the companies they work for an unfair advantage in international trade.

32 c Using nonsexist language

Any language containing sexual stereotypes runs the risk of alienating up to half its potential audience. Several kinds of sex bias arise from habits of thought and language: using masculine terms to refer to people in general; unnecessarily characterizing occupations by gender; providing information about a woman that would not be offered about a man; making nonparallel comparisons between the sexes; and wrongly implying that the audience is exclusively male or female.

■ In pronoun choice

English does not have a singular personal pronoun of indefinite gender. In everyday speech, people often use plural pronouns to avoid the masculine forms: *Everybody had fun on their vacations.* But in writing a sentence like this one where the subject (*everybody*) is actually singular, a singular pronoun must be used. *Everybody had fun on his vacation* is grammatically correct. A sentence like this forces a choice between masculine pronouns such as *his* and feminine pronouns such as *her*.

Until recently, writers and readers alike accepted the generic use of *he, him,* and *his* to refer to singular nouns or pronouns whose gender is unknown, unstated, or irrelevant: *Anyone who believes those promises should have his head examined.* (See 39d.) Those who approve of the use of *he* in such situations say it need not be understood as referring exclusively to males. However, this usage has been disappearing fast, particularly in academic writing, on the grounds that the generic *he* inevitably implies the exclusion of women.

The best strategy is to avoid the exclusion implied by *he*. If you know the gender of the antecedent, you can use the pronoun of the same gender.

■ Every monk has ~~their~~ *his* own room.
  ^

Monks are men, so his *is appropriate.*

You can make the antecedent plural (and look out for other agreement problems).

■ *The doctors have their* ~~Every doctor has his~~ own professional ~~specialty.~~ *specialties.*
  ^   ^

To avoid suggesting that all the doctors had the same specialty, specialty also had to be made plural.

You can use *his or her*. Do this sparingly, as *his or her* becomes monotonous with repetition.

or her
■   A lawyer is only as good as hisₐpreparation.

You can eliminate the pronoun by restructuring the surrounding sentence or sentences. This approach is often the most effective.

Every writer
■   ~~Everyone~~ wrestles with this problemᵢ ~~in his own writing~~.

2 In universal terms

The practice of using *man* and *mankind* to refer to the whole of humanity has fallen into disfavor because it seems to exclude or diminish the female half of the species. Substitute more truly universal terms such as *humanity, the human race, humankind,* or *people.*

3 In occupational terms

In choosing terms for a person's occupation, focus on the occupation, not the person's gender. Otherwise you risk suggesting that gender is a person's most important attribute or that some jobs are "naturally" held by either men or women.

Many occupational terms have a feminine form consisting of the neutral base form and a suffix that indicates the female gender: *actor/actress, author/authoress, poet/poetess, executor/executrix.* Some terms, like *authoress* and *executrix,* are obsolete; others, including *poetess,* appear occasionally but are considered offensive; and still others, such as *stewardess, waitress,* and *actress,* are in the process of changing to more inclusive terms (*flight attendant, server, actor*). As you edit, avoid feminine forms and describe a person solely by occupation, not gender.

Occupational terms that end in *-man* imply that everyone who engages in that profession is a man. Sex-neutral substitutes for many occupations are readily available.

BIASED	MORE NEUTRAL
statesman	diplomat
mailman	letter carrier, mail carrier
policeman	police officer
fireman	fire fighter
businessman	executive, businessperson

Similarly, do not use language that implicitly assumes that an occupation determines a person's gender — that all flight attendants, nurses, secretaries, or teachers are female or that all airline pilots, business executives, or bronco busters are male.

■ The physician was assisted by a ~~male~~ nurse, who helped prepare the patient for surgery.

4 In descriptions

Treat the sexes equally. As you edit, notice comments about a woman's appearance or family life. If you would not have made the same comments about a man in a similar context, delete them.

■ Dr. Jones, ~~mother of three,~~ was named to the hospital's peer review board.

5 In comparisons

Whenever you use a pair of terms for male and female, make sure that the terms are directly comparable. The phrase *man and wife*, for example, identifies one partner as independent (*man*) and the other in terms of her relation (*wife*) to him. Edit it as *man and woman* or *husband and wife*. Similarly, look out for terms like the following, which pair male and female on unequal terms: *men's room/ladies' room* (change *ladies'* to *women's*); *the British novelists Dickens and Jane Austen* (add *Charles* before Dickens or delete *Jane*); *Dr. Morgenstern and Anne Williamson* (use a title and no first name for each or add a first name and delete the title for *Morgenstern*).

6 In addressing your audience

Unless you are sure that only men or only women will read your writing, do not address your audience as if it were of a single gender.

■ When you buy a house, ~~your wife~~ *you* will have to get used to a new kitchen.

■ **EDITING 3: EXPLORATION**

The following are excerpts from three political statements from earlier centuries, when ideas about the roles of the sexes and sexism in language were very different. To whom do you think Jefferson is referring? How about Lincoln? Is either statement ambiguous, open to more than one interpretation? How do you think Stanton interpreted Jefferson's text? In what ways is her use of male and female terms different from Jefferson's? In what ways is it similar to Jefferson's?

"When in the Course of human events, it becomes necessary for one people to dissolve the political bands which have connected them with another, . . . a decent respect to the opinions of mankind requires that they should declare the causes which impel them to the separation.

"We hold these truths to be self-evident, that all men are created equal, that they are endowed by their Creator with certain unalienable Rights. . . . That to secure these rights, Governments are instituted among Men deriving their just powers from the consent of the governed."

THOMAS JEFFERSON, DECLARATION OF INDEPENDENCE (1776)

"Four score and seven years ago our fathers brought forth on this continent, a new nation, conceived in liberty, and dedicated to the proposition that all men are created equal."

ABRAHAM LINCOLN, GETTYSBURG ADDRESS (1863)

"When, in the course of human events, it becomes necessary for one portion of the family of man to assume among the people of the earth a position different from that which they have hitherto occupied, . . . a decent respect to the opinions of mankind requires that they should declare the causes that impel them to such a course.

"We hold these truths to be self-evident: that all men and women are created equal; that they are endowed by their Creator with certain inalienable rights; . . . that to secure these rights governments are instituted, deriving their just powers from the consent of the governed."

ELIZABETH CADY STANTON, DECLARATION OF SENTIMENTS (1848)

■ **EDITING 4: PRACTICE**

Edit the following passage, eliminating any biased language that may be offensive to readers. More than one edited version is possible. Be ready to explain your editing choices.

All of the old people at White Pines Residence agree that there couldn't be a better place for them to live. The modern residence has been designed to meet their every need, and in some ways it resembles a spa more than an old-age home. For one thing, the food is terrific. Every meal offers at least one exotic dish, always cooked to perfection. This isn't surprising, considering that the chef was born in Paris. In the medical area, facilities and services are first rate. A doctor is on call around the clock to provide care to all of the residents, many of whom suffer from cancer. With the handicapped in mind, doorways have been built that are wide enough for a cripple's wheelchair to pass through, and ramps are familiar sights, both inside and outside. Staff members have been carefully chosen for both their experience with old people and their personalities. They are all extremely popular with the residents. One of the best loved is a male nurse who always makes time in his busy schedule to read to the blind residents. Another nurse is a former actress; she has arranged for a local theater group to perform regularly at the residence. In addition, volunteers from the local college visit with the residents, providing them with companionship and friendship. Like so many old people, the residents at White Pines enjoy spending time with young people and telling stories about their youth. State-of-the-art facilities are not cheap, however, and White Pines is no exception; the cost of the facility may explain the high percentage of Jewish residents. To judge from the level of satisfaction among the residents, however, it is money well spent.

■ EDITING 5: APPLICATION

Read through a paper you are working on, looking for examples of biased language. Are there any characterizations that might be considered stereotypical? If so, can you supply specific details to support your use of the stereotypes? Or should they be eliminated? Have you used any labels to describe groups of people? Would these labels be acceptable to the people themselves? Have you used male pronouns to refer to both genders? Can you find any other examples of sexist language? If you discover such stereotypes or biased language in your paper, consider carefully why you might have written that way in the first place and how you can avoid it in the future. Then edit the relevant passages to eliminate the biased language. How does the edited version compare with the original?

Editing Grammar

465

An **independent clause** includes a **subject** and a **predicate** and can stand alone as a complete sentence because it expresses a complete idea.

┌────── Subject ──────┐ ┌────── Predicate ──────┐
Professional athletes can earn huge salaries.

A sentence can contain two complete ideas, but they must be joined in a clear, conventional way: with a comma and a coordinating conjunction; with a semicolon alone; with a semicolon and a conjunctive adverb or transitional phrase; or with a colon. These markers tell readers that a new idea is about to be presented and clarifies the relationship between the ideas.

┌───────────── Independent clause ─────────────┐ ┌────── Independent
Professional athletes can earn huge salaries, yet some of them want

clause ──────┐
still more.

In this example the comma and the coordinating conjunction *yet* indicate that a new independent clause, with its own subject and predicate, is about to begin. They prevent misreading by limiting the number of possible ways the sentence can proceed from that point.

Two independent clauses joined without such a marker make a **fused sentence** (also called a **run-on** or **run-together sentence**). Readers get no warning when one independent clause ends and another begins.

Using a comma and a coordinating conjunction 467

FUSED SENTENCE

┌─────────────── Independent clause ──────────────┐ ┌──────
Professional athletes can earn huge salaries some

Independent clause ──────────────────┐
are paid millions of dollars a year.

COMMON CAUSES OF SENTENCE ERRORS

Comma splices and fused sentences, sometimes called **sentence errors,** often occur when two clauses express ideas closely linked in the writer's mind. Understanding why sentence errors occur can help you learn to recognize them in your own writing. Here are several common situations that often lead to sentence errors.

1. The second clause offers an example, explanation, or elaboration.

■ The tribes gathered every summer along the banks of the river, they
to
fished and hunted and picked berries.

2. The second clause contrasts the meaning of the first.

■ Everyone was asked to express an opinion on the plans, Mr. Johnson
but
was out of town.

3. The subject of the second clause is a pronoun that renames the subject of the first clause.

■ The professor asked us to write our thoughts down. he said just to
He
write whatever came to mind as fast as we could.

4. A conjunctive adverb or transitional phrase is incorrectly used to join two sentences.

■ I remember playing with Ernest and Mike, in fact, I can hardly remember playing with anyone else.

Two independent clauses joined (or "spliced") only by a comma make a **comma splice.**

COMMA SPLICE   Professional athletes can earn huge salaries, some are paid millions of dollars a year.

Seeing the comma not followed by a conjunction, readers may expect what follows to be part of the first clause rather than the beginning of a new clause.

As you edit your writing, watch for sentences that contain two independent clauses; check to see that you have joined them in an acceptable way.

■ Professional athletes can earn huge salaries, *but* ₍ₐ₎million-dollar contracts are the exception, not the rule.

■ Professional athletes can earn huge salaries₍ₐ₎*; in fact,* some are paid millions of dollars a year.

■ Professional athletes can earn huge salaries /₍ₐ₎: Barry Bonds, for example, signed with the San Francisco Giants for $43 million over six years.

As these edited sentences show, there are three ways to join two independent clauses in a single sentence:

■ Use a comma and a coordinating conjunction.

■ Use a semicolon (either alone or with a conjunctive adverb or transitional phrase).

■ Use a colon when the second clause explains or illustrates the first.

Other ways to repair a comma splice or a fused sentence may involve greater changes or rewording:

■ Divide the sentence into two sentences.

■ Subordinate one clause to the other.

■ Rewrite the sentence as one independent clause.

How you choose to correct a fused sentence or comma splice depends on the meaning you wish to convey, the length of the sentence, and the rhythm and wording of surrounding sentences.

| **33** | **a** | **Using a comma and a coordinating conjunction** |

The **coordinating conjunctions** *and, but, yet, so, for, or,* and *nor* join equal grammatical elements and specify a relationship between them, such as addition (*and*), contrast (*but, yet*), causation (*so, for*), and choice (*or, nor*). (See Chapter 26.) If the ideas in two independent clauses are equally important and their relationship can be adequately expressed by a coordinating conjunction, you can join them with a coordinating conjunction preceded by a comma. (See 44a.)

- The cyclone was especially savage, *and* it struck a particularly vulnerable area.

- Maya Angelou has worked as an actress and director, *but* her greatest success came as an autobiographer and poet.

EDITING I: PRACTICE

Edit each fused sentence or comma splice using a comma and a coordinating conjunction. More than one editing option is available to you. Be ready to explain your editing choices.

David Halberstam writes about many of the events of our time, *and* he has received numerous awards for his work.

1. The praise that David Halberstam has received for his nonfiction writing is due in large part to his blunt style he always says what he means.

2. He was critical of the media's involvement in the 1988 presidential election, he said so openly.

3. In his writing he not only identifies the point he is trying to make, he also proceeds to solidify and clarify it.

4. He leads the reader through his thought processes, rarely is any point unsubstantiated.

5. He feels strongly about his subjects he seems to become very involved with them.

---

33 **b**   **Using a semicolon**

1 **Semicolon alone**

A **semicolon** following an independent clause signals that what follows is also an independent clause whose meaning is of equal importance to the first. (See 45a.) Joining two clauses with a semicolon alone is appropriate only when the clauses are closely related and the relationship is clear. If they are not closely related, you probably should make them separate sentences. (See 33d.) If the relationship is not clear, a conjunction is probably needed to clarify it.

■ For years the Federal Communications Commission has advocated legislation to allow competitive auctions for broadcast licenses;so far Congress has refused.

Semicolons are especially useful in sentences that contain more than two independent clauses.

■ The sculpture was monstrous;its surface was rough and pitted, and its colors were garish.

The semicolon helps clarify the relationship among the three clauses. The second and third clauses together illustrate the point made in the first clause and are roughly comparable to it.

Although an independent clause following a semicolon is essentially a complete sentence, it never begins with a capital letter. (See 51a.)

There are two cases in which commas used alone to join independent clauses do not create comma splices and so do not need to be replaced with semicolons. The first is when the clauses are very short, closely related, and parallel in form:

I washed the clothes, I dusted the furniture, I fed the children.

Commas are also used to introduce the brief questions or statements known as **tag sentences:**

A semicolon would look odd here, wouldn't it?

2 Semicolon with a conjunctive adverb or transitional expression

Unlike a coordinating conjunction, a **conjunctive adverb** (*finally, however, therefore*) or a **transitional expression** (*in fact, for example*) cannot be used with a comma to join two independent clauses. Conjunctive adverbs and transitional expressions require a stronger mark of punctuation, a semicolon. (See the box on this page for a list of conjunctive adverbs; see 25c for a list of transitional expressions.)

■ The rebel forces were never completely defeated; moreover, they still control several strategic highland passes.

Some writers mistake conjunctive adverbs for coordinating conjunctions (*and, but, or,* and so on). One way to tell the difference is to note that, like other adverbs, a conjunctive adverb often can be moved to different spots within a sentence, while a coordinating conjunction cannot be moved.

✔ **CONJUNCTIVE ADVERBS**

accordingly	incidentally	now
also	indeed	otherwise
anyway	instead	similarly
besides	likewise	still
certainly	meanwhile	subsequently
consequently	moreover	then
conversely	namely	therefore
finally	nevertheless	thus
furthermore	next	undoubtedly
hence	nonetheless	whereas
however		

CONJUNCTIVE ADVERB

Yes   The mayor presented her budget plans; *however*, the
             council had its own ideas.

Yes   The mayor presented her budget plans; the council,
             however, had its own ideas.

COORDINATING CONJUNCTION

Yes   The mayor presented her budget plans, *but* the coun
             cil had its own ideas.

No   The mayor presented her budget plans, the council,
             but, had its own ideas.

Note that a conjunctive adverb that introduces an independent clause must be followed by a comma; within the clause it must be set off by commas. A transitional expression that introduces an independent clause should be followed by a comma if the expression consists of several words. If the transitional expression consists of a single word, a comma is optional. (See 44b and 44e.)

EDITING 2: PRACTICE

Edit each fused sentence or comma splice using either a semicolon alone or a semicolon with a conjunctive adverb or transitional expression. More than one editing option is available to you. Be ready to explain your editing choices.

> **John McPhee, a contemporary writer of nonfiction, is an extremely prolific writer; he has published twenty-one works in twenty-one years.**

1. John McPhee's "The Headmaster" focuses on Boyden's methods of running a boarding school, it includes several humorous anecdotes of how Boyden made Deerfield Academy a success.

2. Boyden is the only named character no one else shares the stage.

3. Throughout the story, McPhee's own voice is silent, he lets the anecdotes speak for themselves.

4. McPhee describes some of Boyden's unorthodox policies for example there were no formal rules.

5. McPhee does not merely state that Boyden's policies worked, instead he lets the reader infer this.

33 **C**   **Using a colon**

When the second of two independent clauses explains, elaborates, or illustrates the first, you may use a **colon** to join the clauses.

■ This year's team is surprisingly inexperienced/ : seven of the players are juniors and six are sophomores.

When the first independent clause introduces the second, and the second conveys the main point of the sentence, some writers capitalize the first word after the colon. But capitalization is optional; a lowercase letter after a colon is always correct. (See Chapter 46 and 51a.)

My mother gave me one important piece of advice: Never wear plaids with stripes.

■ **EDITING 3: PRACTICE**

Edit each fused sentence or comma splice using a colon.

Ben and Jerry's business has expanded tremendously/ : sales have grown and it has become a franchise.

1. Ben and Jerry are known for their support of environmental causes, they recycle their plastic spoons and all recyclable paper trash.
2. The company is "one percent for peace," one percent of all sales goes toward supporting peacekeeping efforts worldwide.
3. They have an innovative way of generating business from time to time they give out free ice cream.
4. Ben and Jerry's is a great place to work, the co-workers are friendly, and sometimes employees get to take home free ice cream.
5. Ben and Jerry sought a location for their factory that would meet their specific demands, easy access to transportation, fresh water, and a high-quality work force were all important factors.

33 d Writing separate sentences

Sometimes the two independent clauses in a comma splice or fused sentence read better as two separate sentences, especially when one clause is much longer than the other or when the two clauses are dissimilar in structure or meaning. Separating them often puts more emphasis on the second clause than there was before.

■ **The president outlined his administration's new economic strategy on the same day that war broke out in the Middle East, . Almost ~~almost~~ no one noticed his announcement.**

EDITING 4: PRACTICE

Edit each fused sentence or comma splice by separating it into two sentences.

Even though Justice Thurgood Marshall had said many times that he would never retire from the Supreme Court, in 1991 he did, . Everyone ~~everyone~~ was surprised.

1. Thurgood Marshall, one of the most important figures in twentieth-century American life, died in 1993 he was eighty-four years old.

2. Marshall gained recognition due to the 1954 Supreme Court decision *Brown* v. *Board of Education*, it was a landmark in American history.

3. Not everyone was happy with the decision that put an end to the "separate but equal" system of racial segregation, much turmoil followed.

4. Marshall was excluded from the all-white law school that later honored him, they named the library after him.

5. America was deep in the Great Depression when Marshall began his career as a lawyer times were very tough economically.

33 e Subordinating one clause to the other

If the relationship between two ideas in a comma splice or fused sentence is close but cannot be expressed by a coordinating conjunction or a conjunctive adverb, you may need to use **subordination.** (See 26e–g.) Subordination makes one idea logically dependent on another idea. A subordinated clause cannot stand on its own as a complete sentence; it becomes a **dependent clause.** Dependent clauses are introduced by a **subordinating conjunction** such as *after, as, although, because, if, than, whenever,* or *while* or by a **relative pronoun** such as *who, which,* or *that.* (See Chapter 26 for lists of subordinating conjunctions and relative pronouns).

To correct a comma splice or fused sentence through subordination, first you must decide what relationship you want to establish between your ideas. If one idea is dependent on the other, put it in a dependent clause. The idea in the independent clause should be the one that is more important to the meaning of your passage.

■ ~~The~~ rain had frozen as it hit the ground ˄ the streets were slick with glare ice. *(Because the ... ground,)*

■ The committee ˄ studied the issue ~~it~~ decided to recommend allowing the group to participate. *(that)*

■ **EDITING 5: PRACTICE**

Edit the following passage to eliminate fused sentences and comma splices by subordinating clauses as appropriate. More than one edited version is possible. Be ready to explain your editing choices.

Darkness falls the animals begin to settle down for the night. The horses all have their favorite places to sleep, they sleep standing. The chickens have already settled into the shed, occasionally they give off a muffled coo. The piglets playfully scampered all day now they lie quietly in a comfortable pile in the corner of their pen. Everything is quiet, little scratching, scurrying sounds can be heard from the feed room. The mice have come out, they believe they are the true owners of the barn. To a mouse a barn must resemble a cornucopia of hay, oats, and other delicacies, its other residents are all messy eaters. Three of the mice gnaw at the corner of a sack of rolled oats. The three are thinking of nothing but oats around the corner of the door creeps the cat.

| 33 | **f** | **Rewriting the sentence as one independent clause** |

When the two independent clauses in a fused sentence or comma splice are closely related in meaning, often they can be collapsed into one clause. If the two clauses have the same subject, you can drop the second subject and form a compound predicate in a single independent clause.

■ This book held my attention, *and* ~~it~~ gave a lot of information about the colonial period.

Since book *and* it *refer to the same thing, one of them can be dropped. The result is one independent clause with the compound predicate* held *and* gave.

You can also turn one clause into a modifier phrase.

■ The huge chestnut oak cast a heavy blanket of shadow on the ground beneath it, ~~it~~ dwarf*ing* a few saplings.

■ Bobbie Ann Mason, *my favorite author,* writes interesting stories about off-beat characters. ~~She is my favorite author.~~

■ **EDITING 6: PRACTICE**

Edit each fused sentence or comma splice by making it a single independent clause. More than one editing option is available to you. Be ready to discuss your editing choices.

T. S. Eliot considered *Hamlet,* ~~was~~ written by William Shakespeare, ~~T. S. Eliot considered it~~ one of his lesser plays.

1. *Hamlet* is the most popular of Shakespeare's plays, more has been written about it than any other drama.

2. Shakespeare fused several similar plots, he created a new one that is just a little different.

3. One theme in the play is revenge another used is madness.

4. A third theme is crisis, it is created in the play by Hamlet's mother through her sin with Hamlet's uncle.

5. All three themes are familiar ones Shakespeare's blending of them makes them fascinating.

■ EDITING 7: PRACTICE

Edit the following passage to eliminate fused sentences and comma splices using any strategy discussed in this chapter. Be ready to discuss your editing changes.

Expanding the airport will generate more flights, more flights will bring more travelers and money into the region. Each traveler spends an average of $7 in the airport on goods and services, when parking and ground transportation is added, the total approaches $25. The report said that developing the local economy would benefit the area, it said that air travel would make traffic problems worse on roads around the airport. According to the report, expanding the airport offers many advantages, including providing jobs, making travel more convenient, and boosting the economy. However, the expansion plan faces some problems, it would cost $17 million and it would have to be built on land that might be valuable as wetlands. Opponents of the airport expansion appeared before the port commission, saying that new runways would endanger the nesting grounds of several rare migratory birds. The Department of Environmental Quality studied the bird migration patterns it said that the fifteen acres of wetlands in question were home to at least nineteen different species. The Southeast Region Chamber of Commerce has supported the airport expansion, claiming that the plan could create dozens of new jobs, the chamber president called those jobs more important than a few ducks.

■ EDITING 8: APPLICATION

Examine your own recent writing to see whether you have used any fused sentences or comma splices. If you have, is there any pattern to your errors? Can you see why you made these mistakes? Edit any fused sentences or comma splices you found, and think about how best to identify and correct these errors in your future editing.

Perhaps you remember from grade school that a sentence "starts with a capital letter and ends with a period." Is every such group of words a sentence? As the character Sportin' Life says in *Porgy and Bess*, "It ain't necessarily so." A group of words punctuated as a sentence that is not grammatically complete is called a **fragment**.

> No one knew why it happened. *Or even what had happened.*

Fragments may lack subjects, verbs, or both. They occur often in everyday speech and in informal writing that attempts to capture the rhythms of everyday speech. However, in your academic writing you should generally avoid them; most instructors regard sentence fragments as unacceptable writing errors. The problem with a fragment is its incompleteness. A sentence expresses a complete idea, but a fragment neglects to tell the reader either what it is about (the subject) or what happened (the verb). When you edit your writing, examine each sentence to be sure it is grammatically complete. In almost all cases, you should edit fragments to create complete sentences.

As you edit to eliminate sentence fragments, you should do the following:

- Learn to recognize and eliminate phrase fragments.

- Learn to recognize and eliminate dependent clause fragments.

- Know how to use sentence fragments for special effects.

34 **a** **Recognizing and editing phrase fragments**

A complete sentence, or **independent clause,** includes a subject and a verb. A group of words that lacks one or both is called a **phrase.** To edit a phrase fragment, you must decide which element is missing. Then you have two choices.

■ Provide the missing element or elements to make the fragment a complete sentence.

■ Find an appropriate subject or verb in a nearby sentence and incorporate the fragment into that sentence.

Incorporating a fragment into an adjoining sentence often simply means repunctuating the sentence and the fragment as one sentence; indeed, many fragments are nothing more than punctuation errors.

Phrases lacking verbs

Some fragments that lack verbs can be easily repaired by supplying a verb.

■ A fleet of colorful fishing boats at␢anchor in the bay.
                                    rocked

An **appositive** is a noun or pronoun that renames or further identifies a preceding noun or pronoun.

> Symbolism is a very important technique in Alice Walker's "Everyday Use," *a story that shows cultural differences between generations.*

An appositive standing on its own lacks a verb and so is a phrase fragment.

FRAGMENT   I was in the library when I saw him. *The new student from Hong Kong.* He was looking up something in the card catalog.

To eliminate an appositive fragment, you can often attach it to a sentence that contains the noun or pronoun the appositive renames.

I was in the library when I saw him. ~~The~~ *the* new student from Hong Kong. He was looking up something in the card catalog.

The phrase the new student from Hong Kong *restates* him, *so it can be punctuated as part of the preceding sentence.*

✔ RECOGNIZING FRAGMENTS

A group of words can fail to form a complete sentence (or an independent clause) for one of these reasons: it may lack a verb, a subject, or both. Even if a group of words contains a verb and a subject, it may contain a subordinating word or phrase, which turns it into a dependent clause. If you're unsure whether a group of words is a fragment, ask yourself the following questions.

1. Does it contain a verb? If not, it is a **phrase fragment.** (See 34a1 and 34a3.)

> In the old orchard we found three apple trees. *Each of the same variety.*

A gerund, an infinitive, or a participle without a helping verb cannot serve as the main verb of a sentence. (See 34a3.)

2. Does it contain a subject? If not, it is a **phrase fragment.** (See 34a2 and 34a3.)

> During the night the protesters talked quietly and slept. *And prayed.*

Certain sentences in the imperative mood (commands, orders, and requests) do not require explicit subjects: *Come at noon.* The subject is understood to be *you*, so an imperative sentence is not considered a fragment. (See 35g.)

3. Does it contain a subordinating word or phrase? If a group of words contains both a subject and a verb but is introduced by a subordinating conjunction (*until, because, after,* and so on) or a relative pronoun (*who, that, which*) it is a **dependent clause** and cannot stand alone as a complete sentence. (See 26e and 34b.)

> The student council will probably support the measure. *Although it is unlikely really to do much good.*

Sometimes the appositive can replace the noun or pronoun it names, becoming the subject or object of a nearby sentence.

■ I was in the library when I saw him. The new student from Hong Kong. ~~He~~ was looking up something in the card catalog.

■ I was in the library when I saw ~~him.~~ ^the^ ~~The~~ new student from Hong Kong. He was looking up something in the card catalog.

In the first edited version, the appositive has become the subject of the following sentence. In the second version, it has become the object in the preceding sentence.

Lists and examples lacking verbs should not be punctuated as complete sentences. Usually a list elaborates a more general term, so attach the list to the sentence containing the term, using a colon or a dash.

■ Taking the boat out alone for the first time, I tried to think of everything my father had showed me over the summer ^: center-^ ~~.Center-~~ board, halyards, jib sheets, main sheet, tiller, and telltales.

Following a colon, the first word of a list that is not a complete sentence is not capitalized. (See 46b.)

■ Katharine Hepburn has influenced a whole generation of current screen actresses ^, such^ ~~. Such~~ as Meryl Streep, Glenn Close, Sigourney Weaver, and Kathleen Turner.

2 Phrases lacking subjects

A **compound predicate** contains two or more verbs that share the same subject.

Air pollution *hampers* our productivity and *destroys* our health.

If one part of a compound predicate is punctuated as a full sentence, the result is a fragment—one with a verb but no subject.

FRAGMENT Out of control, the careening truck hit the guardrail. *And spilled chickens and feathers halfway across the Utah landscape.*

To edit such a fragment, look for a way to reunite the stranded predicate with its subject.

■ Out of control, the careening truck hit the guardrail/~And~ ^and^ spilled chickens and feathers halfway across the Utah landscape.

Truck *is the subject of both* hit *and* spilled. *A comma is not used between the two parts of the compound predicate. (See 44j.)*

If the verb in a compound predicate fragment merits its own sentence, you can also create a new subject for the stranded verb.

■ Few employees interviewed held the company president in high regard. ~Or~ ^Even fewer^ believed he could bring the business back to profitability.

3 Phrases lacking both verbs and subjects

Prepositional phrase fragments

A **preposition**—*at, between, by, through, to, under, with,* and so on—connects a noun or pronoun (called the **object** of the preposition) to another part of a sentence. A preposition, its object, and any related modifiers together constitute a **prepositional phrase.** The following sentence contains two prepositional phrases:

We interviewed a dozen workers *at the plant* and spoke as well *with several managers.*

A prepositional phrase contains neither a verb nor a subject. If it is punctuated as a sentence, it is a phrase fragment.

PREPOSITIONAL PHRASE FRAGMENT Last month I visited Detroit's Institute of Arts. *With my mother.* We saw a wonderful collection of Impressionist paintings.

ESL **PREPOSITIONS OF TWO OR MORE WORDS**

Most prepositions consist of one word (*with*, *in*, *for*), but some consist of two, three, or four words. Here is a list of common multiple-word prepositions.

according to	for the sake of
along with	in contrast with
as a result of	in favor of
as compared with	in spite of
aside from	instead of
as for	on account of
as well as	regardless of
because of	relative to
contrary to	up until
due to	with respect to
except for	with the exception of

Fragments introduced by multiple-word prepositions are often more difficult to spot than those introduced by one-word prepositions. Whenever you use one of these prepositions in your writing, make sure the phrase it introduces is attached to an independent clause.

■ Our basketball team was not picked for the invitational tournament/ ~~In~~ ,in

spite of our winning record, which we worked hard to attain.

Because it lacks so much information, a prepositional phrase fragment usually should be attached to a nearby sentence. Look for an idea related to the fragment and attach the fragment to the sentence containing that idea.

■ Last month I visited Detroit's Institute of Arts/ ~~With~~ with my mother.

We saw a wonderful collection of Impressionist paintings.

Although joining a prepositional phrase fragment to a nearby sentence usually works better than supplying both a subject and a verb to make a new sentence, the latter approach can also succeed, especially if you realize that you have left something important unsaid.

I didn't want to go alone, so I went with

■ Last month I visited Detroit's Institute of Arts. ~~With~~ my mother.

We saw a wonderful collection of Impressionist paintings.

Some prepositional phrase fragments contain dependent clauses. Because the dependent clause has both a subject and a verb, it may look as if the fragment is really a sentence. Remember that a subject and verb of a dependent clause cannot function as the main subject and verb of a sentence. (See 34b.)

with

■ Last month I visited Detroit's Institute of Arts/ ~~With~~ my mother,

because she knows all about the Impressionists.

> *The dependent clause* because she knows all about the Impressionists *has both a subject and verb, but the prepositional phrase that contains it is still a fragment.*

Verbal phrase fragments

A complete sentence needs a subject and a **finite verb,** one that changes person, tense, and number to show who performed an action and when. (See Chapter 35.) A **verbal** is a verb form that does not indicate person, tense, or number. The three kinds of verbals are participles, gerunds, and infinitives.

PRESENT PARTICIPLE   We predict an *improving* economy.

PAST PARTICIPLE   The committee turned in its *completed* report.

GERUND   I went *running* around the block.

INFINITIVE   They decided *to volunteer.*

A verbal cannot be the main verb in a sentence. Methods for correcting verbal phrase fragments are much like those for correcting prepositional phrase fragments. If the phrase is used as a modifier, you can join it to the sentence containing the element it modifies.

■ Returning to the lab, he found that the bacterial specimens were

, killed,

dying/ ~~Killed~~, apparently, by some excretion from a wild mold.

> *A participle fragment has been joined to the preceding sentence.*

If the fragment names something mentioned in a nearby sentence, try using the fragment to replace the noun or pronoun it renames.

■ Working in the White House,/ ~~This~~ had been his triumph and his undoing.

A gerund fragment has been eliminated.

■ ~~To have a car of my own. That was all~~ I ever wanted./ ∧
All *was to have a car of my own.*
∧

An infinitive fragment has been eliminated.

To constitute a main verb of a sentence, participles must be used with **auxiliary verbs,** a form of *be* or *have.* (See 35c.) You can often eliminate a participle fragment by joining it to a sentence that already contains a suitable auxiliary verb. Sometimes you can correct it by providing a new subject and auxiliary verb.

■ England's war with the colonies was reported by contemporary journalists,/ ~~And~~ reconstructed by later historians.
and
∧

The participle fragment has been joined to a sentence that contains the auxiliary was.

■ My uncle was singing to his new baby. ~~Cooing~~ back with happy sounds of her own.
The baby was cooing
∧

The participle fragment has been given its own subject and auxiliary.

■ **EDITING 1: PRACTICE**

Edit the following passage to eliminate any fragments, making small changes in wording or punctuation that are necessary for smooth reading. More than one edited version is possible. Be ready to explain your editing choices.

There he stood. In the middle of the public square. Speaking at the top of his lungs about the end of the world. After two or three hours in the hot sun, he rested. Sat down in the shade of the clock tower. He opened his satchel and took out his lunch. A banana. A small can of apple juice. Three cookies and a wedge of cheese. I walked over to talk to him. He looked me right in the eye. For a long moment. Then spoke: "Have a cookie."

| 34 | b | **Recognizing and editing dependent clause fragments** |

A **dependent clause** is a clause introduced by a **subordinating conjunction** (such as *after, although, since, because, when, where, whether*) or a **relative pronoun** (such as *who, which, that*). Even though it contains both a subject and a predicate, a dependent clause cannot stand alone as a sentence. You must attach it to an independent clause or remove the subordinating element. (See 26e–g.)

To check for dependent clause fragments, look for clauses that start with subordinating conjunctions and relative pronouns. Most such clauses will already be attached to an independent clause. Those that are not are fragments.

FRAGMENT   It sounds like a pretty good job. *Although it can't be as good as the jobs some researchers have.*

FRAGMENT   This is my cousin Jacob. *Who has never missed a day of school.*

FRAGMENT   *After the leaves had all fallen.* The trees stood bare.

Sometimes you can edit a dependent clause fragment into a complete sentence simply by removing the word or words that make the clause dependent.

■   ~~After the~~ *The* leaves had all fallen. The trees stood bare.

A dependent clause fragment also can be attached to an adjoining sentence.

■   This is my cousin Jacob, ~~Who~~ *who* has never missed a day of school.

On occasion, you will have to choose which adjoining sentence should take in the dependent clause. Try it each way to determine which meaning better fits the surrounding text.

■   It sounds like an excellent opportunity, ~~Although~~ *although* the starting pay is barely minimum wage. It provides more training than many entry-level jobs.

■ It sounds like an excellent opportunity. Although the starting
pay is barely minimum wage/ˌɪt provides more training than
many entry-level jobs.

The first edit uses the clause starting with although *to qualify the value*
of the opportunity. The second edit uses the clause to stress the value
of the training provided.

See 44b and 44c for punctuation of dependent clauses.

■ **EDITING 2: PRACTICE**

Edit the following paragraph to eliminate dependent clause fragments. More
than one edited version is possible. Be ready to explain your editing choices.

Despite the fact that doctors take an oath to protect life. Many physicians
believe they should be allowed to help patients who want to commit suicide.
They want to do whatever they can to ease the pain of death for those who
are suffering. Because they believe people should be able to die with dignity. In
Europe, although euthanasia is not legal, it is becoming more accepted in some
countries, such as the Netherlands. Which has one of the most liberal policies
in the world. There, specific guidelines allow a doctor to assist in the suicide of
a patient who is terminally ill. As long as the patient requests it.

34 **C** Using sentence fragments for special effects

Writers occasionally use fragments deliberately to create special effects, such as the sound of spoken language. Also, because
their rhythms differ markedly from those of complete sentences,
intentional fragments can create dramatic emphasis. For this reason they abound in advertising copy.

The sun's harsh rays can wrinkle your skin. Even cause cancer.
Introducing the ultraviolet protection of new No-ray Oil. A fluid
that blends smoothly with your skin, penetrating and softening.
To soothe and protect.

Intentional fragments appear in fiction, personal essays, and narratives, and wherever dialogue is reproduced. In the following es-

say, Joan Didion uses sentence fragments to create a dramatic change of rhythm.

> I knew that I was no legitimate resident in any world of ideas. I knew I couldn't think. All I knew then was what I couldn't do. All I knew then was what I wasn't, and it took me some years to discover what I was.
>   Which was a writer.
>   By which I mean not a "good" writer or a "bad" writer, but simply a writer, a person whose most absorbed and passionate hours are spent arranging words on pieces of paper.
>
> JOAN DIDION, "WHY I WRITE"

Fragments are almost never used in most academic writing. If you think a fragment would work well in your writing, consider carefully how it is likely to be interpreted. Will it be seen as an effective stylistic device or just a grammatical error? If you decide to use a fragment, make sure that it seems intentional, not inadvertent. Use it to create emphasis. When your point warrants disrupting readers' expectations, a fragment may be in order. If it works.

EDITING 3: EXPLORATION

Look through popular magazines, essay collections, and other publications written for a general audience and note the use of intentional fragments. In each case, what effect does the fragment have on you, the reader? Defend or criticize the effectiveness of each fragment you find.

EDITING 4: EXPLORATION

Read the following passage, which includes a number of intentional fragments. Identify each fragment and consider its overall effect. What do you think the writer was trying to achieve? Do you think the fragments are effective? To determine the overall effectiveness of the passage, edit it to eliminate all fragments and compare your edited version with the original.

There never was any question whether we would be done. Just how soon. It seemed every time we got ready to close up, another bus load would come in. Tired and hungry. And the boss would say, "Can't turn away money," so we'd pour more coffee. Burn more toast. Crack more eggs. Over and over again. Because we needed the money too.

■ **EDITING 5: PRACTICE**

Edit the following passage to eliminate sentence fragments. Make any small changes in wording that are needed for smooth reading. More than one edited version is possible. Be ready to explain your editing choices.

Ferninand le Menthe Morton was born in New Orleans to a Creole family. Although he took classical piano lessons, he fell in love with another kind of music. Jazz and blues. Which he heard in the part of town called Storyville. In Chicago in the 1920s, he got a recording contract with RCA. He made some records and began calling himself "Jelly Roll." He claimed to have invented jazz. By himself. George G. Wolfe wrote a musical about his life. Called *Jelly's Last Jam* and written as though looking back from the moment of his death.

At the end of his life, Morton came face to face with the contributions of other blacks to jazz. Which he had denied all his life. He also had to confront the heritage he shared with black musicians. He eventually came to accept and understand them. Although he had always thought of himself, a Creole, as different from blacks.

■ **EDITING 6: APPLICATION**

Examine your recent writings for sentence fragments. Do you write one kind of fragment frequently? If so, can you explain why you might tend to make this particular mistake? Practice editing any fragments you find by correcting each one in two or three different ways. Then decide which edited version of each sentence works best in your paper.

Effective writing uses strong verbs that show action. (See 29b.) Equally important is the use of the correct verbs that express the meaning you intend.

In addition to telling readers what action occurs in a sentence, verbs convey a great deal of other information. Verbs help show who performed the action by changing form according to **person:** *I talk. He talks.* They show how many people performed the action by changing **number:** *She sings. They sing.* They show when it occurred by changing **tense:** *He thinks. He thought.* They show the speaker's attitude toward or relation to the action by changing **mood:** *You are an honors student. Be an honors student.* They also show whether the grammatical subject of the sentence acts or is acted upon, by changing **voice:** *She took the picture. The picture was taken.*

To convey the meaning you intend, your verbs need to be correct in all these ways. This is not so difficult as it sounds, however. If you speak English fluently and other people generally understand what you mean, you have probably been using the right person, number, tense, mood, and voice all along, without even realizing it. Problems usually occur because we speak differently than we are expected to write. In casual conversation people often ignore the subtleties of correct usage, or they use gestures, intonation, or other words to help convey meaning precisely. Additionally, what is "correct" varies from community to community. People who grew up speaking a nonstandard dialect may be told their use of verbs is incorrect in formal academic writing.

This chapter gives an overview of **finite verbs,** those that change to show person, number, tense, and mood. Some verb forms, called **verbals,** do not change form to show person or number. (See 64c.) The uses of verbs in the active and passive voice are covered in Chapter 29. For questions of agreement between verbs and subjects, see Chapter 36.

TERMS USED TO DESCRIBE VERBS

Knowing the terms used to describe verbs isn't a prerequisite for speaking good English. The terms given here are useful, though, for describing verb problems and their solutions.

Person indicates who or what performs an action. (See 35a and 35b.)

first person: the one speaking	*I read.*
second person: the one spoken to	*You read.*
third person: the one spoken about	*He reads.*

Number indicates how many people or things perform the action. (See 35a and 35b.)

singular: one	*I think.*
plural: more than one	*We think.*

Tense indicates the time of the action. (See 35d–f.)

present: at this time	*I learn.*
past: before this time	*I learned.*
future: after this time	*I will learn.*

Mood indicates the speaker's attitude toward or relation to the action. (See 35g and 35h.)

indicative: speaker states a fact or asks a question	*You are quiet.*
imperative: speaker gives a command or direction	*Be quiet!*
subjunctive: speaker expresses a desire, wish, or requirement or states a condition contrary to fact	*I would be happier if you were quiet.*

Voice indicates whether the grammatical subject of the sentence performs the action or is acted upon. (See 29c.)

active: the subject acts	*She read the book.*
passive: the subject is acted upon	*The book was read by her.*

In editing for the correct use of verbs, you should do the following.

■ Understand verb forms.

■ Use the standard forms of regular and irregular verbs.

- Use auxiliary verbs correctly.

- Understand verb tenses.

- Use the present tense for habitual or future actions when necessary.

- Use verb tenses in appropriate sequence.

- Understand verb moods.

- Use the subjunctive mood when necessary.

VERB FORMS

35 a Understanding verb forms

Except for the verb *be*, all English verbs have five forms. The **base form,** also called the **plain form** or **simple form,** expresses action occurring now (the present tense) performed by *I, we, you,* or *they: I act. We act. You act. They act.* The other form that expresses present-tense action is the **-s form,** which is used for *he, she,* or *it* (third person singular): *he acts.*

Two verb forms express action that occurred in the past: the **past tense** and **past participle.** The present participle must be used with a form of *be* or *have.* (See 35c.) For **regular verbs,** the past tense and past participle are formed by adding *-d* or *-ed* to the base form: *I acted. I have acted.* Verbs that form the past tense and past participle in other ways are called **irregular.** Often the two past forms of an irregular verb differ from each other: *I knew. I have known.* The past tense and the past participle do not change form according to person or number. That is, the same form is used regardless of who performed the action: *I acted. You acted. He acted. They acted.*

For all verbs, both regular and irregular, the **present participle** is formed by adding *-ing* to the base form: *acting, knowing.* It is used to express continuing action in both the past and the present. Like the past participle, it does not change form according to person and number, and to serve as the main verb of a sentence it must be used with a form of *be.* (See 35c.)

For a discussion of the verb *be*, see 35b4; for more on irregular verbs, see 35b2.

THE FIVE VERB FORMS

The five principal forms of English verbs are the base form, the -s form, the past tense, the past participle, and the present participle. Regular verbs add -d or -ed to form the past tense and past participle. Irregular verbs follow some other pattern. (The irregular verb be has more than five forms. See 35b4. For more on irregular verbs, see 35b2.)

BASE FORM	-S FORM	PAST TENSE	PAST PARTICIPLE	PRESENT PARTICIPLE
Regular				
act	acts	acted	acted	acting
seem	seems	seemed	seemed	seeming
Irregular				
know	knows	knew	known	knowing
eat	eats	ate	eaten	eating
hit	hits	hit	hit	hitting

35 b Using standard verb forms

1 Using -s and -ed forms correctly

The **-s form,** or third-person singular form, for all present-tense verbs except *be* and *have* is formed by adding -s or -es to the base form. The **past tense** of regular verbs is created by adding -d or -ed to the base form.

Speakers of some dialects do not use the -s and -ed endings, and other speakers occasionally drop them in casual speech. But such usage is considered nonstandard in formal writing. As you edit your work, watch for missing -s and -ed endings.

■ Yesterday she ~~walk~~ her dog, Wolf, even though it was raining.
  walked

■ That dog ~~don't~~ ever miss a chance to take a walk.
  doesn't

ESL

GERUNDS AND INFINITIVES AS NOUNS FOLLOWING VERBS

Gerunds and infinitives are called **verbals** because they derive from verbs but do not function as verbs in sentences. A **gerund** is the -ing form of the verb functioning as a noun. An **infinitive** (to plus the base form of the verb) can function as a noun, adjective, or adverb. (A participle, the third type of verbal, cannot function as a noun.)

Gerunds and infinitives used as nouns often appear following verbs. Some verbs can be followed only by gerunds or gerund phrases: I enjoy reading. Other verbs can be followed only by infinitives or infinitive phrases: I plan to read. And a third category of verbs can be followed by either gerunds or infinitives (or gerund phrases or infinitive phrases): I like reading. I like to read.

It is sometimes difficult to remember whether to use a gerund or an infinitive with a particular verb. Here are common verbs in each of the three categories.

1. Verbs that can be directly followed only by a gerund.

admit	deny	miss	resent
appreciate	dislike	postpone	risk
avoid	enjoy	practice	suggest
consider	finish	quit	tolerate
defend	imagine	recommend	understand
delay	include		

2. Verbs that can be directly followed only by an infinitive.

agree	desire	need*	refuse
appear	expect*	offer	remind**
ask*	fail	order**	tell**
choose	help*	persuade**	tend
claim	hesitate	plan	wait
command**	hope	prepare*	want*
convince**	instruct**	pretend	warn**
decide	intend	promise*	wish*
demand			

2 Using irregular forms correctly

Unlike regular verbs, irregular verbs do not form the past tense and past participle by the addition of -d or -ed. The past

* These verbs can be followed directly by an infinitive or they can be separated from the infinitive by a noun or a pronoun:

We *asked to see* the bill.

We *asked* the waiter *to bring* the bill.

** These verbs *must* be separated from the infinitive by a noun or pronoun:

No She will *instruct to swim* the children.

Yes She will *instruct* the children *to swim.*

3. Verbs that can be followed by either a gerund or an infinitive.

advise**	continue	permit**	start
allow**	forget	prefer*	stop
begin	hate	remember	try
cause**	like*	regret	urge**
cease	love		

* When these verbs are followed by an infinitive, they can be followed directly by the infinitive or they can be separated from the infinitive by a noun or a pronoun:

The coach *prefers to recruit* students who can balance their studies and practice.

The coach *prefers* students *to set* their own curfews.

** When these verbs are followed by an infinitive, a noun or pronoun *must* separate the verb from the infinitive:

No The instructor *allows to miss* one class each student.

Yes The instructor *allows* each student *to miss* one class.

tense of *have,* for example, is not *haved* but *had.* The past participle of *eat* is not *eated* but *eaten.*

Some patterns appear in the way irregular verbs form the past tense and past participle. Verbs of one group, including *bet,*

IRREGULAR VERBS

BASE FORM	PAST TENSE	PAST PARTICIPLE
arise	arose	arisen
awake	awoke, awaked	awaked, awoken
be	was, were	been
beat	beat	beaten, beat
become	became	become
begin	began	begun
bend	bent	bent
bet	bet	bet
bind	bound	bound
bite	bit	bitten, bit
blow	blew	blown
break	broke	broken
bring	brought	brought
broadcast	broadcast	broadcast
build	built	built
burst	burst	burst
buy	bought	bought
catch	caught	caught
choose	chose	chosen
cling	clung	clung
come	came	come
cost	cost	cost
creep	crept	crept
deal	dealt	dealt
dig	dug	dug
dive	dived, dove	dived
do	did	done
draw	drew	drawn
drink	drank	drunk
drive	drove	driven
eat	ate	eaten
fall	fell	fallen
feed	fed	fed
feel	felt	felt
fight	fought	fought
find	found	found
flee	fled	fled

✔ **IRREGULAR VERBS (Continued)**

BASE FORM	PAST TENSE	PAST PARTICIPLE
fly	flew	flown
forbid	forbade	forbidden
forget	forgot	forgotten, forgot
forgive	forgave	forgiven
freeze	froze	frozen
get	got	gotten, got
give	gave	given
go	went	gone
grow	grew	grown
hang (suspend)	hung	hung
hang (execute)	hanged	hanged
have	had	had
hear	heard	heard
hide	hid	hidden
hold	held	held
hurt	hurt	hurt
keep	kept	kept
know	knew	known
lay (put)	laid	laid
lead	led	led
leap	leapt, leaped	leapt, leaped
leave	left	left
lend	lent	lent
let (allow)	let	let
lie (recline)	lay	lain
light	lit, lighted	lit, lighted
lose	lost	lost
make	made	made
mean	meant	meant
meet	met	met
mistake	mistook	mistaken
pay	paid	paid
prove	proved	proved, proven
quit	quit	quit
read	read	read
rid	rid	rid
ride	rode	ridden

IRREGULAR VERBS (Continued)

BASE FORM	PAST TENSE	PAST PARTICIPLE
ring	rang	rung
rise	rose	risen
run	ran	run
say	said	said
see	saw	seen
seek	sought	sought
sell	sold	sold
send	sent	sent
set	set	set
shake	shook	shaken
shoot	shot	shot
show	showed	shown, showed
shrink	shrank	shrunk
sing	sang	sung
sink	sank	sunk
sit	sat	sat
sleep	slept	slept
speak	spoke	spoken
spend	spent	spent
spin	spun	spun
spit	spit, spat	spit, spat
spring	sprang	sprung
stand	stood	stood
steal	stole	stolen
stick	stuck	stuck
sting	stung	stung
stink	stank, stunk	stunk
strike	struck	struck, stricken
swear	swore	sworn
swim	swam	swum
swing	swung	swung
take	took	taken
teach	taught	taught
tear	tore	torn
tell	told	told
think	thought	thought
throw	threw	thrown

✔ **IRREGULAR VERBS (Continued)**

BASE FORM	PAST TENSE	PAST PARTICIPLE
wake	woke, waked	woken, waked
wear	wore	worn
win	won	won
write	wrote	written

bid, burst, cast, cut, hit, and *quit,* do not change form for the base, past tense, and past participle. Vowel changes provide another pattern: *ring, rang, rung; sing, sang, sung; drink, drank, drunk.* Nevertheless, these patterns are not reliable. The past tense of *think* is not *thank,* nor is its past participle *thunk;* both past and past participle are *thought.*

The forms of irregular verbs cannot easily be predicted; they must be memorized. As an aid in your editing, consult the accompanying chart or a dictionary, which lists the forms of irregular verbs. Be aware of irregular verbs in your writing, and make an effort to memorize the forms of verbs that give you trouble. Then be sure to edit carefully.

■ She ~~seen~~ her mistake immediately.
    saw

■ I had ~~knowed~~ all along that she would.
    known

3 **Using *sit* and *set* and *lay* and *lie* correctly**

The forms of *sit* and *set* and of *lie* and *lay* can cause particular problems because the verbs in each pair have similar sounds and are related in meaning. To distinguish between them, remember that *sit* and *lie* never take direct objects (they are **intransitive** verbs), while *set* and *lay* always take direct objects (they are **transitive**). *Sit* means "to be seated"; *set* means "to put or place." *Lie* means "to recline"; *lay,* "to put or place."

500 Selecting correct verbs

INTRANSITIVE   People *sit* outside when it's warm.

I *lie* down.

TRANSITIVE   We *set* the books on the table.

Every morning I *lay* the mail on her desk.

Part of the confusion between *lay* and *lie* comes from the similarity of their other forms. And the forms of *lie* meaning "to tell a falsehood" are also similar.

BASE FORM	PAST TENSE	PAST PARTICIPLE	PRESENT PARTICIPLE
lie (recline)	lay	lain	lying
lay (put or place)	laid	laid	laying
lie (tell a falsehood)	lied	lied	lying

4 Using *be* correctly

For every other English verb, the base form is used for the present tense with *I*, *you*, *we*, and *they*. For *be*, however, the present-tense forms are different from the base form: *I am. You are. We are. They are.* Because *be* has so many forms, be especially careful in your editing to use the correct form.

■ These books ~~was~~ *were* due back to the library last week.

Some speakers use the base form *be* instead of the correct present-tense form, and some drop the verb entirely. Such usage is regarded as nonstandard in formal writing. Edit carefully to avoid it in writing.

■ He ~~be~~ *is* happy watching television.

■ They *are* ready for the test today.

It is also nonstandard to use the base form *be* as an auxiliary (see 35c) with the past or present participle.

■ I ~~be~~ *am* working harder this semester than last semester.

The past participle *been* should always be preceded by a form of the auxiliary *have*.

■ We been walking for about two hours now.
have
∧

THE FORMS OF *BE*

The most irregular verb in English is *be*, which has three forms in the present tense and two forms in the past tense.

	SINGULAR	**PLURAL**
PRESENT	I *am*	we *are*
	you *are*	you *are*
	he, she, it *is*	they *are*
PAST	I *was*	we *were*
	you *were*	you *were*
	he, she, it *was*	they *were*

These are the principal parts of *be*:

BASE FORM	***-s* FORM**	**PAST TENSE**	**PAST PARTICIPLE**	**PRESENT PARTICIPLE**
be	is	was, were	been	being

■ **EDITING 1: PRACTICE**

Edit the following passage, using the correct *-s* and *-ed* forms and irregular forms of verbs.

The waiter setted down two hot chocolates topped with whipped cream at the table where we sat. The bell over the door rung repeatedly as a steady stream of hungry diners enter. The winter sun shined brightly through the large glass panes next to us as we drunk our hot chocolate. I be resting comfortably in the corner of the booth when suddenly I beheld the woman at the next table as she sprung up and walk toward the door. I gave my companion a questioning look and asked, "What do you think she meaned by that?"

35 c Using auxiliary verbs

Understanding auxiliary verbs

To express some meanings, the main verb of a sentence needs the aid of one or more **auxiliary verbs** (also known as **helping verbs**). The auxiliary and the main verb together form a **verb phrase.**

```
                verb phrase
           auxiliary  main verb
Tyler has been working.
```

The most common auxiliary verbs are forms of *be*, *have*, and *do*. They help form certain tenses (see 35d–f), add emphasis, ask questions, make negative statements, and form the passive voice.

PRESENT PROGRESSIVE	The student council *is considering* what to do next.
EMPHASIS	They *do want* to go to the conference.
QUESTION	*Has* he *received* the blueprints?
NEGATIVE STATEMENT	He *does* not *intend* to leave without them.
PASSIVE VOICE	The blueprints *were delivered* on Friday.

The auxiliary verbs *can, could, may, might, must, shall, should, will,* and *would* are used with a main verb to express condition, intent, permission, possibility, obligation, and desire. Known as **modal auxiliaries,** they do not change form for person, tense, number, or mood. A modal auxiliary cannot be used alone as a main verb; it must appear with the base form of a verb, unless the base form can be inferred from context.

> Staying in touch with friends *can become* difficult for the elderly.
>
> *Can* she *dance?* Yes, she *can.*

A modal auxiliary can be used with the base form of another auxiliary (not a modal) and a participle to form certain tenses. (See 35d–f.)

> Anyone with so high a fever *should be seen* by a doctor.

ESL **PHRASAL MODALS**

In addition to one-word modal auxiliary verbs (*can*, *should*), English also has **phrasal modals** consisting of more than one word.

PHRASAL MODAL	MEANING
be able to	possibility, ability
be allowed to	permission, possibility
be going to	future action, obligation, intent
be supposed to	obligation
had better	obligation
have to	obligation
have got to	obligation
ought to	obligation
used to	habitual past action

Unlike one-word modals, most of these phrasal modals change form to show number, person, and tense. The main verbs following them do not change form.

She *has to* take the bus today.

They *have to* take the bus today.

The phrasal modals *had better* and *used to* do not change form:

We *used to* spend time in the library every day.

You *used to* spend time in the library every day.

---

2 **Using auxiliary verbs correctly**

In standard English, a present participle (*running, believing*) or an irregular past participle (*gone, forgotten*) cannot function as the main verb of a sentence unless it is preceded by a form of auxiliary verb *be* or *have*. (See 35d–f.) In some dialects participles serve alone as main verbs, but as you edit your writing you should always check that participles are accompanied by auxiliary verbs.

■ Gina Wilcox *is* running for the state legislature.

■ She *has* spoken to several campus groups about her campaign.

A form of *be* is needed to create the passive voice; the main verb alone is not enough. As you edit, make sure you have used an auxiliary if you are using the passive voice. (See 29c.)

■ Wilcox ^*is*^ seen by many as having a good chance to win.

In some dialects, *don't* (for *do not*) is used with a third-person singular subject to make a negative statement: *She don't want to finish the assignment.* However, this usage is considered nonstandard in formal writing. In your editing, be sure to use *doesn't* (for *does not*) with third-person singular subjects.

■ She ~~don't~~ ^*doesn't*^ want to finish the assignment.

The correct use of *be* as an auxiliary is covered in 35b4.

■ **EDITING 2: PRACTICE**

Complete the following sentences by supplying an appropriate auxiliary verb in each blank. Some sentences may have more than one possible answer. Be ready to discuss your editing choices. Example:

In 1865, Lucie Wheeler decided that she _____ *should* establish a home for destitute children.

I. Children were taught the rudiments of education while they _____ receiving religious instruction.

2. After the home _____ destroyed by a fire around the turn of the century, Wheeler hoped that enough money _____ be raised to build a new center.

3. A new home _____ built where up to seventy children _____ reside while they waited, hoping that they _____ be adopted.

4. Around World War I, the administration provided agricultural training to the children so that they _____ grow their own food.

5. In the 1950s, the administration decided to hire social workers and psychologists who _____ further serve the children's needs.

6. The center _____ still growing today, and family therapy sessions _____ begun.

VERB TENSES

35 d Understanding verb tenses

The **tense** of a verb places action in time and shows how the action relates in time to other actions. The three **simple tenses** place action in the present, past, or future. Notice that the future tense is expressed with the use of a modal auxiliary, *will*.

PRESENT   He *looks* happy today.

PAST   He *looked* a little depressed yesterday.

FUTURE   He *will look* different ten years from now.

ESL **VERBS THAT DO NOT HAVE A PROGRESSIVE FORM**

Dynamic verbs express actions, processes, or events. A dynamic verb can usually be used in a progressive *-ing* form to express an action in progress: *I am walking through the park.*

Stative verbs express attitudes, conditions, or relationships. A stative verb cannot usually be used in a progressive *-ing* form.

■   *believe*
I am believing your story.
      ʌ

Here are some common stative verbs.

admire	dislike	like	see
agree	doubt	look	seem
appear	hate	love	smell
believe	have	need	sound
belong	hear	own	taste
contain	imagine	possess	think
cost	include	prefer	understand
disagree	know	remember	want

Be aware that many of these verbs can be used as dynamic verbs, to express activities or processes. In these cases, they can be used in a progressive form: *He is thinking about his assignment. I am including two papers in this envelope.*

The three **perfect tenses** indicate action *completed by a specific time*. They also are divided into present, past, and future. The **present perfect** tense relates actions that were completed in the past. It can also indicate past action continuing into the present.

PRESENT PERFECT   She *has looked* for the file already.

PRESENT PERFECT   She *has looked* for it every day this week.

The **past perfect** tense indicates action completed before another past action took place.

PAST PERFECT   She *had looked* for the file ten times before she found it.

The **future perfect** tense indicates action that will be completed at some specific time in the future.

FUTURE PERFECT   Once she goes through the last drawer, she *will have looked* everywhere.

The three **progressive tenses** describe *continuing action* in the present, past, or future. The **present progressive** tense describes continuous or ongoing action in the present.

PRESENT PROGRESSIVE   She *is anticipating* the holidays.

The **past progressive** tense describes continuous or ongoing action in the past, although not always with a specified conclusion: *She was looking well this morning* (and still is).

PAST PROGRESSIVE   Before her father's illness, she *was anticipating* the holidays.

The **future progressive** tense describes continuous or ongoing action in the future, often dependent on some other action or condition.

FUTURE PROGRESSIVE   Once her father is better, she *will be anticipating* the holidays again.

The three **perfect progressive tenses** describe action *continuing up to a specific time of completion* in the present, past, or future. The **present perfect progressive** tense describes ongoing action that began in the past and continues in the present.

PRESENT
PERFECT
PROGRESSIVE
He *has been looking* for a job since August.

The **past perfect progressive** tense describes continuing action that was completed before some other action.

PAST PERFECT
PROGRESSIVE
Before he found work, he *had been looking* for a job since August.

The **future perfect progressive** tense describes continuous action that will be completed at some future time.

FUTURE
PERFECT
PROGRESIVE
Come August, he *will have been looking* for a job six months.

■ **EDITING 3: PRACTICE**

Edit the following passage twice, changing the verbs first to the present tense and then to the future tense.

For one week at the beginning of each semester sororities opened their houses to prospective members. The women took their best dresses off their hangers and carefully painted on their makeup. Along with frozen hair went frozen smiles. Hundreds of young women moved from house to house where they were looked over and judged. For some women this was an exciting time; for others it was humiliating and degrading.

35 **e** | **Using the present tense for habitual or future actions and universal truths**

The present tense usually indicates action happening now, at this instant: *I feel tired.* But the present tense has some other conventional uses, which you should be aware of as you edit.

The present tense expresses habitual or regular actions.

I *run* three miles every weekday morning.

It can also indicate a future action, when used with other words that express futurity.

He *is speaking* tomorrow night.

The present tense can be used to state a universal truth—that is, scientific fact or a definition. (Also see 35f1.)

Newton showed that the moon's orbit *is* an effect of gravity.

Jarosite *is* a hydrous sulfate of iron and potassium.

The **literary present tense** is customarily used to discuss literary or artistic works.

Flannery O'Connor's characters *are* often sinners, rarely saints.

If you use the literary present, check that you have used it consistently.

■ In *The Tempest*, the wizard Prospero seems to control the very heavens. As Shakespeare ~~described~~ *describes* him, he ~~had~~ *has* extraordinary powers.

35 **f** Using verb tenses in appropriate sequence

The dominant or governing verb tense in a piece of writing affects the choice of tense for nearly every verb. "If a melody in a major key is transposed into a minor key," Theodore M. Bernstein writes in *The Careful Writer*, "it is not just the first few notes that are modified; almost every phrase that follows undergoes change." In other words, all the verbs throughout a passage must relate logically to the governing tense. This section deals with using tenses consistently within sentences. Techniques for maintaining logical consistency throughout a passage are discussed in 42a.

The tense of the main verb in the independent clause frequently dictates the tense of any dependent-clause verbs or verbals in the sentence. For example, the present-tense sentence *I think that I am lost* becomes *I thought that I was lost* in the past tense. It would make no sense to say *I thought that I am lost.*

The relationship between the main verb in a sentence and other verbs or verbals is called the **normal sequence of tenses.** Many combinations of verb tenses are possible, but each has to make logical sense in terms of the events it describes.

present **future**
I think that you will enjoy this movie.

present **present**
I think that you like foreign films.

present **past**
I think that you misunderstood me.

Your choice of tense in a dependent clause or verbal depends on your intended meaning, and it is limited only by logic. Changing the tense of any verb in a sentence can change the meaning of the sentence. As you edit, check that such changes make sense.

1 Sequence with habitual actions and universal truths

When the dependent clause expresses a habitual action or a universal truth, the verb in the dependent clause remains in the present tense regardless of the tense in the independent clause. (See 35e.)

He *told* me he *works* for Teledyne.

Copernicus *demonstrated* that the earth *revolves* around the sun.

Notice that this use of the present tense distinguishes between statements accepted as true and assertions that may or may not be true.

He *told* me he *worked* for IBM, but I *learned* later that he *works* for Teledyne.

Only the second independent clause uses the present tense works *because only it expresses a habitual action.*

2 Sequence with direct and indirect quotation

Verbs in a **direct quotation** are not affected by the tense of other verbs in the sentence. The words within quotation marks should be precisely the words the speaker used, regardless of tense.

Nancy *said,* "My dog *is* chasing a squirrel!"

ESL

TRANSFORMING DIRECT QUOTATIONS TO INDIRECT QUOTATIONS

You must make certain changes when you transform a direct quotation into an indirect quotation.

VERBS

You must often change the tense of quoted verbs in transforming a direct quotation to an indirect quotation.

DIRECT QUOTATION	INDIRECT QUOTATION
Present tense	*Past tense*
He said, "They *are* tired."	He said that they *were* tired.
Past tense	*Past perfect tense*
She said, "They *lost* their keys."	She said that they *had lost* their keys.
Present perfect tense	*Past perfect tense*
He said, "She *has written* a great short story."	He said that she *had written* a great short story.

Some modal auxiliary verbs change from present tense to future or past tense.

DIRECT QUOTATION	INDIRECT QUOTATION
can	could
may	might
must, have to	had to
will	would
He said, "They *can* watch television."	He said that they *could* watch television.

However, when you express someone else's words using **indirect quotation,** or **indirect discourse,** you should paraphrase, changing person and tense to make the quotation grammatically compatible with the rest of the sentence. (See 43a5.)

■ Nancy said that her dog ̶i̶s̶ *was* chasing a squirrel.

PRONOUNS

In some cases, you may have to change pronouns when you transform a direct quotation into an indirect quotation. Pay attention to meaning when considering these changes.

DIRECT QUOTATION	**INDIRECT QUOTATION**
She said, "*I* was wrong."	She said that *she* had been wrong.
She said to me, "*You* can sing."	She said that *I* could sing.
She said to them, "*You* can sing."	She said that *they* could sing.

FOR QUESTIONS

When a direct quotation is a question, you may need to change the word order or add a word such as *if* or *whether* when transforming it into an indirect quotation.

DIRECT QUOTATION	**INDIRECT QUOTATION**
She asked, "What *is the answer?*"	She asked what *the answer was.*
He asked, "*Is this correct?*"	He asked *if* that *was correct.*

FOR COMMANDS AND REQUESTS

When a direct quotation that is a command or a request is transformed into an indirect quotation, it should be introduced with a verb such as *tell*, *order*, or *ask* and should contain an infinitive. It may also need to specify who was given the command or request.

DIRECT QUOTATION	**INDIRECT QUOTATION**
I said, "Don't get up."	I *told him* not *to get* up.
She said, "Please leave."	She *asked him to leave.*

3 **Sequence with infinitives and participles**

The tense of an infinitive or a participle must be in proper sequence with the tense of a main verb. The base form of a verb preceded by *to* is the **present infinitive** (*to know*), sometimes called simply the **infinitive.** Use the present infinitive to show action occurring at the same time as or later than the action of the main verb.

Some children *like to play* with educational toys.

The liking and the playing take place at the same time.

The committee *plans to vote* on the proposal next week.

The voting takes place later than the planning.

The **perfect infinitive** consists of the past participle preceded by *to have*: *to have known*. The perfect infinitive generally indicates action that occurred before the action of the main verb.

I seem to have misplaced my bank machine card.

The **present participle,** the *-ing* form of the verb, shows action taking place at the same time as the action of the main verb.

Working feverishly, he *wrote* late into the night.

The **present perfect participle,** *having* plus the past participle, shows action completed before that of the main verb.

Having worked feverishly all night, at dawn he *saw* the sunrise.

The **past participle** can show action taking place at the same time as or completed before the action of the main verb.

Guided by instinct, the birds *returned* as usual on March 19.

The guiding and the returning take place at the same time.

Born in 1917, John F. Kennedy *became* the country's youngest president in 1961.

John Kennedy was born before he became president.

▨ EDITING 4: PRACTICE

Edit the following passage, using appropriate verb tenses and putting them in a logical sequence. More than one edited version is possible. Be ready to explain your editing choices.

Many people thought that it will never happen, but Los Angeles has finally opened a subway system. Perhaps you imagine that the name L.A. will never be associated with public transit, because it was practically synonymous with the word *automobile*. When questioned, some people say that the new system, although it is modest so far, can be a turning point for the city. If you have visited New York, which has more than 450 stations and hundreds of miles of tracks, you will realize that the new system is quite small. On opening day, supporters of the new system had said that they hoped to have put the city's dollars toward building stations rather than freeways.

VERB MOODS

The **mood** of a verb expresses the speaker's attitude toward or relation to the action described. The **indicative mood** is used for statements of fact and opinion and for questions — for things that have happened or will happen.

He *believes* that the theory *is* valid.

When did she *graduate*?

The **imperative mood** is used for commands, orders, or directions — for things the speaker wants to happen. It consists of the base form of the verb and usually omits the subject, which is understood to be *you*.

Sit down and *fill* out these documents.

Knead the dough until it forms a ball.

The **subjunctive mood** expresses wishes, desires, requirements, and conditions that the speaker knows not to be factual. The **present subjunctive** is simply the base form of the verb for all persons and numbers.

I asked that she *leave* early to avoid traffic.

The **past subjunctive** is the same as the simple past tense for all verbs except *be*, which uses *were*.

514 Selecting correct verbs

If you *donated* a million dollars, your alma mater would name a building after you.

If she *were* a millionaire, how would she behave?

The **perfect subjunctive** uses the past perfect tense (*had* with the past participle).

If he *had caught* the bear, he would have been very sorry.

35 h Using the subjunctive mood

1 In standard idiomatic expressions

The subjunctive appears in some idiomatic expressions such as *long live the queen*, *if I were you*, *as it were*, and *far be it from me*. As with other idioms, take care to word these phrases in the customary way if you use them.

2 After *as if, as though,* or *if*

In dependent clauses beginning with *as if* and *as though*, which always specify conditions that are not factual, use the past or perfect subjunctive.

■ He screamed as though the house ~~was~~ *were* on fire.

When a dependent clause beginning with *if* describes a condition contrary to fact, use the past or perfect subjunctive.

■ If only it ~~was~~ *were* sunny, he would be happy.

Note, however, that when the *if* clause expresses an actual condition, the subjunctive is not needed.

If it *was* sunny, he was happy.

To suggest that the *if* clause expresses something uncertain, rather than untrue, use the indicative rather than the subjunctive.

■ If she ~~were~~ *was* awake, she probably heard the doorbell.

3 With *might, could, should,* and *would*

When one of the modal auxiliaries that express conditionality
— *might, could, should, would* — is used without another auxiliary
in an independent clause, the verb in the dependent clause can be
either a subjunctive verb — *I would go if they invited me* — or an
indicative verb using a conditional modal auxiliary — *I would go if
they would invite me.* However, if the dependent clause verb is a
form of *be,* you must use the subjunctive.

■ I would go if there ~~would be~~ a good reason.
  were

If the auxiliary verbs in the independent clause are *might
have, could have, should have,* or *would have* (the conditional perfect), the dependent clause must use the perfect subjunctive, not
another conditional modal auxiliary.

■ The president could have won if he ~~would have~~ fought harder.
  had

4 To express a wish, a requirement, or a request

Use the past or perfect subjunctive in dependent clauses expressing wishes, which are usually contrary to fact. (Sometimes
the relative pronoun *that* introducing the dependent clause is
omitted.)

■ I wished there ~~was~~ some way to help them.
  had been

Dependent clauses following verbs stating requirements —
such as *demand, insist, require, recommend, request, suggest,
specify,* and *ask* — should use the present subjunctive.

■ Courtesy requires that he comes in formal attire.

■ Barbara insisted she ~~goes~~ alone.
  go

The subjunctive makes a request sound a little more formal,
and therefore perhaps a little more polite, than the indicative or
the imperative.

SUBJUNCTIVE	We ask that you *be* seated.
INDICATIVE	We ask you *to be* seated.
IMPERATIVE	*Be* seated.

■ EDITING 5: PRACTICE

Edit the following passage, using subjunctive verb forms wherever appropriate.

He opens the refrigerator door and catches sight of the single slice of birthday cake. If only it was not the last piece of cake! A voice inside his head demands that he does not eat it. "If it is not my birthday, I should not eat the last piece of cake," he thinks. But a second voice insists that he helps himself. "If it was my birthday, I would not mind if someone else eats it," he reasons. His conscience prevails. He sighs, closes the refrigerator door, and wishes that he has never even come into the kitchen.

■ EDITING 6: PRACTICE

Edit the following passage, using the correct form, tense, and mood of each verb. More than one edited version is possible. Be ready to explain your editing choices.

In the early years of this century, the Constitution stated that women cannot vote. Suffragists wished that every woman citizen was able to vote and they strived to amend the Constitution so that no state can deny any citizen the right to vote on account of sex. For this to happen, the Constitution required that three-quarters of the states were in favor of the amendment. Many of the arguments against women's suffrage strike us as absurd now. Some people argued that women do not understand the business world; others said that the cost of elections will go up. If women would get the vote, some worried, next they would want to hold office. Some felt that a woman is represented by her husband and that when he voted it was as though she was voting. Some also feared that a vote for women will be a step toward feminism, which many people consider a radical and dangerous idea.

■ EDITING 7: APPLICATION

Examine your recent writing for misused verb forms, tenses, and moods. Is there one kind of verb error that you make most often? If so, think about how best to identify your verb errors when you edit your work. Practice editing sentences with incorrect verbs.

Verbs and their subjects must agree, or correspond, in person and number. A singular subject requires a singular verb; a plural subject requires a plural verb. Such **agreement,** especially in long sentences like this one in which many words separate the subject from the main verb, helps the reader interpret relations between the parts of the sentence. On seeing a singular subject, such as *agreement,* in the previous sentence, readers expect the main verb, in this case *helps,* to be singular.

Though the idea of subject-verb agreement is simple, applying it is not easy in every circumstance. To solve problems of agreement, you usually need to first identify the subject and then determine whether the subject is singular or plural. Here are some guidelines to follow when editing for subject-verb agreement:

- Ignore words between the subject and the verb.

- Correctly identify the subject when it follows the verb.

- Correctly identify the subject of a linking verb.

- Determine whether subjects joined by *and* are singular or plural.

- Determine whether subjects joined by *or* and *nor* are singular or plural.

- Determine whether collective nouns are singular or plural.

- Determine whether indefinite pronouns such as *everything* and *some* are singular or plural.

- Determine whether relative pronouns such as *who, which,* and *that* are singular or plural.

- Determine whether subjects that refer to amounts are singular or plural.

- Use singular verbs with noun phrases and noun clauses.

- Use singular verbs with titles and with words used as words.

- Use singular verbs with singular subjects that end in -s.

- Use plural verbs with troublesome plurals.

36 **a** Ignoring words between subject and verb

When a verb follows its subject immediately, it is usually easy to tell whether the verb should be singular or plural. When other words fall between the subject and the verb, confusion can arise.

PRINCIPLES OF SUBJECT-VERB AGREEMENT

Matters of agreement often come down to a single letter: s. Most English nouns form plurals by adding -s or -es.

SINGULAR	PLURAL
house	houses
rock	rocks
box	boxes

Most present-tense, third-person singular verbs end in -s or -es.

I
you } think
we
they

she
he } thinks
it

The verbs *have* and *be* also end in -s in the third-person singular: *he is, she has.*

A simple rule of thumb can guide you through many agreement problems: If the subject ends in -s or -es (is plural), the verb probably shouldn't; if the verb ends in -s or -es (is singular), the subject probably shouldn't.

The mansions seem elegant and sophisticated.

The mansion seems elegant and sophisticated.

One exception to this rule is nouns with irregular plurals: *children, men.* These plural nouns still require a verb without an -s or -es: *The children walk home.* Another exception is nouns that end in -s but are singular: *Politics is a dirty business.* (See 36l.)

Finding the subject when it follows the verb 519

In long sentences, many words can appear between subject and verb. Restating the sentence in its simplest form — its subject and verb — can help clarify your choice.

People interested in helping reelect an incumbent representative typically *volunteer/volunteers* time as well as money.

Reduced to its subject and verb, the sentence reads, *People volunteer*; both subject and verb are clearly plural.

Often, the intervening words are **prepositional phrases,** groups of words introduced by a preposition such as *of* or *with.*

The bowl of apples *is/are* very tempting.

Is the subject of the verb the singular *bowl* or the plural *apples*? One way to decide is to analyze the role of each word. Once we determine that *of apples* is a prepositional phrase, it is clear that *bowl* is the subject, so the verb should be singular, *is: The bowl of apples is very tempting.*

Intervening phrases that begin with such words as *including, as well as, along with, together with,* and *in addition to* are not part of a compound subject. (See 36d.) You should ignore them in making decisions about subject-verb agreement. It helps to think of them as parenthetical asides.

■ Mr. Johnson, along with his children, ~~were~~ *was* waiting outside.

36 b **Finding the subject when it follows the verb**

In some sentences the subject follows the verb.

Underneath the freeway overpasses *huddle/huddles* a ramshackle collection of cardboard shelters.

Mentally restoring normal word order to the sentence can help you find the subject.

A ramshackle *collection* of cardboard shelters *huddles* underneath the freeway overpasses.

The subject is collection, *which is singular, so* huddles *is correct.*

In questions, part of the verb almost always precedes the subject. As you edit, look for the subject after the verb, and make sure the verb agrees with it.

Are those *seats* next to you empty?

Without the help of his friends, *is Juan* able to finish on time?

Expletives are words such as *it*, *here*, and *there* that introduce a sentence with inverted word order. *Here* and *there* are never subjects, so you must look for the subject elsewhere in the sentence.

There *are* a million *stories* in the Naked City.

When *it* is used in an expletive construction, it is considered the grammatical subject of the sentence. Because *it* is singular, it is always followed by a singular verb.

It is administrators who want this change, not students.

36 C Finding the subject of a linking verb

Linking verbs include *be*, *become*, *seem*, and verbs describing sensations — *appear*, *look*, *feel*, *taste*, *smell*, and *sound*. They link the subject of a sentence to an element, called a **complement,** that renames or identifies the subject. It helps to think of a linking verb as an equal sign between two equivalent terms.

Angela *is* captain.	Angela = captain
That *looks* difficult.	that = difficult

The term on the left, before the equal sign, is the subject; the term on the right, after the equal sign, is the subject complement.

      subject   subject complement
My paper is "Eliot's Rite of Spring."

        subject   subject complement
"Eliot's Rite of Spring" is my paper.

As you edit, remember that the verb in such a sentence should always agree with the subject, the term before the verb.

■ His parents ~~is~~ *are* the one thing that makes him happy.

■ **EDITING 1: PRACTICE**

Edit the following passage to make verbs agree with their subjects. Take special care when identifying the subject.

Canada, along with Europe and many cities in the United States, have found great success in curbing the spread of AIDS through needle exchange programs. These kinds of programs is an effective way to slow down the spread of the virus among intravenous drug users. There are many who are convinced that providing addicts with clean needles does not result in increased drug use. Others, who think that such programs encourage the use of drugs and sends the wrong message to young people, remains firmly opposed. To this group, free needles and free drug use is one and the same. But, supporters of the idea points out, one of the most important parts of needle exchange programs are educating users about the dangers of sharing needles. After all, intravenous drug users is a segment of the population with an especially high rate of HIV infection, which causes AIDS. And the spread of AIDS and other infectious diseases are a matter of concern for all people.

---

36 d   Making verbs agree with subjects joined by *and*

When the conjunction *and* links two or more parts of a subject, it creates a **compound subject.** (Also see 36e.) Such a subject is almost always considered plural and requires a plural verb.

Peter and Patrick *play* on the lacrosse team.

This rule has several important exceptions. When the two elements joined by *and* are regarded as a single entity, the subject is considered singular and requires a singular verb.

■ Red beans and rice ~~are~~ *is* my favorite dish.

522 Making subjects and verbs agree

If all parts of a compound subject refer to the same person or thing, a singular verb is appropriate.

■ My friend, my partner, and my mentor ~~have~~ *has* brought wisdom and courage to this firm.

The writer is referring to one person who is all three things to her.

Each affects the verb differently depending on how it is used. When singular elements joined by *and* are preceded by *each*, the resulting structure is singular.

■ Each river, brook, and stream in the county ~~have~~ *has* suffered pollution.

However, when *each* comes after such a compound subject rather than before it, the subject is plural.

■ The musician and the singer each deserves special praise.

---

36 e | Making verbs agree with subjects joined by *or* and *nor*

When the conjunction *or, nor, either . . . or, neither . . . nor,* or *not only . . . but also* links two or more elements of a subject, it creates a **compound subject.** (Also see 36d.) When one element of the subject is singular and another is plural, convention dictates that the verb agree with the part of the subject closer to it.

Neither the police officers nor the district attorney *believes* him.

Neither the district attorney nor the police officers *believe* him.

If a singular verb sounds awkward, try rearranging the subject to put the plural part closer to the verb.

■ *One* ~~Two crabs or one~~ lobster *or two crabs make* ~~makes~~ an excellent dinner.

■ **EDITING 2: PRACTICE**

Edit the following sentences to make verbs agree with their compound subjects. Circle the number of any sentence that is correct. Example:

$$\overset{is}{}$$
Either the chief inspector or his assistant ~~are~~ mistaken.

1. Neither the butler nor the chauffeur behave oddly in front of the police.

2. Each man and woman is under suspicion.

3. Not only the time of death but also the choice of weapons figure into the equation.

4. A telephone call or a message sent beyond the premises are forbidden during the investigation.

5. Motive and alibi each matters in an investigation.

6. The inspector and the coroner disagrees.

7. The sum and substance of the investigation are interrogation.

36 f | **Making verbs agree with collective nouns**

Collective nouns (such as *couple, flock, crowd, herd,* and *committee*) refer to groups of people or things. They can cause confusion because the words themselves have a singular form even though they refer to several individuals. Whether a collective noun takes a singular or plural verb depends on whether the members of the group are seen as acting as individuals or as one unit. If the members of a group act individually, use a plural verb.

The jury *have* returned to their homes.

If such a construction sounds awkward to you, try replacing the subject with one that is clearly plural.

The members of the jury *have* returned to their homes.

If an action is taken by an entire group together as a unit, use a singular verb.

The navy *trains* at sea.

ESL **VERB AGREEMENT WITH NONCOUNT NOUNS**

Count nouns name persons, places, or things that can be counted: *one apple, two oranges*. **Noncount nouns** refer to things that can't be counted: mass nouns, abstract concepts, emotions, or qualities.

MASS NOUNS	ABSTRACT CONCEPTS	EMOTIONS	QUALITIES
equipment	behavior	anger	confidence
furniture	education	happiness	honesty
homework	health	love	integrity
money	knowledge	surprise	sincerity

Noncount nouns are usually used only in the singular and therefore take singular verbs. In English these words usually have no plural form.

■ Public transportation*s* in Atlanta ~~make~~ *makes* getting around the city easy.

■ ~~These informations~~ *This information* about subject-verb agreement ~~are~~ *is* intended to help with your editing.

The collective noun *number* can cause special problems. The expression *the number* refers to a group as a single unit, so it needs a singular verb. The expression *a number* means "several" or "more than one," so it needs a plural verb.

The number of times I have been wrong *is* quite small.

A number of visitors *have* complimented the park management on the new trail markers.

---

36 g **Making verbs agree with indefinite pronouns**

In most cases, whether a pronoun is singular or plural depends on whether the word or words it refers to are singular or plural. In the sentence *My uncle enjoys fishing, and he often goes on fishing trips,* the pronoun *he* is singular (and takes a singular verb, *goes*) because it refers to a singular noun, *uncle.* An **indefinite pronoun,** however, often does not refer to a specific person or thing. Most indefinite pronouns are either always singular or always plural.

ESL **VERB AGREEMENT WITH QUANTIFIERS**

1. *Few* and *a few*
Few means "not many" or "not enough." *A few* means "some," "several," or "a small number." *Few* and *a few* take plural verbs.

> Many law students are taking the bar exam today. A few *have* taken it in other states.

> Few *have* failed it more than once.

2. *Little* and *a little*
Little means "not much" or "not enough." *A little* means "some" or "a small amount." *Little* and *a little* take singular verbs.

> Doctors have done much research on heart disease. However, little *has* been done with women as subjects.

> Be careful pouring that hot sesame oil. A little *goes* a long way.

3. *Most of the* and *most*
Most of the (or *most of*) means "the majority of" and is followed by a plural count noun, a noncount noun, or a pronoun. It takes a plural verb when it is followed by a plural noun or pronoun, and a singular verb when it is followed by a noncount noun or a singular pronoun. *Most* is an adjective or a pronoun that is singular or plural depending on the noun or pronoun it modifies or refers to.

PLURAL	Most of the dogs in the neighborhood *bark* in the morning.
PLURAL	Most dogs *are* tied while their owners are at work.
SINGULAR	Most of the violence on TV *is* unnecessary.
SINGULAR	Most *is* treated as harmless by TV producers.

SINGULAR   Everybody *has* heard that old joke already.

PLURAL   Luckily, few of the passengers *were* injured.

Although pronouns such as *everybody* and *someone* are singular, many people have a tendency in everyday speech to treat them as if they were plural in order to avoid sexist language: *Everybody has their mind made up.* This is grammatically incorrect. See 32c for a full discussion of this problem and its solutions.

    Some, any, all, more, most, what, and *none* can be either singular or plural depending on what they mean. If the pronoun renames a person or thing mentioned elsewhere (its antecedent), the number of that person or thing determines the number of the pronoun.

Of the *time* that remained, more *was* spent in arguing than in

making decisions.

Of the *hours* that remained, more *were* spent in arguing than in

making decisions.

As you edit, try mentally recasting the sentence without the indefinite pronoun, using *it* or *they* if necessary to determine whether the pronoun is singular or plural.

Some of the children *is/are* eager to leave.

They *are* eager to leave.

All is plural when it means the total number in a group; it is singular when it means "everything" or "the only thing."

All *are* required to take the foreign language examination.

All I have *is* a rough idea of how I want to proceed.

None standing alone is always singular: *None was injured.* Followed by a prepositional phrase, *none* can be singular or plural, depending on the phrase.

None of the herd *was* missing.

None of the birds *were* gone.

However, some experts argue that because *none* means *not one* or *no one*, only the singular is strictly correct: *None of the birds was gone.*

✔ COMMON INDEFINITE PRONOUNS

ALWAYS SINGULAR

someone	anyone	no one	everyone	either
somebody	anybody	nobody	everybody	neither
something	anything	nothing	everything	each
				much
				one

EITHER SINGULAR OR PLURAL

some	any	none	all	more
				most
				what

ALWAYS PLURAL

few	both	several	many

---

36 h
Making verbs agree with *who, which,* and *that*

To decide whether a verb following the **relative pronouns** *who, which,* or *that* should be singular or plural, find the word for which the pronoun stands (its antecedent).

■ Barbara and Robin, who wants̸ to join the team, will meet with the coach.

Who *stands for* Barbara and Robin, *so the verb should be the plural* want.

slips
■ A bale of shingles that s̶l̶i̶p̶ off the roof could hurt someone.
 ^

That *refers to* bale, *so* slips *is singular.*

Relative pronouns can be particularly troublesome when they follow the construction *one of the* or *the only one of the*. If the pronoun refers to *one*, it is singular; if it refers to whatever comes after *one of the* or *the only one of the*, it is plural.

One of the *areas* that *have* suffered is voter participation.

The only *one* of the women who *disagrees* is Maria.

■ EDITING 3: PRACTICE

Edit the following sentences to make verbs agree with collective noun subjects, indefinite pronoun subjects, and relative pronoun subjects. Circle the number of any sentence that is correct. Example:

> The review of the photographs, which *is* ~~are~~ very enthusiastic, might attract more visitors to the museum.

1. The pictures in the exhibit, which are open every night, feature children from Third World countries.

2. Many of the children photographed in Mexico was casualities of the earthquake.

3. Most people find that it is the look of sadness on their faces that are most moving.

4. The best of the photographers, who spend three months every year in Southeast Asia, has won numerous awards.

5. The museum committee has a variety of opinions on the exhibit.

6. Adding photography exhibits to the museum was one of many good ideas of the curator, who is herself a photographer.

7. Much of her energy are spent in finding good exhibits and soliciting contributions from patrons.

36 i Making verbs agree with subjects that refer to amounts

Words that describe amounts of time, money, distance, measurement, or percentage can take singular or plural verbs. As with collective nouns, the number depends on whether the subject is considered as a group of individuals (plural) or as a single unit or sum (singular).

Four hours *have* passed since we saw each other last.

The hours pass one at a time, individually.

Fifteen minutes *is* too long to keep the boss waiting.

The minutes here are a block of time, a unit.

Using singular verbs with noun phrases and noun clauses

A **noun phrase** is any phrase (group of related words lacking a subject or a verb) that serves as a noun in a sentence. A **noun clause** is any clause (group of related words that has a subject and a verb) that serves as a noun in a sentence. Some noun phrases begin with an infinitive (*to go*) or a gerund (*going*); this type of noun phrase is always singular. All noun clauses are singular.

PHRASE   *To sail the seven seas* was her lifelong dream.

CLAUSE   *That he would not consider our suggestions* was surprising.

Using singular verbs with titles and with words used as words

The titles of books, plays, and movies are treated as singular even if they are plural in form. The name of a company or firm is also singular.

"Shake, Rattle and Roll" *was* by Bill Haley and the Comets.

General Motors *is* an important employer in Michigan.

In discussing a word itself, use a singular verb even if the word is plural.

Hyenas was what my father lovingly called us children.

36 l Using singular verbs *with* singular subjects that end in *-s*

Words such as *statistics, politics, economics, athletics, acoustics,* and *aesthetics* seem to be plural because they end in -s. However, they take singular verbs when used in a general sense to mean a field of study, a body of ideas, or a profession. Such words are plural when referring to specific instances, activities, or characteristics.

> Economics *is* sometimes called "the dismal science."

> The economics of the project *make* no sense.

Words that refer to an ailment such as *shingles* or *measles* are usually singular. So is the word *news*.

> Measles *is* spreading because of a lapse in vaccinations.

> This news *is* encouraging.

36 m Using plural verbs with troublesome plurals

Words such as *media* and *data* look like singular words in English, but they are Latin plurals and should take plural verbs. The corresponding singular forms are *medium* and *datum*. Look out too for *curriculum* and *curricula, criterion* and *criteria, phenomenon* and *phenomena*. The use of *data* as singular is gaining ground, especially in reference to computers, but you should avoid it in writing.

■ The media sometimes fail$ to give a complete picture of complex events.

■ The experimental data support$ the theory you advanced.

Dictionaries list the preferred plural and singular forms of these and other words of foreign origin.

> **ESL** **SOME NOUNS THAT TAKE PLURAL VERBS**
>
> Some collective nouns are derived from adjectives and refer to a group of people: *the wealthy, the homeless, the elderly*. These nouns are considered plural and take plural verbs.
>
> The young often *ignore* the advice of their elders.
>
> The noun *people* is always plural. To indicate one, use *person*.
>
> People *are* wondering who will be the next governor.
>
> That person *is* wondering when to register to vote.
>
> The noun *police* is always plural. It never refers to only one person. Likewise, *the police* is always plural. In English, the article *a* is never used before *police*. To indicate one, use *police officer*.
>
> Police *have* been stationed in front of the courthouse all afternoon.
>
> A police officer *is* always on duty inside the courthouse.

Nouns like *pants, sunglasses, binoculars,* and *scissors* refer to single objects but take plural verbs.

■ The binoculars ~~was~~ *were* very useful for spotting birds.

When the construction *pair of* is used, the verb is singular.

■ The pair of pants you wanted ~~are~~ *is* ready.

■ **EDITING 4: PRACTICE**

Edit the following sentences by making verbs agree with their noun phrase or noun clause subjects, subjects that are titles or words used as words, or troublesome singular or plural subjects. Circle the number of any sentence that is correct. Example:

Studying for classes ~~are~~ *is* easier when I enjoy the reading assignments.

1. Politics are not a field that I find interesting, but I do enjoy my world literature course.

2. Dostoyevsky's *Crime and Punishment* are exactly the sort of novel I would choose to read on my own.

3. That a young man would commit a murder for the reasons Dostoyevsky describes seems unthinkable to me.

4. To make interesting contributions to the weekly class discussions are one of my goals.

5. *Witticisms* are what I would like my classmates to call my comments.

■ EDITING 5: PRACTICE

Edit the following passage to make verbs agree with their subjects. More than one edited version is possible. Be ready to explain your editing choices.

The county employees and volunteers who run the prison education program focuses on illiteracy. Statistics shows that among prison inmates nationwide, some 60 percent is illiterate, and neither substance abuse programs nor vocational training seem as effective as literacy education in limiting the return of repeat offenders. The core of the program, therefore, are reading and writing skills. Each employee and volunteer go through a three-week training program in literacy education. If they can demonstrate sufficiently high reading levels, inmates may also train to become tutors; by doing so, most earns points toward early probation. Tutoring for all participants takes place not only one on one but also in groups, and there is within each group inmates at various levels of reading proficiency. Even inmates who have never achieved any academic success learns without feeling intimidated. Current data shows a high rate of success.

■ EDITING 6: APPLICATION

Examine a paper you are working on to find any verbs that do not agree with their subjects. What kinds of mistakes did you make? Is there one sort of mistake that you make more than others? If so, why do you think this is? Edit any sentences that had subject-verb agreement errors, and think about how best to avoid or edit these problems in the future.

Adjectives and adverbs modify — that is, they describe, identify, or limit the meaning of other words. **Modifiers** can enrich description, changing a simple sentence like *The explorers were lost* into an expressive one like *The explorers were thoroughly, hopelessly, horribly lost.* For modifiers to function effectively in your writing, you must use them carefully and correctly. You must decide whether an adjective or an adverb is grammatically appropriate and form negatives, comparatives, and superlatives according to convention.

Although adjectives and adverbs are the most familiar and descriptive modifiers, **articles** (*a, an, the*), **possessives** (*Michael's, my*), **phrases** and **clauses** (*knife that he used*), and even **nouns** (*music* critic, *tool* belt) can be used as modifiers. This chapter describes the correct uses of adjectives and adverbs; for discussions about using the other types of modifiers, Chapters 29, 38, and 64.

As you edit, examine your adjectives and adverbs carefully and make sure to do the following:

- Choose an adjective or adverb according to what it modifies.

- Use adjectives after linking verbs.

- Choose correctly between commonly confused modifiers.

- Avoid double negatives.

- Use comparatives and superlatives correctly.

37 **a** **Choosing adjectives or adverbs**

Adjectives modify nouns and pronouns.

> **noun** **noun**
> Annette is an *excellent* editor who has a *sharp* eye for
>
> **noun** **noun**
> *vague* statements and *awkward* prose.

> **pronoun**
> She is *careful, thorough,* and *diplomatic.*

Adverbs modify verbs, adjectives, other adverbs, and sometimes whole clauses.

> **verb** **adjective**
> She *often* works with *truly* terrible manuscripts and
>
> **adjective** **verb**
> *nearly always* improves them *greatly.*

> **clause**
> *Amazingly,* she loves her job.

Many adjectives and adverbs are formed by adding **suffixes,** or endings, to other words. (See 31c.) Adjectives are often formed by adding *-able, -ful, -ish,* and many other endings to nouns and verbs: *acceptable, beautiful, foolish.* Many adverbs are formed by adding *-ly* to an adjective: *nearly, amazingly, brilliantly.*

In speaking, some people substitute adjectives for adverbs ending in *-ly: It fit real well* rather than *It fit really well.* If you sometimes speak this way, take care when editing to use adverbs to modify verbs, adjectives, or other adverbs. Use adjectives only to modify nouns and pronouns.

■ They were ~~full~~ *fully* aware that they would be reported.

The *-ly* suffix is not a reliable guide to identifying a word as an adverb. A number of adjectives end in *-ly: brotherly, friendly, lovely.* Also, many adverbs do not end in *-ly: often, always, later.* Still other words can be used as either adjectives or adverbs, even though some of these also have *-ly* adverb forms as well. *Slow* can be an adjective or an adverb; *slowly* is always an adverb. If you are in doubt about whether you have chosen the correct form of an adjective or adverb, consult a dictionary. (Also see 37c.)

■ **EDITING I: PRACTICE**

Edit the following sentences, using an adjective or an adverb when each is needed. Example:

Working with wood can be a lovely and rewardingly~~ly~~ pastime for those who truly enjoy using their hands.

I. Measuring correct is the most important part of woodworking.
2. You have to measure real carefully, but it is likely to pay off in the end.
3. For fine work, measure close. Use a pencil that marks clean.
4. Then you have to cut straight and true. Leave just a part of your mark showing, and the piece should fit perfect.
5. Any good woodworker can give you handily suggestions like these.

37 b   Using adjectives after linking verbs

Confusion about whether to use an adjective or an adverb arises occasionally with **linking verbs** such as *be, become, feel, seem, appear, look, smell, taste,* and *sound.* A modifier after a linking verb modifies the subject of the verb, not the verb itself, so the modifier should be an adjective, not an adverb. (See 37c.)

■ I felt bad~~ly~~ about not being able to help.

An adverb may modify an adjective after a linking verb.

ADJECTIVE MODIFYING NOUN   The hamburger tasted *odd.*

ADVERB MODIFYING ADJECTIVE   The hamburger tasted *oddly* sour.

Some of these verbs can also express action, in which case they do not function as linking verbs. A word that modifies such a verb should be an adverb.

LINKING VERB   The ghost of Hamlet's father *appears* anxious.

ACTION VERB   The ghost of Hamlet's father *appears* suddenly.

■ **EDITING 2: PRACTICE**

Edit the following sentences, using adjectives and adverbs correctly after linking verbs. Circle the number of any sentence that is correct. Example:

poorly
The team played so ~~poor~~ that they felt badly about it afterward.
     ∧

I. The coach sounds odd philosophical about the team's loss.

2. The players all seemed sadly disappointed.

3. How can they become happily?

4. The other team looked really nicely in their new uniforms and they played good enough to win the game.

5. The winners feel excitedly about their victory. All agree that even after a friendly game victory tastes deliciously.

| 37 | c | **Choosing between commonly confused modifiers** |

Several pairs of modifiers frequently cause writing problems, either because they are commonly confused in everyday speech or because their meanings are closely related. If you know you tend to misuse some of these, you may want to use your computer's search function to locate every instance of the potentially incorrect modifiers so that you can evaluate their use.

Bad and *badly*

In standard English, *bad* is always an adjective, *badly* always an adverb. Although they are commonly interchanged in speech, you should be sure to use them correctly in writing, especially after linking verbs.

bad.
■ She looked as though she felt ~~badly.~~
     ∧

badly
■ They were playing so ~~bad~~ that I left at halftime.
     ∧

Good and *well*

Good and *well* also are often confused in conversation, partly because they share the same comparative and superlative forms:

good, better, best; well, better, best. (See 37e.) *Good* is always an adjective. *Well* can be either an adjective or an adverb. As an adjective, *well* means "healthy," the opposite of *ill.* As an adverb, *well* means, among other things, "satisfactorily" or "skillfully." In editing, be careful that you have not used *good* as an adverb or *well* as an adjective meaning "satisfactory."

■   She sings ~~good~~ *well* enough to get the lead.

■   My hat looked ~~well~~ *good* on my mother.

Real and really

Real and *really* have related meanings, but *real* is properly used as an adjective meaning "genuine, true, not illusory": *She trembled and wondered whether the ghost was real. Really* is an adverb meaning "truly" or "very." Even if you sometimes use *real* as an adverb in speech, be careful as you edit to use *really* to modify adjectives and adverbs.

■   He usually speaks ~~real~~ *really* slowly.

Less and fewer

Less and *fewer* are both adjectives, but they are used differently. Use *less* to describe something considered as a whole unit: *less hope, less misery, less money.* Use *fewer* for quantities that can be counted: *fewer dreams, fewer problems, fewer dollars.*

■   The house would lose less heat if ~~less~~ *fewer* windows were open.

37   d   Avoiding double negatives

In English, one negative modifier (*no, not, never,* and so on) is sufficient to change the meaning of a sentence. Although the double negative is common in some dialects, particularly when one of the negatives is a contraction, as you edit you should be sure to make negative statements with only one negative modifier.

■   I didn't have ~~no~~ *any* money.

■   I ~~didn't have~~ *had* no money.

ESL **USING NEGATIVES: *NOT* VS. *NO***

In expressing negation, use *not* in the following situations:

■ To make a verb phrase negative
I do *not* agree with the author's opinion.

■ With forms of *any* or with number modifiers
There are *not any* places to sit in the theater.

There is *not one* place to sit in the theater.

■ To negate the indefinite pronouns *everybody* and *everyone*
Not everyone would have dealt with that problem as well as you did.

To emphasize negation, you can use *no* in front of a noun instead of *not* in a verb phrase.

NEGATIVE   I do *not* see *any* reason to assume he is lying.

EMPHATIC NEGATIVE   I see *no reason* to assume he is lying.

Adverbs like *hardly*, *barely*, and *scarcely* have negative meanings, so using *no* or *not* with them creates a double negative.

■ I ~~don't~~ have hardly any money.

Occasions do arise when you need to retain a double negative to make a positive statement.

His prospective father-in-law called Rothwell a bankrupt and a spendthrift, but Rothwell said it was *not* true that he had *no* money.

EDITING 3: PRACTICE

Edit the following passage, using the correct form of any commonly confused modifiers and correcting any double negatives.

Things have been going real bad for the homeless in recent weeks. First, the city shut its main shelter. Later, a charity soup kitchen ran out of money. Every year the city seems to have more needy people and less dollars to help them. A more comprehensive program would mean less women and children sleeping on the street. Many of these people cannot hardly read or write good enough to get a job that pays good. With only a shelter to live in it's hard for them to feel well about themselves. They eat bad and they sleep bad, so it isn't no wonder that they feel bad too.

37 e Using comparatives and superlatives correctly

The basic form of an adjective or adverb, called the **positive form,** describes a quality or property: *large, delicious, late, graciously.* The **comparative form,** which usually ends in *-er* or is preceded by *more,* makes a comparison between two people or things.

She arrived *later* than I did but was greeted *more graciously.*

The **superlative form,** usually ending in *-est* or preceded by *most,* also makes a comparison, but it does so among three or more people or things.

Of all their guests, she always arrived *latest* and was greeted *most graciously.*

As you edit, keep in mind that your choice of a comparative or a superlative modifier gives readers an important clue about the nature of the comparison.

Of the brothers, Joe was the *stronger* athlete.

Of the brothers, Joe was the *strongest* athlete.

The first sentence says that there are only two brothers, while the second indicates that there are at least three brothers.

If you are using a computer, you can use the search function to help you edit for all the issues covered in 37e. Having the computer find every instance of the words *more, most, less,* and *least* and the letter combinations *er* and *est* will show you where you have used comparatives and superlatives and allow you to evaluate their correctness. Note that if you have the computer search for the letter combinations *er* and *est,* it will also find words such as *swimmer* and *testing.*

> **ESL**
>
> ## ARTICLES WITH COMPARATIVES AND SUPERLATIVES
>
> When a comparative adjective is used by itself, do not use any article (*a, an,* or *the*).
>
> This house is *larger* than the other one.
>
> **DEFINITE ARTICLE *THE***
> Use *the* when a comparative or superlative adjective is followed by a specific noun or pronoun renaming a specific noun.
>
> This house is *the larger one.*
>
> This house is *the largest one.*
>
> The use of *the* is optional when the comparative or superlative adjective is used without a noun but the noun is implied.
>
> Of the two houses, which one is *the larger?* [Implied: *the larger house.*]
>
> Of the two houses, which one is *larger?*
>
> **INDEFINITE ARTICLES *A/AN***
> Use *a* or *an* with comparative adjectives modifying a noun that is not specific.
>
> I've never seen *a larger* grapefruit.
> *The grapefruit mentioned is any grapefruit, not a specific grapefruit.*
>
> Use *a* or *an* with superlative adjectives only if the superlative has the meaning "very."
>
> That was *a most refreshing* glass of grapefruit juice.
> *The meaning is "very refreshing."*

1 Forming regular comparatives and superlatives

Most one-syllable adjectives and adverbs add *-er* and *-est* to form comparatives and superlatives: *smarter, closest.* Adjectives of three or more syllables, adjectives ending in *-ful,* adverbs of two or more syllables, and most adverbs ending in *-ly* generally use *more* and *most* to form comparatives and superlatives: *more impressive,* *most hopeful, most often, most sharply.* With other two-syllable adjectives, the choice is often yours (*happiest, most happy; luckiest, most lucky*), although the *-er* and *-est* endings are more common.

Negative comparisons are formed using *less* for comparatives and *least* for superlatives: *less often, least hopeful.*

 IRREGULAR ADJECTIVES AND ADVERBS

POSITIVE	COMPARATIVE	SUPERLATIVE
good	better	best
well	better	best
bad	worse	worst
badly	worse	worst
ill	worse	worst
many	more	most
much	more	most
some	more	most
little*	less	least

* Little in the sense of "not much" is irregular. Little in the sense of "small" is regular: She wanted a little dog, but mine is littler than hers, and my cousin's is littlest of all.

---

2 Forming irregular comparatives and superlatives

A few adjectives and adverbs form comparatives and superlatives in irregular ways. Take care to memorize them, especially if English is not your first language.

■ Paul did ~~gooder~~ *better* on the test than I did.

■ She said she felt ~~weller~~ *better* today.

3 Avoiding double comparatives and superlatives

When forming comparatives, use either *-er* or *more*, not both. When forming superlatives, use either *-est* or *most*, not both.

■ After eating he felt ~~more~~ better.

4 **Using only the positive form of absolute modifiers**

Some modifiers, called **absolutes,** do not logically form comparatives or superlatives because their positive form already implies the superlative. Words such as *perfect, unique, equal, essential, final, total,* and *absolute* should not be intensified. As you edit, make sure that you have not used *more* or *most* with such words.

■ The turbo engine makes this car ~~even more~~ unique.

■ EDITING 4: PRACTICE

Edit the following passage, using the correct comparative and superlative forms of adjectives and adverbs. More than one edited version is possible. Be ready to explain your editing choices.

How do American students compare with students in other countries? In general, studies show that Americans do worser on tests. Scores on SATs and other standardized tests have been dropping more steadilier over the past decade in the United States. Perhaps we need to take a more closer look at what can be done to make our nation's young people gooder students. Perhaps it is time to admit that the more traditional methods of teaching may not be most perfect. To perform more well, students need to learn more than mere memorization skills; they have to learn the bestest way to study and how best to apply what they learn. With a new approach, perhaps students will find that learning takes lesser time and can even be funner.

■ EDITING 5: PRACTICE

Edit the following passage, using adjectives and adverbs correctly. More than one edited version is possible. Be ready to explain your editing choices.

The fall leaves that had looked so colorfully had turned a more duller color and fallen from the trees weeks ago, leaving the woods grayer and more lonelier. The most sharpest, bitterest wind blew against me as I walked down the dirt road. I had to admit that I was likely to feel badly tomorrow. My hands felt warmly inside my woolen gloves, but I didn't have no hat. My ears felt raw, and the inside of my head throbbed bad.

I felt happier when I saw the large red building with its well-maintained outbuildings. The air smelled pungently: manure, feed, and animal smells were mixed together indistinguishable. I went over to the horse stalls in the barn, where real fragrant wood chips covered the dirt floor, strewn there to absorb the odors of the barn. The horses, covered up good in their colorful blankets, seemed peaceful in their stalls. The warm air felt heavenly and, exhaustedly, I unzipped my jacket and sat down on the floor. I didn't know of no better place to get off my feet and rest for a while.

EDITING 6: APPLICATION

Examine your own recent writing to see whether you have incorrectly used any adjectives or adverbs. Is there one kind of mistake that you make most often? If so, think about how best to eliminate incorrect use of adjectives and adverbs when you edit your work. Edit any sentences that contain such mistakes.

In English, word order is important to meaning. Word order makes the difference between *The man ate the fish* and *The fish ate the man.* In writing, word order problems often involve **modifiers:** adjectives, adverbs, and phrases or clauses used as adjectives and adverbs. Within a sentence, there may be more than one possible place to put a modifier, but if it is not positioned so that it unambiguously modifies the element it should, readers may misinterpret the sentence. *They want just her to sing this song* means something different from *They want her to sing just this song.* Modifiers that seem to modify the wrong thing are called **misplaced.** Those that are ambiguous about what they modify are called **squinting.** Those that have no element to modify sensibly are called **dangling.** Finally, modifiers that come between sentence elements that should not be separated are called **disruptive.**

In editing to position modifiers appropriately, do the following:

■   Reposition misplaced modifiers.

■   Clarify which element is modified by a squinting modifier.

■   Eliminate dangling modifiers.

■   Find a better position for any disruptive modifier.

38 a Repositioning misplaced modifiers

Modifiers separated from the words they are supposed to modify can be misleading. Because readers naturally assume that the modifier modifies the nearest grammatically acceptable element, a **misplaced modifier** is often interpreted as modifying an element other than the one the writer intended.

We wanted our ordeal to end *desperately.*

Unless the writer intended that things turn out badly, the adverb *desperately* is misplaced. When the adverb is placed next to the verb it modifies, *wanted*, the sentence makes more sense: We *desperately wanted our ordeal to end.*

When editing, check for misplaced modifiers by being alert to unintended meanings.

■ He took a frog ^*in a glass jar* to biology class ~~in a glass jar~~.

It seems unlikely that biology class was held in a glass jar.

A **limiting modifier** (such as *almost, even, hardly, just, merely, nearly, only, scarcely,* and *simply*) limits the meaning of the word it modifies by creating an implicit contrast: to say that *only* A is true implies that B and C are not. Readers understand a limiting modifier to modify the sentence element that directly follows it. Consider the difference in meaning created in the following sentences by moving the limiting modifier *just.*

Just the children applauded the conductor.

Only the children, not the adults, applauded.

The children *just* applauded the conductor.

They applauded but did nothing else.

The children applauded *just* the conductor.

The children applauded the conductor and no one else.

A limiting modifier should almost always be placed directly before the word it modifies. As you edit, watch for misplaced limiting modifiers, particularly those that precede a verb when they actually modify a noun following the verb.

■ She ~~almost~~ waited until ^*almost* the last minute.

If you are using a computer in your editing, you may want to use the search function to find every instance of common limiting modifiers such as *only, almost,* and *just* in your paper so that you can evaluate the placement of each one.

■ EDITING I: PRACTICE

Edit the following passage, moving any misplaced modifiers. More than one edited version is possible. Be ready to explain your editing choices.

Most people assume that black bears hibernate all winter incorrectly. During the winter, although sleeping deeply, a true state of hibernation is not achieved by black bears. Their body temperature only drops a little, and one can wake up a black bear with just a little effort. Preparing to sleep for several months, a very large amount of food is eaten by the bears. This way, they can store fat and feed off it all winter while they are sleeping. The female surprisingly gives birth to her young at this time.

38 b Clarifying squinting modifiers

A **squinting modifier** seems to modify two things at once. A squinting modifier is usually found between the sentence element that the writer intended it to modify and some other element — and it seems to look in both directions at once.

Students who follow directions *consistently* score well on standardized tests.

What occurs consistently, the following of directions or the scoring well on tests?

To edit a squinting modifier, first determine which sentence element you want it to modify, and then reposition it or otherwise rearrange the sentence so that no other interpretation is possible.

■ Students who *consistently* follow directions ~~consistently~~ score well on standardized tests.

■ Students who follow directions ~~consistently~~ score *consistently* well on standardized tests.

38 c Eliminating dangling modifiers

A **dangling modifier** is a modifier that cannot be attached logically to anything in the sentence. Either the sentence element that the modifier is intended to modify does not appear in the sentence, or it does not appear in a grammatically appropriate form. Readers interpret a dangling modifier as modifying the nearest grammatically acceptable element, which may not be the one the writer had in mind. Often a dangling modifier consists of a prepositional phrase or verbal phrase at the beginning of a sentence.

> *Running through the rain*, our clothes got soaked.

> *Clearly, it was we who were running through the rain, not our clothes. But we does not appear in the sentence, only our, a form that cannot be modified by the modifier.*

In a sense, it is the reader who is left dangling, wondering what the writer means. To correct a dangling modifier, you must introduce a subject that logically can be modified or change the form of an existing element. Then place it directly after the modifier. Sometimes you must supply a new verb as well.

■ Running through the rain, ‸*we got* our clothes ~~got~~ soaked.

■ Having completed her research, ‸*she earned an A on* the paper‸ ~~earned her an A~~.

■ Still digging out from Thursday's fourteen-inch snowfall, ‸*residents prepared for* another big storm ~~was~~ due early Sunday.

When the main clause is in the passive voice, an introductory phrase often has no subject to modify. One solution is to place the sentence in the active voice. (See 29c.)

■ To study the effects of cigarette smoking, ‸*researcher have forced* monkeys ~~have been forced~~ to inhale the equivalent of a hundred cigarettes a day.

■ **EDITING 2: PRACTICE**

Edit the following passage, clarifying squinting modifiers and eliminating dangling modifiers. More than one edited version is possible. Be ready to discuss your editing choices.

Examining the patient death rates of more than fifty doctors, the results were compared by a panel to a statistical average. Having a better than average rate, a minus score was entered for those doctors. A positive score was entered for those who had worse than average rates. Consisting of only the doctors with positive scores, the panel released a list of names to a local newspaper. After reading the article, a protest was lodged by the county medical society. Doctors who criticized the study strongly argued that the scoring was biased.

38 d Moving disruptive modifiers

If you place a modifier so that it disrupts the flow of a sentence, you may confuse readers or distract, inadvertently, their attention from your meaning. In the previous sentence, for example, there are several better places for *inadvertently*. **Disruptive modifiers** include those that split an infinitive, those that divide a verb phrase, and those that needlessly separate major sentence elements.

▮ Modifiers that split an infinitive

An **infinitive** consists of the word *to* and the base form of the verb: *to fly, to grow, to achieve.* Whenever possible, avoid placing words between the word *to* and the verb. Such a construction, called a **split infinitive,** occurs fairly frequently in speech but can seem awkward in writing.

whenever possible.
■ He promised to ~~whenever possible~~ avoid splitting infinitives./ˇ

Sometimes, however, it is difficult to find a natural-sounding place for the modifier.

The director wanted to *vividly* re-create a bullfight for the theater audience.

Some readers would not be bothered by a split infinitive in such a case. But knowing that some instructors and other readers consider any split infinitive a mark of carelessness, you might choose to edit the sentence to eliminate the infinitive altogether.

■ The director ~~wanted to vividly re-create~~ *planned a vivid re-creation of* a bullfight for the theater audience.

ESL **PLACEMENT OF ADVERBS WITHIN VERB PHRASES**

When an adverb is used between elements of a verb phrase, it usually appears after the first auxiliary verb.

Our baseball stadium has *rarely* been filled to capacity this season.

In questions, the adverb appears after the first auxiliary verb and the subject and before the other parts of the verb.

In the past, have you *usually* found yourself writing a paper the day before it's due?

When *not* is used with another adverb, it should appear directly after the first auxiliary verb and before the other adverb when *not* is being used to negate that adverb.

This newspaper does *not usually* put sports news on the front page. [*Not* negates *usually*; *not usually* means "seldom."]

Not should appear after the adverb when *not* is being used to negate the action expressed by the main verb.

The senators have *often not* paid much attention to those who elected them. [*Not* negates *paid.*]

---

2 **Modifiers that split a verb phrase**

A **verb phrase** consists of one or more auxiliary verbs, such as a form of *be* or *have*, and a participle or the base form of a verb: *had been formed, does happen.* Most instructors will accept a single adverb (or *not* plus another adverb) placed between the elements of a verb phrase.

> Although he was far from India, Columbus's landing had *irrevocably* changed the New World.

However, an intervening phrase or clause will be considered disruptive.

■ ~~The Roanoke colony had,~~ ^Bby the time a supply ship arrived four
the Roanoke colony had ^
years later, disappeared without a trace.
^

3 **Modifiers that separate major sentence elements**

Placing modifiers often means balancing conflicting goals. On the one hand, major sentence elements such as subjects, verbs, objects, and complements need to be placed near each other so that their relationships are clear. On the other hand, a modifier that modifies a sentence element needs to be placed close to that element and thus risks disrupting one of those relationships. These two considerations must often be balanced.

A long modifier falling between a subject and a verb, between a linking verb and a subject complement, or between a verb and its object can cause readers to forget where the sentence was heading.

■ *Because of her great popularity with audiences,*
^Mary Pickford/ ~~because of her great popularity with audiences,~~
became the first silent film actor to be publicized by name.

■ *never a stronghold of slavery,*
Kentucky was/^even though it had residents who fought for the
Confederacy during the Civil War,/~~never a stronghold of slavery.~~
^

■ ~~African American spirituals influenced~~ ^Tthrough their distinctive
African American spirituals ^ *influenced*
harmonic and rhythmic elements, ^the development of most
twentieth-century popular music.

Some modifiers may seem disruptive while others in grammatically similar situations may not. The following sentence, although similar in structure to the previous one, probably will strike you as perfectly readable.

> The partial success of Ross Perot's candidacy suggests, *at least to some analysts*, that Americans are eager for new political choices.

Because even grammatically similar examples like these must be handled differently, no sweeping rule can be made about where to put modifier phrases and clauses. When deciding where to put a modifier clause or phrase, try to minimize disruption and yet place the modifier so that what it modifies is clear.

▉ EDITING 3: PRACTICE

Edit the following passage, moving disruptive modifiers for easier reading. More than one edited version is possible. Be ready to discuss your editing choices.

The writers and editors at *The New Yorker* use specific tactics to effectively fire their information at a very specific audience — educated middle- and upper-class individuals who work and play in New York City. The authors attempt through skillful use of sophisticated vocabulary, varied and complex sentence structure, and stimulating content to capture this readership. Their methods have in almost all instances given the readers what they want, namely the greatest amount of information in the fewest number of words. The magazine has been able to very easily fill, in the world of the written word, a niche. Its pages can be said to be brimming with well-documented material. It has become, for its comments regarding world issues, hints on the latest happenings in the Big Apple, and light-hearted quips, well regarded.

▉ EDITING 4: PRACTICE

Edit the following passage, eliminating dangling, disruptive, and squinting modifiers. More than one edited version is possible. Be ready to explain your editing choices.

Striking millions of Americans, some people only are afflicted by insomnia occasionally, while other people live with it for several years. Having experienced mild, occasional sleeplessness, your insomnia shouldn't be considered a major concern. The causes from which it stems most often are quite simple. Having something troubling or exciting on your mind, exerting too much physical or mental activity before bedtime, having a mild fever, drinking too much caffeine, or eating a heavy meal, sleeplessness might occur. Changing your schedule or surroundings, insomnia can also result. The way to best ensure a good night's sleep is to consistently follow a few simple steps. Try to go to bed at the same time every night. Sleep on a comfortable bed in a dark room. Realizing that it is still, after twenty minutes, hard to fall asleep, it is helpful for you to get up and do something, such as read, until you feel drowsy. And remember to always avoid caffeine and heavy foods as well as strenuous activity before bedtime.

■ EDITING 5: APPLICATION

Read through a paper you are working on, and see if you have used any misplaced, squinting, or dangling modifiers. Do you have many problems with modifier placement? Is there one type of mistake you make frequently? Edit any sentences that have misplaced, squinting, or dangling modifiers, and think about how best to identify and correct these mistakes in your future editing.

Pronouns substitute for nouns, noun phrases, or other pronouns. The word for which a pronoun substitutes is called its **antecedent.** To substitute clearly and correctly, personal pronouns should **agree** with, or correspond to, their antecedents in three possible ways.

First, personal pronouns should agree with their antecedents in **number** — singular or plural.

A *pronoun* is singular if *it* has a singular antecedent.

Pronouns are plural if *they* have plural antecedents.

Second, personal pronouns should agree with their antecedents in **person** — first (*I, we, my, our*) second (*you, your*), or third (*he, she, it, they, his, her, its, their*).

When the *tree* fell down, *it* shook the forest.

When *Joan* fell down, *she* hurt *her* back.

Third, singular personal pronouns should agree with their antecedents in **gender** — feminine, masculine, or neuter.

Mrs. Shah held the door for *her* husband.

Mr. Shah thanked *his* wife.

The most common problems of pronoun-antecedent agreement involve number — determining whether antecedents are singular or plural. In editing for pronoun-antecedent agreement, you should do the following:

- Make pronouns agree with antecedents joined by *and.*
- Make pronouns agree with antecedents joined by *or* or *nor.*
- Make pronouns agree with antecedents that are collective nouns.

■ Make pronouns agree with antecedents that are indefinite pronouns.

Many questions of pronoun-antecedent agreement require the same kinds of analysis used in determining subject-verb agreement. See Chapter 36 for more on subject-verb agreement.

Also see Chapter 40 for advice about making antecedents of pronouns clear, Chapter 41 for a discussion of pronoun case, and 64b for a complete list of the various types of pronouns.

39 a Making pronouns agree with antecedents joined by *and*

A **compound antecedent** has two or more parts joined by a conjunction such as *and, or,* or *nor: you and I, ducks or geese, neither rain nor snow.* When *and* links elements, it unifies them into a group that is considered plural, so a pronoun that refers to a compound antecedent joined by *and* should be plural as well.

The book and the folder are in *their* proper place on the shelf.

There are a few exceptions. A compound antecedent preceded by *each* or *every* takes a singular pronoun. (Also see 39d.) When the parts of a compound antecedent refer to the same person or thing, the pronoun should be singular. Also, when the elements linked by *and* constitute a single entity, use a singular pronoun.

Each book and folder is in *its* proper place.

As my *editor and immediate supervisor, she* oversees my work.

Beans and rice is my favorite dish. *It* is always nice on cold days.

39 b Making pronouns agree with antecedents joined by *or* and *nor*

The conjunctions *or* and *nor* can also join antecedents to form a **compound antecedent.** When both elements are singular, a pronoun that refers to the compound antecedent is singular.

Either *hunger* or bad *weather* will take *its* toll on the soldiers.

When one element of a compound antecedent is singular and the other is plural, a pronoun clearly cannot agree with both of them. The convention is that the pronoun agree with the antecedent closer to it.

Either the supply problems or the bad *weather* will take *its* toll.

If following this convention seems awkward in a particular sentence, try putting the plural part of the antecedent nearer to the pronoun.

Either the bad weather or the supply *problems* will take *their* toll.

39 **C** Making pronouns agree with collective nouns

Collective nouns such as *couple, flock, crowd, herd,* and *committee* often cause agreement problems because they are singular in form, yet they refer to groups or collections that can be regarded as plural. Take your cue from the intended meaning of the sentence. Use a plural pronoun if members of the group are acting separately.

The *crew* gather *their* belongings and prepare to leave the ship.

Use a singular pronoun if the group acts as a unit.

The *flock* arose in flight and made *its* way to the shelter of the trees.

If your paper uses a particular collective noun such as *audience* or *committee* frequently, you may want to use your word processor's search function to find every instance of this word. This will make it easier for you to determine whether you have any problems with pronoun-antecedent agreement in these cases.

EDITING I: PRACTICE

Edit the following passage by making pronouns and antecedents agree. Be especially careful about compound and collective antecedents.

Both the supervisor and her new assistant, James, are unhappy with his mutual arrangement. The supervisor admits that each regular task and special assignment is given the attention they deserve, but her assistant takes too much time to complete each one. The rest of the staff say it agrees with her. What does the assistant say in his own defense? As a junior person and a new member of the staff, he finds it difficult to handle new projects on their own and would like more help from his supervisor. He worries that someday either his irritation or his frustrations will make itself heard.

39 d Making pronouns agree with indefinite pronouns

An **indefinite pronoun** is a pronoun that does not require an explicit antecedent. In the sentence *Everyone likes ice cream,* for example, the pronoun *everyone* needs no other words to explain who is meant. This can make it difficult to determine whether an indefinite pronoun that serves as the antecedent for another pronoun is singular or plural.

Some indefinite pronouns are always singular: *anyone, everyone, someone, anybody, everybody, somebody, anything, everything, something, either, neither, each, nothing, much, one, no one.* Pronouns that refer to them should be singular as well.

> *Everybody* is glad when *his* days at the Longwood Academy for Boys are over.

These pronouns remain singular even when followed by a prepositional phrase with a plural object.

> *Either* of the cats could have left *its* toy mouse here.

Be careful when *each* is used with compounds joined by *and.* When it precedes such a compound, *each* is an indefinite pronoun and the subject of the clause. When it follows such a compound, *each* is an adjective, and the compound itself is the subject of the clause. The pronoun that follows should agree with the subject of the clause.

INDEFINITE PRONOUN   *Each* man and boy sits on *his* chair.

ADJECTIVE   The *man and boy* each sit on *their* chairs.

AVOIDING THE GENERIC *HE*

A singular indefinite pronoun (such as *someone* or *anyone*) does not specify gender, yet a singular personal pronoun that refers to the indefinite pronoun must specify gender (*he, she*). Writers and readers once accepted the masculine pronoun *he, him,* or *his* in such cases, but in recent years many people have come to feel that this use of *he* in a generic sense implicitly excludes women. There are four ways to avoid the generic *he*.

1. If there is no doubt about the gender of the antecedent, use a pronoun of the same gender.

■ Anyone who wants to be an operatic soprano must train ~~their~~ *her* voice

carefully.

2. Make the antecedent plural. If you do, look out for other words in the sentence that need to be made plural as well.

■ ~~Everyone~~ *All the singers* know~~s~~ their ~~part~~ *parts.*

3. Use *his or her.* Do so sparingly, as *his or her* becomes monotonous with repetition.

■ Everyone knows ~~their~~ *his or her* part.

4. Rewrite to eliminate the personal pronoun.

■ Everyone has ~~done their best~~ *worked* to help the recital succeed.

For a more detailed discussion of avoiding biased and sexist language, see Chapter 32.

Other indefinite pronouns are always plural: *few, many, both, several.*

Few of the students have completed *their* work.

Still other indefinite pronouns can be singular or plural depending on context: *some, any, all, more, most, none.*

In a survey of young voters, *some* said *they* were conservative.

Some *refers to* voters, *so both* some *and the pronoun* they *are plural.*

The money is still in the safe. *Some* is still in *its* bags.

Some *refers to* money, *so both* some *and the pronoun* its *are singular.*

If you know you have difficulties with pronoun-antecedent agreement when using any of these indefinite pronouns, you may want to use your computer's search function to find every instance of the troublesome pronoun. This will simplify the task of making sure you have used the pronoun correctly throughout your paper.

■ **EDITING 2: PRACTICE**

Edit the following passage by making pronouns and their indefinite pronoun antecedents agree. More than one edited version is possible. Be ready to explain your editing choices.

Almost everyone knows that they can consult a thesaurus if they want to find a synonym for a given word. Some say that it is useful for improving his or her writing and public speaking. Many say that they use it to increase his or her vocabulary. A thesaurus can be a very good source for somebody who has a general idea in mind but needs a specific word or phrase. However, no one should rely too heavily on the thesaurus as a way for them to become a good writer. The best advice for someone is that they should concentrate on building a strong vocabulary first and consult a thesaurus second.

■ **EDITING 3: PRACTICE**

Edit the following passage by making pronouns agree with their antecedents. (You may have to change some verbs and nouns as well.) More than one edited version is possible. Be ready to explain your editing choices.

Changes in facial hair, a higher or a lower voice, and a decreased sex drive: this is some of the side effects of taking steroids. Yet many continue in their use of this dangerous drug. Athletics is ever more competitive and athletes are always striving to be the best he or she can be. In a race, mere seconds are a long time to an athlete when they mean the difference between a gold and a silver medal. Perhaps the athlete does not know what harm they are doing to their bodies. There is no physical addiction to steroids; any addiction to it is psychological and based on the fact that athletes like what they see. Unfortunately, the athlete cannot always see what lies ahead for them. Ben Johnson and some others should count himself lucky. All Johnson lost was a gold medal and the chance to compete again. Benjamin Ramirez was not so lucky. Nor were the many like him who lost his life.

■ **EDITING 4: APPLICATION**

Read through a paper you are working on, and see if there are any pronouns that do not agree with their antecedents. Can you see why you made the mistakes you did? Edit any sentences with pronoun agreement problems, and think about how best to identify such problems in your future editing.

Pronouns serve as stand-ins for nouns, noun phrases, or other pronouns. To be effective, a pronoun must clearly refer to the word it stands for. When you write *she*, you do not want readers to be asking, "Who?" Readers should know that you are talking about Maya Angelou or Joan of Arc or whomever.

The word for which a pronoun substitutes is called its **antecedent** (from the Latin roots meaning "to go before"). Although antecedents normally appear before pronouns that refer to them, sometimes they follow the pronouns. In either case, there must be no conflicting choices to confuse readers. As you edit your writing to clarify pronoun reference, be sure to do the following:

■   Make sure a pronoun clearly refers to a single antecedent.

■   Place a pronoun close to its antecedent.

■   Provide an explicitly stated antecedent.

■   Use *it*, *they*, and *you* carefully.

■   Avoid overusing *it*.

■   Choose *who*, *which*, or *that* according to the antecedent.

■   Eliminate unneeded pronouns.

Also see Chapter 39 for advice about making pronouns agree with their antecedents, Chapter 41 for a discussion of pronoun use, and 64b for a complete list of the various types of pronouns.

40 a Making each pronoun refer to a single antecedent

A pronoun that has more than one possible antecedent can create a confusing sentence.

Marco met Roger as *he* arrived at the gym.

Who was arriving, Marco or Roger? Because *he* could refer to either, the sentence offers the reader more than one meaning but no clue as to which is correct. Edit such a sentence so that the pronoun has only one possible antecedent. You can eliminate the pronoun, if the result does not seem too awkward.

■ Marco met Roger as ~~he~~ Roger arrived at the gym.

You can also edit the sentence to place the pronoun closer to one antecedent.

■ As Marco ~~met Roger as he~~ arrived at the gym/, he met Roger.

Verbs like *said* and *told* can create confusion about antecedents because they appear often in sentences involving more than one person. When editing such a sentence, you can often use a direct quotation.

■ Barbara told Ramona , "You ~~that she~~ passed the test."

■ **EDITING 1: PRACTICE**

Edit the following passage by making each pronoun refer clearly to a single antecedent. More than one edited version is possible. Be ready to explain your editing choices.

Diane spotted Laura as she was beginning her regimen of stretching exercises. It was twenty minutes before the race was due to begin. Diane told Laura that she thought she would win the race. She was just plain faster. Laura responded that she had a good chance, but that she was going to be tough to beat. Nodding in agreement, Diane shook hands with Laura. "Good luck," she said. "Have a good race."

40 **b**　**Placing pronouns close to antecedents**

The closer a pronoun appears to its antecedent, the better. If many words intervene, the reader may lose the connection between antecedent and pronoun. This is particularly important when a pronoun precedes its antecedent. In the following passage, by the time readers get to *he* in the fourth sentence, they may have forgotten *Galileo* as the antecedent. When a long intervening passage threatens to break the connection between antecedent and pronoun, find a place to introduce the pronoun earlier, or use the antecedent again.

■   In the seventeenth century, the Italian scientist Galileo

Galilei upset the Catholic church by publishing a scientific pa-

per asserting that the earth revolved around the sun. That asser-

tion contradicted contemporary church belief, which held that

the earth was the center of the universe. The paper also violated

a papal order ~~of~~ *that Galileo had accepted* sixteen years earlier not to "hold, teach, or de-

fend" such a doctrine. Under pressure from the church, ~~he~~ *Galileo* re-

canted his theory of the earth's motion, but even as he recanted

he is said to have whispered *"Eppur si muove"* ("Nonetheless it

moves").

40 c   Providing explicit antecedents

In general, a pronoun's antecedent should always be explicitly stated. (Indefinite pronouns, such as *somebody, everybody,* and *no one,* are exceptions. See 39d.) A pronoun whose antecedent is merely implied may confuse readers.

Interviews with several television news people made *it* seem like a fascinating career.

What does *it* stand for? A reader might guess that it stands for *television news reporting,* since this is a possible career, but *television news reporting* does not appear in the sentence. To edit such a sentence, substitute a noun for the pronoun, use another pronoun that can refer to something already explicit in the sentence, or provide a clear antecedent for the pronoun.

■   Interviews with several television news people made ~~it~~ *reporting* seem like

a fascinating career.

ESL **USING *THIS* AND *THAT***

The demonstrative adjectives *this* and *that* mean "near" and "far," respectively. This concept of distance can apply to space.

This vase right here is a better choice than *that* one in the back of the store.

The concept can also apply to time.

That article I showed you last week was very technical. *This* book I just found is more readable.

1 Making pronouns refer to grammatically acceptable antecedents

An antecedent must be a noun, a noun phrase, or another pronoun. It cannot be the possessive form of a noun or an adjective or other modifier. As you edit, make sure that any pronoun refers to a grammatically acceptable antecedent that is explicitly stated in the sentence.

among the committee members

■ The ~~committee's~~ bitter argument ₍reflected badly on all of them.

A possessive form of a noun or pronoun can be an antecedent, however, if the pronoun that refers to it is also possessive.

The *committee's* argument reflected badly on all of *its* members.

2 Supplying explicit antecedents for *this, that,* and *which*

Words like *this* and *that* can be either **demonstrative adjectives** or **demonstrative pronouns.** As pronouns they stand alone (*This is real; that is an imitation*). Confusion can arise when the antecedent of a demonstrative pronoun could be either a clause or a smaller element within the clause.

No one has suggested taxing health care. *This* is unlikely.

What is unlikely, the taxing of health care or the chance that any-one would suggest it? You can usually clarify the reference by re-stating the antecedent that you intend.

■ No one has suggested taxing health care. This is unlikely. *tax*

When *which* and *that* introduce clauses, they are called **rela-tive pronouns.** Usually, a relative pronoun introduces a clause that immediately follows the pronoun's antecedent.

This book, *which* I heartily recommend, is out of print.

If other elements intervene or if the relative pronoun has more than one possible antecedent, confusion can result. To clarify, you can provide an unambiguous antecedent, or you can replace *which* or *that* with another construction.

■ She took the situation seriously, which I found laughable. *a response*

■ She took the situation seriously, ~~which~~ I found laughable. *though* *it*

If you are using a computer to edit your paper, you may want to use the search function to locate every instance of the pro-nouns *this, which,* and *that.* This will make it easier for you to en-sure that these pronouns always have explicit antecedents.

■ EDITING 2: PRACTICE

Edit the following passage by making all pronouns refer to explicit antecedents. More than one edited version is possible. Be ready to explain your editing choices.

The fraternity house that I visited was not as neat inside as I had ex-pected from knowing them. Its old and worn furniture may have made it look worse than it was, but I for one didn't feel like sitting down on any of the couches. The fraternity brothers made it sound like the best thing in the world to be a part of. Downstairs there was a huge crowd. The brothers said that most nights a long line to get food stretches out into the hall, with everybody pushing to get to the front. This is typical. The brothers were all pretty nice, but at one point in the evening they had a toast to the crowd and they threw garbage on everyone at the party, which I didn't think was too nice.

40 d Replacing a vague *it*, *they*, or *you*

In casual speech, people often use *it*, *they*, and *you* with no definite antecedent. In academic writing, however, such indefinite uses of *it*, *they*, and *you* should be avoided in favor of more specific constructions.

■ ~~It said on~~ the news this morning~~,~~ that the game was canceled.

According to — inserted before; *,* inserted after "morning"

■ ~~They~~ tow away any car that is illegally parked.

The police — inserted

■ If the weather doesn't clear, ~~you~~ could experience flooding.

local residents — inserted

You may be used to refer specifically to the reader (as in *You should use specific nouns whenever possible*), but for academic writing, do not use *you* to mean "people in general." One way to avoid *you* is to use an indefinite pronoun such as *one* or *someone*, which refers to an unspecified third person.

40 e Avoiding overuse of *it*

The pronoun *it* has three common uses. First, *it* can function as a personal pronoun: *I want to read the book, but Nancy has it.* Second, *it* can be used in an *expletive* construction introducing a sentence in which the subject and verb are inverted: *It is necessary to apologize.* (See 36b.) Third, *it* is used in idiomatic constructions about time, weather, and distance: *It is ten past twelve.* In speech these different senses of *it* are frequently mixed. In conversation no one would notice the slight confusion created. In writing, however, you should avoid using the same word in different senses in the same sentence.

■ ~~It is important to remember~~ that once the concert begins, it will be two hours before ~~it breaks for~~ intermission.

Remember — inserted

If you are using a computer to edit your paper, you may want to use the search-and-replace function to find every use of the word *it* and underline, boldface, or otherwise highlight it. This will allow you to see at a glance how often you have used this pronoun

and will simplify the task of determining whether *it* is the best word choice in each case.

▆ EDITING 3: PRACTICE

Edit the following passage by clarifying all uses of the pronouns *it, they,* and *you.* Make any small changes in wording that are needed for smooth reading. More than one edited version is possible. Be ready to explain your editing choices.

They say that you shouldn't believe everything you read in the newspaper. It is foolish to assume that it is possible for it to be accurate all of the time. You can't expect that there will never be a mistake. Sometimes they get late-breaking stories and have to rush to get them in before it goes to press. Occasionally you can even see contradictions between two articles on the same topic. It will say one thing in one article and then it will say something different in the other. It is when that happens that it is hard for you to know which article you should believe.

40	f	**Choosing *who, which,* or *that* according to the antecedent**

The pronouns *who, which,* and *that* are used similarly, but in different contexts. In general, *who* is used only for people or animals with names; *which* and *that* are used for objects, ideas, unnamed animals, and anonymous people or groups of people.

> Black Beauty is a fictional horse *who* lives in a world that has now disappeared.
>
> This is the policy *that* the administration wants to enforce.
>
> He tried to rope the last steer, *which* twisted to avoid him.
>
> The tribes *that* built these cities have long since vanished.

(The difference between *who, whom,* and *whose* is one of case. See Chapter 41.)

Most writers avoid using *which* to refer to people.

▆ I have met hundreds of actors, of ~~which~~ *whom* he is the funniest.

CHOOSING BETWEEN _WHICH_ AND _THAT_

Whether to use _which_ or _that_ often depends on whether the modifier to be introduced is restrictive or nonrestrictive. A **restrictive** modifier is one that is necessary to identify what it modifies. It can be introduced by either _which_ or _that_ and is never set off by commas.

All of Ann's enormous fortune _that is in the bank_ is five dollars.

The modifier that is in the bank _restricts, or limits, the larger set_ All of Ann's enormous fortune _to the smaller portion in the bank. It implies that she has money elsewhere._

A **nonrestrictive** modifier merely adds more information. It can be introduced only by _which_ and is set off by commas.

All of Ann's money, _which is in the bank_, is five thousand dollars.

The modifier which is in the bank _doesn't limit or help define the subject_ All of Ann's money. _It just gives more information about the subject._

Although some people prefer _that_ for all restrictive modifiers, _which_ is acceptable as well.

When in the course of human events it becomes necessary for one people to dissolve the political bands _which_ have connected them with another . . . a decent respect for the opinions of mankind requires that they should declare the reasons _which_ impel them to the separation. [Italics added.]

DECLARATION OF INDEPENDENCE

Who may introduce either restrictive or nonrestrictive modifiers.

NONRESTRICTIVE   Americans, who tend to eat a richer diet than Europeans, have rising rates of heart disease.

RESTRICTIVE   Americans who curb their appetites for rich foods may live longer than those who don't.

For more on restrictive and nonrestrictive clauses, see 44c.

If using *of which* to refer to an inanimate object results in an awkward construction, you may substitute *whose*.

■ This is an idea ~~the~~ time ~~of which~~ has come.
      whose

■ **EDITING 4: PRACTICE**

Complete the following passage, filling in the blanks with the correct pronoun: *who, which,* or *that.*

    None of the carpenters _____ I know has any use for imported nails. They swear that American-made nails are the only ones _____ are worth using. A nail _____ bends when it is driven in was probably made in Canada, they say. One box of nails, _____ they got from Japan, had heads _____ broke off if they tried to pull them out. There are problems every time the contractor brings them boxes _____ are imported. These men, every one of _____ works with nails every day, believe that they can tell where a nail comes from as soon as they hit it with a hammer. One thing is certain: a bent nail doesn't get that way because a carpenter hit it crooked.

---

40 g   **Eliminating unneeded pronouns**

Speakers of some dialects use a pronoun immediately following its antecedent.

After Ann repaired it, the wagon *it* just seemed to fall to pieces.

ESL   **UNNEEDED PERSONAL PRONOUNS**

In editing, check that you have not used a personal pronoun (*he, her*) and a relative pronoun (*who, whom, which, that*) in the same clause to refer to the same antecedent.

■ I know the teacher whom my sister had ~~him~~ for history.

■ I corrected the errors that you pointed ~~them~~ out to me yesterday.

Including the extra pronoun can help reproduce a colloquial sound in a direct quotation, but in formal writing or paraphrasing, delete the unneeded pronoun.

■ After Ann repaired it, the wagon i̶t̶ just seemed to fall to pieces.

■ EDITING 5: PRACTICE

Edit the following passage by making sure that all pronoun references are clear and that all pronouns are used appropriately. More than one edited version is possible. Be ready to explain your editing choices.

Studies have shown that alcoholism is a major problem in this city, which has a high percentage of unemployed and homeless people. This is true in other metropolitan areas as well. However, it affects not only the down-and-out but also working people, the elderly, and teenagers which have begun to experiment with drinking. We interviewed some social workers, which said that being homeless caused some people to drink. What we learned from interviewing homeless people, though, was that many of those which are homeless now, they were drinking long before they were on the street. Drink hard enough and long enough and you inevitably lose your home, it seems from their experience.

■ EDITING 6: APPLICATION

Read through a paper you are working on. Are any pronoun references unclear? If so, can you see any pattern to the problems you have with pronoun reference? Edit any sentences in which you found pronoun reference problems, and think about how best to identify and correct these mistakes in your future editing.

In speaking, we usually choose between the pronouns *I* or *me* or *my*, *he* or *him* or *his* without even thinking about it. We say *I saw him* rather than *me saw he*, or *my car* rather than *I car*. These changes of form, the grammatical property of nouns and pronouns called **case**, indicate how a word relates to others in the sentence. The **subjective case** (*I*, *he*, or *she*, for example) serves grammatically as a subject, the person or thing that performs the action of a sentence. The **objective case** (*me*, *him*, *her*) is used for an object, the person or thing that receives the action. The **possessive case** (*mine*, *his*, *hers*) shows possession or ownership.

Problems with case can arise in choosing between subjective and objective forms: *I* and *me*, *we* and *us*, *she* and *her*, *who* and *whom*. Often the difficulty arises because technically incorrect patterns that are acceptable in everyday speech (*It is me*) are considered inappropriate in formal writing; to be correct, you must write *It is I*. The key to choosing the correct case is to focus on how a sentence works. To edit for correct pronoun case, you must do the following:

- Check the case of pronouns in compound elements joined by *and*, *or*, or *nor*.

- Check the case of pronouns used as appositives.

- Determine whether you need *us* or *we* before a noun.

- Check the case of pronouns used with verbals.

- Check the case of pronouns after *than* or *as*.

- Determine whether you need *who* or *whom*, *whoever* or *whomever*.

- Use reflexive pronouns only as objects and only when necessary.

> ✔ **PRONOUN CASE**
>
> **PERSONAL PRONOUNS**
>
> | SINGULAR | SUBJECTIVE | OBJECTIVE | POSSESSIVE |
> |---|---|---|---|
> | 1st person | I | me | my/mine |
> | 2nd person | you | you | your/yours |
> | 3rd person | | | |
> | Masculine | he | him | his |
> | Feminine | she | her | her/hers |
> | Neuter | it | it | its |
> | **PLURAL** | | | |
> | 1st person | we | us | our/ours |
> | 2nd person | you | you | your/yours |
> | 3rd person | they | them | their/theirs |
>
> **INTERROGATIVE OR RELATIVE PRONOUNS***
>
> | | SUBJECTIVE | OBJECTIVE | POSSESSIVE |
> |---|---|---|---|
> | | who | whom | whose |
> | | whoever | whomever | — |
>
> *These pronouns are called interrogative pronouns when used to ask questions: *Whose book is that?* They are called relative pronouns when used to introduce dependent clauses: *The writer whose book we read visited the university.*

41 **a** **Choosing case for compound elements**

Joining two or more words by *and, or,* or *nor* — creating a compound element — does not affect their case. Some speakers regularly use the objective case after *and,* a pattern that leads to errors such as *Joe and me talked to him,* even though few would say *Me talked to him.* Others assume that *and me* is always wrong and make errors such as *He talked to Joe and I.* As you edit, determine the correct case of pronouns by identifying whether they are used as subjects or as objects.

1 Subjective case for compound subjects and subject complements

A subject that has two or more parts joined by *and, or,* or *nor* is a **compound subject.** Use the subjective case for each part of a compound subject. When one part of a compound subject is in the first person (*I*), put that part last.

■ Sandy and ~~me~~ pruned the tall white pine.
　　　　　　 I
　　　　　 ∧

USING THE PRONOUN CASES

SUBJECTIVE CASE
　　Use the subjective case (*I, you, he, she, it, we, they, who, whoever*) for the subject of a sentence or of a dependent clause.

　We planted a winter garden.

　James knew *who* would answer.

Also use the subjective case for a subject complement, which follows a linking verb (*be, seem, become, appear*) and renames the subject.

　It is *they* who will benefit most.

OBJECTIVE CASE
　　Use the objective case (*me, you, him, her, it, us, them, whom, whomever*) for the object of a verb or a preposition.

　The judges chose *her* first.

　They awarded the prize to *us*.

POSSESSIVE CASE
　　Use the possessive case to show ownership, possession, or connection. The adjective form (*my, your, his, her, its, their, whose*) is used before a noun.

　This is *my* coat.

　We heard the singer *whose* songs we liked.

The noun form (*mine, yours, his, hers, theirs*) can stand alone, without a noun.

　Hers is the black one.

　I traded *mine* for *his*.

It sometimes helps to simplify the structure by mentally dropping everything except one pronoun: *I pruned the tall white pine.*

A linking verb — such as *be, become, seem, appear* — links its subject to a **complement** that follows the verb and renames the subject. Although in spoken English the objective case is very common in such a sentence, in writing both the subject and the complement should be in the subjective case.

■ The real winners were my father and ~~me~~. *I.*

If you have trouble choosing between the subjective and objective case following a linking verb, try turning the sentence around and simplifying the compound structure to a single pronoun: *I was the real winner.*

2 Objective case for compound objects

An object that has two or more parts joined by *and, or,* or *nor* is a **compound object**. Use the objective case for each part of a compound object, whether it is the object of a verb or of a preposition.

■ The judges chose neither ~~he~~ *him* nor ~~I~~ *me*.

■ I spoke to Nancy and ~~they~~ *them* about the competition.

Sometimes you can clarify your choice of subjective or objective case by mentally dropping all but one pronoun from the compound object: *The judges chose him. The judges chose me. I spoke to them.*

The preposition *between* is used for a choice of two, *among* for a choice of three or more. (See the Glossary of Usage.) As with any preposition, their objects should be in the objective case: *Between him and me we had caught more than a dozen bass. Then we divided them among him, Jack, and me.*

■ EDITING I: PRACTICE

Edit the following sentences, using the appropriate pronoun case for compound subjects and objects. Example:

I
Bob and ~~me~~ like to watch shows from the early days of televi-
^
sion whenever we get a chance.

1. To him and I they provide hours of entertainment and neither he nor me ever seems to tire of them.

2. I don't remember if it was him or me who first started watching them.

3. Others may not appreciate our passion for these shows, but they never seem boring to either he or I.

4. The best ones make me and him laugh every time we see them, and, thanks to the invention of the VCR, him and I can see them over and over.

5. Me and him have seen some shows so many times that we have practically memorized them.

41 b Choosing case for appositive pronouns

An **appositive** is a noun or pronoun that renames a preceding noun. (See 44c.) Pronouns used as appositives must be in the same case as the nouns they rename.

The losers — Mollie, Jimmy, and *I* — all wanted a rematch.

The appositive renames the subject, losers, *so the pronoun is in the subjective case.*

It was her sons, Paul and *he*, who missed their mother most.

The appositive renames the subject complement, sons, *so it is in the subjective case.*

They asked the medalists, Barbara and *me*, to pose for a picture.

The appositive renames medalists, *the object of the verb* asked, *so it is in the objective case.*

To decide between the subjective and objective case in such sentences, it may help to simplify the construction, substituting the appositive pronoun for the noun: *They asked* me *to pose for a picture.*

| **41** | **c** | **Choosing between *us* and *we* before a noun** |

Pronouns immediately followed by nouns can cause confusion, but the correct case depends on whether the pronoun is a subject or an object. (The noun following the pronoun is an appositive renaming the pronoun. See 44c.)

■   *We*
    ~~Us~~ hikers were worried about the weather.

The pronoun is the subject, so the subjective case is correct.

■   *us*
    They told ~~we~~ hikers not to worry about the weather.

The pronoun is an object, so the objective case is correct.

Mentally dropping the noun following *us* or *we* can make the choice clearer: *We were worried about the weather. They told us not to worry about the weather.*

▇ EDITING 2: PRACTICE

Edit the following paragraph, using the appropriate pronoun cases. Watch out for pronouns in compound subjects and objects, pronouns used as appositives, and *us* and *we* before nouns.

    Fishing with our dad, Charley and me hadn't caught any fish all week. We decided it was up to the two of us, him and I, to find some way to catch something. Us two kids borrowed a rowboat and, with him and me rowing, went way out in the middle of the pond. We dropped anchor and began fishing, him out of one side of the boat and I out of the other side. Charley asked me if I was sleepy and I said, "Not me," but then a splash of water woke me, and the boat was rocking. Charley was pulling madly on his rod, and it seemed as if his catch would tip the boat over and he and I with it. It took ten minutes for us, Charley and I, to get that catfish on board. Dad said it was turning out that the real fishers in the family were Charley and me. Dad made both Charley and I feel really proud.

41 d Choosing case with verbals

Participles, gerunds, and infinitives are called **verbals** because they are derived from verbs but cannot function by themselves as verbs in sentences. A **participle** ends in *-ed*, *-en*, or *-ing* and is used with an auxiliary verb or as a modifier. A **gerund** is the *-ing* form of the verb used as a noun. An **infinitive** is the base form of the verb, usually preceded by *to*.

PRESENT PARTICIPLE	A person *waking* at that hour is often groggy.
PAST PARTICIPLE	He was *tired*.
GERUND	*Waking* at that hour can ruin my day.
INFINITIVE	I hate *to wake* so early.

1 Objective case for verbal objects

Verbals can have objects. In the sentence *I like to read books*, for example, the object of the infinitive *to read* is *books*. Choose the objective case for a pronoun that is the object of a verbal.

I saw Robert greeting *him*.

Seeing *her* made the holiday complete.

To know *him* is to love *him*.

2 Objective or possessive case before *-ing* verbals

The choice of pronoun case before an *-ing* verbal depends on whether it is a gerund or a present participle. Which of these sentences is correct?

He heard their shouting.

He heard them shouting.

Either could be correct depending on the intended meaning.

What did he hear? He heard *shouting*.

What did he hear? He heard *them*.

If your answer is *He heard shouting*, then *shouting* is the object of the verb, so it must be a noun, a gerund. Using the possessive *their* would then be correct because it signals that the following word is a noun. If your answer is *He heard them*, then *them* is the object of the verb and *shouting* is only a modifier, a present participle. The objective *them* would then be correct because the pronoun is the object of the verb.

Use the possessive case for pronouns preceding gerunds and the objective case for pronouns preceding present participles.

■ ~~Me~~ *My* leaving made them all sad.

■ He heard ~~my~~ *me* leaving just before midnight.

3 **Objective case before infinitives**

A pronoun that immediately precedes an infinitive should be in the objective case.

They want *her* to help.

It was hard for *him* to agree.

ESL **USING THE OBJECTIVE CASE WITH *MAKE, LET,* AND *HAVE***

When infinitives follow the verbs *make, let,* and *have* (when it means *make*), they are used without the word *to* before them.

The instructor *let* our class *retake* the exam.

Even though these infinitives do not use the word *to*, pronouns used with them should still be in the objective case.

He let *us* retake the exam.

We made *him* tell us the secret.

She had *me* turn the computer on.

| 41 | e | Choosing case after *than* or *as* |

The subordinating conjunctions *than* and *as* often appear in **elliptical constructions** — clauses that have one or more words intentionally omitted. (See 27f.) Understanding exactly what is omitted is the key to choosing the correct case for a pronoun that follows *than* or *as*.

> Alex is as strong as *I/me.*

Restore the omitted word *am* at the end of the sentence, and it is easy to choose the correct pronoun: *Alex is as strong as I am.*
Sometimes the omitted words will call for the possessive case:

> Jen's luggage weighs as much as *mine* [my luggage].

The subjective case could also be meaningful in this sentence:

> Jen's luggage weighs as much as *I* [weigh].

But the objective case, *me,* would not be correct in any sense here.
By using the correct case, you can help the reader understand sentences that offer more than one possibility for the omitted words.

> My sister has more respect for her friends than *I* [have].

> My sister has more respect for her friends than [she has for] *me.*

If you are using a computer, you may want to use the search function to locate every use of the words *than* and *as* in your paper and evaluate the correctness of any pronouns used with them.

▮ EDITING 3: PRACTICE

Edit the following sentences, using the correct pronoun case after *than* and *as.* Circle the number of any sentence that is correct. Example:

> As the main DJ at our college radio station, Sue has more air
> time than ~~me~~. I.

I. I consider myself just as good an announcer as her.

2. Me playing the latest hits has contributed to my success.

3. Surveys show that her programs appeal to a wider audience than me.

4. The other station in town would like we to be less popular.

5. We give out more free tickets to performances than them.

6. One thing is for sure: we don't play as much dull music as they.

---

41 **f** **Choosing between *who* or *whom***

The distinction between *who* and *whom* and between *whoever* and *whomever* has all but disappeared from everyday speech, so your "ear" for the correct form may be of little help. Yet failing to use *whom* or *whomever* for the objective case is a mistake in formal writing. When you encounter one of these pronouns, remember to use *who* and *whoever* for subjects, *whom* and *whomever* for objects.

As a test, answer a question posed by *who* or *whom* with a sentence using *he* or *him*. *Who/whom got here first? He got here first. Who/Whom do you trust? I trust him.* Use *who* when the answer uses *he* and *whom* when it uses *him.*

1 **To introduce questions**

Who, whom, whoever, and *whomever* are **interrogative pronouns** when they introduce questions. If the pronoun is the subject of the question, use *who* or *whoever: Who is going? Whoever could be calling at this hour?* When the pronoun is the object of the verb, use *whom* or *whomever: Whom did you see? Whomever did he want?* Also use *whom* or *whomever* when the pronoun is the object of a preposition: *To whom are you speaking?*

■ ~~Whom~~ *Who* had the authority to enter the building at night?

Test: He *had the authority. Use* Who.

■ ~~Who~~ *whom* did you admit to the building?

Test: You *did admit* him. *Use* Whom.

580 Choosing the correct pronoun case

■ To ~~who~~ *whom* did you give authority to enter the building?

Test: You did give authority to him. *Use* whom.

Be particularly careful about prepositions left at the end of a question. Pronouns that are objects of such prepositions still need to be in the objective case: *Whom did you give it to?* Moving the preposition so that it appears just before its object can make the choice clear: *To whom did you give it?*

If you are using a computer for your editing, you may want to use the search function to find every instance of the pronouns *who, whom, whoever,* and *whomever* in your paper and evaluate the correctness of each one. Hint: If you search for [*space*]-*w-h-o*, with no space after the *o*, the computer will find all four pronouns with one search, although it will also locate words such as *whose* and *whole.*

2 In dependent clauses

Who, whom, whoever, and *whomever* are **relative pronouns** when they introduce dependent clauses. Use *who* and *whoever* when the pronoun is the subject of its clause, *whom* and *whomever* when it is the object of its clause. The case of the pronoun is determined by its function in the dependent clause, not by anything in the surrounding sentence.

I know a man *who* hates dogs and children.

Who *is the subject of the clause* who hates dogs and children.

That woman, *whom* I met last week, is quite charming.

Whom *is the object of* met, *even though it renames the subject of the main clause,* woman.

As with interrogative pronouns, the question test can help you choose the correct case. Turn the dependent clause into a question introduced by the pronoun, and then answer that question with a personal pronoun. If the answer uses *he* (subjective case), then *who* is correct. If the answer uses *him* (objective case), then *whom* is correct.

■ I want a list of everyone ~~whom~~ *who* visited the plant today.

Test: Who/Whom *visited the plant?* He *did, so use* who.

■ The police will interrogate ~~whoever~~ *whomever* the foreman accuses.

Test: Who/Whom *does the foreman accuse? The foreman accuses* him, *so use* whomever.

EDITING 4: PRACTICE

Edit the following passage, using *who*, *whom*, *whoever*, and *whomever* correctly.

Whomever was it who said that the shortest distance between two points is a straight line? I don't know, but it was certainly someone wise. This maxim implies directness, and anybody whom is trying to write effectively should keep these words in mind. Karen Branch, who is featured regularly in my favorite magazine, knows how to be direct and get to the point. Right at the start, Branch makes the content of an article perfectly clear to whomever is reading it. By avoiding rambling musings and cute anecdotes she gives to the reader who she is addressing only the facts — the what, where, when, how, and whom. Everyone who reads her articles, whomever they are, admires her for her integrity.

41 g   Using reflexive pronouns as objects

The pronouns *myself, yourself, himself, herself, itself, ourselves, yourselves,* and *themselves* are called **reflexive pronouns.** A reflexive pronoun reflects the action of the verb back toward its subject, making it clear that the object and the subject of the verb are one in the same: *I looked at myself in the mirror.*

A reflexive pronoun is never used as a subject. This error is most common when the subject should be *I* or *me.*

■ My friend and ~~myself~~ *I* plan to attend.

If you know you tend to make this mistake, you can use your computer's search function to locate every instance of the word *myself* so that you can evaluate the correctness of each one.

(Note that these same pronouns can serve as intensive pronouns. See 64b.)

A reflexive pronoun should be used as the object of a verb when the subject and the object of the verb name the same person or persons.

■ John cut ~~him~~ *himself* with the scissors.

> *Himself makes it clear that the person who has been cut is the same as the person who did the cutting.*

■ John cut ~~myself~~ *me* with the scissors when he handed them to me.

> *The subject of the verb* cut *is John. The words* myself *and John do not name the same person, so* myself *is incorrect.*

A reflexive pronoun should be used as the object of a preposition when it and an earlier noun or pronoun in the sentence name the same person or persons.

■ I speak only for ~~me,~~ *myself,* not for my roommate.

> *Myself is correct because* I *precedes it in the sentence.*

■ As for Phyllis and ~~myself,~~ *me,* we want to work in radio.

> *Myself is incorrect because* I *does not precede it.*

■ EDITING 5: PRACTICE

Edit the following passage, using the appropriate pronoun cases throughout.

In the memories of my siblings and myself, our house used to be surrounded by a forest on three sides. Us children — my three brothers and me — used to hunt for snakes and salamanders in the woods by overturning the rocks that they lived under. One of the best hunting grounds for ourselves was the land to the south of our yard. When I was eight years old, I saw a garter snake catch a frog and devour it whole. It eating the frog upset my brothers and I terribly. Us, with our childish minds, thought that snakes were nasty, cruel creatures and that frogs were clearly nicer than them. Now that I am grown up, I realize that the snake eating the frog was not an act of cruelty. Snakes eat frogs to survive just as frogs eat insects. Each creature on earth lives and dies according to the natural order of things.

■ **EDITING 6: APPLICATION**

Examine a paper you are working on to see if you have used inappropriate pronoun cases. Is there one kind of error that you make most often? If so, think about how to best identify the problem when you edit your work. Edit sentences in which you have made any pronoun case errors.

Making Sentences Consistent and Complete

Readers are like bus riders; they like to know where they are being taken. A good writer respects readers' expectations the same way that a good driver keeps passengers comfortable: by avoiding unneeded detours and sudden changes of destination. As you edit, check that your sentences are consistent and complete by doing the following:

■ Make sure sentences include no unnecessary or distracting shifts.

■ Make subjects and predicates relate to one another grammatically and logically.

■ Make sure sentences include everything necessary to express ideas clearly.

42 a Avoiding unnecessary shifts

Readers generally expect continuity in the point of view and in references to time throughout a piece of writing. Within sentences, readers expect a logical consistency in the person and number of subjects (see Chapter 36), in the forms of verbs (see Chapter 35), and in the way quotations are reproduced. A change in any of these elements is called a **shift.** Often a writer's meaning requires a shift, such as a change of subject from third person to first person or from singular to plural.

As *Gibson* limped around the bases, *we* in the stands erupted in frenzy.

However, a shift in verb tense in the same sentence would be unnecessary and confusing: *As Gibson limped around the bases, we in the stands erupt in frenzy.* Such unnecessary shifts disrupt effective communication.

■ Shifts in person and number

We refer to ourselves in the **first person** (*I, we*), to our audience in the **second person** (*you*), and to other subjects in the **third person** (*he, she, it, one, they*). Unnecessary shifts in person often arise in sentences about groups or about unidentified people. Some writers shift unnecessarily to the second person, particularly when trying to make a comprehensive statement. To avoid unnecessary shifts to the second person, use *you* in formal writing only when referring specifically to the reader. (See 28c.)

■ The chemistry students learned that ~~you~~ *they* had to be careful with
^

certain combinations of chemicals.

■ As one enters the building, ~~you see~~ *one sees* little evidence of the fire.
^

Unnecessary shifts in **number** — from singular to plural and vice versa — generally occur when a writer has used a singular noun or pronoun of indeterminate gender (*engineer, one*) and then uses a plural pronoun to refer to it, perhaps to avoid the appearance of sexism. (See 32c and 39d.) As you edit, you can avoid such shifts by making the antecedent plural or by substituting a singular pronoun.

■ ~~A child~~ *Children* should listen to their parents.
^

■ A person should listen to ~~their~~ *his or her* own parents.
^

■ Shifts in tense

Tense places the action of the verb in time: *Today I go. Yesterday I went. Tomorrow I will go.* Different verbs in a sentence or paragraph may logically use different tenses to reflect actions occurring at different times. (See 35d–f.)

We *will play* tennis before we *eat* breakfast but after we *have had* our coffee.

As you edit, however, watch for unnecessary or illogical shifts in tense. The tense you select to describe most of the actions in your paper is called the **governing tense.** Once you establish it, do not use another tense without a good reason.

- When the letter arrived, it ~~says~~ *said* nothing about the contract.

The **literary present tense** is used to describe literature or art. (See 35e.) Once you have established the present as your governing tense in such a discussion, be sure to maintain it.

- In *The Glass Menagerie*, Tom realizes how trapped he is after the Gentleman Caller ~~departed~~ *departs*.

ESL **SHIFTING TENSE WITHIN A PARAGRAPH**

Sometimes it is necessary to shift from one verb tense to another within a paragraph when you support or comment on an idea. The following are some acceptable reasons for shifting tense.

FROM PRESENT TENSE TO PAST TENSE
- To provide background information
- To support a claim with an example from the past
- To compare a present situation with a past one

Here is an example of supporting a claim with an example from the past:

> Truly dedicated writers *find* time to write regardless of the circumstances. Austen *wrote* most of her novels in short bursts of activity between receiving visitors and taking care of household duties.

FROM PAST TENSE TO PRESENT TENSE
- To express a comment, opinion, or evaluation

> On May 6, the town council *voted* against the school bond. Their decision *is* unfortunate.

---

3 Shifts in mood

English verbs are used in one of three moods. The **indicative mood** is used for statements and questions: *Rain fell. Did you* *hear*? The **imperative mood** expresses commands, orders, or directions: *Close the door.* The **subjunctive mood** expresses wishes or statements that are known to be not factual: *He wishes she were friendlier. If I were a millionaire, I'd be happy.* (See 35g–h.)

As you edit, watch for unnecessary shifts from the imperative to the indicative, particularly in instructions.

■ First cover your work surface with newspapers, and then ~~you~~ make sure your materials are within easy reach.

It is often correct to use the subjunctive mood and the indicative mood in the same sentence. In the following sentences, the verbs in the independent clauses (*wishes* and *would be*) are in the indicative, while the verbs in the dependent clauses (*were* in both cases) are in the subjunctive.

My professor *wishes* that I *were* more diligent.

The world *would be* a nicer place if everyone *were* as kind as you.

However, watch for and edit out any shifts from the subjunctive to the indicative or imperative that do not make sense.

■ The contract requires that you be in Denver on July 1 and that you ~~will~~ be in Houston on August 1.

4 **Shifts in voice and subject**

The subject of an **active voice** verb performs the verb's action: *He hit the ball.* The subject of a **passive voice** verb is acted upon: *The ball was hit by him.* (See 29c.)

If a sentence has two verbs with the same subject, a shift of voice can be acceptable.

The students *completed* the project and *were given* first prize.

The verbs shift from active (completed) *to passive* (were given) *but have the same subject,* students. *The shift is acceptable because it keeps the focus on the subject.*

A shift from the active to the passive voice (or vice versa) is usually distracting and unnecessary when it requires a shift in subject as well.

■ As we peered out of the tent, *we saw* the waning moon ~~was seen~~ through the trees.

5 Shifts between direct and indirect quotation

Direct quotation, sometimes called **direct discourse,** reproduces someone's exact words, which are enclosed in quotation marks.

"I love my wife," he insisted.

Indirect quotation or **indirect discourse** is a paraphrase of someone else's words; it is not placed in quotation marks. (See Chapter 17.)

He insisted that *he loved his wife.*

As you edit, watch for shifts from indirect to direct quotation that are not clearly indicated. Either use indirect quotation consistently or rewrite the sentence so that the direct quotation is introduced by a new verb and enclosed in quotation marks.

■ He insisted that he loved his wife and *wondered* why ~~did~~ she *had* ~~have~~ to die~~?~~ .

■ He insisted that he loved his wife and *cried, "Why* ~~why~~ does she have to die? *"*

Avoid using one verb to introduce both an indirect quotation and a complete sentence of direct quotation. You have three editing choices: use indirect quotation in both instances, quote less than the full sentence directly, or start a new sentence.

■ Dr. Ryan claims that the play was composed before 1600 and *that it* ~~"It~~ *was certainly written by* ~~shows the clear hand of~~ Shakespeare."

■ Dr. Ryan claims that the play was composed before 1600 and ~~"It~~ *"* shows the clear hand of Shakespeare."

■ Dr. Ryan claims that the play was composed before 1600 ~He says,~ ~and~ "It shows the clear hand of Shakespeare."

EDITING 1: EXPLORATION

Throughout the following excerpt from his essay "Computers," Lewis Thomas uses the pronouns *you* and *we* inconsistently. Consider what effect Thomas hoped to achieve with this unconventional use of pronouns. Do you think he was effective?

"It would be nice to have better ways of monitoring what we're up to so that we could recognize change while it is occurring, instead of waking up as we do now to the astonished realization that the whole century just past wasn't what we thought it was, at all. Maybe computers can be used to help in this, although I rather doubt it. You can make simulation models of cities, but what you learn is that they seem to be beyond the reach of intelligent analysis; if you try to use common sense to make predictions, things get more botched up than ever. This is interesting, since a city is the most concentrated aggregation of humans, all exerting whatever influence they can bring to bear. The city seems to have a life of its own. If we cannot understand how this works, we are not likely to get very far with human society at large."

EDITING 2: PRACTICE

Edit the following sentences to avoid distracting or awkward shifts. Some sentences have more than one possible answer. Be ready to explain your editing choices. Circle the number of any sentence that is correct. Example:

Oral exams can be the hardest ~thing a student faces.~ *things students face. They* ~You~ work so hard to be ready, and then ~you~ *they* can just stand up there and freeze.

1. The entire freshman class did well on their exam.

2. We were given one hour for the examination, and do not use any books.

3. We were told first to review the instructions, and then you can begin to answer the questions.

4. The professor said, "The examination will conclude in one hour," and that we had to answer all of the questions in two out of three sections.

5. After the exam was over, the professor tells us it counts for half of the final grade.

6. When a student completes the exam and puts down their pen, they often feel a great sense of relief that it is over.

7. One student works through the questions too quickly and many mistakes are made.

8. The marking of the exams is up to the teaching assistant, but they don't usually assign the final grade.

42 b Eliminating mixed constructions

The term **mixed construction** applies to sentences that begin one way and then take a sudden, unexpected turn, so that readers are unsure what they mean. One kind of mixed construction uses a grammatically unacceptable element as a subject or predicate. Another kind of mixed construction links subject and verb in an illogical way.

■ Making subjects and predicates grammatically acceptable

Some grammatically mixed sentences have inappropriate elements as subjects. For example, in English a prepositional phrase cannot be the subject of a sentence. To edit such a sentence, either convert the prepositional phrase into something that can be a subject or supply a new subject for the sentence.

■ ~~By listening~~ *Listening* closely and paying attention to nonverbal signals helps a doctor make a fuller diagnosis.

■ ~~By~~ listening closely and paying attention to nonverbal signals *A doctor can make a fuller diagnosis by* . ~~helps a doctor make a fuller diagnosis.~~

A modifier clause also cannot be the subject of a sentence. A modifier clause begins with a subordinating conjunction such as *after, before, when, where, while, because, if, although,* and *unless.* To edit a sentence that has a modifier clause as a subject, provide a new subject for the sentence.

The doctor's status as
▮ ~~Because the doctor is~~ an expert does not mean a patient should
⌃
never question a diagnosis.

The subject is now status *rather than the modifier clause beginning
with* Because.

Another kind of grammatically mixed sentence uses an inappropriate element as a predicate. A dependent clause cannot contain the main verb of a sentence. To edit such a sentence, you
must either supply a new verb or change the sentence so that a
verb already present can function as the main verb.

▮ The fact that most patients are afraid to ask questions, ~~which~~
gives doctors complete control.

Removing which *turns* gives *into the main verb.*

2 Making subjects and predicates logically compatible

Another form of mixed sentence combines elements that do
not quite fit logically. Although the intent of such a sentence is
usually clear, something is wrong at the level of literal meaning.
As you edit, if you sense that some elements do not go together,
reduce your sentence to its most basic elements — subject and
verb — to see where the problem lies.

Most
▮ ~~The opinion of most~~ people believe that dogs make better pets
⌃
than cats.

Reduce the sentence to subject and verb: The opinion *cannot* believe;
people *can. So* people *makes a more logical subject.*

The
▮ ~~The increase in the~~ number of cat owners in the United States
⌃
has doubled since 1960.

The increase *hasn't* doubled; *the* number *of cat owners has.*

■ Repeat offenders whose licenses have already been suspended
have their licenses
for drunk driving will ~~be~~ revoked.
   ∧

It is not offenders who will be revoked, but rather their licenses.

A subject complement, which renames the subject following a linking verb such as *is*, *seems*, or *appears*, must rename or comment on the subject to be logical. If it does not, the result is a mixed construction.

■ My father's favorite kitchen appliance is ~~using~~ our microwave oven.

The basic elements of subject, linking verb, and complement are appliance is using, *which is not logical. The edited version, with* oven *as the complement renaming* appliance, *makes sense.*

3 Eliminating faulty predication

A type of mixed construction called **faulty predication** is both ungrammatical and illogical. It uses a modifier clause, especially one introduced by *when*, *where*, or *because*, as a subject complement following a linking verb such as *is*. Such a construction is ungrammatical because a modifier cannot rename a subject. It is illogical because a person or thing (the subject) cannot be *when*, *where*, or *because*.

Reserve *where* and *when* clauses for references to location or time, not for concepts or conditions.

based on the reproduction of
■ Pop art is ~~where an artist reproduces~~ images from commercial
   ∧
products and the popular media.

In sudden-death
■ ~~Sudden-death~~ overtime ~~is when~~ the game is extended until one
   ∧   ∧
team scores.

Perhaps the most common type of faulty predication occurs in sentences with *the reason* as the subject and a modifier clause introduced by *because* as a subject complement. Whenever you see *the reason is because*, find a way to restate the subject or to turn the complement into a noun clause, usually beginning with *that*.

■ The reason little has been done to solve the problem is ~~because~~ *that*
the committee is deadlocked.

■ *Little*
~~The reason little~~ has been done to solve the problem ~~is~~ because
the committee is deadlocked.

■ EDITING 3: PRACTICE

Edit the following passage by eliminating mixed constructions. More than one
edited version is possible. Be ready to explain your editing choices.

The dissatisfaction of community members often charges that important
decisions are made behind closed doors, or at least doors without welcome
signs. The reason is because many feel it is their right to have information
ahead of time about the decisions made at town meetings. Local newspapers
usually have summaries of town affairs, but some say they are never totally accurate or very thorough. By feeling that they don't have to check with members of the community before voting on every issue means the local officials
are confident of their own opinions. Being an elected official is when you make
certain decisions on behalf of the members of the community.

42 c Finishing incomplete sentences

Sentences can be incomplete for several reasons. An elliptical
construction, in which the writer deliberately omits some words,
may leave out too many. Comparisons may be incomplete or illogical. Or writers may leave out words in haste or from inattention.

■ Adding necessary words to elliptical constructions

When writers use **elliptical constructions,** they intentionally
omit words that readers can be expected to understand. Elliptical
structures are usually used in parallel constructions. For example, in the sentence *The sky seemed gray and the day gloomy,* the
verb *seemed* has been omitted before *gloomy.* (See 26h–j, 27f.)
When you use an elliptical construction, you must make sure that
the words omitted are identical to the words already used in the
other part of the parallel. Otherwise readers may be confused
about your meaning.

594 Making sentences consistent and complete

■ Her hair shone brilliantly, and her eyes~were~ radiant.

> *The second clause requires a different verb from the verb in the first clause,* shone, *so the second verb cannot be omitted.*

For the sake of clarity, consider repeating conjunctions and prepositions, especially in long parallel structures.

■ The project was designed to measure how drinking alters metabolism and ~how~ it affects a person's body chemistry.

2 Making comparisons complete

Comparisons must completely and explicitly state the persons or things involved. Beware, for example, of inadvertently equating a person with a thing.

■ Many of Melville's novels are superior to Cooper~Cooper's.~

> Novels *cannot be compared to* Cooper; *they must be compared to* Cooper's (*novels*).

Also, do not leave readers in doubt about what you are comparing.

■ It seems that Goodall likes apes more than ~she likes~ other people.

> *Does she like apes more* than she likes *other people,* or more than *other people do? Rather than make readers choose, state the comparison clearly and completely.*

For more on comparisons, see 37e and 41e.

3 Checking for missing words

Little words like *the, a, an, is, was, in, at, to,* and *that* are easy to omit, either in haste or in the interest of brevity. As you edit your paper, check carefully that you have not omitted necessary words.

■ When she told me ~to~ meet her at the office, I ~was~ sure she meant her office.

■ Little words are easy to omit, either in haste or ⟨in⟩ the interest of brevity.

Since when you read silently your eye has a tendency to "fill in" what it expects to see, a good way to check for missing words is to read your writing aloud.

▣ EDITING 4: PRACTICE

Edit the following passage by adding any necessary words to elliptical structures, making all comparisons complete and adding all necessary words that may have been inadvertently omitted. More than one edited version is possible. Be ready to explain your editing choices.

It's important to keep in mind that the children at the community center are individuals. No child's problems are the same as another. Change is difficult for everyone, children more so. Some of the children here are severely emotionally disturbed. The goal of the center is assess each child's needs to discover those who need a lot of attention and those who need less attention. For youths who are severely emotionally disturbed, their disturbance is an invisible handicap and becomes more apparent at stressful times. The behavior ranges of emotionally disturbed children are wider than adults. The social workers give the children's lives a sense of structure, the schedule stability.

▣ EDITING 5: PRACTICE

Edit the following passage, making all of the sentences consistent and complete. More than one edited version is possible. Be ready to explain your editing choices.

I'll bet that most people sit down to their dinner between six and seven o'clock each night. You can tell because that's when the infuriating salespeople from the local paper call. He pretends that I already have a subscription, and then he'll ask you, "Was your paper delivered on time today?" or whether it was late. It is especially annoying is where they ask the same question every time. And they think that if you say, "No, I'm not a subscriber," somehow I will agree to listen to their sales pitch. What makes it even worse is a terrible newspaper. If they were trying to sell me the *New York Times* would be a different story.

EDITING 6: APPLICATION

Examine a paper you are working on, and see if you have written any sentences that are inconsistent or incomplete. Is there one kind of mistake that you make frequently? Can you see why you might have made this mistake? Edit any sentences that are inconsistent or incomplete, and think about how best to avoid these problems in the future.

Editing for
Punctuation

The full stop at the end of every written sentence requires one of three marks of punctuation: a **period,** a **question mark,** or an **exclamation point.** Each mark tells a reader that the group of words leading up to it forms a complete sentence and that the following words begin a new sentence. (See Chapter 34 for advice on determining whether a group of words is a complete sentence.)

The choice of which mark to use at the end of a sentence depends largely on the meaning the sentence expresses. In fact, sometimes the only clue to the meaning of a sentence is the end punctuation: *They won. They won? They won!*

As you edit, be aware of the following guidelines for conventional use of end punctuation:

- Use periods after statements, mild commands, polite requests, and indirect questions.

- Use periods in some abbreviations.

- Use question marks after direct questions.

- Use exclamation points after exclamations, strong commands, and interjections.

43 a Using periods at the ends of sentences

The period is the most frequently used mark of end punctuation. Use a period at the end of a statement or a mild command. A period may be used after a polite request in the form of a question.

The administration has canceled classes.

Do not attempt to drive to school this morning.

Would you please sit down.

Use a period, not a question mark, after an indirect question. (See 42a5 and 43c.)

■ I wonder who made the decision? .
                                   ∧

When an abbreviation containing a period falls at the end of a sentence, use a single period to end the sentence.

■ Her flight leaves at 6:15 A.M./

---

43 **b** **Using periods with abbreviations**

Use a period in most abbreviations. When an abbreviation stands for more than one word, do not put a space between the parts of the abbreviation (*U.S.*).

Mr., Mrs., Ms.	A.M., P.M.	U.S., U.K.
Dr., Rev., Msgr.	sec., min., hr.	B.C., B.C.E., A.D.
Atty., Gov., Sen.	wk., mo., yr.	etc., e.g., i.e., vs., ca.
B.A., M.A., Ph.D.	in., ft., yd., mi.	p., para., fig., vol.
R.N., M.D.	Mon., Tues., Wed.	St., Ave., Rd.
Jr., Sr.	Jan., Feb., Mar.	

Initials, without periods, are used for the names of government agencies, organizations, corporations, and other entities: *FBI, CIA, EPA, IRS, LAPD, NCAA, CBS, IBM, SAT.* Many other familiar initial abbreviations are also written without periods: *NYC, TV, VHS, FM, RFD.* Periods are not used with shortened forms of words: *lab, grad, premed, champ, max, tech.* Periods are never used in **acronyms,** which are abbreviations made up of initials and pronounced as words: *NASA, NATO, HUD, AIDS, UNICEF.* (See Chapter 55 for more on abbreviations and acronyms.)

■ **EDITING 1: PRACTICE**

Edit the following sentences by using periods correctly.

Carlos is an excellent student who excels in every one of his classes — history, geography, mathematics, etc./

1. Because he is so interested in the 5th century BC, Carlos usually does well on ancient history tests.

2. He especially likes the period ca 455–430 B.C., when Athenian culture was at its height.

3. The note on the board reads: "For tomorrow's test, please read Chapter 7 (pp 100–133)."

4. Rob asks if he can borrow Carlos's notes to study for the test?

5. Rob sometimes wonders how much studying will be enough?

43 C Using question marks

The question mark is used for questions and to convey doubt or uncertainty. Use a question mark at the end of every direct question. Direct questions are usually signalled either by a word like *what*, *where*, or *why* (interrogative pronouns) or by inverted word order, with the verb before the subject.

Where is Times Square?   How can I get there?

Can I take the subway?   Do you know the fare?

In informal writing, some questions may use normal word order, as if they were statements. Use question marks if you want these sentences to be read as questions.

■ I looked at my exam. I'd gotten an A/ I couldn't believe it.
                                        ^?

A polite request in the form of a question can end in either a question mark or a period. (See 43a.)

A sentence with a dependent clause is a direct question if the independent clause is a question. If the independent clause is not a question, then the sentence is a statement containing an **indirect question** and should not be punctuated as a question. (See 42a5 and 43a.)

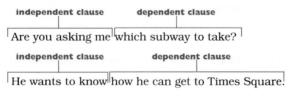

independent clause   dependent clause

Are you asking me which subway to take?

independent clause   dependent clause

He wants to know how he can get to Times Square.

A sentence that ends with a **tag question** takes a question mark, even if the independent clause is in declarative word order. (See 44f for the use of commas with tag questions.)

■ This train goes to Times Square, doesn't it/.

Use a question mark for a direct question in quotation marks, even if it is within a declarative sentence. (See 48g.) The question mark is enclosed within the quotation marks and is not followed by any other end punctuation.

■ "Have we missed the train," she wailed?.

Direct questions in a series may each be followed by a question mark, even if they are not all complete sentences. Capitalizing them is optional if they are not complete sentences, but be consistent. (See 51a.)

Where did Mario go? Did he go to the library? the cafeteria?

Dashes are used to set off words within a sentence. If a group of words between dashes constitutes a direct question, a question mark should be used with them. (See 49b.)

Use a question mark in parentheses to indicate uncertainty about a specific fact such as a date or the correct spelling of a word.

(?)

■ The plays of Francis Beaumont, 1584–1616, were as popular in their day as Shakespeare's.

Do not use question marks in parentheses to suggest sarcasm or irony.

■ Some people think it is funny (?) to humiliate others.

■ EDITING 2: PRACTICE

Edit the following sentences by using question marks correctly.

"You say that by learning another language a person can learn a lot about another culture," I asked.

602 **End punctuation**

1. I wonder how long it takes to be able to think in a different language?

2. What is the best way for me to learn to speak French. Converse with my friends. Go to the language lab. Go to France?

3. The best way to learn to speak another language is to speak it as often as possible, isn't it.

4. Some students think it's entertaining (?) when classmates make mistakes.

5. You know, don't you, that we learn by making mistakes.

43 d Using exclamation points

The exclamation point is used to convey emphasis and strong emotion such as surprise or disbelief. Use an exclamation point for exclamations, strong commands, interjections, and emphatic sentences in the forms of statements or questions.

What a mess!

Stop the train!

Wow! It's getting late!

Was that train fast!

An exclamation point in a direct quotation is enclosed within the quotation marks and is not followed by any other end punctuation. (See 48a, 48g.)

■ "Ouch!" my brother cried. "That hurts!"

Dashes are used to set off words within a sentence. If a group of words between dashes constitutes an exclamation, an exclamation point may be used with them. (See 49b.)

Do not use exclamation points to indicate amazement or sarcasm.

■ The judges selected Carl (!) to represent us in the regional competition.

In most writing, exclamation points should be used sparingly, even though some skilled writers use them generously.

And yet once in the air the non-com had his own standards. He was determined to remain as outwardly cool as the pilot, so that when the pilot did something that truly petrified him, he would say nothing; instead, he would turn silent, catatonic, like a zombie. Perfect! *Zombie.* There you had it, compressed into a single word with all of the foregoing. I'm a hell of a pilot! I shoot dice with death! And now all of you fellows know it! And I haven't spoken of that unspoken stuff even once!

TOM WOLFE, *THE RIGHT STUFF*

Because exclamation points signal emphasis, they make demands on readers' attention and energy — your writing will lose effectiveness if you use too many of them. If a passage of your writing uses more than a couple, pick the most important exclamation point and leave it in place. Replace the others with periods. You may want to use your computer's search and replace function to find and reconsider each exclamation point.

■ EDITING 3: EXPLORATION

Find four or five examples of popular writing that overuse exclamation points. A good place to start your search is in advertising in newspapers or magazines. What effect do the exclamation points have?

■ EDITING 4: PRACTICE

Edit the following sentences by using exclamation points correctly. Some sentences have more than one possible answer. Be ready to discuss your editing choices.

Our mother told us to be careful/ not to slip on the ice when we were running for the bus.

1. "Be careful," she called out as we hurried down the icy driveway.
2. "Oh! No! Here comes the bus now. Hurry up."
3. "Too late. Now we'll have to walk to school."
4. "Are you crazy!? It's a four-mile walk to school."
5. "Don't tell me you can't walk four miles?" I exclaimed.

◼ EDITING 5: PRACTICE

Edit the following by using all end punctuation correctly. More than one edited version is possible. Be ready to explain your editing choices.

What a morning. I wonder if you ever had the kind of morning when everything seems to go wrong? First I overslept (!) because my alarm clock didn't go off Then I was hurrying to make my class and I tripped and fell and skinned my knee. I rushed into the classroom and saw my classmates clearing off their desks and taking out clean sheets of paper? I asked someone whether we were having a test? She whispered back, "Don't you remember. It's our Roman history test. On the collapse of the empire!" Of course. How could I have forgotten. "When was that," I whispered. "It was 133–31 BC," she whispered back. Then Professor Martin wanted to know why I wasn't sitting down? Was I planning to join the rest of the class today. "What else can I do now?," I muttered under my breath as I took my seat. "All right, everybody," he said. "On your mark. Get set. Go. Start writing."

◼ EDITING 6: APPLICATION

Examine a paper you are working on to see if you have misused periods, question marks, or exclamation points. Is there one kind of end punctuation that you consistently use incorrectly? Think about why you tend to make the mistakes you do. Edit any sentences that have incorrect end punctuation.

44 | Commas

The most frequently used mark of punctuation is the **comma.** Readers obtain a guide to the phrasing in a written sentence when they see a comma, just as they do when they hear a brief pause in a spoken sentence. While a period signals the full stop at the end of a complete sentence, a comma shows how a sentence is divided into distinct but connected parts. By showing which words are related and which are separate, commas help readers understand the meaning of a sentence.

Some conventional uses of the comma are strictly required; some are not required but are nearly always expected. Other uses of commas are optional and may be used at your discretion. When in doubt about whether to use an optional comma, remember that using a comma creates a pause, a break in the flow of words, while leaving out the comma keeps the reader moving as quickly as possible.

As you edit your work, the following guidelines will help you use commas correctly and effectively:

- Use commas before coordinating conjunctions that join independent clauses.

- Use commas to set off introductory elements.

- Use commas to set off nonrestrictive modifiers and appositives.

- Use commas between items in a series and between coordinate adjectives.

- Use commas to set off parenthetical elements.

- Use commas to set off elements of contrast, tag sentences, and words of direct address.

- Use commas with quotations.

- Use commas with numbers, dates, names, and addresses.

- Use commas to prevent misreading.

- Avoid misusing commas.

44	a	Using commas before coordinating conjunctions joining independent clauses

An independent clause is a group of words that contains a subject and a predicate and that can stand alone as a complete sentence. A **compound sentence** contains two or more independent clauses. If those clauses are joined with a **coordinating conjunction** (*and, or, but, for, nor, yet, so*), use a comma before the coordinating conjunction.

We must act quickly, or the problem will continue.

She wanted to participate, but her time was limited.

A dependent clause is a group of words containing both a subject and a predicate that cannot stand alone as a complete sentence. A **compound-complex sentence** contains one or more dependent clauses and two or more independent clauses. Use a comma before the conjunction joining the independent clauses.

The farmers ate lunch at 10:00, and they rested in the shade whenever they were hot.

When two independent clauses are very short, especially when they are related in meaning or are parallel in structure, the comma between them may be omitted.

The sun rose and the fog lifted.

You may also separate the parts of a compound sentence or a compound-complex sentence with a semicolon, either alone or with a conjunctive adverb. (See 45a.)

Do not use a comma without a coordinating conjunction to join independent clauses. The result is an error known as a **comma splice.** (See Chapter 33.)

■ His hobby is raising geese, *and* he proudly displays the blue ribbons they have won at the state fair.

Do not use a comma before a coordinating conjunction joining two dependent clauses.

■ When the board meets/ and when the vote is officially recorded, the decision will be final.

A **compound predicate** contains two or more verbs that have the same subject. Do not use a comma before a coordinating conjunction joining the parts of a compound predicate.

■ He said that the government was weak,/ and claimed that the generals were self-serving.

■ **EDITING 1: PRACTICE**

Edit the following sentences, using commas correctly with coordinating conjunctions joining independent clauses. Circle the number of any sentence that is correct. Example:

The highway department sets speed limits on state roads and highways, and it determines standards for intersecting roads.

1. Every new business or residence along a highway needs an access road but first the highway department must approve its design and location.
2. The developer of a new housing development or commercial center must complete an application, and must submit it for the highway department's review.
3. The standards for sight distances and markings are very clearly described in the regulations so a developer can tell if a driveway is acceptable.
4. The minimum sight distances vary with the speed limit and the grade of the road and the standards for driveway construction vary with the expected volume of traffic.
5. The highway department does not have to permit a driveway that does not meet its standards or that would require modifications to the roadway.

<table>
<tr><td>**44**</td><td>**b**</td><td>**Using commas after introductory elements**</td></tr>
</table>

An introductory element is a clause, phrase, expression, or word that precedes and introduces an independent clause. In most cases, a comma should separate the introductory element from the independent clause.

An **adverb clause** is a dependent clause beginning with a subordinating conjunction (*when, because, if,* and so on). Always use a comma after an introductory adverb clause.

> *When Elizabeth I assumed the throne of England in 1558,* the country was in turmoil.

A **phrase** is a group of related words that lacks a subject, a predicate, or both. In most cases, an introductory phrase should be followed by a comma.

PREPOSITIONAL PHRASE	*In every taste test,* the subjects chose the new flavor over the old.
INFINITIVE PHRASE	*To do the job properly,* they need more time.
PARTICIPIAL PHRASE	*Taking a cue from her instructor,* the nervous student eased the car into the parking spot.
ABSOLUTE PHRASE	*His dream of glory having been destroyed,* the boxer died an embittered man.

The comma is optional when the phrase is no more than two or three words and when its absence will not cause confusion: *In 1963 an assassin's bullet shocked the world.* However, a comma is always correct in these situations and may be preferred by some instructors.

Do not use a comma after an introductory phrase when the word order of the sentence is inverted so that the verb precedes its subject.

■ With the changing colors of fall/comes the time for cider.

> *In this sentence,* time *is the subject and* comes *is the verb.*

Do not use a comma after an introductory phrase that functions as the subject of the sentence, not a modifier.

■   Hearing that song/ evokes warm memories.

In this sentence, hearing that song *is the subject.*

Introductory **expressions** and **words** need to be separated from the independent clause by a comma.

ADJECTIVE	*Angered,* the bull charged once more.
ADVERB	*Surprisingly,* the chef was not disenheartened.
CONJUNCTIVE ADVERB	*Nevertheless,* taxes must be raised.
TRANSITIONAL EXPRESSION	*In fact,* most students prefer studying in the library.
INTERJECTION	*Yes,* we need to improve our parks.

(See 44e for the use of commas with a conjunctive adverb, interjection, or transitional expression that is not at the beginning of a sentence.)

■   **EDITING 2: PRACTICE**

Edit the following passage, using commas after introductory elements.

When she met Alfred Stieglitz Georgia O'Keeffe was studying at the Art Students League. Then twenty years old O'Keeffe visited Stieglitz's famous 291 gallery and became acquainted with the pioneering photographer. About eight years later she sent some drawings to a friend and the friend showed them to Stieglitz. Without asking her permission he hung them in his gallery. She demanded that he take them down, but he did not. Nearly a year later he mounted a solo exhibit of her work, and their alliance was fully established.

44	**c**	**Using commas to set off nonrestrictive modifiers and appositives**

A modifier or an appositive is **restrictive** if it provides information that readers must have in order to understand the meaning of the word or words modified. It "restricts" or limits the meaning of the word or words modified from a general group to a more specific one.

Students *who are late* will be prohibited from taking the exam.

The modifier who are late *is restrictive because it identifies a specific group of students: not all students will be prohibited from taking the exam, only those who are late.*

A modifier or an appositive is **nonrestrictive** if it provides additional information but is not essential to the meaning of the word or words it modifies.

Bus drivers, *who are generally underpaid*, work long hours.

The modifier who are generally underpaid *is nonrestrictive because it tells the reader more about* bus drivers *but does not identify a specific group of bus drivers.*

Commas are used to set off nonrestrictive modifiers but not restrictive ones. Often, the only clue to whether a modifier is restrictive or nonrestrictive — and to the writer's meaning — is how the sentence is punctuated.

The driver was late, and the children *who were already on the bus* were impatient to leave.

This modifier is not set off by commas, so it is understood as restrictive. The sentence is about only those children who were already on the bus; it implies that there were more children who were not yet on the bus.

The driver was late, and the children, *who were already on the bus*, were impatient to leave.

This modifier is set off by commas, so it is understood as nonrestrictive. The sentence is about all the children. The modifier clause adds additional information (the children were on the bus) but does not restrict the general group to a more specific one.

For this reason, it is important to evaluate modifiers carefully to see whether they are restrictive or nonrestrictive and to punctuate them accordingly.

To determine whether a modifier is restrictive or nonrestrictive, try omitting it. Omitting a nonrestrictive modifier usually will not change the basic meaning of a sentence, but omitting a restrictive one will.

RESTRICTIVE

Athletes who want a short cut take steroids.

Athletes take steroids.

These two sentences have very different meanings; the modifier is restrictive.

NONRESTRICTIVE

Olympic athletes, who are in excellent physical condition, usually perform well on this test.

Olympic athletes usually perform well on this test.

These two sentences mean about the same thing; the modifier is nonrestrictive.

Another way to see whether a modifier is restrictive or nonrestrictive is to ask a question about the identity of the subject of the clause. If the answer requires the information contained in the modifier, the modifier is restrictive.

RESTRICTIVE

A cat that neglects to groom itself will have matted fur.

What will have matted fur?

A cat that neglects to groom itself.

NONRESTRICTIVE

A cat, which is a nocturnal mammal, hunts small rodents.

What hunts small rodents?

A cat.

Clauses

A clause is a group of words that has both a subject and a predicate. A clause beginning with *that, where, which, who, whom,* or *whose* is an adjective clause. A clause beginning with a subordinating conjunction such as *because, after,* and *if* is an adverb clause. Adjective clauses can be either restrictive or nonrestrictive; adverb clauses are usually restrictive. Use commas to set off nonrestrictive clauses.

RESTRICTIVE CLAUSE

The team *that scores the most points* will receive a special prize.

NONRESTRICTIVE CLAUSE

The dinner party, *which had been carefully planned*, was a great success.

Many writers use *that* at the beginning of restrictive clauses and *which* at the beginning of nonrestrictive clauses. Although *that* should never introduce a nonrestrictive clause, *which* may be used to introduce a restrictive clause.

A clause that modifies a proper noun is almost always nonrestrictive.

■ Col. John Glenn⸍who was a famous astronaut⸍is now a U.S. Senator.

> There is only one Col. John Glenn, so the modifier only provides additional information; it does not identify a specific Col. John Glenn.

A clause that modifies a noun preceded by a possessive pronoun is usually nonrestrictive.

■ Her pen⸍which cost less than two dollars⸍writes better than mine.

> The specific pen is already identified by the words her pen; the modifier does not limit the meaning any further.

A clause that modifies an indefinite pronoun, such as *someone*, *anyone*, or *nobody*, is always restrictive.

■ Anyone/ who visits the National Air and Space Museum,/ can touch a piece of the moon.

2 Phrases

A phrase is a group of related words lacking a subject, a verb, or both. Use commas to set off nonrestrictive phrases.

RESTRICTIVE PHRASES

A house *destroyed by fire* is a terrible sight.

The bucket *for the fertilizer* was sitting in the shed.

NONRESTRICTIVE PHRASES

This book, *written by an authority on camping*, provides much valuable information on tents.

The executive, *with all his power*, still felt inferior.

3 Appositives

An appositive is a noun or phrase that immediately follows a noun and renames it. Appositives can be either restrictive or nonrestrictive. Use commas to set off nonrestrictive appositives.

RESTRICTIVE APPOSITIVES

Former president *Theodore Roosevelt* was an avid hunter and explorer.

My sister *Margaret* often talked to me about literature.

The last sentence implies that the speaker has more than one sister.

NONRESTRICTIVE APPOSITIVES

Theodore Roosevelt, *the former president*, was an avid hunter and explorer.

My sister, *Margaret*, often talked to me about literature.

The last sentence implies that the speaker has only one sister.

■ EDITING 3: PRACTICE

Edit the following passage, using commas correctly with nonrestrictive modifiers and appositives.

A personal computer that essential tool of college work is not just a necessity but a requirement on many campuses. Many schools that once did not require computers have changed their policies. Even these schools the late entries into the personal computer age have mainframe computers for business or scientific applications but usually these are not readily available to large numbers of undergraduate students. The move to computers is happening nearly equally in engineering and humanities departments both of which can put computers to good use although they use them in entirely different ways. In requiring students to own personal computers colleges have had to specify the kind of computer students should use. Colleges then have had to teach students how to use them which has not always been easy.

44	d	**Using commas between elements in a series and between coordinate adjectives**

A **series** consists of three or more words, phrases, or clauses that are equal in grammatical form and in importance. A coordinating conjunction (*and, or, but, nor, so, for, yet*) usually precedes the final element in the series. Use a comma after each element in the series except the last.

He studied all of the notes, memos, letters, and reports.

To accelerate smoothly, to stop without jerking, and to make complete turns require many hours of driving practice.

He reported that some economists believe the recession is over, that some believe it continues, but that most agree a slow recovery is under way.

Sometimes a series is punctuated without the comma that would normally precede the coordinating conjunction: *Participants in the peace talks included Israelis, Palestinians and Syrians.* This style is common in newspapers. It is acceptable in academic writing when there is no chance of confusion or ambiguity, but using the final comma is generally preferred.

When individual elements of a series include commas, you can help readers avoid confusion by separating the elements with semicolons instead of commas. (See 45b.)

Use commas to separate coordinate adjectives. **Coordinate adjectives** are two or more adjectives that modify the same noun: *warm, sunny day.* Coordinate adjectives are independent of each other in meaning and in their relationship to the noun.

To see whether adjectives are coordinate, try inserting *and* between them or reversing their order. If the resulting sentence still makes sense, the adjectives are coordinate and require commas.

ADJECTIVES COORDINATE

Yes   He put on a clean, pressed shirt.

Yes   He put on a clean and pressed shirt.

Yes   He put on a pressed, clean shirt.

ADJECTIVES NOT COORDINATE

Yes   I found five copper coins.

No   I found five and copper coins.

No   I found copper five coins.

Do not use a comma between coordinate adjectives and the noun they modify.

■   They walked with delicate, deliberate/steps across the ice.

    EDITING 4: PRACTICE

Edit the following sentences, using commas correctly between items in a series and between coordinate adjectives. Circle the number of any sentence that is correct. Example:

> **Burlington International Airport, like any other airport, has a tower, a radar room,and many safety devices.**
>   ∧

1.   Inside the airport are a comfortable lounge, three departure gates, and a restaurant.
2.   The airport leases the space to a number of customers, including airlines car rental agencies food concessions and gift shops.
3.   The airport's representative explained that the airport is run like larger airports that it leases out its buildings and that it takes a percentage of the profits made by the independent businesses.
4.   The majority of air travel at the airport is between Boston Newark and Chicago, although travel is by no means limited to these three, major cities.
5.   Over the next ten years, the airport hopes to replace the few, remaining pre-1950s buildings with large modern facilities.

44 e   Using commas to set off parenthetical elements

A parenthetical element is a word, phrase, or clause that interrupts a sentence but does not materially affect its meaning. A parenthetical element may appear at the beginning, middle, or end of a sentence. The meaning of the sentence is not changed if a parenthetical element is moved from one place to another.

Surprisingly enough, none of the bicycles were stolen.

None of the bicycles, surprisingly enough, were stolen.

None of the bicycles were stolen, surprisingly enough.

If a parenthetical element appears at the beginning of a sentence, it should be followed by a comma, like any other introductory element. (See 44b.) If a parenthetical element appears in the middle of a sentence, set it off with a pair of commas; if it appears at the end of a sentence, set it off with a single comma.

Common sentence elements that are treated parenthetically include **transitional expressions** (*indeed, for example, in addition*), **conjunctive adverbs** (*however, furthermore, therefore*), and **interjections** (*alas, oh, hey*).

ESL   **PARENTHETICAL EXPRESSIONS**

Parenthetical expressions in English are often used by writers to comment on what is being said. For example, *surprisingly* and *fortunately* tell the reader that the writer thinks the facts expressed are surprising or fortunate. The expressions *to be honest* and *frankly* tell the reader that the writer is being honest or frank.

Parenthetical expressions may be placed in various parts of the sentence and should be separated from the rest of the sentence with commas. Here are some common parenthetical expressions.

clearly	I imagine	regrettably
fortunately	I suppose	sadly
frankly	I think	to be frank
honestly	it is hoped	to be honest
I believe	obviously	unfortunately

One Saturday, for example, we had marshmallows for breakfast.

The commissioner was not amused by the report, however.

The novice ballplayers were, alas, doomed from the start.

If a conjunctive adverb is being used to join two independent clauses, you must use a semicolon rather than a comma before it. Otherwise, you will create a **comma splice.** (See Chapter 33 and 45a.)

Parentheses and dashes may also be used to set off parenthetical elements. (See 49a and 49b.)

◼ EDITING 5: PRACTICE

Edit the following sentences, using commas correctly with parenthetical expressions. Circle the number of any sentence that is correct. Example:

You must always take care to turn in your work when it is due; of course⌃you might not always be finished.

I. "Is today in fact the day the papers are due?" I have heard that question more often than I choose to remember let me tell you.

2. Since weekly papers are due every Monday, it should come as no surprise although it often does when Monday rolls around with such relentless regularity.

3. Just this morning, for example, some students asked me whether I might allow them to turn in Monday's paper on Tuesday.

4. "Certainly," I replied. I added however that today's essay submitted tomorrow should be worth at least as much as yesterday's newspaper delivered today.

5. "However, there is you should know one important difference between a newspaper company and me. A newspaper company on the one hand gives credit for a paper that is one day late, while I on the other hand do not."

Using commas to set off elements of contrast, tag sentences, and words of direct address

You may use commas with **elements of contrast** — words, phrases, or clauses that emphasize a point by describing what it is not or by citing an opposite condition.

The experience was illuminating, but unnerving, for everyone.

The class started on Tuesday, not on Wednesday.

The article mentioned where he obtained his degree, but not when he received it.

Use a comma before a **tag sentence,** which consists of a noun or pronoun, a verb, and possibly modifiers placed at the end of a sentence to express or elicit an opinion. Tag sentences may be statements or questions.

You received my application in time, I hope.

They meet every Monday, don't they?

Set off words of **direct address** with commas. Words of direct address identify the person or group to whom a sentence is directed. They can appear at the beginning, middle, or end of a sentence.

Lilith, I hope you are well.

That, my friends, is not the end of the story.

We appreciate your generous contribution, Dr. Collins.

■ **EDITING 6: PRACTICE**

Edit the following sentences, using commas correctly to set off elements of contrast, tag questions, and words of direct address. Circle the number of any sentence that is correct. Example:

Independence⌄not reliance on their sons and daughters⌄is the goal of many elderly people today.

1. Most people over seventy-five own their homes my friends not because they have a lot of money but because they purchased them years ago, when housing prices were low.

2. Often elderly people who want to be independent have to live in conditions they consider less than ideal don't they?

3. The children of the elderly, not the elderly themselves, tend to worry about illnesses and accidents.

4. The growing numbers of people over age eighty-five are in better not worse condition than their predecessors.

5. Given that they are in better condition, many are able if not eager to live alone.

44 g Using commas with quotations

If a direct quotation is within another sentence, it may be accompanied by **attributory words,** words that identify the speaker or the writer of the quoted words. Use commas to set off attributory words, whether they appear before, after, or in the middle of the quotation. (A comma before attributory words goes *inside* the quotation marks.)

Montaigne said, "Many things seem to us greater in imagination than in reality."

"Self-approval is acquired mainly from the approval of other people," states Mark Twain.

"When I went to kindergarten and had to speak English for the first time," writes Maxine Hong Kingston, "I became silent."

When the quotation is a question or an exclamation and the attributory words appear after the quotation, conclude the quotation with a question mark or an exclamation point alone. (See 43c and 43d.)

■ "What does the latest survey show?" Marion asked.

■ "The news is terrific!" Vince shouted.

Do not use commas when the quotation is preceded by *that* or when the quotation is part of the grammatical structure of the sentence.

■ He closed by saying that "time will prove us right."

■ According to him, coffee lovers have "reason to lift their cups in celebration."

Do not use commas with indirect discourse.

■ Emerson wrote that/we should trust ourselves.

(See Chapter 48 for more on punctuating quotations.)

■ **EDITING 7: PRACTICE**

Edit the following sentences, using commas correctly with quotations. Example:

At the final race of the regatta, Isabella asked her friend Danielle⸴
^

"Do you think we are going to win the race?"/

I. "I don't know" Danielle replied "but I think that Terry has a good chance."

2. "Did Dolores say anything about the current," Danielle inquired? "Where is it strongest?"

3. Isabella replied "The current is strongest in the deepest part of the channel, but the seaweed in the shallow parts can really slow the boat down."

4. As the gun went off, Isabella muttered "If we lose this race, then all the time and effort that we spent will be for nothing!"

44 h Using commas with numbers, dates, names, and addresses

Numerous rules and conventions govern the use of commas with numbers, dates, names, and addresses. As you edit, make sure you have followed accepted practices and have used commas consistently throughout your paper.

I Numbers

For numbers of five digits or more, use a comma after every third digit, starting from the right. In four-digit numbers, the comma is optional.

The highway sign listed the city's population as 79,087.

Some 2700 [*or* 2,700] species have found homes in the nature preserve.

Do not use a comma in years with four digits, with page numbers, or with numbers in addresses.

> That example is found on page 1269.

> In 1990 we moved to 21001 Southern Boulevard.

(For information on when to use figures or words for numbers, see 54a.)

2 Dates

When a date giving month, day, and year is part of a sentence, use a comma before and after the year.

> Louis Armstrong was born on July 4, 1900, in New Orleans.

Don't use commas when only the month and year are given in a date or when the day precedes the month.

> The letter was dated 6 April 1882.

> The war broke out in August 1914 and ended in November 1918.

3 Names

Use commas to set off a title or abbreviation following the name of a person.

> Joyce B. Wong, M.D., supervised the CPR training session.

> Renee Dafoe, vice president, welcomed the new members.

> Edwin M. Green, Jr., was the first speaker.

Do not use commas to enclose roman numerals following a name: *Frank T. Winters III*. (For more on abbreviations used with names, see 55a.)

4 Addresses

When a full address is given in a sentence, use a comma to separate each element, but do not use a comma before or after the postal zip code.

Please note that my address will be 169 Elm Street, Apartment 4, Boston, Massachusetts 02116 as of July 6.

When an address is in block form, as at the top of a letter or on the front of an envelope, do not use a comma at the end of each line.

If the city and state are given in a sentence, use a comma before and after the state.

She was born in Lexington, Kentucky, and raised in New York.

(For information on using abbreviations in addresses, see 55c.)

■ EDITING 8: PRACTICE

Edit the following sentences, using commas correctly with numbers, dates, names, and addresses. Example:

> **In the week before Christmas, the mail-order company where I worked filled 84,567 orders.**

1. I started my job in February, 1993, and the last day I worked was January 15 1994.

2. During that time, I answered 3456 calls and sold merchandise worth more than $200000.

3. The worst customers are the ones with names like Jane Jones Ph.D. or John Johnson, III, who insist on having their titles appear on all their mail.

4. You may write to my former employer at this address: National Mail-Order Products, 19123 Fifth Avenue New York New York 10001.

5. With $1500 in my savings account, I do not need to worry about getting another job until March 1994.

44 i Using commas to prevent misreading

Commas are often used to make a sentence clear even when they are not required by any specific rule. Use a comma that is otherwise unnecessary when it helps to prevent misreading.

We will all pitch in, in the event of a problem.

Soon after, a policeman came to the door.

Those who can't, change their minds.

In 1990, 256 people were tested.

■ **EDITING 9: EXPLORATION**

Try to make up two or three sentences that are awkward, confusing, or humorous without commas. Read them to your classmates to see if they are able to understand them. Examples:

In the winter time seems to stand still.
Before she had taken the wrong bus to get to the museum.
Help yourself to a lot of food and drink sparingly.

44 j Avoiding misuses of commas

Misused commas can distract your readers and cloud your meaning. Throughout this chapter, misuses of the comma have been mentioned in the sections describing the correct usage. This section summarizes the most common misuses. If you frequently use unnecessary commas, you may want to use your computer's search function to locate all commas in your paper and evaluate each one.

■ Avoid putting commas between subjects and verbs, verbs and objects or complements, or objects and complements

A single comma should never separate a subject from its verb, a verb from its object, a linking verb from its complement, or an object from its complement.

■ A season of drought,/worried the farmers.

■ The agreement entails,/training the part-time staff.

■ The laid-off workers seem,/surprisingly understanding.

■ The extra pay made him,/quite happy.

A pair of commas, such as those used to set off parenthetical elements and nonrestrictive modifiers, may separate these elements.

> David Hill, the chief researcher, developed the method.

2 Avoid misusing commas with compound elements

Do not use a comma between the parts of a compound subject, a compound verb, a compound object, a compound complement, or a compound object of a preposition. Similarly, do not use a comma to separate two dependent clauses.

■ The members of the senior class/ and their parents were invited.

■ Maria quickly turned off the lights/ and locked the door.

■ Sean put the books on the shelf/ and the pens in the drawer.

■ The weather was unbearably hot/ and much too humid.

■ Gina tried to save more/ and spend less.

■ The rule applies to students who have maintained their grades/ and who have paid all their fees.

Commas are used to separate the parts of a compound sentence. (See 44a.)

3 Avoid using commas with restrictive modifiers or appositives

Commas are used to set off only nonrestrictive modifiers and appositives, not restrictive ones. (See 44c.)

■ The information/ that we requested/ has arrived.

4 Avoid using single commas when a pair of commas is needed

Nonrestrictive modifiers, parenthetical elements, words of direct address, attributory words, and elements of contrast must be set off by a pair of commas when they appear in the middle of a sentence. Do not fail to include both commas.

■ This book‸which he has read three times, is slightly tattered.

■ Carla, on the other hand‸is always on time.

■ Do you think‸Alex, that you could hurry a bit?

In many cases, years, states, and titles and abbreviations used with names must also be set off by a pair of commas when they appear in the middle of a sentence. (See 44h.)

5 Avoid misusing commas with relative pronouns and subordinating conjunctions

A single comma should never separate a relative pronoun or a subordinating conjunction from the dependent clause it introduces.

■ He stated that/ home accidents are the cause of most childhood injuries.

■ Our legislators have no idea how to proceed because/ we have not come to a consensus.

A pair of commas, such as those used to set off parenthetical elements, may separate these elements.

We found that, according to the latest data, the population had doubled.

6 Avoid misusing commas in series or with coordinate adjectives

Do not use a comma before the first element or after the last element in a series, unless another rule makes it necessary.

■ The primary colors are/ red, yellow, and blue.

■ They went to London, Paris, and Rome/ on their last trip.

Do not put a comma between the final coordinate adjective and the noun it modifies.

■ His old, blue/ boat was finally ready for the water.

Do not put a comma between adjectives that are not coordinate.

■ Andy bought a new/ leather jacket to wear on his motorcycle.

■ EDITING 10: EXPLORATION

Read the following excerpt from an essay by Isak Dinesen. What is the effect of the many commas in the opening paragraph? Are any of them unnecessary? Copy the paragraph, eliminating any unnecessary commas. Then read it aloud, comparing it to Dinesen's version. Why, do you think, did Dinesen use commas this way?

"Just at the beginning of the long rains, in the last week of March, or the first week of April, I have heard the nightingale in the woods of Africa. Not the full song: a few notes only, — the opening bars of the concerto, a rehearsal, suddenly stopped and again begun. It was as if, in the solitude of the dripping woods, some one was, in a tree, tuning a small cello. It was, however, the same melody, and the same abundance and sweetness, as were soon to fill the forests of Europe, from Sicily to Elsinore."

ISAK DINESEN, "SOME AFRICAN BIRDS"

■ EDITING 11: PRACTICE

Edit the following passage by deleting any unnecessary commas.

All of the students who live in the co-op on campus, work together, to keep the place clean. It usually takes about half an hour to clean the dorm, and each person cleans twice a month. The job of the "whip" is, to make sure the cleaning is done. If the job has not been done, when the whip checks it, the student, who is responsible, is given a demerit point. Students must accumulate fewer than three demerit points, or be forced to move out of the co-op. If the whip says that, a job has been done poorly, the student has to do it again. Cleaning up after others, is not a lot of fun, but I have to admit that, the co-op is the cleanest dorm on campus.

▉ EDITING 12: PRACTICE

Edit the following passage, using commas correctly.

In recent years growing numbers of distinguished, economics experts have presented a disturbing if not totally grim financial forecast for the United States and the world. In fact some predict a total, global, economic collapse before December 31 1999. Anyone, who listens to their dire predictions, might wonder if they are just trying to sell their wares or if there is some validity to their forecasts. A number of sources point out, that there are increasing numbers of financial failures which they say are the first sign of the impending collapse. Banks provide the mechanism for the flow of money and money flow is very complicated. There are two, main resources, where banks get their money for credit, the Federal Reserve System, and their depositors' savings accounts. They prefer the latter which requires them to pay less interest. In these supposedly dire economic times many banks are becoming involved in mergers, a development that economic forecasters see as another sign of collapse.

▉ EDITING 13: APPLICATION

Examine a paper you are working on and look for misused or omitted commas. Is there one kind of mistake that you make consistently? If so, think about how best to identify misused commas or places where you have omitted commas when you edit your work. Edit any sentences in which you have misused or omitted commas.

While a comma marks a pause within a sentence, a **semicolon** marks a stop within a sentence. The stop is not as forceful as the one indicated by a period between sentences. However, the semicolon tells readers that what precedes it is complete and that what follows is also complete and closely related. The semicolon marks the division between sentence elements of equal rank; it is not used to introduce, enclose, or end a statement.

Although using a period or a comma is often mandatory, using a semicolon is often a choice; in certain situations it may be an alternative to either a period or a comma.

As you edit your work, the following guidelines will help you use semicolons correctly and effectively:

- ■ Use semicolons between independent clauses.

- ■ Use semicolons to separate items in a complex series.

- ■ Use semicolons sparingly.

- ■ Avoid misusing semicolons.

45 a Using semicolons between independent clauses

An **independent clause** is a group of words that contains a subject and a predicate and that can stand alone as a complete sentence. Two or more such clauses may be joined with a comma and a coordinating conjunction (*and, or, but, for, nor, yet, so*). (See 44a.) They may also be joined with a semicolon.

Use a semicolon to join independent clauses to indicate that the clauses are closely related. A semicolon is often used when the relationship between clauses is one of contrast or contradiction.

The storm raged all night; most of us slept fitfully, if at all.

Most dogs aim to please their owners; cats are more independent.

Use a semicolon between independent clauses joined with a **conjunctive adverb** (*however, furthermore, therefore*) or a **transitional expression** (*for example, on the other hand*). (See 33b2.)

Many in the community were rightly angered; however, they lacked a forceful spokesperson to promote their cause.

The contract was approved; indeed, no one questioned any of the stipulated restrictions.

You may use a semicolon with a coordinating conjunction to join complex or lengthy independent clauses.

If the weather clears, we plan to leave at dawn; and if it doesn't, George, Hillary, and Norman, each of whom has other commitments, will have to forgo the rest of the trip.

Do not use a coordinating conjunction with a semicolon to join simple independent clauses.

■ Hundreds of volunteers assisted in the cleanup effort; ~~and~~ many worked from dawn to dusk.

(For more on joining independent clauses, see Chapter 26.)

EDITING 1: EXPLORATION

In the next few essays, stories, or textbook chapters you read, pay close attention to how the authors use semicolons. Collect a few examples that seem to you particularly effective. Edit them to eliminate the semicolons. How does this change the effect or sense of the sentences?

EDITING 2: PRACTICE

Edit the following sentences, using semicolons as necessary to join independent clauses. Example:

The treatment team at Connelly Center puts together an individual program for each child with the full awareness of the child/; indeed, the child helps set his or her personal goals.

1. The center provides a very structured environment for the children, for example, there are rules to follow and expectations to meet.

2. For some emotionally disturbed children, school is a very difficult place, with its emphasis on adaptability, attentiveness, and obedience, yet the structure of a school environment benefits the children greatly.

3. When children act inappropriately, teachers try to reassure them that they still care for them, but children have to take responsibility for their actions.

4. Their ultimate goal is to prepare students for successful reintegration into the educational mainstream, consequently, they teach the academic and social skills necessary to be successful at school.

5. The teachers develop a suitable program for each child, discuss the program with the child's parents, and, with their approval, implement the program, but the child is the one who determines the success of the program.

45 b Using semicolons in complex series

Items in a series are generally separated by commas. (See 44d.) In some situations, however, you can prevent confusion by separating the elements with semicolons instead.

Use a semicolon between elements in a series when at least one element of the series includes a comma.

> The candidates for the award are Maria, who won the essay competition; Elaine, the top debater; and Shelby, who directed several student productions.

Some writers use a semicolon to separate a series of long verb phrases or dependent clauses even when they contain no internal commas.

> As a nation, we need to understand why regional conflicts occur; how they are rooted in the power vacuum that followed the fall of the Soviet Union; and what kinds of responses we can offer in this new and different world.

As with commas, a series should not be preceded or followed by a semicolon unless another rule requires it. (See 44j.)

■ **EDITING 3: PRACTICE**

Edit the following sentences, using semicolons as necessary in complex series. Circle the number of any sentence that does not need semicolons. Example:

> **Our vacation to New England included trips to Mystic, Connecticut‖; Ogunquit, Maine╱;Boston, Massachusetts╱;and Keene, New Hampshire.**

1. Several different craft can be seen on the Charles River, including sculls rowed by students from the universities in the area, canoes, rowboats, which can be rented for a small fee, and motorboats.

2. To get to know a new place quickly, obtain a detailed map of the area you plan to visit, walk to as many places as possible, always wearing shoes with good soles, and talk to the residents, provided they look friendly.

3. If you go to Boston's Museum of Fine Arts, don't miss the Paul Revere silver, the Egyptian mummies, the Athenian vases, and the terrific collection of paintings, including works by Gauguin, Degas, Monet, van Gogh, and Whistler.

4. If you really want to fit in, ask someone where the locals eat, find out how to get there, using public transportation, of course, and get to your destination without even consulting your subway map.

5. New England has produced some of the greatest writers in America: Henry David Thoreau, who wrote *Walden*, Henry Wadsworth Longfellow, whose house on Brattle Street in Cambridge is a historic landmark, and Nathaniel Hawthorne, a resident of Salem, Massachusetts, and author of *The Scarlet Letter*.

45 c Using semicolons sparingly

As a stylistic device, the semicolon can be overused, creating a monotonous sameness of rhythm and sentence structure. (See Chapter 27 for advice on varying sentences.) Save the semicolon for the sentences in which it is most effective.

■ Tax incentives can distort the economy; ̶f̶o̶r̶ For example, real estate tax shelters helped create the glut of empty office buildings that forced developers into bankruptcy and caused a banking crisis due to defaults on loans. More tax breaks are not the answer; they would only create more distortion. Politicians, however, compete to think up special tax cuts; it must be an election year.

The editing reserves the semicolon to set up the statement that requires the most emphasis.

If you are using a computer to edit your paper, you may want to use the search function to locate all instances of semicolons. This will allow you to see how often you have used semicolons and will simplify the task of changing ineffective semicolons to other marks of punctuation.

45 d Avoiding misuses of semicolons

The semicolon always separates sentence elements of equal rank. If you find a semicolon not serving that purpose in your writing, either revise the sentence or use other punctuation.

Do not use a semicolon to separate an independent clause and a dependent clause. Use a comma or edit the sentence to eliminate the subordinating word that introduces the dependent clause.

■ Even though my head continued to hurt, we sat in the emergency room for an hour.

■ He ran down the block to the old mailbox; ~~where~~ he dropped his letter into the slot.

Do not use a semicolon to separate an independent clause and a phrase.

■ Having failed in my endless search of old files and musty records, I longed for a simpler research assignment.

Do not use a semicolon to introduce a list. A colon is the correct mark of introduction. (See 46a.)

■ It was a fine old house, but it needed work⁞plaster repairs, wallpaper, light fixtures, paint, and a thorough cleaning.

■ EDITING 4: PRACTICE

Edit the following sentences by replacing any incorrectly used semicolons with the correct mark of punctuation or rewording the sentence. Some sentences can be edited in more than one way. Circle the number of any sentence that is correct. Be ready to explain your editing choices. Example:

Farley Mowat's books are not depressing⁞ though they do make one think about the role of humans in the universe.

1. His writing abounds with examples of the greedy nature of human beings; however, it does not convey a sense of helplessness.
2. Mowat clings to a spark of hope that it is not too late for humans to develop a respectful attitude toward our planet and the animals that inhabit it; although he regards humans as covetous.
3. A self-designated advocate for nonhuman animals, Mowat reveals the precariousness of the relationship between humans and animals; with unforgiving honesty for the most part.
4. He can be delightfully witty when describing a positive and healthy relationship but also merciless in his condemnation; especially when it is destructive and exploitative, as it is more often than not.
5. After describing the harsh conditions in the village of Burgeo in the north of Newfoundland, he reveals the lure of the place; abundant fish, seals, dolphins, and whales.

■ EDITING 5: PRACTICE

Edit the following passage, using semicolons correctly. More than one edited version is possible. Be ready to explain your editing choices.

What I like best about Spalding Gray's writing is that it is so personal. He tells the reader not only what happened, but also how he felt. Although some of the experiences he writes about are somewhat out of the ordinary; he always manages to find something everyone can relate to. Gray is not just a writer, though. He's also a monologist and an actor. He did not write down his first ten monologues, the first of which was an exercise in his acting class. Instead, he simply told them over and over. In fact, when Gray first started writing down his stories; he found it very difficult. He felt as if he had lost his personal voice and rhythm. He decided in the end to rework the transcripts of his monologues from his performances and put them into writing. Luckily, he was successful. He managed to preserve his unique and personal quality, and now, whether his story is told in person or on the page; it is absolutely riveting.

EDITING 6: APPLICATION

Examine a paper you are working on to see if you have overused semicolons or overlooked opportunities to use them effectively. Is there one kind of mistake you consistently make? If so, think about how best to identify misused semicolons and places where you might use them effectively when you edit your work. Edit any sentences in which you need to improve the use of semicolons.

Like the semicolon, the **colon** indicates a stop within a sentence. As a mark of introduction, the colon alerts the reader that the information preceding it is illustrated by what follows. The colon is also required as a mark of separation in certain other situations, such as in writing the time of day in numerals.

As you edit your work, the following guidelines will help you use colons correctly and effectively:

- Use a colon to introduce explanations, examples, lists, and quotations.

- Use colons to separate elements when writing the time of day, titles, biblical citations, and salutations in letters and memos.

- Avoid misusing colons.

46 a | Using colons as marks of introduction

Use a colon to introduce an explanation, example, list, or quotation. The colon used this way must be preceded by an **independent clause,** which contains a subject and a verb and can stand alone as a complete sentence.

An explanation or example can be a single word, a phrase, or a clause.

He has but one objective: success.

Only one task remains: to prepare the final report.

The budget agreement erected a wall between defense and education: No money was to be transferred between the two.

Some writers capitalize the first word of an independent clause following a colon if it conveys the main point of the sentence. Such capitalization is optional; a lowercase letter is always correct.

Use a colon to introduce a list that follows an independent clause. Frequently, an independent clause before a list will contain expressions such as *the following* or *as follows*.

Almost everything you buy travels to you by truck: paper products, food, medicine, even pickup trucks.

To complete the dish, proceed as follows: transfer the meat to a warm platter, arrange the cooked vegetables around it, ladle on some of the sauce, and sprinkle with chopped parsley.

In some cases, a dash may be used to introduce a list. (See 49b.)

Use a colon to introduce a quotation formally when an independent clause precedes the quotation.

As he left, he quoted Puck's final lines from *A Midsummer Night's Dream*: "Give me your hands, if we be friends, / And Robin shall restore amends."

A long quotation set off from main text in block format may also be preceded by a colon. (See 48a.) Use a comma before a quotation if the words preceding it do not constitute an independent clause. (See 44g.) See Chapter 48 for more on punctuating quotations.

46 b Using colons as marks of separation

Use colons to separate the numerals expressing hours, minutes, and seconds.

Court convened promptly at 9:00 A.M.

The winning car's official elapsed time was 2:45:56.

Use a colon to separate a main title from a subtitle.

Blue Highways: A Journey into America

"A Deep Darkness: A Review of *Out of Africa*"

Use a colon in biblical citations to separate the numerals designating chapter and verse.

Isaiah 14:10

Use a colon following the salutation of a business letter and in the heading of a memo.

Dear Mr. Nader:

To: Alex DiGiovanni
From: Paul Gallarelli
Subject: 1993 budget

Colons are also used to separate elements in bibliographies and reference lists. (See Part VII.)

46 c Avoiding misuses of colons

Do not use a colon as a mark of introduction if the material preceding it is not an independent clause.

■ To obtain a good grade⁄,attend all classes and turn in all assign-
^
ments on time.

Do not use a colon to introduce a quotation if the material preceding it is not an independent clause. In most cases, you should change the colon to a comma. (See 44g.)

■ As the song from *South Pacific* puts it⁄,"You've got to be care-
^
fully taught."

Do not use a colon as an introductory mark when it separates a verb and its object or complement.

■ For lunch, he usually eats⁄ fruit, salad, or yogurt.

■ My favorite fruits are⁄ peaches, grapes, and bananas.

Do not use a colon as an introductory mark when it separates a preposition from its object.

■ She has traveled to⁄ New Orleans, San Francisco, and Boston.

Do not use a colon following introductory and transitional expressions such as *for example, such as, like,* and *especially.*

■ The show included a number of unusual pets, including̸ igua-
nas, raccoons, a civet, and a black widow spider.

Do not use more than one colon in a sentence.

■ Wesley's visit always meant gifts: records, magazines, and
books̸ pirate tales, mystery stories, and epic poems.
    ^of

The colon is a very powerful and rather formal mark of punctuation. Do not overuse it. If you find that you use colons frequently in your writing, you may want to use your computer's
search function to find all the colons in your paper. This will allow
you to see how often you have used colons and will simplify the
task of changing ineffective colons to other marks of punctuation.

▨ EDITING I: EXPLORATION

The following excerpt from an essay by Lewis Thomas is exceptional in its use
of colons. Read the passage and consider whether the colons are effective.

"I am old enough by this time to be used to the notion of dying,
saddened by the glimpse when it has occurred but only transiently knocked
down, able to regain my feet quickly at the thought of continuity, any day. I
have acquired and held in affection until very recently another sideline of an
idea which serves me well at dark times: the life of the earth is the same as
the life of an organism: the great round being possesses a mind: the mind
contains an infinite number of thoughts and memories: when I reach my time I
may find myself still hanging around in some sort of midair, one of those small
thoughts, drawn back into the memory of the earth: in that peculiar sense I
will be alive."

LEWIS THOMAS, "LATE NIGHT THOUGHTS ON LISTENING
TO MAHLER'S NINTH SYMPHONY"

▨ EDITING 2: PRACTICE

Edit the following sentences, using colons correctly. Example:

The first chore assigned to me as crewmate on a whale watch
was not very exciting̸ Cleaning the bathroom.
                      ^:

I. One thing is certain, the new person on the job always has to do the worst chores.

2. Given the terrible weather of the last few days, I was relieved by what I saw out in the distance, a nice, calm ocean.

3. I stepped on the deck and spoke these words from Melville's *Moby Dick*, "Call me Ishmael."

4. The sight of my first whale made me think of Jonah 1.17–2.10.

5. Finally, I began the job I had been hired to do, preparing snacks and beverages in the galley.

6. We spotted various kinds of whales on the excursion, right whales, humpback whales, finback whales, and minke whales.

7. There is one thing whale watch enthusiasts should always remember to do, wear rubber-soled shoes.

8. The people on the deck wore clothes to keep them dry ponchos and garbage bags.

9. When we returned to land at 6.00, I wanted nothing more than to go home and sleep.

10. One more chore awaited me, however, scrubbing the slime off the sides of the boat.

■ EDITING 3: APPLICATION

Examine a paper you are working on for misused or omitted colons. Is there one kind of mistake in using colons that you consistently make? If so, think about how best to identify misused colons or places where you have omitted colons when you edit your work. Edit any sentences in which you have misused or omitted colons.

The **apostrophe** is primarily used to show the possessive form of a noun or pronoun. It is also used to indicate certain unusual plural forms and to show where a letter has been dropped in forming a contraction. (In some cases, it may also be used to represent a single quotation mark. See Chapter 48.)

As you edit your work, the following guidelines will help you use apostrophes correctly:

- Use apostrophes to form the possessives of nouns and indefinite pronouns.

- Use apostrophes to form plurals of words used as words, of letters, and of numbers.

- Use apostrophes to form contractions.

- Avoid confusing plurals and contractions with possessives.

47 a Using apostrophes to form the possessive case of nouns and indefinite pronouns

The **possessive case** of a noun or pronoun shows ownership or an association between the noun or pronoun and other words in the sentence. To form the possessive case, nouns and some indefinite pronouns add an apostrophe and -s or add just an apostrophe. Personal pronouns — I, you, he, she, it, we, they — show the possessive case by changing form in other ways. (See 64b.)

Use an apostrophe and -s to form the possessive of any noun that does not end in -s.

Whoopie Goldberg's new movie is one of her best.

She has always been an advocate for children's rights.

For plural nouns ending in -s, add only an apostrophe to form the possessive.

They owe her several *months'* pay.

The *Clintons'* visit to Japan was covered in all the newspapers.

For singular nouns ending in -s, it is always correct to form the possessive by adding both an apostrophe and -s. Some writers prefer to use only the apostrophe for proper nouns ending in -s to indicate the possessive is not pronounced with an additional syllable. Whichever style you choose, be sure to use it consistently throughout your paper. (You may want to use your computer's search function to make sure you have punctuated all such possessives in the same manner.)

Don't waste the *class's* time.

The company produced *Yeats's* [or *Yeats'*] cycle of plays about the Irish hero Cuchulain.

Use an apostrophe and -s on only the last word to form the possessive of a hyphenated or unhyphenated compound noun.

◼ He borrowed his mother's-in-law's car.

◼ The secretary's of state ,office certified the election results.

Use an apostrophe and -s on only the last noun when nouns joined by *and* are considered a unit and are jointly in possession.

◼ My aunt's and uncle's anniversary party was a disaster.

When nouns joined by *and* are considered individuals in separate possession, add the apostrophe and -s to each noun: *The documentary compared Aretha Franklin's and Diana Ross's early careers.*

An **indefinite pronoun** is a pronoun that does not require an antecedent. Use an apostrophe and -s to form the possessive case of some indefinite pronouns, including *someone, anybody, no one, one,* and *another.*

Someone's umbrella was left in the assembly hall.

It is *no one's* business but mine.

Do not use an apostrophe and *-s* to form the possessive of the indefinite pronouns *all, any, both, each, few, many, most, much,
several, some,* and *such.* Indicate the possessive by using a preposition such as *of,* or use a pronoun that has a possessive
form.

■ The syllabus for the Dickinson and Crane seminar requires that
we read ~~both's~~ *the* complete works, ∧ *of both.*

■ With so many applicants, we find it difficult to provide a personal response to ~~each's~~ *everyone's* questions. ∧

■ **EDITING I: PRACTICE**

Edit the following sentences, using apostrophes correctly to form the possessive forms of nouns and indefinite pronouns. Circle the number of any sentence that is correct. Example:

In almost ~~everyones~~ *everyone's* opinion, the blizzard that struck late last ∧
winter was the worst one in decades.

1. The childrens spirits lifted when they saw the snow accumulating, since
they knew it was their local school boards' tendency to close for inclement
weather.

2. To many peoples' surprise, schools were open.

3. The storms' gale force winds howled for hours, and their strength caused
a branch of my neighbors' oak tree to snap.

4. Stranded passenger's cars could be seen dotting the turnpike, abandoned
in the storms' white-out conditions.

5. For most people, it will be several day's work to extricate their cars from
the snow and ice.

6. The various cities' snow removal budgets were depleted even before the
blizzard's first flakes fell.

7. The day before the storm hit, grocery store's long checkout lines attested
to everyones expectations that they would be snowed in for a long time.

8. The storm's devastation could be seen from New England to Florida. Without a doubt it caused the eastern state's worst damage of the century.

47 b   Using apostrophes to form certain plurals

Use an apostrophe and *-s* to form the plural of a word discussed as a word.

There are two *perhaps*'s in that sentence.

Use an apostrophe and an *-s* to form the plural of letters, numbers, and symbols.

The word *occurrence* is spelled with two *r*'s.

Some children have difficulty learning to write *8*'s.

A row of ***'s marks the spot in my paper where I'm having trouble.

Do not use an apostrophe when a number is spelled out.

■ **All the bills I have are one's and five's.**

As shown in these examples, a word, number, or letter is usually set off by italics or underlining when it stands for itself and not for the concept it usually symbolizes. (See 53e.) However, the apostrophe and the *-s* are not italicized or underlined.

An apostrophe and *-s* may be used to form the plural of centuries and decades expressed in figures. The letter *-s* alone is also correct. Whichever style you choose, be consistent throughout your paper. You may want to use your computer's search function to find all occurrences and make sure you have punctuated them consistently. Do not use an apostrophe when the century or decade is expressed in words.

the 1800s   the 1800's
the 60s   the 60's
the sixties

Use an apostrophe and *-s* for plurals of abbreviations ending with periods. Use *-s* alone for abbreviations without periods.

My science professor has earned two Ph.D.'s.

Like all politicians, she has some IOUs.

(See Chapter 55 for more on abbreviations.)

47 c Using apostrophes to form contractions

A **contraction** is a word in which one or more letters are intentionally omitted and replaced by an apostrophe. In everyday speech many words are shortened for convenience. The word most frequently shortened is *not: have not* becomes *haven't* and so on. Other words often contracted are *is* (*'s*), *are* (*'re*), *has* (*'s*), and *have* (*'ve*). The following list shows the correct use of the apostrophe in some common contractions.

cannot	can't	does not	doesn't
do not	don't	would not	wouldn't
will not	won't	was not	wasn't
she would	she'd	it is	it's
who is	who's	you are	you're
I am	I'm	they are	they're
let us	let's	we have	we've
there is	there's	she has	she's

In dialogue, an apostrophe may also be used to show the omission of one or more letters in a single word in order to represent more accurately the speaker's pronunciation: *s'pose, readin'.*

An apostrophe is sometimes used to show that digits have been dropped from a number, especially a year: *the class of '85.*

Be aware that contractions and other shortenings help create an informal tone. (See Chapter 28.) They should be avoided in most formal academic writing. One exception to this guideline is the word *o'clock* (from *of the clock*), which is always acceptable.

■ EDITING 2: PRACTICE

Edit the following sentences, using apostrophes correctly to form contractions. Example:

>   *you're*   *you'll*
> If ~~your~~ a fan of the outdoors, ~~youll~~ enjoy exploring the Hudson
>   *isn't*
> River Valley, which ~~isnt~~ far from New York City.

1. In the summer there's a boat that takes passengers from the city to Bear Mountain, where hiking enthusiasts wont be disappointed.

2. The views from the mountain's 1300-foot summit cant be surpassed; youll see wilderness stretching out before your eyes in every direction.

3. A trip to the country wouldnt be complete without a stop at Buddy's Café n Deli.

4. Hyde Park is home to FDR's country mansion, which has been preserved as it was when he died in 45.

5. You cant go wrong in the Hudson River Valley if what you like is stunning scenery, great hiking possibilities, and rich history.

47 d Avoiding misuses of apostrophes

Do not confuse plurals with possessives. In most cases, an apostrophe is not needed to form the plural of a noun. (For exceptions, see 47b.)

■ Although they presented themselves as an ideal family, the Reagan/s were not always close to their children.

If you sometimes confuse plural and possessive forms, double-check each instance as you edit. Refer to both 50a and the box in this section showing the pattern of plural and possessive forms.

Do not confuse contractions with possessives. The possessives *its*, *whose*, *your*, and *their* are frequently mistaken for the contractions *it's*, *who's*, *you're*, and *they're*, and vice versa. If you sometimes confuse these pairs, examine each occurrence of these words when editing (perhaps with the aid of your computer's search function) to be sure you have used the right one. As a test in each case, try inserting a substitute. If you see a contraction such as *you're*, you should be able to substitute its spelled-out form, in this case *you are*, without destroying the meaning.

You're late. *You are* late.

If you see a possessive form such as *its* or *your*, you should be able to rearrange the sentence to substitute the prepositional phrase *of it* or *of you*.

Can you hear *its* sound? Can you hear the sound *of it*?

If either of these tests results in nonsense, you have confused a possessive with a contraction.

> ✔ **PLURAL AND POSSESSIVE FORMS**
>
> | SINGULAR | SINGULAR POSSESSIVE | PLURAL | PLURAL POSSESSIVE |
> |---|---|---|---|
> | school | school's | schools | schools' |
> | box | box's | boxes | boxes' |
> | class | class's | classes | classes' |
> | Duvalier | Duvalier's | Duvaliers | Duvaliers' |
> | Jones | Jones's | Joneses | Joneses' |
>
> When spoken, the plural, the singular possessive, and the plural possessive sound the same for most words. In writing, the spelling and the placement of the apostrophe help readers distinguish among the three forms.

■ EDITING 3: PRACTICE

Edit the following sentences, being careful to distinguish plurals, contractions, and possessives. Example:

> **Charles Dickens's brief experience of a debtor's prison with it̸'s deplorable conditions had a profound effect on him.**

1. Its perhaps surprising to learn that Dickens didn't start out as a novelist; instead, he trained as a lawyer's clerk.

2. The author, who's literary career began during the 1830s, started out writing for magazines' under the pseudonym "Boz."

3. Society's evil, corruption, and crime were concerns to Dickens, and their frequently found as themes throughout his novels.

4. They're style and structure were affected by the fact that Dickens wrote his novel's for publication in monthly installments.

5. Dickens's first novel was *Pickwick Papers*, who's monthly installments were accompanied by plates created by a popular artist.

■ EDITING 4: EXPLORATION

Apostrophes are often misused in advertising copy. Sometimes even the name of the company omits an apostrophe where we would expect one. Wendys, for instance, is printed without an apostrophe, whereas McDonald's uses one. Is there a reason that some companies use an apostrophe while others do not? Make a note of three or four examples of misused apostrophes in advertising. Good places to look are in newspapers and magazines, on the sides of commercial vehicles, and on storefronts.

■ EDITING 5: PRACTICE

Edit the following passage, using apostrophes correctly.

In ancient Athens, after some of the Acropolis' early buildings were destroyed by the Persians during the Persian War, the Athenian leader Pericles decided to rebuild many of the structures on the citys' chief fortress and sanctuary. The Parthenon was begun in 447 B.C. From anyones point of view, the columns of the temple appear to be straight, but in fact their built with a slight outward bulge. Its a subtle optical effect added for appearances sake. It works, too: one really cant tell that they arent straight. A huge amount of the Athenians's financial resources were used to rebuild the Parthenon, and to the Athenians it became a symbol of they're strength in the ancient world.

■ EDITING 6: APPLICATION

Examine a paper you are working on for misused or omitted apostrophes. Is there one kind of mistake in using apostrophes that you consistently make? If so, think about how best to identify misused apostrophes or places where you have omitted apostrophes when you edit your work. Edit any sentences in which you have misused or omitted apostrophes.

Quotation can be a powerful tool. With quotations, you can document exactly what was said at a crucial time, portray people speaking to each other, clarify an idea you are analyzing, or enlist an expert's support for an argument you are making.

Using another person's exact words is called **direct quotation.** When you quote directly, you must tell readers you are doing so by indicating the source and by enclosing the exact words you use in quotation marks. Restating someone else's idea in your own words is called **paraphrasing** or **indirect quotation.** When quoting indirectly, you must still identify the source but you do not use quotation marks. (For more on identifying sources, see Chapter 17.)

Quotation marks are also used to distinguish certain words, such as titles and foreign expressions, from the main body of the text. Italics are used for this purpose as well. (See Chapter 53.)

In written American English, **double quotation marks** (" ") identify quotations, titles, and so on, and **single quotation marks** (' ') identify quotations within quotations (or titles within titles). In print and in handwriting, a distinction is made between an opening quotation mark (") and a closing quotation mark ("). Most typewriters and personal computers, however, use the same mark at both ends of a quotation. Similarly, many typewriters and computers use an apostrophe (') for both the opening and closing single quotation mark.

The guidelines for presenting quotations vary somewhat from discipline to discipline. This chapter follows the conventions of the Modern Language Association, the authority for papers written in the languages and literature. For information on this and other disciplinary styles, see Chapters 59–63.

As you edit your work, the following guidelines will help you use quotation marks correctly:

■ Use quotation marks to indicate brief direct quotations.

■ Use quotation marks for dialogue.

■ Use ellipsis points and brackets to indicate changes in quotations.

■ Use quotation marks for certain titles.

■ Use quotation marks for translations, specialized terms and coinages, ironic uses, and some nicknames.

■ Use other punctuation marks conventionally with quotation marks.

■ Avoid misusing quotation marks.

48 a   Using quotation marks for brief direct quotations

Brief direct quotations are enclosed in quotation marks. Brief quotations are those of up to four typed lines of prose or up to three lines of poetry. If a parenthetical citation of the source is provided, place it after the closing quotation marks but before the period.

> In <u>Lives under Siege</u>, Ratzenburger argues that "most adolescents are far too worried about the next six months and far too unconcerned about the next sixty years" (84).

When quoting poetry, use a slash preceded and followed by a single space to indicate line breaks. (See 49e.)

> Shakespeare concludes Sonnet 18 with this couplet: "So long as men can breathe or eyes can see, / So long lives this, and this gives life to thee."

Longer direct quotations are set off from the main text in **block format.** Start a new line for the quotation, indent all lines of the quotation ten spaces, and do not use quotation marks. If the words introducing a block quotation form a complete sentence, they are usually followed by a colon, although a period is also acceptable. (See 46a.) If the introductory words do not constitute a complete sentence, a comma or no punctuation at all is used, depending on context. If a parenthetical citation of the source is provided, place it two spaces after the final mark of end punctuation.

> A recent editorial describes the problem:
>
> > In countries like the United States, breast-
> > feeding, though always desirable, doesn't
> > mean the difference between good and poor
> > nutrition--or life and death. But it does in
> > developing countries, where for decades
> > infant food manufacturers have been
> > distributing free samples of infant formulas
> > to hospitals and birthing centers. (Daily
> > Times 17)
>
> The editorial goes on to argue that the samples last
> only long enough for the mothers' own milk to dry up;
> then the mothers find they cannot afford to buy the
> formula.

As this example shows, single paragraphs or parts of paragraphs in block format do not use paragraph indents. If you are quoting from two or more paragraphs, indent the first line of each new paragraph three additional spaces.

When quoting poetry, reproduce as precisely as possible the line breaks, indents, spacing, and capitalization of the original.

> In Patience, W. S. Gilbert has the character Reginald
> Bunthorne proclaim,
>
> > This air severe
> > > Is but a mere
> > > > Veneer!
> >
> > This cynic smile
> > > Is but a wile
> > > > Of guile! (5-10)

If a quotation appears within a quotation, use single quotation marks for the inner quotation.

```
After the election, the incumbent said, "My opponent
will soon learn, as someone once said, 'You can't
fool all of the people all of the time.'"
```

If a quotation appears within a quotation displayed in block format, use double quotation marks for the inner quotation.

■ EDITING I: EXPLORATION

In your own writing or in professional writing, look for examples of quotations taken from other sources. Locate at least one example that uses quotation marks within text and one that uses block format set off from text. Rewrite each example using the alternative format. How do the different ways of presenting the information affect the readability of the passages?

■ EDITING 2: PRACTICE

Edit the following sentences, using quotation marks correctly with brief direct quotations. Example:

> **Describing the atmosphere at the White House under the Clinton administration, an anonymous aide said,"It's a lot less uptight than it was under previous administrations."**

1. "Nobody even bothers to get dressed up to see the president, one senator said. That takes a little getting used to for those of us older senators."

2. "Even though Clinton holds the highest office in the country, he has never told us "You have to call me Mr. President now," " said a former campaign organizer.

3. "The president keeps such long hours that the White House kitchen stays open until late at night," one adviser said. And the food is really good, too."

4. "If I had to choose one word to describe the atmosphere under the new administration, I'd have to say "unpredictable," a recent visitor said.

5. "An Elvis impersonator entertained here last week," a visitor added. Like my friend said, this White House is "a lot less uptight" than it ever was.

48 b Using quotation marks for dialogue

To reproduce dialogue, either real or fictional, use quotation marks and a new paragraph to show every change of speaker. Once the pattern is established, readers can tell who is speaking even if every quote does not have attributory words.

> "Early parole is not the solution to overcrowding," the prosecutor said. "We need a new jail."
> The chairman of the county commission asked, "How do you propose we should pay for it?"
> "Increase taxes if you must, but whatever you do, act quickly."

If one speaker's words continue for more than a single paragraph, use quotation marks at the beginning of each new paragraph but at the end of only the last paragraph.

(See 44g for advice about using commas to set off the attributory words that identify the speaker.)

▪ EDITING 3: APPLICATION

Look through some of your recent papers and locate a passage that could have been written in dialogue. Edit the passage to turn it into dialogue, following the guidelines described in this section.

48 c Using ellipsis points and brackets to indicate changes to quotations

Quotation marks tell readers that you are reproducing the words of your source exactly. Yet you must sometimes modify quotations for brevity or clarity. The only permissible changes to a quotation are deletions that shorten the original without changing its meaning, minor changes to make a quotation grammatically compatible with the sentence in which it appears, and insertions of your own words for the purpose of clarification.

To indicate an omission within a quotation, use **ellipsis points,** three periods each preceded and followed by a space. (See 49c.) To indicate words that have been added or changed, use **brackets:** [ ]. (See 49d.)

48 d **Using quotation marks for certain titles**

Use quotation marks for titles of brief poems, short stories, essays, book chapters and parts, magazine and journal articles, episodes of television series, and songs. Italics are used to indicate titles of longer works such as books, magazines, journals, television series, recordings, films, and plays. (See 53a for a comparison of the uses of italics and quotation marks for titles.)

The Beatles' *Sgt. Pepper's Lonely Hearts Club Band* includes the song "A Day in the Life."

If the title of a part of a work or series is generic rather than specific — for example, Chapter 6 — do not use either quotation marks or italics.

The titles of sacred works, parts of sacred works, and ancient manuscripts are not enclosed in quotation marks or italicized: the Bible, the Talmud; Genesis; the Book of Kells. The titles of public documents also appear without quotation marks or italics: the Constitution, the Gettysburg Address.

 TITLES WITHIN TITLES

Use the following models as a guide to presenting titles within other titles. These same guidelines apply to other words that normally are indicated by quotation marks or italics (such as foreign words or quotations) when they appear in titles.

1. A title enclosed in quotation marks within an italicized title:

"A Curtain of Green" and Other Stories

2. An italicized title within a title enclosed in quotation marks:

"Morality in Death of a Salesman"

3. A title enclosed in quotation marks within another title enclosed in quotation marks:

"The Symbolism in 'Everyday Use'"

4. An italicized title within another italicized title:

Modern Critics on Hamlet and Other Plays

Use single quotation marks to indicate quoted material that is part of a title enclosed in double quotation marks.

We read "'This Is the End of the World': The Black Death" by historian Barbara Tuchman.

Do not use quotation marks around your own titles placed at the beginning of your essays, poems, or stories. Titles are indicated by quotation marks only when they are referred to in text. You should, however, indicate any part of your title that is itself a quotation or a title.

An Analysis of the "My Turn" Column in *Newsweek*

■ EDITING 4: PRACTICE

Edit the following sentences, using quotation marks correctly with titles. Circle the number of any sentence that is correct. Example:

Jeff read a review of *Six Degrees of Separation* in ~~The Theater~~, a
"The Theater"
column in *The New Yorker* magazine, and he wants to see the play tonight.

1. Jan prefers to stay at home and finish reading *A View from the Woods*, one of the stories in Flannery O'Connor's *Everything that Rises Must Converge.*
2. As usual, Kim will be watching *Star Trek* reruns on television. Her favorite episode is Who Mourns for Adonis?
3. Erik will spend the evening reading "Why I Write," an essay that Orwell wrote the year *after* he published his novel *Animal Farm.*
4. Alan wants to stay home and study Thomas Hardy's poem *At the Word "Farewell."*
5. Jeff decides to stay at home and listen to his jazz records. He always turns up the volume when the song *Basin Street Blues* comes on.

48 e Using quotation marks for translations, specialized terms, ironic usages, and nicknames

When a foreign word or phrase is translated into English, the translation may be enclosed in quotation marks. (Parentheses may also be used for this purpose; see 49a. The foreign word or phrase is italicized; see 53c.)

> I've always called Antonio *fratellino*, or "little brother," because he is twelve years younger than I.

A specialized term or new coinage is often introduced in quotation marks when it is first defined. (When the definition itself is considered parenthetical, it can be set off by commas, parentheses, or dashes. See 44e, 49a, 49b.)

> The ecology of this "chryocore" — a region of perpetual ice and snow — has been studied very little.

> He called the new vegetable a "broccoflower," a yellow-green cross between broccoli and cauliflower.

If a word is used in an ironic sense — that is, with a meaning opposed to its literal one — you can call attention to the intended effect by putting the word in quotation marks, but use this technique sparingly in academic writing.

> Jonathan Swift's essay "A Modest Proposal" offers a quick "solution" to Ireland's poverty and overpopulation: eat the children.

An unusual nickname may be enclosed in quotation marks at first mention.

> When I joined the firm, the president was a man named Garnett E. "Ding" Cannon.

With common nicknames, such as Don, Dick, or Jackie, there is no need to use quotation marks or even to include the nickname on first reference.

---

48 **f** **Using other punctuation with quotation marks**

When a word is to be followed by both a quotation mark and by another mark of punctuation, confusion sometimes arises as to which punctuation mark should come first. The format rules in these cases are guided partly by logic and partly by convention.

(For information on using brackets and ellipses with quotation marks, see Chapter 49.)

1 Periods and commas

Periods and commas go inside quotation marks. (See Chapter 43 and 44g for the uses of periods and commas with quotations.)

> After Gina finished singing "Memories," Joe began to hum "The Way We Were."

> "Denver is usually warm in the spring," he said, "but this year it's positively hot."

> *The second comma is not inside quotation marks because it follows an attributory word rather than a quoted word. See 44g.*

2 Colons and semicolons

Colons and semicolons go outside quotation marks. (See 46a for the use of colons to introduce quotations.)

> The sign read "Closed": there would be no cold soda for us today.

> In 1982, Bobbie Ann Mason wrote "Shiloh"; it is considered one of her finest works.

3 Question marks, exclamation points, and dashes

Question marks, exclamation points, and dashes go inside the quotation marks if they are part of the quotation, outside the quotation marks if they are not. (See 43c, 43d, and 49b for the uses of these punctuation marks with quotations.)

> "Would you like some fruit?" Phil asked.

> Was it you who said "We're sorry"?

> He began singing "Oklahoma!" and doing a square dance.

> I can't believe you've never read "The Lottery"!

> "Hold on a minute. I can't hear — "

> Emma's first word — "dada" — caused her father to beam.

If the logic of a sentence dictates that a question mark or exclamation point appear directly next to a comma or period, keep the stronger mark of punctuation (the question mark or exclamation point) and delete the weaker one (the comma or period).

■ As soon as we heard someone shout "Fire!|" we began to run toward the exit.

■ **EDITING 5: PRACTICE**

Edit the following sentences, adding quotation marks as needed and making sure that other punctuation marks are used correctly. Example:

"All right," Sam said, "Maybe experiments on animals do serve a
^   ^   ^
purpose. But, I suggest, the price is too high."
                                      ^

1. What you don't understand, Dr. Burton explained, is that with animal research, we can test hypotheses and isolate variables. She sighed. Let me tell you about — she started to say.

2. I don't deny that animal research can yield valuable information, he interrupted. My problem is about whether it is morally defensible.

3. "Morally defensible!" she exclaimed. We're talking about saving lives! Because animal research leads to medical breakthroughs that benefit human beings, she added, I would call it a necessary evil.

4. "Just because we humans have a superior intellect, Sam suggested, does not mean that we should exploit less intelligent animals."

5. She replied I think we should draw a distinction not between more intelligent and less intelligent animals, but between human and nonhuman animals.

6. There is a distinction, Sam agreed. Humans are the only animals with a conscience. Knowing that, we should listen to that conscience, he added.

---

48 g | **Avoiding misuses of quotation marks**

Do not use quotation marks to indicate emphasis. Emphasis should generally be created by the structure and rhythm of your sentences. (See Chapter 27.) In some cases, italics may be used for emphasis. (See 53d.)

■ He was guilty of a /felony,/ not a misdemeanor.

Avoid using quotation marks to call attention to a slang term or to a term you think is overused or funny. If you are uncomfortable using such a term without quotation marks, you should probably substitute another.

■ Several of these companies should be placed in a /hall of shame/ for their employment practices.

Be sure always to use quotation marks in pairs and to include only quoted words within them. You may want to use your computer's search function to help you check for this common mistake. Have the computer find the first quotation mark, then move the cursor through the quotation — checking each word to make sure it's part of the quotation — until you reach the closing quotation mark. Repeat this process until you have gone completely through your paper.

■ "There are always a few students who boycott the assembly," he said, "but that's no reason for us to call it off."

■ EDITING 6: PRACTICE

Edit the following passage to make sure that quotation marks and related punctuation are used correctly.

With the election in 1992 of Bill Clinton, the first baby boomer president, many people were excited by the possibility of change. One of the many baby boomers in the electorate said, "finally, I can really identify with the leader of my country." "I think he's going to effect some real changes." For the first time, America had a president who grew up listening to the "The White Album," who read "Rolling Stone" magazine, who even named his daughter after *Chelsea Morning*, a popular song from the seventies. His running mate, Al Gore, also had concerns that they shared, especially an interest in environmental issues, which earned him the nickname Ozone Man in Republican circles. The Bush administration's attitude at the "Earth Summit," an international conference held in June 1992 to discuss environmental issues, had disappointed many voters. Already impatient for change on a number of other issues, voters looked to the Clinton-Gore team to be the voice of their environmental concerns as well.

■ EDITING 7: APPLICATION

Examine a paper you are working on to see if you have incorrectly punctuated any quotations. Is there one kind of mistake in punctuating quotations that you consistently make? If so, think about how best to identify misused quotation marks or places where you have omitted quotation marks when you edit your work. Edit any sentences in which you have incorrectly punctuated quotations.

Parentheses, dashes, ellipsis points, brackets, and slashes each have such specific uses that the need for them arises infrequently. If you can use these marks of punctuation where they are appropriate and resist using them when they are not, they will bring a certain polish and flair to your writing. If you use them incorrectly or too much, they will call attention to themselves and distract from your meaning.

As you edit your work, the following guidelines will help you use these marks of punctuation correctly and effectively:

■ Use parentheses to enclose and deemphasize nonessential information.

■ Use dashes to enclose and emphasize nonessential information in a sentence, to indicate contrast, and to indicate a pause or interruption.

■ Use ellipsis points to indicate the omission of words in direct quotations or to indicate a pause or interruption.

■ Use brackets to indicate changes to or comments on direct quotations and to enclose material already within parentheses.

■ Use slashes to separate lines of quoted poetry, to indicate alternatives, and to separate certain figures.

49 a Using parentheses

Parentheses enclose elements within a sentence that would otherwise be interruptive: explanations, examples, asides, and supplementary information. Parentheses create a strong break and tend to deemphasize the enclosed material. Commas and dashes may also be used to enclose parenthetical material, but they are used in different circumstances. (See the box in 49b for guidance on choosing among commas, parentheses, and dashes.) Parentheses are also used to set off numbers in a list. Parentheses are distracting, so use them sparingly.

■ Enclosing explanations, examples, and asides

Use parentheses to enclose explanations, examples, and asides within a sentence.

> Relatives of famous people now famous themselves include Mariel Hemingway (niece of Ernest), Angelica Huston (daughter of John), and Michael Douglas (son of Kirk).

> He had graduated with high honors (or so he said) and moved to New York to begin a lucrative career in marketing.

Parentheses are often used to set off the date of an event or the dates of a person's birth and death.

> *The Oxford English Dictionary* was first published under the editorship of James A. H. Murray (1888–1933).

A question mark enclosed in parentheses is used to indicate doubt about a date or fact.

> The house was built in 1726(?) and appears on the land survey of 1733.

When a translation is given for a specialized term or foreign word, the translation is often enclosed in parentheses. (Commas, quotation marks, and dashes may also be used for translations. See 44e, 48e, 49b. A foreign word appears in italics. See 53c.)

> English also borrowed the Dutch word *koekje* (cookie).

2 Enclosing cross-references and citations

Use parentheses to enclose cross-references to other parts of your paper.

> The map (p. 4) shows the areas of heaviest rainfall.

Also use parentheses to identify references and sources for quotations that you use in your paper.

Nick Carraway felt unsettled to see Gatsby at the end of his dock beckoning in the direction of a "single green light" (21).

(See 48a for more information about citing sources for quotations and Chapters 59–63 for documentation styles in various disciplines.)

3 Enclosing numbers or letters in a list

Use parentheses to enclose numbers or letters used to introduce items in a list within a sentence.

The dictionary provides (1) pronunciation, (2) etymology, (3) past meanings, and (4) usage citations for almost 300,000 words.

4 Using other punctuation with parentheses

Never place a comma directly before a set of parentheses. If the words before the parenthetical material require a comma, the comma should be placed after the parentheses.

■ His favorite American authors include Mark Twain, Emily Dickinson, (he always refers to her as "my favorite recluse"),and Zora Neale Hurston.

If the words enclosed by parentheses form a complete sentence, the punctuation depends on the context. If the parenthetical sentence is not enclosed within another sentence, the first word is capitalized and end punctuation is placed before the last parenthesis.

The Countess of Dia is almost forgotten today. (She was quite well known in her own time.)

If a parenthetical sentence is within another sentence, no period is used, and the first word is not capitalized.

Uncle Henry (he is my mother's brother) has won many awards for his poetry.

If a parenthetical sentence within another sentence is a question or an exclamation, a question mark or exclamation point is used, but the first word is not capitalized.

After a brief visit to Detroit (why did I ever leave home?) I was headed back to Philadelphia.

Alexandra grabbed the ball from the Doberman's mouth (yikes!) and then ran as fast as she could.

ESL   **PLACEMENT OF PUNCTUATION**

Only a few kinds of punctuation can begin a line in English: ellipsis points, an opening quotation mark, an opening parenthesis, and an open bracket. All other types of punctuation should be placed within or at the end of a line.

If you are using a word processor with a "wraparound" screen or a "soft return" feature, the word processor will avoid most problems for you automatically, as long as you have not incorrectly inserted a space before a mark of punctuation.

Some word processors, however, will break a line in the middle of a set of ellipsis points or a dash represented by two hyphens, putting part of the punctuation on one line and part on the next. You can correct these by inserting "hard returns" to start the next line either with the complete set of ellipsis points or with a word followed by a dash.

■ **EDITING 1: PRACTICE**

Edit the following sentences, inserting parentheses where appropriate and deleting parentheses that are unnecessary. You may need to make other changes in punctuation. Some sentences can be edited in more than one way. Be ready to explain the changes you made. Example:

> The first railroad constructed in the United States was the Baltimore and Ohio₍1830₎

1. In Europe, railroads were a major factor in the Industrial Revolution, see pp. 300–24.

2. England was the first country to open a public railroad, called "railway" by the British.

3. The first railroad to carry passengers began running in England in 1825 — ?.

4. In some cases railroads grew on top of smaller tracks that were already in place in various industries, for example, in mining.

5. U.S. railroads were built to take advantage of the commerce and industry in the newly settled West, in those days Ohio was considered the West.

6. The rails were laid on wood, later concrete, cross ties (Modern railroads use continuous welded rails).

49 b Using dashes

Dashes serve many of the same purposes as parentheses — that is, they set off explanations, examples, asides, and supplementary information that would otherwise interrupt the flow of the sentence. They tend to emphasize the material they set off. Unlike parentheses, dashes are not always used in pairs. Dashes can also be used to emphasize contrast and to indicate interruptions and pauses in speech.

Dashes are not as interruptive as parentheses, but they do break the flow of a sentence. In some cases, it also becomes difficult for readers to tell what is inside and what is outside a pair of dashes. For these reasons, use dashes sparingly.

On the typewriter, use two hyphens with no space on either side to create a dash.

```
A dash--when you use one--should look like this.
```

Use dashes to set off explanations, examples, or asides within sentences.

At first we did not notice the rain — it began so softly — but soon we were soaked through.

Of all the oddities in Richard's apartment, the contents of the bathtub — transistors, resistors, circuit boards, and odd bits of wire — were the strangest of all.

She donates a considerable sum to Georgetown University — her alma mater — every year.

Use dashes to emphasize contrast.

We have all read the novels of British and American writers, but few of us know even the titles of novels by German or Spanish writers — not to mention those by Asian or African writers.

CHOOSING AMONG COMMAS, PARENTHESES, AND DASHES

Commas, parentheses, and dashes can all be used to set off nonessential material within a sentence. Use commas when the material being set off is closely related to the rest of the sentence. (See Chapter 44.)

A dusty plow, the kind the early Amish settlers used, hung on the wall of the old barn.

Use parentheses when the material being set off is not closely related to the main sentence and when you want to deemphasize it. (See 49a.)

Two young boys found an old plow (perhaps as old as the first Amish settlement) hidden in an unused corner of the barn.

Use dashes when the material being set off is not closely related to the main sentence and when you want to emphasize it. (See 49b.)

The old plow — the one his great-grandfather had used — was still in good working order.

In dialogue, use dashes to indicate a pause, interruption, or abrupt change.

"Well, I guess I was a little late — OK, an hour late."

"Hold on," she shouted, "while I grab this — "

"Nothing is so exciting as seeing an eagle — there's one now!"

If the words enclosed by dashes within a sentence form a sentence, do not capitalize the first word of the inner sentence or use a period. If the enclosed sentence is a question or an exclamation, you may use a question mark or an exclamation point, but do not capitalize the first word.

■ Ward and June Cleaver — who can forget their orderly world‸—
never once question their roles in life.

■ My cousin Eileen — ~~She~~ *she* was from Ireland/ — brought a strange flute with her when she came to visit.

Do not use a comma with a dash.

■ With so many things happening at once — graduation, a new job/ — Joan felt that she had become a different person.

Avoid using more than two dashes in a sentence.

■ He never told his father about his dreams — he couldn't explain them — but silently began to make plans /, plans that would one day lead him away from this small town.

■ EDITING 2: EXPLORATION

Read the following excerpt from an essay by Joyce Carol Oates. Do you think that the author's use of parentheses and dashes is effective?

"The mystique of high-performance cars has always intrigued me with its very opacity. Is it lodged sheerly in speed? — mechanical ingenuity? — the 'art' of a finely tuned beautifully styled vehicle (as the mere physical fact of a Steinway piano constitutes 'art')? — the adrenal thrill of courting death? Has it primarily to do with display (that of male game fowl, for instance)? Or with masculine prowess of a fairly obvious sort? (Power being, as the cultural critic Henry Kissinger once observed, the ultimate aphrodisiac.)"

JOYCE CAROL OATES, " 'STATE OF THE ART CAR': THE FERRARI TESTAROSSA"

■ EDITING 3: PRACTICE

Edit the following passage, deleting dashes where they are not effective. More than one edited version is possible. Be ready to explain your editing choices.

Jamaica Kincaid's most openly opinionated — and, to my mind, best — book — *A Small Place* — is a social critique of her home island — Antigua. In this book, her voice — humble yet strong, and sometimes filled with anger — speaks for her people. Her feelings — stemming from years of living in Antigua in the aftermath of British imperialism — are expressed in a simple — yet beautiful — manner.

49 **c** **Using ellipsis points**

Ellipsis points are three periods, each preceded and followed by a space. They are used to mark an **ellipsis,** the deliberate omission of words from a direct quotation. Quotations are generally shortened either to make a passage more emphatic or to reduce it to a usable length. (See Chapter 17 and 48c.) Ellipsis points can also be used in dialogue to show a pause or interruption or to create a dramatic pause in informal writing.

Consider the following paragraph from Betty Edwards's *Drawing on the Right Side of the Brain.*

> Drawing is not really very difficult. *Seeing* is the problem, or, to be more specific, shifting to a *particular way of seeing.* You may not believe me at this moment. You may feel that you are seeing things just fine and that it's the drawing that is hard. But the opposite is true, and the exercises in this book are designed to help you make the mental shift and gain a twofold advantage: first, to open access by *conscious volition* to the right side of your brain in order to experience a slightly altered mode of awareness; second, to see things in a different way. Both will enable you to draw well.

Use three ellipsis points to indicate an omission within a sentence.

> Edwards tells the reader, "You may feel that . . . it's the drawing that is hard."

If the omission comes after the end of a complete sentence, use four periods: one period to end the sentence and three to indicate the omission.

> Edwards addresses the reader directly with a provocative assertion: "Drawing is not really very hard. . . . You may not believe me at this moment."

If the end of the quotation you select is also the end of a sentence in the original, use no ellipsis points. If you stop quoting before the end of a sentence in the original, however, insert the ellipsis points to show that the sentence continues.

Edwards acknowledges, "You may feel that you are seeing things just fine and that it's the drawing that is hard. But the opposite is true. . . ."

The first period marks the end of a complete sentence, even though true *was in the middle of a sentence in the original passage.*

Ellipsis points are not necessary when quoting words that are obviously not a complete sentence.

Edwards offers the reader paths to "a slightly altered mode of awareness."

If you omit a whole line or more when quoting poetry, indicate the omission by using ellipsis points for the length of a line.

She walks in beauty, like the night
. . . .
And all that's best of dark and bright
Meet in her aspect and her eyes.

It is never acceptable to omit words such that the meaning of the quoted passage is changed.

■   "Drawing is not ⌒ really very difficult," Edwards tells us.

In dialogue, ellipsis points can be used to indicate a paused or interrupted speech. In informal writing, they can be used to create a pause for dramatic effect.

"The panther tracks come from that direction, . . . but where do they go after that?" he wondered.

For a moment there was silence . . . followed by a rush as the cat bolted from the underbrush.

EDITING 4: PRACTICE

Using ellipsis points, edit the following paragraph to shorten it for a paper on racism. More than one edited version is possible. Be ready to explain your editing choices.

"Until we label an out-group it does not clearly exist in our minds. Take the curiously vague situation that we often meet when a person wishes to locate responsibility on the shoulders of some out-group whose nature he cannot specify. In such a case he usually employs the pronoun 'they' without an antecedent. 'Why don't they make these sidewalks wider?' 'I hear they are going to build a factory in this town and hire a lot of foreigners.' 'I won't pay this tax bill; they can just whistle for their money.' If asked 'who?' the speaker is likely to grow confused and embarrassed. The common use of the orphaned pronoun *they* teaches us that people often want and need to designate out-groups (usually for the purpose of venting hostility) even when they have no clear conception of the out-group in question. And so long as the target of wrath remains vague and ill-defined specific prejudice cannot crystalize around it. To have enemies we need labels."

GORDON ALLPORT, "THE LANGUAGE OF PREJUDICE"

49 d Using brackets

Brackets are square parentheses that look like this: [ ]. They are used to enclose material added to or changed within direct quotations. (See Chapter 17 and 48c.) They can also be used to enclose comments about quotations and to enclose material that is already inside parentheses. If your typewriter or printer does not have brackets, you can write them in by hand.

Consider this passage from an article entitled "Interview with a Sparrow" by E. B. White.

> As yet the onset of Spring is largely gossip among the sparrows. Any noon, in Madison Square, you may see one pick up a straw in his beak, put on an air of great business, twisting his head and glancing at the sky. Nothing comes of it. He hops three or four times and drops both the straw and the incident.

In quoting from this passage, it would be permissible to make small changes and indicate them with brackets in order to clarify the meaning of a reference or of a word or to make the quoted words grammatically compatible with the text surrounding it.

> E. B. White describes just such a spring day: "Any noon, in Madison Square, you may see [a sparrow] pick up a straw in his beak, put on an air of great business, twisting his head and glancing at the sky."

> E. B. White describes a sparrow on a spring day: "Any noon, in Madison Square [in New York City], you may see one pick up a

straw in his beak, put on an air of great business, twisting his head and glancing at the sky."

White concludes by noting that the bird "[hopped] three or four times and [dropped] both the straw and the incident."

If you have added italics (or underlining) to a quoted word in order to emphasize it, inform the reader that the italics are yours by enclosing the words "italics added" in brackets at the end of the passage. (See 53d.)

Did Woolf succeed in making a radical departure from the conventional realism of the British novel? Philip Rahv, in his essay "Mrs. Woolf and Mrs. Brown," argues that she did not. "The ultimate *failure* of Virginia Woolf's experiments might perhaps be explained by going back to her initial conception of reality as an old lady in a railway carriage called Mrs. Brown. [Italics added.]

Brackets can be used to indicate an error in quoted material that was present in the original. By enclosing the word *sic* (Latin for "such") in brackets directly after the error, you inform the reader that you see the error but are not responsible for it.

In its statement, the commission said that its new health insurance program "will not effect [sic] the quality of medical care for county employees."

Generally, you should only do this if the error is significant or if you want to call attention to it. Small mistakes in spelling or punctuation can be corrected, and historical or British spellings can be presented without remark.

Within parentheses, use brackets where you would otherwise use parentheses.

Theodore Bernstein explains that a person who feels sick is *nauseated*: "A person who feels sick is not nauseous any more than a person who has been *poisoned* is *poisonous* (*Dos, Don'ts and Maybes of English Usage* [New York: Times, 1977])."

■ **EDITING 5: PRACTICE**

Edit the following passage, using brackets correctly.

According to the findings of a new study, people who smoke may be hurting not only themselves. "It (tobacco smoke) can be just as detrimental to nonsmokers as to smokers," a spokesperson for the study told reporters. "In fact, secondhand smoke may be even more dangerous," she added, "since they (nonsmokers) are inhaling it without a filter." This latest finding adds to the growing list of the dangers of cigarette smoking. (See the related article on the effects of smoking on fetal development (p. 14).)

49 e Using slashes

A **slash** (/) is a slanted line, also known as a **solidus** or **virgule,** that is used to separate lines of poetry quoted in text, to indicate alternative choices, and to separate figures in certain situations.

Use a slash, preceded and followed by a space, to mark the end of a line of poetry incorporated in text.

> Shakespeare opens *The Passionate Pilgrim* with a seeming paradox: "When my love swears that she is made of truth, / I do believe her, though I know she lies."

(See 48a for more on quoting poetry.)

A slash is used to separate alternatives in expressions such as *an either/or situation, a pass/fail grading system,* and *the president and/or the Congress.* In this usage, no space comes before or after the slash. In formal writing, however, the preferred method is to write out the combination — a pass or fail grading system — when this is possible, rather than to use the slash.

Use a slash to separate month, day, and year in a date given entirely in figures (*7/16/94*) and to separate the numerator and the denominator in a typed fraction that is written in figures (*1/16, 2-3/4*). Note that if the fraction appears in a mixed number, a hyphen is used to separate the whole number from the numerator of the fraction.

EDITING 6: EXPLORATION

Locate two or three examples of professional writing that includes slashes used to present alternatives. Have the authors used the slashes correctly? Do you think that the information has been presented in the best way possible? Is there a better way to present it?

▨ EDITING 7: PRACTICE

Edit the following paragraph, using parentheses, dashes, and brackets correctly. More than one edited version is possible. Be ready to discuss your editing choices.

When you're in the business of selling something, whether it be books or balloons you find out pretty quickly that the market isn't stationery (sic). That means you have to keep moving, too. But how do you find new markets for your product? You should know from the outset that learning about them isn't easy for many reasons, such as the following: a: you might not have personal contacts for example, acquaintances to give you leads, b: you might not have much money for research, c: you might not be very knowledgeable about a certain area, and d: there might not be much information about them (new markets) when you start selling your product. There are thank goodness! a few things you can do to offset the difficulties, though. Keep up with the professional journals and handbooks there's a new one available every month, it seems. And remember to keep smiling, your biggest sale ever could be right around the corner!

▨ EDITING 8: APPLICATION

Examine a paper you are working on for misused or omitted parentheses, dashes, ellipsis points, brackets, and slashes. Is there one kind of error that you make often? If so, think about how best to identify this problem when you edit your work. Edit any sentences in which you have misused or omitted punctuation marks.

Editing Mechanics

The spelling of English words seems sometimes to defy reason. The complexity arises in part because some words sound exactly the same even though they are spelled differently (*their, there, they're*). The same sound may be represented in different letter combinations — as with the long *e* sound in *meet, seat, concrete, petite, conceit,* and *piece.* Conversely, the same letter or letter combination can represent different sounds — such as the *a*'s in *amaze;* the *g*'s in *gorgeous;* and the *ough* in *tough, though,* and *through.*

English spelling reflects the language's many etymological sources. (See 31a for more on the history of the English language.) As English has absorbed words from other languages, it has assumed or adapted their spellings; thus the spelling of a word in English often cannot be determined simply by its pronunciation.

Misspellings can seriously undermine a writer's credibility and, in some cases, can lead readers to misunderstand. *Always* check a good dictionary whenever you are in doubt about how to spell a word. As you edit for spelling, do the following:

- Check for commonly confused words.

- Know and use basic spelling rules.

- Take steps to improve your spelling.

50 a Checking for commonly confused words

Checking for homonyms

Homonyms are words with the same sound but different meanings: *great, grate; fair, fare.* During drafting or revision, writers commonly confuse homonyms such as *their* for *there* or *they're*

CONFUSING CONTRACTIONS

The words on the left are contractions; the words on the right are not. It's easy to make a spelling error by confusing these words, so be careful when you use them.

it's (it is)	its (of it)
they're (they are)	their (of them)
	there (at that place)
who's (who is)	whose (of whom)
you're (you are)	your (of you)

and *write* for *right* or *rite*. During editing, writers must check carefully to make sure they've chosen the right word in each case.

Memory aids can help you distinguish between some homonyms. For example, *piece*, what you slice a pie into, has a *pie* in it, whereas *peace* does not. Knowing word origin or related words can also help. *Rite* is related to *ritual*, in the sense of ceremony. *Write* is descended from an Old English word, *writan*, meaning "to scratch, draw, or engrave." Sometimes examining roots, prefixes, and suffixes is helpful. *Foreword* (the introduction to a book) is a *word* at the *fore*, or *front*; *forward*, or "to the front," is a direction, with a root common to *toward* and *homeward*.

2 Checking for one-word/two-word pairs

Some words can be written either as one word or two: *Maybe Phil is finished. Phil may be finished.* For some words, the spelling depends on meaning.

all ready (completely prepared)	already (previously)
all together (all in one place)	altogether (thoroughly)
all ways (all methods)	always (at all times)
a lot (a large amount)	allot (distribute, assign)
every day (each day)	everyday (ordinary)
may be (could be)	maybe (perhaps)
some time (an amount of time)	sometime (at some unspecified time)

✔ **HOMONYMS AND OTHER SIMILAR-SOUNDING WORDS**

accept (receive)	except (leave out)
access (approach)	excess (too much)
adapt (change)	adopt (choose)
affect (influence)	effect (result)
allude (suggest)	elude (escape)
allusion (suggestion)	illusion (deception)
altar (church table)	alter (change)
ascent (climb)	assent (agree)
bazaar (market)	bizarre (weird)
birth (childbearing)	berth (place of rest)
board (plank, food)	bored (drilled, uninterested)
born (given birth to)	borne (carried)
break (smash, split)	brake (stopping device)
canvas (fabric)	canvass (examine)
capital (city, wealth)	capitol (building)
censor (prohibit)	sensor (measuring device)
cite (mention)	sight (vision)
coarse (rough)	course (way or path)
complement (make complete)	compliment (praise)
conscience (moral judgment)	conscious (aware)
council (committee)	counsel (advice, adviser)
cursor (on a computer display)	curser (swearer)
diary (daily book)	dairy (farm)
desert (dry land)	dessert (sweet food)
dissent (disagreement)	descent (movement down)
dual (having two parts)	duel (fight)
dye (color)	die (perish)
elicit (draw forth)	illicit (improper)
eminent (noteworthy)	imminent (impending)
exercise (activity)	exorcise (drive out)
fair (just)	fare (food)
faze (disturb)	phase (stage)
formerly (at an earlier time)	formally (according to pattern)
forth (forward)	fourth (follows third)
forward (to the front)	foreword (preface)
gorilla (ape)	guerrilla (fighter)
hear (perceive)	here (in this place)
heard (perceived)	herd (group)
heroin (drug)	heroine (principal character)

hole (opening)	whole (entire)
holy (sacred)	wholly (entirely)
horse (animal)	hoarse (rough)
immigrate (come in)	emigrate (leave)
know (be aware)	no (not yes)
lead (metal)	led (guided)
lesson (instruction)	lessen (reduce)
lightning (electric flash)	lightening (making less heavy)
meat (food)	meet (encounter)
miner (excavator)	minor (young person)
pair (two)	pear (fruit)
passed (went by)	past (earlier time)
peace (absence of war)	piece (part, portion)
peer (look)	pier (pillar)
plain (simple)	plane (flat surface)
pray (ask, implore)	prey (feed upon)
principle (rule)	principal (chief person, sum)
quiet (silent)	quite (really, positively)
rain (precipitation)	reign (rule, authority)
right (proper)	rite (ritual)
road (path)	rode (past of *ride*)
scene (stage, setting)	seen (perceived)
sense (perception)	since (from that time)
shone (past of *shine*)	shown (displayed)
stationary (not moving)	stationery (writing paper)
straight (not curved)	strait (narrow place)
tack (angle of approach)	tact (sensitivity, diplomacy)
taut (tight)	taught (past of *teach*)
than (word of comparison)	then (at that time)
threw (past of *throw*)	through (by way of)
to (in the direction of)	too (also)
waist (center of body)	waste (squander)
weak (feeble)	week (seven days)
wear (carry on the body)	where (in what place)
weather (atmospheric conditions)	whether (if, in case)
which (what one)	witch (sorceress)
write (inscribe, record)	wright (builder)

For others, the spelling depends on how the word is used.

> Patricia will try to *work out* her frustrations by exhausting herself at her afternoon *workout*.
>
> *The two words* work out *are a verb; the word* workout *is a noun.*

If you are in doubt as to whether a word should be spelled as one word or two, consult a dictionary. If the word does not appear in the dictionary, it is not spelled as one word. Remember that *cannot* is always spelled as one word.

3 Checking for words with similiar spellings

Misspellings often occur with words that are spelled and pronounced similarly. Sometimes the words are closely related in meaning.

advice (noun)	advise (verb)
breath (noun)	breathe (verb)
chose (past tense)	choose (present tense)
cloths (fabrics)	clothes (garments)
device (noun)	devise (verb)
envelope (noun)	envelop (verb)
human (of people)	humane (merciful)
later (after more time)	latter (in final position)
prophecy (noun)	prophesy (verb)

In other cases the confusion arises because the only spelling difference is in the prefix or suffix: *perspective, prospective; personal, personnel.* If you have trouble with words like these, remembering differences in pronunciation can help you distinguish the correct spelling of the word you intend.

The British spelling of some words differs from the American: *centre* (British), *center* (American); *labour* (British), *labor* (American). British spellings are also used widely in other countries, including Australia, New Zealand, Canada, and India. Instructors in the United States prefer American spellings. If you think you tend to use British spellings or if you are unsure which is the preferred spelling, consult a dictionary.

PRONUNCIATION VERSUS SPELLING

Pronunciation is sometimes a poor guide to spelling. If you try to spell the following words exactly as you say them, you will probably misspell some of them. As you edit words such as these, it may help to pronounce them mentally according to their *spelling*, not as you would normally say them.

accident*a*lly	memento	re*l*evant
arctic	mischiev*ous*	roo*m*mate
ari*th*metic	nuc*l*ear	san*d*wich
a*th*lete	possibly	simi*l*ar
can*d*idate	preju*d*ice	surprise
environment	(noun)	temperature
extra*o*rdinary	prejudice*d*	tentative
February	(adjective)	use*d* to
in*t*erference	prob*a*bly	usu*a*lly
laboratory	pronun*c*iation	veteran
library	quantity	We*d*nesday
literature	re*a*ltor	win*t*ry
mathematics	recognize	

■ EDITING I: PRACTICE

Edit the following passage, looking for commonly confused words.

"Were just about to have our desert. Would you care to join us?"

"Thanks allot, but no. I've all ready eaten — a four-coarse meal."

"Oh, just have one small peace of pie. You can have it plane, without any topping."

"It looks extrordinary, but to tell you the truth, I'm a little afraid of the affect it'll have on my waste. I've been trying to loose weight; my cloths are getting so tight that I can hardly breath."

"Are you getting any exorcise? That's probly the best way to lose weight."

"We'll, I never was much of an athalete, as you know. I have a stationery bike, but I just can not seem to motivate myself to workout. I always seem to find an excuse to put it off until latter."

"I no just what you mean. It's really difficult. And than when I don't exorcise, I have such a guilty conscious."

"Heres an idea: Why don't we lesson our guilt, and meat tomorrow morning at the tennis courts?"

"Alright! Your on!"

50 b   Using basic spelling rules

1 Remembering the *ie/ei* rule and its exceptions

You may already be familiar with the rule about using "*i* before *e*": Put *i* before *e* except after *c*, or when it sounds like "ay" as in *neighbor* and *weigh*. In most cases the rule holds true.

> *i* **before** *e*: belief, field, friend, mischief, niece, patience, piece, priest, review, shield, view
>
> *ei* **after** *c*: ceiling, conceit, conceive, deceit, deceive, receipt
>
> *ei* **sounding like "ay":** eight, feign, freight, sleigh

There are, however, several common exceptions to remember.

> *ie* **after** *c*: ancient, conscience, financier, science, species
>
> *ei* **not after** *c* **or sounding like "ay":** caffeine, codeine, counterfeit, either, feisty, foreign, forfeit, height, leisure, neither, seize, weird

2 Adding suffixes according to spelling rules

A **suffix** is a syllable or sound attached to the end of a word to change its meaning and, sometimes, its part of speech: *tap* + *-ed* =

USING *-CEDE, -CEED,* AND *-SEDE*

Because they have similar sounds, the syllables *-cede, -ceed,* and *-sede* are often confused. The most common is *-cede,* as in *accede, concede, intercede, precede, recede,* and *secede. -Ceed* appears in the words *exceed, proceed,* and *succeed. -Sede* appears only in the word *supersede.*

tapped, align (verb) + *-ment* = *alignment* (noun). (See 31c.) Adding a suffix can sometimes cause changes in the spelling of the base word. In addition, some suffixes are commonly confused with one another. You must attend to both of these concerns when you edit your writing for spelling. (A **prefix** is a sound or syllable attached to the beginning of a word. Adding a prefix almost never causes a spelling change in the base word. However, some prefixes require the use of hyphens; see 52b.)

Suffixes after words ending in y

When adding most suffixes to a word ending in *y*, change the *y* to *i* if the letter before the *y* is a consonant; keep the *y* if the letter before the *y* is a vowel.

CONSONANT BEFORE *y*	friendly + -er	= friendlier
	happy + -ly	= happily
	merry + -ment	= merriment
VOWEL BEFORE *y*	convey + -ed	= conveyed
	annoy + -ance	= annoyance
	pay + -ment	= payment

A few exceptions to this rule involve very short words ending in *y*, such as *dryly, wryly, shyly; daily, gaily.*

If the suffix starts with *i*, the *y* never changes to *i*.

SUFFIX STARTING WITH *y*	apply + -ing = applying
	baby + -ish = babyish

Proper nouns ending in *y* do not change spellings when adding suffixes (for example, *McCarthyism, Kennedyesque*). (See 50b3 for rules about plurals of words ending in *y*.)

Suffixes after words ending in e

In some cases, when a suffix is added to a base word ending in *e*, the final *e* of the base word is dropped. If the suffix begins with a consonant, do not drop the final *e* of the base word.

SUFFIX STARTING WITH CONSONANT	sure + -ly	= surely
	polite + -ness	= politeness
	hate + -ful	= hateful
	state + -ment	= statement

There are a few exceptions to this rule, which should be memorized: *acknowledgment, argument, judgment, duly, truly, wholly, awful, ninth.*

If the suffix begins with a vowel, usually drop the final *e* of the base word.

SUFFIX STARTING WITH VOWEL	admire + -able = admirable
	insure + -ing = insuring
	dance + -er = dancer

There are two major exceptions to this rule. First, the *e* is retained in certain cases to prevent misreading: *dye + ing = dyeing* (not *dying*). Second, if the suffix starts with *a* or *o*, the *e* is retained when it is needed to signal a soft *c* (sounding like *s*, not *k*) or a soft *g* (sounding like *j*). A vowel other than *e* or *i* after a soft *c* or *g* would change it to a hard *c* or *g*.

BASE WORD WITH SOFT *c* OR *g*	enforce + -able = enforceable
	outrage + -ous = outrageous

Suffixes after words ending in a consonant

Usually a suffix added to a word ending in a consonant requires no spelling change. Sometimes, the consonant ending the base word is doubled.

If a suffix beginning with a consonant is added to a word ending in a consonant, simply add the suffix, even if this results in a double letter.

SUFFIX STARTS WITH CONSONANT	cup + -ful = cupful
	defer + -ment = deferment
	open + -ness = openness
	girl + -like = girllike

If a suffix beginning with a vowel is added to a word ending in a consonant, whether to double the final consonant of the base word depends on two things: where the stress is in the base word and what letters precede the final consonant of the base word.

If the stress in the base word is on a syllable other than the last one, do not double the final consonant.

STRESS NOT ON LAST SYLLABLE	barter + -ing = bartering
	benefit + -ed = benefited
	danger + -ous = dangerous

One exception to this rule is *format: formatting, formatted.*

If the final consonant of the base word follows another consonant or two vowels, do not double the final consonant.

FINAL CONSONANT FOLLOWS CONSONANT	hurt + -ing = hurting doubt + -ed = doubted might + -y = mighty
FINAL CONSONANT FOLLOWS TWO VOWELS	cool + -ed = cooled fuel + -ing = fueling sweep + -er = sweeper

If the base word is stressed on the last syllable (or if it is a one-syllable word) and if the final consonant is preceded by a single vowel, double the final consonant.

slap + -ed = slapped	refer + -al = referral
hop + -ing = hopping	occur + -ence = occurrence
abet + -or = abettor	admit + -ing = admitting

If the base word is stressed on the last syllable but adding the suffix changes the pronunciation so the stress of the base word is no longer on the final syllable, do not double the final consonant: *defer* + *ence* = *deference*.

-ly or -ally

The suffix *-ly* or *-ally* turns a noun into an adjective or an adjective into an adverb. Add *-ally* to words that end in *ic*. An exception is *publicly*.

automatically	characteristically
basically	dynamically

Add *-ly* to words that do not end in *ic*.

absolutely	differently
actually	instantly

Most other words that end in *-ally* are formed by adding *-ly* to the adjective suffix *-al: nation, national, nationally*. When adding *-ly* to a word that ends in *l*, keep both *l*'s: *real* + *ly* = *really*.

3 Forming plurals according to spelling rules

Most English nouns are made plural by adding -s: *book, books; page, pages*. There are, however, many exceptions. Fortunately, most of these follow the general rules described here.

General rules for plurals

Nouns ending in *ch*, *s*, *sh*, or *x*, usually are made plural by adding -*es*.

church, churches   glass, glasses   wish, wishes   box, boxes

Nouns ending in *y* are made plural by adding -*s* if the letter before the *y* is a vowel. Otherwise, the plural is formed by changing the *y* to *i* and adding -*es*.

day, days   dairy, dairies
alloy, alloys   melody, melodies

Nouns ending in *o* are often made plural by adding -*s*.

video, videos   trio, trios   duo, duos
burro, burros   Latino, Latinos   inferno, infernos

However, several nouns ending in *o* preceded by a consonant always form their plurals by adding -*es*: *embargo, embargoes; hero, heroes; potato, potatoes; tomato, tomatoes; veto, vetoes.* Other nouns ending in *o* may take either -*s* or -*es* in forming the plural: *zero, zeros, zeroes; volcano, volcanos, volcanoes; tornado, tornados, tornadoes; cargo, cargos, cargoes.*

Many writers find that they usually need to refer to a dictionary for the accepted plural form of words ending in *o*.

Nouns ending in *f* change the *f* to *v* and add -*es* to make the plural in some cases.

leaf, leaves   calf, calves   half, halves
self, selves   loaf, loaves   thief, thieves

Other nouns ending in *f* simply add -*s*.

brief, briefs   chief, chiefs   proof, proofs
belief, beliefs reef, reefs   oaf, oafs

Still others form the plural either way: *hoof, hooves, hoofs.*

Some nouns ending in *fe* change the *f* to *v* before adding *-s*: *wife, wives; life, lives; knife, knives*. But not all nouns ending in *fe* follow this pattern: *safe, safes; fife, fifes; strife, strifes*.

Irregular and unusual plural forms

A few nouns are made plural without adding an *-s* or *-es*.

child, children	foot, feet	goose, geese
man, men	mouse, mice	woman, women

A handful of words have the same form for singular and plural: *moose, moose; sheep, sheep; series, series*.

Many loan words are made plural according to the rules of their original language. Words borrowed from Latin that end in *-us* form their plurals by changing the ending to *-i*: *alumnus, alumni; radius, radii*. Words from Latin that end in *-a* add *-e*: *alumna, alumnae; alga, algae*. Words from Latin that end in *-um* change the ending to *-a*: *datum, data; medium, media*. Words from Greek that end in *-on* change to *-a*: *criterion, criteria*. Greek words ending in *-is* change the ending to *-es*: *analysis, analyses; crisis, crises*.

However, some loan words have Anglicized plurals that are more widely accepted than their original Latin or Greek plurals: *stadiums* rather than *stadia, podiums* rather than *podia*. Some foreign plurals are regarded as singular in English because the true singular form is so rare: *The agenda is brief*.

Plurals of proper nouns

In general, proper nouns form plurals by adding *-s* or *-es*. Adding *-s* when forming the plural does not create an extra syllable in pronunciation: *the Clintons, the Kennedys, several Toms*. When the plural is pronounced with one more syllable than the singular, add *-es*. This usually occurs with proper nouns that end in *ch, s, sh, x*, or *z*: *the Bushes, the Joneses, the Koches, the Katzes*. Do not use an apostrophe to indicate the plural of a proper name.

Plurals of compound nouns

A compound noun consists of two or more words regularly used together. If the compound is written closed, that is, as one word, make the last part plural: *newspapers, henhouses, notebooks*. An exception to this is the word *passersby*.

If a compound noun is written open, as separate words, or if it is hyphenated, make plural the word that expresses the central idea. Usually this is the noun: *attorneys general, brothers-in-law.* If there is more than one noun, make plural the one that expresses the central idea: *bath towels, ladies-in-waiting.*

▊ EDITING 2: PRACTICE

Edit the following passage, using basic spelling rules to eliminate misspelled words.

Early in my senior year of high school, I had to make the very tough decision about where I wanted to go to college. I sent away for brochures and catalogs from a number of schools, and when I recieved them, I leaved threw them to get some ideas of colleges that offerred programs in the engineering feild. I was hopping to get into one of the colleges or universitys in the Midwest, specificly in the state of Michigan. I looked into attendding the University of Michigan, and I saw that it had quite an extensive engineering program. I have an aunt who majorred in mechanical engineering at the University of Michigan, so she is very knowledgable about the program. She told me that it is basicly a very good program but that it is also a lot of work. The curriculum offers many different courses leading to a bachelor of sceince degree. Some of the major subjects are design, solid and fluid mechanics, manufactureing processes and systems, and thermodynamics. In addition to these courses, six courses in the humanitys and social sceince feilds are required. After considerring it for a week, I decided that the University of Michigan was where I would go to get my college education.

50 c Working to improve your spelling

Whenever you encounter a new word, note its spelling. If you look it up in the dictionary, note its origin and its root. A dictionary with information on word history, or etymology, is useful if not essential for improving your spelling.

Keep a personal spelling list. Whenever you misspell a word or look one up to check its spelling, add it to the list. Writing the word will help you remember it. If the word shares a root, prefix, or suffix with other words you already know, that will help you remember the meaning as well as the spelling. You can use a few pages in your journal for your spelling list. If you use a word processor when editing your papers, you may also want to keep a list of words you frequently misspell in a special file on your computer disk. This will make it easy for you to use the search-and-replace function to locate and correct words you often misspell.

If you have a word processing program, use its spell-checking routine to proofread your papers. It will tell you when you have transposed or dropped letters, as in *concieve* for *conceive* or *goverment* for *government*. If you have the right word but have spelled it incorrectly, the computer will point it out to you. However, if your spelling is correct but you have chosen the wrong word, computer spelling aids are worthless. If you confuse *to, too,* and *two,* or *its* and *it's,* the spell checker will not find your error. You must proofread your work even if you used a spell checker.

◼ **EDITING 3: APPLICATION**

Keep a word list for one week. Look up in a dictionary any unfamiliar words that you encounter in your reading or writing, noting the origin and spelling of each word. Record these words on your word list. At the end of the week, review your list of words. Have a friend give you a spelling test, and cross off the words you get right. Start a new list with any you miss.

Capital letters are conventionally used to indicate the beginning of a sentence and to distinguish names, titles, and certain other words. Two special instances of capitalization apply to one-letter words. Always capitalize the first-person singular pronoun *I*. Also capitalize the interjection *O*, used in prayers and to express wonder or surprise: *O best beloved*; *Forgive us, O Lord*. (For information on the capitalization of abbreviations, see Chapter 55.)

As you edit for capitalization, make sure to do the following:

- Capitalize the first word of a sentence.

- Capitalize quotations and lines of poetry as required.

- Capitalize proper nouns and their derivatives.

- Capitalize titles appropriately.

51 a **Capitalizing the first word of a sentence**

Use a capital letter at the beginning of a sentence or a deliberate sentence fragment. Capital letters help readers recognize where each sentence starts.

Alfred enjoyed working in the garden. And in the conservatory.

In a series of fragmentary questions, most writers capitalize the first letter of each fragment, although it is equally acceptable to use lowercase for each fragment.

What, we wondered, was the occasion? A holiday? Someone's birthday?

Whichever style of capitalization you choose, be sure to use it consistently throughout your paper.

Two independent clauses can be joined with a colon: *He decided to work as a carpenter's apprentice that summer: he needed the money.* (See 33c.) When the first clause introduces the second, which contains the main point, you may capitalize the first letter of the clause following the colon. (See Chapter 46.) A numbered list of sentences following a colon should always be capitalized.

> His philosophy can be reduced to three basic rules: (1) Think for yourself. (2) Take care of your body. (3) Never hurt anyone.

Capitalize the first word of a complete sentence within parentheses if it is not inside another sentence. The first word of a sentence set off by dashes or by parentheses within another sentence is not capitalized.

> Congress attacked sex discrimination in sports with a 1972 law called Title IX. (Changes added in 1974 are called the Bayh amendments.)
>
> Title IX (the name refers to a section of U.S. civil rights law) has changed collegiate sports a great deal over twenty years. On many campuses Title IX has increased the number of competitive sports offered to women — even opponents of the law agree this is true — but its effect on men's sports is more difficult to assess.

---

51 **b** **Capitalizing quotations and lines of poetry**

 Quotations

Capitalize the first word of a quotation if it is the first word of the sentence you are writing or if it is the first word of the sentence by the original speaker or writer.

> "We'd like to talk to you about the budget for women's sports," Jeannine told the athletic director. "Ryan has the first question."
>
> Ryan asked, "How many sports are offered?"

Do not capitalize the first word of a continuation of a quotation interrupted by attributory words.

> "Indeed," Mr. Kott responded, "we field men's and women's teams in track, swimming, tennis, and golf."

Do not capitalize the first word of a quotation if the word does not begin a sentence of yours or a sentence in the original.

> Recognizing details familiar from his childhood, E. B. White feels "the same damp moss covering the worms in the fishing can."

When quoting from published sources, you may have to change the capitalization of the original to fit your sentence. If you use a capital letter where the original has a lowercase letter, or a lowercase letter where the original has a capital, use brackets to show the change. (See 49d.)

2 Capitalizing quotations from poetry

When quoting poetry, always follow the capitalization of the original.

> The poem opens with Frost's usual directness and rhythmic formality: "Whose woods these are, I think I know. / His house is in the village, though." Compare this to Lucille Clifton's offhanded "boys / i don't promise you nothing . . ."

(See Chapters 48 and 49 for more on punctuating quotations.)

51 c Capitalizing proper nouns and their derivatives

Proper nouns name particular persons, places, or things: *John Smith*, *Atlantic Ocean*, *Mercedes*. In general, proper nouns should be capitalized. Note that any articles, coordinating conjunctions, and prepositions in a proper name are not capitalized.

If you find that you have incorrectly capitalized a name once in your paper, it is likely that you have made the same mistake elsewhere. Use your computer's search-and-replace function to find all such errors and replace them with correctly capitalized names. Be careful, however, when searching for words whose capitalization depends on context, such as *ocean* in *the Atlantic Ocean* and *the vast ocean*. You may want to have the computer stop at each use of the word so you can decide whether or not it should be changed.

Individual people and animals

Capitalize names and nicknames of individual people and animals, except for people who expressly want their names to be spelled with lowercase letters. Rules for spelling surnames containing words such as *van, de, la,* and so on vary from language to language and case to case. Consult a biographical dictionary or the biographical section of a regular dictionary for the conventional spelling of a particular name.

Eleanor Roosevelt	Catherine the Great
Karl Marx	e. e. cummings
Snoopy	Vincent van Gogh
Buffalo Bill	Martin Van Buren

Capitalize words describing family relationships only when they are used as names: *The family gave a party for Mother and Aunt Carol. My mother and my aunt are twins.*

Religions and religious terms

Capitalize the names of religions, members of a religion, religious sects, deities, and sacred works.

Judaism, Jews	Christianity, Christians
Roman Catholic	Protestant
God	Allah
the Koran	the Bible

Nationalities, ethnic groups, and languages

Capitalize the names of nationalities, ethnic groups, and languages.

French	Chinese	Hindustani
Chicano	Slavic	Latin

Titles

Capitalize formal and courtesy titles and their abbreviations when used before a name and not set off by commas.

Sir Edmund Hillary	Senator Dianne Feinstein
President Bill Clinton	Prof. Cox
Pope John Paul II	Dr. Wu
Ms. Taggart	Mr. Patten

Lowercase such titles when used alone or separated from the name by commas: *my physics professor, Alice Cox.*

You may capitalize titles not followed by a name when they indicate high station or office: *the President of the United States.* Derivatives of titles are not capitalized: *presidential, professorial.*

Months, days of the week, and holidays

Capitalize the names of months, the days of the week, and holidays, but not numbers or seasons.

August 12, 1914	summer
Tuesday, the twentieth of April	spring
Arbor Day	winter

Geographic names

Capitalize the names and nicknames of cities, states, countries, provinces, regions, bodies of water, and other geographical features.

Little Rock, Arkansas	the Western Hemisphere
France	the Midwest
the Grand Canyon	the Atlantic Ocean
the Windy City	the Rockies

Capitalize common nouns like *river, avenue, street,* and *square* when they are part of a place name, but use lowercase letters when they are preceded by two or more proper nouns: *Arlington Street* but *Bleecker and MacDougal streets.*

Although direction words are capitalized when they name a region (*the South*), they are not when they indicate compass directions: *We headed south on U.S. 61.*

Institutions, organizations, and businesses

Capitalize the names of institutions, organizations, and businesses.

Oberlin College	the Internal Revenue Service
the United Nations	Congress
the English Department	Planned Parenthood
Procter & Gamble	the Veterans of Foreign Wars

Be sure to capitalize only the proper name of an institution, not a generic term referring to it: *Oberlin is ranked among the best small colleges in the country.*

Words such as *company, incorporated,* and *limited* and their abbreviations are capitalized when they are used as part of a business's formal name: *Jones Brothers Limited.* They are not capitalized when they are not part of the formal name: *The company is on the verge of bankruptcy.*

Historical documents, events, and periods

Capitalize the names of historical documents (including legislative acts) and well-known events or periods. Many writers also capitalize the names of major movements in art, music, literature, and philosophy.

the Constitution	the Norman Conquest
the Stone Age	World War II
the Stamp Act	the Renaissance
the Romantic poets	Public Law 100-13
an Impressionist painter	the Modern movement

Ships, aircraft, spacecraft, and trains

Capitalize the names of individual vehicles. (See 53b for guidelines on italicizing names of vehicles.)

the U.S.S. *Constitution*	the *Spirit of St. Louis*
the *Challenger*	the Orient Express

Derivatives of proper nouns

Adjectives and other words derived from all the proper nouns just discussed are capitalized, except where noted otherwise.

Newtonian	Texan
Marxist	American

Prefixes before such derivatives are not capitalized: *neo-Marxist, anti-American.* (See 52b for information on hyphenating prefixes before proper adjectives.)

Words derived from proper nouns that have taken on independent meanings often are no longer capitalized: *french fries, herculean, quixotic, ohm, vulcanization.*

51 d Capitalizing titles

For the title of a book, play, essay, story, poem, movie, television program, piece of music, or work of art, capitalize the first word, the last word, and all other words except articles (*the, a, an*), coordinating conjunctions (*and, or, for, but, nor, so, yet*), and prepositions (*in, on, with, by, upon, at, between,* and so on).

Pride and Prejudice	"What I Did for Love"
The Taming of the Shrew	*Beauty and the Beast*
"Why I Live at the P.O."	*Nude Descending a Staircase*

Follow the same rule for subtitles, including capitalizing the first word: *An Architecture for Democracy: The Bellmont Civic Center.*

If a title contains words joined by a hyphen, both words usually are capitalized, with the exception of articles, conjunctions, and prepositions (*The One-Minute Grammarian; The Social History of the Jack-in-the-Box*).

(See 48d and 53a on the use of quotation marks and italics for titles.)

■ EDITING 1: PRACTICE

Edit the following passage, using capital letters according to the guidelines in this chapter.

The renaissance, a term that means "rebirth," began in italy in the mid-fourteenth century and spread throughout western Europe by the middle of the sixteenth century. and what a time of rebirth! With the help of numerous patrons of the arts, such as the Medici Family in Florence, learning, literature, and the arts flourished. Lorenzo de' Medici was the influential patron of the great artist Botticelli, whose works include *The birth of Venus* and *La primavera.* (the works of Botticelli became great favorites of the Pre-Raphaelites.)

The pursuit of literature and the arts was also fostered by Popes, such as Pope Nicholas V. Petrarch and Boccaccio were among the first writers to become interested in secular literature. Before the renaissance, most of the literature read in their christian society had been related to the church. During the Renaissance, an interest in reading latin and greek literature grew, and many people put their energy into collecting manuscripts, often ransacking monastic libraries throughout europe to obtain them. Countless old manuscripts are now housed in many of the great museums and libraries of the world, including the British museum.

The Renaissance was also a turning point in philosophy and science. Galileo and Copernicus, for example, made great discoveries in the field of astronomy.

◼ EDITING 2: APPLICATION

Examine a paper you are working on for mistakes in capitalization. Is there one kind of mistake in using capitalization that you consistently make? If so, think about how best to identify words that should and should not be capitalized when you edit your work. Edit any sentences in which you have made capitalization mistakes.

52 Hyphenation

The hyphen helps readers understand how words are to be read. A hyphen can link two words, or two parts of a word, that might otherwise be seen as separate. A hyphen can also separate two parts of a word, such as a prefix and a base word, that might be misleading or hard to read if written as one word. Finally, hyphens have conventional uses in numbers, fractions, and units of measure.

As you edit for hyphens, make sure to do the following:

- Hyphenate words that are divided at the ends of lines.

- Hyphenate after certain prefixes.

- Hyphenate certain compound words.

- Hyphenate some fractions, numbers, and units of measure.

52 a Hyphenating words at the ends of lines

If a word is too long to fit at the end of a line, you can divide it in two parts, using a hyphen at the end of the first part to signal to readers that the word continues on the next line. It is better not to divide words, but if you must, be sure to do so at an acceptable point. Whenever you are in doubt about where to hyphenate a word, consult a dictionary. The divisions in the entry word indicate where it may be hyphenated at the end of a line. Here are six helpful guidelines.

1. Divide only between syllables. On encountering a hyphen at the end of a line, a reader must pause before reading the rest of the word. Make sure that pause falls at a natural point, one that corresponds to a break between pronounced syllables. One-syllable words such as *eighth*, *through*, *dreamed*, and *urged* cannot be divided without suggesting an incorrect pronunciation.

2. Do not leave just one letter on a line. A reader encountering an *i-* at the end of a line, for example, has no indication whether that *i* is pronounced as in *idea* or *idiot*. Thus a word like *icon* cannot be divided, and a word like *iambic* can only be divided *iam-bic*, not *i-ambic*.

3. Divide at prefixes or suffixes. Rather than divide base words, divide after a prefix or before a suffix, to leave both parts recognizable: not *an-tibody* but *anti-body*; not *ea-gerness* but *eager-ness*.

4. Divide between compounds. The most natural place to divide a compound word like *motherland* is where its parts join: *mother-land*, *sword-fish*. Divide a hyphenated compound word (such as *self-esteem* or *son-in-law*) at the hyphen.

5. Take care with double letters. A word with an internal double letter usually divides between the letters: *syl-la-ble*, *wil-low*. If a base word ends with a double letter, keep the double letter together and divide before a suffix: *access-ible*, *assess-ment*. If, however, the final consonant is doubled only when the suffix is added, put the second consonant with the suffix: *cut*, *cut-ting*; *abet*, *abet-ting*. (See 50b.)

6. Double-check your computer's hyphenation. Many computer word processing programs can automatically hyphenate a document as you write or as a final step just before printing. Some programs refer to a dictionary contained in a computer file for permissible hyphenation; others hyphenate by using criteria similar to those just discussed. In either case, the computer's decisions about hyphenation may be less than perfect. If you choose not to hyphenate any words, most programs allow you to turn off hyphenation. If you take advantage of your computer's ability to hyphenate, be sure to double-check its decisions.

▪ **EDITING I: PRACTICE**

Indicate the best place for hyphenating each of the following words. If a word contains more than two syllables, indicate all possible hyphenation points. Not all these words can be hyphenated. You may want to use a dictionary to check your hyphenation.

1.	coordinated	**6.**	minibus
2.	acquitted	**7.**	ignite
3.	preparedness	**8.**	overcast
4.	width	**9.**	commitment
5.	crossbones	**10.**	antidote

52 b Hyphenating after some prefixes

Most words that include prefixes are written without hyphens: *disembark*. However, in some words a hyphen is used after the prefix to prevent misreading. When in doubt as to whether a prefix needs a hyphen after it, consult your dictionary. The following guidelines cover most of the common uses of hyphens following prefixes.

When a prefix is attached to a capitalized word or to a date, use a hyphen: *pre-Cambrian, pre-1990*. (Note that the prefix itself is usually not capitalized.)

A prefix attached to a term with more than one word needs a hyphen: *post-World War II, anti-labor union*.

A few prefixes such as *all-, ex-, self-*, and *quasi-* almost always use hyphens: *all-inclusive, ex-convict, self-hypnosis*. (Note that *-self* used as a suffix never takes a hyphen: *myself, herself*.)

When a prefix ends with the same letter that begins the base word, a hyphen can be used: *anti-intellectual, co-ownership*. However, the hyphen has been dropped from many such words: *cooperate, preexisting, unnatural*. Because the use of hyphens in such words is unpredictable, it is usually best to check a dictionary.

A hyphen is occasionally used to distinguish between two different words spelled with the same letters, especially when there is a strong chance of a misreading.

We asked them to *refund* our money.

Congress will *re-fund* [fund again] the program for another year.

When two prefixes separated in a sentence by a conjunction apply to the same base word, add a hyphen after both prefixes.

We compared the *pre- and post-election* analyses.

52 c Hyphenating compound words

Two or more words used as a single unit form a **compound word.** Many compounds are written as one word, sometimes called a closed compound: *workhorse, schoolteacher*. Other compounds are written as two words, or open compounds: *hope chest, lunch break, curtain rod*. Still others, like *great-grandson, mother-in-law*, and *stick-in-the-mud*, are hyphenated compounds.

Compound nouns that are spelled as one word or that are hyphenated can be found in the dictionary. If you are in doubt as to how to spell a compound noun, check the dictionary. If you do not find the compound there, write it as an open compound. In general, most compound nouns formed of more than two words are hyphenated: *jack-of-all-trades.*

A **compound adjective** consists of two or more modifiers that function together as a single adjective before a noun. Compound adjectives are usually hyphenated: *a long-blooming peony, a late-night party.* This makes it clear that the group of words includes two or more modifiers and a one-word noun rather than a single modifier and a compound noun. For example, compare the meanings of the following sentences.

Mr. Donovan is an old car collector.

He is an old person who collects cars.

Mr. Donovan is an old-car collector.

He is a person who collects old cars.

This sort of clarification is unnecessary when a group of modifiers come after the noun it modifies, so no hyphen is needed.

The *well-liked* teacher has become a civic leader.

The teacher, who is *well liked,* has become a civic leader.

If the compound adjective is so well established as a noun that misreading is unlikely, no hyphen is needed: *post office box* (not *post-office box*), *high school student* (not *high-school student*).

No hyphen is ever used between an adverb ending in *-ly* and the adjective it modifies: *a highly motivated employee, a strongly worded statement.*

| 52 | d | **Hyphenating numbers, fractions, and units of measure** |

Hyphenate two-word numbers from twenty-one to ninety-nine. Do not hyphenate before or after *hundred, thousand,* or *million.*

fifty-seven   twenty-two hundred
two hundred fifty-seven   six hundred twenty thousand

Remember that long numbers are often easier to read when expressed in figures. (See 54a.)

A hyphen is used between the numerator and denominator of a spelled-out fraction unless one of them is already hyphenated.

one-half   two-thirds
twenty-one fiftieths

When a number includes a unit of measure (feet, inches, miles, pounds), hyphenate modifiers but not nouns.

An ordinary dump truck has a *nine-cubic-yard* bed.

Only a gardener would delight in *nine cubic yards* of manure.

When expressing a person's age, hyphenate the construction *five-year-old* as a noun and as a modifier, but do not hyphenate *five years old.*

A hyphen can be used to suggest a range between numbers: *1987–90, 120–140 times a year.* However, readers generally find it clearer if the range is described in words: *from 1987 to 1990; between 120 and 140 times a year.* Do not combine the two methods: *they attended the college from 1987 to 1990* (not *from 1987–1990*).

■ EDITING 2: PRACTICE

Edit the following passage, hyphenating all words where necessary and deleting unnecessary hyphens. You may have to consult a dictionary.

Twenty five years ago, Massachusetts was in a state of steady decline. The economy of the pre 1970s had been built upon industries that were now out of date and rundown. Un-employment was on the rise, and the future looked grim for the state's residents. But early in the 1970s, the situation began to improve, as Massachusetts embarked on what became known as the "Massachusetts Miracle." Thanks to an ex-plosion of high tech industries and products such as mini-computers, the economy started to turn around dramatically. Pre-existing industries began to die out, and the economy boomed with new industries, new companies, and new jobs for thousands of previously-unemployed workers. With more hightech companies than any-where in the country except California's well known Silicon Valley, Massachusetts became one of the wealthiest states. Its prosperity seemed neverending. Literally thousands of companies were started in Massachusetts from 1973–1988.

■ EDITING 3: APPLICATION

Examine a paper you are working on for hyphenation mistakes. Is there one kind of mistake in using hyphens that you consistently make? If so, think about how best to remember hyphenation rules when you edit your work. Edit any sentences in which you have misused or omitted hyphens.

Most books, magazines, and academic papers use a roman typeface for the main body of the text. The sentence you are reading
now, for example, is set in roman type. An italic typeface — *which
looks like this* — can then be used to distinguish certain words
from the main body of the text, usually to indicate that they must
be interpreted in a slightly different manner.

If you are writing a paper with a typewriter or using a computer that does not have an italic typeface, indicate words that
would be italicized by underlining them, like this: <u>Underlining and
italicizing are equivalent.</u>

As you edit for italics, make sure to do the following:

- Italicize certain titles.

- Italicize the names of most individual vehicles.

- Italicize foreign words that have not been adopted into English.

- Italicize words to indicate emphasis.

- Italicize words, letters, and numbers used as words.

53 a   Italicizing titles

Italicize the titles of books, plays, operas and other long musical works, movies, recordings, newspapers, magazines, television
or radio series, long poems considered to be independent works,
and works of art. Use quotation marks rather than italics for titles
that are subdivisions of a larger work. For example, put quotation
marks around the song title "Nature Boy" from Natalie Cole's
recording *Unforgettable.* (See 48d for more on using quotation
marks for titles.)

The titles of sacred works, parts of sacred works, and ancient
manuscripts are not italicized: the Bible, the Talmud; Genesis; the

Book of Kells. The titles of public documents also appear without italics: the Constitution, the Declaration of Independence.

The Modern Language Association style for academic papers suggests neither capitalizing nor italicizing the article (*a*, *an*, or *the*) in the name of a newspaper or magazine, even if the newspaper or magazine includes it in its own name, as does [*The*] *New York Times*. Nevertheless, publications, like most of us, prefer to be addressed by the names they have chosen. So consider following a publication's own style when writing about, for, and especially *to* one.

(For information on titles within titles, see 48d.)

 ITALICS AND QUOTATION MARKS FOR TITLES

ITALICS	QUOTATION MARKS
Holy the Firm (book)	"Newborn and Salted" (chapter)
	"Gift of the Magi" (short story)
Goblin Market and Other Poems (poetry collection)	"Goblin Market" (poem)
Song of Roland (long poem considered an independent work)	
Oklahoma! (musical)	"Oklahoma!" (song)
Carmen (opera)	
Nick of Time (long musical recording)	
Rhapsody in Blue (long musical composition)	
The Simpsons (television series)	"Homer Meets Godzilla" (episode)
Silence of the Lambs (movie)	
Waiting for Godot (play)	
New Republic (magazine)	"Icy Words on Global Warming" (article)
New York Times (newspaper)	"The Tariff Party" (article)
The Boating Party (painting)	
Reclining Nude (sculpture)	

53 **b** **Italicizing the names of individual trains, ships, airplanes, and spacecraft**

Italicize the official names of individual trains, ships, airplanes, and spacecraft.

the *Shasta Daylight* (train)   *Spirit of St. Louis* (airplane)
the U.S.S. *Arizona* (ship)   *Voyager* (spacecraft)

Do not italicize names that apply to a whole class or series of vehicles: a Polaris rocket, a Trident nuclear submarine.

53 **c** **Italicizing foreign words**

English is full of words borrowed from other languages. Words such as *moccasin*, *rococo*, *hors d'oeuvres*, and *burro* have become a familiar part of the language and require no special treatment.

We rode the burros into the canyon.

However, words that have been borrowed more recently may be unfamiliar to the reader and should be distinguished by italics.

"*Bon appétit!*" she said as we started our meal.

One way to tell whether a word has become part of the language is to look it up in the dictionary. If a word or term is in the dictionary and there is no indication that it is usually written in italics, you may use roman type. If the word is not in the dictionary, using italics is usually safer. (Be sure to consult a recent dictionary, as these categories change quickly.)

Always italicize a foreign word or phrase that you are introducing for the first time.

The Hawaiian word for that smooth, ropelike lava is *pahoehoe*.

The Latin names used to classify plants and animals by genus and species are also italicized: *Cypripedium acaule*. (Note that the genus name is capitalized but the species name is not.)

53 d Italicizing for emphasis

Italics can be used to indicate that a certain word should receive special emphasis within a sentence.

> Some 90% of executive men but only 35% of executive women have children by the age of 40. The *automatic* association of all women with babies is clearly unjustified.
>
> FELICE N. SCHWARTZ, "MANAGEMENT WOMEN AND THE NEW FACTS OF LIFE"

Be careful not to overuse italics for emphasis; if many words in a passage are italicized, the use of italics loses its impact. Also avoid using italics as a shortcut when you can create the proper emphasis through other means. (See Chapter 27.)

You can use italics in quotations to call attention to a precise word in the original source. If you italicize to add emphasis in a quoted passage, tell readers so by enclosing a phrase such as "Italics added" within brackets at the end of the passage. (See 49d.)

53 e Italicizing words, letters, and numbers used as words

Whenever you use a word, letter, or number to stand only for itself rather than the concept it usually symbolizes, use italics.

> By the term *liberal*, he meant anyone who disagreed with him.
>
> Every time I type quickly, I begin to substitute *y* for *u*.
>
> Because he read the *1* as a *7*, his calculations were incorrect.

■ EDITING I: PRACTICE

Edit the following passage, making sure words are italicized according to convention.

Before planting a garden it is a good idea to consult a reputable source for tips on successful gardening. Many newspapers, such as the New York Times, have a weekly column devoted to gardening. There are also many useful books, such as "A Guide to Growing Gorgeous Greenery," with its especially helpful introductory chapter, *Plan before You Plant.*

First a gardener should learn about the different types of plants. Annuals is the term given to plants that complete their lifetime in one year; the term *perennials* is used for plants that grow back every year. Many annuals are popular with gardeners, especially the Begonia semperflorens and the Petunia hybrida.

Another issue for gardeners to consider is pesticides. Environmentally conscious gardeners are not opposed to pesticides *per se*, but they use only organic pesticides, which derive from *natural* rather than *synthetic* substances.

Gardening books are useful sans doute, and they may prevent the worst *faux pas* in the garden, but in the end there is no one way to make a garden — chacun à son goût!

■ **EDITING 2: APPLICATION**

Examine a paper you are working on for mistakes in italicizing. Is there one kind of mistake in using italics that you consistently make? If so, think about how best to remember which words to italicize when you edit your work. Edit any sentences in which you have misused or omitted italics.

Many techniques of analysis and persuasion depend on numbers. When you research, you identify the numbers that accurately describe your findings. When you write, you find or develop numbers that support your position. When you edit, you must ensure that numbers are presented effectively and clearly. Clarity is important because numbers can be confusing to many people. The more numbers and the more different kinds of numbers used in a piece of writing, the more likely readers are to become confused or intimidated.

As you edit for the use of numbers, make sure to do the following:

- Choose between words and figures for numbers according to the situation.

- Use figures when required by convention.

---

54 a **Choosing between figures and words according to context**

Conventions for choosing between figures and words for numbers vary according to discipline. The guidelines given here cover most nontechnical writing (including writing in literature and other humanities) and most technical writing (including writing in the social and natural sciences). For more information, consult the style guide of your discipline. (See Chapters 59–63.)

In scientific and technical writing, most numbers, especially measurements or statistics, are written in figures.

The pressure increased by 3 kilograms per square centimeter.

Fewer than 1/10 of the eggs failed to hatch.

The test pilots all reported lightheadedness in turns exceeding 4g.

In general, nontechnical academic writing, write out in words the numbers one hundred and below as well as all fractions. (See 52d about using hyphens in numbers.)

thirty universities

three-fourths of the class

For numbers over one hundred, write out round numbers if they can be expressed in two words. Otherwise, use figures.

five hundred students	517 students
more than fifty thousand trees	52,317 trees

It is sometimes clearer to express very large round numbers using a combination of words and figures: *The Census Bureau says that the U.S. population exceeds 250 million.*

In both technical and nontechnical writing, treat consistently any numbers that readers must compare with each other. If you must use figures for one number according to a particular rule, use them as well for the other numbers in that category.

■ In Midville last year, ~~eighty-seven~~ 87 cats and 114 dogs were

destroyed by the humane society.

In both nontechnical and technical writing, use words for any number that begins a sentence. If you think writing out a long number at the beginning of a sentence is awkward, rewrite the sentence.

■ ~~547~~ *Five hundred forty-seven* students attended the concert.

■ *Attending the concert were* 547 students. ~~attended the concert.~~

The following cases, by convention, require the use of figures, even in nontechnical writing.

ESL **SINGULAR AND PLURAL FORMS OF NUMBERS**

When the word for a number is used as a plural noun without another number before it, use the plural form of the word. You may also need to use the word *of* after it.

The news report said there were only a few protesters at the nuclear power plant, but we saw *hundreds*.

Dozens of geese headed south today.

When the word for a number is preceded by another number, use the singular form of the word, and do not use *of* with it.

There were approximately *two hundred* protesters.

At least *three dozen* geese flew over the lake today.

When a word expressing a unit of weight, money, time, or distance is used with the word for a number as a hyphenated adjective, always use the singular forms for both words.

That movie lasted *three hours*.

It was a *three-hour* movie.

In dates

11 April 1994
July 16, 1896

the year 1357 B.C.E.
A.D. 914

In addresses

2551 Polk Street, Apt. 3
San Francisco, CA 94109

With abbreviations and symbols

3500 rpm
65 mph
74%

37°C
$62.23
53¢

In discussions that use numbers infrequently, you may use words to express percentages and amounts of money if you can do so in two or three words: *seventy-four percent* and *fifty cents*, but not *sixty-two dollars and twenty-three cents*. If you use words for the number, be sure to use words for "percent," "dollars," and "cents" rather than the symbols for these concepts.

For time

12:15 A.M.   2330 hours

Note that numbers used with *o'clock, past, to, till,* and *until* are generally written out as words: *at seven o'clock, twenty past one.*

For decimal fractions

2.7 seconds   35.4 miles

For cross-references and citations

Chapter 56   line 25
volume 3, pages 13–17   act 3, scene 2

(See Chapters 59–63 for specific documentation formats.)

ESL   PUNCTUATING NUMBERS

Numbering systems throughout the world differ in their use of punctuation. Some numbering systems use a period to mark divisions of thousands, so that *ten thousand* is written 10.000. In the United States, commas are used to mark divisions of thousands.

In 1989, the population of Ecuador was 10,262,271.

In the United States, the period is used as a decimal point to separate whole numbers from decimal fractions.

Seven and a half can also be written 7.5.

◼ EDITING 1: PRACTICE

Edit the following passage, making sure all numbers are handled appropriately for nontechnical writing.

At 10 o'clock this morning, after a seven-hour journey, the peacekeeping force turned back when stopped by a crowd of 300 demonstrators. At least

1/4 of the angry demonstrators were armed, and they claimed to have more than three thousand rounds of ammunition. The 33 trucks left the area and drove toward the nearest town sixty miles to the west. The peacekeeping force had been carrying food and medicine for the more than thirteen thousand five hundred sick and wounded citizens. That number will probably grow, with temperatures expected to drop below twenty degrees later this month.

■ EDITING 2: APPLICATION

Examine a paper you are working on for numbers that you have handled incorrectly. Is there one kind of mistake in using numbers that you consistently make? If so, think about how best to remember how to handle numbers when you edit your work. Edit any sentences in which you have handled numbers incorrectly.

Abbreviations are frequently used in tables, footnotes, endnotes, and bibliographies to help readers proceed through the material quickly and easily. (Documentation and its acceptable abbreviations are discussed in Chapters 59–63.) They are also used quite often in scientific and technical writing. With a few exceptions, however, you should avoid abbreviations in the body of a general, nontechnical essay, paper, or report. This chapter discusses abbreviations that are acceptable in nontechnical text.

When you want to use an abbreviation, you must ask yourself three questions. First, is the abbreviation appropriate for the paper you're writing? Second, have you used it in a way that will be easy for readers to understand? Third, have you correctly punctuated and capitalized it? Be guided by the conventions of the discipline and genre in which you are writing and by the guidelines presented in this chapter.

The search-and-replace function available with most word processing programs can simplify the task of ensuring that you have correctly spelled, punctuated, and capitalized all abbreviations. If you have abbreviated a word or term incorrectly once, it is likely that you have made the same mistake elsewhere in your paper. You can ask the computer to search for all such incorrect abbreviations and replace them with correct abbreviations.

Additionally, the spell-checking programs available with most word processors will stop at an unusual abbreviation and ask you whether you've spelled it correctly; some spell checkers may query all abbreviations. This is a good way for you to see if you've used an abbreviation that may be unfamiliar to your readers.

As you edit, remember that in some cases you may do the following:

■ Abbreviate titles and degrees.

■ Abbreviate with numbers and symbols.

ABB **55** **a**

Abbreviating titles and degrees 713

- Abbreviate in addresses.

- Abbreviate common Latin terms.

- Use initials and acronyms.

55 **a** Abbreviating titles and degrees

Personal or courtesy titles such as *Mr.*, *Mrs.*, *Dr.*, and *St.* may be abbreviated when they precede a full name. For each word that is abbreviated, capitalize the first letter only and put a period after the word. Two exceptions are the abbreviations LL.D. (for a doctorate in law) and LL.B. (for a bachelor degree in law). If there is more than one word in the abbreviation, usually you should write them together, with no space in between.

Mr. Samuel Taylor Darling	Dr. Ellen Hunter
St. Francis of Assisi	Prof. Karen Greenberg
Gen. Colin Powell	Gov. Betty Roberts
Rep. Tom Foley	Sen. Bill Bradley
the Rev. Martin Luther King, Jr.	

Never abbreviate *president* or *mayor*. (Note that *Miss* is not an abbreviation, so it is written without a period. The courtesy title *Ms.* ends with a period even though it is not an abbreviation.)

When *Mr.*, *Mrs.*, and *Dr.* appear before a surname only, they are still abbreviated. Most writers spell out other titles before a surname used alone.

Mr. Wang	Professor Greenberg
Dr. Gallaher	Senator Bradley

Whenever titles appear apart from a name, they are spelled out.

- Raisha Goldblum has been named assistant ~~prof.~~ *professor* of chemistry.

Titles or degrees such as *Esq.*, *M.D.*, *LL.D.*, *J.D.*, and *Ph.D.* that follow a name are always abbreviated, as are generational titles such as *Jr.* and *Sr.* They are set off by commas in a sentence:

He talked to Thomas Burke, Jr., and Karen Burke. Do not use both *Dr.* and a degree.

■ ~~Dr.~~ Barry Qualls, Ph.D., will speak at commencement.

55 **b** Abbreviating numerals and symbols

Use *A.M.* and *P.M.* (or *a.m.* and *p.m.*), for *ante meridiem* and *post meridiem*, with specific times of day. Using either capital letters or lowercase letters is fine, but be consistent. Use *B.C.* and *A.D.*, for *before Christ* and *anno Domini*, for calendar years; to avoid a religious reference, many writers substitute *B.C.E.* (*before Common Era*) and *C.E.* (*Common Era*). Notice that only *A.D.* precedes the year.

3:45 P.M.   A.D. 376 (or 376 C.E.)

425 B.C. (or 425 B.C.E.)

Other acceptable abbreviations in nontechnical text are *F* for degrees Fahrenheit and *C* for degrees Celsius in temperatures, *no.* or *No.* for *number*, and *mph* for *miles per hour*.

The prime minister's official residence is No. 10 Downing Street.

California has a speed limit of 65 mph for cars and 55 mph for trucks.

In scientific or technical writing, abbreviations for units of measure are acceptable with figures. They are usually used without periods.

To 750 ml of this solution was added 200 mg of sodium cyanate.

Most units of measure may be abbreviated on second mention if they are adequately defined at the first mention. (If you place your cursor at the beginning of your computer file, the search function can easily locate the first use of an abbreviation.)

ABB **55** **C**

The engine develops maximum torque at 2900 revolutions per minute (rpm). Peak power is achieved at 6500 rpm.

Symbols are often used with abbreviations. Symbols acceptable in nontechnical writing include those for degrees (°), percents (%), and dollars ($), when they are used with figures denoting specific quantities. Spell out the words for symbols when they are used without figures. Always use *and* rather than an ampersand (&).

By definition, 100°C equals 212°F, the boiling point of water.

The bill came to $35.99.

He dreamed about what he would do with a million dollars.

55 **C** **Abbreviating geographic names**

Abbreviate geographic names when addressing a piece of mail. For state names, use the U.S. Postal Service abbreviations, which have two capital letters and no periods. For other abbreviations, capitalize the first letter only and put a period after the word.

Lila Branch
100 W. Glengarry Dr.
Birmingham, MI 48009

When presenting a full address in text, spell out everything but the state name. When presenting less than a full address, spell out everything.

His address was 1109 West Green Street, Harrisburg, PA 17102.

She was born in Harrisburg, Pennsylvania.

Geographic names that are always abbreviated include *DC* (for the District of Columbia) and *USSR*. The abbreviation *U.S.* can be used as an adjective but not as a noun.

(See 44h for information on using commas with place names and in addresses.)

✔ **STATE ABBREVIATIONS**

Use these U.S. Postal Service abbreviations (capitalized, with no periods) for the names of the fifty states and the District of Columbia only on mail, in full addresses in text, or in documentation.

STATE	ABBRE-VIATION	STATE	ABBRE-VIATION
Alabama	AL	Missouri	MO
Alaska	AK	Montana	MT
Arizona	AZ	Nebraska	NB
Arkansas	AR	Nevada	NV
California	CA	New Hampshire	NH
Colorado	CO	New Jersey	NJ
Connecticut	CT	New Mexico	NM
Delaware	DE	New York	NY
District of	DC	North Carolina	NC
Columbia		North Dakota	ND
Florida	FL	Ohio	OH
Georgia	GA	Oklahoma	OK
Hawaii	HI	Oregon	OR
Idaho	ID	Pennsylvania	PA
Illinois	IL	Rhode Island	RI
Indiana	IN	South Carolina	SC
Iowa	IA	South Dakota	SD
Kansas	KS	Tennessee	TN
Kentucky	KY	Texas	TX
Louisiana	LA	Utah	UT
Maine	ME	Vermont	VT
Maryland	MD	Virginia	VA
Massachusetts	MA	Washington	WA
Michigan	MI	West Virginia	WV
Minnesota	MN	Wisconsin	WI
Mississippi	MS	Wyoming	WY

55 d Abbreviating common Latin terms

The following abbreviations for common Latin terms are not generally used in text but can be used in documentation or notes. (See Chapters 59–63.)

ABB **55** e

Using initials and acronyms 717

ABBREVIATION	LATIN	MEANING
c. or ca.	*circa*	about
cf.	*confer*	compare
e.g.	*exempli gratia*	for example
et al.	*et alii*	and others
etc.	*et cetera*	and so forth
ibid.	*ibidem*	in the same place
i.e.	*id est*	that is
N.B.	*nota bene*	note well
vs. or v.	*versus*	against (used in legal case names)

55 e **Using initials and acronyms**

Initials or **initial abbreviations** consist of the first letter of each word in a phrase or name, such as *IMF* for International Monetary Fund, *U.K.* for the United Kingdom, or *CD* for compact disc. An **acronym** is a word consisting of initials and pronounced as a word: *NATO* for North Atlantic Treaty Organization, *UNICEF* for United Nations International Children's Emergency Fund. Both initials and acronyms consist entirely of capital letters.

When abbreviating a person's name, normally use a period and a space after each initial: *T. S. Eliot.* Some people are conventionally referred to by initials without periods or spaces: *JFK, LBJ.* Others prefer to have no spaces between their initials. Always follow the conventions that have been established for a particular individual or the individual's preferences. Some abbreviations for countries use periods but no spaces: *U.S., U.K.* Most other initial abbreviations are written with neither periods nor spaces between the letters. Acronyms are never spelled with periods or spaces. If you are in doubt as to the spelling or punctuation of an initial abbreviation or acronym, consult a dictionary.

Unfamiliar initials or acronyms can bewilder readers. If you read that NATO and the IMF told the CIS to cut its deficit as a percentage of GNP, would you understand what the writer was saying? Before using an initial abbreviation or an acronym, decide whether it will be familiar to your readers and whether it is essential to your writing. Most can easily be avoided, for example, by substituting a general term like *the Commonwealth* for *CIS.*

If you are using an initial abbreviation or acronym that might be unfamiliar to your readers, provide the full name at the first mention in your text followed by the abbreviation or acronym in parentheses. (If you are using a computer, you can use the search function to quickly locate the first mention.) In later references you can then use just the abbreviation or acronym.

> World commerce is governed in large part by a set of treaties called the General Agreement on Tariffs and Trade (GATT).

■ **EDITING 1: EXPLORATION**

Look for examples of abbreviations in your textbooks as well as in popular writing in magazines, newspapers, and fiction. Does the use of abbreviations in both types of writing follow the rules outlined in this chapter? Why do you think words have been abbreviated as they have in each kind of writing?

■ **EDITING 2: PRACTICE**

Edit the following passage, using abbreviations correctly.

Although the United States Constitution is supposed to guarantee equal rights to all people regardless of color, in the first half of this century most African Americans in the southern U.S. lived in deplorable conditions. E.g., African Americans had to use separate washrooms, and they could not attend schools with whites. Not until the 1940s did the United States Supreme Court finally begin to outlaw practices that deprived African Americans of their rights. One small step toward equality was made when representatives from the National Association for the Advancement of Colored People (N.A.A.C.P.) persuaded the Court that maintaining separate schools for African Americans and whites was not equal. In 1954, under Chief Justice Earl Warren of Calif., the Court ordered the desegregation of schools in the U.S. Despite the new legislation, however, the southern states still resisted integration, and only Senator Lyndon Johnson from TX and two sen. from Tenn. (Estes Kefauver and Albert Gore, Senior) were in favor of desegregating the schools. Racial conflict raged throughout the southern states over the issue of integration; one area of conflict was Little Rock, Ark., where resistance was so great that the National Guard had to be used to enforce integration. Even this drastic step did not solve the problem, however, and the struggle for equal education and other civil rights for African Americans went on for many years.

ABB **55** **e**

Using initials and acronyms 719

EDITING 3: APPLICATION

Examine a paper you are working on for misused or omitted abbreviations. Is there one kind of mistake in using abbreviations that you consistently make? If so, think about how, in editing your work, you might best remember to abbreviate words correctly. Edit any sentences in which you have made errors in abbreviating.

Whether you are handing in a paper to an instructor, sending a business letter, or submitting an article for publication, a finished appearance that follows accepted guidelines helps make a positive first impression. For college papers, first learn and follow any format guidelines your instructor provides. Then, consider the style of your discipline. (See Chapters 59–63 for detailed discussions of specific styles.) Finally, follow the guidelines in this chapter.

Proofreading, the process of checking for errors, involves looking yet again at writing you already have read several times. The key to proofreading is to see what is *actually* on the page rather than what you *intended* to put there. Plan to proofread twice: once on the final edited draft from which you prepare your final manuscript, and once on the final manuscript itself.

As you prepare your final manuscript, make sure to do the following:

- Use effective proofreading techniques.

- Make corrections using standard proofreading marks.

- Make sure your manuscript is neat and legible.

- Position margins, titles, and page numbers correctly.

- Indent and space according to convention.

56 a Using effective proofreading techniques

The purpose of proofreading is primarily to find and correct small typographical errors of punctuation or mechanics. Of course, if you notice serious problems with effectiveness or grammar at this stage, you should correct them as well. Keeping a list in your journal of the kinds of errors you find may help you avoid them in the future. If you found several misused apostrophes in your last paper, for example, look carefully at apostrophes in the current paper. Here are some useful techniques to help you proofread.

Proofreading on hard copy

If you have been composing on a word processor, print a hard copy to use for proofreading. You will be surprised how many errors or awkward passages leap out at you from the printed page, no matter how many times you have read them on the screen. As you find each error or needed change, you may want to make your correction on the computer screen immediately, or you may find it more efficient to make all changes on the hard copy before going back to enter them on the screen.

Reading aloud

A good way to get a fresh perspective on your writing is to read it aloud. As suggested in earlier chapters, one test of good writing is whether it sounds clear and natural when read aloud. Reading aloud is also an effective way to find dropped words and incorrect punctuation.

Reading with a partner

Another way to get a pair of fresh eyes is to borrow someone else's. Ask a friend to proofread your final draft for any errors, omissions, or passages that seem unclear. Having another person read your work aloud is a good way to check for awkward wordings, usage problems, and unclear punctuation.

Reading backward

In proofreading for spelling, the idea is to read the manuscript one word at a time. In practice, this is hard to do, as most people read at the level of phrases and sentences. To avoid being distracted by meaning, read the text backward, starting at the last word and proceeding to the first. Some writers use a ruler to help focus on one line at a time; other writers use a pencil to point out each word.

Using a computer spell checker

If your word processor has a spell-checking function, use it. However, be aware that it can only tell you when you have misspelled a word, not when you have used the wrong word (such as *their* for *there*) or left one out. On the other hand, a computer does read every word letter for letter, and it will never make the mistake of seeing what it expects to see instead of what is there. If you question a spelling suggested by your computer, check your dictionary. (See Chapter 50 for more on spelling and using a spell checker.)

56 b | Using standard proofreading marks

When you find an error, mark your paper using the proofreading marks listed here. You can then incorporate the changes as you prepare your final manuscript. If you find errors in the final manuscript itself, you may also use these marks to make correc-

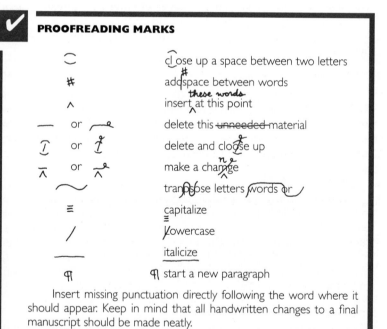

✔ PROOFREADING MARKS

⌒	close up a space between two letters
#	add space between words
∧	insert *these words* at this point
— or ℯ	delete this ~~unneeded~~ material
⟁ or ⟁	delete and close up
∧ or ∧	make a change
∼	transpose letters words or
≡	capitalize
/	lowercase
___	italicize
¶	¶ start a new paragraph

Insert missing punctuation directly following the word where it should appear. Keep in mind that all handwritten changes to a final manuscript should be made neatly.

tions; however, if you have to make more than two corrections on a page, you should probably rewrite or retype the page.

▉ EDITING 1: EXPLORATION

Reflect on your usual practices when it comes to proofreading your papers. Do you proofread them at all? How do you go about proofreading? Do your methods of proofreading produce good results? Are your papers returned to you with proofreading errors marked?

▉ EDITING 2: PRACTICE

Proofread the following passage, correcting all errors in spelling, grammar, punctuation, and mechanics. Use standard proofreading marks.

Marian Anderson, who died in 1993, was the first black opera singer to preform at the Metropoliton Opera (1955), and she became an inspiracion to generations of black performers thoughout the U.S. Yet she was not able to make a name for herself in her own county until late in her life because of raical discrimmination. Althrough her grate talent was recognised early in her life (she won a voice contest in New York in 1925,) she could not get any rolls in opera, and her carrer was going nowhere. In the 1930s, Anderson decided to go to Europe to perform, and she quicky became an international singing star. When she returned to the U.S. and was invited to sing in Washington, DC, the D.A.R. (Daughters of the American Revolution) denied her acess to Constitution Hall, it's national headquarters. Eleanor Roosvelt (along with several other women) resined from the D.A.R. over this disgracefull incident, and she aranged for Anderson to perform outside at the Lincoln Memorial. 75,000 people came to hear Anderson sing, and her peformence in front of Lincolns statute became a powerful cymbal of the civil right's movement.

56	**c**	**Making the final manuscript neat and legible**

For a final manuscript, use 8" × 11" white bond paper of medium weight. Do not use very light paper, onionskin, or so-called erasable paper, all of which are hard to handle and make writing corrections or comments difficult. Printing from a computer generally gives the most legible results. Corrections are also easy, as you can reprint a single page if necessary. Typing yields good results too, but accuracy is harder to achieve than with a computer. Some instructors will accept short papers written by hand.

Some computer printouts can be hard to read. If you have a dot matrix printer, make sure it is printing at its highest possible quality and darkest impression. If your printer's output is faint and hard to read, try to find a true letter-quality printer for your final manuscript, or hire someone who has better equipment. If your printer uses continuous paper, remove the perforated edges, separate the pages, and put them in the proper order. Make sure your final manuscript is double-spaced and use a standard typeface, not script or italics.

If you type your manuscript, double space it. Use a standard typeface, not script or italics. Make sure the ribbon is fresh and the typewriter keys clean. With a self-correcting typewriter, you can save time and effort by making corrections before removing each page from the typewriter. Otherwise use lift-off film or correction fluid. Some instructors will accept standard proofreading marks if there are no more than two per page. (See 56b.)

Before submitting a handwritten paper, make sure it will be acceptable to your instructor. Write in blue or black ink on white ruled paper, using only one side. Do not use legal-size paper or paper torn from a spiral binder. Some instructors may ask that you write on every other line to make your paper more legible and to leave room for corrections or comments. If your handwriting is hard to read, write very carefully or consider having your paper typed. Keep in mind that a handwritten paper, no matter how neat, will seem less formal than a typed paper; try to submit a typed final manuscript whenever you can.

Some symbols, such as brackets and accent marks, may not be available on your typewriter or word processor. Add any such symbols to your final manuscript neatly by hand using dark blue or black ink.

56 **d** **Positioning margins, titles, and page numbers**

Each manuscript page should have left, right, top, and bottom margins of one inch.

For most college papers, the title and identification information are included on the first text page rather than on a title page. Start at the top left margin and, without indenting, write your name, your instructor's name, the course title, and the date the paper is due, each on a separate double-spaced line.

On the next double-spaced line, center the title of the paper, following the rules for capitalizing and punctuating titles. Do not underline your title or put it in quotation marks. Double-space again before beginning the body of the text. (See 18a for an example of an opening page using this format.)

If your instructor requires a separate title page, follow his or her guidelines or those of your discipline. (See 18b and 18c for examples of title pages using MLA and APA formats.)

Each page of your manuscript, including the first, should be numbered in the upper right-hand corner about one-half inch from the top of the page. If your paper has a separate title page, begin numbering with the first page of the text if you are using the MLA style. To avoid confusion should papers get shuffled, you can also include your last name or an abbreviated title just before the page number, separated by a single space. Do not use slashes, parentheses, or periods. (See Chapter 18 for models.) Most word processors can automatically insert the page number at the top of the page when printing.

56 e Indenting and spacing

- Indent the first word of each paragraph five spaces.

- Space once after each word.

- Space twice after any punctuation that ends a sentence.

- Space once after a comma or a semicolon.

- Space once after a colon. (Some styles call for two spaces after a colon, but MLA style calls for one space.)

- Do not space after an opening quotation mark, parenthesis, or bracket or before a closing quotation mark, parenthesis, or bracket.

- Do not space between quotation marks and a period, a question mark, or an exclamation point.

- Do not space between single and double quotation marks.

- Do not space after a hyphen except in a suspended construction: *The rest of the staff are half- and quarter-time employees.*

- Do not space on either side of a dash, which on a typewriter or word processor consists of two hyphens with no spaces between.

- Space before and after a slash only when you use it to separate lines of poetry quoted within your text. (See 48a.)

- To display quotations of more than four typed lines, use block format. (See 48a.)

- Underlining spaces between underlined words is optional, but be consistent throughout the manuscript.

EDITING 3: APPLICATION

Before you hand in your next paper, take the time to make sure that you have followed all of the conventions of format and style discussed in this chapter. Pay attention to the indentation and spacing, as well as the positioning of the various elements on the page (margins, titles, page numbers, and so on). Make sure that you have corrected all typographical errors and that your paper is neat and legible.

PART SEVEN

Writing across the Curriculum

Writing is considered "good" according to how well it communicates with its intended audience. In college your audience will vary from discipline to discipline. Although all of your instructors will value good writing, each area of study has its own set of criteria by which writing is judged. This chapter provides a broad outline of these different criteria and points to some important similarities for writing across the curriculum.

As a rule, knowledge in the humanities focuses on texts and on individual ideas and speculations, personal insights, and imaginative connections. Interpretation in the humanities is thus relatively subjective. Accordingly, good writing in the humanities is characterized by personal involvement, lively language, and speculative or open-ended conclusions.

In contrast, knowledge in the social and physical sciences is likely to focus on data and on ideas and information that can be verified through measuring and testing. Interpretation in these disciplines attempts to be objective. Accordingly, good writing in the social and physical sciences downplays personal involvement and is as precise and conclusive as possible.

But boundaries between the disciplines are not absolute. For example, at some colleges history is considered one of the humanities; at others it is classified as a social science. Geography is a social science when it looks at regions in terms of how people live, but a physical science when it investigates the properties of rocks and glaciers. Anthropology emphasizes the personal and imaginative study of individual cultures, but is classified as social science. Business, engineering, education, and natural resources all draw on numerous disciplines for their sources of knowledge.

The field of English includes not only the study of literature, but also literary theory and history; not only composition, but also creative and technical writing. In addition, English departments often include linguistics, journalism, folklore, women's studies, Afro-American studies, and sometimes speech, film, and communications. In other words, within even this one discipline, you might be asked for several distinct kinds of writing: personal experience essays for a composition course; interpretations for a literature course; abstracts for a linguistics course; short stories for a creative writing course.

Consequently, any observations about the different kinds of knowledge studied in college and the differing conventions for writing about them are only generalizations. The more carefully you study any one discipline, the more complex it becomes and the harder it is to make a generalization that doesn't have numerous exceptions.

57 b — Understanding similarities among the disciplines

Although within different disciplines writing varies according to the subject and method of investigation, certain principles about writing hold true across all of the academic disciplines.

1 Knowledge

Each field of study attempts to develop knowledge about a particular aspect of the physical, social, or cultural world. For example, history courses focus on human beings living in particular time periods; sociology courses focus on human beings in groups; psychology courses focus on the operation and development of the individual human mind. In writing for a particular course, keep in mind the larger purpose of its field of study, especially in selecting, introducing, and concluding your investigation.

2 Method

Each field of study has accepted methods of investigation. Perhaps the best known is the scientific method, used in most of the physical and social sciences. Briefly stated, one who uses the scientific method first asks a question, then poses a possible answer (a hypothesis), then carries out experiments to disprove this answer, and finally, if it cannot be disproved, concludes that the answer is correct. However, while research in the social sciences follows this scientific pattern, some disciplines, such as anthropology, rely instead on the more personal approach of ethnographic study. Literary research may be formal, historical, deconstructive, and so on. It is important to recognize that every discipline has its accepted — and its controversial — methods of study. Any conclusions you arrive at in writing should reflect that awareness.

3 Evidence

Any claim you make about the subject of your study needs to be supported by evidence. If, in order to identify an unknown rock, you scrape it with a known rock in the geology laboratory, the scratch marks of the harder on the softer will be part of your evidence to support your claims about the unknown rock. If you analyze a character in a novel based on her monologue in Chapter 3, the words in Chapter 3 will be part of your evidence to support your interpretation. If you conduct a survey of students on your campus to examine college study habits, the findings of your survey will be part of your evidence to support your conclusions. In other words, although the nature of evidence varies greatly between disciplines, needing it in every discipline is a constant. Many kinds of evidence will come from sources you consulted to make an assertion and will need clear documentation. (Chapters 59–62 provide detailed guidelines for documenting sources in various disciplines.)

4 Accuracy

In every discipline, the value of care, precision, and correctness cannot be overstressed. Every discipline has its own specialized vocabulary for talking about knowledge — you are expected to use terms precisely and to spell them correctly. In addition, each discipline has developed forms in which to report information. You should know the difference in form between a literary analysis in English, a research report in sociology, and a laboratory report in chemistry. Each discipline also values conventional correctness in language. Your writing must reflect standard use of grammar, punctuation, and mechanics.

Essay examinations are common writing assignments in the humanities, but they are important in the social and physical sciences as well. Such exams require students to sit and compose responses to instructors' questions about information, issues, and ideas covered in the course. Instructors assign essay exams instead of "objective" tests (multiple choice, matching, true/false) because they want students to go beyond identifying facts and to demonstrate mastery of concepts covered in the course.

The best preparation for taking an essay exam is a thorough knowledge of the course subject matter. If you have attended all classes, done all assignments, and read all texts, you should be in good shape for such writing. If you have also kept journals, annotated textbooks, discussed course material with other students, and posed possible essay exam questions, you should be in even better shape for such writing. Equally important is your strategic thinking about the course and its syllabus. If the course has been divided into different topics or themes, anticipate a general question on each one covered; if it has been arranged chronologically, expect questions focusing on comparisons or cause and effect relations within a particular period or across periods. Consider, too, the amount of class time spent on each topic or work, and pay proportionately greater attention to emphasized areas.

There is no substitute for careful preparation. However, using writing strategies will enhance your presentation of information in an exam. This chapter outlines suggestions for writing these high-pressure exams.

58 a Understanding the question

1 Read the whole examination

Before answering a single question, read over the whole exam to assess its scope and focus. Answering three of four questions in

50 minutes requires a different approach than answering, say, five of eight questions in 75 minutes. If you have a choice, plan to answer those questions that provide a good demonstration of your knowledge of the whole course rather than two or more that might result in repetitive writing. Finally, decide which questions you are best prepared to answer, and respond to those first (budgeting your time to allow you to deal fully with the others later). Starting with the questions you know best warms you up intellectually and often triggers knowledge about the others in the process.

2 Attend to direction words

Once you decide which questions you will answer, analyze each one before you begin to write. Read the question two or three times. Underline the direction words in the question, those that identify the task you are to carry out. (See Chapter 4 for more on direction words.)

Define or **identify** asks for the distinguishing traits of a term, subject, or event, but does not require an interpretation or judgment. Use appropriate terminology learned in the course. For example, "Define John Locke's concept of *tabula rasa*" is best answered using some of Locke's terminology along with your own.

Describe may ask for a physical description ("Describe a typical performance in ancient Greek theater"), or it may be used more loosely to request an explanation of a process, phenomenon, or event ("Describe the culture and practices of the mound builders"). Such questions generally do not ask for interpretation or judgment but require abundant details and examples.

Summarize asks for an overview or a synthesis of the main points. Keep in mind that "Summarize the impact of the Battle of Gettysburg on the future conduct of the war" asks only that you hit the highlights; avoid getting bogged down in too much detail.

Compare and contrast suggests that you point out both similarities and differences, generally between two subjects but sometimes among three or more. Note that questions using other direction words may also ask for comparison or contrast: "Describe the differences between the works of Monet and Manet."

Analyze asks that you write about a subject in terms of its component parts. The subject may be concrete ("Analyze the typical seating plan of a symphony orchestra") or abstract ("Analyze the ethical ramifications of Kant's categorical imperative"). In general, your response should look at one part at a time.

Interpret asks for a definition or analysis of a subject based on internal evidence and your own particular viewpoint: "Interpret Flannery O'Connor's short story 'Revelation' in terms of your understanding of her central religious and moral themes."

Explain asks what causes something or how something operates. Such questions may ask for an interpretation and an evaluation. "Explain the function of color in the work of Picasso," for example, clearly asks for interpretation of the artist's use of color; although it does not explicitly ask for a judgment, some judgment might be appropriate.

Evaluate or **critique** asks for a judgment based on clearly articulated analysis and reasoning. "Evaluate Plato's concept of the ideal state" and "Critique the methodology of this experiment," for example, ask for your opinions on these topics. Be analytical as you lead up to your judgmental verdict, and don't feel that your verdict must be completely one-sided. In many cases, you will want to cite more experienced judgments to back up your own.

Discuss or **comment on** is a general request, which allows considerable latitude. Your answers to questions such as "Discuss the effects of monetarist economic theories on current third world development" often let you demonstrate what you know especially well. Use terms and ideas as they have been discussed during the course, and add your own insights with care and thoughtfulness.

58 b   Writing a good answer

◼ Plan and outline

Take one or two minutes per question to make a quick outline of your answer. If asked, for example, to compare and contrast three impressionist painters, decide in advance which three you will write about and in what order. Granted, as you start writing, other ideas will come to you and you should use those. But starting with an organizational plan often allows you to write more effectively: you can alert the reader to your intention to discuss "three reasons" or "four main differences" — suggesting a greater command of the subject. As you create an outline, you can plan to build up to your most important points rather than discussing them randomly.

2 Write with specific detail, examples, and illustrations

Remember, most good writing contains specific information that lets readers see for themselves the evidence for your position. Use as many supportive specifics as you can; memorize them as you prepare for the exam so they can be recalled accurately as needed. Dates, names, titles, and statistics alone may not be worth much, but when embedded as evidence in an essay that also contains strong reasoning, these specifics make the difference between good and mediocre answers.

3 Provide context

In answering a question posed by an instructor who is an expert in the field, it is sometimes tempting to assume your instructor does not need a full explanation and to answer too briefly. However, in a test situation you are being asked to demonstrate how much *you* understand. Briefly explain any concepts or terms that are central to your answer. Take the time to fit any details into the larger scheme of the subject. View each question as an opportunity to show how much you know about the subject.

4 Use the technical terminology of the discipline

Be careful not to drop in names or terms gratuitously, but if names and terms have been an integral part of the course, use them in your answer. Make sure you define them, use them appropriately, and spell them correctly. Essay exams also test your facility with the language and concepts peculiar to a particular discipline. For example, you should know that terms such as *perspective* and *foreground* have technical meanings in the visual arts whereas their meaning is more general or metaphoric in history.

5 Write to persuade

No matter what the question asks, write as though you were trying to convince a skeptic. See your answer as an act of persuasion in which you need to marshal evidence to be believed. Even when responding to less analytical questions that ask you to describe, define, or discuss, formulate your answer to be as convincing as possible. At the same time, remember that many situations and issues are not black or white. When you answer a question, alert your reader that you are aware of this grayness. In fact, one of the marks of more sophisticated learners is their understanding that every issue has several sides to it. Be assertive and knowledgeable, but neither arrogant nor wishy-washy.

6 Budget your time

Ideally, you should allow yourself a few minutes at the end of the exam period to reread and proofread your answers. In reality, this is not always possible. If you find yourself running out of time, outline answers to questions you do not have time to finish; you may be given partial credit.

This chapter describes the aims, style, forms, and documentation conventions required for most kinds of writing required of courses in English, comparative literature, and foreign languages where the primary focus is on the study of texts. Many specialized areas — such as film and cultural studies — also follow the conventions described here.

59 a The aims of writing in languages and literature

Language and literature courses are concerned with reading and writing about texts such as poems, novels, plays, and essays written by published authors, as well as by students. (The term *text* is defined broadly to encompass films, visual arts, advertisements — anything that can be read and interpreted.)

What sets literary studies apart from most other disciplines — including others in the humanities — is the attention devoted to all elements of written language. In these courses, writing is not only the *means* of study but often the *object* of study as well: works are examined for their form and style as well as their content. Texts are read, listened to, discussed, and written about in order to discover what they are, how they work, what they mean, and what makes them exceptional or flawed. Moreover, literary studies often draw on ideas from other disciplines. For instance, reading a single nineteenth-century novel, such as Charles Dickens's *David Copperfield* can teach readers a little about sociology, psychology, history, geography, architecture, political science, and economics as well as the aesthetics of novel writing.

When you write in language and literature, you can examine texts from a variety of perspectives. You can focus on a text's ideas, authors, formal qualities, or themes. You can also consider the culture that produced the text, the text's relationship to other

The style of writing in languages and literature 737

texts, the text's place in history, and the politics of the text. In general, there are four basic activities you can engage in with a text.

1   You can **appreciate** texts. You can write about the most moving or interesting features, the beauty or strangeness of the setting, the character with whom you identify, the plot as it winds from beginning to end, or the turns and rhythms of the language.

2   You can **analyze** texts, asking questions such as "How is it put together?" or "How does it work?" Analysis involves looking at a text's component parts (chapters) and the system that makes it work as a whole (plots), defining what they are, describing what they are like, and explaining how they function.

3   You can **interpret** texts, asking questions such as "What does it mean?" "How do I know what it means?" and "Why was it made?" Interpretations often vary widely from reader to reader and may provoke quite a bit of disagreement.

4   You can **evaluate** texts, asking questions such as "How good is it?" "What makes it worth reading?" and "How does it compare to other texts?" These are questions of judgment, based on criteria that might differ considerably from person to person. For example, you might judge a poem good because its pattern of rhythm and imagery is pleasing (aesthetic criteria). Another reader may praise the same poem because it subverts common assumptions about power relationships (political criteria) and a third because it evokes fond childhood memories (personal criteria); however, a fifth reader might dismiss the poem as sentimental (philosophical criteria), and a sixth find it weak in contrast to another poet's work (comparative criteria).

All of these activities come together when you are asked to write **critical essays** about the literature you read. (See 59c.) Learning to be critical — to think, read, and write critically — is one of the goals of all literary study. (See Chapter 12.) Critical essays answer questions such as, Is the idea or text clear? What does it mean? Is it true? Is the argument sound?

| 59 | b | **The style of writing in languages and literature** |

Writing in languages and literature demands clarity, variety, and vitality to create a strong connection between the writer and reader. Direct, unpretentious language and an engaging tone are valued over obscure terminology and an artificially formal style. Readers look for sophistication of thought expressed in a lively, readable, and imaginative way. Observing the standard conventions of grammar, punctuation, and mechanics is also expected.

All that said, great freedom and variety of style are allowed in language and literature study, more perhaps than in any other discipline. Because literary studies center so closely on the multitude of ways readers approach texts, writing can range from the highly personal to the highly theoretical, from deeply impressionistic to sharply rational, from journalistic to experimental. Indeed, a single essay may knit together all these styles.

As a student, much of the writing you do in language and literature may be relatively conventional in style — asserting a thesis with supporting textual evidence and reasoned insight. But do not be surprised if you find yourself responding in different styles and voices for different kinds of assignments.

| **59** | **c** | **Common forms of writing in languages and literature** |

As discussed in 59a, four common aims of writing about texts are appreciation, analysis, interpretation, and evaluation. Given any one of these aims, the essays you are assigned in language and literature courses are likely to fall into two categories: those in which you focus on one or more texts in terms of your own responses, without consulting any other outside sources; and those in which you research and synthesize additional material in coming to your own conclusions about a particular text or texts. (See Chapter 12 for more on writing about texts.)

█ Essays that focus on a writer's responses

When you write to focus on your own responses to a text, you may be expected to do so subjectively and to acknowledge and include your experiences, cultural background, and gender in your analysis. Or you may be asked to respond objectively, based exclusively on the way a text is put together, its form, and its imagery. (See 12d.) Either way, be sure to quote from the work directly, whenever doing so can help clarify a point you are making.

Aim to go beyond summarizing the text or what may have already been covered in class discussions. Your particular insights into what a text means, how it works, and how well it works should constitute the body of any such paper. Your conclusions may be tentative and exploratory rather than assertive and conclusive, but they should always represent a careful, detailed reading.

2 Essays that incorporate secondary sources

Assignments that ask you to go beyond a primary text to consider secondary source material require you to read, evaluate, and synthesize what other critics have said about a work. In doing so, be careful not to let your sources overwhelm your own insights and viewpoint. You will be expected to develop your own thesis based on your close reading of the work, and to introduce secondary sources as a way of supporting, expanding, or contrasting your views with those of other critics.

You may also be required (or choose) to consult other kinds of sources: biographies, letters, journals, and interviews about the writer; studies and documents that provide historical or social context of the text; popular responses to the text; or recordings and dramatizations of the text. Your use of such sources should serve to help develop and support a thesis or point of view that is ultimately your own. (See 59d for more on synthesizing sources.)

Samples of papers about literary texts appear in Chapters 12 and 18.

59 d Documentation and format conventions: MLA guidelines

The Modern Language Association (MLA) system is the preferred form for documenting research sources in the languages and literature. The MLA system requires that all sources be briefly documented in text by an identifying name and page (generally in parentheses) and that there be a Works Cited section at the end of the paper listing full publication information for each source cited. (The MLA system is explained in detail in the *MLA Handbook for Writers of Research Papers* [3rd ed. New York: MLA, 1988], the book on which the information in this chapter is based.)

DOCUMENTATION AND FORMAT CONVENTIONS: MLA GUIDELINES

17. Anonymous book
18. Government document
19. Dissertation

Documenting Periodicals
20. Article, story, or poem in a monthly or bimonthly magazine
21. Article, story, or poem in a weekly magazine
22. Article in a daily newspaper
23. Article in a journal paginated by volume
24. Article in a journal paginated by issue
25. Editorial
26. Letter to the editor and reply
27. Review

Documenting Other Sources
28. Pamphlet
29. Cartoon
30. Computer software program
31. Film or videocassette
32. Personal interview
33. Published or broadcast interview
34. Unpublished lecture, public address, or speech
35. Personal or unpublished letter
36. Published letter
37. Map
38. Performance
39. Recording
40. Television or radio broadcast
41. Work of art

Documenting More Than One Source by the Same Author
42. Subsequent source by the same author

The MLA system provides a simple, economical, and thorough way to identify the sources used by writers in research papers. Footnotes and endnotes are used to provide additional explanatory information by the author, but not to cite information provided by external sources (see 59d2). Whenever possible, include explanatory information in the text itself and limit the use of foot-notes or endnotes. Pay careful attention to the mechanics of documentation, so that readers can readily identify, understand, and locate your sources.

■ Conventions for in-text citations

In-text citations identify ideas and information borrowed from other writers. They also refer readers to the end of the paper where they will find complete publication information about each original source (Works Cited). The languages and literature are not primarily concerned with when something was written but focus instead on writers and the internal qualities of texts. In-text citations of the MLA system, therefore, feature author names, text titles, and page numbers. MLA style is economical, providing only as much information in the text as readers need to find complete information in the Works Cited. Following are some examples of how in-text citation works; see 59d3 for the format of entries in the Works Cited. (See Chapters 12 and 18 for sample papers using this style of documentation.)

1. Single work by one or more authors

When you quote, paraphrase, or summarize an author, you must include in the text of the paper the author's last name and the page or pages on which the original information appeared. Page numbers are inserted parenthetically (do not use the word *page* or abbreviations *p.* or *pp.*); authors' names may be mentioned in the sentence or included parenthetically preceding the page number(s).

Lewis Thomas explains simply and elegantly why bacteria endanger the human organism (74-79).

Exotoxins make bacteria dangerous to humans (Thomas 76).

Note that a parenthetical reference at the end of a sentence comes before the period. There is no punctuation between the author's name and the page number(s).

If a work cited is by **two or three authors,** the parenthetical reference must include all the names: (Rombauer and Becker

715), (Child, Bertholle, and Beck 215). For works by **more than three authors,** you may list all the authors or, to avoid awkwardness, use the first author's name and add "et al." (for the Latin *et alia* meaning "and others") without a comma: (Britton et al. 395).

2. Two or more works by the same author

If your paper includes references to two or more works by the same author, your citation needs to distinguish the work to which you are referring. To do so, either mention the title in your sentence or include a shortened version of the title (usually the first one or two important words) in your parenthetical citation.

According to Lewis Thomas in Lives of a Cell, many bacteria only become dangerous if they manufacture exotoxins (76).

Many bacteria only become dangerous if they manufacture exotoxins (Thomas, Lives 76).

Note that if a parenthetical citation includes both the author's name and a title identification, the two are separated by a comma; there is no comma between the title identification and the page number.

3. Unknown author

When an author is unknown, identify the complete title in your sentence or include a shortened version of the title in the parenthetical citation along with the page number.

According to Statistical Abstracts, the literacy rate for Mexico stood at 75% in 1990, up 4% from census figures ten years earlier (374).

The literacy rate for Mexico stood at 75% in 1990, up 4% from census figures ten years earlier (Statistical 374).

4. Corporate or organizational author

When no author is listed for a work published by a corporation, organization, or association, indicate the group's full name in any parenthetical reference: (Florida League of Women Voters 3). When such names are long, cite the group in your sentence and put only the page number in parentheses.

5. Authors with the same last name

When you cite works by two or more authors with the same last name, include each author's first name either in your sentence or the parenthetical citation: (Janice Clark 51).

6. Works in more than one volume

When your sources include more than one volume of a multivolume work, indicate the pertinent volume number for each citation by placing it before the page number, followed by a colon and one space: (Hill 2: 70). If your sources include only one volume of a multivolume work, you need not specify the volume number in your in-text citation, but do so in your Works Cited list.

7. One-page works

When you cite a work that is only one page long, it is not necessary to include the page number parenthetically. Author or title identification is sufficient for readers to find the exact page number on your Works Cited list.

8. Quote from an indirect source

When a quotation or any information in your source is originally from another source, use the abbreviation "qtd. in."

```
Lester Brown of Worldwatch feels that international
agricultural production has reached its limit and
that "we're going to be in trouble on the food front
before this decade is out" (qtd. in Mann 51).
```

9. Literary works

In citing classic prose works that are available in various editions, provide additional information (such as chapter number or scene number) for readers who may be consulting a different edition. Use a semicolon to separate the page number of your source from this additional information: (331; bk. 10, ch. 5). In citing poems, use only line numbers, indicating that you are doing so by including the word *line* or *lines* in the first reference.

```
In "The Mother," Gwendolyn Brooks remembers ". . .
the children you got that you did not get" (line 1);
children that "never giggled or planned or cried"
(30).
```

Cite verse plays using act, scene, and line numbers, separated by periods: (*Hamlet* 4.4.31–39.)

10. More than one work in a citation

To cite more than one work in a single parenthetical reference, separate them with semicolons: (Aronson, *Golden Shore* 177; Didion 49–50).

11. Long quote set off from text

For quotes of four or more lines, which are set off from the text by indentation, the parenthetical citation follows any end punctuation and is not followed by a period.

2 Conventions for endnotes and footnotes

MLA style uses notes only to offer comments, explanations, or information that cannot be accommodated in the text of the paper, to cite several different sources, or to comment on sources. In general, omit additional information unless it is necessary for clarification or justification of the text.

If notes are necessary, insert a raised (superscript) numeral at the reference point in the text; the note itself should be introduced by a corresponding raised numeral and indented.

TEXT WITH SUPERSCRIPT

```
The standard ingredients for guacamole include
avocadoes, lemon juice, onion, tomatoes, coriander,
salt, and pepper.¹ Hurtado's poem, however, gives this
traditional dish a whole new twist (lines 10-17).
```

NOTE

```
        ¹ For variations see Beard 314, Egerton 197,
Eckhardt 92, and Kafka 26. Beard's version, which
includes olives and green peppers, is the most
unusual.
```

The references listed in this note would appear in the Works Cited.

Notes may come at the bottom of the page on which the text reference appears (as footnotes) or be included, double-spaced, on a separate page as endnotes at the end of the paper (before the Works Cited), with the title *Note* or *Notes*. (For examples of format and use of endnotes, see the student paper in Chapter 18. For more on the format for footnotes, see 60d3.)

3 **Conventions for Works Cited**

All sources mentioned in a paper should be identified on a concluding list of Works Cited. The Works Cited page should follow specific rules for formatting and punctuation so that the reader can readily find information.

Format. After the final page of the paper, title a separate page "Works Cited," an inch from the top of the page, centered, but not underlined and not in quotation marks. (If you are required to list all the works you have read in researching the topic, title the list "Works Consulted.") Number the page, following in sequence from the last page of your paper.

Double-space between the title and first entry. Begin each entry at the left margin, and indent the second and subsequent lines of an entry five spaces. Double-space both between and within entries. If the list runs to more than a page, continue the page numbering in sequence but do not repeat the Works Cited title.

Order of entries. Alphabetize your list of entries according to authors' last names. For entries by an unknown author, alphabetize according to the first word of the title (excluding an initial *A*, *An*, or *The*).

Format for entries. There are many variations on the following general formats, given the additional information needed to identify various kinds of sources. The following formats are the three most common.

GENERAL FORMAT FOR BOOKS

GENERAL FORMAT FOR JOURNAL ARTICLES

```
                 two spaces          two spaces        one space
                     |                   |                 |
        Author(s).  | "Article Title."  | Journal Title  |volume
Indent 5 ————number |(year of publication):|inclusive page
  spaces            └────────┐              |
        numbers.   one space                 one space
```

GENERAL FORMAT FOR MAGAZINE AND NEWSPAPER ARTICLES

```
                 two spaces          two spaces        one space
                     |                   |                 |
        Author(s).  | "Article Title."  | Publication Title|date
Indent 5 ————of publication:|inclusive page numbers.
  spaces                  one space
```

Authors. Authors are listed last name first, followed by a comma and the rest of the name as it appears on the publication. A period follows the full name of the author. When a work has more than one author, the subsequent names are listed first name first and are separated by a comma. When more than one work is included by the same author, substitute three hyphens for the name in entries after the first.

Titles. Titles and subtitles are listed fully and capitalized as in the original. Underline titles of entire books and periodicals; put quotation marks around the titles of essays, poems, and so forth, that are part of a larger work. A period follows a book title or article title; no punctuation follows a journal, magazine, or newspaper title.

Places of publication. For books, the city of publication is always given. If there are several cities listed on the title page or copyright page, give only the first. If the name of the city could be unfamiliar or confusing to your readers, also include an abbreviation for the state or country. A comma separates the city from the state or country; a colon separates the place of publication from the publisher.

Publishers. Abbreviate publisher's names as discussed under Abbreviations. If the title page indicates that a book is published under an imprint (for example, Arbor House is an imprint of William Morrow), list both imprint and publisher, separated by a hyphen (Arbor-Morrow). For books, a comma separates the publisher from publication date.

Dates and page numbers. For books and periodicals, give only the year of publication. The year for books is followed by a period; the year for periodicals is within parentheses and followed by a colon. For dates of newspapers, use no commas to separate elements, and put the day before the month (25 May 1954). For magazines and newspapers, the date is followed by a colon. Inclusive page numbers are separated by a hyphen with no spaces (36-45); use all digits for second page numbers up to 99 and the last two digits only for numbers above 99 (130-38) unless the full sequence is needed for clarity (198-210). If subsequent pages do not follow consecutively (as in a newspaper), follow the final consecutive page with a plus sign (39+, 52-55+).

Abbreviations. State and country names are abbreviated using country or state postal abbreviations when used to identify the city of publication. Publishers' names are abbreviated by dropping the words *Press, Company*, and so forth ("Blair" for "Blair Press"); by using only the first in a series of names ("Farrar" for "Farrar, Straus & Giroux"); and by using only the last name of a person ("Abrams" for "Harry N. Abrams"). "University Press" is abbreviated "UP" (Columbia UP; U of Chicago P). In periodical dates, all months are abbreviated to the first three letters followed by a period (Apr., Dec.), except May, June, and July, which are never abbreviated. For a book, if no publisher or date of publication is given, use the abbreviations "n.p." or "n.d."

Following are examples of the Works Cited format for a variety of specific types of sources. For a sample Works Cited list, see Chapter 18.

DOCUMENTING BOOKS

1. Book by one author

Thomas, Lewis. <u>Lives of a Cell: Notes of a Biology</u>
    <u>Watcher</u>. New York: Viking, 1974.

2. Book by two or three authors

Fulwiler, Toby, and Alan Hayakawa. <u>The Blair Handbook</u>.
    Boston: Blair-Prentice, 1994.

Names after the first are identified first name first, and the final name is preceded by "and."

3. Book by more than three authors

Britton, James, et al. The Development of Writing
Abilities (11-18). London: Macmillan Education,
1975.

If there are more than three authors, you have the option of using the Latin abbreviation *et al.* ("and others") or listing all authors' names in full as they appear on the title page.

4. Book by a corporation, association, or organization

U.S. Coast Guard Auxiliary. Boating Skills and
Seamanship. Washington, DC: Coast Guard Auxiliary
National Board, 1988.

Alphabetize by the name of the organization.

5. Revised edition of a book

Hayakawa, S. I. Language in Thought and Action. 4th ed.
New York: Harcourt, 1978.

6. Edited book

Hoy, Pat C., II, Esther H. Shor, and Robert DiYanni, eds.
Women's Voices: Visions and Perspectives. New York:
McGraw, 1990.

7. Book with an editor and author

Britton, James. Prospect and Retrospect. Ed. Gordon
Pradl. Upper Montclair, NJ: Boynton, 1982.

8. Book in more than one volume

Waldrep, Tom, ed. Writers on Writing. 2 vols. New York:
Random, 1985-88.

When separate volumes were published in different years, include inclusive dates.

9. One volume of a multivolume book

Waldrep, Tom, ed. <u>Writers on Writing</u>. Vol. 2. New York:
    Random, 1988.

When each volume has an individual title, list the volume's full
publication information first, followed by series information (number of volumes, dates).

Churchill, Winston S. <u>Triumph and Tragedy</u>. Boston:
    Houghton, 1953. Vol 6. of <u>The Second World War</u>. 6
    vols. 1948-53.

10. Translated book

Camus, Albert. <u>The Stranger</u>. Trans. Stuart Gilbert.
    New York: Random, 1946.

11. Book in a series

Magistrale, Anthony. <u>Stephen King, The Second Decade:</u>
    <u>Danse Macabre to The Dark Half</u>. Twayne English
    Authors Ser. 599. New York: Twayne-Macmillan, 1992.

Add series information after the title. Book titles within a title are
not underlined.

12. Reprinted book

Hurston, Zora Neal. <u>Their Eyes Were Watching God</u>. 1937.
    New York: Perennial-Harper, 1990.

Add original publication date after the title; then cite current edition information.

13. Introduction, preface, foreword, or afterword in a book

Holroyd, Michael. Preface. <u>The Naked Civil Servant</u>. By
    Quentin Crisp. New York: Plume-NAL, 1983.
Odell, Lee. Foreword. <u>Writing across the Disciplines:</u>
    <u>Research into Practice</u>. Art Young and Toby
    Fulwiler, eds. Upper Montclair, NJ: Boynton, 1986.

14. Work in an anthology or chapter in an edited collection

Donne, John. "The Good-Morrow." The Metaphysical Poets.
Ed. Helen Gardner. Baltimore: Penguin, 1957. 58.

Gay, John. The Beggar's Opera. British Dramatists from
Dryden to Sheridan. Ed. George H. Nettleton and
Arthur E. Case. Carbondale: Southern Illinois UP,
1975. 530-65.

Lispector, Clarice. "The Departure of the Train."
Trans. Alexis Levitin. Latin American Writers:
Thirty Stories. Ed. Gabriella Ibieta. New York:
St. Martin's, 1993. 245-58.

Enclose the title of the work in quotation marks unless the work
was originally published as a book, in which case it should be underlined. At the end of the entry, add inclusive page numbers for
the selection. When citing two or more selections from one anthology, list the anthology separately under the editor's name. Selection entries will then need to include only a cross-reference to the
anthology entry.

Donne, John. "The Good-Morrow." Gardner 58.

15. Periodical article reprinted in a collection

Emig, Janet. "Writing as a Mode of Learning." College
Composition and Communication 28 (1977): 122-28.
Rpt. in The Web of Meaning. Ed. Janet Emig. Upper
Montclair, NJ: Boynton, 1983. 123-31.

Include the full citation for the original periodical publication, followed by "Rpt. in" (Reprinted in) and the book publication information. Include inclusive page numbers for both sources.

16. Article in a reference book

"Behn, Aphra." The Concise Columbia Encyclopedia. 1983
ed.

Miller, Peter L. "The Power of Flight." The
Encyclopedia of Insects. Ed. Christopher O'Toole.
New York: Facts on File, 1986. 18-19.

If the article is signed, begin with the author's name. For commonly known reference works, full publication information and editors' names are unnecessary. Page and volume numbers are unnecessary when entries are arranged alphabetically.

17. Anonymous book

The World Almanac and Book of Facts. New York: World

    Almanac-Pharos, 1993.

Alphabetize by title, excluding an initial *A*, *An*, or *The*.

18. Government document

United States. Central Intelligence Agency. National

    Basic Intelligence Fact Book. Washington: GPO,

    1980.

If the author is identified, begin with that name. If not, begin with the government (country or state), followed by the agency or organization. The Government Printing Office is abbreviated GPO.

19. Dissertation

Kitzhaber, Albert R. "Rhetoric in American Colleges."

    Diss. U of Washington, 1953.

Put the title in quotation marks. Include the university name and the year. For a published dissertation, underline the title and add publication information as for a book, including the order number if the publisher is University Microfilms International UMI.

DOCUMENTING PERIODICALS

20. Article, story, or poem in a monthly or bimonthly magazine

Linn, Robert L., and Stephen B. Dunbar. "The Nation's

    Report Card Goes Home." Phi Delta Kappan Oct. 1990:

    127-43.

Abbreviate all months except May, June, and July. Hyphenate months for bimonthlies (July-Aug. 1993). Do not list volume or issue numbers.

21. Article, story, or poem in a weekly magazine

Updike, John. "His Mother Inside Him." New Yorker 20
     Apr. 1992: 34-36.

The publication date is inverted.

22. Article in a daily newspaper

Brody, Jane E. "Doctors Get Poor Marks for Nutrition
     Knowledge." New York Times 10 Feb. 1992, natl. ed.:
     B7.

"Redistricting Reconsidered." Washington Post 12 May
     1992: B2.

If it is unsigned, begin with the article's title. Give the name of the
newspaper as it appears on the masthead, but drop any introductory *A*, *An*, or *The*. If the city is not in the name, it should follow
the name in brackets: El Diario [Los Angeles]. Include with the
page number the letter that designates any separately numbered
sections; if sections are numbered consecutively, list the section
number (sec. 2) before the colon, preceded by a comma.

23. Article in a journal paginated by volume

Harris, Joseph. "The Other Reader." Journal of Advanced
     Composition 12 (1992): 34-36.

If page numbers are continuous from one issue to the next
throughout the year, include only the volume number and year,
not the issue number or month.

24. Article in a journal paginated by issue

Tiffin, Helen. "Post-Colonialism, Post-Modernism, and the
     Rehabilitation of Post Colonial History." Journal
     of Commonwealth Literature 23.1 (1988): 169-81.

If each issue begins with page 1, include the volume number followed by a period and the issue number. Do not include the
month of publication.

25. Editorial

"Price Support Goes South." Editorial. Burlington Free
     Press 5 June 1990: A10.

If signed, list the author's name first.

26. Letter to the editor and reply

Kempthorne, Charles. Letter. <u>Kansas City Star</u> 26 July
    1992: A16.

Massing, Michael. Reply to letter of Peter Dale Scott.
    <u>New York Review of Books</u> 4 March 1993: 57.

27. Review

Kramer, Mimi. "Victims." Rev. of <u>'Tis Pity She's a</u>
    <u>Whore</u>. New York Shakespeare Festival. <u>New Yorker</u>
    20 Apr. 1992: 78-79.

Rev. of <u>Bone</u>, by Faye Myenne Ng. <u>New Yorker</u> 8 Feb. 1992:
    113.

If a review is unsigned and untitled, list as "Rev. of ____"; alphabetize by the name of the work reviewed. If the review is unsigned
but titled, begin with the title. If the review is of a performance,
add pertinent descriptive information such as director, composer,
or major performers.

DOCUMENTING OTHER SOURCES

28. Pamphlet

Cite as you would a book.

29. Cartoon

Roberts, Victoria. Cartoon. <u>New Yorker</u> 13 July 1992:
    34.

MacNelly, Jeff. "Shoe." Cartoon. <u>Florida Today</u>
    [Melbourne] 13 June 1993: 8D.

30. Computer software program

<u>Fastfile</u>. Computer software. Computerworks, 1992. MS-
    DOS, disk.

List title first if the author is unknown. Name the distributor and
the year published. List other specifications (such as the operating

system, the units of memory, and the computer on which the program can be used) as helpful.

31. Film or videocassette

```
Casablanca. Dir. Michael Curtiz. With Humphrey Bogart
    and Ingrid Bergman. Warner Bros., 1942.
```

Begin with the title followed by the director, the studio, and the year released. Including the names of lead actors and other personnel following the director's name is optional. If your essay is concerned with a particular person's work on a film, lead with that person's name.

```
Lewis, Joseph H., dir. Gun Crazy. Screenplay by Dalton
    Trumbo. King Bros., 1950.
```

32. Personal interview

```
Holden, James. Personal interview. 12 Jan. 1993.
Morser, John. Professor of Political Science, U of
    Wisconsin. Telephone interview. 15 Dec. 1993.
```

Begin with the interviewee's name, and specify the kind of interview and the date. Identify the individual's position if it is important to the purpose of the interview.

33. Published or broadcast interview

```
Steinglass, David. Interview. Counterpoint 7 May 1970:
    3-4.
Lee, Spike. Interview. Tony Brown's Journal. PBS.
    WPBT, Miami. 20 Feb. 1993.
```

Begin with the interviewee's name. Include appropriate publication information for a periodical or book, and appropriate broadcast information for a radio or television program.

34. Unpublished lecture, public address, or speech

```
Graves, Donald. "When Bad Things Happen to Good Ideas."
    National Council of Teachers of English Convention.
    St. Louis, 21 Nov. 1989.
```

Begin with the speaker, followed by the title (if any), the meeting (and sponsoring organization if needed), the location, and date. If untitled, use a descriptive label (such as *Speech*) with no quotation marks.

35. Personal or unpublished letter

Friedman, Paul. Letter to the author. 18 Mar. 1992.

Begin with the name of the letter writer, and specify the letter's audience. Include the date written if known, the date received if not. To cite an unpublished letter from an archive or private collection, include information that locates the holding (for example, "Quinn-Adams Papers. Lexington Historical Society. Lexington, KY.").

36. Published letter

Smith, Malcolm. "Letter to Susan Day." 15 Apr. 1974.
    The Collected Letters of Malcolm Smith. Ed. Sarah
    Smith. Los Angeles: Motorcycle Press, 1989. 23.

Cite published letters like a selection from an anthology. Specify the audience in the letter title. Include the date of the letter immediately following its title. Also include the page number(s) following the publisher information. In citing more than one letter from a collection, cite only the entire work and list dates and individual page numbers in the text.

37. Map

Northwest United States. Map. Seattle: Maps Unlimited,
    1978.

Cite as you would a book by an unknown author. Underline the title and identify it as a map or chart.

38. Performance

Rumors. By Neil Simon. Dir. Gene Saks. Broadhurst
    Theater, New York. 17 Nov. 1988.
Bissex, Rachel. Folk Songs. Flynn Theater, Burlington,
    VT. 14 May 1990.

Identify the pertinent details such as title, place, and date of performance. If you focus on a particular person (such as the director or conductor), lead with that person's name. For a recital or individual concert, lead with the performer's name.

39. Recording

```
Marley, Bob, and the Wailers.  "Buffalo Soldier."
     Legend.  Island Records, 422 846 210-4, 1984.
Mahler, Gustav.  Symphony no. 5.  Compact disc.  Cond.
     Seiji Ozawa.  Boston Symph. Orch.  Philips, 432 141-
     2, 1991.
```

Depending on the focus of your essay, begin with the artist, composer, or conductor. Enclose song titles in quotation marks, followed by the recording title underlined. (Do not underline musical compositions identified only by form, number, and key.) Specify the recording format. End with the company label, the catalog number, and the date of issue.

40. Television or radio broadcast

```
"Emissary."  Star Trek: Deep Space Nine.  Teleplay by
     Michael Pillar.  Story by Rick Berman and Michael
     Pillar.  Dir. David Carson.  Fox.  WFLX, West Palm
     Beach, FL.  9 Jan. 1993.
```

If the broadcast is not an episode of a series or the episode is untitled, begin with the program title. Include the network, the station and city, and the date of broadcast. Including other information (such as narrator, writer, director, performers) depends on the purpose of your citation.

41. Work of art

```
McIntyre, Linda.  Colors.  Art Inst. of Chicago.
Holbein, Hans.  Portrait of Erasmus.  The Louvre, Paris.
     Page 148 in The Louvre Museum.  By Germain Bazin.
     New York: Abrams, n.d.
```

Begin with the artist's name. Follow with the title, and conclude with the location. If your source is a book, give pertinent publication information.

DOCUMENTING MORE THAN ONE SOURCE BY THE SAME AUTHOR

42. Subsequent source by the same author

Thomas, Lewis. <u>Lives of a Cell: Notes of a Biology
Watcher</u>. New York: Viking, 1974.

---. <u>The Medusa and the Snail: More Notes of a Biology
Watcher</u>. New York: Viking, 1979.

This chapter describes the aims, style, forms, and documentation conventions associated with the disciplines in the humanities other than languages and literature: history, philosophy, religion, the fine arts. The endnote or footnote system of documentation described in 60d differs substantially from the MLA documentation system (see Chapter 59) used in languages and literature studies.

60 a The aims of writing in the humanities

The purpose of studies in the humanities is to understand the human experience as expressed and interpreted in a variety of media. History examines the many documents produced by a civilization that provide clues to how its people thought and lived. Philosophy and religion examine the nature of humanity by scrutinizing texts produced by past thinkers and prophets. Studies in art and communications examine texts that are often nonverbal, including paintings, sculptures, and films.

In all humanities disciplines, writing is a primary means of interpreting meaning. Classes such as history and philosophy spend a lot of time reading texts, reading about texts, listening to lectures based on texts, and writing texts that demonstrate an understanding of historical or philosophical knowledge.

Studies in languages and literature and in the other humanities have much in common. In both disciplines, texts are analyzed, interpreted, and evaluated. (See 59a.) However, texts in history, philosophy, and the other humanities are more often a stepping-stone toward defining a broader context, a larger issue, or a fuller understanding of some aspect of human life or thought. They are seen as documents to be argued with.

Issues in the humanities seem matters of interpretation and debate rather than absolute truths. When you write papers in any of the humanities, be sure that your interpretations, inferences, and opinions are carefully reasoned and well supported so that your work will be believed.

60 b The style of writing in the humanities

In the humanities, variety and vitality of expression are important, as are direct language and sophistication of thought. Because writing in the humanities is often explicitly argumentative, your tone should be fair and objective, presenting issues or positions reasonably, completely, and with a minimum of bias and subjectivity. Writing neutrally and analytically encourages readers to take your ideas seriously. When you treat a text objectively, even one with which you disagree, you lay the foundation for strong and believable criticism. Treating texts, ideas, or people fairly invites readers to listen more carefully when you do interpret or evaluate them in a critical fashion.

Although you should try to write objectively in the humanities, understand that the stylistic rules in the humanities are more variable than in most social science and science writing. In many of the humanities, individuality and uniqueness of expression are highly prized.

60 c Common forms of writing in the humanities

Two common forms of writing in the humanities include the critical analysis (or review) and the research paper.

1 Critical analyses and reviews

As with language and literature studies, writing about texts in the other humanities requires analysis, interpretation, and evaluation. (See 59c.) However, essays in the humanities generally focus on nonliterary works and the persuasiveness or relevance of the ideas expressed in these texts.

Critical analyses require a thorough and objective summary of the ideas expressed in a text, which often involves less direct quotation than an evaluation of the work. Question connections among ideas, underlying assumptions, and contradictions within the text; and note persuasive or enlightening arguments. Your thesis may be tentative or qualified, but it should be a clear assertion of a well-reasoned viewpoint.

Reviews most often focus on contemporary interpretations of events, ideas, or works. For example, you might review a dramatized version of a historic event or a biographical analysis of an artist's work. You will need to express an overall judgment based on your analysis of both strengths and weaknesses of your subject.

2 Research papers

Most research papers in the humanities require a synthesis of primary sources (such as original documents, historical accounts, and statements of ideas) and secondary sources (what other writers have said about those primary sources). The aim may be analytical (for example, tracing the effect of a particular invention on a society's economic or cultural life) or argumentative (for example, positing a radically different interpretation of a philosopher's beliefs). Whatever your aim, remember that the best research papers demonstrate originality of thought, suggest new insights, and point to further areas of study.

60 **d** Documentation and format conventions: endnotes and footnotes

The note system for documenting sources has a long scholarly tradition. This system continues to be the most widely used documentation system in the humanities because, although it is somewhat more cumbersome for writers and scholars than contemporary in-text citation systems, it is the least obtrusive form of documentation for readers. (See the end of this chapter for sample pages using this style of documentation.)

1 Conventions for marking citations

Each time you summarize, paraphrase, or quote source material in your text, you need to mark it by inserting a raised (superscript) Arabic number immediately after the sentence or clause that contains the information. The superscript number must

DOCUMENTATION AND FORMAT CONVENTIONS: ENDNOTES AND FOOTNOTES

Documenting Books: First Reference

1. Book by one author
2. Book by two or more authors
3. Revised edition of a book
4. Edited book and one volume of a multivolume book
5. Translated book
6. Reprinted book
7. Work in an anthology or chapter in an edited collection
8. Article in a reference book
9. Anonymous book

Documenting Periodicals: First Reference

10. Article, story, or poem in a monthly or bimonthly magazine
11. Article, story, or poem in a weekly magazine
12. Article in a daily newspaper
13. Article in a journal paginated by volume
14. Article in a journal paginated by issue
15. Review

Documenting Other Sources: First Reference

16. Personal interview
17. Personal or unpublished letter
18. Work of art

Documenting Subsequent References to the Same Work

19. Subsequent references to a work

follow all punctuation except dashes. Each new reference to source material requires a new number, and numbers are arranged consecutively throughout the text.

Frank Lloyd Wright's "prairie style" was characterized initially by the houses he built around Chicago "with low horizontal lines echoing the landscape."[1] Vincent Scully

```
sees the suburban building lots for which Wright was
designing as one of the architect's most important
influences.²
```

Each superscript number corresponds to a note, either at the end of the paper or at the foot of the page on which the number appears.

```
    ¹ "Wright, Frank Lloyd," The Concise Columbia
Encyclopedia, 1st ed.

    ² Vincent Scully, Architecture: The Natural and the
Manmade (New York: St. Martin's, 1991) 340.
```

2 Conventions for positioning notes and including a bibliography

Endnotes are typed as a single list at the end of a text. In terms of formatting, endnotes are easy to deal with because they can be typed up last on a single sheet of paper, without calculating the space needed at the bottom of a page for footnotes. In addition, using endnotes allows writers to add or delete notes with little fuss, because changes affect primarily the endnote page, rather than the entire text. (Many word processing programs format and number notes automatically, which makes the difference in difficulty between the two systems negligible.)

The **endnote page** follows the last page of text, and it and any subsequent pages are numbered in sequence with the paper. Title the first page "Notes" (without quotation marks, centered, and one inch from the top of the page). Double-space before the first entry, within entries themselves, and between entries. Order entries consecutively according to the note numbers as they appear in your paper.

Footnotes are convenient for readers because, instead of turning to the back of a paper, article, or chapter to check a numbered source, they can find the information at a glance. Each footnote appears at the bottom of the page on which the citation is made, four lines below the last line of text.

Some instructors require a separate, alphabetically arranged list of sources, or **bibliography,** in addition to endnotes or footnotes. If so, follow the MLA guidelines for a list of Works Cited. (See 59d3.) If you are asked to include all sources consulted for the paper in your bibliography, you may head the list "Works Consulted."

3 Conventions for endnote and footnote format

Different style manuals offer a number of minor variations for the format of endnotes and footnotes. The following guidelines are based on the *MLA Handbook for Writers of Research Papers.* (*The Chicago Manual of Style* and Kate Turabian's *A Manual for Writers of Term Papers, Theses, and Dissertations* also describe endnote and footnote documentation.)

Numbers and spacing. Each entry is preceded by a superscript Arabic number that is indented five spaces and followed by a space. Any subsequent lines for an entry begin at the margin. Double-space endnotes throughout. Single-space individual footnotes and double-space between footnotes.

Authors. All authors' names are listed first name first, and first names are spelled out in full.

Punctuation. Authors' names and all titles are separated by commas. Book publication information and periodical dates are enclosed in parentheses. Colons separate the place of publication from the publisher; commas separate the publisher from the date. Colons also separate periodical dates from page numbers. All entries end with a period.

Page numbers. Every entry for a book or periodical should end with the page number(s) on which the cited information can be found.

The following are examples of the most common citations required in undergraduate humanities papers. (See 59d3 for information about titles, publishers' names, dates and page numbers, and abbreviations, and for more on what information to include in entries.)

DOCUMENTING BOOKS: FIRST REFERENCE

I. Book by one author

[1] Lewis Thomas, Lives of a Cell: Notes of a Biology Watcher (New York: Viking, 1974) 76.

2. Book by two or more authors

[2] Toby Fulwiler and Alan Hayakawa, <u>The Blair Handbook</u> (Boston: Blair-Prentice, 1994) 234.

For three or more authors, follow each name with a comma.

3. Revised edition of a book

[3] S. I. Hayakawa, <u>Language in Thought and Action</u>, 4th ed. (New York: Harcourt, 1978) 77.

4. Edited book and one volume of a multivolume book

[4] Tom Waldrep, ed., <u>Writers on Writing</u>, vol. 2 (New York: Random, 1988) 123.

5. Translated book

[5] Albert Camus, <u>The Stranger</u>, trans. Stuart Gilbert (New York: Random, 1946) 12.

6. Reprinted book

[6] Zora Neal Hurston, <u>Their Eyes Were Watching God</u> (1937; New York: Perennial-Harper, 1990) 231-32.

7. Work in an anthology or chapter in an edited collection

[7] John Donne, "The Good-Morrow," <u>The Metaphysical Poets</u>, ed. Helen Gardner (Baltimore: Penguin, 1957) 58.

8. Article in a reference book

[8] "Behn, Aphra," <u>The Concise Columbia Encyclopedia</u> 1983 ed.

No page number is needed for an alphabetically arranged book. Begin with the author of the entry, if listed.

9. Anonymous book

[9] <u>The World Almanac and Book of Facts</u> (New York: World Almanac-Pharos, 1993).

DOCUMENTING PERIODICALS: FIRST REFERENCE

10. Article, story, or poem in a monthly or bimonthly magazine

[10] Robert A. Linn and Stephen B. Dunbar, "The Nation's Report Card Goes Home," Phi Delta Kappan Oct. 1990: 127-43.

11. Article, story, or poem in a weekly magazine

[11] John Updike, "His Mother Inside Him," New Yorker 20 Apr. 1992: 34.

12. Article in a daily newspaper

[12] Jane E. Brody, "Doctors Get Poor Marks for Nutrition Knowledge," New York Times 10 Feb. 1992, natl. ed.: B7.

[13] "Redistricting Reconsidered," Washington Post 12 May 1992: B2.

13. Article in a journal paginated by volume

[14] Joseph Harris, "The Other Reader," Journal of Advanced Composition 12 (1992): 34-36.

14. Article in a journal paginated by issue

[15] Helen Tiffin, "Post-Colonialism, Post-Modernism, and the Rehabilitation of Post Colonial History," Journal of Commonwealth Literature 23.1 (1988): 169-81.

15. Review

[16] Mimi Kramer, "Victims," rev. of 'Tis Pity She's a Whore, New York Shakespeare Festival, New Yorker 20 Apr. 1992: 78-79.

DOCUMENTING OTHER SOURCES: FIRST REFERENCE

16. Personal interview

[17] John Morser, personal interview, 15 Dec. 1993.

17. Personal or unpublished letter

¹⁸ Paul Friedman, letter to the author, 18 Mar. 1992.

If in a collection, give any pertinent information after the date.

18. Work of art

¹⁹ Hans Holbein, <u>Portrait of Erasmus</u>, The Louvre, Paris, page 148 in <u>The Louvre Museum</u>, by Germain Bazin (New York: Abrams, n.d.).

DOCUMENTING SUBSEQUENT REFERENCES TO THE SAME WORK

19. Subsequent references to a work

The second and any subsequent times you refer to a source, include only the author's last name and the page number(s).

²⁰ Thomas 99.

If more than one work is cited by the same author, include an abbreviated title of each work in subsequent notes.

²¹ Thomas, <u>Lives</u> 76.
²² Thomas, <u>Medusa</u> 129.

The traditional Latin abbreviations *ibid.* ("in the same place") and *op. cit.* ("in the work cited") are little used in contemporary scholarly writing.

60 e   Sample page with endnotes

recorded "in exultant tones the universal neglect that
had overtaken pagan learning."[2] It would be some time,
however, before Christian education would replace
classical training, and by the fourth century, a lack of
interest in learning and culture among the elite of
Roman society was apparent. Attempting to check the
demise of education, the later emperors established
municipal schools, and universities of rhetoric and law
were also established in major cities throughout the
Empire.[3]

Notes

[1] Rosamond McKitterick, The Carolingians and the
Written Word (Cambridge: Cambridge UP, 1983) 61.

[2] J. Bass Mullinger, The Schools of Charles the
Great (New York: Stechert, 1911) 10.

[3] James W. Thompson, The Literacy of the Laity in
the Middle Ages (New York: Franklin, 1963) 17.

[4] O. M. Dalton, introduction, The Letters of
Sidonius (Oxford: Clarendon, 1915) cxiv.

[5] Pierre Riche, Education and Culture in the
Barbarian West (Columbia: U of South Carolina P, 1976) 4.

[6] Riche 6.

[Notes continue.]

Kelly 5

The Teatro Olimpico was completed in 1584, the
statues, inscriptions, and bas-reliefs for the <u>frons-
scena</u> being the last details completed. Meanwhile,
careful plans were made for an inaugural which was to be
a production of <u>Oedipus</u> in a new translation.[10] Final
decisions were made by the Academy in February of 1585
for the seating of city officials, their wives, and
others, with the ruling that "no masked men or women
would be allowed in the theatre for the performance."[11]

The organization of the audience space was "unique
among Renaissance theaters, suggesting . . . its
function as the theater of a 'club of equals' rather
than of a princely court."[12] The Academy is celebrated
and related to Roman grandeur by the decoration over the
monumental central opening, where its motto, "Hoc Opus,"
appears.[13] It is difficult to make out the entrances

[10] J. Thomas Oosting, <u>Andrea Palladio's Teatro
Olimpico</u> (Ann Arbor: UMI Research Press, 1981) 118-19.

[11] Oosting 120.

[12] Marvin Carlson, <u>Places of Performance: The
Semiotics of Theater Architecture</u> (Ithaca: Cornell UP,
1989) 135.

[13] Simon Tidworth, <u>Theaters: An Architectural and
Cultural History</u> (London: Praeger, 1973) 52.

61 | Writing in the Social Sciences

This chapter describes the aims, style, forms, and documentation conventions associated with disciplines in the social sciences: psychology, sociology, anthropology, political science, and economics. The system of documentation described here is based on guidelines published by the American Psychological Association (APA).

61 | a | The aims of writing in the social sciences

The social sciences examine the fundamental structures and processes that make up the social world. Sociology examines social groups; political science examines the politics of social organizations; anthropology examines social cultures; economics examines the allocation and distribution of resources among social groups; and psychology examines the mind as both a biological and social construction. The social sciences use methodical and systematic inquiry to examine and analyze human behavior, commonly asking questions such as the following:

- What is society? Can it be isolated and observed? Can it be described?

- How do social and psychological systems function? What forces hold them together or lead to their breakdown?

- Why do social organizations and individuals behave the way they do? Can governing laws be identified, explained, and understood?

Most writing in the social sciences explains findings based on factual research — either the empirical research of firsthand observation and experimentation or the comprehensive reading that results in a literature review. Social scientists must also *interpret* their factual findings. As with any other field of academic study, individual interpretations and opinions must be carefully reasoned and based on clear evidence that is objectively presented.

As a student in the social sciences, you will be writing for professors and graduate students who are themselves social scientists and who are knowledgeable about the concepts and information you present. They will expect current, accurate information that is presented concisely and interpreted reasonably.

61 **b** **The style of writing in the social sciences**

Effective writing in the social sciences must have clear organization. Connections among ideas should be explicitly stated. Language is expected to be precise — informal diction is discouraged. However, social science writing need not be dull or dry. Readers of the social sciences look for clarity, smoothness, and economy of expression. Writers should therefore avoid unnecessary jargon, wordiness, and redundancy. As you write and revise, keep the following guidelines in mind.

1   Write from a third-person point of view. (First-person experience is considered inappropriate for conveying empirical data because, in calling attention to the writer, it detracts from the information.)

2   Use the past tense to describe methods and results ("Individuals responded by . . ."); use the past or past perfect tense for literature reviews ("The study resulted in . . . ," "Jones has suggested . . ."); use the present to report established knowledge or discuss conclusions ("The evidence indicates . . ."). Use tenses consistently.

3   Use the technical language of the discipline correctly, but avoid excessive jargon. Use plain, direct language. Choose synonyms with care.

4   Include graphs, charts, and illustrations when they convey information more readily than words. Label them clearly.

5   Incorporate numbers, statistics, and equations clearly and accurately. Include explanations.

61 **c** **Common forms of writing in the social sciences**

Two common forms of social science writing are reports of original research and reviews of published research.

Research reports

Empirical studies are common in the social sciences. In political science, a study might be based on an opinion poll about an election; in psychology, on the effects of a particular stimulus on behavior. The conventional form for research reports varies somewhat from discipline to discipline. However, many social science reports use the following basic structure.

Title page. The title should offer a concise summary of the paper and identify the theoretical issues or variables under study. Center the title on the page, and underneath it type your name, your instructor's name, the course, title, and the date.

Abstract. An abstract is a brief (100 to 150 words) summary of the study and its results. It should be concise but comprehensive and self-contained. It is best written after you complete the text itself. The abstract page follows the title page.

Introduction. Begin the report with an introduction that defines the problem you set out to study and outlines your research strategy. In your introduction you should discuss the background of the problem. Include a brief literature review of any previously reported studies of the problem or issue. End by discussing your own purpose and rationale for the study and stating your hypothesis. The introduction has no heading.

Methods. The next section (headed "Methods") explains how your study was conducted. This section is often divided into three subsections: *subjects* (describing the type, number, and selection of participants in the study); *apparatus* (including any materials or statistical programs and their function); and *procedure* (summarizing the steps involved in conducting the study).

Results. In this section (headed "Results"), report the findings and conclusions of your study. Include any findings that do not support your hypothesis. Use tables to present your results when doing so is clearer or more concise than a description in words. In this section, remain descriptive, not interpretive or evaluative.

Discussion. In this final section (headed "Discussion") interpret what the results mean. Begin with a statement of whether or not your study supported your hypothesis. Consider what it contributes to understanding the problem you set out to study. You may speculate on any theoretical implications or implications for further experiments. (This is the only section of a formal report in which the first person may be appropriate, as you may want to identify an opinion or theory as your own.)

References. List all references cited in the report. (See 61d3.)

2 Literature reviews

In addition to being included as part of research reports, literature reviews (sometimes called surveys) are often written as independent documents. Preparing a literature review will expose you to knowledge generated by social science methodology as well as acquaint you with the conventions of experimentation and documentation.

Reviews are generally written in the style of an essay, with one paragraph devoted to each article surveyed. While the precise form, length, and name of these papers may vary slightly in each discipline, they will generally contain the following parts.

Title. Create a title that concisely describes the subject area that is surveyed in the paper.

Introduction. Begin the report with a brief introduction to the subject and a chronological listing of the articles reviewed.

Summary. Summarize the main conclusion of each article reviewed. Include brief quotations that succinctly state the researchers' findings and some suggestion of your interpretation of their implications.

Conclusion. Conclude the report with a cumulative summary of the survey. Assess the most important articles in the review and suggest possible implications for further research.

References. List all articles cited in the report. (See 61d3.)

---

61 **d** **Documentation and format conventions: APA guidelines**

Most disciplines in the social sciences (along with education and business) use a name-and-date system of documentation. In these disciplines, in-text citations highlight date of publication because the currency of the published material is considered of primary importance. A complete discussion of this system is available in the *Publication Manual of the American Psychological Association,* 3rd ed. (Washington, DC: American Psychological

> ✔ **DOCUMENTATION AND FORMAT CONVENTIONS:**
> **APA GUIDELINES**
>
> **CONVENTIONS FOR IN-TEXT CITATIONS (61d1)**
> **1.** Single work by one or more authors
> **2.** Two or more works by the same author published in the same year
> **3.** Unknown author
> **4.** Corporate or organizational author
> **5.** Authors with the same last name
> **6.** Quote from an indirect source
> **7.** More than one work in a citation
> **8.** Long quote set off from text
>
> **CONVENTIONS FOR FOOTNOTES (61d2)**
>
> **CONVENTIONS FOR THE REFERENCE LIST (61d3)**
> Documenting Books
> **1.** Book by one author
> **2.** Book by two or more authors
> **3.** Book by a corporation, association, or organization
> **4.** Revised edition of a book
> **5.** Book with an editor
> **6.** Book in more than one volume
> **7.** Translated or reprinted book
> **8.** Chapter or article in an edited book
> **9.** Anonymous book
> **10.** Government document
>
> Documenting Articles in Periodicals
> **11.** Magazine article
> **12.** Newspaper article
> **13.** Article in a journal paginated by volume
> **14.** Article in a journal paginated by issue
>
> Documenting Other Sources
> **15.** Film, recording, and other nonprint media
> **16.** Report available from an information service
>
> Documenting Multiple Sources by an Author
> **17.** Sources by the same author

Association, 1983). (See Chapters 11 and 18 for examples of this style of documentation.)

■ Conventions for in-text citations

The following are examples of how to cite sources in text.

I. Single work by one or more authors

When you quote, paraphrase, or summarize source material in your text, include both the author's last name and the date of the source. For direct quotations, also include specific page numbers. Dates and page numbers are generally inserted parenthetically; authors' names may be mentioned in text or included in the parenthetical citation.

Exotoxins make some bacteria dangerous to humans (Thomas, 1974).

According to Thomas (1974), "Some bacteria are only harmful to us if they make exotoxins" (p. 76).

We only need fear some bacteria "if they make exotoxins" (Thomas, 1974, p. 76).

If a work cited is by **two authors,** always cite both names.

Smith and Hawkins (1990) agree that all bacteria-producing exotoxins are harmful to humans.

All known exotoxin-producing bacteria are harmful to humans (Smith & Hawkins, 1990).

Note that authors' names are joined by the word *and* in text but by an ampersand (&) when cited parenthetically.

If a work cited is by **three to five authors,** identify all authors by last name the first time source is cited. Identify the first author followed by "et al." ("and others") for subsequent references.

The most recent study supports the belief that alcohol abuse is on the rise (Dinkins, Dominic,

```
Smith, Rogers, & White, 1989). . . . When homeless
people were excluded from the study, the results were
the same (Dinkins et al., 1989).
```

When a source is by **six or more authors,** identify only the first author, followed by "et al." in all references.

2. Two or more works by the same author published in the same year

To distinguish two or more works published in the same year by one author or author team, follow the date with a lowercase letter: (Smith, 1989a, 1989b). These letters correspond to the alphabetized listing by title that appears in the reference list.

3. Unknown author

When an author is unknown, identify the work by using the first two or three words of the title.

```
Statistical Abstracts (1991) reports the literacy
rate for Mexico at 75% for 1990, up 4% from census
figures 10 years ago.

Many researchers now believe that treatment should
not begin until other factors have been dealt with
("New Evidence Suggests," 1987).
```

4. Corporate or organizational author

When referencing a work by a corporation, association, or organization, spell out the name either in text or parenthetically. However, if the entity has a readily identifiable abbreviation, spell out the name fully only the first time, and include the abbreviation immediately following in brackets; for subsequent references, use only the abbreviation: (American Psychological Association [APA], 1980), (APA, 1980).

5. Authors with the same last name

To avoid confusion in citing two or more authors with the same last name, include each author's initials in every citation: (J. Clark, 1986), (T. H. Clark, 1989).

6. Quote from an indirect source

Indicate when a quotation or any information in your source is originally from another source with the words "cited in."

```
Lester Brown of Worldwatch believes international
agricultural production has reached its limit and
that "we're going to be in trouble on the food front
before this decade is out" (cited in Mann, 1993, p.
51).
```

7. More than one work in a citation

To cite more than one work by the same author in a single parenthetical reference, list the dates of the works in chronological order, separated by commas: (Thomas, 1974, 1979). To cite works by different authors, list them in alphabetical order, separated by semicolons: (Miller, 1990; Webster & Rose, 1988).

8. Long quote set off from text

For quotes of forty or more words, which are set off from the text by indentation, the parenthetical citation follows any end punctuation and is not followed by a period.

2 Conventions for footnotes

Footnotes are used to provide additional information that cannot be worked into the main text. They should be as brief as possible; when the footnote information is extensive, it is better to include it as an appendix. Footnotes should be numbered consecutively. The notes should appear on a page headed "Footnotes" after the reference list. Notes are double-spaced, and the first line of each note is indented five spaces.

3 Conventions for the reference list

All works mentioned in a paper should be identified on a reference list according to the following general rules.

Format. After the final page of the paper, title a separate page "References." Center the title an inch from the top of the page, but do not underline or place within quotation marks. Number the page, following in sequence from the last page of the paper.

Double-space between the title and the first entry. Begin each entry at the left margin, and indent the second and subsequent lines of an entry three spaces. Double-space both between and within entries. If your list runs to more than a page, continue listing in sequence, but do not repeat the title "References."

Order of entries. Alphabetize your list of references according to authors' last names, using the first author's last name for works by multiple authors. For entries by an unknown author, use the first word of the title (excluding an initial *A*, *An*, or *The*) when alphabetizing.

Format for entries. There are several variations on general formats; the following, however, are the three most common.

GENERAL FORMAT FOR BOOKS

Author(s). (Year of publication). <u>Book title</u>. City of

publication: Publisher.

GENERAL FORMAT FOR JOURNAL ARTICLES

Author(s). (Year of publication). Article title. <u>Journal

Title</u>, <u>volume number</u>, inclusive page numbers.

GENERAL FORMAT FOR MAGAZINE AND NEWSPAPER ARTICLES

Author(s). (Year, month of publication). Article title.

<u>Publication Title</u>, inclusive page numbers.

Authors. Authors are listed last name first, followed by a comma and the author's initials. When a work has more than one author, all authors are listed in this way. The last author's name is preceded by an ampersand (&). A period follows the author's name.

Titles. Complete titles and subtitles of books and articles are listed, but only the first word of the title and subtitle and proper nouns are capitalized. Book titles are underlined. Article titles are neither underlined nor placed in quotation marks. A period follows the title.

Journal titles are capitalized following APA style (capitalize *all* words of four letters or more in titles) and underlined. Volume numbers for journals are also underlined. Roman numerals are converted to Arabic numerals. A comma follows the title.

Publishers. Publishers' names are listed in shortened form, omitting words like "Company." The names of university presses and organizations are spelled out fully. (See 59d3.) For books, a colon separates the city of publication from the publisher.

Dates and page numbers. For issue dates of magazines and newspapers, use commas to separate the year from the month and day: (1954, May 25). Enclose publication dates in parentheses. Inclusive page numbers are separated by a hyphen with no spaces: 361-375. (APA style uses full sequences for pages and dates.) If pages do not follow consecutively (as in newspapers), include subsequent page numbers after a comma: pp. 1, 16. Note that the page numbers for magazine and newspaper articles are preceded by "pp."; those for journal articles are not.

Abbreviations. State and country names are abbreviated when used to identify the city of publication. U.S. postal abbreviations are used for states. Months are not abbreviated.

Following are examples of the reference list format for a variety of specific types of sources.

DOCUMENTING BOOKS

1. Book by one author

Steinbach, R. A. (1968). <u>Pain: A psychophysiological analysis</u>. New York: Academic Press.

2. Book by two or more authors

Hanushek, E. A., & Jackson, J. E. (1977). <u>Statistical methods for social scientists</u>. New York: Academic Press.

Include all authors' names, last name first, with an ampersand ("&") before the last author. In the reference list, all authors' names are spelled out regardless of number.

3. Book by a corporation, association, or organization

American Psychiatric Association. (1983). <u>Publication manual of the American Psychological Association</u> (3rd ed.). Washington, DC: Author.

Alphabetize corporate authors by the corporate name, excluding articles *A, An,* and *The.* Note that when the corporate author is also the publisher, the publisher is designated as "Author."

4. Revised edition of a book

Mussen, P. H., Conger, J. J., & Kagan, J. (1969). <u>Child development and personality</u> (rev. ed.). New York: Harper & Row.

5. Edited book

Rorty, A. O. (Ed.). (1980). <u>Explaining emotions</u>. Berkeley: University of California Press.

If there is more than one editor, use the abbreviation "Eds."

6. Book in more than one volume

Waldrep, T. (Ed.). (1985-1988). <u>Writers on writing</u> (Vols. 1-2). New York: Random House.

For a work with volumes published in different years, indicate the range of dates of publication. In citing only one volume of a multi-volume work, indicate only the volume cited.

Waldrep, T. (Ed.). (1988). <u>Writers on writing</u> (Vol. 2). New York: Random House.

7. Translated or reprinted book

Freud, S. (1950). <u>The interpretation of dreams</u> (A. A. Brill, Trans.). New York: Modern Library-Random House. (Original work published 1900)

Use the date of the publication of the translation or reprint in parentheses after the author's name. Indicate original publication date parenthetically at the end of the citation, with no period. Parenthetically cite the information in the text: (Freud 1900/1950).

8. Chapter or article in an edited book

Rosch, E. (1978). Principles of categorization. In E. Rosch & B. B. Lloyd (Eds.), <u>Cognition and categorization</u> (pp. 27-48). Hillsdale, NJ: Erlbaum.

The chapter or article title is not underlined or enclosed in quotation marks. Editors' names are not inverted. List inclusive page numbers parenthetically.

9. Anonymous book

Stereotypes, distortions and omissions in U.S. history
    textbooks. (1977). New York: Council on Interracial
    Books for Children.

10. Government document

Central Intelligence Agency. (1980). National basic
    intelligence factbook. Washington, DC: U.S. Government
    Printing Office.

DOCUMENTING ARTICLES IN PERIODICALS

In citing periodical articles, follow the same format in listing authors' names as for books.

11. Magazine article

Shigaki, J. S. (1983, May). Child care practices in Japan
    and the United States. Young Children, pp. 13-24.

For nonprofessional periodicals, include the year and month after the author's name.

12. Newspaper article

Redistricting reconsidered. (1992, May 12). The
    Washington Post, Sec. B, pp. 2, 7.

If the article continues onto another page, include the second page number as well as the first. If the article has an author, list the author's name, followed by the date in parentheses, and then the article title.

13. Article in a journal paginated by volume

Hernstein, R. J. (1970). On the law of effects. Journal
    of Experimental Analysis of Behavior, 3, 116-129.

If page numbers are continuous between volumes in a year, use only the volume number, underlined, following the periodical title. Use inclusive page numbers.

14. Article in a journal paginated by issue

Lowther, M. A. (1977). Career change in mid-life: Its

impact on education. Innovator, 8(7), 1, 9-11.

Include the issue number in parentheses if each issue of a journal is paginated separately.

DOCUMENTING OTHER SOURCES

15. Film, recording, and other nonprint media

Flaherty, R. (Director). (1934). Man of Aran [Film].

London: Gainsborough Studios.

Include the name or names of those with primary responsibility for the production, identify the medium in brackets, and indicate the location and name of the distributor. Other identifying information (such as a retrieval number) should be provided parenthetically.

16. Report available from an information service

Spolsky, B. (1981). Navajo language maintenance: Six-

year-olds in 1969 (Navajo Reading Study Program Report

No. 5). Albuquerque: University of New Mexico. (ERIC

Document Reproduction Service No. ED 043 004)

Include the service and the document number parenthetically.

DOCUMENTING MULTIPLE SOURCES BY AN AUTHOR

17. Sources by the same author

Two or more works by the same author (or the same author team listed in the same order) are listed chronologically by year of publication with the earliest first. Any such works published in the same year are arranged alphabetically by title, and a lowercase letter follows the date. In either case, full identification of author(s) is given each time.

Bandura, A. (1969). <u>Principles of behavior modification</u>.
New York: Holt, Rinehart, and Winston.

Bandura, A. (1977a). Self-efficacy: Toward a unifying
theory of behavioral change. <u>Psychological Review</u>, <u>84</u>,
191-215.

Bandura, A. (1977b). <u>Social learning theory</u>. Englewood
Cliffs, NJ: Prentice-Hall.

List references by the same first author working with different
coauthors under the first author's name, alphabetizing by the last
name of the second author. Lead such lists with any works by the
first author alone.

This chapter describes the general aims and style of scientific writing, and provides an overview of common forms and specialized documentation systems shared by the scientific community. If you write extensively in the sciences, consult one of the more detailed style manuals listed in 62d.

62 a The aims of writing in the sciences

Scientific study examines the fundamental structures and processes of the natural world. In analyzing particular phenomena and organisms, scientists ask questions such as the following.

- What is it? Can it be isolated and observed? How can it be described?

- How does it function? What forces are in operation? How can these forces be explained?

- Why does it function the way it does? Can governing principles be identified, explained, and understood? Can predictions be made?

- What can be learned about other phenomena or organisms based on the evidence of particular studies?

Scientists approach and attempt to answer such questions using the **scientific method** of observation, prediction, experimentation, and analysis.

Observation. A chemist notices, for example, that when liquid A is mixed with liquid B, the solution of the two (C) has a higher temperature than A or B alone.

Prediction. Based on this observation, the chemist predicts that whenever these amounts of A and B are mixed together, C will always have a higher temperature. This prediction is called a

hypothesis — a preliminary generalization or explanation based on the observed phenomena.

Experimentation. To test the hypothesis, the chemist devises an experiment (in this example, the mixing of the two liquids under controlled conditions), watches the results, and carefully notes what happens.

Analysis and conclusions. The results of the experiment may lead the scientist to conclude, "Yes, when specific amounts of A and B are mixed, reaction C occurs." This finding can be shared with other scientists and could provide the basis for further hypotheses. If the results are different from the hypothesis, new questions must be asked and new hypotheses formulated to explain why the results differed from the initial observations.

Writing plays a central role throughout the investigative and experimental process. To develop a hypothesis, scientists record observations, questions, and possible explanations. In conducting an experiment, scientists take full and accurate notes to keep a running account of methods, procedures, and results. To understand the significance of the results, scientists wrestle with it in writing. To communicate their findings, scientists report or publish the results so other scientists can read about them.

Most science writing reports the results of observation or discovery, either by firsthand experimentation or a library search. Scientific writing does not report the writer's opinions, values, or feelings; it aims for objectivity and accuracy. When you write in the sciences, try to separate your observations from your expectations or biases. Record what you see and hear and what the instruments tell you, not what you hope to discover. Keep in mind that your primary purpose is to present information accurately — not to persuade, argue, or entertain.

62 b The style of writing in the sciences

Most science writing seeks to convey information specifically, directly, economically, and accurately. But this does not mean that the style of all science writing is uniform. For example, the form and style of a laboratory report is quite different from the laboratory notebook on which it is based. An article in *Scientific*

American (written for a general readership) is quite different from one in *The Journal of Chemical Education* (written for college chemistry instructors). In writing in the sciences, keep the goals of clarity and directness in mind.

1   Choose simple rather than complex words when the meaning is the same, and use disciplinary terminology carefully and accurately.

2   Prefer simple to complex sentences.

3   Maintain a third-person point of view, to avoid the pronoun *I*. Use the passive voice when necessary to describe procedures: *The liquids were brought to a temperature of 35° C.*

4   Use the present tense to refer to established knowledge or to discuss conclusions. Use the past tense to describe methods and results.

5   Insert subheadings to help readers predict what is coming.

6   Include tables and figures when they can help explain your methods or results. Label each of these clearly, and mention them at appropriate points in the text.

62 c   Common forms of writing in the sciences

Scientific reports have set forms that allow readers to locate information in predictable places. Two common forms of writing in college science courses are laboratory notebooks and laboratory reports.

1 Laboratory notebooks

Lab notebooks are journals that scientists keep to monitor day-to-day laboratory work and experimentation. They are kept to record data — dates, times, temperatures, quantities, measurements — as well as to aid memory and keep records. Lab notebooks are also used to speculate about the meaning of the data. These privately kept notes serve as the basis for the information made public in formal laboratory reports.

When using a laboratory notebook, keep the following in mind.

■ Lab notebooks are usually bound with numbered pages rather than looseleaf pages. This unalterable order is meant to guarantee an accurate record of exactly what happened in the laboratory and when it happened.

■ Double-entry lab notebooks, with a vertical line down the center of each page, are especially useful. Data can be recorded on the left; the space to the right can be used for notes and speculations about the data.

■ Lab notebooks must be complete and detailed. It is crucial to record all information about an experiment or observation.

2 Laboratory reports

One of the major forms of writing in laboratory science courses is the laboratory report. A lab report describes exactly what happened in an experiment. The reader of a lab report should be able to replicate (or duplicate) an experiment by following the information in the report. While *labs* (as they are commonly called) vary slightly in format conventions from discipline to discipline, they all follow the following basic structure.

Introduction. The first section of the report defines the reasons for conducting the particular study, summarizes the findings of previous studies (a literature review), and states the researcher's hypothesis.

Methods and materials. Sometimes called "Procedure," this section details how the experiment was conducted and identifies all the equipment used. The experimental design is explained, and the methods of observation and measurement are described.

Results. In this section, the researcher reports the specific factual findings of the study; describing the data and patterns that emerged, but refraining from any judgment or interpretation.

Discussion. The final section of a laboratory report examines whether or not the results support the hypothesis. It may be somewhat speculative and focus on the possible implications and limitations of the experiment and its results. It may also point out the relationship of the current study to other researchers' results, suggest further hypotheses that could be tested, and draw theoretical conclusions.

Your instructor may also require an **abstract,** a highly abbreviated summary of the report. Although an abstract is placed at the beginning of the report, it is usually the last section written.

If you have mentioned published sources in your report, you will need to include a list of **references cited.** (See 62d2.)

62	d	**Documentation and format conventions: number system**

The number system of documentation is used in the applied sciences (chemistry, computer science, mathematics, and physics); the life sciences (biology, botany, zoology); and the medical sciences (medicine, nursing, general health). (See the end of this chapter for sample pages using this style of documentation.)

1 Conventions for number citation

In the number system of citation, writers alert readers to the use of other sources by citing a number, either in parentheses or superscript, that corresponds to a numbered list of sources at the end of the paper. Math and life science disciplines generally prefer parenthetical numbers; chemistry, physics, the medical fields, and computer science disciplines generally prefer superscript numbers.

If an author's name is used in the sentence, place the number in parentheses or in superscript immediately following the name.

```
Linhoffer (3) reported similar results.

Linhoffer[3] reported similar results.
```

If no author's name is used in the sentence, place the number immediately following the use of the source material. In using parenthetical numbers, science writers have the option of including the author's last name before the number in the parentheses: (Smith, 3).

The numbers cited in the text are organized either sequentially or alphabetically. In **sequential arrangement,** the first source mentioned in text is numbered "1," the second source mentioned is numbered "2," and so on. Any subsequent reference to the source is given the same number. (Sequential arrangement is preferred in chemistry, computer science, physics, the life sciences, and medicine.)

In **alphabetical arrangement,** numbers are assigned according to the alphabetical order of the authors' last names on the reference page. For example, a reference to an author named Smith, even if it is the first source cited in the text, might be accompanied by the number "12" because eleven other names on the list of references precede Smith alphabetically. (Alphabetical arrangement is preferred by mathematics.)

When using the sequential system, number your bibliography sequentially as you write, and continue to use the same number each time you cite that authority. When using the alphabetical system, arrange your bibliography alphabetically, and number accordingly.

2 Conventions for the list of references

The "Literature Cited" or "References" section provides publication information for all sources cited in the text. Sources are arranged either sequentially (according to their first reference in the text) or alphabetically (by author's last name).

Each scientific discipline has a unique format for documenting sources. Select the style appropriate to your discipline, or consult your instructor.

Life sciences

Biology, botany, zoology, anatomy, and physiology follow the documentation system recommended in the *CBE Style Manual,* rev. 5th ed. (Chicago: Council of Biology Editors, 1983). Number in-text citations sequentially in parentheses. The list of references is titled "Literature Cited," "References Cited," or "References," and uses the following general styles.

BOOK ENTRIES

```
1. Winfree, A. T. The timing of biological clocks.
   2nd ed. New York: Scientific American Library;
   1987:102-110.
```

Titles are not underlined, and only the first word is capitalized. The publisher is followed by a semicolon. The date is followed by a colon (no space), if page numbers are included.

PERIODICAL ENTRIES

> 2. Brown, S. G.; Wagsten, M. V. Socialization
>   processes in a female lowland gorilla. Zoo Biol.
>   5:269-280; 1986.

Neither article nor journal title is in quotation marks or underlined. There are no spaces between volume and page numbers. If an issue number is required, place it immediately after the volume number in parentheses.

Chemistry

Documentation style in chemistry is based on the American Chemical Society's *The ACS Style Guide: A Manual for Authors and Editors* (Washington, DC: American Chemical Society, 1986). In-text citations are made with superscript numbers and are arranged either sequentially or by author name and date. Entries on the reference list, titled "Literature Cited," use the following general styles.

BOOK ENTRIES

> 1. Siggia, S.; Hanna, J. G. <u>Quantitative Organic
>   Analysis via Functional Groups</u>, 4th ed.; R. E.
>   Krieger: Malabar, FL, 1988; pp. 55-60.

PERIODICAL ENTRIES

> 2. Scott, J. M. W. <u>J. Chem. Ed</u>. 1992,69,600-602.

Article titles are not included. If an issue number is required, place it immediately after the volume number in parentheses. There are no spaces between date, volume, and page numbers for periodicals. Use all digits for page sequences.

Physics

Physics follows the style of the *AIP Style Manual*, 4th ed. (New York: American Institute of Physics, 1990). Number in-text citations sequentially using superscript. The reference page, entitled "References," uses the following styles.

BOOK ENTRIES

[1] Pagels, H. R. <u>Perfect Symmetry: The Search for the Beginning of Time</u> (Bantam, New York, 1986), pp. 78-86.

PERIODICAL ENTRIES

[2] Crawford, F. S. Am. J. Phys. 60, 751-752 (1992).

Article titles are not included. If issue numbers are required, place them immediately after the volume number in parentheses and follow with a comma. The date comes last.

63 Writing in Business

This chapter describes the aims, style, and common forms of writing in the business and professional world. Like writing in the social and physical sciences, business writing puts a premium on information; like writing in the humanities, it is highly influenced by the relation between writer and reader.

63 a The aims of writing in business

The guiding objectives of successful companies are efficiency, accuracy, and responsibility: procedures are designed to involve minimal wasted time and energy, care is taken to avoid errors, and transactions are conducted fairly.

Communication in business mirrors these precepts. Writing in business is primarily practical and instrumental, because its goal is to get things done. In terms of efficiency, it should be simple, direct, and brief; in terms of accuracy, it should convey correct information and conform to standard conventions; in terms of responsibility, it should be honest and courteous.

Business writers must be aware of their audience. They must ask, To whom is the communication being written? What information do they already have? What else do they need to know? What does this communication need to include in order to have its intended effect? What, if any, secondary audience is likely to read this communication? Business writers must also be concerned about presentation. To make a good impression, any piece of writing must be neat, clean, and correct.

63 b The style of writing in business

Writing in business should be clear, direct, economical, and conventional. In general, the preferred tone is objective and fairly formal (although when addressing someone you know well, a more personal, informal tone may be appropriate). For most business writing, the following guidelines should be considered.

1 Get to the main point immediately. Avoid unnecessary information or repetition. Keep in mind that in business your reader's time — as well as your own — is valuable.

2 Write in simple, direct language. Keep your sentences as straightforward and readable as possible.

3 Choose the active voice rather than the passive.

4 Use technical terminology or jargon sparingly. Write out complete names of companies, products, and titles. Explain any terms that could be misunderstood.

5 Avoid emotional or potentially offensive language, and try to maintain a level of courtesy even when lodging a complaint. Avoid sexist construction.

6 Use numbers or descriptive headings when needed to help readers locate information quickly.

7 Use graphs, charts, and other illustrations when they convey information more clearly than words would.

63 **c** **Common forms of writing in business**

Common forms of writing in business include letters, résumés, and memos.

1 **Business letters**

Business letters commonly request, inform, or complain, in many cases to an audience unknown to the letter writer. State the purpose clearly and provide all information needed to make responding easy for the reader.

Business letters are typed on 8 1/2" × 11" paper, one side only. Most business letters use block format, in which every element of the letter is typed flush with the left margin and paragraphs are not indented. All business letters include the following elements.

Heading. The sender's address (but not name) and the date are typed single-spaced approximately one inch from the top of the first page of the letter. Spell out all street and town names and months in full; abbreviate state names using the standard postal abbreviations. Zip codes should be included.

Business Letter: Block Format on Letterhead

Doyle Advertising Services
1011 Oakhollow Road
Norman, Oklahoma 73071   **LETTERHEAD**
405-555-1966 telephone
405-555-1982 fax

October 11, 19XX   **DATE**

Ms. Tamara Blackburn
Marketing Director
Tamlyn Foods   **INSIDE**
6850 Amberly Way   **ADDRESS**
Cordova, TN 38018

Dear Ms. Blackburn: **GREETING**   **BODY, UNINDENTED**

Tony Adamo, your account representative, asked that I
give you an update about the direct mail campaign for
Tamlyn's Muffin Chips.

During the week of September 1, our direct mail
contractor sent mailings to approximately 7,500 homes in
the Oklahoma City/Little Rock test markets. As you know,
these mailings contained a sample-size package of the
chips, along with a postage-paid questionnaire that
recipients could return to receive a cents-off coupon
for other Tamlyn products.

As of October 9, 2,267 questionnaires had been returned,
a very high response rate. We are currently compiling
the questionnaire results and should have a formal
report ready for you by October 15. The cents-off
coupons will be mailed out October 22.

If you have any other questions, please give me a call
at extension 557.

Sincerely,   **CLOSING**

Casey Dorris   **SIGNATURE**

Casey Dorris
Direct Mail Coordinator

If you are using letterhead stationery, type the date two line spaces below the letterhead address.

Inside address. Type the recipient's address two or more line spaces below the heading (depending on how much space is needed to center the letter on the page). Include the person's full name (and a courtesy title, if appropriate), followed by his or her position (if needed), the name of the division within the company, the company name, and the full street, city, and state address.

When writing an unknown person, always try to find out the name, perhaps by calling the company switchboard. If this is impossible, use an appropriate title (*Personnel Director* or *Claims Manager*, for example) in place of a name.

Greeting. Type the opening salutation two line spaces below the inside address (*Dear Dr. Jones, Dear James Wong*) followed by a colon. If you and the recipient are on a first-name basis, it is appropriate to use only the first name. If you do not know the recipient's name, use *To Whom It May Concern:* or some variation of *Dear Claims Manager:* or *Attention: Director of Marketing* (the latter without a second colon). Avoid the old-fashioned *Dear Sir* or *Dear Sir or Madam.*

Body. Begin the body of the letter two line spaces below the greeting. Single-space within paragraphs; double-space between paragraphs. If your reason for writing is clear and simple, state it directly in the first paragraph. If it is absolutely necessary to detail a situation, provide background, or supply context, do so in the first paragraph or two, and then move on to describe your purpose in writing.

If your letter is more than a page long, type the addressee's last name, the date, and the page number flush with the margin of each subsequent page.

Closing. Type the complimentary closing two spaces after the last line of the body of the letter. The most common closings are *Sincerely, Cordially, Yours truly, Respectfully yours* (formal), and *Best regards* (informal). Capitalize only the first word of the closing; follow it with a comma.

Signature. Type your full name, including any title, four line spaces below the closing. Sign the letter with your full name (or just first name if you have addressed the recipient by first name) in blue or black ink in the space above your typed name.

Additional information. You may provide additional brief information below your signature, flush with the left margin. Such

Cover Letter

405 Martin Street
Lexington, Kentucky 40508   **HEADING**
February 10, 19XX

Barbara McGarry, Director
Kentucky Council on the Arts
953 Versailles Road   **INSIDE ADDRESS**
Box 335
Frankfort, Kentucky 40602

Dear Ms. McGarry: **GREETING**   **BODY, UNINDENTED**

John Huff, one of my professors at the University of
Kentucky, recommended that I write to you regarding
openings in the Council's internship program this
summer. I would like to apply for one of these positions
and have enclosed my résumé for your consideration.

As you will note, my academic background combines a
primary concentration in business administration with a
minor in the fine arts. My interest in the arts goes back
to childhood when I first heard a performance by the
Lexington Symphony, and I have continued to pursue that
interest ever since. My goal after graduation is a
career in arts administration, focusing on fundraising
and outreach for a major public institution.

I hope you'll agree that my experience, particularly my
work with the local Community Concerts association, is
strong preparation for an internship with the Council. I
would appreciate the opportunity to discuss my
qualifications with you in greater detail.

I will call your office within the next few weeks to see
about setting up an appointment to meet with you. In the
meantime, you can reach me at the above address or by
phone at 555-4033.

Thank you for your attention.

Sincerely,   **CLOSING**

Chris Aleand   **SIGNATURE**

Chris Aleandro

enc.   **ADDITIONAL INFORMATION**

Résumé

Chris Aleandro
405 Martin Street
Lexington, Kentucky 40508
(606) 555-4033

Objective: Internship in arts administration.

Education

University of Kentucky: 1991 to present.
Currently a sophomore majoring in business administration with a minor in art history. Degree expected May 1995.

Henry Clay High School (Lexington, KY): 1987 to 1991.
College preparatory curriculum, with emphasis in art and music.

Related Work Experience

Community Concerts, Inc.: 1992 to present.
Part-time promotion assistant, reporting to the local director. Responsibilities include assisting with scheduling, publicity, subscription/ticketing procedures, and fundraising. Position involves general office duties as well as heavy contact with subscribers and artists.

Habitat for Humanity: September to November 1993.
Co-chaired campus fundraising drive that included a benefit concert, raising $55,000.

Art in the Schools Program: 1991 to 1993.
Volunteer, through the Education Division of the Lexington Center for the Arts. Trained to conduct hands-on art appreciation presentations in grade school classrooms, visiting one school a month.

Other Work Experience

Record City: 1991 to 1993 (part time and summers).
Sales clerk and assistant manager in a music store.

Special skills: Wordperfect 5.1; desktop design of brochures, programs, and other materials.

References

Professor John Huff	Ms. Joan Thomas
School of Business	Community Concerts,
Administration	Inc.
The University of Kentucky	1200 Fayette Street
Lexington, KY 40506	Lexington, KY 40513
(606) 555-3110	(606) 555-2900

information may include recipients of copies of the letter (*cc Jennifer Rodriguez*); the word *Enclosures* (or the abbreviation *enc.*) to indicate you are also enclosing additional material mentioned in the letter; and, if the letter was typed by someone other than the writer, the writer's initials and the typist's initials (*TF/jlw*).

2 Résumés

A résumé is a brief summary of an applicant's qualifications for employment. It outlines education, work experience, and other activities and interests so a prospective employer can decide quickly whether or not an applicant is a good prospect for a particular job. Try to tailor your résumé for the position you are seeking by emphasizing experience that is most relevant to the position. Preparing a résumé on a computer lets you revise it easily and quickly.

Generally, a résumé is sent out with a cover letter that introduces the applicant, indicates the position applied for, and offers additional information that cannot be accommodated on the résumé itself. Examples of a résumé and cover letter appear on the preceding pages.

Résumés should be brief and to the point, preferably no more than a page long (if relevant experience is extensive, more than one page is acceptable). Résumé formats vary in minor ways, but most include the following information.

Personal information. Résumés begin with the applicant's name, address, and phone number, usually centered at the top.

Objective. Many résumés include a line summarizing the applicant's objective, naming either the specific job sought or describing a larger career goal.

Education. Most first-time job applicants list their educational background first, since their employment history is likely to be fairly limited. Name the last two or three schools attended (including dates of attendance and degrees), starting with the most recent. Indicate major areas of study, and highlight any relevant courses. Also consider including grade point average, awards, and anything else that shows you in a good light. When employment history is more detailed, educational background is often included at the end of the résumé.

Work experience. Starting with the most recent, list all relevant jobs, including company name, dates of employment, and a brief job description. Use your judgment about listing jobs where you had difficulties with your employer.

Special skills or interests. It is often useful to mention special skills, interests, or activities that provide additional clues about your abilities and personality.

References. Provide the names, addresses, and phone numbers of two or three people — teachers, supervisors, employers — whom you trust to give a good reference for you. (Make sure you get their permission first.) You may want to conclude with the line "References available on request."

63 **d** **Documentation and format conventions**

The format and style of documentation for business reports usually follow the guidelines of the American Psychological Association. (See 61d.)

A Grammar Reference

The **sentence,** a group of words expressing a complete thought, is the basic unit of speech and writing. Sentence **grammar** describes how sentences are organized and structured and describes the function of each word in a sentence. Understanding grammar can help you identify and improve areas of possible confusion or misreading. It can help you find places where nonstandard structures or usages may distract attention from meaning.

In English, there are two main approaches to sentence grammar. Both describe the role of a word in a sentence depending on its meaning, its form, and its position. The first approach looks at an individual word and asks, "What 'kind' of word is it?" This question leads to a discussion of words as **parts of speech:** nouns, pronouns, verbs, adjectives, adverbs, prepositions, conjunctions, and interjections. This chapter discusses words as parts of speech.

The second approach to sentence grammar examines the organization of a sentence to determine the role of words and phrases within it. It asks, "What function does each word or group of words serve in the sentence?" This analysis leads to a discussion of the basic **elements of a sentence:** the subject and the predicate (including objects and complements) and groups of words called phrases and clauses. Chapter 65 discusses words and word groups as elements of a sentence.

The part of speech of a word depends on its meaning and position in a sentence. Indeed, some words may appear as one part of speech in one context and as another part of speech in another. The word *ride,* for example, can be either a verb or a noun.

NOUN	They *ride* their horses.
VERB	They went for a *ride.*

To tell what part of speech a word is, you must look not only at the word itself, but also at its relation to other words in the sentence.

64 a Nouns

Nouns are words that name persons, animals, places, things, or ideas: *woman, Lassie, Grand Canyon, tree,* and *virtue* are all nouns.

1 Kinds of nouns

Proper nouns are the names of particular people, animals, places, or things: *Marie Curie, Black Beauty, Kentucky, USS Constitution, Catholicism.* Proper nouns are almost always capitalized. (See 51c.) Nouns that can apply to any member of a class or group are **generic nouns** or **common nouns:** *scientist, horse, state, ship, religion.* They are generally not capitalized.

Nouns that refer to things that can be seen, heard, touched, smelled, or tasted are called **concrete nouns:** *butterfly, telephone, ice, fudge.* Those that refer to ideas or concepts that cannot directly be sensed are **abstract nouns:** *beauty, communication, temperature, temptation.* (See 29a for suggestions about using concrete and abstract nouns.)

Nouns that refer to one or more individual items that can readily be counted are called **count nouns:** *one book, two books.* Count nouns are usually concrete nouns, though some are abstract nouns: *one idea, several ideas.* Nouns referring to entities that cannot be counted individually are called **mass nouns** or **noncount nouns:** *sand, water, fudge.* These are seldom made plural, except occasionally in a poetic sense: *the sands of time.* The things denoted by mass nouns are counted only as part of a more complex phrase: *grains of sand, pails of water, pieces of fudge.* Most abstract nouns are mass nouns.

Nouns like *crowd, couple,* and *flock* that refer to groups of similar things are called **collective nouns.**

2 Singular and plural nouns

Nouns that refer to a single individual are **singular:** *boy, town, box.* Those that refer to two or more are **plural:** *boys, towns,* *boxes.* Most nouns add *-s* or *-es* to the singular to create the plural. A few nouns change spelling in other ways to form the plural: *goose, geese; child, children; man, men; medium, media.* And a few stay the same regardless of number: *sheep, sheep.* Mass nouns (see 64a1) are almost never plural. (See Chapter 50 for more on forming plurals.)

3 Possessive forms of nouns

Nouns change form to show possession, ownership, or connection, usually by adding an apostrophe and an *-s: the king's son, the town's mayor.* A noun that has changed form in this way is said to be in the **possessive case.** (For more on case, see 64b2.) Possession or connection can also be expressed by using an *of* phrase: *son of the king, mayor of the town.* (See 47b for guidelines on forming possessives of plural nouns and nouns that end in *-s.*)

64 b Pronouns

The word **pronoun** means "for noun," and as the derivation suggests, a pronoun is a word that substitutes for a noun or another pronoun. The word for which the pronoun stands is called its **antecedent** or **referent.**

       antecedent   **pronoun**
Sean helped Ramona paint her room.

    pronoun   **antecedent**
Because of its construction, the boat was unsinkable.

Usually an antecedent appears before the pronoun, as in the first example. Sometimes the antecedent follows shortly after the pronoun, as in the second example. Pronouns with no clear antecedents can cause readers confusion and frustration. (See Chapter 40.) A pronoun must agree with (or correspond to) its antecedent in terms of person, number, and gender. (See Chapter 39.)

1 Kinds of pronouns

Personal pronouns

Personal pronouns, such as *me, you, their,* and *it,* refer to specific people, animals, places, things, or ideas.

I asked *you* to buy *it.*

Personal pronouns change their form depending on their role in the sentence. They change form to show **person,** a quality that indicates the relationship of the person or thing named by the pronoun to the writer or speaker. First-person pronouns refer to the speaker or writer directly: *I, we.* Second-person pronouns refer to those being addressed: *you.* Third-person pronouns refer to someone other than the speaker or writer or those being addressed: *he, she, it, they.*

Personal pronouns change form to show **number.** They are either singular (*I, he, she, it*) or plural (*we, they*). The pronoun *you* does not change to show number; it is the same whether it is plural or singular.

Singular personal pronouns change form to show **gender.** They are either masculine (*he*), feminine (*she*), or neuter (*it*).

Personal pronouns change form to show **case.** (See 64b2.)

Indefinite pronouns

Indefinite pronouns, such as *anyone, everybody, something, many, few,* and *none,* are called "indefinite" because they do not require an antecedent. That is, they do not need to refer to a specific person, animal, place, thing, or idea. Often they are used to denote a quantity.

Many are called, but *few* are chosen.

Indefinite pronouns change form to indicate the possessive case the same way that nouns do, by adding an apostrophe and an -*s*: *anyone's idea, everyone's preference.* They do not change form to show person, number, or gender. Most are either always singular (*someone*) or always plural (*many*). A few can be either singular or plural, depending on the context. (See 36g.)

Demonstrative pronouns

Demonstrative pronouns, such as *this, that, these,* and *those* are used to identify or point out a specific person, place, or thing.

This is the largest one we have.

Demonstrative pronouns change form to show number: *this* and *that* are singular, and *these* and *those* are plural.

These words are demonstrative pronouns only when they are not immediately followed by a noun. If they are directly followed by a noun, they are adjectives: *I enjoyed reading this book.*

Relative pronouns

A relative pronoun, such as *who, whom, which,* or *that,* introduces a dependent clause and "relates" that clause to an antecedent elsewhere in the sentence.

He chose the tool *that* worked best.

Some relative pronouns are indefinite: *whoever, what, whatever, whichever.* They have no specific antecedents: *Take whatever you want.* Relative pronouns change form to show case. (See 64b2.) (For more on relative pronouns and dependent clauses, see 26e–g.)

Interrogative pronouns

Interrogative pronouns, such as *who, what,* and *whose,* are used to ask questions.

Who is there?

Interrogative pronouns change form to show case. (See 64b2.)

Reflexive and intensive pronouns

Pronouns ending in *-self* or *-selves,* such as *myself, yourself,* and *themselves,* are **reflexive pronouns** when they refer back to, or "reflect," the subject of the sentence.

Dave cut *himself* while shaving.

The same pronouns are called **intensive pronouns** when they are used to emphasize, or "intensify," an antecedent.

I talked to the president *herself.*

Unlike reflexive pronouns, intensive pronouns can be omitted without changing the sense of the sentence: *I talked to the president.*

Reflexive and intensive pronouns change form to show person, number, and gender, just as personal pronouns do.

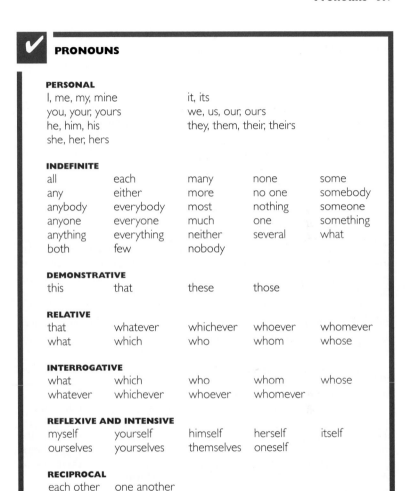

✔ **PRONOUNS**

PERSONAL

I, me, my, mine	it, its
you, your, yours	we, us, our, ours
he, him, his	they, them, their, theirs
she, her, hers	

INDEFINITE

all	each	many	none	some
any	either	more	no one	somebody
anybody	everybody	most	nothing	someone
anyone	everyone	much	one	something
anything	everything	neither	several	what
both	few	nobody		

DEMONSTRATIVE

this	that	these	those

RELATIVE

that	whatever	whichever	whoever	whomever
what	which	who	whom	whose

INTERROGATIVE

what	which	who	whom	whose
whatever	whichever	whoever	whomever	

REFLEXIVE AND INTENSIVE

myself	yourself	himself	herself	itself
ourselves	yourselves	themselves	oneself	

RECIPROCAL

each other	one another

Reciprocal pronouns

The reciprocal pronouns are *each other* and *one another*. They are used to describe an action or state that is shared between two people, animals, places, things, or ideas.

The investigators helped *one another* with the research.

Reciprocal pronouns have possessive forms: *each other's*, *one another's*. Otherwise, they do not change form.

2 Pronoun case

Personal pronouns, indefinite pronouns, and the relative or interrogative pronouns *who* and *whoever* change form according to case. **Case** indicates the role a word plays in a sentence, whether it is a subject, an object, or a possessive. (For more on subjects and objects, see 65a and 65c.)

subject	possessive	object
Anne took	Betty's book away from	Michelle.
She took	hers away from	her.

The three cases are the subjective case, the objective case, and the possessive case. Nouns change form to show the possessive case, usually by adding an apostrophe and -s to the end of the word. (See 64a.) Nouns in the subjective case and the objective case have the same form. Personal pronouns and the relative or interrogative pronouns *who* and *whoever* change form to show all three cases. Indefinite pronouns change form to show the possessive case by adding an apostrophe and -s, as nouns do.

SUBJECTIVE		OBJECTIVE		POSSESSIVE	
Singular	**Plural**	**Singular**	**Plural**	**Singular**	**Plural**
I	we	me	us	my, mine	our, ours
you	you	you	you	your, yours	your, yours
he	they	him	them	his	their, theirs
she	they	her	them	her, hers	their, theirs
it	they	it	them	its	their, theirs
who		whom		whose	
whoever		whomever			

The **subjective case** indicates that a pronoun is the subject of a clause or is a subject complement.

We should leave now.

It was *she who* wanted to leave.

The **objective case** indicates that a pronoun is the object of a verb, a preposition, or a verbal.

Whom did they choose?

The judging seemed unfair to *us*.

Seeing *her* made the holiday complete.

The **possessive case** indicates possession, ownership, or connection. Possessive personal pronouns occur in two forms. The adjective form (*my, your*) modifies a noun or gerund. The noun form (*mine, yours*) stands alone as a subject or complement.

That is *my* hat.

The hat is *mine*.

(For more on choosing pronoun case, see Chapter 41.)

64 **c** Verbs

A **verb** describes an action or state of being.

The logger *chops* the tree.

The air *is* fragrant with the scent of pine.

The verb of a sentence changes form to show person, number, tense, voice, and mood. The **person** indicates who performed the action. The **number** indicates how many people performed the action. The **tense** indicates when the action was performed. The **voice** indicates whether the grammatical subject of the sentence acts or is acted upon. The **mood** indicates the speaker's reaction to or opinion of the action.

PERSON	I write, she writes
NUMBER	he sings, they sing
TENSE	she argues, she argued
VOICE	she *read* the book, the book *was read*
MOOD	I *am* a millionaire, if I *were* a millionaire

A verb with a specific person and number is called a **finite verb.** A verb form without these properties is called a **verbal.** (See

64c5.) For complete information on verb person, number, tense, and mood, see Chapter 35. For information on verb voice, see 64c4.

In addition to one-word verbs, English has many **phrasal verbs** or **multiple-word verbs.** These consist of a verb plus a **particle,** a word that may serve as a preposition in other contexts but which is so important to the meaning of the phrasal verb that it is considered a part of it. Both the verb and the particle are necessary to convey the meaning of the phrasal verb, and that meaning usually cannot be determined by examining the parts individually. In the sentence, *That performance came off very well,* for example, *came off* is a phrasal verb; its meaning (*succeeded*) is not easy to determine by considering the separate meanings of the words *come* and *off.*

◼ Auxiliary verbs

One sentence may have several verbs in it. The verb that expresses the action or state of the subject of the sentence is the **main verb.**

main verb
After swimming for an hour, he decided to go home.

In some cases, the main verb of a sentence is preceded by one or more **auxiliary verbs** (or **helping verbs**). Together, the main verb and its auxiliaries form a **verb phrase.**

verb phrase
auxiliary verb   main verb
My oldest sister was doing a crossword puzzle.

Forms of the verbs *be, do,* and *have* are the most common auxiliary verbs. These auxiliaries are used to form certain tenses, add emphasis, ask questions, make negative statements, and form the passive voice. These verbs can also stand alone as main verbs. When used as auxiliaries, these verbs change to show person, number, and tense.

Certain auxiliary verbs, called **modal auxiliaries** or **modals,** add to the verb the meanings of desire, intent, permission, possibility, or obligation. Modals are not usually used alone as main verbs. English has both one-word modals and phrasal modals (or multiple-word modals).

ONE-WORD MODALS

can	may	must	should	would
could	might	shall	will	

PHRASAL MODALS

be able to	be supposed to	have got to
be allowed to	had better	ought to
be going to	have to	used to

The one-word modals do not change form to show person, number, or tense: *I can sing, and you can dance.* Most of the phrasal modals do change form to show person, number, and tense: *I am able to sing, and you are able to dance.* The phrasal modals *had better, ought to,* and *used to* do not change form.

2 **Transitive and intransitive verbs**

Some verbs require a **direct object,** a word or words that indicate who or what received the action of the verb. (See 65c.)

direct object
|
She threw the ball.

A verb that has a direct object is a **transitive verb.** A verb that does not have a direct object is an **intransitive verb.** Many verbs may be transitive or intransitive, depending on the context.

TRANSITIVE   Joey *grew* tomatoes last summer.

INTRANSITIVE   The tomatoes *grew* rapidly.

3 **Linking verbs**

Linking verbs include *be, become, seem,* and verbs describing sensations — *appear, look, feel, taste, smell, sound,* and so on. They link the subject of a sentence to an element, called a **subject complement,** that renames or identifies the subject. Subject complements can be nouns or adjectives. (See 65d.)

It may help to think of a linking verb as an equal sign linking two equivalent terms.

Sue is nice.	Sue = nice
They felt tired.	they = tired
Jake was a recent graduate.	Jake = a recent graduate

4 Voice

Most transitive verbs may be used in either the active or the passive voice. In a sentence using the **active voice,** the subject of the sentence is the person or thing performing the action or state expressed by the verb. In a sentence using the **passive voice,** the subject of the sentence is the person or thing acted upon.

ACTIVE   The woman pushes the baby carriage.

PASSIVE   The baby carriage is pushed by the woman.

The passive voice is formed by using the past participle of the verb with a form of the verb *be* as an auxiliary verb. (See 64c1.) The object of the sentence in the active voice becomes the subject of the passive voice sentence. The subject of the active voice sentence, if it appears at all in the passive voice sentence, is usually an **agent** following the preposition *by: Movies are often seen by teenagers.* Some passive voice sentences do not have agents: *Movies are often seen at night.*

5 Verbals

A **verbal** is a verb form that does not change form to show person or number. There are three types of verbals.

1 **Infinitives:** the base form of the verb, usually preceded by the word *to*

2 **Gerunds:** the *-ing* form of the verb functioning as a noun

3 **Participles:** either the past participle (usually ending in *-ed* or *-d*) or the present participle (ending in *-ing*)

The infinitive changes form to show tense.

PRESENT INFINITIVE   *To sing* at Carnegie Hall is her ambition.

PAST INFINITIVE   *To have sung* so well last night is something you should be proud of.

After prepositions and certain verbs, the *to* of an infinitive does not appear: *He did everything except wash the floor. She let them visit their cousins.*

A verbal can function as a noun, an adjective, or an adverb, but it cannot function as the main verb of a sentence or clause.

NOUN   *Jogging* is a great form of exercise.

ADJECTIVE   We had *boiled* eggs for breakfast.

ADVERB   This machine was designed *to self-destruct.*

Verbals can form **verbal phrases** by taking objects, complements, and modifiers. For more on verbal phrases, see 65e.

---

64 d   Adjectives and adverbs

Adjectives and **adverbs** modify — that is, they further describe, identify, or limit the meaning of other words. They have many similar properties, so sometimes adjectives and adverbs are grouped together as **modifiers.** The difference between them lies in what they modify. Adjectives modify nouns, pronouns, or phrases and clauses used as nouns.

The tourist spotted *scarlet* tanagers. [Modifies noun *tanagers.*]

They were *beautiful.* [Modifies pronoun *they.*]

To see them would be *delightful.* [Modifies phrase *to see them.*]

Adverbs modify verbs, adjectives, verbals, or other adverbs; they can also modify clauses or entire sentences.

His judgment was made *hastily.* [Modifies verb *was made.*]

The feathers are *quite* beautiful. [Modifies adjective *beautiful.*]

Writing *well* takes practice. [Modifies verbal *writing.*]

She sings *very* nicely. [Modifies adverb *nicely.*]

Surprisingly, the band played for hours. [Modifies entire sentence.]

See 37a for more on distinguishing adjectives and adverbs.

Adjectives and adverbs come in three **degrees:** positive, comparative, and superlative. A modifier that makes no comparison is known as the **positive** form. A **comparative** adjective or adverb makes a comparison between two things. A **superlative** adjective or adverb distinguishes among three or more things.

POSITIVE   He lives in an *old* house.

COMPARATIVE   It is *older* than mine.

SUPERLATIVE   It is the *oldest* house in the county.

See 37e for more on forming comparatives and superlatives.

Kinds of adjectives

Adjectives that describe qualities or attributes are called **descriptive adjectives:** *gray* sky, *beautiful* garden. Adjectives that do not describe qualities but instead identify or specify the words they modify are called **limiting adjectives:** *this* sky, *my* garden.

Many types of words can serve as limiting adjectives. The words *a, an,* and *the* are **articles** and are classified as adjectives. The word *the* is called the **definite article** because it identifies, or "defines," precisely which person or thing is being referred to. The words *a* and *an* are called **indefinite articles.** The choice between *a* and *an* depends on the initial sound of the following word: *a* precedes a consonant sound or a long *u* sound (*a monster, a university*) and *an* precedes any other vowel sound (*an apron*). Several types of **pronouns** can serve as limiting adjectives.

PERSONAL   She is going to buy *her* dog today.

RELATIVE   She hasn't decided *which* dog she will take.

DEMONSTRATIVE   She likes *that* dog very much.

INDEFINITE   But *every* dog looks good to her.

These words are considered adjectives only when they are directly followed by a noun. (See 64a1.) **Numbers** can also be limiting adjectives when they are directly followed by a noun: *two dogs.*

Adjectives derived from proper nouns are called **proper adjectives:** *Alaskan, Shakespearean, British.* Like proper nouns, proper adjectives are always capitalized. (See 51c.)

Sometimes a noun is used as an adjective without any change of form. Such a noun is called a **noun modifier.**

He works as a *masonry* contractor and employs six *stone* masons.

The police dispersed the rioters with a *water* cannon.

2 Kinds of adverbs

In addition to the usual kind of descriptive adverb (*quickly, often*) there are several special groups of words that are classified as adverbs. The **negators** *no* and *not* are considered adverbs. **Conjunctive adverbs,** such as *however* and *therefore*, are words that modify an entire clause and express its relationship to another clause. (For a list of common conjunctive adverbs, see Chapter 26.) **Relative adverbs,** such as *where*, *why*, and *when*, introduce adjective or adverb clauses. (See 65f.)

NEGATOR	We were *not* ready.
CONJUNCTIVE ADVERB	*However*, the train was leaving.
RELATIVE ADVERB	We were visiting the house *where* I grew up.

64 e Prepositions

Words such as *to, with, by,* and *of* are **prepositions.** In addition to one-word prepositions such as these, English has several **phrasal prepositions** or **multiple-word prepositions,** which are made up of two or more words: *because of, except for, instead of.*

A preposition shows the relationship between a noun or pronoun — the **object** of the preposition — and other words in the sentence. The preposition, its object, and any associated modifiers are together called a **prepositional phrase.** In the sentence *I sat on the bed*, for example, *on* is a preposition, *bed* is the object of the preposition, and *on the bed* is a prepositional phrase. (For more on prepositional phrases, see 65e.)

A word is a preposition only if it introduces a phrase containing an object. Words that are commonly used as prepositions may also function as adverbs and as particles (parts of phrasal verbs).

PREPOSITION	I looked *up* the street.
ADVERB	The woman looked *up*.
PARTICLE	He looked *up* the word in the dictionary.

(For more on adverbs, see 64d. For more on phrasal verbs, see 64c.)

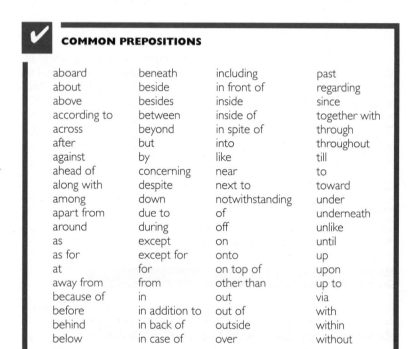

✔ COMMON PREPOSITIONS

aboard	beneath	including	past
about	beside	in front of	regarding
above	besides	inside	since
according to	between	inside of	together with
across	beyond	in spite of	through
after	but	into	throughout
against	by	like	till
ahead of	concerning	near	to
along with	despite	next to	toward
among	down	notwithstanding	under
apart from	due to	of	underneath
around	during	off	unlike
as	except	on	until
as for	except for	onto	up
at	for	on top of	upon
away from	from	other than	up to
because of	in	out	via
before	in addition to	out of	with
behind	in back of	outside	within
below	in case of	over	without

64 f Conjunctions

The word **conjunction** comes from Latin words meaning "join" and "with." Conjunctions join two or more words, phrases, or clauses with one another. The **coordinating conjunctions** — *and*, *but*, *or*, *nor*, *for*, *so*, and *yet* — imply that the elements linked are equal or similar in importance.

Bill *and* I went shopping.

The bus will take you to the market *or* to the theater.

Correlative conjunctions always appear in pairs: *either . . . or, neither . . . nor, both . . . and, not only . . . but also, whether . . . or.* Correlative conjunctions join pairs of similar words, phrases, or clauses.

Neither Jack *nor* his brother was in school this morning.

She *not only* sings *but also* dances.

Subordinating conjunctions, such as *after, before, when, where, while, because, if, although,* and *unless,* introduce ideas in dependent clauses that are less important to the point of the passage than the ideas in main or independent clauses. (See 26e for a complete list of subordinating conjunctions.)

While you finish sewing, I will start dinner.

I left *because* I was angry.

Conjunctive adverbs, such as *however, therefore,* and *furthermore,* link independent clauses. The clauses they link must be separated by a semicolon or a period. (See 33b2 and 45a.)

I am finished; *therefore,* I am going home.

64 g Interjections

Interjections are words inserted, or "interjected," into a sentence. They may show surprise, dismay, or strong emotion. They most often appear in speech or dialogue, and their presence often calls for an exclamation point.

Ouch! That pipe is hot!

Gosh, you're muddy all over!

Yes, it does.

The principal elements of a sentence are the subject and the predicate. In general, the **subject** names who or what performs the action of the sentence or, if there is no action, whom or what the sentence is about. (Exceptions are sentences with verbs in the passive voice or the imperative mood. See 64c4.) The subject consists of a noun, a pronoun, or another word or group of words that can serve as a noun, along with all of its modifiers. The **predicate** contains the verb of the sentence, along with its objects, its modifiers, and any words that refer back to it. Both subject and predicate can be one word or many:

predicate

subject |

Rain fell.

subject   predicate

A women in a yellow raincoat ran to catch the bus.

As in these examples, the subject usually comes at the beginning of a sentence and the predicate at the end. Sometimes, as in questions, the subject may follow part of the predicate.

predicate

subject

Do you know a good roofing contractor?

Simple subject. The simple subject of a sentence is the person or thing that acts, is described, or is acted upon. Usually this is a noun or pronoun, but it can also be a verbal, a phrase, or a clause that is used as a noun.

NOUN   Long *shadows* crept along the lawn.

PRONOUN   *He* looked exactly like a cowboy.

VERBAL   *Singing* pleases Alan.

PHRASE   *To work hard* is our lot in life.

CLAUSE   *That LeeAnn could dance* amazed us all.

Complete subject. The complete subject consists of the simple subject and all words that modify or directly relate to it. Elements of a complete subject can be adjectives, adverbs, phrases, or clauses.

> *Winning the last game of a dreadful season that included injuries, losing streaks, and a strike* was small consolation to the team.

In this example, the simple subject is the gerund *Winning. The last game* is the object of *Winning;* the prepositional phrase *of a dreadful season* modifies *game;* and the clause *that included injuries, losing streaks, and a strike* modifies *season.*

Compound subject. A compound subject includes two or more subjects linked by a coordinating conjunction such as *and* or *or.*

> *Books, records, and videotapes* filled the room.

Implied subject. An implied subject is one that is not stated directly but may be understood.

> Come to the meeting to learn about the preschool program.

In this example, the subject is understood to be *you.* Commands with verbs in the imperative mood often have the implied subject you.

65 **b**   **Predicates**

Simple predicate. The simple predicate consists of the main verb of the sentence and any auxiliaries.

> The candidate who wins the debate *will win* the election.

Complete predicate. The complete predicate consists of the simple predicate and all words that modify or directly relate to it. Objects and complements are part of the predicate. Modifiers, including phrases, clauses, and single words, are part of the predicate if they modify the verb, object, or complement.

The farmer *gave the pigs enough food to last the weekend.*

The verb *gave* is the simple predicate. *Food* is the direct object of the verb and *pigs* is the indirect object of the verb. The words *the* and *enough* modify *pigs* and *food*, respectively. The phrase *to last the weekend* also modifies *food*.

Compound predicate. The following sentence has four verbs with the same subject.

At the beach we *ate* our picnic, *swam* in the surf, *read* to each other, and *walked* on the sand.

Ate, slept, read, and *walked* all have the subject *we.* A predicate in which two or more verbs have the same subject is a compound predicate.

65 **c** **Objects of verbs**

A **direct object** completes the meaning of a transitive verb.

The company paid its *workers* a day early.

Without the direct object *workers* and its modifiers, this sentence would be incomplete. If you read *The company paid,* you would not think it was a complete sentence, expressing a complete thought. You would ask, *Whom or what did the company pay?* Asking a *Whom?* or *What?* question about the subject and verb of a sentence is a good way to find its direct object. (For more on transitive verbs, see 64c2.)

An **indirect object** is a person or thing to whom (or for whom) the action of the verb is directed. It must be a noun or a pronoun that precedes the direct object. It cannot be accompanied by a preposition (or it becomes the object of the preposition, not the object of the verb).

indirect object   direct object
The quarterback threw Lionel Fischer the ball.

To find an indirect object, identify the verb and the direct object and ask *To or for whom?* or *To or for what?* The answer is the indirect object. *He threw the ball to whom?* He threw it to *Lionel Fischer.*

A **complement** renames or describes a subject or an object. A complement can be a noun, a pronoun, or an adjective.

A **subject complement** renames or describes the subject of a sentence. It follows a **linking verb,** a verb such as *be, become, seem,* or *appear.* (See 64c3.) A linking verb can be thought of as an equal sign, linking two equivalent terms. Whatever is on the left of the equal sign, before the linking verb, is the subject; whatever is on the right is the subject complement.

subject   subject complement
⌐My mother's uncle⌐is ⌐the factory foreman.⌐
subject   subject complement
⌐The factory foreman⌐is⌐my mother's uncle.⌐

An **object complement** appears following a direct object, modifying it or renaming it.

Tonight we will paint the town *red.*

In this example, the adjective *red* describes the direct object *town.*

A noun or pronoun used as a complement is sometimes called a **predicate noun.** An adjective used as a complement is sometimes called a **predicate adjective.**

A group of related words lacking a subject, a predicate, or both is a **phrase.**

Verb phrase

A verb phrase consists of the main verb of a clause and its auxiliaries. It functions as the verb of a sentence.

verb phrase
The college⌐has been having⌐a difficult year.

Noun phrase

A noun phrase consists of a noun, a pronoun, or an infinitive or gerund serving as a noun, and all its modifiers.

noun phrase

⌐The venerable and well-known institution⌐is bankrupt.

Noun phrases may function as subjects, objects, or complements.

SUBJECT	*The college's president* is distraught.
OBJECT	He addressed *the board of trustees*.
COMPLEMENT	They became *a terrified mob*.

Modifier phrase

A modifier phrase is any phrase that functions in a sentence as an adjective or an adverb. Prepositional phrases, infinitive phrases, participial phrases, and absolute phrases can be modifier phrases. Appositive phrases are sometimes considered modifier phrases.

Prepositional phrase

A prepositional phrase consists of a preposition, its object, and any related modifiers.

prepositional phrase

The new book was hailed⌐with great fanfare.⌐

A prepositional phrase may function as an adjective or an adverb.

ADJECTIVE	He knows the difficulty *of the task*.
ADVERB	She arrived *at work* a little early.

Verbal phrase

A verbal phrase is one that contains a verbal plus any objects, complements, or modifiers. There are three kinds of verbals: infinitives, gerunds, and participles. (See 64c5.)

An **infinitive phrase** is one built around an infinitive, the base form of the verb usually preceded by *to*. Infinitive phrases can function as nouns, adjectives, or adverbs. When they function as nouns, they are usually subjects, complements, or direct objects.

NOUN *To raise a family* is a lofty goal.

ADJECTIVE He has the duty *to protect his children.*

ADVERB My father worked *to provide for his family.*

A **gerund phrase** is one built around a gerund, the *-ing* form of a verb functioning as a noun. Gerund phrases always function as nouns; they are usually subjects, subject complements, direct objects, or the objects of prepositions.

SUBJECT *Studying these essays* takes a lot of time.

SUBJECT COMPLEMENT The key to success is *reading all the assignments.*

DIRECT OBJECT My roommate likes *reading novels.*

OBJECT OF PREPOSITION She can forgive me *for preferring short stories.*

A **participial phrase** is one built around a participle, either the past participle (usually ending in *-ed* or *-d*) or the present participle (ending in *-ing*). A participial phrase always functions as an adjective.

ADJECTIVE *Striking a blow for freedom,* the Minutemen fired the "shot heard round the world."

Appositive phrase

An appositive appears directly after a noun or pronoun and renames or further identifies it. (See 41b and 44c3.)

appositive phrase

Ralph Nader, a long-time consumer advocate, supports the new auto emissions proposal.

Absolute phrase. An absolute phrase modifies an entire sentence or clause. It consists of a noun or pronoun and a participle, together with any accompanying modifiers, objects, or complements.

absolute phrase

The work done, the boss called for a celebration.

65 **f** Clauses

Any group of related words with a subject and a predicate is a **clause.** A clause that can stand alone as a complete sentence is called an **independent clause** or a **main clause.**

The moon rose.

The best candidate will win the election.

A clause that cannot stand by itself as a complete sentence is called a **dependent clause** or a **subordinate clause.** It is dependent because it is introduced by a subordinating word, usually either a subordinating conjunction (such as *because, when, unless*) or a relative pronoun (such as *who, which,* or *that*). (For lists of subordinating conjunctions and relative pronouns, see 26e.)

The little girl laughed *when the moon rose.*

I know *that the best candidate will win the election.*

Dependent clauses must be joined to independent clauses. They can be classified by the role they play in the sentence: they may be used as nouns, adjectives, or adverbs.

Noun clause

A noun clause is used as a noun would be — as a subject, an object, or a subject complement. A noun clause is usually introduced by a relative pronoun (such as *who, what,* or *which*) or by the subordinating conjunctions *how, when, where, whether,* or *why.*

SUBJECT	*What I want* is a good job.
DIRECT OBJECT	In class we learned *how we should write our résumés.*
OBJECT OF PREPOSITION	We wondered to *whom we should send them.*
SUBJECT COMPLEMENT	English history is *what I know best.*

Adjective clause

An adjective clause modifies a noun or pronoun elsewhere in the sentence. Most adjective clauses begin with relative pronouns such as *who, whose,* or *that.* They can also begin with the relative adverbs *when, where,* or *why.* Adjective clauses are sometimes called **relative clauses.**

Because adjective clauses and noun clauses are introduced by similar words, they are often confused. Remember that a noun clause functions as a noun, while an adjective clause modifies a noun or pronoun. To determine if a dependent clause is an adjective clause, look for the noun or pronoun it modifies. Usually, an adjective clause directly follows the word it modifies.

The book ⌐that you reserved⌐is now available.

The graduating seniors, ⌐who had just completed their exams,⌐ were full of high spirits.

Adjective clauses, along with adverb clauses, are also known as **modifier clauses.**

Adverb clause

An adverb clause modifies a verb, an adjective, an adverb, or an entire clause. Adverb clauses tell when, where, why, or how, or they specify a condition. They are introduced by subordinating conjunctions (such as *although, than,* or *since*).

The fish ride the tide⌐as far as it will carry them!

Now they can be caught more easily⌐than at any other time!

Adverb clauses, along with adjective clauses, are also known as **modifier clauses.**

Elliptical clauses

Clauses with words deliberately omitted are called elliptical clauses. The word left out of an elliptical clause may be the relative pronoun or subordinating conjunction introducing it, or it may be part of the predicate.

The man [that] I saw had one black shoe.

Marcia is as tall as I [am].

Understanding how sentences are put together is particularly useful in editing for effectiveness and grammar. Sentences can be classified in two ways: by function and by grammatical structure. They can also be described in terms of their sentence patterns.

66 a   Classifying sentences by function

Declarative sentences make statements.

The road is long.

The Pirates have won the Eastern Division.

The normal word order for a declarative sentence is subject followed by predicate, although this order is occasionally inverted: *At the top of the hill stood a tree.* (See 66c.)

Interrogative sentences ask questions.

Who goes there?

Is there life on Mars?

Can pigs really fly?

An interrogative sentence can be introduced by an interrogative pronoun, as in the first example. (See 64b.) Or the subject can follow part of the verb, as in the second and third examples.

Imperative sentences make commands or requests.

Drive slowly.

Signal before changing lanes.

In commands, the subject is *you*; it is usually not stated but is implied: [*You*] *drive slowly.* The verb form used is always the base form.

Exclamatory sentences exclaim (and usually end with an exclamation point).

Oh, how I hate to get up in the morning!

See 27c for more on the uses of these different types of sentences.

66 b Classifying sentences by grammatical structure

Sentences are classified by grammatical structure according to how many dependent and independent clauses they contain. (See 65f.)

A **simple sentence** consists of a single independent clause and no dependent clause. Some simple sentences are brief. Others, if they contain modifier phrases or compound subjects, verbs, or objects, can be quite long.

Marmosets eat bananas.

Benny and Griselda, marmosets at our local zoo, eat at least fifteen bananas a day, in addition to lettuce, nuts, and sometimes each other's tails.

A **compound sentence** has two or more independent clauses and no dependent clause.

> **independent**
> **independent**
> ⌐They grew tired of waiting,⌐so they finally hailed a taxicab.⌐

A **complex sentence** contains one independent clause and at least one dependent clause.

> **independent**
> **dependent**
> ⌐The students assemble outside⌐when the bell rings.⌐

A **compound-complex sentence** contains at least two independent clauses and at least one dependent clause.

> **independent**
> ⌐The first motorcyclists to finish never ordered anything to eat;⌐
> **independent**
> **dependent**
> ⌐they just sat quietly⌐until their hands stopped shaking.⌐

66 c Understanding sentence patterns

Most independent clauses are built on one of five basic patterns. (See Chapter 65 for more on the sentence elements mentioned here.)

The simplest pattern has only two elements, a subject and a verb (S-V).

s   v
Rain fell.

Even when expanded by modifying phrases, the basic pattern of an independent clause may still be only subject-verb.

s   v
⌜Heavy tropical rain⌝ ⌜fell⌝ Tuesday and Wednesday in the Philippines, causing mud slides and killing hundreds of people.

In this example, *Tuesday and Wednesday in the Philippines* modifies the verb; *causing mud slides and killing hundreds of people* modifies the subject.

The next simplest pattern includes a subject, a verb, and a direct object (S-V-DO).

s   v   DO
Gloria read ⌜the book.⌟

s   v   DO
Robins eat worms.

A third pattern is subject, verb, indirect object, and direct object (S-V-IO-DO).

s   v   IO   DO
⌜The committee⌝sent⌜the mayor⌝⌜its report.⌟

s   v   IO   DO
⌜The waiter⌝brought her⌜an appetizer.⌟

A fourth pattern is subject, verb, and subject complement (S-V-SC).

     s   **v** **sc**

⌐The commissioner⌐seems worried.

  s v   **sc**

She is a⌐Republican.⌐

  The fifth basic pattern is subject, verb, direct object, and object complement (S-V-DO-OC).

     s **v** **DO**   **OC**

⌐His friends⌐call him⌐an achiever.⌐

   s   **v** **DO** **OC**

That makes him proud.

Glossary of Usage

This glossary provides information about words that are frequently confused, words that are often used incorrectly, and words that are not considered appropriate for formal academic writing. If you are unsure about how to use a word or are having trouble choosing between words, try to find that word or words here.

Like any other aspect of editing, good usage is usually more than a matter of clear-cut distinctions and unvarying rules. On the one hand, some usages described here would be considered incorrect by any knowledgeable speaker or writer in any context. For example, *discreet* means "prudent" and *discrete* means "separate"; no one who knows that these are two different words would argue that they are interchangeable. On the other hand, some usages are considered acceptable by some authorities but not by others. For example, some writers prefer to use *farther* only when referring to physical distances and *further* only when referring to the more abstract distances of time, quantity, or degree. However, respectable writers have been using them interchangeably for hundreds of years. To decide what is appropriate for your writing, carefully consider the expectations of your audience. In most cases, instructors will appreciate your using words as carefully and precisely as possible. This glossary identifies distinctions among words to enable you to do this.

Some of the usages described in this glossary are acceptable or common in contexts other than formal academic writing. For example, **nonstandard** usages (such as *anyways* instead of the standard *anyway*) reflect the speech patterns of a particular community but do not follow the conventions of the dominant American dialect. **Colloquial** usages (such as *flunk* meaning "to fail" or *awfully* meaning "very") are often heard in speech but are usually considered inappropriate for academic writing. **Informal** usages (such as using *can* and *may* interchangeably) may be acceptable in some papers, but not in formal research essays or argument papers. Except where otherwise noted, the usages recommended in this glossary are those of standard written English as found in formal academic papers.

a, an   Use *a* before words that begin with a consonant sound (*a boy, a hero, a shining star*), even if the first letter of the word is a vowel (*a useful lesson*). Use *an* before words that begin with a vowel sound (*an antelope, an hour, an umbrella*).

a while   See *awhile, a while.*

accept, except   *Accept* is a verb meaning "to receive" or "to approve" (*I accept your offer of a ride*). *Except* is a verb meaning "to leave out" or "to exclude" (*He excepted all vegetables from his list of favorite foods*) or a preposition meaning "excluding" or "leaving out" (*He liked everything on the menu except the vegetables*).

adapt, adopt   *Adapt* is a verb meaning "to adjust" or "to accommodate"; it is usually followed by *to* (*It is sometimes hard to adapt to college life*). *Adopt* is a verb meaning "to take into a relationship" (*My parents decided to adopt another child*) or "to take and use as one's own" (*I have adopted my roommate's habits*).

adverse, averse   *Adverse* is an adjective meaning "unfavorable" or "unpleasant," generally used to describe a thing or situation (*Adverse weather forced us to cancel the game*). *Averse*, also an adjective, means "opposed to" or "feeling a distaste for" and usually describes feelings about a thing or situation; it is usually followed by *to* (*We are averse to playing on a muddy field*).

advice, advise   *Advice* is a noun meaning "recommendation" or "information given" (*My advice is to study hard*). *Advise* is a verb meaning "to give advice to," "to warn," or "to inform" (*I advise you to study hard*).

affect, effect   *Affect* is a verb meaning "to influence" or "to produce an effect" (*That movie affected me deeply*). *Affect* is also used as a noun meaning "feeling" or "emotion," especially in psychology. *Effect* is commonly used as a noun meaning "result," "consequence," or "outcome" (*That movie had a profound effect on me*); it is also sometimes used as a verb meaning "to make happen" or "to bring about" (*Dr. Johnson effected important changes as president*).

aggravate   *Aggravate* is a verb meaning "to make worse" (*Careless exercise can aggravate back problems*). *Aggravate* is sometimes used colloquially to mean "to irritate" or "to annoy," but in formal writing use *irritate* or *annoy* (*I was irritated by my neighbors' loud stereo; my irritation was aggravated when they refused to turn it down*).

all ready, already   *All ready* means "fully prepared" (*The children were all ready for bed*). *Already* means "previously" (*The children were already in bed when the guests arrived*).

all right, alright   The two-word spelling is preferred; the one-word spelling is considered incorrect by many.

all together, altogether   *All together* means "everyone gathered" or "all in one place" (*The animals were all together in the ark*). *Altogether* means "thoroughly" or "completely" (*The ark was altogether too full of animals*).

allude, elude   *Allude* is a verb meaning "to refer to something indirectly"; it is usually followed by *to* (*Derek alluded to the rodent infestation by mentioning that he'd bought mousetraps*). *Elude* is a verb meaning "to escape" or "to avoid" (*The mouse eluded Derek at every turn*).

allusion, illusion   *Allusion* means "an indirect reference" or "the act of alluding to, or hinting at, something" (*Derek's allusion to lunchtime was not lost on his companions*). *Illusion* is a noun meaning "misapprehension" or "misleading image" (*Mr. Hodges created an optical illusion with two lines*).

a lot   *A lot* should be written as two words. Although *a lot* is used informally to mean "a large number" or "many," avoid using *a lot* in formal writing (*The prisoners had many* [not *a lot of*] *opportunities to escape*).

already   See *all ready, already.*

alright   See *all right, alright.*

altogether   See *all together, altogether.*

a.m., p.m. or A.M., P.M.   These abbreviations should be used only with numbers to indicate specific times (6:30 P.M.). In formal usage, do not substitute them for *morning, afternoon, evening,* or *night.*

among, between   *Among* should be used when discussing three or more individuals (*It was difficult to choose among all the exotic plants*). *Between* is generally used when discussing only two individuals (*There were significant differences between the two candidates*).

amount, number   *Amount* should be used to refer to quantities that cannot be counted or cannot be expressed in terms of a single number (*Fixing up the abandoned farmhouse took a great amount of work*). *Number* is used for quantities that can be counted (*A large number of volunteers showed up to clean out the abandoned farmhouse*).

an   See *a, an.*

and etc.   *Etc.* is an abbreviation for the Latin *et cetera,* which means "and so forth"; adding *and* to this term is redundant. Use *etc.* alone; but see *etc.*

and/or   *And/or* is used in technical and legal writing to connect two terms when either one or both apply (*Purchasers must select type and/or size*). Avoid this awkward phrasing by using the construction "*a* or *b* or both" (*Students may select chemistry or physics or both*).

anxious, eager   *Anxious* is an adjective meaning "worried" or "uneasy" (*Lynn is anxious about her mother's surgery*); it should not be confused with *eager*, which means "enthusiastic," "impatient," or "marked by strong desire" (*Lynn is eager* [not *anxious*] *for her mother's recovery*).

anybody, anyone, any body, any one   *Anybody* and *anyone* are singular indefinite pronouns that refer to an unspecified person (*Anybody may apply for the new scholarship. Anyone on the hill could have seen our campfire*). *Any body* and *any one* are noun phrases consisting of the adjective *any* and the noun *body* or the pronoun *one*; they refer to a specific body or to a single member of a group (*Any body of water has its own ecosystem*). The phrase *any one* consists of the pronoun *one* modified by the adjective *any*, and it refers to a specific person or thing within a group (*Each child may select any one toy from the toy box*).

anyplace, anywhere   In formal writing, do not use *anyplace*; use *anywhere* instead (*We could not find the game piece anywhere* [not *anyplace*]).

anyways, anywheres   Use the standard terms *anyway* and *anywhere* in writing.

as   *As* may be used to mean "because" (*We did not go ice skating as the lake was no longer frozen*), but only if no confusion will result. For example, *We canceled the meeting as only two people showed up* could mean that the meeting was canceled at the moment when the two people showed up or because only two showed up. For the latter meaning, *because* would be clearer. Also see *since*.

as, as if, like   Although all these terms are used to indicate comparisons, *like* should be used only as a preposition followed by a noun or noun phrase (*Ken, like his brother, prefers to sleep late*). In formal writing, *like* should not be used as a conjunction linking two clauses. Use *as* or *as if* instead (*Anne talks as if* [not *like*] *she has read every book by Ernest Hemingway*). Also use *as* to express an equivalence (*Mike served as master of ceremonies*); use *like* when comparing items that are similar but not equivalent (*Beth, like Gabe, sang an original song in the show*).

assure, ensure, insure   *Assure* is a verb meaning "to reassure" or "to convince," and it is generally followed by a direct object that names a person or persons (*The lawyer assured her client that the case was solid*). *Ensure* and *insure* both mean "to make sure, certain, or safe," but *insure* generally refers to financial certainty (*John hoped his college degree would ensure him a job, preferably one that would insure him in case of injury or illness*).

as to   Do not use *as to* as a substitute for *about* (*We had questions about* [not *as to*] *the company's affirmative action policies*).

averse   See *adverse, averse.*

awful, awfully   *Awful* is an adjective meaning "inspiring awe or reverence." In formal writing, do not use it to mean "disagreeable" or "objectionable." Similarly, the adverb *awfully* means "in an awe-inspiring way"; in writing, do not use it in the colloquial sense of "very."

awhile, a while   The one-word form *awhile* is an adverb that can be used to modify a verb (*We rested awhile*). Only the two-word form *a while*, a combination of the article *a* and the noun *while*, can be the object of a preposition (*We rested for a while*).

bad, badly   *Bad* is an adjective, so it must modify a noun or follow a linking verb, such as *be, feel,* or *become* (*John felt bad about holding the picnic in bad weather*). *Badly* is an adverb, so it must modify a verb (*Pam played badly today*).

being as, being that   *Being as* and *being that* are nonstandard expressions for *because* (*Anna withdrew from the tournament because* [not *being as*] *her shoulder was injured*).

beside, besides   *Beside* is a preposition meaning "by the side of" or "next to" (*The book is beside the typewriter*). *Besides* can be used as a preposition meaning "other than" or "in addition to" (*No one besides Linda can build a good campfire*). *Besides* can also be used as an adverb meaning "moreover," "furthermore," or "in addition" (*The weather is bad for hiking; besides, I have a cold and do not feel up to it*).

between   See *among, between.*

breath, breathe   *Breath* is a noun (*I had to stop to catch my breath*); *breathe* is a verb (*It became difficult to breathe at higher elevations*).

bring, take   The verb *bring* should be used to describe movement from a distant place to or toward a nearer place; the verb *take* should be used to describe movement away from a place (*Dr. Gavin asked us to bring our rough sketches to class; she said we may take them home after class*).

burst, bust   *Burst* is an irregular verb meaning "to break open, apart, or into pieces." Its past tense and past participle are both *burst*; the past-tense form *bursted* is nonstandard and should not be used in academic writing (*Lee burst the balloon with the point of a pen*). *Bust* is an informal verb with many meanings, including "to burst," "to break," "to demote," "to tame," and "to arrest"; it should be avoided in formal writing.

but, however, yet   Each of these words should be used alone, not in combination (*We finished painting the house, but* [not *but however*] *there is still much work to do*).

but that, but what   *But that* and *but what* are wordy and nonstandard ways of saying *that*, usually in expressions of doubt; use *that* alone in writing (*I doubt that* [not *but that* or *but what*] *we will finish by summer*).

can, may   In informal usage, *can* and *may* are often used interchangeably to indicate permission. But in formal writing, only *may* should be used this way (*May I borrow your dictionary?*). *May* is also used to indicate possibility (*It may snow tomorrow*). In formal writing, *can* should be used only to indicate ability (*I can see much better with my new glasses*).

cannot   *Cannot* should always be written as one word (*I cannot* [not *can not*] *believe you ate the entire cake*).

capital, capitol   *Capital* is an adjective meaning "punishable by death" (*capital punishment*) or used to refer to uppercase letters (*A, B*). It is also a noun meaning "accumulated wealth" (*We will calculate our capital at the end of the fiscal year*) or "a city serving as a seat of government" (*Albany is the capital of New York*). *Capitol* is a noun for the building in which lawmakers meet (*The civics class toured the capitol last week*).

censor, censure   *Censor* can be a noun or verb referring to the removal of material that is considered objectionable or harmful. *Censure* is a verb meaning "to blame or condemn sternly" (*Plans to censor song lyrics have been censured by groups that support free speech*).

cite, site   *Cite* is a verb meaning "to quote for purposes of example, authority, or proof" (*Tracy cites several legal experts in her paper on capital punishment*). *Site* is usually used as a noun meaning "place or scene" (*Today we poured the foundation on the site of our future home*).

climactic, climatic   *Climactic* is an adjective derived from the noun *climax*; it refers to a moment of greatest intensity (*In the climactic scene of the play, the murderer's identity is revealed*). *Climatic* is an adjective derived from the noun *climate*; it refers to weather conditions (*Some people fear that climatic changes are a sign of environmental dangers*).

cloth, cloths; clothe, clothes   *Cloth* is a noun meaning "fabric"; *cloths* is its plural (*Glass should be cleaned with a soft cloth*). *Clothe* is a verb meaning "to dress" or "to provide with clothing"; *clothes* is a noun for clothing (*It is getting more expensive to clothe children properly; the cost of washing clothes is rising too*).

compare to, compare with   *Compare to* means "to liken" or "to represent as similar" (*Jim compared our new puppy to an unruly child*).

Compare with means "to examine to discover similarities or differences" (*We compared this month's ads with last month's*).

complement, compliment   *Complement* is a verb meaning "to fill out or complete" or "to fit with"; it is also a noun meaning "something that completes or fits with" (*The bouquet of spring flowers complemented the table setting*). *Compliment* is a verb meaning "to express esteem or admiration" or a noun meaning "an expression of esteem or admiration" (*Russ complimented Nancy on her choice of flowers*).

compose, comprise   *Compose* is a verb meaning "to constitute or make up"; *comprise* is a verb meaning "to include or contain" (*Last year's club comprised fifteen members; only eight members compose this year's club*).

conscience, conscious   *Conscience* is a noun referring to a sense of right and wrong (*His conscience would not allow him to lie*). *Conscious* is an adjective meaning "marked by thought or will" or "acting with critical awareness" (*He made a conscious decision to be more honest*).

contact   *Contact* is often used informally as a verb meaning "to get in touch with," but it should not be used this way in formal writing. Use a verb such as *write* or *telephone* instead.

continual, continuous   *Continual* is an adjective meaning "recurring" or "occurring repeatedly" (*Liz saw a doctor about her continual headaches*). *Continuous* is an adjective meaning "uninterrupted in space, time, or sequence" (*Eventually we grew used to the continuous noise of machinery*).

council, counsel   *Council* is a noun meaning "a group meeting for advice, discussion, or government" (*The tribal council voted in favor of the new land rights law*). As a noun, *counsel* means "advice" or "a plan of action or behavior" (*The priest gave counsel to the young men considering the priesthood*). *Counsel* may also be used as a verb meaning "to advise or consult" (*The priest counseled the young man*).

criteria   *Criteria* is the plural form of the noun *criterion*, which means "a standard on which a judgment is based" (*Many criteria are used in selecting a president; some feel that a candidate's personal life is not an appropriate criterion*).

data   *Data* is the plural form of the noun *datum*, which means "a fact" or "a result in research." Some writers and speakers now use *data* as both a singular and a plural noun; in formal usage it is still better to treat it as plural (*The data indicate that a low-fat diet may increase life expectancy*).

different from, different than   In general, *different from* is preferred to *different than* (*Hal's taste in music is different from his wife's*). But *different than* may be used to avoid awkward constructions (*Hal's* *taste in music is different than* [instead of *different from what*] *it was five years ago*).

differ from, differ with   *Differ from* means "to be unlike" (*This year's parade differed from last year's in many ways*). *Differ with* means "to disagree with" (*Stephanie differed with Tom over which parade was better*).

discreet, discrete   *Discreet* is an adjective meaning "prudent" or "modest" (*Most private donors were discreet about their contributions*). *Discrete* is an adjective meaning "separate" or "distinct" (*Professor Roberts divided the course into four discrete units*).

disinterested, uninterested   *Disinterested* is an adjective meaning "unbiased" or "impartial" (*It will be difficult to find twelve disinterested jurors for such a highly publicized case*). *Uninterested* is an adjective meaning "indifferent" or "unconcerned" (*Most people were uninterested in the case until the police discovered surprising new evidence*).

don't   *Don't* is a contraction for *do not*; it should not be used as a contraction for *does not*. The contraction for *does not* is *doesn't* (*He doesn't* [not *don't*] *know where she's living now*).

due to   *Due to* is an adjective phrase that is generally used after forms of the verb *be* (*The smaller classes were due to a decline in enrollment*). In formal writing, *due to* should not be used as a prepositional phrase meaning "because of" (*Class size decreased because of* [not *due to*] *a decline in enrollment*).

each   When used as a pronoun, *each* is singular (*Each goes in its own place*).

eager   See *anxious, eager*.

effect   See *affect, effect*.

e.g.   *E.g.* is the abbreviation for the Latin phrase *exempli gratia*, which means "for example." In formal writing, use a full English expression, such as *for example* or *for instance*.

elicit, illicit   *Elicit* is a verb meaning "to draw forth" or "to bring out" (*The investigators could not elicit any new information*). *Illicit* is an adjective meaning "unlawful" or "not permitted" (*The investigators were looking for evidence of illicit drug sales*).

elude   See *allude, elude*.

emigrate, immigrate   *Emigrate* means "to leave one's country to live or reside elsewhere"; it is often followed by *from* (*His grandparents emigrated from Russia*). *Immigrate* means "to come into a new country to take up residence"; it is often followed by *to* (*His grandparents immigrated to the United States*).

eminent, imminent   *Eminent* is an adjective meaning "lofty" or "prominent" (*Her operation was performed by an eminent surgeon*). *Imminent* is an adjective meaning "impending" or "about to take place" (*The hurricane's arrival is imminent*).

ensure   See *assure, ensure, insure*.

enthused, enthusiastic   *Enthused* is the past-tense form of the verb *enthuse*. In formal writing, *enthused* should not be used as an adjective; use *enthusiastic* instead (*Barb is enthusiastic* [not *enthused*] *about her music lessons*).

equally as good   This is a redundant phrase; use *equally good* or *as good as* instead.

especially, specially   *Especially* is an adverb meaning "particularly" or "unusually" (*The weather was especially cold this winter*). *Specially* is an adverb meaning "for a special reason" or "in a unique way" (*The cake was specially prepared for Sandy's birthday*).

etc.   *Etc.* is the abbreviation for the Latin expression *et cetera*, which means "and so forth." In formal writing it is best not to end a list with *etc.*; if you want to indicate that you are leaving items out of a list, use *and so on* or *and so forth* instead.

eventually, ultimately   Although these words are often used interchangeably, *eventually* means "at an unspecified later time," while *ultimately* means "finally" or "in the end" (*He knew that he would have to stop running eventually, but he hoped that he would ultimately win a marathon*).

everybody, everyone, every body, every one   *Everybody* and *everyone* are singular indefinite pronouns that refer to an unspecified person (*Everybody wins in this game*). *Every body* and *every one* are noun phrases consisting of the adjective *every* and the noun *body* or the pronoun *one*; they refer to each individual body or each single member of a group (*Every one of these toys must be picked up*).

except   See *accept, except*.

expect   *Expect* is a verb meaning "to anticipate or look forward to." Though it is sometimes used colloquially to mean "to think or suppose," avoid this usage in formal writing (*I suppose* [not *expect*] *I should go study now*).

explicit, implicit   *Explicit* is an adjective meaning "perfectly clear, direct, and unambiguous" (*Darrell gave me explicit directions to his house*). *Implicit* is an adjective meaning "implied" or "revealed or expressed indirectly" (*His eagerness to see me was implicit in his cheerful tone of voice*).

farther, further   Although these words are often used interchangeably, some writers prefer to use *farther* to refer to physical distances (*Boston is farther than I thought*) and *further* to refer to quantity, time, or degree (*We tried to progress further on our research project*).

fewer, less   *Fewer* is an adjective used to refer to people or items that can be counted (*Because fewer people came to the conference this year, we needed fewer programs*). *Less* is used to refer to amounts that cannot be counted (*We also required less space and less food*).

finalize   Many writers avoid using *finalize* to mean "to make final" or "to finish." It is best to use an alternative phrasing (*We needed to complete* [not *finalize*] *the plans by June*).

firstly, secondly, thirdly   These expressions are awkward; use *first, second, third*, and so on instead.

flunk   *Flunk* is a colloquial word for the verb "to fail"; it should not be used in formal writing.

former, latter   *Former* is used to refer to the first of two people, items, or ideas being discussed, *latter* to refer to the second (*Monet and Picasso were both important painters; the former is associated with the impressionist school, the latter with cubism*). *Former* and *latter* should not be used when referring to more than two people, items, or ideas.

further   See *farther, further*.

get   The verb *get* has many colloquial uses that should be avoided in formal writing. Examples include *get* meaning "to provoke or annoy" (*He gets to me*), "to start" (*We should get going on this project*), or "to become" (*She got worried when he didn't call*). *Have got to* should not be used in place of *must* (*I must* [not *have got to*] *finish by five o'clock*).

goes, says   The verb *goes* is sometimes used colloquially for *says*, but avoid this usage in formal writing (*When the coach says* [not *goes*] *"Now," everybody runs*).

good and   *Good and* should not be used for *very* in formal writing (*My shoes were very* [not *good and*] *wet after our walk*).

good, well   *Good* is an adjective; it should not be used in place of the adverb *well* in formal writing (*Mario is a good tennis player; he played well* [not *good*] *in the tournament*).

hanged, hung   *Hanged* is the past-tense and past-participle form of the verb *hang* meaning "to suspend by the neck until dead" (*Two Civil War prisoners were hanged at this spot*). *Hung* is the past-tense and past-participle form of the verb *hang* meaning "to suspend" or "to dangle" (*All her clothes were hung neatly in the closet*).

hardly, scarcely   *Hardly* and *scarcely* are adverbs meaning "barely," "only just," or "almost not." Phrases like *can't scarcely* and *not hardly* are double negatives and should not be used in formal writing; use *hardly* or *scarcely* alone (*I can scarcely* [not *can't scarcely*] *keep my eyes open*).

has got, have got   These are colloquial expressions; in formal writing use simply *has* or *have* (*He has* [not *has got*] *his books arranged alphabetically*).

have, of   The auxiliary verb *have* (not *of*) should be used in verb phrases beginning with modal auxiliaries such as *could, would,* and *might* (*We could have* [not *of*] *gone to the concert*).

he/she, his/her   When you require both female and male personal pronouns in formal writing, use *she or he* (or *he or she*) and *his or her* (or *her or his*) (*Someone left her or his* [not *her/his*] *umbrella on the porch*).

herself, himself, itself, myself, ourselves, themselves, yourself, yourselves   These are reflexive or intensive pronouns and should be used only to reflect the action of a sentence back toward the subject (*He locked himself out of the apartment*) or to emphasize the subject (*I myself have no regrets*). Do not use these pronouns in place of personal pronouns such as *I, me, you, her,* or *him* (*He left an extra key with Bev and me* [not *myself*]).

hisself   *Hisself* is nonstandard; always use *himself.*

hopefully   *Hopefully* is an adverb meaning "in a hopeful manner" (*The child looked hopefully out the window when he heard a car door slam*). In formal writing, do not use *hopefully* to mean "I or we hope that" or "It is hoped that" (*I hope that* [not *Hopefully*] *Bob will remember his camera*).

however   See *but, however, yet.*

hung   See *hanged, hung.*

i.e.   *I.e.* is an abbreviation for the Latin phrase *id est,* which means "that is." In formal writing, use the expression *that is* instead of the abbreviation (*Hal is a Renaissance man; that is* [not *i.e.*], *he has many varied interests*).

if, whether   Use *if* in a clause that refers to a conditional situation (*I will wear my new boots if it snows tomorrow*). Use *whether* (or *whether or not*) in a clause that expresses or implies an alternative (*I will decide whether to wear my boots when I see what the weather is like*).

illicit   See *elicit, illicit.*

illusion   See *allusion, illusion.*

immigrate   See *emigrate, immigrate.*

imminent   See *eminent, imminent.*

implicit   See *explicit, implicit.*

imply, infer   *Imply* is a verb meaning "to express indirectly" or "to suggest"; *infer* is a verb meaning "to conclude" or "to surmise" (*Helen implied that she had time to visit with us, but we inferred from all the work on her desk that she was really too busy*).

incident, instance   *Incident* refers to a specific event or occurrence (*Gayle reported the incident to the police*). *Instance* means "example" or "case" (*It was the third instance of theft that week*).

incredible, incredulous   *Incredible* is an adjective meaning "hard to believe"; *incredulous* is an adjective meaning "skeptical" or "unbelieving" (*My parents were incredulous when I told them the incredible story*).

individual   *Individual* should be used only when stressing the distinctness of a single person; in formal writing it should not be used in place of the noun *person* (*Objections were raised by several persons [not individuals] at the meeting*).

infer   See *imply, infer.*

ingenious, ingenuous   *Ingenious* is an adjective meaning "resourceful" or "clever" (*Elaine came up with an ingenious plan for surprising Dave*). *Ingenuous* is an adjective meaning "innocent" or "simple" (*It was a surprisingly deceptive plan for such an ingenuous person*).

in regards to   *In regards to* is an incorrect combination of two phrases, *as regards* and *in regard to* (*In regard to [or As regards; not in regards to] the first question, please refer to the guidelines you received*).

inside, inside of; outside, outside of   The prepositions *inside* and *outside* should not be followed by *of* (*The suspect is inside [not inside of] that building*).

instance   See *incident, instance.*

insure   See *assure, ensure, insure.*

interact with, interface with   Both of these verb phrases are examples of technical jargon; avoid them in formal writing.

irregardless, regardless   *Irregardless* is often used, mistakenly, in place of *regardless* (*We will have the party regardless [not irregardless] of the weather*).

is when, is where   Avoid these awkward expressions in formal writing to define terms (*Sexual harassment refers to* [not *is when someone makes*] *inappropriate sexual advances or suggestions*).

its, it's   *Its* is the possessive form of the pronoun *it*; *it's* is a contraction for *it is* (*It's hard to tear a baby animal away from its mother*).

itself   See *herself, himself.* . . .

kind, sort, type   *Kind, sort,* and *type* are singular nouns; each should be used with *this* (not *these*) and a singular verb (*This kind of mushroom is* [not *These kind of mushrooms are*] *very expensive*). The plural forms — *kinds, sorts,* and *types* — should be used with *these* and with a plural verb (*These three types of envelopes are the only ones we need*).

kind of, sort of   In formal writing, avoid using the colloquial expressions *kind of* and *sort of* to mean "somewhat" or "rather" (*My paper is rather* [not *kind of*] *short; my research for it was somewhat* [not *sort of*] *rushed*).

later, latter   *Later* means "after some time"; *latter* refers to the second of two people, items, or ideas (*Later in the evening Jim announced that the latter of the two guest speakers was running late*). See *former, latter.*

lay   See *lie, lay.*

lead, led   As a verb, *lead* means "to go first" or "to direct"; as a noun, it means "front position" (*Hollis took the lead in organizing the files*). *Lead* is also a noun for the metallic element. Be careful not to confuse this form of *lead* with *led*, which is pronounced the same way; *led* is the past-tense and past-participle form of the verb *lead.*

learn, teach   *Learn* means "to gain knowledge or understanding"; *teach* means "to cause to know" or "to instruct" (*Tonight James will teach* [not *learn*] *us a new dance step; I hope we can learn it quickly*).

leave, let   *Leave* means "to depart"; it should not be used in place of *let*, which means "to allow" (*When you are ready to leave, let* [not *leave*] *me give you a ride*). The expressions *leave alone* and *let alone*, however, may be used interchangeably (*I asked Ben to leave* [or *let*] *me alone while I worked on my paper*).

led   See *lead, led.*

less   See *fewer, less.*

liable, likely   *Liable* means "inclined" or "tending," generally toward the negative (*If you do not shovel the sidewalk you are liable to fall on* *the ice*). *Liable* is also a legal term meaning "responsible for" or "obligated under the law" (*The landlord is liable for the damage caused by the leak*). *Likely* is an adjective meaning "probable" or "promising" (*The school board is likely to cancel classes if the strike continues*).

lie, lay   The verb *lie* meaning "to recline" or "to rest in a horizontal position" has the principal forms *lie, lay, lain*. *Lie* should not be confused with the transitive verb *lay*, which means "to put or set down" and is followed by an object; the principal forms of *lay* are *lay, laid, laid* (*Lay the blanket on this spot and lie down*; *She laid the book next to the spot where he lay on the bed*).

like   See *as, as if, like*.

likely   See *liable, likely*.

loan   *Loan* is a noun meaning "money lent at interest" or "something lent for temporary use." In formal writing, do not use *loan* as a verb; use *lend* instead (*Though the bank is willing to lend me the money, I am not prepared to take out such a large loan*).

loose, lose   *Loose* is an adjective meaning "not securely attached"; it should not be confused with the verb *lose*, which means "to misplace," "to fail to keep," or "to undergo defeat" (*Be careful not to lose that loose button on your jacket*).

lots, lots of   *Lots* and *lots of* are colloquial expressions meaning "many" or "much"; avoid them in formal writing (*The senator has much* [not *lots of*] *support; she is expected to win many* [not *lots of*] *votes*).

man, mankind   These terms were once used to refer to all human beings. Now such usage is considered sexist; use terms such as *people, humanity,* and *humankind* instead (*What has been the greatest invention in the history of humanity* [not *mankind*]?).

may   See *can, may*.

may be, maybe   *May be* is a verb phrase (*Charles may be interested in a new job*); *maybe* is an adverb meaning "possibly" or "perhaps" (*Maybe I will speak to him about it*).

media   The term *media*, frequently used to refer to various forms of communication, including newspapers, magazines, television, and radio, is the plural form of the noun *medium*; it takes a plural verb (*Some people feel that the media were responsible for the candidate's loss*).

moral, morale   *Moral* is the message or lesson of a story or experience (*The moral is to treat others as you wish to be treated*). *Morale* is the mental condition or mood of a person or group (*The improvement in the weather lifted the crew's morale*).

most   In formal writing, do not use *most* to mean "almost" (*Prizes were given to almost* [not *most*] *all the participants*).

Ms.   Use *Ms.* — not *Miss* or *Mrs.* — as the title accompanying a woman's name, unless the woman you are addressing has indicated a preference for a different title (*Dear Ms. Smith*).

myself   See *herself, himself.* . . .

neither   The pronoun *neither* is singular (*Neither of my parents is able to come this weekend*).

nor, or   *Nor* should be used with *neither* (*Neither Paul nor Sara guessed the right answer*); *or* should be used with *either* (*Either Paul or Sara will have to drive me home*).

number   See *amount, number.*

of   See *have, of.*

off of   Use *off* alone; *of* is not necessary (*The child fell off* [not *off of*] *the playground slide*).

OK, O.K., okay   All three spellings are acceptable, but this colloquial term should be avoided in formal writing (*John's performance was all right* [or *adequate* or *tolerable*; not *okay*], *but it wasn't his best*).

on, upon   Use *on*, not *upon*, following verbs like *depend* (*My plans for next semester depend on* [not *upon*] *my grades this semester*).

on account of   In formal writing, avoid *on account of* to mean "because of" (*The course was canceled because of* [not *on account of*] *lack of interest*). Also see *due to.*

one   When *one* is used as a pronoun meaning "a person," use *one* or *one's* (not *he or she* or *his or her*) in subsequent references (*One must be careful not to reveal one's* [not *his or her*] *secrets too quickly*).

or   See *nor, or.*

ourselves   See *herself, himself.* . . .

outside, outside of   See *inside, inside of; outside, outside of.*

passed, past   *Passed* is the past-tense form of the verb *pass* (*She passed here several hours ago*). *Past* may be an adjective or a noun referring to a time before the present (*She has forgotten many details about her past life*).

per   The Latin term *per* should be reserved for commercial or technical use (*miles per gallon, price per pound*); it should be avoided in other formal writing (*Kyle is now exercising three times each* [not *per*] *week, in accordance with* [not *per*] *his doctor's advice*).

percent, percentage   The term *percent* (or *per cent*) refers to a specific fraction of one hundred; it is always used with a number (*We* *raised nearly 80 percent of our budget in one night*). Do not use the symbol % in formal writing. The term *percentage* is more general and is not used with a specific number (*We raised a large percentage of our budget in one night*).

perspective, prospective   *Perspective* is a noun meaning "a view"; it should not be confused with the adjective *prospective*, meaning "potential" or "likely" (*Mr. Harris's perspective on the new school changed when he met his son's prospective teacher*).

personal, personnel   *Personal* is an adjective meaning "individual" or "private"; it should not be confused with *personnel*, which refers to a group of people employed by an organization (*Our company's personnel department keeps all employees' personal information in confidential files*).

phenomena   *Phenomena* is the plural of the noun *phenomenon*, meaning "an observed fact, occurrence, or circumstance" (*Last month's blizzard was an unusual phenomenon; there have been several such phenomena this year*).

plenty   *Plenty* means "full" or "abundant"; in formal writing, do not use it to mean "very" or "quite" (*The sun was quite* [not *plenty*] *hot on the beach today*).

plus   *Plus* is a preposition meaning "increased by" or "with the addition of" (*With wool socks plus your heavy boots, your feet should be warm enough*). Do not use *plus* to link two independent clauses; use *besides* or *moreover* instead (*Brad is not prepared for the advanced class; moreover* [not *plus*], *he can't fit it in his schedule*).

p.m., P.M.   See *a.m., p.m.* or A.M., P.M.

precede, proceed   *Precede* is a verb meaning "to go or come before"; *proceed* is a verb meaning "to move forward or go on" or "to continue" (*The bridal attendants preceded the bride into the church; when the music started, they proceeded down the aisle*).

pretty   In formal writing, avoid *pretty* to mean "quite" or "somewhat" (*Dave is quite* [not *pretty*] *tired this morning*).

principal, principle   *Principal* is an adjective meaning "first" or "most important"; it is also a noun meaning "head" or "director" or "an amount of money" (*My principal reason for visiting Gettysburg was my interest in the Civil War. My high school principal suggested the trip*). *Principle* is a noun meaning "a rule of action or conduct" or "a basic law" (*I also want to learn more about the principles underlying the U.S. Constitution*).

proceed   See *precede, proceed.*

prospective   See *perspective, prospective.*

quotation, quote *Quotation* is a noun, and *quote* is a verb. Avoid using *quote* as a noun (*Sue quoted Jefferson in her speech, hoping the quotation* [not *quote*] *would have a powerful effect on her audience*).

raise, rise *Raise* is a transitive verb meaning "to lift" or "to increase"; it takes a direct object (*The store owner was forced to raise prices*). *Rise* is an intransitive verb meaning "to go up"; it does not take a direct object (*Prices will rise during periods of inflation*).

rarely ever Do not use *rarely ever* to mean "hardly ever"; use *rarely* alone (*We rarely* [not *rarely ever*] *travel during the winter*).

real, really *Real* is an adjective meaning "true" or "actual" (*The diamonds in that necklace are real*). *Really* is an adverb, used informally to mean "very" or "quite"; do not use *real* as an adverb (*Tim was really* [not *real*] *interested in buying Lana's old car*). In formal writing, it is generally best to avoid using *really* altogether.

reason is because *Reason is because* is redundant; use *reason is that* or *because* instead (*The reason I am late is that* [not *because*] *I got stuck in traffic. Yesterday I was late because* [not *The reason I was late yesterday was because*] *I overslept*).

reason why *Reason why* is redundant; use *reason* alone (*The reason* [not *The reason why*] *we canceled the dance is that no one volunteered to chaperone*).

regardless See *irregardless, regardless*.

regretful, regrettable *Regretful* is an adjective meaning "sorrowful for what is lost or gone"; it should not be used interchangeably with the adjective *regrettable*, which means "causing or inspiring feelings of sorrow or remorse" (*Anne felt regretful when her youngest child left for college; it was regrettable that no one tried to comfort her*).

relate to Do not use *relate to* in formal writing to mean "appreciate" or "understand" (*I can understand* [not *relate to*] *your sadness*).

relation, relationship *Relation* is a connection or association between things; *relationship* is a connection or involvement between people (*The analyst explained the relation between investment and interest. The relationship between a mother and child is complex*).

respectfully, respectively The adverb *respectfully* means "in a respectful manner" (*The children listened to their teacher respectfully*). The adverb *respectively* means "in the order given" (*The sessions on Italian, French, and Spanish culture are scheduled for Tuesday, Wednesday, and Thursday, respectively*).

rise See *raise, rise*.

says See *goes, says*.

scarcely   See *hardly, scarcely*.

secondly   See *firstly, secondly, thirdly*.

sensual, sensuous   *Sensual* is an adjective meaning "arousing or exciting the senses or appetites"; it is often used in reference to sexual pleasure (*His scripts often featured titillating situations and sensual encounters*). *Sensuous* is a more general adjective meaning "experienced through or affecting the senses," although it generally refers to aesthetic enjoyment or pleasure (*Her sculpture was characterized by muted colors and sensuous curves*).

set, sit   *Set* is a transitive verb meaning "to put" or "to place"; it takes a direct object, and its principal forms are *set, set, set* (*Mary set her packages on the kitchen table*). *Sit* is an intransitive verb meaning "to be seated"; it does not take a direct object, and its principal forms are *sit, sat, sat* (*I sat in the only chair in the waiting room*).

shall, will   In the past, *shall* (instead of *will*) was used as a helping verb with the first-person subjects *I* and *we*. Now *will* is acceptable with all subjects (*We will invite several guests for dinner*). *Shall* is generally used in polite questions (*Shall we go inside now?*) or in legal writing (*Jurors shall refrain from all contact with the press*).

since   *Since* should be used to mean "continuing from a past time until the present" (*Carl has not gone skiing since he injured his knee*). Do not use *since* to mean "because" if there is any possibility that readers will be confused about your meaning. For example, in the sentence *Since she sold her bicycle, Lonnie has not been getting much exercise, since* could mean either "because" or "from the time that." Use *because* to avoid confusion.

sit   See *set, sit*.

site   See *cite, site*.

so, so that   The use of *so* to mean "very" or "extremely" can be vague; it is generally better to follow *so* with a *that* clause of explanation (not *Gayle was so depressed*, but *Gayle was so depressed that she found it hard to get out of bed in the morning*).

somebody, someone, something   These singular indefinite pronouns take singular verbs (*Somebody calls every night at midnight and hangs up; I hope something is done about this problem soon*).

someplace, somewhere   Do not use *someplace* in formal writing; use *somewhere* instead (*The answer must lie somewhere* [not *someplace*] *in the text*).

some time, sometime, sometimes   The phrase *some time* (an adjective and a noun) means "a length of time" (*We have not visited our* *grandparents in some time*). *Sometime* is an adverb meaning "at an indefinite time in the future" (*Let's get together sometime*); *sometimes* is an adverb meaning "on occasion" or "now and then" (*Sometimes we get together to talk about our assignments*).

sort   See *kind, sort, type.*

stationary, stationery   *Stationary* is an adjective meaning "standing still" or "not moving" (*All stationary vehicles will be towed*). *Stationery* is a noun meaning "writing materials" (*Karen is always running out of stationery because she writes so many letters*).

supposed to, used to   Both of these expressions consist of a past participle (*supposed, used*) followed by *to*. Do not use the base forms *suppose* and *use* (*Ben is supposed* [not *suppose*] *to take the garbage out; he is used* [not *use*] *to his mother's reminders by now*).

sure, surely   In formal writing, do not use the adjective *sure* to mean "certainly" or "undoubtedly"; use the adverb *surely* or *certainly* or *undoubtedly* instead (*It is certainly* [or *surely*; not *sure*] *cold today*).

sure and, try and   *Sure and* and *try and* are colloquial expressions for *sure to* and *try to*, respectively; avoid them in formal writing (*Be sure to* [not *and*] *come to the party; and try to* [not *and*] *be on time*).

tack, tact   *Tack* as a noun means, among other things, "a short, sharp-pointed nail" and "a course of action, especially one differing from an earlier course." It should not be confused with the noun *tact*, which means "taste" or "sensitivity" (*The teacher decided to try a different tack* [not *tact*] *with his students. John displayed great tact in not mentioning Betsy's mistake*).

take   See *bring, take.*

teach   See *learn, teach.*

than, then   *Than* is a conjunction used in comparisons (*Dan is older than Eve*). *Then* is an adverb meaning "at that time" or "immediately or soon afterward" (*First pick up the files and then deliver them to the company office*).

that   See *that, which*; and *which, who, that.*

that, which   A clause introduced by *that* is always a restrictive clause; it should not be set off by commas (*The historical event that interested him most was the Civil War*). Many writers use *which* only to introduce nonrestrictive clauses, which are set off by commas (*His textbook, which was written by an expert on the war, provided useful information*); however, *which* may also be used to introduce restrictive clauses (*The book which offered the most important information was an old reference book in the library*).

their, there, they're *Their* is the possessive form of the pronoun *they* (*Did they leave their books here?*). *There* is an adverb meaning "in or at that place" (*No, they left their books there*); it may also be used as an expletive with a form of the verb *be* (*There is no time to look for their books*). *They're* is a contraction of *they are* (*They're looking all over for their books*).

theirselves *Theirselves* is nonstandard; always use *themselves* (*They pushed themselves* [not *theirselves*] *to run an extra mile*).

themselves See *herself, himself*. . . .

then See *than, then.*

thirdly See *firstly, secondly, thirdly.*

'til, till, until *Till* and *until* are both acceptable spellings; *'til*, however, is a contraction and should be avoided in formal writing (*We will work until we are finished; you should not plan to leave till then*).

to, too, two *To* is a preposition, often used to indicate movement or direction toward something (*Nancy is walking to the grocery store*). *Too* is an adverb meaning "also" (*Sam is walking too*). *Two* is a number (*The two of them are walking together*).

toward, towards *Toward* is generally preferred, but both forms are acceptable.

try and See *sure and, try and.*

type In colloquial speech, *type* is sometimes used alone to mean "type of," but avoid this usage in formal writing (*What type of* [not *type*] *medicine did the doctor prescribe?*). Also see *kind, sort, type.*

ultimately See *eventually, ultimately.*

uninterested See *disinterested, uninterested.*

unique *Unique* is an adjective meaning "being the only one" or "having no equal." Because it refers to an absolute, unvarying state, it should not be preceded by a word that indicates degree or amount (such as *most, less,* or *very*) (*Her pale blue eyes gave her a unique* [not *very unique*] *look*). The same is true of other adjectives that indicate an absolute state: *perfect, complete, round, straight,* and so on.

until See *'til, till, until.*

upon See *on, upon.*

usage, use The noun *usage* means "an established and accepted practice or procedure" (*He consulted the glossary whenever he was unsure of the correct word choice or usage*). Do not substitute it for the noun *use* when the intended meaning is "the act of putting into service" (*The park guidelines forbade the use* [not *usage*] *of gas grills*).

used to　See *supposed to, used to*.

utilize　The verb *utilize*, meaning "to put to use," is often considered inappropriately technical for formal writing; it is generally better to use *use* instead (*We were able to use* [not *utilize*] *the hotel kitchen to prepare our meals*).

wait for, wait on　*Wait for* means "to await" or "to be ready for." *Wait on* means "to serve"; in formal writing they are not interchangeable (*You are too old to wait for* [not *on*] *your mother to wait on you*).

way, ways　Do not use *ways* in place of *way* when referring to long distances (*Los Angeles is a long way* [not *ways*] *from San Francisco by car*).

well　See *good, well*.

where　*Where* is nonstandard when used in place of *that* (*I read that* [not *where*] *several of the company's plants will be closed next summer*).

where . . . at, where . . . to　*Where* should be used alone, not in combination with *at* or *to* (*Where did you leave your coat?* [not *Where did you leave your coat at?*] *Where are you going next?* [not *Where are you going to next?*]).

whether　See *if, whether*.

which　See *that, which*.

which, who, that　Use the relative pronoun *which* to refer to places, things, or events; use *who* to refer to people or to animals with individual qualities or given names; use *that* to refer to places, things, or events or to groups of people (*The parade, which was rescheduled for Saturday, was a great success*; *The man who* [not *which*] *was grand marshal said it was the best parade that he could remember*). *That* is also occasionally used to refer to a single person (*Beth is like the sister that I never had*).

who　See *which, who, that*.

who, whom, whoever, whomever　Use *who* and *whoever* for subjects and subject complements; use *whom* and *whomever* for objects and object complements (*Who revealed the murderer's identity? You may invite whomever you wish*).

who's, whose　*Who's* is a contraction of *who is* (*Who's coming for dinner tonight?*). *Whose* is the possessive form of *who* (*Whose hat is lying on the table?*).

will   See *shall, will.*

-wise   The suffix *-wise* indicates position or direction in words such as *clockwise* and *lengthwise.* In formal writing, do not add it to words to mean "with regard to" (*My personal life is rather confused, but with regard to my job* [not *jobwise*], *things are fine*).

yet   See *but, however, yet.*

your, you're   *Your* is the possessive form of the pronoun *you* (*Your table is ready*); *you're* is a contraction of *you are* (*You're leaving before the best part of the show*).

yourself, yourselves   See *herself, himself. . . .*

Glossary of Terms

absolute   A modifier indicating a quality that cannot be made larger or smaller (*entire, unique, superior*). An absolute does not have a comparative or superlative form. See 37e.

absolute phrase   A phrase that consists of a noun or pronoun and a participle and that modifies an entire sentence, not just one part of it. See 65e.

abstract word   A word referring to something that cannot be perceived by one of the five senses: *liberty, education, exciting.* See 29a, 64a.

active voice   See *voice.*

acronym   An abbreviation that forms a word out of the initials of the name or title that it shortens: *LILCO, MoMA, MADD.* See 55e.

adjective   A modifier that describes nouns and pronouns. There are three types of adjectives: **descriptive** (*green, tall*), **proper** (*Italian, Buddhist*), and **limiting** (*few, all, a, the*). See also *article* and *modifier.* See 29a, Chapter 37, Chapter 38, 64d.

adjective clause   A dependent clause introduced by a relative pronoun (*who, which, that*) and functioning as an adjective. See 65f.

adverb   A modifier that describes a verb, adjective, another adverb, or a whole sentence. See also *modifier.* See 29a, Chapter 37, Chapter 38, 64d.

adverb clause   A dependent clause introduced by a subordinating conjunction and functioning as an adverb. See 65f.

agreement   Grammatical correspondence in number, person, and gender between subjects and their verbs and between pronouns and their antecedents. See Chapter 36, Chapter 39.

analogy   See *figurative language.*

analytical essay   See *interpretive essay.*

antecedent   A noun, noun phrase or clause, or pronoun that a pronoun replaces. Pronouns agree with their antecedents in person, number, and gender. Also called *referent.* See also *agreement, gender, number,* and *person.* See Chapter 39, Chapter 40, 64b.

appositive   A word or phrase placed next to a noun or pronoun and used to describe or rename it: *Cliff, an old family friend, always helps out at harvest time.* See 41b, 44c.

argumentative research   Research undertaken to collect information to support a thesis. See also *informational research.* See 14b.

argumentative thesis   See *thesis.*

argument paper   An essay whose purpose is to persuade readers of one side of an issue or one answer to a question. See also *interpretive essay, position paper.* See Chapter 12.

article   *A, an* **(indefinite articles),** or *the* **(definite article).** Considered adjectives and also called *determiners.* See 64d.

attributory words   Words that indicate the person quoted in a direct quotation: *I said, Jonathan wrote.*

audience   The readers to whom a piece of writing is directed. See Chapter 5.

automatic phrase   A phrase that is used habitually but adds little to a sentence's meaning. See 30b.

auxiliary verb   A form of the verb *be, do,* or *have* or the verb *can, could, may, might, must, shall, should, will,* or *would.* An auxiliary verb together with a main verb or a participle constitutes a verb phrase. Also called *helping verb.* See 35c, 64c.

base form   The first-person, singular, present-tense form of a verb: *go, stop, sit, stand.* Also called *plain form* or *simple form.* See 35a.

biased language   Writing in which meaning is expressed by connotation rather than by direct statements of opinion, fact, inference, or evidence. See Chapter 32.

bibliography   A complete list of works on a topic or sources consulted in conducting research. See 15b, 60d.

brainstorming   An invention and discovery technique in which the writer makes a list of possible solutions to a problem or answers to a question. See 7a.

bureaucratese   Jargon or pretentious language that is typical of governmental or institutional writing. See *doublespeak, euphemism.*

case   The form of a pronoun that shows whether it functions as a subject **(subjective case)** or an object **(objective case)** or whether it indicates ownership **(possessive case).** Nouns change form only to show ownership (possessive case). See Chapter 41, 47a, 64a, 64b.

cause-and-effect analysis   A writing strategy in which the writer identifies the action or actions (cause) that bring about a certain condition (effect). See 10d.

chronological order   See *sequence of events.*

claim   A statement or assertion made in support of an argument. The argument's central claim is its *thesis.* A **counterclaim** is a claim made against the thesis. See 11a.

classification and division   A writing strategy in which the writer puts things or people in a category or class with similar things or people (classification) and identifies the constituent parts of something (division). See 10d.

clause   A group of words that includes both a subject and a predicate. See also *dependent clause, independent clause.* See 65f.

cliché   An expression used so often and for so long that it is no longer striking, vivid, or meaningful. See 31j.

clustering   An invention and discovery technique in which ideas are grouped nonlinearly, with relationships among them indicated by lines and circles. See 7g.

collaborating   Working as a group with other writers. See Chapter 22, 23d.

collective noun   A singular noun that names a group of things or people: *fleet, team, family.* See 36f, 39c, 64a.

colloquialism   A term or expression used in spoken language but not precise enough or understandable enough for formal writing. See 31g.

command   See *imperative sentence.*

comma splice   The joining of two independent clauses with only a comma. See Chapter 33.

common noun   A noun that names a general person, place, or thing. Also called *generic noun.* See also *proper noun.* See 51c, 64a.

communicative writing   Writing whose primary purpose is to communicate information and ideas. The most common communicative purposes are to recount an experience, to report information, to explain an idea, and to argue a position. See 4b.

comparative form   See *modifier.*

comparison and contrast   A writing strategy in which the writer describes similarities between two or more things or people (comparison) and then the differences between them (contrast). See 10d.

complement   A word or phrase that renames a subject or object. A **subject complement** is an adjective or noun that follows a linking verb and renames the subject: *Tom is patient.* An **object complement** is an adjective or noun that follows an object and renames it: *They named him captain.* See also *linking verb.* See 36c, 37b, 44j, 65d.

complete predicate See *predicate.*

complete subject See *subject.*

complex sentence A sentence that includes one independent clause and one or more dependent clauses. See 26e, 27c, 66b.

compound adjective Two or more modifiers working as a unit with a single meaning: *freeloading, self-sufficient.* See 52c.

compound noun Two or more words joined to create a noun: *football, trash can, jack-in-the-box.*

compound predicate Two or more predicates that share a subject and that are joined by a coordinating conjunction: *My uncle Ron shaved and got dressed.* See also *predicate.* See 65b.

compound sentence A sentence containing two or more independent clauses and no dependent clauses: *I went to John's house, but he wasn't home.* See 26a, 27c, 66b.

compound subject Two or more subjects that share a predicate and that are joined by a coordinating conjunction: *Her dog and her cat got sick.* See also *subject.* See 36d–e, 39a–b, 41a, 65a.

compound-complex sentence A sentence containing two or more independent clauses and at least one dependent clause: *While you were gone, your mother called and the sink overflowed.* See 27c, 66b.

conclusion The final section of a paper, in which the writer usually summarizes what has gone before and makes general statements about the topic that are needed to complete its purpose. See 19c, 24c, 24d.

concrete word A word referring to something that can be perceived by the senses: *loud, sharp, computer.* See 29a, 64a.

conjunction A word or pair of words that joins two sentence elements and sets up a relationship between them. A **coordinating conjunction** joins elements of equal grammatical weight: *and, but, or, nor, so, for, yet.* A **correlative conjunction** is a pair of words that joins grammatically equivalent elements: *both . . . and, either . . . or, neither . . . nor, not only . . . but also, whether . . . or.* A **subordinating conjunction** introduces a dependent clause and indicates its relationship to an independent clause. Subordinating conjunctions include *although, because, when,* and *while.* See also *conjunctive adverb.* See Chapter 26, 33a, 36d, 36e, 39a, 39b, 41a, 64f.

conjunctive adverb A conjunctive adverb, together with a semicolon, joins two independent clauses. It can also be used alone in an independent clause to express its connection to another independent clause. See 25c, 26e, 44b, 64e, 64f.

connotation   A word's associations in addition to its literal meaning. See also *denotation*. See 31d.

context   Background information provided for readers to understand a whole work. See 5b, 11c.

contraction   A word or phrase shortened by the omission of one or more letters, which are replaced with an apostrophe. See 28c, 47c.

contrast   See *comparison and contrast*.

coordinate adjectives   Two or more adjectives with distinct meanings modifying a noun or pronoun separately: *The tired, discouraged, disgusted ballplayer slumped on the bench.* Coordinate adjectives are separated by commas. See also *cumulative adjectives*. See 44d.

coordinating conjunction   See *conjunction*.

coordination   The grammatical connection of two or more ideas to give them equal emphasis and importance. See Chapter 26.

correlative conjunction   See *conjunction*.

counterclaim   See *claim*.

count noun   A noun that names something that can be counted by unit or instance: *fifty laps, thirty-nine flavors, two apples.* See also *mass noun*. See 64a.

creative writing   Writing whose primary purpose is the creation of a text that is enjoyable and rewarding in and of itself, apart from the information or ideas it conveys. Fiction, poetry, and drama are commonly identified as creative writing, but all writing can be creative. See 4c.

critical essay   See *interpretive essay*.

critical reading   An analysis of an author's assumptions, ideas, arguments, and conclusions to better understand them, test them, and determine their meaning in an overall sense. See Chapter 2.

cumulative adjectives   Two or more adjectives that build on one another and together modify a noun: *The unsightly green chair had been in the family for five generations.* See also *coordinate adjectives*.

cumulative sentence   A sentence in which the main idea is stated at the beginning. See also *periodic sentence*. See 27c.

dangling modifier   A modifier, often a participle or participial phrase that does not modify a clearly stated noun or pronoun: *Driving down the highway, the radar detector went off.* See 38c.

declarative sentence   A sentence that presents facts or assertions. See 27c, 66a.

deductive reasoning Reasoning in which a general statement supports a conclusion about a specific case: *All cats purr. Rex is a cat. Rex must purr.* See also *inductive reasoning.* See 11f.

definition A writing strategy in which the writer describes something so that it can be distinguished from similar things. See 10d.

definite article See *article.*

degree See *modifier.*

demonstrative adjective See *demonstrative pronoun.*

demonstrative pronoun A pronoun that distinguishes its antecedent from similar things: *this, that, these, those.* When the word precedes a noun, it is a **demonstrative adjective:** *these apples.* See 64b.

denotation A word's literal meaning. See also *connotation.* See 31d.

dependent clause A clause containing a subject and a verb but introduced by a subordinating conjunction or a relative pronoun. A dependent clause cannot constitute a complete sentence. Also called *subordinate clause.* See 26e, 27c, 30c, 33e, 34b, 65f.

description A writing strategy in which the writer creates an image of something using words that appeal to the five senses. See 10d.

determiner See *article.*

direct address A word or phrase that indicates a person or persons spoken to: *Don't forget, Amy, to lock the door.* See 44f.

direct discourse See *quotation.*

direct object See *object.*

direct question A sentence that asks a question and ends with a question mark: *Will you marry me?* See also *indirect question, tag sentence.* See 43c.

direct quotation See *quotation.*

discovery writing Writing whose primary purpose is to uncover ideas and information stored in the writer's memory. See also *invention.* See 4a, Chapter 7.

disruptive modifier A modifier placed in such a way as to make the phrase or clause it modifies difficult to follow. See also *split infinitive.* See 38d.

division See *classification and division.*

documentation The practice and procedures for crediting and identifying source materials used in research writing. See 17c, 59d, 60d, 61d, 62d.

double negative   The nonstandard use of two negative modifiers that, in effect, cancel each other out. See 37d.

doublespeak   An extreme form of euphemism that purposely describes things so they seem the opposite of what they actually are. See 30f.

drafting   The stage of the writing process in which the writer begins to produce a text. The complete text is called a **draft;** each subsequent revision of the piece of writing is considered a new draft. See also *editing, revising.* See 3c.

editing   The stage of the writing process in which the writer improves a draft by making sentences and words more clear, powerful, and precise. See also *revising.* See 3f.

effect   See *cause-and-effect analysis.*

effectiveness   The quality of writing that makes it clear, interesting, and readable.

ellipsis   The omission of one or more words from a quoted phrase or clause. An ellipsis must be indicated by ellipsis points (. . .). See also *elliptical construction.* See 49c.

elliptical construction   A phrase or clause from which one or more words are omitted and are assumed to be understood: *I ordered the shrimp; Angelo, the lobster.* See 26j, 27f.

euphemism   A polite term substituted for something considered unpleasant or impolite. See 30f.

evidence   Information presented in support of an argument. The most important types of evidence are facts, examples, inferences, informed opinions, and personal testimony. See 11e.

exclamatory sentence   A sentence that expresses strong feeling and that usually ends with an exclamation point. See 27c, 66a.

explanatory paper   An essay whose purpose is to present information and ideas that will help readers understand the subject. Sometimes called *informative paper, expository paper,* or *report.* See Chapter 10.

expletive construction   A sentence beginning with *it* or *there* (called an *expletive* when used in this manner), followed by a form of the verb *be* and the subject of the sentence: *There is a delay on Route 24 this morning.* See 29b, 30c.

expository paper   See *explanatory paper.*

fallacy   Weak or incorrect logic or reasoning. See 11e.

faulty predication   A mixed construction in which the subject and verb do not make sense together. See 42b.

field research   Research conducted outside of the library by **interviewing** people who have information about a topic or by **observing** people and activities related to the topic. See Chapter 16.

figurative language   Any use of language that makes surprising comparisons or describes things in unexpected ways. The main types of figurative language are analogy, hyperbole, metaphor, paradox, personification, simile, and understatement. See 31i.

finite verb   A verb that changes form to indicate person, number, tense, and mood. See also *verbal*. See 34a, Chapter 35, 64c.

first person   See *point of view*.

fragment   A word group that is grammatically incomplete but that is punctuated as a sentence. See Chapter 34.

freewriting   An invention and discovery technique in which the writer writes quickly without stopping. See 7b.

fused sentence   Two or more independent clauses joined without any punctuation or a conjunction. See Chapter 33.

gender   (1) The categorization of a noun or pronoun as masculine, feminine, or neuter. See also *agreement*. See Chapter 39. (2) The categorization of a person as male or female. See Chapter 32. Pronouns must agree with their antecedents in gender.

general   Categorization of a word or statement that includes or refers to an entire group, type, or category. See also *specific*. See 29a.

generality   A very broad generalization that is essentially meaningless or empty. See 30a.

generalization   A conclusion based on a number of specific facts or instances. Sometimes called *inference*. When a generalization becomes so broad as to be empty or meaningless, it is called a *generality*. See 11f, 30a, 32a.

gerund   The *-ing* form of a verb functioning as a noun: *Painting is her life*. See also *present participle, verbal*. See 34a, 35b, 64c.

gerund phrase   A gerund, its modifiers, complements, and objects. See 65e.

grammar   A system for describing how sentences are organized and structured. See Chapter 23, Chapter 64.

helping verb   See *auxiliary verb*.

homonym   Words that sound alike but have different spellings and meanings. See 31e.

hyperbole   See *figurative language*.

idiom   A customary phrase or usage that does not make literal sense or follow strict rules. See 31f.

imperative mood   See *mood.*

imperative sentence   A sentence that gives an order or instruction. Also called *command.* See 27c, 66a.

implied subject   A subject that is not stated but that can be inferred from context. In imperative sentences (commands), the subject *you* is usually implied: *Shut the door.* See also *subject.* See 65a.

indefinite article   See *article.*

indefinite pronoun   A pronoun that refers to a nonspecific person or thing and therefore does not have a clear antecedent: *anybody, no one, everything, some, none.* See 36g, 39b, 64b.

independent clause   A clause that contains a subject and a predicate that can stand alone as a complete sentence because it is not introduced by a subordinating word. Also called *main clause.* See also *dependent clause.* See Chapter 33, Chapter 34, 65f.

indicative mood   See *mood.*

indirect discourse   See *quotation.*

indirect object   See *object.*

indirect question   A sentence that reports a question, usually in a dependent clause, and ends with a period: *She asked if I would marry her.* See also *direct question, tag sentence.* See 43c.

indirect quotation   See *quotation.*

inductive reasoning   Reasoning in which specific facts support a probable general conclusion: *The alarm has rung at 8:30 on the past five mornings. The alarm will probably ring at 8:30 this morning.* See also *deductive reasoning.* See 11f.

inference   See *generalization.*

infinitive   The base form of a verb preceded by *to.* An infinitive functions as a noun, adverb, or adjective. See also *verbal.* See 34a, 35b, 64c.

infinitive phrase   An infinitive, its modifiers, and its objects or complements. See 65e.

informational research   Research undertaken to collect information needed to answer a research question. See also *argumentative research.* See 14b.

informational thesis   See *thesis.*

informative paper   See *explanatory paper.*

intensive pronoun   A pronoun ending in *-self* or *-selves* placed next to its antecedent for emphasis: *I myself prefer steak*. See also *reflexive pronoun*. See 41g, 64b.

interjection   A term inserted into a sentence or standing alone that expresses strong feeling or reaction: *wow, jeepers*. See 64g.

interpretive community   Any group that shares a set of beliefs or approaches to analyzing, discussing, and interpreting ideas. See 12d.

interpretive essay   An essay whose purpose is to analyze a text and present a persuasive interpretation. Sometimes called *analytical essay, critical essay, literary interpretation,* or *review essay*. See Chapter 12.

interrogative pronoun   A pronoun used to introduce a question: *who, whose*.

interrogative sentence   A sentence that asks a question. See also *direct question, indirect question, tag sentence*. See 27c, 66a.

interview   See *field research*.

intransitive verbs   See *transitive and intransitive verbs*.

invention   Writing or other activities undertaken to help the writer develop solutions to questions and problems encountered in the writing process. See also *discovery writing*. See Chapter 7.

inverted word order   The placement of words in a sentence in an unexpected sequence for emphasis. The most common inverted order is verb before subject. See 27c.

invisible writing   An invention and discovery technique in which the writer uses a word processor for freewriting but darkens the screen so that the words on it are invisible. See 7c.

irony   See *figurative language*.

irregular verb   A verb that does not follow the usual *-d* or *-ed* pattern in spelling its past tense and past participle. See also *regular verb*. See 35b.

issue   A topic that can be argued about, often stated in the form of a question. It raises a real question that has at least two distinct answers, one of which the writer is interested in advocating. See 11b.

jargon   Terms and expressions that arise within a specialty or field, often essential language for people in that field but not understood by others. See 31h.

journal   A record of a person's thoughts and ideas on any aspect of life, work, or studies. See Chapter 8.

level of formality A quality of language created by word choice and sentence structure and ranging from the very formal (or ceremonial) to the familiar. Also called *register*. See 28c.

limiting modifier A modifier that distinguishes the word modified from other similar things. See 38a, 64d.

linking verb A verb that connects a subject to a complement, a word that renames or describes the subject. See also *complement*. See 36c, 37b, 64c.

literary interpretation See *interpretive essay.*

literary present The present tense used to describe the events of a literary work. See 35e.

looping An invention and discovery technique in which the writer creates a series of freewritings, each building on the most important idea uncovered in the previous one. Sometimes called *loop writing.* See also *freewriting.* See 7d.

mass noun A noun that names something concrete that cannot be counted and given a number: *silver, tobacco, information.* Also called *noncount noun.* See also *count noun.* See 64a.

mechanics The standardized features of written language, other than punctuation, that are used to clarify meaning. Elements of mechanics are spelling, capitalization, hyphenation, and italics. See Chapter 23.

metaphor See *figurative language.*

misplaced modifier A modifier that is placed in a sentence so that it is unclear what it describes or which word it modifies. See 38a.

mixed construction A sentence that combines two or more types of sentence structures that do not fit together grammatically. See 42b.

mixed metaphor An implied comparison in which unrelated elements are introduced from a different implied comparison: *We're all in the same boat, and the wing is broken.* See also *figurative language.* See 31i.

modal auxiliary An auxiliary verb that does not change form for person or number. The one-word modals are *can, could, may, might, must, shall, should, will,* and *would.* See 35c, 64c.

modifier A word or group of words that describes a noun, verb, phrase, or clause. The most common modifiers are adjectives and adverbs. Modifiers have three degrees: **positive,** which simply states a quality (*He worked hard*); **comparative,** which compares the degree of that quality between two persons or things (*He worked harder than his* *sister*); and **superlative,** which compares the degree of the quality among three or more persons or things (*He worked <u>hardest</u> of all the company's employees*). See Chapter 37, Chapter 38, 64d.

modifier clause   A dependent clause that functions as an adjective or adverb. See 65f.

modifier phrase   A phrase that functions as an adjective or adverb. See 65e.

mood   The characteristic of a verb used to indicate whether it is stating fact **(indicative),** giving an order or instruction **(imperative mood),** or expressing a wish or condition contrary to fact **(subjunctive).** See 35g, 64c.

nominalization   The construction of a noun from a verb root plus a suffix: *estrange* plus *-ment* equals the nominal *estrangement.* See 29b.

nonfinite verb   See *verbal.*

nonrestrictive clause   See *restrictive and nonrestrictive clause.*

nonsexist language   See *sexist language.*

noun   A word that names a person, animal, place, or idea. See also *common noun, proper noun, count noun, mass noun.* See 64a.

noun clause   A dependent clause that functions as a noun (as a subject, object, or complement). See 65f.

noun cluster   A group of words consisting of a noun and several other nouns used as modifiers: *hardwood maple ballroom floor.* See 29b.

noun phrase   A noun and its modifiers functioning as a noun. See 65e.

number   The characteristic of a noun, pronoun, or verb that indicates whether it is *singular* (referring to one person or thing) or *plural* (referring to more than one). See also *agreement.* See Chapter 36, Chapter 39, 64a, 64b, 64c.

object   A noun, pronoun, or noun phrase or clause that receives the action of or is influenced by a verb, a verbal, or a preposition. A **direct object** receives the action of a verb or verbal: *She read the newspaper.* An **indirect object** indicates to or for whom or what the action of the verb is directed: *She gave him the newspaper.* The **object of a preposition** follows a preposition: *The newspaper had a story about the peace plan.* The preposition, its object, and any associated modifiers together form a **prepositional phrase:** *The newspaper had a story about the peace plan.* See 64e, 65c, 65e.

objective case   See *case.*

objective stance   See *stance.*

observation   See *field research.*

opening   The beginning of an essay, which establishes the subject, the tone, and sometimes the theme or thesis of the essay. See 19c, 24c, 24d.

outline   Organized list showing the points made about a topic, the information supporting each point, and the organization of this material. Outlining is useful as an invention and discovery technique, a means of organizing materials before drafting, and a revision technique. See 7f, 19c, and 14b.

paradox   See *figurative language.*

paragraph   A group of sentences about a single topic. Good paragraphs are unified, coherent, and well organized. See Chapter 25.

parallelism   Repetition of a grammatical element or structure — a word, phrase, clause, sentence, or paragraph — for emphasis. See 26h–j.

paraphrase   A restatement of the ideas of a written or spoken source in the writer's own words. See also *quotation, summary.* See 17b.

parenthetical element   A word or word group that comments on or adds information to a sentence but that is not part of the sentence structure and does not alter the meaning of the sentence. Parenthetical elements appear between parentheses, commas, or dashes. See 44e, 49a, 49b.

participial phrase   A present or past participle, including its modifiers, that functions as an adjective. See 65e.

particle   See *phrasal verb.*

past participle   A verb form created by adding *-d* or *-ed* to the base form in regular verbs. In irregular verbs the past participle is formed differently for each verb. Used with an auxiliary verb it can function as a main verb in a sentence. Used without an auxiliary verb, it functions as a modifier. See also *verbal.* See 34a, 35a, 35d, 64c.

passive voice   See *voice.*

past tense   See *tense.*

perfect progressive tense   See *tense.*

perfect tense   See *tense.*

periodic sentence   A sentence in which the main idea is placed at the end. See also *cumulative sentence.* See 27c.

person   The characteristic of a noun, pronoun, or a verb that indicates whether the subject or actor is the one speaking (**first person:** *I, we*) spoken to (**second person:** *you*), or spoken about (**third person:** *he, she, it, they*). See 35a, Chapter 36, Chapter 39, 64a, 64b, 64c.

personal experience paper   A common college writing assignment whose purpose is to recount a specific event experienced by the writer in an interesting and enlightening manner. See Chapter 9.

personal pronoun   A pronoun that refers to a particular person, group, or thing. See 64b.

personification   See *figurative language*.

perspective   The vantage point from which a paper is written. Perspective is established through point of view, tense, emphasis, and level of formality. See also *point of view, stance, tone*. See 9d, 10f, 12d.

persuasion   See *argument paper*.

phrasal preposition   A group of words that work together as a single preposition: *except for, according to*. See 64d.

phrasal verb   A verb with more than one word. Phrasal verbs are formed by combining a one-word verb with one or more **particles** such as *to* or *off*. Together, the verb and the particle(s) create a meaning that is distinct from that of the original verb: *come to, come off*. Also called *two-word verb* or *multiple-word verb*. See 31f, 64c.

phrase   Two or more words that do not include a subject and a verb but that work as a grammatical unit, serving as a noun, verb, adjective, or adverb. See also *absolute phrase, modifier phrase, noun phrase, object, verb phrase, verbal phrase*. See 65e.

plagiarism   Any use of someone else's ideas or words without explicit and complete documentation or acknowledgment. See 17c.

plain form   See *base form*.

plural   See *number*.

point of view   An indication of the writer's proximity to or distance from his or her material. See also *person*. See 28b.

position paper   A type of argument paper that sets forth a position on an issue of local or national concern. See Chapter 12.

positive form   See *modifier*.

possessive case   See *case*.

predicate   The part of a sentence that specifies action or being. The **simple predicate** is the main verb of the sentence. The **complete predicate** is the simple predicate plus its modifiers, objects, and complements. See also *compound predicate*. See 65b.

predicate adjective An adjective functioning as a complement. See also *complement.*

predicate noun A noun functioning as a complement. See also *complement.*

prefix A word segment attached to the beginning of a word root to change its meaning. See 31c.

preposition A word that connects a noun or noun phrase (the **object** of the preposition) to another word, phrase, or clause and conveys a relation between the elements connected. See also *object*. See 64e.

prepositional phrase See *object.*

present participle A verb form created by adding *-ing* to the base form. Used with auxiliary verbs, it forms the progressive tenses. Used without an auxiliary verb, it is a modifier and functions as an adjective or it is a gerund and functions as a noun. See also *verbal*. See 34a, 35a, 35d, 64c.

pretentious language Excessively formal, old-fashioned, or complicated words and expressions used not for their appropriateness but to impress the reader. See 30e.

primary and secondary sources A primary source contains firsthand information and raw data on a topic. Many of the sources consulted in field research are primary sources. A secondary source contains interpretations of and arguments about firsthand information and raw data. Many of the sources consulted in library research are secondary sources. See 14b.

progressive tense See *tense.*

proofreading The final stage in a writing project; it involves rereading the final draft to catch small errors such as typographical errors, misspellings, and incorrect capitalization. See 56a, 56b.

pronoun A word used in place of a noun or noun phrase. See also *agreement, antecedent, demonstrative pronoun, intensive pronoun, interrogative pronoun, personal pronoun, reciprocal pronoun, reflexive pronoun, relative pronoun.*

proper adjective See *adjective.*

proper noun A name of a particular person, place, animal, organization, or thing. Proper nouns are capitalized. See also *common noun*. See 51c, 64a.

punctuation A system of standardized marks used in written material to clarify meaning. The marks of punctuation used most often in English are the period, the exclamation point, the question mark, the comma, the semicolon, the colon, the apostrophe, quotation marks, the slash, the dash, ellipsis points, parentheses, and brackets. See Chapter 23.

purpose   The reason for generating a piece of writing; the goal a writer wants to accomplish through writing. Three general purposes for writing are to discover, to communicate, and to create. See Chapter 4.

quotation   The reproduction of a writer's or speaker's exact words. In **direct quotation** (or **direct discourse**), a writer reproduces another person's words exactly and places them in quotation marks. In **indirect quotation** (or **indirect discourse**), a writer rephrases another person's words and integrates them grammatically and logically into his or her own sentence. See also *paraphrase, summary*. See 17b.

reciprocal pronoun   A two-word pronoun that refers to one part of a plural antecedent: *each other, one another*. See 64b.

recounting experience   See *personal experience paper*.

referent   See *antecedent*.

reflective essay   A common college writing assignment in which the writer reflects on a significant subject, raises questions about it, and speculates on possible answers but does not provide a strong argument. Sometimes called simply an *essay*. See Chapter 13.

reflexive pronoun   A pronoun ending in *-self* or *-selves* whose antecedent is the subject of the sentence it appears in: *I could kick myself*. See also *intensive pronoun*. See 41g, 64b.

regionalism   A form of language use that is common in one geographic area but not used elsewhere.

regular verb   A verb that forms its past tense and past participles by adding *-d* or *-ed* to the base form. See also *irregular verb*. See 35b.

relative adverb   An adverb that introduces an adjective clause. Common relative adverbs are *when, where*, and *how*. See 64d.

relative clause   A dependent clause that functions as an adjective. See 65f.

relative pronoun   A pronoun that introduces a dependent noun or adjective clause: *who, whose, which, what*. See 64b.

report   See *explanatory paper*.

reporter's questions   A set of questions that reporters use in gathering information and that can be used by any writer as an invention and discovery technique: *Who? What? Where? When? Why? How?* Also called *journalist's questions*. See 7e.

research essay   A common college writing assignment in which students conduct research and write about their findings. Research essays are generally longer, require more extensive research, use a more formal style and format, and take more time than other papers. Sometimes called *research paper* or *research report*. See Chapter 14.

researching   The stage of the writing process in which the writer gathers information and ideas about which to write. Research is a part of all writing assignments except those written completely from personal experience. See also *argumentative research*, *field research*, *informational research*, *research essay*. See 3d.

research question   The question that research is designed to answer. See 14a.

responding   The act of offering comments on a writer's material, ideas, or drafts. See *collaborating*, *writing groups*. See Chapter 22.

restrictive and nonrestrictive clause   *Restrictive clauses* are adjective clauses that limit the nouns they modify and are essential to the meaning of a sentence: *I bought the books that were assigned.* Restrictive clauses are not set off from the words they modify with commas. *Nonrestrictive clauses* do not limit the nouns they modify and are not essential to the meaning of a sentence: *The assigned books, which were on a special shelf, cost sixty dollars.* Nonrestrictive clauses are not set off with commas. See 40f, 44c.

review essay   See *interpretive essay*.

revising   The stage of the writing process in which the writer improves a draft by making changes to its direction, focus, argument, information, organization, or other important features. Revision generally occurs at the level of ideas. See also *editing*. See 3e.

root   The part of a word that stays the same as the word changes form with the addition of prefixes and suffixes. *Route* is the root of *routing, routine, reroute*. See 31c, 50b.

second person   See *point of view*.

secondary source   See *primary and secondary source*.

sentence   A group of words containing a subject and a predicate and conveying a comprehensible, complete idea or thought.

sequence of events   The order in which events are related in an essay. The most straightforward sequence of events is *chronological order*, which presents events in the same order in which they happened. Another sequence of events is the *flashback*, in which earlier events are related after later ones. See 9f.

series   A list of words, phrases, or clauses separated by commas or semicolons. See 26h, 44d.

sexist language   Any language in which assumptions about gender are embedded: *policeman, each must do his best.* Nonsexist alternatives are *police officer* and *his or her best.* See Chapter 32.

shift   Any change in verb tense, number, or person within a sentence or between sentences that results in confusion for the reader. See 42a.

simile   See *figurative language.*

simple form   See *base form.*

simple predicate   See *predicate.*

simple sentence   A sentence that contains one independent clause. See 66b.

simple subject   See *subject.*

simple tense   See *tense.*

singular   See *number.*

slang   Colorful, irreverent expressions coined by small groups to describe their worlds and relationships. Slang is not appropriate in formal writing.

specific   Categorization of a word or statement that refers to a single, particular thing. See also *general.* See 29a.

split infinitive   A construction in which words intervene between the infinitive marker *to* and the infinitive verb. See 38d.

squinting modifier   An ambiguously placed modifier that does not clearly modify one sentence element but could modify more than one. See 38b.

stance   The perspective adopted for a particular paper. An **objective stance** focuses on the topic under discussion rather than on the writer's own thoughts and feelings. A **subjective stance** incorporates the writer's thoughts and feelings into the account or analysis. See 12d.

static verb   A verb that expresses a subject's existence rather than action: *be, seem, become.* See 29b.

stereotype   Overgeneralization about a person or group based on gender, race, ethnicity, and so on. See 32a.

style   The distinctive way a writer expresses himself or herself, established primarily through the level of formality and the simplicity or complexity of words, sentences, and paragraphs. See also *level of formality.* See 5b, 6b.

subject   (1) The noun or pronoun that performs the action of the verb, is acted upon by the verb, or is described by the verb. The **sim-**

ple subject is the noun or pronoun alone. The **complete subject** is the noun or pronoun plus its modifiers. See also *compound subject, implied subject.* See 65a. (2) The idea or thing about which a paper is written. See also *topic.*

subject complement   See *complement.*

subjective case   See *case.*

subjective stance   See *stance.*

subjunctive mood   See *mood.*

subordinate clause   See *dependent clause.*

subordinating conjunction   See *conjunction.*

subordination   Connection of two or more ideas (usually clauses) to make one of them dominant and the other or others logically secondary or subordinate. See 26e–g, 33e.

suffix   A word segment attached to the end of a word root to change its meaning or form. See 31c, 50b.

summary   A distillation of a source's ideas into a brief statement phrased in the writer's own words. See also *paraphrase, quotation.* See 17b.

superlative form   See *modifier.*

synonym   Two or more different words with the same meaning.

tag question   See *tag sentence.*

tag sentence   A brief sentence placed at the end of another sentence (after a comma) for the purpose of providing emphasis or eliciting a response. A tag sentence may be either a statement or a question: *Mark cannot join us, I'm afraid. You're tired, aren't you?* See 33b, 44f.

tense   The form a verb takes to show when its action occurs. **Simple tenses** show events that occur in the past, present, or future: *I walked, I am walking, I will walk.* **Perfect tenses** indicate action completed in the past (*had sat*), present (*have sat*), and future (*will have sat*). **Progressive tenses** indicate action happening continuously, and not necessarily ending, in the past (*was sitting*), present (*am sitting*), and future (*will be sitting*). **Perfect progressive tenses** express actions happening over a period of time and then ending in the past (*had been sitting*), the present (*have been sitting*), or in the future (*will have been sitting*). See 35d, 64c.

text   Any symbolic work constructed by humans that is open to interpretation, specifically, written texts such as essays, novels, short stories, plays, and poems. See Chapter 12.

theme   The central idea of a personal or reflective essay. It is not necessarily stated outright but is more often strongly implied.

thesis   A statement, usually made early in a research or persuasive essay, that asserts the point the writer hopes to make in the essay. A **working thesis** is a statement of the point a writer thinks his or her finished essay will make; it is useful in the research and drafting phases of writing and often changes during the writing process. An **argumentative thesis** expresses an opinion about the issue the writer is exploring; the essay then serves to support that opinion. An **informational thesis** presents a factual statement that will be fleshed out with explanation and detail.

tone   The writer's attitude toward the subject and audience conveyed through the piece of writing. Tone is established primarily through word choice, point of view, and level of formality. See also *point of view, level of formality.* See 5b, 5c, Chapter 28.

topic   The specific issue, idea, fact, or situation about which a paper is written. See also *subject.*

topic sentence   The sentence that states the main idea of a paragraph. See 25a.

transitional expression   A word or phrase connecting separate ideas or statements and describing the relationship between them: *for example, as a result.* See 25c, 44b, 44e.

transitive and intransitive verb   A **transitive verb** expresses an action that has an object or recipient; an **intransitive verb** expresses action or being with no object or recipient. Many verbs are both transitive and intransitive; *I walked the dog* (transitive); *I walked to the store* (intransitive). See 64c.

understatement   See *figurative language.*

verb   A word that indicates action or existence, expressing what a subject does or is. See 64c.

verb phrase   A main verb plus any auxiliary verbs. See also *auxiliary verb.* See 65e.

verbal   A verb form that does not function as the main verb of a sentence. See also *gerund, infinitive, past participle, present participle.* See 34a, 35b, 64c.

verbal phrase   A verbal plus its modifiers, objects, and complements. See also *gerund phrase, infinitive phrase, participial phrase.* See 65e.

voice   (1) The sense of the writer conveyed to the reader through a piece of writing. See Chapter 6. (2) In grammar, an attribute of a verb showing whether the action of the verb is performed by the sentence's subject **(active voice)** or is performed on the sentence's subject **(passive voice).** Active: *Mary reads the book*; passive: *The book is read by Mary.* See 29c, 64c.

working thesis   See *thesis*.

writing group   A group of writers who work together to help one another improve their writing. Writers may respond to one another's work or they may collaborate on a piece of writing. See 22e.

writing process   The set of activities writers go through to produce a finished piece of writing. Writing processes vary from person to person and from situation to situation. However, the typical writing process can be described as having five discrete but overlapping stages: planning, drafting, researching, revising, and editing. See Chapter 3.

ESL Index

Index

Editing symbols

ABB	abbreviation **55**	REP	repetitious **30d**
AD	adjective/adverb **37**	S-V AGR	subject-verb agreement **36**
AWK	awkward	SHIFT	distracting shift **42a**
BIAS	biased language **32**	SLANG	slang **31g**
CAP	capital letter **51**	SP	spelling **50**
CASE	pronoun case **41**	SUB	subordination **26e–g**
CLICHÉ	cliché **31j**	T	verb tense **35d–f**
COH	coherence **25c**	TONE	tone **28**
CONCL	conclusion **24c–d**	TRANS	transition **25c**
COORD	coordination **26a–d**	??	unclear
CS	comma splice **33**	U	unity **25a**
D	diction **29a–b, 31**	US	usage glossary
DEV	development **9–13**	VAR	variety **27b–f**
DIR	indirect **30e–f**	VERB	verb **35**
DM	dangling modifier **38c**	VITAL	vitality **29**
DOC	documentation **59–63**	W	wordy **30a–d**
EMPH	emphasis **27a**	WC	word choice **31**
FRAG	sentence fragment **34**	WW	wrong word **31**
FS	fused sentence **33**	’	apostrophe **47**
GR	grammar **64–66**	[ ]	brackets **49d**
HYPH	hyphen **52**	:	colon **46**
INC	incomplete construction **42c**	,	comma **44**
ITAL	italics (underlining) **53**	—	dash **49b**
JARG	jargon **31h**	. . .	ellipsis points **49c**
LC	lowercase letter **51**	!	exclamation point **43d**
LOG	logic **11e**	( )	parentheses **49a**
MIX	mixed construction **42b**	.	period **43a–b**
MM	misplaced modifier **38a–b, d**	?	question mark **43c**
MOOD	verb mood **35g–h**	" "	quotation marks **48**
MS	manuscript form **56**	;	semicolon **45**
NUM	number **54**	/	slash **49e**
OPEN	opening **24a–b**	◡	close up space
¶	paragraph **25**	#	add space
//	parallelism **26h–j**	^	insert
P	punctuation **43–49**	℮	delete
P-A AGR	pronoun-antecedent agreement **39**	∿	transpose
PASS	passive voice **29c**	X	obvious error
REF	pronoun reference **40**		

How to use *The Blair Handbook*

When you identify a concept, strategy, or convention you would like more information about, first locate it in the **brief table of contents** on the inside front cover of the book, the **table of contents** at the beginning of the book, or the **index** at the end of the book. These sources will tell you what page number to turn to. The table of contents will also tell you the chapter and the section within the chapter that contain the information you want.

INFORMATION AT THE TOP OF THE PAGE helps you find the part of the book you need.

SECTION HEADINGS identify chapter number, section letter, and section title for the material that follows.

Chapter number

Page number

Section letter

SYMBOLS correspond to the subject discussed on the page.

SHORTENED TITLES list chapter title on left pages; section on right pages.

EXPLANATIONS provide information on the concept, strategy, or convention.

EXAMPLES WITH HANDWRITTEN CHANGES show problems and their solutions at a glance.

COMMENTS clarify examples.

OTHER EXAMPLES illustrate general principles.

BOLDFACE indicates important terms in the explanation. Many are also included in the Glossary of Terms.

CROSS REFERENCES provide a chapter number and section letter to locate information on a related topic.

BOXES summarize key information for quick reference and review.

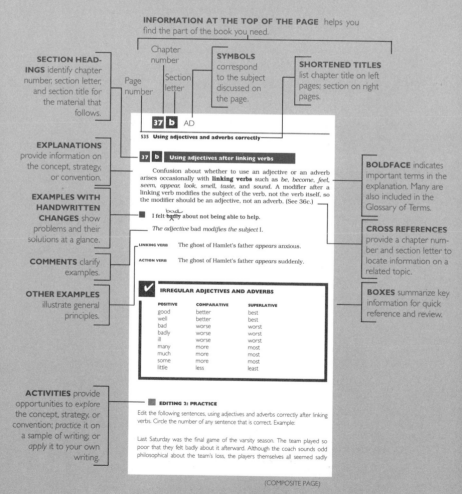

37 b AD

535 Using adjectives and adverbs correctly

37 b Using adjectives after linking verbs

Confusion about whether to use an adjective or an adverb arises occasionally with **linking verbs** such as *be, become, feel, seem, appear, look, smell, taste,* and *sound.* A modifier after a linking verb modifies the subject of the verb, not the verb itself, so the modifier should be an adjective, not an adverb. (See 36c.)

■ I felt ~~badly~~ bad about not being able to help.

The adjective bad *modifies the subject* I.

LINKING VERB   The ghost of Hamlet's father *appears* anxious.

ACTION VERB   The ghost of Hamlet's father *appears* suddenly.

✓ IRREGULAR ADJECTIVES AND ADVERBS

POSITIVE	COMPARATIVE	SUPERLATIVE
good	better	best
well	better	best
bad	worse	worst
badly	worse	worst
ill	worse	worst
many	more	most
much	more	most
some	more	most
little	less	least

■ EDITING 2: PRACTICE

Edit the following sentences, using adjectives and adverbs correctly after linking verbs. Circle the number of any sentence that is correct. Example:

Last Saturday was the final game of the varsity season. The team played so poor that they felt badly about it afterward. Although the coach sounds odd philosophical about the team's loss, the players themselves all seemed sadly

ACTIVITIES provide opportunities to *explore* the concept, strategy, or convention; *practice* it on a sample of writing; or *apply* it to your own writing.

(COMPOSITE PAGE)